STUDENT ACHIEVEMENT SERIES

Foundations of Management

Basics and Best Practices

▶
▶
▶

Robert Kreitner

Arizona State University

W9-CNC-576

▶

▶

▶

▶

Houghton Mifflin Company

Boston   New York

Vice President, Executive Publisher: George Hoffman

Executive Sponsoring Editor: Lise Johnson

Senior Marketing Manager: Nicole Hamm

Senior Development Editor: Joanne Dauksewicz

Senior Project Editor: Nancy Blodget

Art and Design Coordinator: Jill Haber

Cover Design Director: Tony Saizon

Senior Photo Editor: Jennifer Meyer Dare

Senior Composition Buyer: Chuck Dutton

New Title Project Manager: James Lonergan

Marketing Associate: Karen Mulvey

Cover Photo: © Louisa Gould Photography

▶ THIS BOOK IS DEDICATED TO *YOU*, AND YOUR DREAM FOR A BETTER FUTURE. THERE'S NO MAGIC. IT JUST TAKES CHALLENGING GOALS, COURAGE AND ADAPTABILITY, LOTS OF PERSISTENT HARD WORK, AND A LITTLE LUCK TO ACHIEVE MORE THAN YOU CAN IMAGINE. GO FOR IT!

Printed in the U.S.A.

Library of Congress control number: 2007924352

Instructor's edition:
ISBN 13: 978-0-618-92440-0
ISBN 10: 0-618-92440-X

For orders, use student text ISBNs:
ISBN 13: 978-0-618-90737-3
ISBN 10: 0-618-90737-8

1 2 3 4 5 6 7 8 9 – VH – 11 10 09 08 07

Foundations of Management
Basics and Best Practices

Brief Contents

Contents

Instructor's Introduction

Many textbooks are developed to teach the basic fundamentals of management, and these books generally include all of the principles that management professors believe are important for students to learn before entering the "real life" management world. However, it is important to gain other important individual perspectives when developing textbooks so that such learning tools are well rounded and adequately cover the topics that students believe to be important. *Student Achievement Series: Foundations of Management* incorporates these various perspectives by including students, as well as professors, in the development process. In particular, Houghton Mifflin, in using a variety of data collection methods, compiled information from a diverse national sample of professors and students so that this text could be developed to reflect the interests of both groups. This positions the text as one of the first educational management products that considers the needs and interests of professors, while at the same time utilizing extensive student feedback to enhance the "student friendly" nature of the concepts covered. Students and professors have been included in every basic component of this textbook development process including the structure of the text, the evaluation of key material, the development of concepts, and creation of the title and cover design.

Student involvement in the project has been one of the most important elements of the textbook's development process. The feedback provided by these student participants has facilitated the development of a management text that is quite different from other books that are currently available on the market. In particular, students suggested that, in addition to a reasonable price, a textbook should present the material in a manner that facilitates learning both inside and outside the classroom. With all of their interests and activities both inside and outside of school, students prefer texts that provide a useful overview of the material so that they can learn the information well, perform in an exemplary fashion on examinations, and are prepared for the workplace after the college experience. Taking all of these preferences into consideration, this textbook should represent a good value from an educational standpoint—it should satisfy price-sensitive buyers, as well as enhance the efficiency and effectiveness of student learning.

▶ PEDAGOGY

Satisfying these basic interests and preferences can be a challenge, and many textbooks on the market fall below the mark. In particular, some students learn best by focusing on visual aspects of material, while others learn best by reading the material or participating in practical learning exercises, while still other students learn best by reading aloud or listening to MP3s. To respond to these individual learning styles, we established many different methods of content delivery. We also focused on the students' feedback or "wishlist" of items students wanted to see in their textbook program.

Request #1: We want a straightforward text that contains fewer and shorter chapters/sections and offers brief outlines of content rather than long drawn-out paragraphs (preferably in bulleted format).

Student Achievement Series Response:

▌ Our author has worked laboriously to tighten wording, condense chapter coverage, and critically approach each section. In cases where a concept was introduced, then illustrated by more than one example, close attention was paid to whether or not that additional example (or two) was really vital to student comprehension. In most cases the point was clearly made with one example so why add more words to a page at the risk of being redundant? While it is important to make sure that the concept is adequately explained and illustrated, oftentimes students become bored when given example upon example or rewordings of the same material. In addition, content, when appropriate, was transformed from running paragraph text to bullets for clear connectivity and to retain student interest.

▌ Since students commented that they usually skip the boxes and do not deem them integral to concept comprehension, we included only one or two boxed inserts on "Best Practices," because they provide important real-world applications. Opening and Closing Cases were added but closely edited to ensure clarity and succinctness.

1. Working with and through others
2. Achieving organizational objectives
3. Balancing effectiveness and efficiency
4. Making the most of limited resources
5. Coping with a changing environment (see Figure 1.1 on page 6)

Working with and Through Others

Management is, above all else, a social process. Many collective purposes bring individuals together—writing software, building cars, providing emergency health care, publishing books, and on and on. But in all cases, managers are responsible for getting things done by working with and through others.

Aspiring managers who do not interact well with others hamper their careers. This was the conclusion two experts reached following interviews with 62 executives from the United States, United Kingdom, Belgium, Spain, France, Germany, and Italy. Each of the executives was asked to describe two managers whose careers had been *derailed*. Derailed managers were those who had not lived up to their peers' and superiors' high expectations. The derailed managers reportedly had these shortcomings:

▌ Problems with interpersonal relationships

▌ Failure to meet business objectives

▌ Failure to build and lead a team

▌ Inability

price for stepping to the front of the administrative parade. According to one management expert, when you accept a supervisory or managerial position you *lose* your right to do any of the following:

▌ Lose your temper

▌ Be one of the gang

▌ Bring your personal problems to work

▌ Vent your frustrations and express your opinion at work

▌ Resist change

▌ Pass the buck on tough assignments

▌ Get even with your adversaries

▌ Play favorites

▌ Put your self-interests first

▌ Ask others to do what you wouldn't do

▌ Expect to be immediately recognized and rewarded for doing a good job[35]

Request #2: We want to be ready for our exams. We need assessment tools to prepare us for our tests.

Student Achievement Series Response:

▌ A Test Prepper is included at the end of each major section. Each Test Prepper contains true/false and multiple choice questions that are both recall and application based. The answers can be found at the end of each chapter.

▌ In addition, ACE and ACE+ Practice tests can be found in the Online Study Center.

TEST PREPPER 1.1   ANSWERS CAN BE FOUND ON P. 27

True or False?

_____ 1. A key component in the definition of the term *management* is achieving one's personal objectives.

_____ 2. Microsoft automatically qualifies as an "efficient" company if it launches a new product on time.

_____ 3. Globalization is one of the five overarching sources of change for today's managers.

_____ 4. The design-it-in approach to product quality is an out-of-date approach.

_____ 5. E-business involves performing all basic business functions and all organizational support activities on the Internet.

Online Study Center
ACE the Test
ACE Practice Tests 1.1

Multiple Choice

_____ 6. By definition, management is the process of _____ to achieve _____ in a changing environment.
   a. working effectively; key results
   b. solving problems; individual and collective goals
   c. planning; strategic goals
   d. working with and through others; organizational objectives
   e. operating efficiently; success

_____ 7. Researchers found which of these to be the number-one ethical problem in a survey of more than 4,000 employees?
   a. Stealing and theft
   b. Lying to supervisors
   c. Falsifying records
   d. Abusing drugs and alcohol
   e. Sexual harassment

Request #3: We want a Web site that's easy to use and worth our time.

Student Achievement Series Response:

▌ This text is supported by a comprehensive online support tool. Students also let us know that, by far, the most utilized section of a book's supporting Web site is the Quizzing and Testing portion. The Online Study Center (or student Web site) contains a plethora of content for students to follow up on what they've read in the chapter. At the conclusion of each chapter, there is a section that outlines all of the valuable assets found in the Online Study Center. To save students time and energy searching an unorganized site, we have categorized assets on the Web site into three categories:

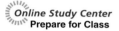 **Online Study Center
Prepare for Class**    **Online Study Center
Improve Your Grade**    **Online Study Center
ACE the Test**

Many valuable assets are found within these three categories. All assets found on the Web site are tied to content within the chapter. Icons appear in the text margins to point students to the Online Study Center, the specific category, and the asset name.

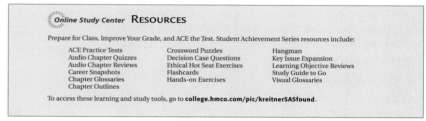

Online Study Center **RESOURCES**

Prepare for Class, Improve Your Grade, and ACE the Test. Student Achievement Series resources include:

ACE Practice Tests	Crossword Puzzles	Hangman
Audio Chapter Quizzes	Decision Case Questions	Key Issue Expansion
Audio Chapter Reviews	Ethical Hot Seat Exercises	Learning Objective Reviews
Career Snapshots	Flashcards	Study Guide to Go
Chapter Glossaries	Hands-on Exercises	Visual Glossaries
Chapter Outlines		

To access these learning and study tools, go to **college.hmco.com/pic/kreitnerSASfound**.

▌ We also repeat the Web site URL on every other page in the text to really drive home the message!

Online Study Center college.hmco.com/pic/kreitnerSASfound

Request #4: We want a text that is visually appealing but uses space economically and with purpose—the longer the book, the heavier it is to carry!

Student Achievement Series Response:

▌ All photographs, cartoons, figures, and tables in this text are included not only to enhance the esthetic appeal of the text but, more important, to illustrate the written words. The captions are closely tied to the illustrations as well as the content being discussed in the text. In addition, art was sized substantially smaller than in other texts to avoid waste in the layout.

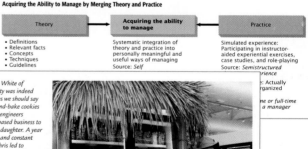

FIGURE 1.5
Acquiring the Ability to Manage by Merging Theory and Practice

Theory	Acquiring the ability to manage	Practice
• Definitions • Relevant facts • Concepts • Techniques • Guidelines	Systematic integration of theory and practice into personally meaningful and useful ways of managing Source: *Self*	Simulated experience: Participating in instructor-aided experiential exercises, case studies, and role-playing Source: *Semistructured*

For entrepreneurs Paula and Chris White of Wrentham, Massachusetts, necessity was indeed the mother of invention. Or perhaps we should say the mother of a great line of slice-and-bake cookies called "600 lb. Gorillas." The two engineers decided Paula should run a home-based business to better care for their infant son and daughter. A year of experimentation in their kitchen and constant tasting that added 20 pounds to Chris led to cookies many customers admit to passing off as homemade.

Request #5: We want cases that cover topics, organizations, or companies to which we can relate.

Student Achievement Series Response:

▌ The author has taken special care to include contemporary companies/organizations and student-friendly topics. For instance, Chapter 10's opener talks about the importance of clear communication and introduces students to Starbucks' Jim Donald, while the Closing Case Study focuses on the multicultural work force.

Jim Donald, CEO of Starbucks: "A Double Shot of Productivity"

I'm kind of a simple guy—brewed coffee, straight black. And I do my own e-mails. If anyone in our company e-mails me or leaves me a voicemail, they get a response, quickly. I'm fanatical about communicating. We have to operate like a store. Nobody likes to wait in line. My Treo is a godsend. I get 200 to 250 e-mails a day, and I respond to 75 percent of them. I'm brief, but that's better than not responding.

I also carry a hardback black binder with me. If someone says something particularly smart or not smart, I write it down so I have actual facts to use when I coach people or give reviews.

Return Calls at Dawn

My day in the office starts around 6 A.M. for one reason only: It's the perfect time to reach out to people. This morning I left a voice-mail for 100 regional managers. I also wrote personal thank-you

CLOSING CASE STUDY

Found in Translation: How to Make the Multicultural Work Force Work

At City Fresh Foods, CEO Glynn Lloyd likes to hire from the neighborhood. And because the 12-year-old food-service company is headquartered in Boston's polyglot Dorchester neighborhood, Lloyd's payroll resembles a mini-United Nations. Some 70 percent of his 65 employees are immigrants, from places like Trinidad, Brazil, Nigeria, the Dominican Republic, and Cape Verde, off the West Coast of Africa. They speak half a dozen languages, not to mention the myriad cultural differences. "Visitors can see that we're a community of people from all over. They pick up on it right away," says Lloyd, 38. "You walk in, and you can feel the vibe of all those places."

Immigrants will account for nearly two-thirds of the country's population growth between now and 2050, according to the U.S. Department of Labor. Minority

the Dominican Republic, sits next to employees who need the Spanish version and translates. Delivery manager Jose Tavares makes notes about his department meetings; his assistant translates them into Portuguese and Spanish for the company's 26 drivers. He's also ready to jump on the phone and solve any problems that might occur when an immigrant driver cannot answer a customer's question. Cotumanama "Toby" Peña—many employees adopt nicknames to further the cause of simplification—learned English words such as "safe" and "out" by watching baseball in his native Dominican Republic and picked up the alphabet from *Sesame Street*. "The English I speak is broken," says Peña, a cook. "For me, it's sometimes better to write things down." (Nonetheless, he often finds himself translating for one of his

Request #6: We want material that we can really use in our current or future careers.

Student Achievement Series Response:

▌ Instead of providing a smattering of exercises at the end of each chapter, the author has been precise in selecting only the most appropriate exercises to include in the text and the Online Study Center. The end-of-chapter case questions give students an opportunity to practice their critical thinking skills. Hands-On Exercises, Decision Cases, and Ethical Hot Seat Exercises can be found in the Online Study Center.

KEY TERMS

accommodative social
    responsibility strategy   *p. 60*
altruism   *p. 61*
amoral managers   *p. 67*
corporate philanthropy   *p. 62*
corporate social responsibility
    p. 55
defensive social responsibility
    strategy   *p. 60*
enlightened self-interest   *p. 61*
ethical advocate   *p. 68*
ethics   *p. 64*
iron law of responsibility   *p. 59*
proactive social responsibility
    strategy   *p. 61*
reactive social responsibility
    strategy   *p. 60*
stakeholder audit   *p. 58*
whistle-blowing   *p. 69*

Online Study Center
Prepare for Class
Chapter Glossary

Improve Your Grade
Flashcards
Hangman
Crossword Puzzles

■ In addition, at the start of each chapter, the author has listed the important terms found within the chapter. These terms are also found in the Online Study Center as glossaries and flashcards. The terms also appear in the text margins to further drive home the importance of understanding the language of management.

---

reactive social responsibility strategy
Denying responsibility and resisting change.

Reaction

A business that follows a **reactive social responsibility strategy** will deny responsibility while striving to maintain the status quo. A case in point involves the charges of "environmental racism" made by local residents against the many petrochemical plants along the Mississippi River near Baton Rouge, Louisiana. Their complaint centered on the fact that industrial pollution tends to be worst in the poorest, typically minority-populated neighborhoods. In response, a Louisiana Chemical Association spokesman said: "There has been a big emphasis on minority training, recruiting, and hiring.... We are trying to reach out to the minority community, to those who live near our plants, to find out what their concerns are. I just think we need to talk more and build up some trust."[14] Widespread mistrust in the affected minority communities presages a wave of lawsuits against the chemical companies.

defensive social responsibility strategy
Resisting additional responsibilities with legal and public relations tactics.

Defense

A **defensive social responsibility strategy** uses legal maneuvering and/or a public relations campaign to avoid assuming additional responsibilities. This strategy has been a favorite one for the tobacco industry, which is intent on preventing any legal liability linkage between smoking and cancer. When European countries showed signs of adopting U.S.-style bans on secondhand smoke, Philip Morris launched a rather odd defensive strategy:

In a Western European ad campaign that backfired, Philip Morris suggested that inhaling secondhand smoke is less dangerous than eating a cookie or drinking milk. The campaign was banned from France after the National Union of Biscuit Makers and the National Committee Against Tobacco Use filed separate suits against Philip Morris.[15]

accommodative social responsibility strategy   Assuming additional responsibilities in response to pressure.

Accommodation

The organization must be pressured into assuming additional responsibilities when it follows an **accommodative social responsibility strategy**. Some outside stimulus, such as pressure from a special-interest group or threatened government

---

We believe that *Student Achievement Series: Foundations of Management* fills an important need in the marketplace by listening to students' requests in order to provide a value-based learning tool, not just another textbook.

▶ ORGANIZATION OF THIS TEXT

The text has been arranged into three basic parts to provide students with a knowledge base of management principles and concepts. Part 1 provides students with an overview of management, including an introduction to the job of managing others in organizations, the role of the environment in management, management's social and ethical responsibilities, and international management. Part 2 covers core administrative processes, including planning and strategy, decision making, designing effective organizations, and maintaining control and improving quality. Part 3 focuses on managing people by highlighting human resource management, effective communication, motivating employees, managing groups and teams, leadership and influence, and managing change and conflict.

In addition to breaking the text into Parts and Chapters, the author has paid a great deal of attention to breaking each chapter into palatable sections. By dividing the chapters into short sections, the content is made more accessible to students. Each section correlates to a learning objective and heading in the chapter outline. The author has taken a systematic approach to structuring the text so that the student will always know where he/she is in the context of the chapter and the text as a whole. The Learning Objectives are reiterated one last time as the last asset in the chapter, the Learning Objective Review. Each individual Learning Objective, major section, and Learning Objective Review section is color coded to divide the text for those who are seeking a more visual connection to the chapter content.

Chapter Outline

▶ THE SOCIAL ENVIRONMENT
Demographics of the New U.S. Workforce
Nagging Inequalities in the Workplace
Managing Diversity

▶ THE POLITICAL-LEGAL ENVIRONMENT
The Politicization of Management
Increased Personal Legal Accountability
Political-Legal Implications for Management

▶ THE ECONOMIC ENVIRONMENT
The Job Outlook in Today's Service Economy,
Where Education Counts
Benefiting from Economic Forecasts
The Challenge of a Global Economy

▶ THE TECHNOLOGICAL ENVIRONMENT
The Innovation Process
Promoting Innovation Through Intrapreneurship

Online Study Center
Prepare for Class
Chapter Outline

3 ▶ *Discuss why the global economy is a vital economic consideration for modern managers.*

2 ▶ *Discuss how the changing political-legal environment is affecting the practice of management.*

1 ▶ *Summarize the demographics of the new U.S. workforce and define the term managing diversity.*

THE SOCIAL ENVIRONMENT

1 ▶ *Summarize the demographics of the new U.S. workforce and define the term managing diversity.*

THE POLITICAL-LEGAL ENVIRONMENT

2 ▶ *Discuss how the changing political-legal environment is affecting the practice of management.*

THE ECONOMIC ENVIRONMENT

3 ▶ *Discuss why the global economy is a vital economic consideration for modern managers.*

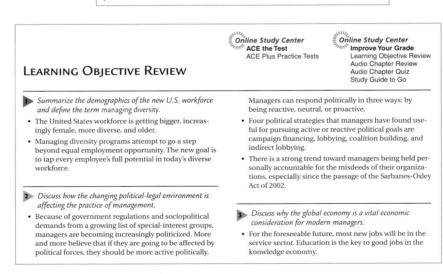

Online Study Center
ACE the Test
ACE Plus Practice Tests

Online Study Center
Improve Your Grade
Learning Objective Review
Audio Chapter Review
Audio Chapter Quiz
Study Guide to Go

LEARNING OBJECTIVE REVIEW

▶ *Summarize the demographics of the new U.S. workforce and define the term managing diversity.*
- The United States workforce is getting bigger, increasingly female, more diverse, and older.
- Managing diversity programs attempt to go a step beyond equal employment opportunity. The new goal is to tap every employee's full potential in today's diverse workforce.

2 ▶ *Discuss how the changing political-legal environment is affecting the practice of management.*
- Because of government regulations and sociopolitical demands from a growing list of special-interest groups, managers are becoming increasingly politicized. More and more believe that if they are going to be affected by political forces, they should be more active politically.

Managers can respond politically in three ways: by being reactive, neutral, or proactive.
- Four political strategies that managers have found useful for pursuing active or reactive political goals are campaign financing, lobbying, coalition building, and indirect lobbying.
- There is a strong trend toward managers being held personally accountable for the misdeeds of their organizations, especially since the passage of the Sarbanes-Oxley Act of 2002.

3 ▶ *Discuss why the global economy is a vital economic consideration for modern managers.*
- For the foreseeable future, most new jobs will be in the service sector. Education is the key to good jobs in the knowledge economy.

▶ SUPPLEMENTS FOR INSTRUCTORS

Student Achievement Series: Foundations of Management includes an extensive bundle of educational materials and activity-based learning tools that help professors teach a principles of management course:

▪ The ***Online Instructor's Resource Manual*** contains chapter objectives, opening case interpretations, a lecture outline, and solutions for the closing case questions. Additional instructor support features include Instructional Tips, Additional Discussion/Essay Questions, Key Issue Expansions, Decision Cases, Cooperative Learning Tools, and appropriate Transparency Masters.

▪ The ***Online Test Bank*** is comprised of close to 2,000 multiple-choice, true/false, and short-answer essay questions. Each question is supplemented with a particular learning objective, page reference, an estimation of difficulty level, and category type (fact or application).

▪ The ***HMTesting™ Instructor CD*** is a computerized version of the Test Bank and enables professors to easily select and/or edit questions to be included on a test master for duplication and distribution. There are also Online Testing and Gradebook features that enable professors to give examinations over their local area network or the World Wide Web, organize course content and procedures, tabulate assignment grades, and calculate student grade statistics.

▪ The ***Online Teaching Center*** is an excellent resource for instructors that offers PowerPoint slides (basic and premium), downloadable Instructor's Resource Manual files, the Video Guide, Classroom Response System materials, and other relevant course content.

▪ A ***DVD Program*** is included with the text to provide realistic examples of the chapter information and to spark students' interest in material. A discussion-based video guide is also offered, which contains discussion questions and activities.

▪ ***BlackBoard® and WebCT®***—these online course management systems include Instructor's Resource Manual files, Test Bank questions, CRS content, video segments, quizzes, various PowerPoint slides, audio chapter summaries and quizzes in MP3 format, and other relevant course content.

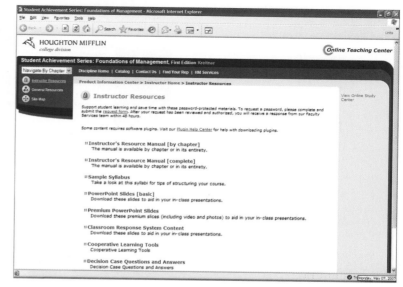

▶ SUPPLEMENTS FOR STUDENTS

▌ The ***Online Study Center*** provides various valuable online assets. As mentioned before, the Online Study Center contains ACE Practice Tests, Video Segments, and much more.

▌ "Your Guide to an 'A'" Media Passkey enables students to access content beyond what is available on the standard Online Study Center. While Chapter 1 is available to all students, the remainder of the chapters contain passkey protected assets. The "Your Guide to an 'A'" Media Passkey is packaged on request with every new textbook. In addition, the "Your Guide to an 'A'" passkey is available for purchase at the bookstore or Houghton Mifflin's eCommerce site for those students using used textbooks. Assets that are housed behind the passkey include:

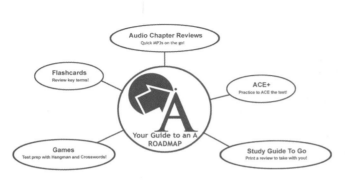

- ACE+ Practice Tests (10 true/false and 10 multiple choice questions with immediate scoring and feedback)
- Downloadable *Study Guide to Go* (a printable packet containing the chapter outline, learning objective review, a comprehensive list of key terms, and sample quiz questions)
- Online Flash *Interactive Skills Self-Assessments* that provide instant feedback and scoring for students wanting to evaluate their personal management competencies
- Audio Chapter Review and Quiz MP3 files (audio chapter summaries and short quizzes)
- Exercises that enhance student learning (Hands-On Exercises, Ethical Hot Seat Exercises, Decision Case Exercises)
- Flashcards (glossary terms in Flash format)

Preface

▶ A Team Approach: Built by Professors and Students, for Professors and Students

Over the past three years Houghton Mifflin has conducted research and focus groups with a diverse cross-section of professors and students from across the country to create the first textbook series that truly reflects what professors and students want and need in an educational product. Everything we have learned has been applied to create and build a brand new educational experience and product model, from the ground up, for our two very important customer bases. *Student Achievement Series: Foundations of Management* is based on extensive professor and student feedback and is specifically designed to meet the teaching needs of today's instructors as well as the learning, study, and assessment goals of today's students. Professors and students have been involved with every key decision regarding this new product development model and learning system—from content structure, to design, to packaging, to the title of the textbook, and even to marketing and messaging. Professors have also played an integral role as content advisers through their reviews, creative ideas, and contributions to this new textbook.

It has long been a Houghton Mifflin tradition and honor to partner closely with professors to gain valuable insights and recommendations during the development process. Partnering equally as closely with students through the entire product development and product launch process has also proved to be extremely gratifying and productive.

▶ What Students Told Us

Working closely with students has been both rewarding and enlightening. Their honest and candid feedback and their practical and creative ideas have helped us to develop an educational learning model like no other on the market today.

Students have told us many things. While price is important to them, they are just as interested in having a textbook that reflects the way they actually learn and study. As with other consumer purchases and decisions they make, they want a textbook that is of true value to them. *Student Achievement Series: Foundations of Management* accomplishes both of their primary goals: it provides them with a price-conscious textbook, and it presents the concepts in a way that pleases them.

Today's students are busy individuals. They go to school, they work, some have families, they have a wide variety of interests, and they are involved in many activities. They take their education very seriously. Their main goal is to master the materials so they can perform well in class, get a good grade, graduate, land a good job, and be successful.

Different students learn in different ways; some learn best by reading, some are more visually oriented, and some learn best by doing through practice and assessment. While students learn in different ways, almost all students told us the same things regarding what they want their textbook to "look like." The ideal textbook for students gets to the point quickly, is easy to understand and read, has fewer and/or shorter chapters, has pedagogical materials designed to reinforce key concepts, has a strong supporting website for quizzing, testing, and assessment of materials, is cost conscious, and provides them with real value for their dollar.

Students want smaller chunks of information rather than the long sections and paragraphs found in traditional textbooks. This format provides them with immediate reinforcement and allows them to assess the concepts they have just studied. They like to read materials in more bulleted formats that are easier to digest than long sections and paragraphs. They almost always pay special attention to key terms and any materials that are boldfaced or highlighted in the text. In general, they spend little time reading or looking at materials that they view as superficial, such as many of the photographs (although they want some photos for visual enhancement) and boxed materials. However, they do want a textbook that is visually interesting, holds their interest, and is designed in an open, friendly, and accessible format. They want integrated study and assessment materials that help them reinforce, master, and test their knowledge of key concepts. They also want integrated Web and technology components that focus on quizzing and provide them with an interactive place to go to for help and assessment. They don't want Web sites that simply repeat the textual information in the book or that provide superficial information that is not primary to the key concepts in the text.

While students learn and study in a variety of different ways, a number of students told us that they often attend class first to hear their professor lecture and to take notes. Then they go back to read the chapter after (not always before) class. They use their textbook in this fashion to not only get the information they need but to also reinforce what they have learned in class. Students told us that they study primarily by using index or flashcards that highlight key concepts and terms, by reading lecture notes, and by using the supporting book Web site for quizzing and testing of key concepts. They also told us that they are far more likely to purchase and use a textbook if their professor actively uses the textbook in class and tells them that they need it.

▶ TAKING WHAT PROFESSORS AND STUDENTS TOLD US TO CREATE *Student Achievement Series: Foundations of Management*

Student Achievement Series: Foundations of Management provides exactly what students want and need pedagogically in an educational product. While other textbooks on the market include some of these features, the *Student Achievement Series* gives us the first textbooks to fully incorporate all of these cornerstones, as well as to introduce innovative new learning methods and study processes that completely meet the wishes of today's students. It does this by:

▮ Being concise and to the point

▮ Presenting more content in bulleted or more succinct formats

▮ Highlighting and boldfacing key concepts and information

▮ Organizing content in more bite-size and chunked-up formats

▮ Providing a system for immediate reinforcement and assessment of materials throughout the chapter

▪ Creating a design that is open, user friendly, and interesting for today's students

▪ Developing a supporting and integrated Web component that focuses on quizzing and assessment of key concepts

▪ Eliminating or reducing traditional chapter components that students view as superficial

▪ Creating a product that is easier for students to read and study

▪ Providing students with a price-conscious product

▪ Providing students with a product they feel is valuable

When we asked students to compare a chapter from this new learning model to chapters from traditional competing textbooks, students overwhelmingly rated this new product model as far superior. In one focus group, ten students were asked to rank each "blind" chapter on a scale from 1 to 5, with 5 being the highest mark. The *Student Achievement Series* received six 5's, while three competing books collectively received two 5's. Students told us that the Student Achievement Series is "very valuable," is "easier to read and easier to study from," is "more modern," and is "more of what [they] want in a text."

▶ PROFESSORS AND STUDENTS: WE COULDN'T HAVE DONE IT WITHOUT YOU

We are very grateful to all the students across the country who participated in one form or another in helping us to create and build the first educational product pedagogically designed specifically for them and their learning and educational goals. Working with these students was an honor, as well as a lot of fun, for all of us at Houghton Mifflin. We sincerely appreciate their honesty, candor, creativeness, and interest in helping us to develop a better learning experience. We also appreciate their willingness to meet with us for lengthy periods of time and to allow us to videotape them and use some of their excellent quotes. We wish them much success as they complete their college education, begin their careers, and go about their daily lives.

STUDENT PARTICIPANTS

Acosta, Pricilla, *University of Texas at Brownsville*
Aiken, Katie, *Miami University*
Albert, Chris, *California State University, Sacramento*
Allen, Laura, *Carroll College*
Araujo, Javier H., *University of Texas at Brownsville*
Arreola, Jose, *University of Texas at Brownsville*
Back, Hillary, *James Madison University*
Barrett, O'Neil, *Borough of Manhattan Community College*
Barron, Joe, *Providence College*
Beal, Laura, *Miami University*
Belle, JaLisha Elaine, *Adrian College, MI*
Bis, Ryan, *Boston University*

Brantley, Gerius, *Florida Atlantic University*
Brewster, Angie, *Boston College*
Brez, Cyleigh, *Miami University*
Bruss, Joy, *Carroll College*
Buchholz, Mike, *James Madison University*
Butters, Amy, *Carroll College*
Calvo, Veronica, *Keiser College*
Campbell, Jessy, *James Madison University*
Chester, Elaine, *Columbus Technical College*
Chimento, Kristin, *Miami University*
Coker, Nadine, *Columbus Technical College*
Connolly, Catie, *Anna Marie College*
Cooper, Angelique, *DePaul University*
Counihan, Mallory, *James Madison University*

Day, Brian, *Georgia State University*
Delaney-Winn, Adam, *Tufts University*
Denton, Justin, *California State University, Sacramento*
DiSerio, Stephanie, *Miami University*
Diz, Rita, *Lehman College*
Dolcemascolo, Christine, *California State University, Sacramento*
Dolehide, Maggie, *Miami University*
Dripps, Matthew, *Miami University*
Duran, Gabriel, *Florida International University*
Espinoza, Giovanni, *Hunter College*
Fahrenbach, Tanya, *Benedictine University*
Faridi, Muneeza, *Georgia State University*
Fischer, Christina, *University of Illinois at Chicago*
Fleming, Linda, *Columbus Technical College*
Frazier, Sharita, *Georgia State University*
Gabri, Holli, *Adrian College, MI*
Gagnon, Danielle, *Boston University*
Gamez, Iris, *University of Texas at Brownsville*
Garza, Brenda, *University of Texas at Brownsville*
Glater, Paulina, *DePaul University*
Gonzalez, Donna, *Florida International University*
Goulet, Michelle, *Carroll College*
Greenbaum, Barry, *Cooper Union*
Griffis, Jill, *Carroll College*
Hall, Rachel, *Miami University*
Harris, Emma, *Miami University*
Hill, Erika, *University of Florida*
Hoff, Joe, *University of Wisconsin–LaCrosse*
Hooser, Ginny, *Western Illinois University*
Huang, Jin, *Georgia State University*
Janko, Matt, *University of Massachusetts–Amherst*
Johnson, Stella, *Columbus Technical College*
Keltner, Travis, *Boston College*
Khan, Javed, *University of Central Florida*
Knowles, Mary, *University of Central Florida*
Konigsberg, Matthew, *Baruch University*
Krouse, Molly, *James Madison University*
Kuhnlenz, Fritz, *Boston University*
Lambalot, Lindsey, *Northeastern University*
Largent, Thomas, *Adrian College, MI*
Lee, Cheng, *University of Wisconsin–LaCrosse*
Lippi, Steven, *Boston College*
Lopez, Henry, *Florida International University*
Ly, Bryant, *Georgia State University*
Lynch, Jessie, *Miami University*
Mancia, Mario, *Georgia State University*
Marcous, Michael, *University of Central Florida*
Marith, Sarah, *Boston University*

Marshall, Nichole, *Columbus Technical College*
Mavros, Nichelina, *Fordham University*
McLean, Chad, *California State University, Sacramento*
McNamara, Meghan, *California State University, Sacramento*
Medina, Jose A., *University of Texas at Brownsville*
Michalos, Marika, *City College of New York*
Miller, Evan, *Parsons School of Design*
Monzon, Fernando, *Miami Dade College*
Nitka, Matt, *University of Wisconsin–LaCrosse*
Noormohammad, Rehan, *Northeastern Illinois University*
Offinger, Caitlin, *Amherst College*
Ortiz, Laura, *University of Texas at Brownsville*
Paredes, Idalia, *University of Texas at Brownsville*
Paruin, John, *Adrian College, MI*
Queen, Durrell, *University of New York*
Rayski, Adrienne, *Baruch University*
Rederstorf, Melonie, *Adrian College, MI*
Regan, Rosanna, *Western Illinois University*
Ringel, Kevin, *Northwestern University*
Rodriguez, Juan F., *University of Texas at Brownsville*
Rodriguez, Uadira, *University of Texas at Brownsville*
Savery, Alison, *Tufts University*
Schaffner, Laura, *Miami University*
Schiller, Raquel, *University of Central Florida*
Schlutal, Aubrey, *James Madison University*
Silgvero, Jesus Javier, *University of Texas at Brownsville*
Silva, Miriam, *University of Texas at Brownsville*
Simkovi, Jordan, *Northwestern University*
Smith, Christine, *James Madison University*
Smith, Karl, *Western Illinois University*
Staley, Ahmad, *Columbus Technical College*
Stenzler, Michael, *University of Central Florida*
Stondal, Adam, *Adrian College, MI*
Teekah, Karissa, *Lehman College*
Thermitus, Patrick, *Bentley College*
Toft, Gregory, *Baruch University*
Tolles, Rebecca, *Miami University*
Tran, Vivi, *University of Central Florida*
Trzyzewski, Sam, *Boston University*
Uribe, Vanessa, *Florida International University*
Vayda, Kristin, *Miami University*
Werner, Michael, *Baruch University*
White, Robert, *DePaul University*
Williams, Jen, *Carroll College*
Wong, Helen, *Hunter College*
Yusuf, Aliyah, *Lehman College*
525 Students in MKTG 431: Principles of Marketing, San Francisco State University

We are equally grateful to all the professors across the country who participated in the development and creation of this new textbook through content reviews, advisory boards, and/or focus group work regarding the new pedagogical learning system. As always, professors provided us with invaluable information, ideas, and suggestions that consistently helped to strengthen our final product. We owe them great thanks and wish them much success in and out of their classrooms.

PROFESSOR PARTICIPANTS AND REVIEWERS

Blakely, Malika, *Georgia State University*
Boeckelman, Keith, *Western Illinois University*
Brown, Paula E., *Northern Illinois University*
Eliason, Robert, *James Madison University*
Fine, Terri Susan, *University of Central Florida*
Fisher, Bruce, *Elmhurst College*
Fox, Mark, *Indiana University South Bend*
Hensley, Kermelle, *Columbus Technical College*
Hladik, Paula, *Waubonsie Community College*
Nalder, Kimberly Love, *California State University, Sacramento*
McConnel, Lisa, *Oklahoma State University*
Peterson, Suzanne, *Arizona State University*
Schultz, Debbie, *Carroll College*
Silver, Gerald, *Purdue University–Calumet*
Thannert, Nancy, *Robert Morris College*
Thomas, Ron, *Oakton Community College*
Thompson, Kenneth, *DePaul University*
Weeks, Benjamin, *St. Xavier University*

▶ A WORD FROM THE AUTHOR

These are challenging and exciting times for all of us. Especially so for managers. Changes are many and varied. A global economy in which world-class quality is the ticket to ride, increased diversity in the work force, the proliferation of technology and e-business, and demands for more ethical conduct promise to keep things interesting. As trustees of society's precious human, material, financial, and informational resources, today's and tomorrow's managers hold the key to a better world. A solid grounding in management is essential to successfully guiding large or small, profit or nonprofit organizations in the twenty-first century. *Student Achievement Series: Foundations of Management,* First Edition, represents an important step toward managerial and personal success. It is a complete, up-to-date, and highly readable introduction to the field of management. This book reflects my thirty years in management classrooms and management development seminars around the world. Its style and content have been shaped by interaction with thousands of students, instructors, reviewers, and managers. All have taught me valuable lessons about organizational life, management, and people in general. *Foundations of Management* integrates classical and modern concepts with a rich array of contemporary real-world examples, cases, exercises, and insightful features.

▶ AN EFFECTIVE TEACHING AND LEARNING PACKAGE

FOR INSTRUCTORS:

- *Online Instructor's Resource Manual.* This resource includes chapter objectives, opening case interpretations, lecture outlines, solutions for the closing cases, and discussion questions for each chapter, as well as learning tools that help faculty expand on the text material. Types of learning tools may include issue expansions, decision cases, cooperative learning tools, and appropriate transparency masters.

- *Online Test Bank.* The Test Bank includes close to 2,000 true-false, multiple-choice, and short answer essay questions. Each question is identified by its corresponding learning objective, estimated level of difficulty, page number, and question type (fact or application). This Test Bank is available on the instructor Web site and course management platforms (BlackBoard/WebCT).

- *DVD.* An expanded video program accompanies the text. Each chapter has its own video designed to illustrate the concepts discussed in the chapter by applying the discussion of the text to real-world case examples. The segments are designed to be shown in the classroom to generate discussion. The video guide for instructors can be found on the instructor Web site and course management platforms (BlackBoard/WebCT).

- *HMTesting™ Instructor CD.* This CD contains electronic Test Bank items. Through a partnership with the Brownstone Research Group, HMTesting—now powered by *Diploma*™—provides instructors with all the tools they need to create, author/edit, customize, and deliver multiple types of tests. Instructors can import questions directly from the Test Bank, create their own questions, or edit existing algorithmic questions, all within *Diploma*'s powerful electronic platform.

- *Online Teaching Center.* This text-based instructor Web site offers valuable resources, including basic and premium PowerPoint slides, downloadable Instructor's Resource Manual files, a video guide, classroom response system content, and much more.

- *BlackBoard®/WebCT®.* This online course management system, powered by BlackBoard, contains Instructor's Resource Manual files, Test Bank pools, a video guide, classroom response system content, video segments, quizzes, discussion threads, basic and premium PowerPoint slides, audio chapter summaries and quizzes (MP3s), homework, and much more.

FOR STUDENTS:

- *Online Study Center.* This text-specific student Web site offers non-passkey protected content such as ACE practice tests, visual glossary terms, career snapshots, outlines, summaries, glossaries (chapter-based and complete), and much more. Content behind "Your Guide to an 'A'" passkey includes ACE+ quizzes, Flashcards, *Study Guide to Go* content, and audio chapter reviews (MP3 chapter summaries and quizzes).

▶ **ACKNOWLEDGMENTS**

Countless students, teachers, colleagues, managers, writers, friends, and relatives all have shaped how I perceive management theory and practice. They, collectively, are the real driving force behind this book. I am grateful for the lessons they have taught me. Thank you so much to M.T. Alabbassi (University of North Florida), Michael Drafke (College of DuPage), Mark G. Fenton (University of Wisconsin, Stout), Leatrice T. Freer (Pitt Community College), Linda Hefferin (Elgin Community College), Valorie Marschall (Spokane Falls Community College), Daniel James Rowley (University of Northern Colorado), G. David Sivak (Westmoreland County Community College), Robert L. Stephens (Macon State), Ray Sumners (Westwood College of Technology), Sean Valentine (University of Wyoming), and Elizabeth White (Orange County Community College). Thank you also to Maria Muto for her contributions to the Instructor's Resource Manual and Carmen Powers (Monroe Community College) for her fine work on the supplements program for this text.

My 32-year partnership with Houghton Mifflin through the years has been productive and enjoyable. I would like to offer a hearty thank you by acknowledging the following key contributors: George Hoffman, Lisé Johnson, Joanne Dauksewicz, Nancy Blodget, Nicole Harris, and Damaris Curran, as well as Stacy Shearer of Xplana Learning.

To Margaret—my wife, best friend, and hiking buddy—thank you for being my center of gravity and for being the wise "first reader" of every page. Our long and durable marriage is indeed a treasure. I also appreciate the attentive supervision in my home office by our two cats, Yahoo and Sweetie Pie. Finally, I would like to thank the thousands of introductory management students I have had the pleasure of working with through the years for teaching me a great deal about tomorrow's managers. Best wishes for a rewarding career in management.

Bob Kreitner

Foundations of Management
Basics and Best Practices

Today's Managers and Entrepreneurs

Tracy Reese is a successful entrepreneur because she has a clear vision of what she wants and is "willing to do whatever is necessary."

1 *Define the term* management *and explain the managerial significance of the terms* effectiveness *and* efficiency.

2 *Identify and briefly explain the eight managerial functions.*

3 *Explain how managers learn to manage.*

Everybody's path is their own. And we all have hurdles to overcome."

—Tracy Reese, Fashion designer and entrepreneur

Chapter Outline

Online Study Center
Prepare for Class
Chapter Outline

4 ▶ *Challenge two myths about small businesses and describe entrepreneurs.*

Tracy Reese Has the Right Design for Both Fashion and Success

Fashion is a bumpy industry. We started out nine years ago, and when we got a huge order from a store, we would all look at each other and say, "Oh, no, how are we going to produce this?" We knew our production facilities were limited and sort of old school. We had to embrace success more, and not be afraid to go forward.

At the beginning, it was very grass roots. I was doing everything myself, making samples and working out of an apartment in Harlem with a sewing machine. I had a freelance patternmaker who would come up to my apartment and work with me during the day. Some days I didn't have train fare, and I would walk 60 blocks back and forth from home and work, or eat ramen noodles for dinner. I've definitely had my phones cut off, electricity, you name it. It was always that choice: do I buy my buttons or do I pay this phone bill?

Online Study Center college.hmco.com/pic/kreitnerSASfound

I started my first company with my dad's money that he raised. I was 23 years old, and it was actually his suggestion. He said, "You've got to do your own thing." That had never honestly crossed my mind. I was happy working for another company and learning the business. He wanted me to have freedom because I don't think he ever really did. He always had to provide, working for Chrysler as a plant manager.

I probably lead by example more than anything. Though I'm not great at it, I've learned to delegate more over the years. But I like knowing that I know how to do those tasks that I'm asking others to do. People at my company know that I'm willing to do whatever is necessary. And I hope as they go down the road, they feel capable of attacking all kinds of situations for themselves.

There are any number of potential things that you can let hold you back, or you can persevere. I choose not to focus on whether or not the industry embraces black people. If I went around every day thinking, I'm not getting attention because I'm black, I wouldn't get anywhere. Everybody's path is their own. And we all have hurdles to overcome.

I think if you talk to most designers in business today, they've been out of business probably more than once. But if it's what you're meant to do, if it's what you desire, you find a way to get back. Fashion is fickle. You're in one minute; you're out the next. And in the moment, you're fragile. But each little setback gives you an opportunity to come back strong.

I'm not looking at today, thinking, "Wow, look at what we've achieved." It probably wouldn't hurt me to enjoy that more, but I'm in a business where everything is about "tomorrow."[1] ■

Tracy Reese is an inspiring example of a modern manager in action. Her overriding goal is to do whatever it takes to achieve her organization's mission in a highly competitive world. Relative to our present challenge to learn more about management, Tracy's story underscores four key realities of managing today:

1. The only certainty today is *change.* Challenging *goals* motivate people to strive for improvement and overcome obstacles and resistance to change.
2. *Speed, teamwork,* and *flexibility* are the orders of the day, from both strategic and operational standpoints. Managers need to be vigilant for *unexpected opportunities,* exploiting them promptly and wisely.
3. Managers at all levels in both small and large organizations need to stay close to the *customer.* Product/service *quality* is the driving force in the battle to stay competitive.
4. Without *continuous improvement* and *lifelong learning,* there can be no true economic progress for individuals and organizations alike.

Keep these managerial realities in mind as you explore the world of management in this text.

Every one of us—whether as an employee, a customer, a stockholder, or a member of the surrounding community—has a direct stake in the quality of management. Joan Magretta, a management consultant who went on to become an editor at *Harvard Business Review,* recently offered this perspective:

Management's business is building organizations that work. Underneath all the theory and the tools, underneath all the specialized knowledge, lies a commitment to performance that has powerfully altered our economy and our lives. That, ultimately, is why management is everyone's business.[2]

In fact, bad management is a major source of stress and a serious threat to our quality of life.[3]

Effective management is the key to a better world, but mismanagement squanders our resources and jeopardizes our well-being. Every manager, regardless of level or scope of responsibility, is either part of the solution or part of the problem. Management or mismanagement—the choice is yours. A basic knowledge of management theory, research, and practice will help prepare you for productive and gainful employment in a highly organized world in which virtually everything is managed.

MANAGEMENT DEFINED

 Define the term management *and explain the managerial significance of the terms* effectiveness *and* efficiency.

We now need to define management, in order to highlight the importance, relevance, and necessity of studying it. **Management** is the process of working with and through others to achieve organizational objectives in a changing environment. Central to this process is the effective and efficient use of limited resources.

Five components of this definition require closer examination:

1. Working with and through others
2. Achieving organizational objectives
3. Balancing effectiveness and efficiency
4. Making the most of limited resources
5. Coping with a changing environment (see Figure 1.1 on page 6)

management   The process of working with and through others to achieve organizational objectives in a changing environment.

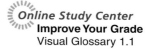
Online Study Center
Improve Your Grade
Visual Glossary 1.1

Working with and Through Others

Management is, above all else, a social process. Many collective purposes bring individuals together—writing software, building cars, providing emergency health care, publishing books, and on and on. But in all cases, managers are responsible for getting things done by working with and through others.

Aspiring managers who do not interact well with others hamper their careers. This was the conclusion two experts reached following interviews with 62 executives from the United States, United Kingdom, Belgium, Spain, France, Germany, and Italy. Each of the executives was asked to describe two managers whose careers had been *derailed*. Derailed managers were those who had not lived up to their peers' and superiors' high expectations. The derailed managers reportedly had these shortcomings:

▮ Problems with interpersonal relationships

▮ Failure to meet business objectives

▮ Failure to build and lead a team

▮ Inability to change and adapt during a transition[4]

FIGURE 1.1

Key Aspects of the Management Process

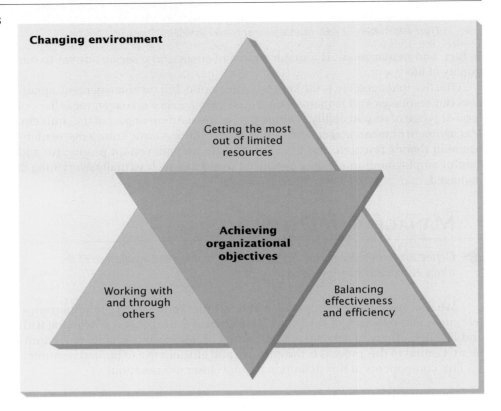

Significantly, the first and third shortcomings involve failure to work effectively with and through others. The derailed managers experienced a number of interpersonal problems; among other things, they were perceived as manipulative, abusive, untrustworthy, demeaning, overly critical, not team players, and poor communicators.

Even managers who make it all the way to the top often have interpersonal problems, according to management consultant Richard Hagberg. His study of 511 chief executive officers led to this conclusion about why managers often fail to inspire loyalty in employees:

> *Many are also hobbled by self-importance, which keeps them from hearing feedback about their own strengths and weaknesses. The head of one large company recently told me about an incident that occurred as he and his wife waited in line to get his driver's license renewed. He was frustrated at how long it was taking and grumbled to his wife, "I have a lot to do. Don't they know who I am?" She replied, "Yeah, you're a plumber's son who got lucky." Her remark really got to him. It drove home how far he had gotten caught up in his sense of self-importance.[5]*

Arrogance, it turns out, is the "kiss of death" when attempting to get things done with and through others. The challenge is to be competent and confident without being arrogant about it.[6]

"When asked to describe their role, new managers typically focus on the rights and privileges that come with being boss. . . . [They] face a rude awakening. . . . They are enmeshed in a web of relationships—not only with subordinates but also with bosses, peers, and others inside and outside the organization, all of whom make relentless and often conflicting demands on them. The resulting daily routine is pressured, hectic, and fragmented."

Source: Linda A. Hill, "Becoming the Boss," *Harvard Business Review,* 85 (January 2007): 51–52.

Question: How willing and able are you to become a manager?

Achieving Organizational Objectives

An objective is a target to be strived for and, one hopes, attained. Like individuals, organizations are usually more successful when their activities are guided by challenging, yet achievable, objectives. From an individual perspective, scheduling a college course load becomes more systematic and efficient when a student sets an objective, such as graduating with a specific degree by a given date.

Although personal objectives are typically within the reach of individual effort, organizational objectives or goals always require collective action. For example, it took more than 10,000 Microsoft Corp. employees five years to create Vista, the Windows operating system launched in 2007.[7]

Organizational objectives also serve later as measuring sticks for performance. Without organizational objectives, the management process, like a trip without a specific destination, would be aimless and wasteful.

Balancing Effectiveness and Efficiency

Distinguishing between effectiveness and efficiency is much more than an exercise in semantics. The relationship between these two terms is important, and it presents managers with a never-ending dilemma. **Effectiveness** entails achieving a stated objective in a timely manner. **Efficiency** enters the picture when the resources required to achieve an objective are weighed against what was actually accomplished. The more favorable the ratio of benefits to costs, the greater the efficiency.

Managers are responsible for balancing effectiveness and efficiency (see Figure 1.2 on page 8). Too much emphasis in either direction leads to mismanagement. On the one hand, managers must be effective by getting the job done.

On the other hand, managers need to be efficient by reducing costs and not wasting resources. Of course, managers who are too stingy with resources may fall short of their objective.

At the heart of the quest for *productivity improvement* (a favorable ratio between inputs and output) is the constant struggle to balance effectiveness and efficiency.[8] Consider how American Airlines stays competitive by studiously managing costs:

> *A big cost is the cost of fuel. American Airlines jets now taxi on one engine instead of two. They figured out how much water (for sinks and toilets) they need per passenger and don't fill the tank as much so planes are lighter. Flying lighter planes saves more than $200 million a year. Just taking magazines off planes, over the course of a year, saves $3 million.*[9]

effectiveness A central element in the process of management that entails achieving a stated organizational objective in a timely manner.

efficiency A central element in the process of management that balances the amount of resources used to achieve an objective against what was actually accomplished.

Making the Most of Limited Resources

We live in a world of scarcity. Those who are concerned with such matters worry not only about running out of nonrenewable energy and material resources but also about the lopsided use of those resources. The United States, for example, with about 5 percent of the world's population, is currently consuming about 25 percent of the world's annual oil production and generating 25 percent of the greenhouse gases linked to global warming.[10]

Although experts and nonexperts alike may quibble over exactly how long it will take to exhaust our nonrenewable resources or come up with exotic new technological alternatives, one bold fact remains. Our planet is becoming increasingly crowded.

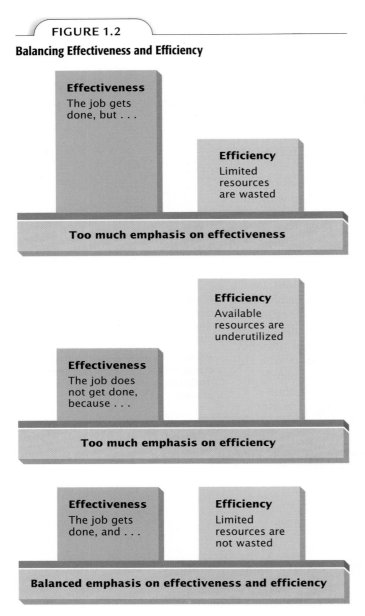

FIGURE 1.2

Balancing Effectiveness and Efficiency

Effectiveness
The job gets
done, but . . .

Efficiency
Limited
resources
are wasted

Too much emphasis on effectiveness

Efficiency
Available
resources are
underutilized

Effectiveness
The job does
not get done,
because . . .

Too much emphasis on efficiency

Effectiveness
The job gets
done, and . . .

Efficiency
Limited
resources are
not wasted

Balanced emphasis on effectiveness and efficiency

Demographers who collect and study population statistics tell us the Earth's human population is growing by 203,024 every day and 6.2 million every month.[11] The present world population of more than 6.5 billion people is projected to reach 9 billion within 70 years. Meanwhile, our planet's carrying capacity is open to speculation.[12] (For up-to-the-minute global and U.S. population statistics, go to www.census.gov/main/www/popclock.html.)

Approximately 83 percent of the world's population in the year 2020 will live in relatively poor and less-developed countries. Developed and industrialized nations, consequently, will experience increasing pressure to divide the limited resource pie more equitably.[13]

Because of their common focus on resources, economics and management are closely related. Economics is the study of how limited resources are distributed among alternative uses. In productive organizations, managers are the trustees of limited resources, and it is their job to see that the basic factors of production—land, labor, and capital—are used efficiently as well as effectively. Management could be called "applied economics."

Coping with a Changing Environment

Successful managers are the ones who anticipate and adjust to changing circumstances rather than being passively swept along or caught unprepared. Employers today are hiring managers who can take unfamiliar situations in stride. *Business Week* recently served up this amusing but challenging profile of tomorrow's managers: "The next generation of corporate leaders will need the charm of a debutante, the flexibility of a gymnast, and the quickness of a panther. A few foreign languages and a keen understanding of technology won't hurt either."[14] Also in the mix are a sense of humor, passion, and the ability to make fast decisions. Chapter 2 provides detailed coverage of important changes and trends in management's social, political-legal, economic, and technological environments. At this point, it is instructive to preview major changes for managers doing business in the twenty-first century (see Table 1.1). This particular collection of changes is the product of five overarching sources of change: globalization, the evolution of product quality, environmentalism, an ethical reawakening, and the Internet revolution. Together, these factors are significantly reshaping the practice of management.

Globalization

Figuratively speaking, the globe is shrinking in almost every conceivable way. Networks of transportation, communication, computers, music, and economics have tied the people of the world together as never before. Companies are having to become global players just to survive, let alone prosper. Here are some striking examples:

TABLE 1.1

The Twenty-First Century Manager: Ten Major Changes

	Moving away from	Moving toward
Administrative role	Boss/superior/leader	Team member/facilitator/teacher/sponsor/advocate/coach
Cultural orientation	Monocultural/monolingual	Multicultural/multilingual
Quality/ethics/environmental impacts	Afterthought (or no thought)	Forethought (unifying themes)
Power bases	Formal authority; rewards and punishments	Knowledge; relationships; rewards
Primary organizational unit	Individual	Team
Interpersonal dealings	Competition; win-lose	Cooperation; win-win
Learning	Periodic (preparatory; curriculum-driven)	Continuous (lifelong; learner-driven)
Problems	Threats to be avoided	Opportunities for learning and continuous improvement
Change and conflict	Resist/react/avoid	Anticipate/seek/channel
Information	Restrict access/hoard	Increase access/share

▌ McDonald's "is the leading global foodservice retailer with more than 30,000 local restaurants serving nearly 50 million people in more than 119 countries each day according to its Web site."[15]

▌ Coca-Cola earns 76 percent of its operating profits from customers outside the United States.[16]

▌ The United States currently imports about 60 percent of its oil, with a higher percentage forecasted.[17]

▌ On the export side, 3M, the maker of Scotch tape and Post-it notes, rings up more than half its sales outside the United States.[18]

On the negative side is the controversial practice of **offshoring**, the outsourcing of jobs from developed countries to lower-wage countries. This practice has been going on for decades. Hundreds of thousands of jobs in the textile, steel, and consumer electronics industries are long gone from the United States, and call-center jobs are going fast. Thanks to the broadband Internet, skilled jobs in areas such as computer hardware and software engineering, architecture, tax return preparation, and medical diagnosis are being outsourced to well-educated workers in India, China, the Philippines, and Russia. A recent study puts the situation in perspective:

offshoring Controversial practice of sending jobs to lower-wage countries.

> Meta Group Inc., a Stamford, Conn., consulting and research firm, says the outsourcing trend will grow by 20 percent per year through 2008 as more U.S. firms focus on cutting labor costs. Meta estimates that 60 percent of U.S. firms will send some technology work abroad by 2008....
>
> "In the bigger picture, one job gain in India does not relate to one job in the United States," said Stan Lepeak of Meta Group.

"The United States might employ fewer programmers here, but it will employ more managers and a variety of other new roles will be created to manage these new relationships."[19]

Conclusion: A good education and marketable skills are the best insurance against having your job offshored to a foreign country. Also, some worry about giant global corporations eclipsing the economic and political power of individual nations and their citizens. Indeed, the annual revenue of Exxon (about $340 billion in 2005) exceeds the gross national product of many countries around the world.

Today's model manager is one who is comfortable transacting business in multiple languages and cultures. There is a rapidly growing army of global managers from all corners of the world, and you can become a member of it through diligent effort and a strong need for personal growth. Chapter 4 is devoted to the topic of international management. The internationally oriented cases and Best Practices features throughout the text are intended to broaden your awareness of international management and cross-cultural dealings.

The Evolution of Product Quality

Managers have been interested in the quality of their products, at least as an afterthought, since the Industrial Revolution. But thanks to U.S. and Japanese quality gurus such as W. Edwards Deming and Kaoru Ishikawa (more about them in Appendix A at **college.hmco.com/pic/kreitnerSASfound**), product/service quality has become both a forethought and a driving force in effective organizations of all kinds. Today's hospitals, hotels, universities, and government agencies are as interested in improving product/service quality as are factories, mines, airlines, and railroads.

In its most basic terms, the emphasis on quality has evolved through four distinct stages since World War II—from "fix it in" to "inspect it in" to "build it in" to "design it in." Progressive managers are moving away from the first two approaches and toward the build-it-in and design-it-in approaches.[20] Here are the key differences:

- *The fix-it-in approach to quality.* Rework any defective products identified by quality inspectors at the end of the production process.

- *The inspect-it-in approach to quality.* Have quality inspectors sample work in process and prescribe machine adjustments to avoid substandard output.

- *The build-it-in approach to quality.* Make *everyone* who touches the product responsible for spotting and correcting defects. Emphasis is on identifying and eliminating *causes* of quality problems.

- *The design-it-in approach to quality.* Intense customer and employee involvement drives the entire design-production cycle. Emphasis is on *continuous improvement* of personnel, processes, and product.

Notice how each stage of this evolution has broadened the responsibility for quality, turning quality improvement into a true team effort. Also, the focus has shifted from reactively fixing product defects to proactively working to prevent them and to satisfying the customer completely. Today's quality leaders strive to exceed, not just meet, the customer's expectations.

A popular label for the build-it-in and design-it-in approaches to quality is *total quality management* (TQM). TQM is discussed in detail in Chapter 8.

Environmentalism

Environmental issues such as deforestation; global warming; depletion of the ozone layer; toxic waste; and pollution of land, air, and water are no longer strictly the domain of campus radicals. Mainstream politicians and managers around the world have picked up the environmental banner. The so-called green movement has spawned successful political parties in Europe and is gaining a foothold in North America and elsewhere. Managers are challenged to develop creative ways to make a profit without unduly harming the environment in the process. Terms such as *industrial ecology* and *eco-efficiency* are heard today under the general umbrella of sustainable development.[21]

Also, cleaning up the environment promises to generate whole new classes of jobs and robust profits in the future. The debate over jobs versus the environment has been rendered obsolete by the need for both a healthy economy *and* a healthy environment. Authors William McDonough and Michael Braungart, while calling for a new industrial revolution, recently offered this fresh new perspective:

> *We see a world of abundance, not limits. In the midst of a great deal of talking about reducing the human ecological footprint, we offer a different vision. What if humans designed products and systems that celebrate an abundance of human creativity, culture, and productivity? That are so intelligent and safe, our species leaves an ecological footprint to delight in, not lament?*
>
> *Consider this: All the ants on the planet, taken together, have a biomass greater than that of humans. Ants have been incredibly industrious for millions of years. Yet their productiveness nourishes plants, animals, and soil. Human industry has been in full swing for little over a century, yet it has brought about a decline in almost every ecosystem on the planet. Nature doesn't have a design problem. People do.*[22]

Encouragingly, researchers recently found 80 percent higher stock market valuations for multinational corporations adhering to strict environmental standards,

Source: By Mike Thompson

compared with those taking advantage of the lax environmental standards often found in less-developed countries.[23] In short, investors tend to reward "clean" companies and punish "dirty" ones.

An Ethical Reawakening

Managers are under strong pressure from the public, elected officials, and respected managers to behave better. This pressure has resulted from disturbing headlines about discrimination, illegal campaign contributions, accounting fraud, price fixing, insider trading, the selling of unsafe products, and other unethical practices. The results of a Gallup poll indicate how bad things had gotten by 2003: "just 17 percent of Americans give execs high marks for honesty and ethics,"[24] a 32 percent drop from the year before.

Ethics and honesty are everyone's concern: *yours, mine,* and *ours.* Every day we have countless opportunities to be honest or dishonest. One survey of more than 4,000 employees uncovered the following ethical problems in the workplace (the percentage of employees observing the problem during the past year appears in parentheses):

- Lying to supervisors (56 percent)
- Lying on reports or falsifying records (41 percent)
- Stealing and theft (35 percent)
- Sexual harassment (35 percent)
- Abusing drugs or alcohol (31 percent)
- Conflict of interest (31 percent)[25]

Because of closer public scrutiny, ethical questions can no longer be shoved aside as irrelevant. The topic of managerial ethics is covered in depth in Chapter 3.

The Internet and E-Business Revolution

Like a growing child, the Internet first crawled, then walked, then ran too fast and fell, and now is running more wisely. In concept, the Internet began as a U.S. Department of Defense (DOD) research project during the Cold War era of the 1960s. The plan was to give university scientists a quick and inexpensive way to share their DOD research data. Huge technical problems such as getting incompatible computers to communicate in a fail-safe network were solved in 1969 at UCLA when researchers succeeded in getting two linked computers to exchange data. The Internet was born. Other universities were added to the Internet during the 1970s, and gradually applications such as e-mail emerged. By 1983, technology made it possible to share complex documents and graphics on the Internet, and the World Wide Web came into existence.[26] Time passed and improvements were made. During the early 1990s, individuals and businesses began to log on to the "Web" to communicate via e-mail and to buy and sell things.

Internet   Global network of servers and personal and organizational computers.

Growth of the **Internet**—the worldwide network of personal computers, routers and switches, powerful servers, and organizational computer systems—has been explosive. No one owns the Web, and anyone with a computer modem can be part of it. Within its digital recesses are both trash and treasure. According to the *Computer Industry Almanac*, "The worldwide number of Internet users surpassed 1 billion in 2005—up from only 45M in 1995 and 420M in 2000. The 2 billion Internet users milestone is expected in 2011."[27] The implications of this massive interconnectedness for managers (and everyone else) are profound and truly revolutionary. Legal, ethical, security, and privacy issues, however, remain largely unresolved. New Web developments from the likes of Yahoo! and Google, MySpace and Facebook, and YouTube and others promise to keep things interesting.[28]

Following the dot-com crash of 2000–2001,[29] the e-business revolution is proceeding in a more measured way and with more realistic expectations.[30] Where their focus before the dot-com crash was primarily on business-to-consumer retailing, Internet strategists are now much more broadly focused. Thus, an **e-business** is one seeking efficiencies via the Internet in all basic business functions—production, marketing, and finance/accounting—and all support activities involving human, material, and financial resources. Craig Barrett, the chairman of Intel, the computer chip giant, explained how his firm evolved into what he calls an "Internet company":

e-business A business using the Internet for greater efficiency in every aspect of its operations.

> . . . for Intel, being an Internet company meant turning ourselves into a 100% e-business from front to back—not just in terms of selling and buying, but also in terms of information transfer, education, and customer interaction. We wanted to improve our competitiveness and our productivity, to streamline our internal operations, and to save some money. We also wanted to show that we can use the technology that we sell to the rest of the world.[31]

Aspects and implications of the Internet and e-business revolution are explored throughout this text, including a discussion of Internet strategy in Chapter 5.

Considering the variety of these sources of change in the general environment, managers are challenged to keep abreast of them and adjust and adapt as necessary.

TEST PREPPER 1.1

ANSWERS CAN BE FOUND ON P. 27

True or False?

_____ 1. A key component in the definition of the term *management* is achieving one's personal objectives.

_____ 2. Microsoft automatically qualifies as an "efficient" company if it launches a new product on time.

_____ 3. Globalization is one of the five overarching sources of change for today's managers.

_____ 4. The design-it-in approach to product quality is an out-of-date approach.

_____ 5. E-business involves performing all basic business functions and all organizational support activities on the Internet.

Online Study Center
ACE the Test
ACE Practice Tests 1.1

Multiple Choice

_____ 6. By definition, management is the process of _____ to achieve _____ in a changing environment.
   a. working effectively; key results
   b. solving problems; individual and collective goals
   c. planning; strategic goals
   d. working with and through others; organizational objectives
   e. operating efficiently; success

_____ 7. Researchers found which of these to be the number-one ethical problem in a survey of more than 4,000 employees?
   a. Stealing and theft
   b. Lying to supervisors
   c. Falsifying records
   d. Abusing drugs and alcohol
   e. Sexual harassment

WHAT DO MANAGERS DO?

 Identify and briefly explain the eight managerial functions.

Although nearly all aspects of modern life are touched at least indirectly by the work of managers, many people do not really understand what the management process involves. Management is much more, for example, than the familiar activity of telling employees what to do. Management is a complex and dynamic mixture of systematic techniques and common sense. As with any complex process, the key to learning about management lies in dividing it into readily understood pieces.

Managerial Functions

For nearly a century, the most popular approach to describing what managers do has been the functional view. It has been popular because it characterizes the management process as a sequence of rational and logical steps. **Managerial functions** are general administrative duties that need to be carried out in virtually all productive organizations. Henri Fayol, a French industrialist turned writer, became the father of the functional approach in 1916 when he identified five managerial functions: planning, organizing, command, coordination, and control.[32] Fayol claimed that these five functions were the common denominators of all managerial jobs, whatever the purpose of the organization. Over the years Fayol's original list of managerial functions has been updated and expanded by management scholars. This text, even though it is based on more than just Fayol's approach, is organized around eight different managerial functions: planning, decision making, organizing, staffing, communicating, motivating, leading, and controlling (see Figure 1.3). A brief overview of these eight managerial functions will describe what managers do and will preview what lies ahead in this text.

Planning

Commonly referred to as the primary management function, planning is the formulation of future courses of action. Plans and the objectives on which they are based give purpose and direction to the organization, its subunits, and contributing individuals.

Decision Making

Managers choose among alternative courses of action when they make decisions. Making intelligent and ethical decisions in today's complex world is a major management challenge.

Organizing

Structural considerations such as the chain of command, division of labor, and assignment of responsibility are part of the organizing function. Careful organizing helps ensure the efficient use of human resources.

Staffing

Organizations are only as good as the people in them. Staffing consists of recruiting, training, and developing people who can contribute to the organized effort.

Online Study Center
Improve Your Grade
Career Snapshot 1.1

managerial functions   General administrative duties that need to be carried out in virtually all productive organizations to achieve desired outcomes.

REALITY CHECK 1.3

In a study of 1,040 managers in 100 rapidly changing organizations, the two leading causes of managerial failure were: "Ineffective communication skills/practices" and "Poor work relationships/interpersonal skills."

Source: Clinton O. Longenecker, Mitchell J. Neubert, and Laurence S. Fink, "Causes and Consequences of Managerial Failure in Rapidly Changing Organizations," *Business Horizons,* 50 (March–April 2007): 145–155.

Question: What do you think is the leading cause of managerial failure?

Communicating

Today's managers are responsible for communicating to their employees the technical knowledge, instructions, rules, and information required to get the job done. Recognizing that communication is a two-way process, managers should be responsive to feedback and upward communications.

Motivating

An important aspect of management today is motivating individuals to pursue collective objectives by satisfying needs and meeting expectations with meaningful work and valued rewards. Flexible work schedules can be motivational for today's busy employees.

Leading

Managers become influential and inspiring leaders by serving as role models and adapting their management style to the demands of the situation. The idea of visionary leadership is popular today.

Controlling

When managers compare desired results with actual results and take the necessary corrective action, they are keeping things on track through the control function. Deviations from past plans should be considered when formulating new plans.

FIGURE 1.3

Identifiable Functions in the Management Process

Controlling · Planning · Decision making · Organizing · Staffing · Communicating · Motivating · Leading · **Managing for effectiveness and efficiency**

Some Managerial Facts of Life (with No Sugar Coating)

Managing is a tough and demanding job today. The hours are long and, at first anyway, the pay may not be generous. Worse yet, managers are visible authority figures who get more than their fair share of criticism and ridicule from politicians and cartoonists.[33] Nevertheless, managing can be a very rewarding occupation for those who develop their skills and persist, as evidenced by American Management Association (AMA) research findings:

▮ Forty-six percent of U.S. managers say they feel more overwhelmed at work today than two years ago, and 22 percent more say they're "somewhat" more overwhelmed.

▮ Half of U.S. managers say they experience stress every day, but an even greater share—63 percent—say they feel enthusiasm for their jobs.[34]

A Hectic Pace

The typical manager's day follows a hectic schedule, with lots of brief communication episodes and interactions. Interruptions and fragmentation are the norm. Henry Mintzberg's classic observational study of top managers led him to conclude: "The manager is overburdened with obligations; yet he cannot easily delegate his tasks. As a result, he is driven to overwork and is forced to do many tasks superficially. Brevity, fragmentation, and verbal communication characterize his work."[35] An even quicker pace is in store for future managers. Those who prefer extended quiet periods of contemplation should seek another line of work.

Managers Lose Their Right to Do Many Things

Mention the word *manager,* and the average person will probably respond with terms like *power, privilege, authority, good pay,* and so on. Although many managers eventually do enjoy some or all of these good things, they pay a significant price for stepping to the front of the administrative parade. According to one management expert, when you accept a supervisory or managerial position, you *lose* your right to do any of the following:

- Lose your temper
- Be one of the gang
- Bring your personal problems to work
- Vent your frustrations and express your opinion at work
- Resist change
- Pass the buck on tough assignments
- Get even with your adversaries
- Play favorites
- Put your self-interests first
- Ask others to do what you wouldn't do
- Expect to be immediately recognized and rewarded for doing a good job[36]

We tell you this not to scare you away from what could be a financially and emotionally rewarding career, but rather to present a realistic picture so you can choose intelligently. Management is not for everyone—it is not for the timid, the egomaniacal,[37] or the lazy. Management requires clear-headed individuals who can envision something better and turn it into reality by working with and through others.

TEST PREPPER 1.2   ANSWERS CAN BE FOUND ON P. 27

True or False?

_____ 1. The chain of command and division of labor are part of management's organizing function.

_____ 2. Staffing and motivating are among the eight basic managerial functions.

_____ 3. The typical manager's day is hectic, with lots of interruptions and brief interactions.

_____ 4. The best part of being a manager is that you can play favorites and be one of the gang.

Multiple Choice

_____ 5. Which managerial function involves taking corrective action after comparing actual results with desired results?
- a. Controlling
- b. Leading
- c. Organizing
- d. Decision making
- e. Staffing

_____ 6. According to Henri Fayol, the French father of the functional approach to management, all managers perform which five functions?
- a. Problem solving, budgeting, planning, motivating, and monitoring
- b. Planning, leading, motivating, communicating, and reviewing
- c. Checking, convincing, innovating, leading, and control
- d. Planning, organizing, hiring, team building, and motivating
- e. Planning, organizing, command, coordination, and control

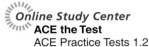

Online Study Center
ACE the Test
ACE Practice Tests 1.2

LEARNING TO MANAGE

3 ▶ *Explain how managers learn to manage.*

Students of management are left with one overriding question: "How do I acquire the ability to manage?" This question has stimulated a good deal of debate among those interested in management education. What is the key, theory or practice? Some contend that future managers need a solid background in management theory acquired through formal education. Others argue that managing, like learning to ride a bicycle, can be learned only by actually doing it. We can leapfrog this debate by looking at how managers learn to manage, understanding how students learn about management, and considering how you can blend the two processes to your best advantage.

How Do Managers Learn to Manage?

We have an answer to this simple but intriguing question, thanks to the Honeywell study, which was conducted by a team of management development specialists employed by Honeywell.[38] In a survey, they asked 3,600 Honeywell managers: "How did you learn to manage?" Ten percent of the respondents were then interviewed for additional insights. Successful Honeywell managers reportedly acquired 50 percent of their management knowledge from job assignments (see Figure 1.4). The remaining 50 percent of what they knew about management reportedly came from relationships with bosses, mentors, and coworkers (30 percent) and from formal training and education (20 percent).

Fully half of what the Honeywell managers knew about managing came from the so-called school of hard knocks. To that extent, at least, learning to manage is indeed like learning to ride a bike. You get on, you fall off and skin your knee, you get back on a bit smarter, and so on, until you're able to wobble down the road. But in the minds of aspiring managers, this scenario raises the question of what classes are held in the school of hard knocks. A second study, this one of British managers, provided an answer. It turns out that the following are considered *hard knocks* by managers:

▪ Making a big mistake

▪ Being overstretched by a difficult assignment

▪ Feeling threatened

▪ Being stuck in an impasse or dilemma

▪ Suffering an injustice at work

▪ Losing out to someone else

▪ Being personally attacked[39]

These situations are traumatic enough to motivate managers to learn how to avoid repeating the same mistakes.

FIGURE 1.4

**The Honeywell Study:
How Managers Learn to Manage**

Source: Data from Ron Zemke, "The Honeywell Studies: How Managers Learn to Manage," *Training,* 22 (August 1985): 46–51.

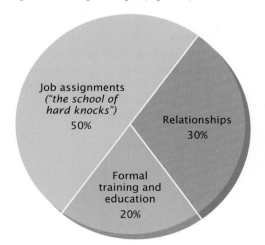

How Can Future Managers Learn to Manage?

As indicated in Figure 1.5, students can learn to manage by integrating theory and practice and observing role models. Theory can help you systematically analyze, interpret, and internalize the managerial significance of practical experience and observations. Although formal training and education contributed only 20 percent to the Honeywell managers' knowledge, they nonetheless represent a needed conceptual foundation. Returning to our bicycle example, a cross-country trip on a high-tech bike requires more than the mere ability to ride a bike. It requires a sound foundation of knowledge about bicycle maintenance and repair, weather and road conditions, and road safety. So, too, new managers who have a good idea of what lies ahead can go farther and faster with fewer foolish mistakes. The school of hard knocks is inevitable.[40] But you can foresee and avoid at least some of the knocks.

Ideally, an individual acquires theoretical knowledge and practical experience at the same time, perhaps through work-study programs or internships. Usually, though, full-time students get a lot of theory and little practice. This is when simulated and real experience become important. If you are a serious management student, you will put your newly acquired theories into practice wherever and whenever possible (for example, in organized sports; positions of leadership in fraternities, sororities, or clubs; and part-time and summer jobs). What really matters is your personal integration of theory and practice.

TEST PREPPER 1.3   ANSWERS CAN BE FOUND ON P. 27

True or False?

_____ 1. According to the Honeywell study, managers learned half of what they knew about managing from formal training and education.

_____ 2. Being overstretched by a difficult assignment was one of the managerial "hard knocks" uncovered by British researchers.

_____ 3. Future managers stand to learn little if anything from theory.

Multiple Choice

_____ 4. In the Honeywell study, which of these was the leading source of knowledge about managing?
  a. Formal training and education
  b. Mentors
  c. Relationships
  d. Peers
  e. Job assignments

_____ 5. Which of these was *not* among the "school of hard knocks" managerial lessons uncovered in the British study?
  a. Feeling threatened
  b. Making a big mistake
  c. Being personally attacked
  d. Losing out to someone else
  e. Experiencing a serious budget shortfall

_____ 6. The author recommends _____ for acquiring the ability to manage.
  a. reading *Business Week* magazine
  b. merging theory and practice
  c. forgetting about academic theories
  d. starting at the very bottom
  e. starting your own business

Online Study Center
ACE the Test
ACE Practice Tests 1.3

FIGURE 1.5

Acquiring the Ability to Manage by Merging Theory and Practice

Theory	Acquiring the ability to manage	Practice

- Definitions
- Relevant facts
- Concepts
- Techniques
- Guidelines

Source: *Textbooks, audiovisual presentations, and formal classroom instruction*

Systematic integration of theory and practice into personally meaningful and useful ways of managing
Source: *Self*

Imitating managerial role models
Source: *Practicing managers*

Simulated experience: Participating in instructor-aided experiential exercises, case studies, and role-playing
Source: *Semistructured classroom experience*

Real experience: Actually managing an organized endeavor
Source: *Part-time or full-time employment as a manager*

SMALL-BUSINESS MANAGEMENT

4 *Challenge two myths about small businesses and describe entrepreneurs.*

Small businesses have been called the "engine" of the U.S. economy. For example, "Sam and Helen Walton began a five-and-dime in 1945 that's now Wal-Mart—the nation's biggest employer, with 1.3 million workers."[41] Small businesses are often too small to attract much media attention, but collectively small businesses around the world are a *huge* and *vibrant* part of the global economy. As evidence, consider these facts about the 5.6 million small businesses in the United States:

- They represent 99 percent of the nation's employers.[42]

- Each year they account for more than one-quarter of the nation's $1.4 trillion in business capital investment.[43]

Interestingly, about 60 percent of them are "microbusinesses" with fewer than five employees, typically operating out of the owner's home. Free-enterprise capitalism is a rough-and-tumble arena where anyone can play, but only the very best survive. The only guaranteed result for those starting their own business is that they will be tested to their limit.[44]

Few would dispute the facts and claims cited above, but agreement on the definition of a small business is not so easily reached. Some of the many yardsticks used to distinguish small from large businesses include the number of employees, level of annual sales, amount of owner's equity, and total assets. For our present purposes, a **small business** is defined as an independently owned and managed profit-seeking enterprise employing fewer than 100 people. (If the small business is incorporated, the owner/manager owns a significant proportion of the firm's stock.)

The health of every nation's economy depends on how well its small businesses are managed. To get a better grasp of the realm of small-business management,

small business An independently owned and managed profit-seeking enterprise with fewer than 100 employees.

For entrepreneurs Paula and Chris White of Wrentham, Massachusetts, necessity was indeed the mother of invention. Or perhaps we should say the mother of a great line of slice-and-bake cookies called "600 lb. Gorillas." The two engineers decided Paula should run a home-based business to better care for their infant son and daughter. A year of experimentation in their kitchen and constant tasting that added 20 pounds to Chris led to cookies many customers admit to passing off as homemade.

we will clear up two common misconceptions, explore small-business career options, and discuss entrepreneurship.

Exploding Myths About Small Business

Mistaken notions can become accepted facts if they are repeated often enough. Such is the case with failure rates and job creation for small businesses. Fortunately, recent research sets the record straight.

The 80-Percent-Failure-Rate Myth

An often-repeated statistic says that four out of five small businesses will fail within five years.[45] This 80 percent casualty rate is a frightening prospect for anyone thinking about starting a business. But a study by Bruce A. Kirchhoff of the New Jersey Institute of Technology found the failure rate for small businesses to be *only 18 percent during their first eight years.*[46] Why the huge disparity? It turns out that studies by the U.S. government and others defined business failures much too broadly. Any closing of a business, whether because someone died, sold the business, or retired, was recorded as a business failure. In fact, only 18 percent of the 814,000 small businesses tracked by Kirchhoff for eight years went out of business with unpaid bills. This should be a comfort to would-be entrepreneurs.

The Low-Wage-Jobs Myth

When it came to creating jobs during the 1980s and 1990s, America's big businesses were put to shame by their small and mid-size counterparts. Eighty percent of the new job growth was generated by the smaller companies; massive layoffs were the norm at big companies.[47] Critics, meanwhile, claimed that most of the new jobs in the small-business sector went to low-paid clerks and hamburger flippers. Such was not the case, according to a Cambridge, Massachusetts, study by researcher David Birch.

After analyzing new jobs created in the United States between 1987 and 1992, Birch found that businesses with fewer than 100 employees had indeed created most new jobs. Surprisingly, however, only 4 percent of those small firms produced 70 percent of that job growth.[48] Birch calls these rapidly growing small companies "gazelles," as opposed to the "mice" businesses that tend to remain very small. For the period studied, the gazelles added more high-paying jobs than big companies eliminated. Gazelles are not mom-and-pop operations. They tend to be computer software, telecommunications, and specialized engineering or manufacturing firms.[49] So, while small businesses do in fact pay on average less than big companies do, they are *not* low-wage havens.[50]

Again, as in the case of failure rates, the truth about the prospects of starting or working for a small company is different—and brighter—than traditional fallacies suggest.

Career Opportunities in Small Business

Among the five small-business career options listed in Table 1.2, only franchises require definition. The other four are self-defining.[51] A franchise is a license to sell another company's products and/or to use another company's name in business. Familiar franchise operations include McDonald's, the National Basketball Association, and Holiday Inn.[52] Notice how each of the career options in Table 1.2 has positive and negative aspects. There is no one best option. Success in the small-business sector depends on the right combination of money, talent, hard work, luck, and opportunity. Fortunately, career opportunities in small business are virtually unlimited. This is especially true for women and minorities, who saw their ranks among business owners soar "31% to more than 4 million from 1997 to 2002,"[53] according to recent figures from the U.S. Census Bureau.

REALITY CHECK 1.4

Advice for entrepreneurs from best-selling author and mountain climber Jim Collins: "First figure out your partners, then figure out what ideas to pursue. The most important thing isn't the market you target, the product you develop, or the financing, but the founding team. Starting a company is like scaling an unclimbed face—you don't know what the mountain will throw at you, so you must pick the right partners, who share your values, on whom you can depend, and who can adapt."

Source: As quoted in Matthew Boyle, "Questions for Jim Collins," *Fortune* (February 19, 2007): 50.

Question: Is Collins right, or should you follow the more typical recommendations to start with an unmet customer need or a great new product idea?

TABLE 1.2

Career Opportunities in Small Business

Small-business career options	Capital requirements	Likelihood of steady paycheck	Degree of personal control	Ultimate financial return
1. Become an independent contractor/consultant	Low to moderate	None to low	Very high	Negative to high
2. Take a job with a small business	None	Moderate to high	Low to moderate	Low to moderate
3. Join or buy a small business owned by your family	Low to high	Low to high	Low to high	Moderate to high
4. Purchase a franchise	Moderate to high	None to moderate	Moderate to high	Negative to high
5. Start your own small business	Moderate to high	None to moderate	High to very high	Negative to very high

---
TABLE 1.3

Contrasting Trait Profiles for Entrepreneurs and Administrators

Entrepreneurs tend to	Administrators tend to
Focus on envisioned futures	Focus on the established present
Emphasize external/market dimensions	Emphasize internal/cost dimensions
Display a medium-to-high tolerance for ambiguity	Display a low-to-medium tolerance for ambiguity
Exhibit moderate-to-high risk-taking behavior	Exhibit low-to-moderate risk-taking behavior
Obtain motivation from a need to achieve	Obtain motivation from a need to lead others (i.e., social power)
Possess technical knowledge and experience in the innovative area	Possess managerial knowledge and experience

Source: From Philip D. Olson, "Choices for Innovation-Minded Corporations," *The Journal of Business Strategy,* 11 (January–February 1990): Exhibit 1, p. 44. Reproduced with permission of Emerald Group Publishing Limited.

Entrepreneurship

entrepreneurship   Process of pursuing opportunities without regard to resources currently under one's control.

According to experts on the subject, "**entrepreneurship** is the process by which individuals—either on their own or inside organizations—pursue opportunities without regard to the resources they currently control."[54] In effect, entrepreneurs look beyond current resource constraints when they envision new possibilities. Entrepreneurs are preoccupied with "how to," rather than "why not." Entrepreneurs, as we discuss next, are risk takers—and all they want is a chance (see Best Practices on page 24).

A Trait Profile for Entrepreneurs

Exactly how do entrepreneurs differ from general managers or administrators? According to the trait profiles in Table 1.3, entrepreneurs tend to be high achievers who focus more on future possibilities, external factors, and technical details. Also, compared with general administrators, entrepreneurs are more comfortable with ambiguity and risk taking. It is important to note that entrepreneurs are not necessarily better or worse than other managers—they are just different.[55] Norm Brodsky, a successful entrepreneur who has founded six businesses, says people need what he calls the X Factor to succeed as an entrepreneur. He explains: "Call it passion, tenacity, stick-to-itiveness, true grit, or just plain stubbornness. Whatever it is and wherever it comes from, it's the most important quality an entrepreneur can have. Ultimately, it determines whether we succeed or fail."[56] Do you have the X Factor?

Entrepreneurship Has Its Limits

Many successful entrepreneurs have tripped over a common stumbling block. Their organizations outgrow the entrepreneur's ability to manage them. In fact, according to "a poll by PriceWaterhouseCoopers, about 40% of CEOs at the fastest-growing companies said that their own ability to manage or reorganize their business could be an impediment to growth."[57] Some refer to this problem as "founder's disease." Moreover, entrepreneurs generally feel stifled by cumbersome and slow-paced bureaucracies. One management consultant praised Microsoft's Bill Gates for knowing his limits in this regard:

> *In January [2000], Gates went from being CEO of the multibillion-dollar business he cofounded to naming himself "chief software architect" and handing over executive responsibility for his company to Steve Ballmer. . . . few people recognized it for what I think it was: a courageous leap into a self-esteem-threatening black hole.*[58]

Entrepreneurs who launch successful and growing companies face a tough dilemma: either grow with the company or have the courage to step aside and turn the reins over to professional managers who possess the necessary administrative traits,[59] such as those listed in Table 1.3.

TEST PREPPER 1.4   ANSWERS CAN BE FOUND ON P. 27

True or False?

_____ 1. Small businesses represent 99 percent of the employers in the United States.

_____ 2. By definition, a small business has fewer than 100 employees.

_____ 3. Eighty percent of small businesses fail within five years.

_____ 4. While small businesses are far more numerous, the 100 largest businesses accounted for most of the job growth in the United States during the 1980s and 1990s.

_____ 5. Entrepreneurs tend to shy away from ambiguity and risk.

Online Study Center
ACE the Test
ACE Practice Tests 1.4

Multiple Choice

_____ 6. What percent of the small businesses tracked for eight years by Kirchhoff went out of business with unpaid bills?
   a. 90   d. 80
   b. 66   e. 50
   c. 18

_____ 7. Which of these is a trait of entrepreneurs?
   a. Obtain motivation from a need to achieve
   b. Focus on the established present
   c. Exhibit low-to-moderate risk-taking behavior
   d. Possess managerial knowledge and experience
   e. Emphasize internal/cost dimensions

Got a Good Business Idea? You've Got 45 Seconds

According to new-venture expert Elton B. Sherwin Jr., entrepreneurs who are trying to raise venture capital should be able to answer these "Seven Sacred Questions" in 45 seconds:

1. What is your product?
2. Who is the customer?
3. Who will sell it?
4. How many people will buy it?

5. How much will it cost to design and build?
6. What is the sales price?
7. When will you break even?

Source: From *Inc.: The Magazine For Growing Companies* by Marc Ballon, "Hot Tips," April 1999. Copyright © 1999 by Mansueto Ventures LLC. Reproduced with permission of Mansueto Ventures LLC via Copyright Clearance Center.

CLOSING CASE STUDY

Jennifer Reingold's (Long) Day on the Managerial Hot Seat

The lightning bolt wasn't a great sign. My first day on the job, and I was already losing control: A string of emails demanded split-second decisions for problems I had only just heard about; I needed to pull together a business-plan presentation for a product I had never laid eyes on; a rabid reporter lurked outside my door. Then, the single, jagged flash shot across my window. I gulped my Diet Dr Pepper. Maybe I wasn't meant to be an executive after all.

Not that I ever really thought I was. Sure, I've been covering management and leadership for 10 years, lambasting and lionizing executives, dismissing their best-laid plans with a few cutting words and anointing their successors with a few sparkling ones. But my actual experience with leading and managing has remained largely theoretical. Ironic? Sure, but I liked that.

Still, we all have to grow up sometime. So when Richard Wellins, an SVP at human-resources consulting firm Development Dimensions International (DDI), invited me to its intensive one-day "operational executive platform"—a simulation used to screen potential job candidates or identify and develop stars already in-house—I jumped at the chance. Over the course of one full day, I'd make strategic decisions, launch a new product, and deal with the challenges a boss typically faces. I'd be thrown curveballs by company brass, employees, customers, and media alike (all role-played by trained assessors). And then I'd receive an unvarnished evaluation of my work, a kind of psychographic leadership report card.

In the days running up to my visit, I logged on to DDI's Assessing Talent portal, which gave me financial and historical information about my fictitious company, Global Solutions, a robotics shop facing tough times in the year 2025. I also took a series of preliminary psych tests, or "leadership inventories," that would be analyzed in conjunction with my performance. Then I received my pseudo identity: Kelly Myers, a new VP whose predecessor at Global had just been canned.

Kelly and I, it turned out, had our work cut out for us: Margins were falling, inventories were rising, and the Jeeves—a robotic valet—had started doing odd things, such as cooking a client's favorite shoes and breaking into hotel rooms in the middle of the night.

The morning of the big day found me chugging coffee in my hotel room and trying to look the part, when the front desk called up to say my car had arrived. "But they're early!" I spat. "I'll be down when I can!" After I hung up on the poor woman, it occurred to me that I might have already blown my first test. Leadership? Yeah. In boot camp, maybe.

In the glass-skinned Pittsburgh headquarters of DDI, I was shown to my new "office." Ah! The faux-wood desk, the paper clips in the drawer, a suspicious box of tissues (would I be needing those?). A pleasant picture of boats distracted me from the view of the parking lot—and from the video camera recording my every move. I was disappointed to note that the workplace of 2025 was as drab as ever.

My email revealed a host of headaches, including a note about the Jeeves from a furious hotel manager and another from my boss: One of my direct reports was resisting the centralization of the sales and marketing functions. "It is imperative that you gain Marty's buy-in," he wrote.

Kelly and I dove in. First up was Marty, whom I motivated, I felt sure, with a deft application of both carrot and stick. Next came the hostile hotelier: I pulled out all the stops trying to placate her, offering a quick (and possibly nonexistent) fix that included temporarily substituting an earlier-generation robot. "This relationship is critical to our company, and we want to make you happy," I purred, adding an eye roll that was promptly captured by the now-forgotten camera.

I suddenly realized I hadn't gotten a single email in hours. "Oh, dear," said the coordinator. It seems there had been a computer glitch, not part of the simulation. When I rebooted, a good dozen emails lay festering in my inbox: Design an agenda for our off-site! Decide whether to move a guy from Asia to the inventory-reduction task force—today! Determine why all of our new-hire MBAs are quitting! Write a business plan by 4 p.m.! And, oh, by the way, you have a TV interview to address concerns that one of our security robots caused a teenager's death.

It was at about this time that the lightning bolt struck. "Not fair," I whined to myself, pining for my messy desk, my writer's block. No time for that now, though—I had a dead teenager on my hands. At least the interview would be a breeze, I figured, given my day job in real life. But when I tried to stay cool, explaining our position on the "unfortunate event," the jerk kept putting words in my mouth.

The rest of the day was a blur. More vile emails. An inspirational voice mail I had to record to introduce Kelly to the staff (in a brilliant, if unauthorized, initiative, I announced $1,000-to-$25,000 bonuses to anyone with "ideas that help the company"). I swore a lot under my breath. And then it was time for the business-plan presentation. Without a clue about how to crunch the production numbers, I had opted to concentrate on the marketing side of the Jeeves product launch—and to talk so much that my boss wouldn't miss the margin calculations or the ad budget. Amazingly, he actually seemed to buy it.

My day finally ended. I left feeling like the white-collar equivalent of Lucille Ball in the chocolate factory.

I didn't think I had been a complete loser, but that just raised the question: If this ink-stained—and untrained—wretch could pass for management material, wasn't this whole exercise suspect? Could it really be worth the $4,000 to $12,000 that more than 1,000 companies have ponied up for DDI's full- or half-day assessments?

Kelly and I cuddled up together in the hotel for a brain-dead evening of reality TV, then returned to DDI the next morning for our results. . . .

To my delight and horror, the tests nailed me cold. My passion for new and different challenges, my hard-working, ambitious side, my love of socializing and interacting with others—all there. But so, too, were my tendency to get snappish at stressful moments and my "low interpersonal sensitivity" (i.e., extreme bluntness). DDI doesn't make yes-or-no job recommendations for candidates. Yet I came away with the strange—and somehow disturbing—conclusion that, warts and all, I could, with a lot of practice and probably a lot of therapy, be Kelly Myers. I didn't have much time to think about that, though. Thankfully, I had a story to write.

Source: From *Fast Company* by Jennifer Reingold, "My (Long) Day at the Top," June 2006. Copyright © 2006 by Mansueto Ventures LLC. Reproduced with permission of Mansueto Ventures LLC via Copyright Clearance Center.

Case Questions

1. How would you rate Jennifer Reingold's (aka Kelly Myers) effectiveness and efficiency? Explain.
2. Which of the eight managerial functions are evident in this case? Explain.
3. In what respects was this a manager's typical day?
4. Based on the trait profiles in Table 1.3 on page 22, did Jennifer Reingold act more like an administrator or an entrepreneur? Explain.

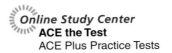

Online Study Center
ACE the Test
ACE Plus Practice Tests

Online Study Center
Improve Your Grade
Learning Objective Review
Audio Chapter Review
Audio Chapter Quiz
Study Guide to Go

LEARNING OBJECTIVE REVIEW

 Define the term management *and explain the managerial significance of the terms* effectiveness *and* efficiency.

- Formally defined, *management* is the process of working with and through others to achieve organizational objectives in a changing environment. Central to this process is the effective and efficient use of limited resources.

- A manager is effective if he or she reaches a stated objective and efficient if limited resources are not wasted in the process.

- Five overarching sources of change affecting the way management is practiced today are:
    - Globalization
    - The evolution of product quality
    - Environmentalism
    - An ethical reawakening
    - E-business on the Internet

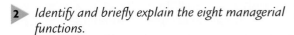 *Identify and briefly explain the eight managerial functions.*

- This text is organized around the following eight managerial functions:
    - Planning (the primary management function involving the formulation of future courses of action)
    - Decision making (choosing among alternative courses of action)
    - Organizing (structuring the organization with a chain of command, division of labor, and assignment of responsibilities)
    - Staffing (recruiting, training, and developing employees)
    - Communicating (a two-way process of sharing needed information)
    - Motivating (getting individuals to pursue collective objectives)
    - Leading (serving as a role model and influencing others to accomplish shared objectives)
    - Controlling (taking corrective action after comparing desired and actual results)

 *Explain how managers learn to manage.*

- Honeywell researchers found that managers learned 50 percent of what they know about managing from job assignments (or the school of hard knocks). The remaining 50 percent of their management knowledge came from relationships (30 percent) and formal training and education (20 percent).

- A good foundation in management theory can give management students a running start and help them avoid foolish mistakes.

- The key to becoming an effective manager is to personally integrate theory, the experience of role models and mentors (borrowed practice), and one's own experience (personal practice).

4 *Challenge two myths about small businesses and describe entrepreneurs.*

- A small business (independently owned and managed profit-seeking company with fewer than 100 employees) is central to a healthy economy.

- Contrary to conventional wisdom, 80 percent of new businesses do not fail within five years. In fact, one large study found only an 18 percent failure rate during the first eight years.

- The belief that small businesses create only low-wage jobs has been shown to be a myth.

- Five career opportunities in the small business sector include:
  - Becoming an independent contractor/consultant
  - Going to work for a small business
  - Joining or buying your family's business
  - Buying a franchise
  - Starting your own business

- Compared with general administrators, entrepreneurs tend to be high achievers who are more future-oriented, externally focused, ready to take risks, and comfortable with ambiguity.

TEST PREPPER ANSWERS

▶ **1.1**
1. F   2. F   3. T   4. F   5. T   6. d   7. b

▶ **1.2**
1. T   2. T   3. T   4. F   5. a   6. e

▶ **1.3**
1. F   2. T   3. F   4. e   5. e   6. b

▶ **1.4**
1. T   2. T   3. F   4. F   5. F   6. c   7. a

Online Study Center RESOURCES

Prepare for Class, Improve Your Grade, and ACE the Test. Student Achievement Series resources include:

ACE Practice Tests	Crossword Puzzles	Hangman
Audio Chapter Quizzes	Decision Case Questions	Key Issue Expansion
Audio Chapter Reviews	Ethical Hot Seat Exercises	Learning Objective Reviews
Career Snapshots	Flashcards	Study Guide to Go
Chapter Glossaries	Hands-on Exercises	Visual Glossaries
Chapter Outlines		

To access these learning and study tools, go to **college.hmco.com/pic/kreitnerSASfound**.

A recent poll found 84 percent of employees are willing to report to a younger manager. This is good news considering it is very common these days.

3 *Discuss why the global economy is a vital economic consideration for modern managers.*

2 *Discuss how the changing political-legal environment is affecting the practice of management.*

1 *Summarize the demographics of the new U.S. workforce and define the term managing diversity.*

Chapter Outline

Online Study Center
Prepare for Class
Chapter Outline

4 ▶ *Describe the three-step innovation process and define the term intrapreneur.*

Welcome to the World of Younger Bosses and Older Workers

So your new boss wasn't even born when you finished high school. Is that going to bother you? Not at all, according to a new study from staffing service OfficeTeam in Menlo Park, Calif. Eighty-four percent of polled employees said they would be comfortable reporting to a manager who is younger than they are; 89 percent said they wouldn't mind supervising an older employee. "For the first time in history, four generations of employees are in the work-force," says Diane Domeyer, executive director of OfficeTeam. "Companies recognize the benefits of having diverse, well-rounded teams, and employees may be just as likely to report to a younger supervisor as an older one." Traci McCready, a principal at the Boston-based Capital H Group, a human capital consulting firm, says she was surprised by how few age-related issues she faced as she climbed the corporate ladder to become a principal— something rare for someone in her mid-30s. "I have come up

Online Study Center college.hmco.com/pic/kreitnerSASfound

Online Study Center
Prepare for Class
Chapter Glossary

Improve Your Grade
Flashcards
Hangman
Crossword Puzzles

through the ranks very quickly," she says. "To be quite honest with you, I anticipated a lot more push-back than I ever received. The only place that I have ever encountered it is my own head."

Furthermore, McCready has faced one of the hypotheticals posed in the survey: She's managed people significantly older than herself. She says age isn't an issue—but respect is. "[Older employees] add so much value. You just have to treat them with respect," she says, adding, "What I find when you're managing someone significantly older than you is that they're going to have a completely different perspective than what you have, and you have to expect that. It's not right or wrong, it's just different."[2] ■

Jeffrey Immelt's comment in the chapter-opening quotation is right on target because ignoring the impact of general environmental factors on management makes about as much sense as ignoring the effects of weather, road, and traffic conditions on high-speed driving. The general environment of management includes social, political-legal, economic, and technological dimensions. Changes in each area present managers with unique opportunities and obstacles that will shape not only the organization's strategic direction but also the course of daily operations. This challenge requires forward-thinking managers who can handle change and figure out the greater scheme of things. For example, in the opening vignette, both younger bosses and the older workers who report to them all need to make adjustments while teaming up to get the job done.

The purpose of this chapter, then, is to prepare you for constant change and help you see the *big picture* by identifying key themes in the changing environment of management.

THE SOCIAL ENVIRONMENT

> **1** *Summarize the demographics of the new U.S. workforce and define the term* managing diversity.

According to sociologists, society is the product of a constant struggle between the forces of stability and change. Cooperation promotes stability, whereas conflict and competition upset the status quo. The net result is an ever-changing society. Keeping this perspective in mind, we shall discuss three important dimensions of the social environment: demographics, inequalities, and managing diversity. Each presents managers with unique challenges.

Demographics of the New U.S. Workforce

demographics   Statistical profiles of population characteristics.

Demographics—statistical profiles of population characteristics—are a valuable planning tool for managers and government policymakers. Foresighted leaders and managers who study demographics can make appropriate adjustments in their strategic, human resource, and marketing plans. Different nations have their own unique population patterns, trends, and challenges. For example, Russia has such a low birthrate that its population is projected to decline from 147 million in

2000 to 111 million in 2050. Japan, Germany, and Italy all face the same prospect, with serious implications for their productivity and national security.[3] The projections in Figure 2.1 are not "blue sky" numbers. They are based on people already born, most of whom are presently working. In short, the U.S. workforce demonstrates the following trends:

FIGURE 2.1

The Changing U.S. Workforce: 2000–2010

Source: Data and bottom figure from U.S. Department of Labor, Bureau of Labor Statistics, "Tomorrow's Jobs," *Occupational Outlook Handbook*, 2002–2003 edition, http://stats.bls.gov.

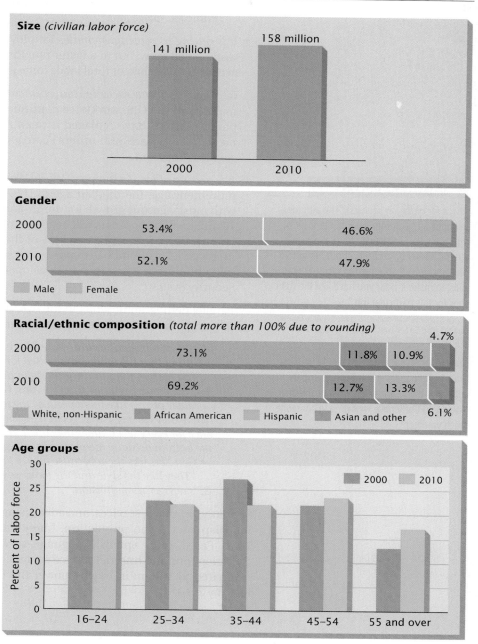

■ *It is getting larger.* As in the previous two decades, the U.S. labor force will continue to grow at a faster rate than the national population. The resulting labor shortage will continue to be a magnet for legal and illegal immigration. According to *Business Week*, immigrants give the U.S. labor force a significant competitive advantage in the global economy:

> The U.S. takes more than 1 million immigrants annually, including illegals. That is one key reason economic growth has averaged 3.7% a year for the past decade. Immigrants have supplied crucial technical and scientific talent, founded thousands of Silicon Valley startups, and helped hold down prices by filling low-wage jobs.[4]

■ *It is getting increasingly female.* Employment opportunities for both men and women will grow, but at a faster rate for women. In the United States women accounted "for 59% of total labor force growth between 1996 and 2006."[5]

■ *It is getting more racially and ethnically diverse.* The white, non-Hispanic majority of the U.S. workforce continues to proportionately shrink, and Hispanics/Latinos have replaced African Americans as the second-largest segment.[6] The "Asians and others" category is the fastest growing, but still the smallest, segment.

■ *It is getting older.* As the post–World War II baby-boom generation moves into retirement age, the median age of U.S. employees will continue to increase, with most vigorous growth for the 55-and-older groups. "In 2011, the bubble of 77 million baby boomers will begin turning 65. By 2050, the 65-and-over population will grow from 12% to 21% of the population, the U.S. Census Bureau predicts."[7] This trend has major (some say troubling) implications for the viability of old-age assistance in developed countries, including the U.S. Social Security System.

Parallel demographic shifts in the overall U.S. population have manufacturers redesigning products. Take refrigerators, for example:

> Just 4% of refrigerators are sold with freezers on the bottom, but GE Appliances is betting that the models are poised for a sales surge.
>
> The bottom freezers are gaining in popularity with two important demographic groups: retirees and Gen Xers, GE says.
>
> Older people like them because the food they reach for most often is up high, where they can see it and get at it. According to GE, consumers open their freezer once for every seven times they open their refrigerator. So having the freezer on the bottom actually means less bending over.
>
> Gen Xers like them because they're different.
>
> "They like the style and the look," says Robert Rogers, marketing manager for GE's refrigeration division.[8]

Similarly, products, services, and advertising are being tailored to the rapidly growing Hispanic/Latino population. Many banks, including Bank of America and Wells Fargo, offer Spanish-language services at their teller windows, ATMs, and telephone and Internet service centers. Businesses cannot afford to ignore the estimated $1 trillion in buying power the U.S. Hispanic/Latino community will have by 2010.[9]

REALITY CHECK 2.1

Advice for older job seekers: "The attitude an applicant takes into the job interview is important. You don't want to treat a manager as 'sonny boy' or talk about the last 26 jobs you've had. You need to focus on your skills, to make it clear you have just the right ones for this particular job."

Source: Jeannette Woodward, as quoted in Amy Dunkin, "You're Older? So Sell your Wisdom," *Business Week* (February 19, 2007): 82.

Questions: What problems would you likely have managing someone your parents' age? If you are older, what problems would you likely have reporting to someone much younger?

Nagging Inequalities in the Workplace

Can the United States achieve full and lasting international competitiveness if a large proportion of its workforce suffers nagging inequalities? Probably not. Unfortunately, women, minorities, and part-timers often encounter barriers in the workplace. Let us open our discussion by focusing on women because their plight is shared by all minorities to varying degrees.

Under the Glass Ceiling

As a large and influential minority, women are demanding—and getting—a greater share of workplace opportunities. Women occupy 50 percent of the managerial and administrative positions in the U.S. civilian workforce. Still, a large inequity remains. Here is a summary of the situation:

> For every dollar a man made in 2003, women made 75.5 cents, the Census Bureau said in its annual report on income. That was down from the record 76.6 cents that women earned vs. men's in 2002. The median income for men working full-time in 2003 was $40,668, not significantly different from the prior year, while the median income for women working full-time was $30,724, down 0.6% from 2002.
>
> While the drop might appear minor, it was the first statistically significant decline in women's incomes since 1995, the Census Bureau said.[10]

Also, according to a recent study, lifetime earnings for women in the United States equal, on average, 44 percent of the lifetime earnings for their male counterparts. Across all job categories—from top business executives to lawyers, physicians, and office workers—the same sort of gender pay gap can be found.[11] This gap has expanded and contracted at various times since the 1950s in the United States, with the shortfall actually *growing* for women managers between 1995 and 2000.[12] In the United States, the gender pay gap can be summed up in two words: *large* and *persistent*. Comparatively well-paid men can grasp the significance of the gender wage gap by pondering the impact on their standard of living of a 25 percent pay cut. Moreover, men who share household expenses with a woman wage earner are also penalized by the gender wage gap.

In addition to suffering a wage gap, women (and other minorities) bump up against the so-called glass ceiling when climbing the managerial ladder.[13] "The **glass ceiling** is a concept popularized in the 1980s to describe a barrier so subtle that it is transparent, yet so strong that it prevents women and minorities from moving up in the management hierarchy."[14] It is not unique to the United States. Consider the situation going into 2007:

glass ceiling The transparent but strong barrier keeping women and minorities from moving up the management ladder.

▌ Among the 1,000 largest companies in the United States, only 2 percent of the chief executive officers and corporate board chairs were women. Researchers project that figure to rise to 4.9 percent by 2010 and to a still puny 6.2 percent by 2016.[15]

▌ "Only about 15% of *Fortune* 500 board members are women—a conspicuously low figure."[16]

Why is there a glass ceiling? According to *Working Woman* magazine, women are being held back by "the lingering perception of women as outsiders, exclusion from informal networks, male stereotyping and lack of experience."[17] Nordstrom, the upscale chain of department stores where women occupy nearly two-thirds of the executive and senior manager positions, is a good role model for breaking the glass ceiling.[18] Another force is also at work here, siphoning off some of the best female executive talent part way up the corporate ladder. Many women are leaving the corporate ranks to start their own businesses. According to the U.S. Small Business Administration's latest data, "In 2002, women owned 6.5 million or 28.2 percent of nonfarm U.S. firms. More than 14 percent of these women-owned firms were employers, with 7.4 million workers and $173.7 billion in annual payroll."[19]

Continuing Pressure for Equal Opportunity

Persistent racial inequality is underscored by the fact that the unemployment rate for African Americans generally is about twice as high as that for whites during both good and bad economic times. "African-Americans tend to be the last to be hired when the economy is booming. That means they also tend to be the first to lose their jobs when a downturn hits."[20] Women, African Americans, Hispanics/Latinos, Native Americans, the physically challenged, and other minorities who are overrepresented in either low-level, low-paying jobs or the unemployment line can be expected to press harder to become full partners in the world of work (see Best Practices on page 49). Equal employment opportunity (EEO) and Affirmative Action are discussed in Chapter 9.

Managing Diversity

Online Study Center
Improve Your Grade
Career Snapshot 2.1

The United States, a nation of immigrants, is becoming even more racially and ethnically diverse. The evidence is compelling:

▌ "Foreign-born workers accounted for 14.8% of the U.S. labor force in 2005, up from 14.5% in 2004. . . . Since 2000, the foreign-born have accounted for nearly half the net gain in the total labor force."[21]

▌ "The country will become a nation of minorities. Whites accounted for about 71% of the population . . . [in 2000,] but by 2050, the number will drop to 53%, blacks will increase one percentage point (to 13.2%), Asians will more than double to 8.9% (from 3.9%), and Hispanics will jump to 24.3% (from 11.8%)."[22]

▌ "California joins New Mexico and half of the 100 largest U.S. cities, as well as numerous counties along the U.S.-Mexico border, where Caucasians do not constitute a clear majority."[23]

▌ *Sonia Perez, National Council of La Raza:* "A third of the Latinos are under 18, so this is going to be the future of the workforce in the U.S."[24]

Accordingly, the U.S. workforce is becoming more culturally diverse. For example, the employees at some Marriott Hotels speak 30 different languages.[25] Some Americans decry what they consider to be an invasion of "their" national and organizational "territories." But many others realize that America's immigrants and minorities have always been a vitalizing, creative, hardworking force.[26] Progressive organizations are taking steps to better accommodate and more fully utilize America's more diverse workforce. **Managing diversity** is the process of creating an organizational culture that enables *all* employees, including women and minorities, to realize their full potential.[27]

managing diversity   Process of helping all employees, including women and minorities, reach their full potential.

More than EEO

Managing diversity builds on equal employment opportunity (EEO) and Affirmative Action programs (discussed in Chapter 9). EEO and Affirmative Action are necessary to get more women and minorities into the workplace. But getting them in the door is not enough. Comprehensive diversity programs are needed to create more *flexible* organizations where *everyone* has a fair chance to thrive and succeed.[28] These programs need to include white males who have sometimes felt slighted or ignored by EEO and Affirmative Action; they, too, have individual differences (opinions, lifestyles, age, and schedules) that deserve fair accommodation. Managing diversity requires many of us to adjust our thinking. According to sociologist Jack McDevitt, "We don't want to have as a goal just tolerating people. We have to *value* them."[29] In addition to being the ethical course of action, managing diversity is a necessity. A nation cannot waste human potential and remain globally competitive.

Promising Beginnings

Among the diversity programs in use today are the following:

- Teaching English as a second language

- Creating mentor programs (an experienced employee coaches and sponsors a newcomer)

- Providing immigration assistance

- Fostering the development of support groups for minorities

- Training minorities for managerial positions

- Training managers to value and skillfully manage diversity

- Encouraging employees to contribute to and attend cultural celebrations and events in the community

- Creating, publicizing, and enforcing discrimination and harassment policies

- Actively recruiting minorities[30]

The scope of managing diversity is limited only by management's depth of commitment and imagination. For example, a supervisor learns sign language to communicate with a hearing-impaired employee. Or a married male manager attends a diversity workshop and becomes aware of the difficulties of being a single working mother. Perhaps a younger manager's age bias is blunted after reading a research report documenting that older employees tend to be absent less often and have lower accident rates than younger ones.[31] Maybe other companies begin to follow Corning's diversity policy, whereby "new employees are no longer encouraged to adopt the dress, style, and social activities of the white male majority."[32]

Be yourself. Race. Ethnicity. Religion. Nationality. Gender. In the end, there's just one variety of human being. The individual. All six billion of us. **Be bullish.**

ml.com

Stockbroker Merrill Lynch uses its famous Wall Street bull to give diversity a boost in this advertisement. (And there's only one race—the human race.)

True or False?

_____ 1. The U.S. workforce is getting older, more diverse, and increasingly female.

_____ 2. Recent years have seen a complete closing of the pay gap between men and women in the U.S. workplace.

_____ 3. According to *Working Woman* magazine, the glass ceiling results from a serious shortage of qualified women for executive positions.

_____ 4. Hispanics/Latinos are unlikely to overtake African Americans as the second largest racial/ethnic segment of the U.S. workforce.

_____ 5. Comprehensive diversity programs are meant only for women and minorities.

Multiple Choice

_____ 6. Which one of these statements about the U.S. workforce is false? It is getting

     a. more racially diverse

     b. less predominantly white, non-Hispanic

     c. smaller

     d. increasingly female

     e. older

_____ 7. If a student from Kenya asked you about the representation of women in senior management positions in the United States, what would be the correct answer?

     a. Moderate and shrinking

     b. Nearly equal to men

     c. Very small and shrinking

     d. Now greater than men

     e. Very small but growing

_____ 8. _____ is the process of creating an organizational culture that enables all employees to realize their full potential.

     a. Issues management

     b. Managing diversity

     c. Constructive conflict

     d. Human asset accounting

     e. Protectionism

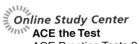

Online Study Center
ACE the Test
ACE Practice Tests 2.1

THE POLITICAL-LEGAL ENVIRONMENT

> **2** Discuss how the changing political-legal environment is affecting the practice of management.

In its broadest terms, *politics* is the art (or science) of public influence and control. Laws are an outcome of the political process that differentiate good and bad conduct. An orderly political process is necessary because modern society is the product of an evolving consensus among diverse individuals and groups, often with conflicting interests and objectives. Although the list of special-interest groups is long and still growing, not everyone can have his or her own way. In a democracy, the political system tries to balance competing interests in a nonviolent manner. Interestingly, today's college students have a renewed taste for politics:

> *After 36 years of a general decline in interest in current affairs among college freshman, new students at four-year colleges appear to be having a political awakening.*
>
> *For the second consecutive year, an annual survey of freshman reveals that an increasing proportion—32.9 percent, up from 31.4 percent . . . [in 2002]— consider following politics a "very important" or "essential" goal.*[33]

Two key pressure points for managers in this area are the politicization of management and increased personal legal accountability.

The Politicization of Management

Prepared or not and willing or not, today's managers often find themselves embroiled in issues with clearly political overtones. Just ask the Walt Disney Company. In 1994 Disney abandoned plans to build a history-oriented theme park in Virginia in the face of public outcry about dishonoring nearby Civil War battlefields.[34] Another political bombshell exploded in 1996. "The Southern Baptist Convention, 16 million members strong, threatened . . . to boycott Walt Disney's parks, movies and products to protest Disney's departure from its 'family-values image.' The chief complaint: Disney gives health benefits to companions of gay employees."[35] This time, Disney did not give in to pressure. Disney's official response: "We question any group that demands that we deprive people of health benefits."[36] Political pressures on management most likely will intensify in the wake of recent corporate scandals that outraged citizens and legislators alike.[37]

General Political Responses

The three general political responses available to management can be plotted on a continuum, as illustrated in Figure 2.2. Managers who are politically inactive occupy the middle neutral zone and have a "wait-and-see" attitude. But few managers today can afford the luxury of a neutral political stance. Those on the extreme left of the continuum are politically active in defending the status quo and/or fighting government intervention. In contrast, politically active managers on the right end of the continuum try to identify and respond constructively to emerging political/legal issues.

In recent years, more and more business managers have swung away from being reactive and become proactive. Why? In short, they view prompt action as a way to avoid additional governmental regulation. The wisdom of choosing a proactive stance is clearly illustrated by the recent experiences of Microsoft and Intel. Both are dominant players in their respective fields of software and computer chips. According to *Harvard Business Review:*

> For years now, Microsoft has been mired in court, facing charges of predatory behavior by the U.S. Department of Justice and the attorneys general of more than a dozen states. It has seen its name and business practices dragged through the mud, its senior executives distracted and embarrassed, and its very future as a single company thrown into doubt.
>
> Intel, in stark contrast, has managed to avoid prolonged, high-profile antitrust cases. It's remained above the fray, its business focus largely undisturbed by trustbusters.

FIGURE 2.2

Management's Political Response Continuum

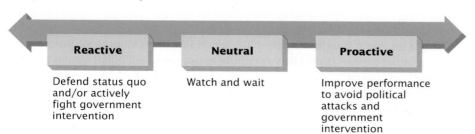

Reactive	Neutral	Proactive
Defend status quo and/or actively fight government intervention	Watch and wait	Improve performance to avoid political attacks and government intervention

> *Intel's success is not a matter of luck. It's a matter of painstaking planning and intense effort. The company's antitrust compliance program, refined over many years, may not receive a lot of attention from the press and the public, but it's been an integral element in the chip maker's business strategy.*[38]

Specific Political Strategies

Whether acting reactively or proactively, managers can employ four major strategies.[39]

1. *Campaign financing.* Although federal law prohibits U.S. corporations from backing a specific candidate or party with the firm's name, funds, or free labor, a legal alternative is available. Corporations can form political action committees (PACs) to solicit volunteer contributions from employees biannually for the support of preferred candidates and parties. Importantly, PACs are registered with the Federal Election Commission and are required to keep detailed and accurate records of receipts and expenditures. Some criticize corporate PACs for having too great an influence over federal politics. But legislators are reluctant to tamper with a funding mechanism that tends to favor those already in office.

2. *Lobbying.* Historically, lobbying has been management's most popular and successful political strategy. Secret and informal meetings between hired representatives and key legislators in smoke-filled rooms have largely been replaced by a more forthright approach. Today, formal presentations by well-prepared company representatives are the preferred approach to lobbying for political support.[40] Despite lobbying reform legislation from the U.S. Congress in response to abuses, loopholes, and weak penalties for inappropriate gifts, it is pretty much business as usual for the 37,000 registered lobbyists in Washington, D.C.[41]

3. *Coalition building.* In a political environment of countless special-interest groups, managers are finding that coalitions built around common rallying points are required for political impact.

4. *Indirect lobbying.* Having learned a lesson from unions, business managers now appreciate the value of grassroots lobbying. Members of legislative bodies tend to be more responsive to the desires of their constituents than to those of individuals who vote in other districts. Employee and consumer letter-writing, telephone, and e-mail campaigns have proved effective. **Advocacy advertising**, the controversial practice of promoting a point of view along with a product or service, is another form of indirect lobbying that has grown in popularity in recent years.

advocacy advertising Promoting a point of view along with a product or service.

Increased Personal Legal Accountability

Recent changes in the political and legal climate have made it increasingly difficult for managers to take refuge in the bureaucratic shadows when a law has been broken. Managers in the United States who make illegal decisions stand a good chance of being held personally accountable in a court of law.

Things got even tougher in July 2002, when President George W. Bush signed into law the Sarbanes-Oxley Act, a sweeping corporate fraud bill driven by an unusually high degree of bipartisan cooperation. The lawmakers were prodded into decisive action by public disgust over the fraud-tainted failures of corporate giants including Enron, Andersen, WorldCom, and Adelphia.

> *The law, which passed the Senate by 99-0 and the House by 423-3, quadruples sentences for accounting fraud, creates a new felony for securities fraud that carries a 25-year prison term, places new restraints on corporate officers, and establishes a federal oversight board for the accounting industry.*
>
> *"No more easy money for corporate criminals, just hard time," the president said. "The era of low standards and false profits is over, no boardroom in America is above or beyond the law."[42]*

This increases the likelihood of managers being held *personally responsible* for the illegal actions of their companies. For example, consider this recent list of executive criminals:

- Bernard Ebbers, former CEO of WorldCom: serving a 25-year prison sentence

- Jeffrey Skilling, former CEO of Enron: serving a 24-year, 4-month prison sentence (not much of a bargain, considering Skilling's estimated $70 million in legal fees)

- Andrew Fastow, former chief financial officer of Enron: serving a 6-year prison sentence

- Dennis Kozlowski, former CEO of Tyco: serving an 8-year, 4-month to 25-year prison sentence

- John Rigas, former CEO of Adelphia Communications: sentenced to 15 years in prison

- Sanjay Kumar, former CEO of Computer Associates: serving a 12-year prison sentence[43]

The trend toward greater legal accountability for managers is spreading to other countries as well.

Source: © 2004 Gary Markstein. Courtesy of *The Milwaukee Journal Sentinel.*

Political-Legal Implications for Management

Managers will continue to be forced into becoming more politically astute, whether they like it or not. Support appears to be growing for the idea that managers can and should try to shape the political climate in which they operate. And the vigilant media and a wary public can be expected to keep a close eye on the form and substance of managerial politics to ensure that the public interest is served. Managers who abuse their political power and/or engage in criminal conduct while at work will increasingly be held accountable.

On the legal side, managers are attempting to curb the skyrocketing costs of litigation. Suing large companies with so-called deep pockets is common practice in the United States today. For example, in a well-publicized class-action suit in 2002, McDonald's was sued for advertising and selling food to children who tend to become overweight and plagued by diabetes and heart disease. No matter how the suit turns out, *Fortune* issued this warning to the food industry:

> *Seasoned lawyers from both sides of past mass-tort disputes agree that the years ahead hold serious tobacco-like litigation challenges that extend beyond fast foods to snack foods, soft drinks, packaged goods, and dietary supplements.[44]*

Not surprisingly, U.S. business leaders are pushing hard for tort reform in which some sort of legislated cap is put on jury awards and damage claims. Trial lawyers are pushing equally hard to squelch any such limitations, citing the need to protect the public. In the meantime:

legal audit Review of all operations to pinpoint possible legal liabilities or problems.

▌ Managers can better prepare their companies and hopefully avoid costly legal problems by performing legal audits. "A **legal audit** reviews all aspects of a firm's operations to pinpoint possible liabilities and other legal problems."[45] For example, a company's human resources department needs to carefully screen job application forms to eliminate any questions that could trigger a discriminatory hiring lawsuit.

alternative dispute resolution Avoiding courtroom battles by settling disputes with less costly methods, including arbitration and mediation.

▌ Another approach, called **alternative dispute resolution** (ADR), strives to curb courtroom costs by settling disagreements out of court through techniques such as arbitration and mediation.[46]

> *The modern ADR phenomenon has led to much greater use of older methods such as arbitration and mediation, as well as the creation of many new methods such as mini-trial, summary jury trial, private judging, neutral evaluation, and regulatory negotiation. Variations and hybrids of these techniques are also commonly found today.*[47]

As a technical point, a third-party arbitrator makes a binding decision, whereas a mediator helps the parties reach their own agreement.

TEST PREPPER 2.2

ANSWERS CAN BE FOUND ON P. 51

True or False?

_____ 1. A "defend status quo" attitude is adopted by managers on the neutral portion of the political response continuum.

_____ 2. Lobbying has been management's most successful political strategy.

_____ 3. With the passage of the Sarbanes-Oxley Act in 2002, executives are more likely to go to jail for their organizational misdeeds.

_____ 4. Legal auditing refers to settling legal disputes outside of court.

Multiple Choice

_____ 5. An attitude adopted by managers on the _____ portion of the political response continuum is "watch and wait."
   a. proactive
   b. anticipatory
   c. reactive
   d. neutral
   e. entrenched

_____ 6. Which political strategy does the timber industry rely on when it presents its case directly to members of Congress prior to votes on land-preservation matters?
   a. Coalition building
   b. Campaign financing
   c. Indirect lobbying
   d. Lobbying
   e. Civil disobedience

_____ 7. What do the various alternative dispute resolution methods such as mediation and arbitration have in common?
   a. Binding decisions by a third party
   b. High cost
   c. Legally questionable
   d. Not available to profit-seeking businesses
   e. Out-of-court settlements

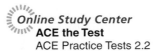
Online Study Center
ACE the Test
ACE Practice Tests 2.2

THE ECONOMIC ENVIRONMENT

 Discuss why the global economy is a vital economic consideration for modern managers.

As stated in Chapter 1, there is a close relationship between economics and management. Economics is the study of how scarce resources are used to create wealth and how that wealth is distributed. Managers, as trustees of our resource-consuming productive organizations, perform an essentially economic function. Three aspects of the economic environment of management that deserve special consideration are jobs, economic forecasts, and the global economy.

The Job Outlook in Today's Service Economy, Where Education Counts

As in other important aspects of life, you have no guarantee of landing your dream job. However, as you move through college and into the labor force, one assumption is safe: you will probably end up with a service-producing job. Why? "According to the [U.S.] Bureau of Labor Statistics, the service economy is expected to account for 19.1 million of the 19.5 million total new wage and salary jobs generated over the 1998–2008 period."[48] Those concerned about having their future jobs outsourced to India, China, and elsewhere can take some comfort in knowing that the service-job category "general managers and operations managers" is one of the most rapidly growing job categories (*and* that it is resistant to being moved offshore).

The traditional notion of the service sector as a low-wage haven of nothing but hamburger flippers and janitors is no longer valid. Well-paid doctors, lawyers, engineers, scientists, consultants, and other professionals are all service-sector employees enjoying the fruits of a good education. Economists at the U.S. Bureau of Labor Statistics see it this way: "Occupations that require a bachelor's degree are projected to grow the fastest, nearly twice as fast as the average for all occupations. All of the 20 occupations with the highest earnings require at least a bachelor's degree. . . . Education is essential in getting a high paying job."[49]

Benefiting from Economic Forecasts

In view of the fact that Congress's economic advisers accurately predicted the U.S. economy's output only one-third of the time between 1980 and 1994,[50] economic forecasting has come under fire lately.[51] One wit chided economic forecasters by claiming they have predicted eight out of the last four recessions! How can managers get some value from the hundreds of economic forecasts they encounter each year?

A pair of respected forecasting experts recommends a *consensus approach.*[52] They urge managers to survey a wide variety of economic forecasts, taking the forecasters' track records into consideration, and to look for a consensus or average opinion. Decisions related to the business cycle can then be made accordingly, and slavish adherence to a single forecast avoided. One sure formula for failure is naively to assume that the future will simply be a replication of the past. In spite of their imperfection, professional economic forecasts are better than no forecasts at all. One economist puts it this way: "Forecasters are very useful, in fact indispensable, because they give you plausible scenarios to help you think about the future in an organized way."[53]

The Challenge of a Global Economy

The global economy is expanding as never before. *Business Week* recently offered this perspective:

> *Since 1995 imports have risen from 12% of gross domestic product to about 17%. And foreign money finances about 32% of U.S. domestic investment, up from 7% in 1995. In other words, the U.S. is more open to the global economy than ever before, and the links run in both directions. Now many of the levers affecting the U.S. economy are located not in Washington but in Beijing, London, and even Mexico City.*[54] *Each of us is challenged to understand the workings and implications of the global economy better because of its profound impact on our lives and work.*

A Single Global Marketplace

Money spent on imported Japanese cars, French perfumes, Colombian coffee, Chinese electronics, New Zealand meat and produce, German beers, and Italian shoes may be evidence of an increasingly global economy. Deeper analysis, however, reveals more profound changes. First, according to John Naisbitt and Patricia Aburdene's landmark book *Megatrends 2000*, "The new global economy ... must be viewed as the world moving from trade among countries to a single economy. One economy. One marketplace."[55] The North American Free Trade Agreement (NAFTA) among Mexico, Canada, and the United States, the 25-nation (as of early 2007) European Union, and the 150-nation (as of early 2007) World Trade Organization (WTO) represent steps toward that single global marketplace. Second, the size of the global economy has expanded dramatically. *Fortune* explains why:

> *... the commercial world has been swelled by the former Soviet empire, China, India, Indonesia, and much of Latin America—billions of people stepping out from behind political and economic walls. This is the most dramatic change in the geography of capitalism in history.*[56]

Third, and an ominous sign to some, the business cycles of countries around the world show signs of converging in concert with the U.S. economy. International Monetary Fund economists recently documented this trend after studying 20 years of economic data from 170 countries: "They found that an increase of one percentage point in the growth of U.S. output per capita was associated with an increase of 0.8 to 1.0 percentage point in the average growth of other countries. Decreases in U.S. output likewise lowered growth elsewhere."[57] The prospect of global expansions and recessions gives new meaning to the old saying, "We're all in the same boat."

Globalization Is Personal

Economic globalization is a huge concept, stretching the limits of the imagination. For instance, try to grasp what it means that more than $1.5 trillion moves through the global banking network in a single day![58] Ironically, globalization is also a very personal matter, affecting where we work, how much we're paid, what we buy, and how much we pay for things. Let us explore two personal aspects of the global economy:

REALITY CHECK 2.3

"... people from countries like China, India and the former Soviet Union, which all once scorned the global market economy, ... are now enthusiastic and increasingly sophisticated participants in it. They are poorer, hungrier and in some cases well trained, and will inevitably compete with Americans and America for a slice of the pie. A Goldman Sachs study concludes that by 2045, China will be the largest economy in the world, replacing the United States."

Source: Fareed Zakaria, "How Long Will America Lead the World?" *Newsweek* (June 12, 2006): 42.

Question: Is this global economic shift a threat, opportunity, or both? Explain.

All sorts of interesting possibilities emerge when high-tech meets the global economy. Here a staff member from Japan's leading mobile phone company, NTT DoCoMo, demonstrates how to get a can of Coke from a vending machine without any cash. Coca-Cola's specially designed machine downloads debit card data via an infrared signal from the buyer's cell phone. One more reason not to lose your cell phone!

1. *Working for a foreign-owned company.* One of the most visible and controversial signs of a global economy is the worldwide trend toward foreign ownership. Consider the case of Japan's Toyota Motor, for example. By 2005, it was the eighth largest company in the world, employing nearly 286,000 people around the globe. Toyota's eight North American factories (with two more under construction) manufactured more than 1.5 million vehicles annually. Those facilities employed more than 38,000 people and helped create at least 190,000 jobs at Toyota's dealerships and suppliers in North America.[59] This sort of cross-border ownership raises fundamental questions. For instance, has the increase in foreign-owned companies in the United States been a positive or a negative? Economists have found positive evidence:

   > *Americans who work in the USA for foreign companies typically make about 10% more than those who work for U.S. companies, just as foreigners who work for U.S. companies abroad make 10% more than domestic workers there, says Gary Hufbauer, senior economist with the Institute for International Economics.*
   > *The reason, Hufbauer says, is that companies with the might to expand globally are the most productive, want the best workers and are willing to pay a premium.*[60]

2. *Meeting world standards.* One does not have to work for a foreign-owned company to be personally impacted by the global economy. Many people today complain of having to work harder for the same (or perhaps less) money. Whether they realize it or not, they are being squeezed by two global economic trends: higher quality and lower wages. The "offshoring" of jobs discussed in Chapter 1 is a major by-product of these trends. Only companies striking the right balance between quality and costs can be globally competitive. Consider this recent reality check from *Business Week:*

   > *"A basic business tenet is that things go to the areas where there is the best cost of production," says Ann Livermore, head of services at Hewlett-Packard Co., which has 3,300 software engineers in India. "Now you're going to see the same trends in services that happened in manufacturing."*
   > *The rise of a globally integrated knowledge economy is a blessing for developing nations. What it means for the U.S. skilled labor force is less clear. At the least, many white-collar workers may be headed for a tough readjustment.*[61]

True or False?

____ 1. The service sector accounts for most of the job growth in the United States.

____ 2. A consensus approach to economic forecasts involves looking for patterns among many forecasts.

____ 3. The global economy has put downward pressure on wages while improving product quality.

Multiple Choice

____ 4. According to U.S. Bureau of Labor Statistics economists, which occupations will grow the fastest in today's economy?
   a. Ones requiring a bachelor's degree
   b. The lowest paying jobs
   c. Jobs requiring at least a master's degree
   d. Truck drivers and autoworkers
   e. Teachers and paralegals

____ 5. What sort of evidence have researchers found about the increase of foreign-owned companies in the United States?
   a. Very negative
   b. A neutral impact
   c. Positive
   d. Nothing conclusive
   e. Slightly negative

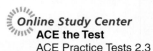
Online Study Center
ACE the Test
ACE Practice Tests 2.3

THE TECHNOLOGICAL ENVIRONMENT

4 ▶ *Describe the three-step innovation process and define the term* intrapreneur.

Technology is a term that ignites passionate debates in many circles these days. Some blame technology for environmental destruction and cultural fragmentation. Others view technology as the key to economic and social progress. No doubt there are important messages in both extremes. See Table 2.1 for technological shifts that are likely to have significant impacts on our lives in the future.

For our purposes, **technology** is defined as all the tools and ideas available for extending the natural physical and mental reach of humankind. A central theme in technology is the practical application of new ideas, a theme that is clarified by the following distinction between science and technology: "Science is the quest for more or less abstract knowledge, whereas technology is the application of organized knowledge to help solve problems in our society."[62] According to the following historical perspective, technology is facilitating the evolution of the industrial age into the information age, just as it once enabled the agricultural age to evolve into the industrial age.

technology All the tools and ideas available for extending the natural physical and mental reach of humankind.

> *Stephen R. Barley, a professor at Cornell's School of Industrial and Labor Relations, builds on the work of others to argue that until recently, "the economies of the advanced industrial nations revolved around electrical power, the electric motor, the internal combustion engine, and the telephone." The development of these "infrastructural technologies" made possible the shift from an agricultural to a manufacturing economy, in the process precipitating "urbanization, the growth of corporations, the rise of professional management. . . ."*

> *Now, Barley writes, the evidence suggests that another shift is taking place, with implications likely to be just as seismic: "Our growing knowledge of how to convert electronic and mechanical impulses into digitally encoded information (and vice versa) and how to transmit such information across vast distances is gradually enabling industry to replace its electromechanical infrastructure with a computational infrastructure."*[63]

Consequently, *information* has become a valuable strategic resource. Organizations using appropriate information technologies to get the right information to the right people at the right time will enjoy a competitive advantage (Internet strategies are discussed in Chapter 5).

Two aspects of technology with important implications for managers are the innovation process and intrapreneurship.

The Innovation Process

Technology comes into being through the **innovation process**, defined as the systematic development and practical application of a new idea.[64] A great deal of time-consuming work is needed to develop a new idea into a marketable product or service. And many otherwise good ideas do not become technologically feasible, let alone marketable and profitable. According to one innovation expert, "only one of every 20 or 25 ideas ever becomes a successful product—and of every 10 or 15 new products, only one becomes a hit."[65] Understanding the innovation process better can help management turn more new ideas into profitable goods and services. Intel's chairman, Craig Barrett, drove this point home by noting: "If you don't invest for the future, you have no future."[66]

innovation process The systematic development and practical application of a new idea.

TABLE 2.1

Science Fiction Is Becoming Reality with These Seven New Technologies

- **Plastic solar cells:** "The new photovoltaics use tiny solar cells embedded in thin sheets of plastic to create an energy-producing material that is cheap, efficient, and versatile."

- **Printable mechatronics:** Researchers are "developing processes that adapt ink-jet printing technology to build ready-to-use products, complete with working circuitry, switches, and movable parts."

- **Memory drugs:** These drugs aim to help people with Alzheimer's and boost healthy peoples' memory by enhancing the brain's neural connections and functions.

- **Perpendicular magnetic storage:** "Today's hard drives store bits of data horizontally, like stalks of freshly cut corn. PMR stores them vertically, like cornstalks standing in a field. With perpendicular storage, each bit occupies less space on the surface of the disc, so more data can be stuffed into a smaller area." This technology also uses less power, thus prolonging battery life.

- **Microfluidic testing:** "Microfluidics is the science of moving fluids through tiny channels the thickness of a human hair. In microfluidic tests, blood, saliva, or urine samples are analyzed after coming into contact with tiny amounts of a chemical reagent."

- **Micro-opticals:** Combining the functions of several present-day chips on one integrated optical chip will make telecommunication faster and less expensive.

- **Software radio:** The goal of this new software is to create wireless communication devices that will work on all mobile networks—anywhere, anytime.

Source: Adapted from G. Pascal Zachary, Om Malik, David Pescovitz, and Matthew Maier, "Seven New Technologies That Change Everything," *Business 2.0,* 5 (September 2004): 82–90.

product technology   Second stage of the innovation process: creating a working prototype.

production technology   Third stage of the innovation process: developing a profitable production process.

innovation lag   Time it takes for a new idea to be translated into satisfied demand.

A Three-Step Process

The innovation process has three steps (see Figure 2.3). First is the conceptualization step, when a new idea occurs to someone. Developing a working prototype is the second step, called **product technology**. This involves actually creating a product that will work as intended. The third and final step is developing a production process to create a profitable quantity-quality-price relationship. This third step is labeled **production technology**. Successful innovation depends on the right combination of new ideas, product technology, and production technology. A missing or deficient step can ruin the innovation process.

Innovation Lag

The time it takes for a new idea to be translated into satisfied demand is called **innovation lag**. The longer the innovation lag, the longer society must wait to benefit from a new idea. For example, fax machines came into wide use in the early 1990s. But the facsimile concept was patented by a Scottish clockmaker named Alexander Bain in 1843—an innovation lag of nearly a century and a half.[67] Over the years, the trend has been toward shorter innovation lags. For example, Britain's Imperial Chemical Industries has "slashed the time it takes to commercialize a technology from the industry norm of more than a decade to only five years."[68]

Shortening Innovation Lag

Reducing innovation lags should be a high priority for modern managers. Innovative companies generally rely on two sound management practices: *goal setting* and *empowerment*. These practices create the sense of urgency necessary for speedier innovation. Medtronic, the Minnesota-based leader in manufacturing heart pacemakers, uses goal setting skillfully. Top management sends a powerful message about promptly getting new ideas to market to its 33,000-plus employees worldwide when it restates the "annual goal of gathering 70% of its sales from products introduced within the past two years."[69] That is a bold commitment!

Empowerment, discussed in Chapter 13, involves pushing decision-making authority down to levels where people with the appropriate skills can do the most good. Software giant Microsoft is strong in this regard, as illustrated by the following story told by the firm's recently retired chief operating officer:

> *I was in a meeting where Bill Gates was quizzing a young manager—dressed in cutoffs, sandals, and a well-worn Microsoft T-shirt—about a new product proposal. After the meeting, I asked Bill, for whom this had been the first significant briefing on the product, what the next step would be. Would the manager*

FIGURE 2.3

The Three-Step Innovation Process

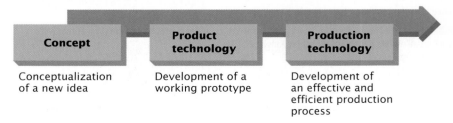

Concept	Product technology	Production technology
Conceptualization of a new idea	Development of a working prototype	Development of an effective and efficient production process

prepare a memo summarizing the arguments, something top management could review before suggesting modifications to his proposal and granting final approval? Bill looked at me and smiled. "No, that's it. The key decisions got made," he said. "Now his group better hustle to implement things—or else."[70]

Another step in the right direction is a practice called **concurrent engineering**. Also referred to as parallel design, concurrent engineering is a team approach to product design, that differs sharply from traditional practice.

concurrent engineering Team approach to product design involving specialists from all functional areas including research, production, and marketing.

Concurrent engineering

▌ Research, design, production, finance, and marketing specialists have a direct say in the product design process from the very beginning.[71]

Traditional engineering

▌ The practice of having a product move serially from research to design, from design to manufacturing, and so on down the line toward the marketplace.

The time to hear about possible marketing problems is while a product is still in the conceptualization stage, not after it has become a warehouse full of unsold goods.

Promoting Innovation Through Intrapreneurship

When we hear someone called an entrepreneur, we generally think of a creative individual who has risked everything while starting his or her own business. Indeed, as we saw in Chapter 1, entrepreneurs are a vital innovative force in the economy. A lesser-known but no less important type of entrepreneur is the so-called *intrapreneur*.

Gifford Pinchot, author of the book *Intrapreneuring*, defines an **intrapreneur** as an employee who takes personal "hands-on responsibility" for pushing any type of innovative idea, product, or process through the organization. Pinchot calls intrapreneurs "dreamers who do." But unlike traditional entrepreneurs, who tend to leave the organizational confines to pursue their dreams, intrapreneurs strive for innovation *within* existing organizations.[72] Intrapreneurs tend to have a higher need for security than entrepreneurs, who strike out on their own. They pay a price for being employees rather than owners. Pinchot explains:

intrapreneur An employee who takes personal responsibility for pushing an innovative idea through a large organization.

> *Corporate entrepreneurs [or intrapreneurs], despite prior successes, have no capital of their own to start other ventures. Officially, they must begin from zero by persuading management that their new ideas are promising. Unlike successful independent entrepreneurs, they are not free to guide their next ventures by their own intuitive judgments; they still have to justify every move.*[73]

Kathleen Synnott, a division marketing manager for Pitney Bowes Inc., is the classic intrapreneur. After seeing the potential of the versatile new Mail Center 2000, a computerized mail-handling and -stamping machine, Synnott became its enthusiastic champion. Just two things stood in her way: change-resistant managers and satisfied customers.

> *During the design process, for instance, Synnott helped protect the original blueprint from execs who wanted to break up the Mail Center 2000 and sell it as upgrading components to Pitney's existing mail-metering machines. She also guided it through a technical maze, insisting on 22 simulations to make sure potential customers liked what they saw. "There were naysayers who didn't think we were ready" for such a system, says Synnott. . . . "But they got religion."*[74]

If today's large companies are to achieve a competitive edge through innovation, they need to foster a supportive climate for intrapreneurs like Synnott. According to experts on the subject, an organization can foster intrapreneurship if it does four things:

- Focuses on results and teamwork
- Rewards innovation and risk taking
- Tolerates and learns from mistakes
- Remains flexible and change-oriented[75]

Our discussions of creativity, empowerment, participative management, and organizational cultures in later chapters contain ideas about how to encourage intrapreneurship of all types.

TEST PREPPER 2.4

ANSWERS CAN BE FOUND ON P. 51

True or False?

_____ 1. Coming up with a bold new idea is "product technology" in the three-step innovation process.

_____ 2. Innovation lag is the time it takes to come up with a radically new idea.

_____ 3. "Intrapreneurs" typically do not quit their present job to pursue an innovative idea.

Multiple Choice

_____ 4. When Sony develops a working prototype for a new product, it has achieved which step in the three-step innovation process?
   a. Conceptual
   b. Production technology
   c. Exploitation
   d. Product technology
   e. Differentiation

_____ 5. _____ refers to the time it takes to turn a new idea into a product that satisfies consumer demand.
   a. Innovation lag
   b. Developmental decay
   c. Creativity lapse
   d. Innovation drag
   e. Demand slack

_____ 6. The term _____ describes an employee in a large company who takes personal responsibility for pushing an innovation through the organization.
   a. entrepreneur
   b. intrapreneur
   c. concurrent engineer
   d. contingent worker
   e. innovation advocate

Online Study Center
ACE the Test
ACE Practice Tests 2.4

How Three Corporate Giants Helped Women Reach the Top

First up is Reynolds American. The tobacco giant is the only *Fortune* 500 company to have women in the CEO and CFO positions, as well as a female COO running its largest subsidiary. Then there's DuPont, where two women run three of the company's five business segments, bringing in $18 billion of DuPont's $27 billion in annual revenues. And Honeywell is unlike any of its competitors in having an equal number of men and women—two apiece—as divisional chief executive officers.

What's going on here? For a start, all three companies are fanatical about measurable results. "We're a performance culture," says Nance Dicciani, president and CEO of Specialty Materials at Honeywell. "The results and how you get them are judged and rewarded accordingly." All companies say they value performance, but Reynolds, DuPont and Honeywell go further, creating the conditions—empirical standards, clear goals, frequent reviews—that enable them to identify and reward high performers, regardless of sex. . . .

Highfliers are not just recognized. They're asked to take the kinds of tough assignments that give them the chance to leap beyond middle management. Reynolds CEO Susan Ivey says her big break came in 1990, when she was asked to take an overseas assignment and given 48 hours to decide. She went for it. The experience, Ivey says, was "broadening in every way." . . .

Then there's the chain-reaction effect. High-level female executives can inspire women throughout the organization and draw new talent. Ivey says Reynolds's new general counsel, E. Julia "Judy" Lambeth, was attracted to the job in part because there were so many women at the top. "It's easy for companies to say they don't have a glass ceiling," says Ivey, "but when you walk in the door here, it's eminently clear that we don't."

Source: Excerpted from Eugenia Levenson, "Leaders of the Pact," *Fortune*, October 16, 2006, p. 189. Copyright © 2006 Time Inc. All rights reserved.

Is EEStor a Pipe Dream or the BIG Breakthrough in Automotive Technology?

Forget hybrids and hydrogen-powered vehicles. EEStor, a stealth company in Cedar Park, Texas, is working on an "energy storage" device that could finally give the internal combustion engine a run for its money—and begin saving us from our oil addiction. "To call it a battery discredits it," says Ian Clifford, the CEO of Toronto-based electric car company Feel Good Cars, which plans to incorporate EEStor's technology in vehicles by 2008.

EEStor's device is not technically a battery because no chemicals are involved. In fact, it contains no hazardous materials whatsoever. Yet it acts like a battery in that it stores electricity. If it works as it's supposed to, it will charge up in five minutes and provide enough energy to drive 500 miles on about $9 worth of electricity. At today's gas prices, covering that distance can cost

$60 or more; the EEStor device would power a car for the equivalent of about 45 cents a gallon.

And we mean power a car. "A four-passenger sedan will drive like a Ferrari," Clifford predicts. In contrast, his first electric car, the Zenn, which debuted in August [2006] and is powered by a more conventional battery, can't go much faster than a moped and takes hours to charge.

The cost of the engine itself depends on how much energy it can store; an EEStor-powered engine with a range roughly equivalent to that of a gasoline-powered car would cost about $5,200. That's a slight premium over the cost of the gas engine and the other parts the device would replace—the gas tank, exhaust system, and drive train. But getting rid of the need to buy gas

CLOSING CASE STUDY (CONTINUED)

should more than make up for the extra cost of an EEStor-powered car.

EEStor is tight-lipped about its device and how it manages to pack such a punch. According to a patent issued in April [2006], the device is made of a ceramic powder coated with aluminum oxide and glass. A bank of these ceramic batteries could be used at "electrical energy stations" where people on the road could charge up.

EEStor is backed by VC firm Kleiner Perkins Caufield & Byers, and the company's founders are engineers Richard Weir and Carl Nelson. CEO Weir, a former IBM-er, won't comment, but his son, Tom, an EEStor VP, acknowledges, "That is pretty much why we are here today, to compete with the internal combustion engine." He also hints that his engine technology is not just for the small passenger vehicles that Clifford is aiming at, but could easily replace the 300-horsepower brutes in today's SUVs. That would make it appealing to automakers like GM and Ford, who are seeing sales

of their gas-guzzling SUVs and pickup trucks begin to tank because of exorbitant fuel prices.

Source: Excerpted from Erick Schonfeld and Jeanette Borzo, "The Next Disruptors," *Business 2.0,* 7, October 2006, pp. 82–83. Copyright © 2006 Time Inc. All rights reserved.

Case Questions

1. Where would you plot EEStor's ceramic power source device on the innovation continuum in Figure 2.3?
2. From a big picture perspective, what are the major arguments for and against an EEStor-powered car?
3. On a scale from 0 (no chance) to 100 (a virtual guarantee), where would you rank the probability that an EEStor-powered car will be a commercial success in the marketplace? Explain.
4. If you were a rich venture capitalist and EEStor's CEO Richard Weir came to you for funding, how much would you be willing to invest? Explain your decision.

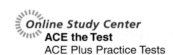

Online Study Center
ACE the Test
ACE Plus Practice Tests

Online Study Center
Improve Your Grade
Learning Objective Review
Audio Chapter Review
Audio Chapter Quiz
Study Guide to Go

LEARNING OBJECTIVE REVIEW

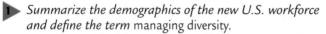

1 ▸ *Summarize the demographics of the new U.S. workforce and define the term* managing diversity.

- The United States workforce is getting bigger, increasingly female, more diverse, and older.
- Managing diversity programs attempt to go a step beyond equal employment opportunity. The new goal is to tap every employee's full potential in today's diverse workforce.

2 ▸ *Discuss how the changing political-legal environment is affecting the practice of management.*

- Because of government regulations and sociopolitical demands from a growing list of special-interest groups, managers are becoming increasingly politicized. More and more believe that if they are going to be affected by political forces, they should be more active politically.

Managers can respond politically in three ways: by being reactive, neutral, or proactive.

- Four political strategies that managers have found useful for pursuing active or reactive political goals are campaign financing, lobbying, coalition building, and indirect lobbying.
- There is a strong trend toward managers being held personally accountable for the misdeeds of their organizations, especially since the passage of the Sarbanes-Oxley Act of 2002.

3 ▸ *Discuss why the global economy is a vital economic consideration for modern managers.*

- For the foreseeable future, most new jobs will be in the service sector. Education is the key to good jobs in the knowledge economy.

- Managers can make timely decisions by taking a consensus approach to economic forecasts.

- Business is urged to compete actively and creatively in the rapidly growing global economy. By influencing jobs, prices, quality standards, and wages, the global economy affects virtually everyone.

4▶ *Describe the three-step innovation process and define the term* intrapreneur.

- A healthy innovation process—which includes conceptualization, product technology, and production tech-

nology—is vital to technological development. Innovation lags must be shortened.

- An intrapreneur is an employee who champions an idea or innovation by pushing it through the organization. Organizations can foster intrapreneurship by focusing on results and teamwork, rewarding innovation and risk taking, tolerating mistakes, and remaining flexible and change-oriented.

TEST PREPPER ANSWERS

▶ **2.1**

1. T   2. F   3. F   4. F   5. F   6. c   7. e
8. b

▶ **2.2**

1. F   2. T   3. T   4. F   5. d   6. d   7. e

▶ **2.3**

1. T   2. T   3. T   4. a   5. c

▶ **2.4**

1. F   2. F   3. T   4. d   5. a   6. b

Online Study Center RESOURCES

Prepare for Class, Improve Your Grade, and ACE the Test. Student Achievement Series resources include:

ACE Practice Tests	Crossword Puzzles	Hangman
Audio Chapter Quizzes	Decision Case Questions	Key Issue Expansion
Audio Chapter Reviews	Ethical Hot Seat Exercises	Learning Objective Reviews
Career Snapshots	Flashcards	Study Guide to Go
Chapter Glossaries	Hands-on Exercises	Visual Glossaries
Chapter Outlines		

To access these learning and study tools, go to **college.hmco.com/pic/kreitnerSASfound**.

Mercado Global was started by two Yale graduates who had the vision to bring the benefits of globalization to poor communities in Guatemala.

1 ▸ *Define corporate social responsibility (CSR), and summarize the arguments for and against it.*

2 ▸ *Identify and describe the four social responsibility strategies, and explain the role of enlightened self-interest in CSR.*

3 ▸ *Summarize the three practical lessons from business ethics research. Then identify and describe at least four of the ten general ethical principles.*

Chapter Outline

Online Study Center
Prepare for Class
Chapter Outline

4 ▶ *Discuss what management can do to improve business ethics.*

From College Students to Global Entrepreneurs

Benita Singh and Ruth DeGolia were still undergraduates in the summer of 2003 when they found their destiny in the village of San Alfonso, on the Pacific coast of Guatemala. Singh and DeGolia, international-studies majors at Yale, were working on their senior theses when they visited the village, which was filled with women who had fled Guatemala during that country's brutal civil war in the 1980s. After two years in refugee camps in Mexico, the women, many of them widowed by the fighting, had been repatriated here, where there was no work and no market for the exquisite woven and beaded handicrafts they produced. "There are only so many tourists, and each one can only buy so much," says DeGolia ruefully. But the women weren't beggars; it was, says Singh, "the first time I'd ever walked into an impoverished [Third World] community where people weren't asking me for money."

Online Study Center college.hmco.com/pic/kreitnerSASfound

Online Study Center
Prepare for Class
   Chapter Glossary

Improve Your Grade
   Flashcards
   Hangman
   Crossword Puzzles

So the two young women filled their suitcases with beaded bags and necklaces and took them back to Yale that fall, where they quickly sold out at a 300 percent markup. By Christmas they were back in Guatemala, laying the groundwork for a nonprofit they named Mercado ("market") Global, which seeks to bring the benefits of globalization to poor communities that until now have seen only the downside, in the collapse of prices for their locally grown crops. With a start-up grant from Echoing Green, a "social entrepreneurship" foundation, Singh and DeGolia organized 15 to 18 cooperatives in villages so remote that many inhabitants don't even speak Spanish, let alone English. The members produce textiles on backstrap looms, hand-painted ceramics and jewelry for the export market. They grossed about $75,000 last year in retail, online and catalog sales; this year, their second, Singh and DeGolia project sales of $600,000, and they are in talks with a major chain about carrying their hand-painted coffee mugs. The money will be used to fund scholarships for children whose parents could not afford the $50 or $60 it costs to send a child to elementary school in rural Guatemala. This year they're sending a computer to each of the cooperatives so the women can keep their books (although only a few can read or write). "We have a very special place in our heart," says Lara Galinsky, a vice president of Echoing Green, "for young people with the audacity, the vision and the energy to see things through." Even in places like San Alfonso.[2] ∎

Countless headlines about executive misconduct and criminal activity at firms such as Enron, Tyco, and WorldCom in recent years have created a strong negative impression about the business world. Unfortunately, news reporters generally overlook the vast majority of managers and entrepreneurs who are upstanding and honest. For example, entrepreneurs Benita Singh and Ruth DeGolia are dedicated to the well-being of less fortunate people. The spirit of their story is what this chapter is all about—management's social and ethical responsibilities. But as Singh and DeGolia's generation moves into positions of leadership, what sort of corporate conduct can we expect in the future? Recent research evidence paints a mixed picture.

∎ "In a new survey [of 13 to 25-year-olds], 61% said they feel personally responsible for making a difference in the world. And more than 75% said companies should join them in this effort."[3]

∎ A survey by Rutgers University "showed 56 percent of upper level business students admitted to cheating in the past year. The reason? Many said they believed it was an accepted practice in business."[4]

Conclusion: Studying this chapter about corporate social responsibility and business ethics will be time well spent for both present and future managers.

SOCIAL RESPONSIBILITY: DEFINITION AND DEBATE

> **1** ► *Define corporate social responsibility (CSR), and summarize the arguments for and against it.*

When John D. Rockefeller was at the zenith of his power as the founder of Standard Oil Company, he handed out dimes to rows of eager children who lined the street. Rockefeller did this on the advice of a public relations expert who believed the dime campaign would counteract his widespread reputation as a monopolist who had ruthlessly eliminated his competitors in the oil industry. The dime campaign was not a complete success, however, because Standard Oil was broken up under the Sherman Antitrust Act of 1890. Conceivably, Rockefeller believed he was fulfilling some sort of social responsibility by passing out dimes to hungry children. Since Rockefeller's time, the concept of social responsibility has matured to the point where many companies today are intimately involved in social programs that have no direct connection with the bottom line. These programs include everything from support of the arts and urban renewal to environmental protection. But like all aspects of management, social responsibility needs to be carried out in an effective and efficient manner.

What Does Social Responsibility Involve?

Social responsibility, as defined in this section, is a relatively new concern of the business community. Like a child maturing through adolescence on the way to adulthood, the idea of corporate social responsibility (CSR) is evolving. Thomas A. Stewart, the editor of Harvard Business Review, recently explained the logic of CSR this way:

> *companies and society are not in different camps; they are in the same boat. Companies cannot thrive in corrupt, enervated, impoverished societies; and the train of social progress will move much faster with locomotives of private enterprise at its head. If you start from the premise that business and society are interdependent, CSR becomes an opportunity, not a duty.*[5]

Not surprisingly, there is wide-ranging disagreement over the exact nature and scope of management's social responsibilities.

Voluntary Action

One expert defined **corporate social responsibility** as "the notion that corporations have an obligation to constituent groups in society other than stockholders and beyond that prescribed by law or union contract."[6] A central feature of this definition is that an action must be *voluntary* to qualify as a socially responsible action. For example, consider this corporate initiative as described by Sir Richard Branson, the legendary British entrepreneur behind the Virgin family of brands including Virgin Atlantic airlines, Virgin Megastores, and Virgin Mobile phone service:

> *At Virgin, we have been engaged for some years in trying to create a business model for the 21st century that takes into account the whole cycle of energy consumption and carbon output, in order to change the balance....*

Online Study Center
Improve Your Grade
Visual Glossary 3.1

REALITY CHECK 3.1

"Dow Chemical is increasing R&D [research and development] in products such as roof tiles that deliver power to buildings and water treatment technologies for regions short of clean water. 'There is 100% overlap between our business drivers and social and environmental interests,' says Dow CEO Andrew N. Liveris."

Source: Pete Engardio, "Beyond the Green Corporation," *Business Week* (January 29, 2007): 56.

Question: Is this just "green talk," for public relations purposes, or is it possible for companies to be both environmentally responsible and profitable?

corporate social responsibility The idea that business has social obligations above and beyond making a profit.

Why wait until you've earned your college degree to become socially responsible? Dental students at Cleveland's Case Western Reserve University have the right idea by volunteering in the surrounding community. Here they clean and seal disadvantaged childrens' teeth in a portable dental office set up in a local school. This sort of university-community partnership is a win-win situation eveyone can smile about.

This project recently culminated in a $3 billion investment plan for the next 10 years in biofuel production, research and development, and other investments in renewable-energy production. The project will also include investment in new technology to dramatically shrink the carbon footprint of our existing transport operations. Since the transport sector is one of the largest consumers of oil, dramatically reducing the amount of oil used in ships, planes, trains and cars, or even replacing oil with nonfossil fuels, is critical to our goals. We think it can happen in our lifetime.[7]

According to our definition and the ten commandments of corporate social responsibility listed in Table 3.1, would you credit Branson with an act of corporate social responsibility? This could be open to debate because his actions, although voluntary, are clearly profit-motivated. But one fact remains: he is dedicated to helping us lessen our dependence on pollution-causing fossil fuels. Importantly, the notion of corporate social responsibility does *not* discard the profit motive. It simply challenges managers to *voluntarily* make the world a better place while pursuing a *legitimate* profit.

A company is *not* being socially responsible when:

▌ It will not respond to societal needs unless lawsuits are initiated or court orders issued.

▌ It files endless court appeals.

▌ It complies reluctantly, or uses public relations ploys in lieu of meaningful action.

An Emphasis on Means, Not Ends

Another key feature of this definition of corporate social responsibility is its emphasis on means rather than ends:

Corporate behavior should not, in most cases, be judged by the decisions actually reached, but by the process by which they were reached. Broadly stated, corporations need to analyze the social consequences of their decisions before they make them and take steps to minimize the social costs of these decisions when appropriate. The appropriate demand to be made of those who govern large corporations is that they incorporate into their decision-making process means by which broader social concerns are given full consideration. This is corporate social responsibility as a means, not as a set of ends.[8]

Unfortunately, social consequences are too often shortchanged in the heat of competitive battle.

Arguments for and Against Corporate Social Responsibility

As one might suspect, the debate about the role of business in society has spawned many specific arguments both for and against corporate social responsibility.[9] A sample of four major arguments on each side reveals the principal issues.

Arguments For

Convinced that a business should be more than simply a profit machine, proponents of social responsibility have offered these arguments:

1. *Business is unavoidably involved in social issues.* As social activists like to say, business is either part of the solution or part of the problem. There is no denying that private business shares responsibility for such societal problems as unemployment, inflation, and pollution. Like everyone else, corporate citizens must balance their rights and responsibilities.
2. *Business has the resources to tackle today's complex societal problems.* With its rich stock of technical, financial, and managerial resources, the private business sector can play a decisive role in solving society's more troublesome problems. After all, without society's support, business could not have built its resource base in the first place.
3. *A better society means a better environment for doing business.* Business can enhance its long-run profitability by making an investment in society today. Today's problems can turn into tomorrow's profits.
4. *Corporate social action will prevent government intervention.* As evidenced by waves of antitrust, equal employment opportunity, and pollution-control legislation, government will force business to do what it fails to do voluntarily.

Arguments like these four give business a broad socioeconomic agenda. Advocates of the socioeconomic model point out that many groups in society besides stockholders have a stake in corporate affairs. Creditors, current and retired employees, customers, suppliers, competitors, all levels of government, the community, and society in general

---

TABLE 3.1

Ten Commandments of Corporate Social Responsibility

I. Thou Shall Take Corrective Action Before It Is Required.
II. Thou Shall Work with Affected Constituents to Resolve Mutual Problems.
III. Thou Shall Work to Establish Industrywide Standards and Self-Regulation.
IV. Thou Shall Publicly Admit Your Mistakes.
V. Thou Shall Get Involved in Appropriate Social Programs.
VI. Thou Shall Help Correct Environmental Problems.
VII. Thou Shall Monitor the Changing Social Environment.
VIII. Thou Shall Establish and Enforce a Corporate Code of Conduct.
IX. Thou Shall Take Needed Public Stands on Social Issues.
X. Thou Shall Strive to Make Profits on an Ongoing Basis.

Source: From Larry D. Alexander and William F. Matthews, "The Ten Commandments of Corporate Social Responsibility," *Business and Society Review*, 50, Summer 1984, pp. 62–66. Reprinted with permission of Blackwell Publishing Ltd.

FIGURE 3.1

A Sample Stakeholder Audit for Wal-Mart, the World's Largest Retailer

stakeholder audit   Identifying all parties possibly impacted by the organization.

have expectations, often conflicting, for management. Some companies go so far as to conduct a **stakeholder audit**.[10] This growing practice involves systematically identifying all parties that could possibly be impacted by the company's performance (for an example, see Figure 3.1). According to this broad socioeconomic view of business, managers have an obligation to respond to the needs of all stakeholders while pursuing a profit.

Arguments Against

Remaining faithful to the more restricted classical economic model of business, opponents of corporate social responsibility rely on the first two of the following four arguments. The third and fourth arguments have been voiced by those who think business is already too big and powerful.

1. *Profit maximization ensures the efficient use of society's resources.* By buying goods and services, consumers collectively dictate where assets should be deployed. Social expenditures amount to theft of stockholders' equity.
2. *As an economic institution, business lacks the ability to pursue social goals.* Gross inefficiencies can be expected if managers are forced to divert their attention from their pursuit of economic goals.
3. *Business already has enough power.* Considering that business exercises powerful influence over where and how we work and live, what we buy, and what we value, more concentration of social power in the hands of business is undesirable.
4. *Because managers are not elected, they are not directly accountable to the people.* Corporate social programs can easily become misguided. The market system effectively controls business's economic performance but is a poor mechanism for controlling business's social performance.

These arguments are based on the assumption that business should stick to what it does best—pursuing profit by producing marketable goods and services. Social goals should be handled by other institutions such as the family, schools, religious organizations, or government. Which set of arguments do you find most convincing? Why?

action, is usually required to trigger an accommodative strategy. For example, consider this 2006 news item:

> *The fast-food industry's frantic race to cook up the first "better-for-you" french fry appears to have been won by Wendy's.*
> *The No. 3 fast-food chain today will announce plans to dump its cooking oil for a blend of non-hydrogenated corn and soy oil containing next-to-no artery-clogging trans fats.*
> *With the new oil—to be rolled out in the USA and Canada. . . .—a large order of Wendy's fries will drop from 7 grams of trans fats to 0.5 grams. And a kids-size portion will drop from 3.5 grams to 0 grams.*[16]

Was Wendy's accommodation necessary and appropriate? You be the judge.

Proaction

A **proactive social responsibility strategy** involves formulating a program that serves as a role model for the industry. Proaction means aggressively taking the initiative. Consider, for example, the community-centered practices of the Washington, D.C., law firm Arnold & Porter: "Lawyers at this firm are socially responsible. Last year they contributed 81,714 attorney pro bono [free] hours (the equivalent of 39 people on a full-time basis), and associates volunteer for six-month stints at the Legal Aid Society."[17] Such generous and trend-setting action qualifies as proactive social responsibility. No surprise then that Arnold & Porter ranked number 54 on *Fortune* magazine's 2006 list of "The 100 Best Companies to Work For."

Corporate social responsibility proponents would like to see proactive strategies become management's preferred response in both good times and bad[18] (see Best Practices on page 70).

proactive social responsibility strategy
Taking the initiative with new programs that serve as models for the industry.

Who Benefits from Corporate Social Responsibility?

Is social responsibility like the old theory of home medicine, "It has to taste bad to be good"? In other words, does social responsibility have to be a hardship for the organization? Those who answer *yes* believe that social responsibility should be motivated by **altruism**, an unselfish devotion to the interests of others.[19] This implies that businesses that are not socially responsible are motivated strictly by self-interest. In short-run economic terms, companies violating pollution laws do indeed save a great deal of money. In contrast, 3M's decision to pull its popular Scotchgard fabric protector spray cans from the marketplace as soon as it became aware of a possible health hazard actually cost the company an estimated $500 million in annual sales.[20] On the basis of these cases alone, one would be hard-pressed to say that social responsibility pays. But research paints a brighter picture.

Online Study Center
Improve Your Grade
Career Snapshot 3.1

altruism Unselfish devotion to the interests of others.

▌ A study of 243 companies over two years found a positive correlation between industry leadership in environmental protection/pollution control and profitability. The researchers concluded: "It pays to be green."[21]

▌ A second study found a good reputation for corporate social responsibility to be a competitive advantage in recruiting talented people.[22]

Enlightened Self-Interest

Enlightened self-interest, the realization that business ultimately helps itself by helping to solve societal problems, involves balancing short-run costs and long-run benefits. Advocates of enlightened self-interest contend that social responsibility

enlightened self-interest A business ultimately helping itself by helping to solve societal problems.

corporate philanthropy Charitable donation of company resources.

expenditures are motivated by profit. Research into **corporate philanthropy**, the charitable donation of company resources ($14 billion in the United States in 2005),[23] supports this contention.

After analyzing Internal Revenue Service statistics for firms in 36 industries, researchers concluded that corporate giving is a form of *profit-motivated advertising*. They went on to observe that "it would seem ill-advised to use philanthropy data to measure altruistic responses of corporations."[24] This profit-motivated advertising thesis was further supported by a study of 130 large manufacturing firms in the United States.

▌ Companies that had committed significant crimes but donated a good deal of money had better responsibility ratings than companies that had committed no crimes but donated very little money.[25]

▌ Still more evidence of corporate philanthropy being profit-motivated advertising is the tactic called *cause-related marketing*. This is an offshoot of advocacy advertising, discussed in Chapter 2. Only in this instance, instead of promoting a point of view or opinion along with their products, advertisers support a worthy cause.

▌ U.S. companies spent about $828 million on cause-related marketing in 2002, up sharply from $125 million in 1990.[26] Typically, customers are urged to buy a product or service because a portion of the proceeds will go to a specified charity. For example, "Use of American Express credit cards generated $22 million for Share Our Strength, a poverty-relief charity, over the four-year life of the Charge Against Hunger program."[27] Clearly, this win-win situation was an act of enlightened self-interest by American Express because it polished the company's reputation while fighting poverty.

An Array of Benefits for the Organization

In addition to the advertising effect, other possible long-run benefits for socially responsible organizations include the following:

▌ Tax-free incentives to employees (such as buying orchestra tickets and giving them to deserving employees)

▌ Retention of talented employees by satisfying their altruistic motives

▌ Help in recruiting talented and socially conscious personnel

▌ Swaying public opinion against government intervention

▌ Improved community living standards for employees

▌ Attracting socially conscious investors

▌ A nontaxable benefit for employees in which company funds are donated to their favorite causes—many companies match employees' contributions to their college alma maters, for example

Social responsibility can be a win-win proposition; both society and the socially responsible organization can benefit in the long run.[28]

REALITY CHECK 3.2

"At many large corporations, a full-time philanthropy staff selects charities to support. For small companies lacking a strategic philanthropic mission, Gratus Capital Management in Atlanta has created CompanyGivingTest.com. The site uses an online questionnaire to help employees find charities from a pool of about 80 nonprofits that Gratus has vetted for soundness."

Source: Dean Foust, "Charity Begins . . . Online," *Business Week* (March 5, 2007): 10.

Question: How do you determine what causes to support with your donations?

TEST PREPPER 3.2

ANSWERS CAN BE FOUND ON P. 73

True or False?

_____ 1. The iron law of responsibility states that "in the long run, those who do not use power in a way that society considers responsible will tend to lose it."

_____ 2. An example of a reactive social responsibility strategy is a blue jeans maker switching to organically grown cotton.

_____ 3. Proaction means aggressively taking the initiative in the corporate social responsibility area.

_____ 4. Managers who believe in enlightened self-interest think that ultimately the best way to help themselves is to help create a better society.

Multiple Choice

_____ 5. According to the iron law of responsibility,
   a. power corrupts.
   b. absolute power is dangerous.
   c. nothing gets accomplished without power.
   d. economic power prevails.
   e. we need to use power responsibly or lose it.

_____ 6. A(n) _____ social responsibility strategy uses legal maneuvering and/or a public relations campaign to avoid assuming additional responsibilities.

   a. accommodation
   b. reactive
   c. defensive
   d. proactive
   e. protective

_____ 7. Aggressively taking the initiative on the social responsibility continuum is called
   a. empowerment.
   b. proaction.
   c. altruism.
   d. reaction.
   e. decentralization.

_____ 8. Researchers found which sort of relationship between industry leadership in environmental protection/pollution control and profitability?
   a. Positive correlation
   b. Negative correlation
   c. Inconsistent
   d. No impact
   e. Inverse

_____ 9. The realization that business ultimately helps itself by helping to solve societal problems defines
   a. profit-motivation.
   b. corporate philanthropy.
   c. ethics.
   d. social-motivation.
   e. enlightened self-interest.

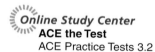
Online Study Center
ACE the Test
ACE Practice Tests 3.2

THE ETHICAL DIMENSION OF MANAGEMENT

3 *Summarize the three practical lessons from business ethics research. Then identify and describe at least four of the ten general ethical principles.*

There is widespread cynicism about business ethics these days.[29] No wonder, considering countless reports of accounting fraud, conflicts of interest, price fixing, illegal mutual fund trading, theft of trade secrets, back dating of stock options, and corporate spying.[30] Subsequent public disgust has surfaced in opinion polls: in one annual survey of corporate reputations, 74 percent said "corporate America's reputation is 'not good' or 'terrible.'"[31] Managers seem to be getting the message. A recent survey of 1,600 executives found 57 percent paying more attention to manager and supervisor ethics.[32] Indeed, the subject of ethics certainly deserves serious attention in management circles.[33]

ethics The study of moral obligation involving right versus wrong.

Ethics is the study of moral obligation involving the distinction between right and wrong.[34] *Business ethics,* sometimes referred to as management ethics or organizational ethics, narrows the frame of reference to productive organizations.[35] But, as a pair of ethics experts has noted, business ethics is not a simple matter:

> Just being a good person and, in your own way, having sound personal ethics may not be sufficient to handle the ethical issues that arise in a business organization. Many people who have limited business experience suddenly find themselves making decisions about product quality, advertising, pricing, hiring practices, and pollution control. The values they learned from family, church, and school may not provide specific guidelines for these complex business decisions. For example, is a particular advertisement deceptive? Should a gift to a customer be considered a bribe, or is it a special promotional incentive? . . . Many business ethics decisions are close calls. Years of experience in a particular industry may be required to know what is acceptable.[36]

With this realistic context in mind, we turn now to a discussion of business ethics research, ethical principles, and the steps that management can take to foster ethical business behavior.

Practical Lessons from Business Ethics Research

Empirical research is always welcome in a socially relevant and important area such as business ethics.[37] It permits us to go beyond mere intuition and speculation to determine more precisely who, what, and why. On-the-job research of business ethics has produced three practical insights for managers: (1) ethical hot spots, (2) pressure from above, and (3) discomfort with ambiguity.

Ethical Hot Spots

In a survey of 1,324 U.S. employees from all levels across several industries, 48 percent admitted to at least one illegal or unethical act (during the prior year) from a list of 25 questionable practices. The list included everything from calling in sick when feeling well to cheating on expense accounts, forging signatures, and giving or accepting kickbacks, to ignoring violations of environmental laws. Also uncovered in the study were the top ten workplace hot spots responsible for triggering unethical and illegal conduct:

- Balancing work and family
- Poor internal communications
- Poor leadership
- Work hours, workload
- Lack of management support
- Need to meet sales, budget, or profit goals
- Little or no recognition of achievements
- Company politics
- Personal financial worries
- Insufficient resources[38]

Pressure from Above

A number of studies have uncovered the problem of perceived pressure to produce results. As we discuss in Chapter 12, pressure from superiors can lead to blind conformity. How widespread is the problem? Very widespread, according to the ethical hot spots survey just discussed:

▌ Most workers feel some pressure to act unethically or illegally on the job (56 percent), but far fewer (17 percent) feel a high level of pressure to do so....

▌ Mid-level managers most often reported a high level of pressure to act unethically or illegally (20 percent). Employees of large companies cited such pressure more than those at small businesses (21 percent versus 14 percent).

▌ High levels of pressure were reported more often by those with a high school diploma or less (21 percent) versus college graduates (13 percent).[39]

By being aware of this problem of pressure from above, managers can (1) consciously avoid putting undue pressure on others and (2) prepare to deal with excessive organizational pressure.

A prime case of pressure from above is the overselling scandal at Sears, Roebuck & Company's automotive centers. According to investigations by the California attorney general's office and a U.S. Senate subcommittee, between 1990 and 1992 Sears systematically pressured auto customers to buy parts and services they didn't need. Many customers across the country complained of having paid hundreds of dollars for unnecessary repair work. Roy Liebman, a California deputy attorney general, told *Business Week*, "There was a deliberate decision by Sears management to set up a structure that made it totally inevitable that the customer would be oversold."[40] Indeed, former Sears employees claimed that intense pressure to boost revenue, a commission pay system tied to actual sales, and unrealistic sales goals forced them to oversell. Sears reworked the goal-setting and commission structure in its auto repair shops only to see similar problems crop up among overzealous bill collectors in its credit card operations. The situation led to a two-year FBI investigation and culminated in a record $60 million fine for bankruptcy fraud in 1999.[41] Excessive pressure to achieve results is a serious problem because it can cause otherwise good and decent people to take ethical shortcuts just to keep their jobs. The challenge for managers is to know where to draw the line between motivation to excel and undue pressure.[42]

Ambiguous Situations

Surveys of purchasing managers and field sales personnel uncovered discomfort with ambiguous situations in which there are no clear-cut ethical guidelines. One result of this kind of research is the following statement: "A striking aspect of the responses to the questionnaire is the degree to which the purchasing managers desire a stated policy."[43] In other words, those who often face ethically ambiguous situations want formal guidelines to help sort things out. Ethical codes, discussed later in this chapter, can satisfy this need for guidelines.

A Call to Action

Corporate misconduct and the foregoing research findings underscore the importance of the following call to action. It comes from Thomas R. Horton, former president and chief executive officer of the American Management Association.

REALITY CHECK 3.3

"When company culture ignores, promotes, or even rewards improper conduct, no amount of employee training on the intricacies of compliance laws will be sufficient to prevent a business disaster."

Source: D Christopher Kayes, David Stirling, and Tjai M. Nielsen, "Building Organizational Integrity," *Business Horizons,* 50 (January–February 2007): 65.

Question: What specific steps should managers take to create an ethical organizational culture?

In my view, this tide can be turned only by deliberate and conscious actions of management at all levels. Each manager needs to understand his or her own personal code of ethics: what is fair; *what is* right; *what is* wrong? *Where is the ethical line that I draw, the line beyond which I shall not go? And where is the line beyond which I shall not allow my* organization *to go?*[44]

Horton's call is *personal.* His words suggest each of us can begin the process of improving business ethics by looking in a mirror.[45]

General Ethical Principles

Your ethical beliefs have been shaped by many factors, including family and friends, the media, culture, schooling, religious instruction, and general life experiences.[46] This section brings our often unspoken and unexamined ethical beliefs out into the open for discussion and greater understanding. It does so by exploring ten general ethical principles. Though we may not know what labels ethics scholars place on them, we use ethical principles both consciously and unconsciously when we deal with ethical dilemmas.[47] Each of the ten ethical principles is followed by a brief behavioral guideline.*

"THE DOG ATE OUR QUARTERLY STATEMENT? I LIKE IT."

Source: Copyright John Caldwell, originally appeared in the *Harvard Business Review.*

1. *Self-interests.* "Never take any action that is not in the *long-term* self-interests of yourself and/or of the organization to which you belong."
2. *Personal virtues.* "Never take any action that is not honest, open, and truthful and that you would not be proud to see reported widely in national newspapers and on television."
3. *Religious injunctions.* "Never take any action that is not kind and that does not build a sense of community, a sense of all of us working together for a commonly accepted goal."
4. *Government requirements.* "Never take any action that violates the law, for the law represents the minimal moral standards of our society."
5. *Utilitarian benefits.* "Never take any action that does not result in greater good than harm for the society of which you are a part."
6. *Universal rules.* "Never take any action that you would not be willing to see others, faced with the same or closely similar situation, also be free to take."
7. *Individual rights.* "Never take any action that abridges the agreed-upon and accepted rights of others."
8. *Economic efficiency.* "Always act to maximize profits subject to legal and market constraints, for maximum profits are the sign of the most efficient production."
9. *Distributive justice.* "Never take any action in which the least [fortunate people] among us are harmed in some way."
10. *Contributive liberty.* "Never take any action that will interfere with the right of all of us for self-development and self-fulfillment."

Which of these ethical principles appeals most to you in terms of serving as a guide for making important decisions? Why? The best way to test your ethical standards and principles is to consider a *specific* ethical question and see which of these ten principles is most likely to guide your *behavior.* Sometimes, in complex situations, a combination of principles will be applicable.

Source: Excerpted from Hosmer, *Moral Leadership in Business,* pp. 39–41. © 1994, McGraw-Hill. Reprinted with the permission of the McGraw-Hill Companies.

TEST PREPPER 3.3

ANSWERS CAN BE FOUND ON P. 73

True or False?

_____ 1. Business ethics involves a simple obligation of choosing right versus wrong.

_____ 2. One of the top-ten workplace hot spots that trigger unethical and illegal conduct is little or no recognition of achievements.

_____ 3. High levels of pressure to act unethically were more often reported by college graduates than by those with a high school diploma or less.

_____ 4. Among the ten general ethical principles are universal rules, personal virtues, and government requirements.

Multiple Choice

_____ 5. Ethics refers to the study of
   a. moral obligation.
   b. social trade-offs.
   c. cross-cultural value conflict.
   d. black-and-white political issues.
   e. economic trade-offs.

_____ 6. Discomfort with _____ was found in surveys of purchasing and sales personnel.
   a. overly specific ethical codes
   b. any type of ethical code
   c. moralistic managers
   d. ambiguous situations
   e. immoral managers

_____ 7. Which statement best represents the general ethical principle of contributive liberty?
   a. Never take any action that violates the law.
   b. Never take any action that is not in the long-term self-interest of yourself.
   c. Never take any action that will interfere with the right of all of us for self-development and self-fulfillment.
   d. Never take any action that does not result in greater good than harm for the society of which you are a part.
   e. Always act to maximize profits subject to legal and market constraints.

Online Study Center
ACE the Test
ACE Practice Tests 3.3

ENCOURAGING ETHICAL CONDUCT

4 ► *Discuss what management can do to improve business ethics.*

Simply telling managers and other employees to be good will not work. Both research evidence and practical experience tell us that words must be supported by action. Four specific ways to encourage ethical conduct within the organization are ethics training, ethical advocates, ethics codes, and whistle-blowing. Each can make an important contribution to an integrated ethics program.

Ethics Training

Managers lacking ethical awareness have been labeled *amoral* by ethics researcher Archie B. Carroll. **Amoral managers** are neither moral nor immoral, but indifferent to the ethical implications of their actions. Carroll contends that managers in this category far outnumber moral or immoral managers.[48] If his contention is correct, there is a great need for ethics training, a need that too often is not adequately met. According to a survey of 1,001 employees in the United States, only 28 percent had received any ethics training during the prior year.[49]

Some say ethics training and education are a waste of time because ethical lessons are easily shoved aside in the heat of competition.[50] For example, Dow Corning's model ethics program included ethics training but did not save the

amoral managers Managers who are neither moral nor immoral, but ethically lazy.

company from accusations that it sold leaky breast implants.[51] Ethics training is often halfhearted and intended only as window dressing. Among the companies that do take ethics training seriously is Medtronic, the Minnesota-based maker of heart pacemakers and other medical technology. Each senior manager at Medtronic must attend a five-day ethics workshop.[52] Hard evidence is lacking that ethics training actually improves behavior. Nonetheless, carefully designed and administered ethics training courses can make a positive contribution. Key features of effective ethics training programs include the following:

- Top-management support
- Open discussion of realistic ethics cases or scenarios
- A clear focus on ethical issues specific to the organization
- Integration of ethics themes into all training
- A mechanism for anonymously reporting ethical violations (e.g., an ethics hotline)
- An organizational climate that rewards ethical conduct[53]

Ethical Advocates

ethical advocate Ethics specialist who plays a role in top management decision making.

An **ethical advocate** is a business ethics specialist who sits as a full-fledged member of the board of directors and acts as the board's social conscience.[54] This person may also be asked to sit in on decision deliberations of top management. The idea is to assign someone the specific role of critical questioner (see Table 3.2 for recommended questions). Problems with groupthink and blind conformity, discussed in Chapter 12, are less likely when an ethical advocate tests management's thinking about ethical implications during the decision-making process.

Codes of Ethics

An organizational code of ethics is a published statement of moral expectations for employee conduct. Some codes specify penalties for offenders. As in the case of ethics training, the number of companies adopting codes of ethics has stalled in recent years.

Recent experience has shown codes of ethics to be a step in the right direction, but not a cure-all.[55] To encourage ethical conduct, formal codes of ethics for an organization's members must satisfy two requirements.

1. They should refer to specific practices such as kickbacks, payoffs, receiving gifts, falsifying records, and making misleading product claims. For example, Xerox Corporation's 15-page ethics code says: "We're honest with our customers. No deals, no bribes, no secrets, no fooling around with prices. A kickback in any form kicks anybody out. Anybody."[56] General platitudes about good business practice or professional conduct are ineffective—they do not provide specific guidance and they offer too many tempting loopholes.

2. An organizational code of ethics should be firmly supported by top management and equitably enforced through the reward-and-punishment system. Selective or uneven enforcement is the quickest way to kill the effectiveness of an ethics code. The effective development of ethics codes and monitoring of compliance are more important than ever in today's complex global economy.[57]

Whistle-Blowing

Detailed ethics codes help managers deal swiftly and effectively with employee misconduct. But what should a manager do when a superior or an entire organization is engaged in misconduct? Yielding to the realities of organizational politics, many managers simply turn their backs or claim they were "just following orders." (Nazi war criminals who based their defense at the Nuremberg trials on this argument ended up with ropes around their necks.) Managers with leadership and/or political skills may attempt to work within the organizational system for positive change.[58] Still others will take the boldest step of all, whistle-blowing. **Whistle-blowing** is the practice of reporting perceived unethical practices to outsiders such as the news media, government agencies, or public-interest groups.[59] Two widely publicized whistle-blowers in recent years are Sherron Watkins, who foresaw Enron's financial collapse, and Coleen Rowley, an FBI agent who went public with allegations of a mishandled terrorist lead.[60]

Not surprisingly, whistle-blowing is a highly controversial topic among managers, many of whom believe it erodes their authority and decision-making prerogatives. Because loyalty to the organization is still a cherished value in some quarters, whistle-blowing is criticized as the epitome of disloyalty. Consumer advocate Ralph Nader disagrees: "The willingness and ability of insiders to blow the whistle is the last line of defense ordinary citizens have against the denial of their rights and the destruction of their interests by secretive and powerful institutions."[61] Still, critics worry that whistle-blowers may be motivated by revenge.

Whistle-blowing generally means putting one's job and/or career on the line, even though the federal government and many states have passed whistle-blower protection acts.[62] The challenge for today's management is to create an organizational climate in which the need to blow the whistle is reduced. Constructive steps include the following:

▌ Encourage the free expression of controversial and dissenting viewpoints.

▌ Streamline the organization's grievance procedure so that problems receive a prompt and fair hearing.

▌ Find out what employees think about the organization's social responsibility policies and make appropriate changes.

▌ Let employees know that management respects and is sensitive to their individual consciences.

▌ Recognize that treating a whistle-blower harshly will probably lead to adverse public opinion.[63]

In the final analysis, individual behavior makes organizations ethical or unethical. Organizational forces can help bring out the best in people by clearly identifying and rewarding ethical conduct.

TABLE 3.2

Twelve Questions for Examining the Ethics of a Business Decision

1. Have you defined the problem accurately?
2. How would you define the problem if you stood on the other side of the fence?
3. How did this situation occur in the first place?
4. To whom and to what do you give your loyalty as a person and as a member of the corporation?
5. What is your intention in making this decision?
6. How does this intention compare with the probable results?
7. Whom could your decision or action injure?
8. Can you discuss the problem with the affected parties before you make your decision?
9. Are you confident that your position will be as valid over a long period of time as it seems now?
10. Could you disclose without qualm your decision or action to your boss, your CEO, the board of directors, your family, society as a whole?
11. What is the symbolic potential of your action if understood? If misunderstood?
12. Under what conditions would you allow exceptions to your stand?

Source: Reprinted by permission of *Harvard Business Review*. From "Ethics Without the Sermon," by Laura L. Nash, November–December 1991. Copyright © 1991 by Harvard Business School Publishing Corporation; all rights reserved.

whistle-blowing   Reporting perceived unethical organizational practices to outside authorities.

TEST PREPPER 3.4   ANSWERS CAN BE FOUND ON P. 73

True or False?

_____ 1. An ethical advocate is assigned the specific role of critical questioner, and he or she may also be asked to sit in on top-management decision deliberations.

_____ 2. An effective code of ethics needs to be stated in general terms rather than getting bogged down in the details of specific behaviors.

_____ 3. The first step to reduce the need for whistle-blowing is encouraging the free expression of controversial and dissenting viewpoints.

Multiple Choice

_____ 4. An amoral manager can be described as one who is
  a. devoted to others.
  b. above criticism.
  c. strictly selfish.
  d. indifferent to ethical implications.
  e. consistently unethical.

_____ 5. Which statement about ethics training is true?
  a. It is a waste of time.
  b. It is becoming less popular.
  c. It lacks hard evidence of effectiveness.
  d. It is practically universal today.
  e. It is out of date.

_____ 6. _____is the practice of reporting perceived unethical practices to outsiders such as the media or government agencies.
  a. Ethical conscience
  b. Whistle-blowing
  c. Devil's advocacy
  d. Functional conflict
  e. Ombudsmanship

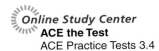
Online Study Center
ACE the Test
ACE Practice Tests 3.4

BEST PRACTICES

Seventh Generation Sets the Standard

Jeffrey Hollender started his career as an entrepreneur in the 1980s with an audio book company that scored with titles like *How to Marry Money*. But he soon had an epiphany, sold his company, moved to Vermont, and joined Seventh Generation, one of the first makers of green consumer products.

Two decades and several crests of ecoconsciousness later, Hollender sees interest in greener living at an all-time high. Indeed, after years of being sold exclusively in health food and specialty stores, Seventh Generation's paper towels, toilet paper, diapers, and cleansers can now be found in chains such as Safeway and Target, spurring annual growth of 30 to 40 percent and driving revenue to more than $60 million.

Seventh Generation stands out for its top-to-bottom commitment to social and corporate responsibility. The company audits manufacturing partners on their environmental and social performance and evaluates its own practices in a corporate responsibility report. And while Hollender admits that Seventh Generation is "not even a fly on the back of a Procter & Gamble," he's proud of what his company has accomplished. "We are making everyone in the consumer products field think about what they do," he says.

Source: From *Inc.: The Magazine For Growing Companies,* "The Green 50: The Pioneers," November 2006. Copyright © 2006 by Mansueto Ventures LLC. Reproduced with permission of Mansueto Ventures LLC via Copyright Clearance Center.

Chiquita Cleans Up Its Act

At first, Dave McLaughlin didn't tell his bosses at Chiquita that he was talking to environmentalists, much less taking their suggestions. After all, the banana company's executives so mistrusted the "greens" that meetings with them often turned into shouting matches. "They would sit at opposite ends of the table," McLaughlin says.

But what began as a dialogue between McLaughlin, then a Chiquita general manager in Costa Rica, and the nonprofit Rainforest Alliance has since cleared a path toward a companywide transformation. Starting in 1992, McLaughlin essentially used his two Costa Rican farms as test beds to rein in environmental abuses. Those changes—and their impact on the bottom line— persuaded Chiquita in 1996 to allot $20 million to overhaul the environmental and employment standards at all of its 127 farms, which employ 30,000 workers in seven Latin American countries. With McLaughlin recently appointed Chiquita's senior director of environmental and social performance, the company is becoming a study in corporate responsibility, rather than a counterexample. "It would be a challenge to find a company that has come so far and so fast," says Chris Wille, sustainable agriculture chief for the Rainforest Alliance, which certifies Chiquita's progress.

For decades the $3.9 billion fruit giant was synonymous with the notion of the rapacious multinational. Farm workers toiled long hours in dangerous conditions, agrochemical runoff contaminated water, and tropical forests were cleared for expansion, says J. Gary Taylor, coauthor of *Smart Alliance*, a book about Chiquita. "We had a problem that could impact our brand," McLaughlin says.

Enter New York–based environmental group Rainforest Alliance, which had previously worked with timber companies in Indonesia to lessen the impact of logging operations. (The nonprofit does not accept donations from companies that it certifies, though they can buy tables at its annual dinner.) In 1992 the Alliance sent banana companies a list of environmental and worker-rights standards required to gain its certification; Chiquita's officials dismissed the proposal as too expensive. Determined, two Rainforest staffers got face time with McLaughlin at one of the Costa Rican farms. By the end of the four-hour visit, McLaughlin realized the environmentalists weren't crazy after all and agreed to work with them.

Four months later McLaughlin told Chiquita executives about his activities up to that point, which included cutting down on agrochemical use, and presented them with a budget for the remaining changes. "Dave had to fight for every penny," says former Chiquita CEO Steve Warshaw, now the COO [chief operating officer] of a financial services firm in Cincinnati. "He was very compelling and persistent."

During the next two years, McLaughlin says, Chiquita spent $40,000 to overhaul the Costa Rican farms. One of the first steps was phasing out the toxic pesticide paraquat, replacing it with the milder glyphosate, and building new warehouses to store the chemicals. McLaughlin began monitoring water quality in rivers and wells and providing workers with better safety equipment. The farms also started recycling programs, turning plastic bags into paving stones for sidewalks.

After letting the Rainforest Alliance inspect McLaughlin's farms, Chiquita decided to replicate the changes throughout the organization; in 2000 it began publishing annual corporate responsibility reports to track the progress. "They were really transparent," says Michelle Lapinski, director of food and agriculture advisory services at the nonprofit Business for Social Responsibility. "When someone admits they weren't perfect, you trust them a little more." Today all 110 of Chiquita's company-owned farms and the vast majority of its independent farms are certified by the Rainforest Alliance. Chiquita now recycles 100 percent of its plastic bags and twine and has reduced pesticide use by 26 percent.

Though the improvements in working conditions aren't nearly as dramatic, things are getting better for Latin American employees, who can now join unions. Disputes with Honduran labor unions in late November [2005] prompted Chiquita to spend two days renegotiating the workers' contracts. In addition, the company has installed showers, lunchrooms, and locker rooms for workers. "Clearly there've been improvements, but it's far from perfect," says Stephen Coats, executive director of U.S. LEAP, which advocates for Latin American worker rights.

Still, Chiquita is just getting started, and the results are beginning to show up on the bottom line. According to spokesman Michael Mitchell, the company now saves $5 million a year on pesticides, while productivity is up 27 percent. "Our CEO said, 'This is the first time I've made an investment decision without having a spreadsheet in front of me, and it's been one of the best,'" McLaughlin says. "I agree totally."

Source: Jennifer Alsever, "Chiquita Cleans Up Its Act," *Business 2.0,* 7, August 2006, pp. 56, 58. Copyright © 2006 Time Inc. All rights reserved.

Case Questions

1. Which arguments *for* corporate social responsibility are evident in this case? Explain with specific examples.
2. Which of the four social responsibility strategies are evident in this case? Explain.
3. What role, if any, does enlightened self-interest play in this case? Explain.
4. Which one of the ten general ethical principles seems to be guiding Dave McLaughlin's actions? Explain.

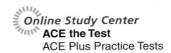
Online Study Center
ACE the Test
ACE Plus Practice Tests

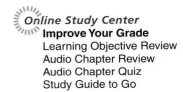
Online Study Center
Improve Your Grade
Learning Objective Review
Audio Chapter Review
Audio Chapter Quiz
Study Guide to Go

LEARNING OBJECTIVE REVIEW

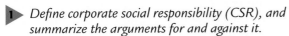 *Define corporate social responsibility (CSR), and summarize the arguments for and against it.*

- Corporate social responsibility is the idea that management has broader responsibilities than just making a profit.
  - A strict interpretation holds that an action must be voluntary to qualify as socially responsible.
  - Accordingly, reluctantly submitting to court orders or government coercion is not social responsibility.
- The arguments for corporate responsibility say businesses are members of society with the resources and motivation to improve society and avoid government regulation.
- Those arguing against it call for profit maximization because businesses are primarily economic institutions run by unelected officials who have enough power already.

2 *Identify and describe the four social responsibility strategies, and explain the role of enlightened self-interest in CSR.*

- Management scholars who advocate greater corporate social responsibility cite the iron law of responsibility.

This law states that if business does not use its socio-economic power responsibly, society will take away that power.

- A continuum of social responsibility includes four strategies: reaction, defense, accommodation, and proaction.
  - The reaction strategy involves denying social responsibility.
  - The defense strategy involves actively fighting additional responsibility with political and public relations tactics.
  - Accommodation occurs when a company must be pressured into assuming additional social responsibilities.
  - Proaction occurs when a business takes the initiative and becomes a positive model for its industry.
- In the short run, proactive social responsibility usually costs the firm money. But, according to the notion of enlightened self-interest, both society and the company will gain in the long run.
- Research indicates that corporate philanthropy actually is a profit-motivated form of advertising.

3 ▶ *Summarize the three practical lessons from business ethics research. Then identify and describe at least four of the ten general ethical principles.*

- Business ethics research has taught these three practical lessons:
    - A large percentage of surveyed workers report engaging in illegal or unethical practices.
    - Perceived pressure from above can erode ethics.
    - Employees desire clear ethical standards in ambiguous situations

- The call for better business ethics is clearly a personal challenge.

- The ten general ethical principles that consciously and unconsciously guide behavior when ethical questions arise are:
    - Self-interests (protect your long-term self-interests)
    - Personal virtues (always be open, honest, and truthful)
    - Religious injunctions (work together for a common goal)
    - Government requirements (always follow the law)
    - Utilitarian benefits (work for the greater good)
    - Universal rules (act as others should)
    - Individual rights (don't hamper the rights of others)
    - Economic efficiency (legally maximize profits)
    - Distributive justice (don't harm the least fortunate)
    - Contributive liberty (don't interfere with others' right to self-fulfillment)

4 ▶ *Discuss what managers can do to improve business ethics.*

- The typical manager is said to be amoral—neither moral or immoral—just ethically lazy or indifferent.

- Management can encourage ethical behavior in the following four ways:
    - Conduct ethics training.
    - Use ethical advocates in high-level decision making.
    - Formulate, disseminate, and consistently enforce specific codes of ethics.
    - Create an open climate for dissent in which whistle-blowing becomes unnecessary.

TEST PREPPER ANSWERS

▶ **3.1**
1. F   2. T   3. T   4. d   5. b   6. d

▶ **3.2**
1. T   2. F   3. T   4. T   5. e   6. c   7. b
8. a   9. e

▶ **3.3**
1. F   2. T   3. F   4. T   5. a   6. d   7. c

▶ **3.4**
1. T   2. F   3. T   4. d   5. c   6. b

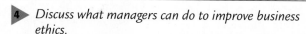

Online Study Center RESOURCES

Prepare for Class, Improve Your Grade, and ACE the Test. Student Achievement Series resources include:

ACE Practice Tests	Crossword Puzzles	Hangman
Audio Chapter Quizzes	Decision Case Questions	Key Issue Expansion
Audio Chapter Reviews	Ethical Hot Seat Exercises	Learning Objective Reviews
Career Snapshots	Flashcards	Study Guide to Go
Chapter Glossaries	Hands-on Exercises	Visual Glossaries
Chapter Outlines		

To access these learning and study tools, go to **college.hmco.com/pic/kreitnerSASfound**.

International Management

Thanks to the wireless Internet, Ivko Maksimovic, a Serb who lives in the Dominican Republic, can work from the beach as the chief technology officer of San Francisco–based Vast.com.

1 *Describe the six-step internationalization process, and distinguish between a global company and a transnational company.*

2 *Explain from a cross-cultural perspective the difference between high-context and low-context cultures, and identify at least four of the GLOBE cultural dimensions.*

3 *Explain what Hofstede's research has to say about the applicability of American management theories in foreign cultures, and summarize the leadership lessons from the GLOBE project.*

"I've always thought of travel as a university without walls." [1]
—Anita Roddick, British Founder of the Body Shop

Chapter Outline

Online Study Center
Prepare for Class
Chapter Outline

4 ▶ *Discuss why U.S. expatriates fail and what can be done about it, and summarize the situation of North American women on foreign assignments.*

Doing Business from a Beach in the Dominican Republic

When working in the tropical sun becomes too much for Ivko Maksimovic, the lanky Serbian heads to one of the Dominican Republic's pristine white-sand beaches. He first gathers up a black hat, mosquito repellent, and a bottle of drinking water. Along with those essentials, he starts stuffing his black backpack with a tangle of computer cords, an extra laptop battery, a spare 160-gigabyte hard drive, and an EVDO card to connect to the Caribbean country's 3G broadband network. Finally, he adds a battered ThinkPad, a Skype-ready headset, and a cable lock to lash all the gear to a tree when he decides to take a swim. "It's very cool to think about important stuff while you fight the waves," Maksimovic says.

Maksimovic, 29, is the CTO [chief technology officer] of Vast.com, a startup search company based in San Francisco. He lives in the Dominican Republic because it's warm and far from Serbia's troubles. He works for Vast because his bosses think he's the best person for the job, and it doesn't matter much where he is physically as long as he has a broadband connection.

Online Study Center college.hmco.com/pic/kreitnerSASfound

Online Study Center
Prepare for Class
Chapter Glossary

Improve Your Grade
Flashcards
Hangman
Crossword Puzzles

Between sessions in the surf pondering the arcana of coding on a May afternoon, Maksimovic chats with Vast's main development team in Belgrade by instant message and checks in with a colleague in Ireland through e-mail. The rest of the executive team dials in from San Francisco for a rare spoken conversation using a Skype-enabled speakerphone. Recently back from a trip to the Dominican Republic himself, Vast CEO Naval Ravikant can't resist asking his CTO what he's wearing. "Short pants," Maksimovic says. "And nothing else." The three people in the fogbound San Francisco office let out a collective groan. "I wish we were there too," says Ravikant, a serial entrepreneur who co-founded comparison-shopping service Epinions.

Vast launched a year ago in its present form and now employs 25 people who work across five time zones, four nations, and two continents—all of which makes it a particularly striking example of a growing breed of startup that can best be described as a micro-multinational. According to the United Nations, in 1990 there were about 30,000 multinational companies. Today there are more than 60,000, and while the number of multinational companies continues to grow, their average size is falling. As micro-multinationals proliferate, they're creating an entirely new form of corporate organization—one with powerful advantages for startups and entrepreneurs.

Like Exxon or IBM, these multinational startups operate all over the world, pursuing talent and markets wherever they find them. Unlike their corporate big brothers, which historically expanded internationally via acquisitions or after tapping out markets close to home, micro-multinationals are global from day one. A big reason is money, but the benefits go beyond building a company on the cheap. Micro-multinationals are designing new corporate cultures and processes to compete in an increasingly global economy. Bound together by broadband and jet planes, they're startups all the same, run with the same fervor and energy as any garage-born company.

This is not offshoring as the term is commonly understood, although it is an outgrowth of it. Micro-multinationals aren't just moving operations from high-rent locales like Silicon Valley to Bangalore and other bargain-rate boomtowns. From the get-go, micro-multinationals open up shop and recruit skilled workers where it makes sense to do so. Are the ace coders in Estonia? Hire 'em. The COO [chief operating officer] would rather live in Sydney than Sunnyvale? So be it. The visionaries see Mongolia as a natural market for the planned product? Sign up some sales reps on the steppes. In short, these are true distributed companies; they're not merely handing off the scut work to overseas electronics sweatshops. "This is core stuff, very advanced technology," Ravikant says. "We are building a company in a way that wouldn't have been possible even two years ago."[2] ∎

Profit opportunities, such as those being exploited by the far-flung techies at Vast.com, are moving from country to country as never before, intensifying international competition. At the heart of this swirl of commerce, technology, and talent is a business tradition dating back further than one might think:

> In the antique shops of Shanghai's old French quarter, amid the German cameras, American radios, Russian crystal and other relics of a vanished past, lie tarnished reminders of just how long the world economy has been a global economy: rough-cast taels of South American silver and smooth-worn Mexican silver dollars.
>
> It was in 1571 that modern global commerce began, argues Dennis O. Flynn, head of the economics department of the University of the Pacific in Stockton, Calif. That year, the Spanish empire founded the city of Manila in the Philippines to receive its silver-laden galleons that made their way across the vast Pacific Ocean from the New World. The metal was bound not for Spain, but for imperial China. For the first time, all of the world's populated continents were trading directly—Asia with the Americas, Europe and Africa, and each with the others. They were highly interdependent: when silver depreciated in later decades, world-wide inflation ensued.
>
> "Some economists think the global economy is a World War II thing," says Prof. Flynn. "That just demonstrates an ignorance of history."[3]

Both air travel and modern information technology have made the world a seemingly smaller place. A third globe-shrinking force that is steadily gaining momentum is *corporate globalism*. By creating global organizations and networks, this third force promises to be a leading contributor to the emergence of a smaller world with many similarities.

Striking evidence of the modern global marketplace is everywhere today. Take a trip to your local supermarket and you will likely find grapes from Chile, oranges from Australia, meat from Argentina, wines from France and South Africa, cheese from Italy, and seafood from Thailand. A look at the labels on your clothes will yield names like Mexico, Vietnam, Bangladesh, India, and China. This sort of world-wide interdependence is simply business as usual in our global economy, which is projected to grow from $26 trillion in 1994 to $48 trillion in 2010. Over the same period, world trade is expected to quadruple, from $4 trillion to $16.6 trillion![4]

Like any other productive venture, an international corporation must be effectively and efficiently managed. Consequently, **international management**, the pursuit of organizational objectives in international and cross-cultural settings, has become an important discipline. Indeed, Nancy Adler, a leading international management scholar at Canada's McGill University, sees it this way: "Managing the global enterprise and modern business management have become synonymous."[5] The purpose of this chapter is to define and discuss multinational and global corporations, stimulate global and cross-cultural awareness, and discuss the need for cross-cultural training.

GLOBAL ORGANIZATIONS FOR A GLOBAL ECONOMY

▶ 1   *Describe the six-step internationalization process, and distinguish between a global company and a transnational company.*

Many labels have been attached to international business ventures over the years. They have been called international companies, multinational companies,

---

REALITY CHECK 4.1

"According to the Office of the United States Trade Representative, 95 percent of the world's consumers reside outside the United States. Some of those people have holes in their lives the exact size and shape of your product. . . .

"If you're not up to serving your globalizing clients, someone else will be."

Source: Excerpted from Leigh Buchanan, "Going Global," *Inc.,* 29 (April 2007): 88–90.

Question: How would you respond to a fellow student (or a manager) who made the following statement? *"Globalization* is an over-used buzzword that doesn't affect me."

international management   Pursuing organizational objectives in international and cross-cultural settings.

Online Study Center
Improve Your Grade
Visual Glossary 4.1

Online Study Center college.hmco.com/pic/kreitnerSASfound

Today's global economy is a lively mix of old and new. That is especially evident in Dubai, United Arab Emirates. Here we see a busy traditional open-air market, while just a few miles away, a world-class multicultural commercial and residential complex is growing out of the desert sand. With its oil reserves soon to be depleted, Dubai is rapidly diversifying its economy around trade, finance, medical care, education, and tourism.

global companies, and transnational companies. This section clarifies the terminology confusion by reviewing the six-stage internationalization process as a foundation for contrasting global and transnational companies.

The Internationalization Process

There are many ways to do business across borders. At either extreme, a company may merely buy goods from a foreign source or it may actually buy the foreign company itself. In between is an internationalization process with identifiable stages. Companies may skip steps when pursuing foreign markets, so the following sequence should *not* be viewed as a lock-step sequence.

Stage 1: Licensing

Companies in foreign countries are authorized to produce and/or market a given product within a specified territory in return for a fee.[6] For example, under the terms of a ten-year licensing agreement, South Korea's Samsung Electronics will get to use Texas Instruments' patented semiconductor technology for royalty payments exceeding $1 billion.[7]

Stage 2: Exporting

Goods produced in one country are sold to customers in foreign countries. Exports amount to a large and growing slice of the U.S. economy.[8]

Stage 3: Local Warehousing and Selling

Goods produced in one country are shipped to the parent company's storage and marketing facilities located in one or more foreign countries.

Stage 4: Local Assembly and Packaging

Components, rather than finished products, are shipped to company-owned assembly facilities in one or more foreign countries for final assembly and sale.

Stage 5: Joint Ventures

A company in one country pools resources with one or more companies in a foreign country to produce, store, transport, and market products, with the resulting profits/losses shared appropriately. Joint ventures, also known as *strategic alliances* or *strategic partnerships*, have become very popular in recent years.[9] Fuji Xerox is a prime example of a successful international joint venture.

> *Joint ventures are usually formed to ensure a fast and convenient entry into a complex foreign market. That's particularly the case in Japan, where convoluted distribution systems, tightly knit supplier relationships and close business-government cooperation have long encouraged foreign companies to link up with knowledgeable local partners.*
>
> *But in truth, these joint ventures don't often last long. And they sometimes flop, occasionally spectacularly. The reasons for failure can include disagreements over strategy, struggles over operational control or even simple spats over each partner's level of effort.*
>
> *But Fuji Xerox, a 34-year-old joint venture between Xerox Corp., Stamford, Conn., and Tokyo-based Fuji Photo Film Co., has avoided all that. In contrast to the turmoil at many other joint ventures, Fuji Xerox not only has been bedrock stable, but also has grown into a major strategic asset for both companies.*[10]

Indeed, the strength of the Fuji Xerox joint venture was underscored in 2001 when a financially struggling Xerox sold half of its 50 percent share to Fuji, while all other aspects of the venture remained intact.[11]

International joint ventures/strategic alliances have tended to be fruitful for Japanese companies but disappointing for American and European partners.

> *Gary Hamel, a professor at the London Business School, regards partnerships as "a race to learn": The partner that learns fastest comes to dominate the relationship and can then rewrite its terms. Thus, an alliance becomes a new form of competition. The Japanese excel at learning from others, Hamel says, while Americans and Europeans are not so good at it.*[12]

Experts offer the following recommendations for successful international joint ventures/strategic alliances. First, exercise *patience* when selecting and building trust with a partner that has compatible (but not directly competitive) products and markets. Second, *learn* as fast and as much as possible without giving away core technologies and secrets. Third, establish firm *ground rules* about rights and responsibilities at the outset.[13]

Stage 6: Direct Foreign Investments

Typically, a company in one country produces and markets products through wholly owned subsidiaries in foreign countries. Global corporations are expressions of this last stage of internationalization.

Cross-border mergers are an increasingly popular form of direct foreign investment.[14] A cross-border merger occurs when a company in one country buys an entire company in another country. Unfortunately, cross-border mergers are not a quick and easy way to go global.

> *On top of the usual challenges of acquiring a company—paying a fair price, melding two management teams, and capturing the elusive "synergy" that's supposed to light up the bottom line—special risks and costs attach to cross-border mergers. They often involve wide differences in distance, language, and culture that can lead to serious misunderstandings and conflicts. . . .*
>
> *According to a study of cross-border mergers among large companies by consultants McKinsey & Co., nearly 40% end in total failure, with the acquiring company never earning back its cost of capital.[15]*

TABLE 4.1

Corporate Giants Worldwide

Company	Home country	Industry	2005 sales (U.S.$, billions)
Petrobrás	Brazil	Petroleum products	56
BP	Britain	Petroleum products	268
Nokia	Finland	Electronics	42
DaimlerChrysler	Germany	Motor vehicles	186
Fiat	Italy	Motor vehicles	58
Toyota Motor	Japan	Motor vehicles	186
Pemex	Mexico	Petroleum products	83
ING	Netherlands	Insurance	138
Samsung Electronics	South Korea	Electronics	79
Nestlé	Switzerland	Food products	75
General Electric	United States	Electrical equipment/ Financial services	157

Source: Adapted from data in "Global 500: World's Largest Corporations," *Fortune* (July 24, 2006): 113–126.

From Global Companies to Transnational Companies

The difference between global companies and transnational companies is the difference between actual and theoretical. That is to say, transnational companies are evolving and represent a futuristic concept while global companies, such as the giants in Table 4.1 do business in many countries simultaneously.

Global companies

▪ Global companies have global strategies for product design, financing, purchasing, manufacturing, and marketing.

▪ By definition, a **global company** is a multinational venture centrally managed from a specific country.[16]

▪ For example, even though Coca-Cola earns most of its profit outside the United States, it is viewed as a U.S. company because it is run from a powerful headquarters in Atlanta, Georgia. The same goes for McDonald's, Ford, IBM, and Wal-Mart, with their respective U.S. headquarters.[17]

Transnational companies

▪ A **transnational company**, in contrast, is a global network of productive units that have a decentralized authority structure and no distinct national identity.[18]

▪ Transnationals rely on a blend of global and local strategies, as circumstances dictate. They adopt local values and practices whenever possible because, in the end, all *customer contacts* are local.

▪ Ideally, managers of transnational organizations "think globally, but act locally." Managers of foreign operations are encouraged to interact freely with their colleagues from around the world. Once again, this type of international business venture exists mostly in theory, although some global companies are moving toward transnationalism.

▪ For example, consider L. M. Ericsson, the Swedish telecommunications equipment manufacturer. As reported in *Business Week*, "Ericsson . . . moved its European headquarters to London to escape Sweden's high personal-income taxes, and to be closer to investors and customers."[19] Ericsson's decision to relocate its headquarters was not constrained by national identity, but rather guided by business and financial considerations.

Significantly, many experts are alarmed at the prospect of immense "stateless" transnational companies because of the unresolved political, economic, and tax implications. If transnational companies become more powerful than the governments of even the largest countries in which they do business, who will hold them accountable in cases of fraud, human rights violations, and environmental mishaps?[20]

global company A multinational venture centrally managed from a specific country.

Source: Copyright www.CartoonStock.com

transnational company A futuristic model of a global, decentralized network with no distinct national identity.

TEST PREPPER 4.1

ANSWERS CAN BE FOUND ON P. 101

True or False?

_____ 1. Buying a foreign company is the only way to do international business.

_____ 2. Foreign direct investment is the first stage in the internationalization process.

_____ 3. Experts suggest that patience is important for successful international joint ventures.

_____ 4. A transnational company, by definition, is a multinational venture centrally managed from a specific country.

Multiple Choice

_____ 5. _____ is not one of the stages of the internationalization process.
   a. A joint venture
   b. Bilateral cooperation
   c. Local assembly and packaging
   d. Exporting
   e. Direct foreign investment

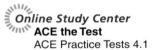

Online Study Center
ACE the Test
ACE Practice Tests 4.1

_____ 6. International joint ventures have tended to be fruitful for _____ companies but disappointing for _____partners.
   a. European; Japanese
   b. African; Japanese
   c. North American; Latin American
   d. Japanese; American
   e. American; European

_____ 7. Which of the following best characterizes a transnational company?
   a. Centralized authority and distinct national identity
   b. Decentralized authority and distinct national identity
   c. Decentralized authority and no distinct national identity
   d. Centralized authority and no distinct national authority
   e. Part centralized and part decentralized authority with a distinct national identity

Online Study Center
Improve Your Grade
Career Snapshot 4.1

TOWARD GREATER GLOBAL AWARENESS AND CROSS-CULTURAL COMPETENCE

2 *Explain from a cross-cultural perspective the difference between high-context and low-context cultures, and identify at least four of the GLOBE cultural dimensions.*

Americans in general and American business students and managers in particular are often considered too narrowly focused for the global stage. Boris Yavitz, former dean of Columbia University's Graduate School of Business, observed that, "unlike European and Asian managers, who grow up expecting to see international service, U.S. executives are required to prepare only for domestic experience, with English as their only language."[21] This state of affairs is slowly changing as business and economies continually globalize. To compete successfully in a dynamic global economy, present and future managers need to develop their international and cross-cultural awareness[22] (see Table 4.2 on page 84). In this section we examine attitudes toward international dealings and explore key sources of cultural diversity.

Are the people of the world becoming more alike or more different? The theory of convergence says we will become more similar than different, because of global business, travel, telecommunications, media, and entertainment. Oppositely, the theory of divergence points toward a world of expanding differences, because of cultural tribalization and the growing gap between rich and poor. A third perspective, crossvergence, *says nations will evolve their own unique blends of domestic and foreign practices. This mobile-phone store in the West African country of Côte d'Ivoire illustrates convergence.*

Beware of an Ethnocentric Attitude

Managerial success in today's global economy often hinges on one's attitude about foreign people, practices, and ideas. An ethnocentric attitude can be a huge roadblock in international dealings.[23]

Managers (and employees) with an **ethnocentric attitude** are home-country-oriented. Home-country personnel, ideas, and practices are viewed as inherently superior to those from abroad. Foreign nationals are not trusted with key decisions or technology. Home-country procedures and evaluation criteria are applied worldwide without variation. Proponents of an ethnocentric approach to management say that it makes for simpler and more tightly controlled organizations. Critics say ethnocentrism is narrow-minded, demeans other cultures, and is self-defeating.

In U.S.-Japanese business relations, ethnocentrism cuts both ways. Procter & Gamble failed to do its cultural homework when it ran a series of advertisements for Pampers in Japan. Japanese customers were bewildered by the ads, in which a stork carried a baby, because storks have no cultural connection to birth in Japan.[24] Similarly, Japanese companies operating in the United States seem to be out of touch with the expectations of American managers. In a survey of American

ethnocentric attitude View that assumes the home country's personnel and ways of doing things are best.

One in One Hundred

If you were in a group of one hundred people that represented the makeup of the world, what would the people around you look like? Where would they come from, what language would they speak, what religion would they practice, and would they have enough to eat?

From Asia	61
From China	21
From India	17
From Africa	13
From Europe	12
From the U.S.	5
From Australia and New Zealand	1
Who speak a Chinese dialect	22
Who speak English	9
Who speak Hindi	8
Females	50
Males	50
Christians	32
Non-Christians	68
Muslims	19
Buddists	6
Jew	1
Who have enough to eat	30
Old enough to read	88
Old enough to read, but cannot read at all	17
Teacher	1

managers employed by 31 such companies, the common complaint was too few promotions and too little responsibility.[25]

Ethnocentric attitudes can also cause problems in ethnically diverse countries, such as the United States, where Hispanics/Latinos are projected to be nearly one-quarter of the population by 2050, and 12 percent of the population presently speaks Spanish.[26] Miller Brewing Co. tripped over this problem:

> *Rey Perez, a sales manager at Chicago Beverage Systems, recalls an attempt by Miller to reach Hispanic consumers. Management pushed a Tejano music-based marketing strategy, similar to one that had succeeded in Texas. "We told them it wouldn't work," says Perez. "Tejano isn't as big among Mexicans in Chicago." It failed miserably.[27]*

In fact, U.S. Hispanics and Latinos trace their roots to 22 different countries.[28]

The Cultural Imperative

Culture has a powerful impact on people's behavior.[29] For example, consider the everyday activity of negotiating a business contract.

> *To Americans, a contract signals the conclusion of negotiations; its terms establish the rights, responsibilities, and obligations of the parties involved. However, to the Japanese, a company is not forever bound to the terms of the contract. In fact, it can be renegotiated whenever there is a significant shift in the company's circumstances. For instance, an unexpected change in governmental tax policy, or a change in the competitive environment, are considered legitimate reasons for contract renegotiation. To the Chinese, a signatory to an agreement is a partner with whom they can work, so to them the signing of a contract is just the beginning of negotiations.[30]*

Cross-cultural business negotiators who ignore or defy cultural traditions do so at their own risk. That means they risk not making the sale, losing a contract, or failing to negotiate a favorable deal. Therefore, a sensitivity to cross-cultural differences is imperative for people who do business in other countries. Indeed, cross-cultural sensitivity is vital to *each* of us on a daily basis because we live in a world where three out of every 100 people (more than 175 million total) live outside the country of their birth.[31]

In this section, we define the term *culture*, identify basic cultural dimensions, and explore important cross-cultural differences.

Culture Defined

culture   A population's taken-for-granted assumptions, values, beliefs, and symbols, which foster patterned behavior.

Culture is the pattern of taken-for-granted assumptions about how a given collection of people should think, act, and feel as they go about their daily affairs.[32] Regarding the central aspect of this definition—*taken-for-granted assumptions*—pioneering anthropologist Edward T. Hall noted:

Much of culture operates outside our awareness; frequently, we don't even know what we know. . . . This applies to all people. The Chinese or the Japanese or the Arabs are as unaware of their assumptions as we are of our own. We each assume that they're part of human nature. What we think of as "mind" is really internalized culture.[33]

In Chapter 7, *organizational* culture is called the social glue that binds members of an organization together. Similarly, at a broader level, societal culture acts as a social glue made up of norms, values, attitudes, role expectations, taboos, symbols, heroes, beliefs, morals, customs, and rituals. Cultural lessons are imparted from birth to death via role models, formal education, religious teachings, and peer pressure.

Cultural undercurrents make international dealings immensely challenging. According to Fons Trompenaars and Charles Hampden-Turner, the Dutch and English authors of the landmark book *Riding the Waves of Culture:*

International managers have it tough. They must operate on a number of different premises at any one time. These premises arise from their culture of origin, the culture in which they are working, and the culture of the organization which employs them.

In every culture in the world such phenomena as authority, bureaucracy, creativity, good fellowship, verification, and accountability are experienced in different ways. That we use the same words to describe them tends to make us unaware that our cultural biases and our accustomed conduct may not be appropriate, or shared.[34]

Are U.S. Global Corporations Turning the World into a Single "Americanized" Culture?

Protesters at World Trade Organization and global economic summit meetings in recent years have decried the growing global reach of McDonald's and other American corporate giants. They predict a homogenizing of the world's unique cultures into a so-called McWorld, where American culture prevails. Although emotionally appealing, these concerns are *not* supported by evidence according to University of Michigan researchers who have been tracking cultural values in 65 societies for more than 20 years. Citing evidence from their ongoing World Values Survey, the researchers recently concluded:

The impression that we are moving toward a uniform "McWorld" is partly an illusion. The seemingly identical McDonald's restaurants that have spread throughout the world actually have different social meanings and fulfill different social functions in different cultural zones. Eating in a McDonald's restaurant in Japan is a different social experience from eating in one in the United States, Europe, or China.

Likewise, the globalization of communication is unmistakable, but its effects may be overestimated. It is certainly apparent that young people around the world are wearing jeans and listening to U.S. pop music; what is less apparent is the persistence of underlying value differences.

In short, economic development will cause shifts in the values of people in developing nations, but it will not produce a uniform global culture. The future may look like McWorld, but it won't feel like one.[35]

Cultural roots run deep, have profound impacts on behavior, and are not readily altered.

High-Context and Low-Context Cultures

People from European-based cultures typically assess people from Asian cultures such as China and Japan as quiet and hard to figure out. Conversely, Asians tend to view Westerners as aggressive, insensitive, and even rude. True, language differences are a significant barrier to mutual understanding. But something more fundamental is involved, something cultural. Hall prompted better understanding of cross-cultural communication by distinguishing between high- and low-context cultures.[36] The difference centers on how much meaning one takes from what someone actually says or writes versus who the other person is.

High-context cultures

high-context cultures   Cultures in which nonverbal and situational messages convey primary meaning.

▎ In **high-context cultures**, people rely heavily on nonverbal and subtle situational messages when communicating with others. The other person's official status, place in society, and reputation say a great deal about the person's rights, obligations, and trustworthiness.

▎ In high-context cultures, people do not expect to talk about such "obvious" things. Conversation simply provides general background information about the other person.

▎ In high-context Japan, the ritual of exchanging business cards is a social necessity, and failing to read a card you have been given is a grave insult. The other person's company and position determine what is said and how. Arab, Chinese, and Korean cultures also are high-context.

Low-context cultures

low-context cultures   Cultures in which words convey primary meaning.

▎ People from **low-context cultures** convey essential messages and meaning primarily with words. Low-context cultures in Germany, Switzerland, Scandinavia, North America, and Great Britain expect people to communicate their precise intended meaning. While low-context people do read so-called body language, its messages are secondary to spoken and written words.

▎ Legal contracts with precisely worded expectations are important in low-context countries such as the United States. However, according to international communications experts, "in high-context cultures the process of forging a business relationship is as important as, if not more important than, the written details of the actual deal."[37] This helps explain why Americans tend to be frustrated with the apparently slow pace of business dealings in Japan. For the Japanese, the many rounds of meetings and social gatherings are necessary to collect valuable contextual information as a basis for judging the other party's character. For the schedule-driven American, anything short of actually signing the contract is considered a pointless waste of time. *Patience* is a prime virtue for low-context managers doing business in high-context cultures.

Nine Dimensions of Culture from the GLOBE Project

The GLOBE (Global Leadership and Organizational Behavior Effectiveness) project was conceived by Robert J. House, a University of Pennsylvania researcher. Beginning with a 1994 meeting in Calgary, Canada, the GLOBE project has grown to encompass an impressive network of over 150 researchers from 62 countries. It is a massive ongoing effort in which researchers assess organizations in their own cultures and languages with standardized instruments to collect data from around the world, building a comprehensive model. If things go as intended, the resulting data base will yield important new insights about both similarities and differences across the world's cultures.[38] More importantly, it promises to provide practical guidelines for international managers. Thanks to the first two phases of the GLOBE project, we have a research-based list of key cultural dimensions (see Table 4.3 on page 88).

Interestingly, according to one GLOBE research report, mid-level managers in the United States scored high on assertiveness and performance orientation and moderately on uncertainty avoidance and institutional collectivism.[39]

Other Sources of Cultural Diversity

Managers headed for a foreign country need to do their homework on the following cultural variables to avoid awkwardness and problems.[40] There are no rights or wrongs here, only cross-cultural differences.

▎ *Individualism versus collectivism.* This distinction between "me" and "we" cultures deserves closer attention because it encompasses two of the nine GLOBE cultural dimensions in Table 4.3. People in **individualistic cultures** focus primarily on individual rights, roles, and achievements.[41] The United States and Canada are highly individualistic cultures. Meanwhile, people in **collectivist cultures**—such as Egypt, Mexico, India, and Japan—rank duty and loyalty to family, friends, organization, and country above self-interests. Group goals and shared achievements are paramount to collectivists; personal goals and desires are suppressed. Importantly, individualism and collectivism are extreme ends of a continuum, along which people and cultures are variously distributed and mixed. For example, in the United States, one can find pockets of collectivism among Native Americans and recent immigrants from Latin America and Asia. This helps explain why a top-notch engineer born in China might be reluctant to attend an American-style recognition dinner where individual award recipients are asked to stand up for a round of applause.

▎ *Time.* Anthropologist Hall referred to time as a silent language of culture. He distinguished between monochronic and polychronic time.[42] **Monochronic time** is based on the perception that time is a unidimensional straight line divided into standard units, such as seconds, minutes, hours, and days. In monochronic cultures, including North America and northern Europe, everyone is assumed to be on the same clock, and time is treated as money. The general rule is to use time efficiently, be on time, and above all, do not waste time. In contrast, **polychronic time** involves the perception that time is flexible, elastic, and multidimensional.[43] Latin American, Mediterranean, and Arab cultures are polychronic. Managers in polychronic cultures such as rural Mexico see no problem with loosely scheduled, overlapping office visits. A monochronic American, arriving ten minutes early for an appointment with a regional Mexican official, resents having to wait another 15 minutes. The American perceives the Mexican official as slow and insensitive. The Mexican believes the American is self-centered and impatient.[44] Different perceptions of time are responsible for this collision of cultures.

individualistic cultures   Cultures that emphasize individual rights, roles, and achievements.

collectivist cultures   Cultures that emphasize duty and loyalty to collective goals and achievements.

monochronic time   A perception of time as a straight line broken into standard units.

polychronic time   A perception of time as flexible, elastic, and multidimensional.

TABLE 4.3

Nine Cultural Dimensions from the GLOBE Project

Dimension	Description	Countries scoring highest	Countries scoring lowest
Power distance	Should leaders have high or low power over others?	Morocco, Argentina, Thailand	Denmark, Netherlands, South Africa (black sample)
Uncertainty avoidance	How much should social norms and rules be used to reduce future uncertainties?	Switzerland, Sweden, Germany (former West)	Russia, Hungary, Bolivia
Institutional collectivism	To what extent should society and institutions reward loyalty?	Sweden, South Korea, Japan	Greece, Hungary, Germany (former East)
In-group collectivism	To what extent does the individual value loyalty to their family or organization?	Iran, India, Morocco	Denmark, Sweden, New Zealand
Assertiveness	How aggressive and confrontational should one be with others?	Germany (former East), Austria, Greece	Sweden, New Zealand, Switzerland
Gender equality	How equal are men and women?	Hungary, Poland, Slovenia	South Korea, Egypt, Morocco
Future orientation	How much should one work and save for the future, rather than just live for the present?	Singapore, Switzerland, Netherlands	Russia, Argentina, Poland
Performance orientation	How much should people be rewarded for excellence and improvement?	Singapore, Hong Kong, New Zealand	Russia, Argentina, Greece
Humane orientation	How much should people be encouraged to be generous, kind, and fair to others?	Philippines, Ireland, Malaysia	Germany (former West), Spain, France

Sources: Adapted from discussions in Mansour Javidan and Robert J. House, "Cultural Acumen for the Global Manager: Lessons from Project GLOBE," *Organizational Dynamics,* 29 (spring 2001): 289–305; Robert House, Mansour Javidan, Paul Hanges, and Peter Dorfman, "Understanding Cultures and Implicit Leadership Theories Across the Globe: An Introduction to Project GLOBE," *Journal of World Business,* 37 (spring 2002): 3–10; and Mansour Javidan, Robert J. House, and Peter W. Dorfman, "A Nontechnical Summary of GLOBE Findings," in Robert J. House, Paul J. Hanges, Mansour Javidan, Peter W. Dorfman, and Vipin Gupta, eds. *Culture Leadership, and Organizations: The GLOBE Study of 62 Societies* (Thousand Oaks, Calif.: Sage, 2004), pp. 29–48.

▌ *Interpersonal space.* People in a number of cultures, including Arabs and Asians, prefer to stand close when conversing. An interpersonal distance of only six inches is very disturbing to a northern European or an American, accustomed to conversing at arm's length. Cross-cultural gatherings in the Middle East often involve an awkward dance as Arab hosts strive to get closer while their American and European guests shuffle backward around the room to maintain what they consider to be a proper distance.

As always, these are exciting and turbulent times in the Middle East, where ethnic, religious, and cultural traditions collide with modern ways. Here Kuwaiti women demonstrate for broader rights in front of their nation's Parliament in Kuwait city. Expatriates working in countries such as Kuwait need to be fully aware of cross-cultural and religious differences if they are to get the job done.

▌ *Language.* Foreign language skills are the gateway to true cross-cultural understanding. Translations are not an accurate substitute for conversational ability in the local language.[45] Consider, for example, the complexity of the Japanese language:

> *Japanese is a situational language and the way something is said differs with the relationship between speaker, listener, or the person about whom they are speaking; their respective families, ages, professional statuses, and companies all affect the way they express themselves.*
>
> *In this respect, Japanese isn't one language but a group of them, changing with a dizzying array of social conventions with which Americans have no experience. Japanese people are raised dealing with the shifting concepts of in group/out group, male and female speech patterns, appropriate politeness levels, and humble and honorific forms of speech. An unwary student, armed only with a few years of classroom Japanese, can pile up mistakes in this regard very quickly.[46]*

Foreign-language instructors who prepare Americans for foreign assignments have noted these recent trends: an increase in demand for Brazilian Portuguese and Mandarin Chinese and a decrease in demand for Japanese. Spanish remains the most widely studied foreign language, followed by French and German.[47]

▌ *Religion.* Awareness of a business colleague's religious traditions is essential for building a lasting relationship. Those traditions may dictate dietary restrictions, religious holidays, and Sabbath schedules, which are important to the devout and represent cultural minefields for the uninformed. For instance, the official day of rest in Iran is Thursday; in Kuwait and Pakistan it is Friday.[48] In Israel, where the official day off is Saturday, "Burger King restaurants—unlike McDonald's—do not offer cheeseburgers in order to conform to Jewish dietary laws forbidding mixing milk products and meat."[49]

True or False?

_____ 1. An ethnocentric CEO from France would insist that French be spoken in all the firm's world-wide offices.

_____ 2. Culture involves actual behavior, not taken-for-granted assumptions about behavior.

_____ 3. Researchers from the University of Michigan concluded that the world is indeed moving toward a uniform "McWorld," where American culture prevails.

_____ 4. People are expected to communicate their precise intended meaning through written and spoken words in low-context cultures, such as the United States and Germany.

_____ 5. The nine cultural dimensions form the GLOBE project include two types of collectivism.

_____ 6. The appropriate interpersonal distance is about 18 inches when transacting face-to-face business anywhere in the world.

Multiple Choice

_____ 7. In _____ organizations, authority and decision making are headquarters-centered.
   a. polycentric
   b. regiocentric
   c. geocentric
   d. transnational
   e. ethnocentric

_____ 8. Culture is best described as
   a. the meaning of life.
   b. prejudice.
   c. universal language.
   d. taken-for-granted assumptions.
   e. one's native language.

_____ 9. _____ is (are) vital to communication in high-context cultures.
   a. Being on time
   b. Nonverbal and situational cues
   c. Being polite
   d. Having family ties
   e. Written contracts

_____ 10. Which of these is *not* one of the GLOBE project's nine cultural dimensions?
   a. Assertiveness
   b. Power distance
   c. Future orientation
   d. Religious orientation
   e. In-group collectivism

_____ 11. The concept of monochronic time is best described as
   a. standardized.   d. multidimensional.
   b. flexible.   e. variable.
   c. relaxed.

Online Study Center
ACE the Test
ACE Practice Tests 4.2

COMPARATIVE MANAGEMENT INSIGHTS

3 *Explain what Hofstede's research has to say about the applicability of American management theories in foreign cultures, and summarize the leadership lessons from the GLOBE project.*

comparative management The study of how organizational behavior and management practices differ across cultures.

Comparative management is the study of how organizational behavior and management practices differ across cultures. In this comparatively new field of inquiry, as in other fields, there is disagreement about theoretical frameworks and research methodologies. Nevertheless, some useful lessons have been learned. In this section, we focus on:

1. The applicability of American management theories in other cultures
2. Leadership lessons from the GLOBE Project

Made-in-America Management Theories Require Cultural Translation

In the 1970s, Geert Hofstede, a Dutch organizational behavior researcher, surveyed 116,000 IBM employees from 40 different countries.[50] He classified each of his 40 national samples according to four different cultural dimensions. Hofstede found a great deal of cultural diversity among the countries studied. For example, employee needs were ranked differently from country to country.

The marked cultural differences among the 40 countries led Hofstede to recommend that American management theories should be adapted to local cultures rather than imposed on them. As we can see in Appendix A at **college.hmco.com/pic/kreitnerSASfound/students**, many popular management theories were developed within the U.S. cultural context. Hofstede believes that it is naive to expect those theories to apply automatically in significantly different cultures. For example, American-made management theories reflecting Americans' preoccupation with individualism are out of place in collectivist countries such as Mexico, Brazil, and Japan, where individualism is discouraged.

Hofstede's research does not attempt to tell international managers *how* to apply various management techniques in different cultures. However, it does present a convincing case for the cultural adaptation of American management theory and practice. In turn, Americans would do well to culturally adapt any management theories and practices acquired from other cultures.

Lessons in Leadership from the GLOBE Project

The huge 62-nation data base compiled by the GLOBE researchers provides valuable insights about the applicability of leadership styles around the world. As listed along the top of the matrix in Figure 4.1 on page 92, the GLOBE researchers focused on the following five different leadership styles:

■ *Charismatic/value-based:* a visionary person who inspires high performance by exhibiting integrity and decisiveness

■ *Team-oriented:* an administratively competent person and team builder who diplomatically emphasizes common purposes and goals

■ *Participative:* a person who actively involves others in both making and carrying out decisions

■ *Humane-oriented:* a compassionate, generous, considerate, and supportive person

■ *Self-protective:* a self-centered and status-conscious person who tends to save face and stir conflict[51]

The GLOBE leadership matrix in Figure 4.1 rates these five leadership styles as most acceptable, moderately acceptable, and least acceptable for ten cultural clusters.

According to the matrix, the charismatic/value-based and team-oriented leadership styles have the greatest cross-cultural applicability. The self-protective leadership style definitely is *not* acceptable, regardless of the cultural setting. Humane-oriented leaders are perceived around the world as being only moderately acceptable, except within the southern Asia cultural cluster. This is probably because humane-oriented leaders are perceived in most cultures as not pushing hard enough to achieve goals and solid results. The picture for participative leadership is mixed, despite its general popularity in North and South America and in Germanic, Latin, and Nordic Europe.[52]

Overall conclusion: International managers need a full repertoire of leadership styles in a culturally diverse world, and they need to be flexible enough to use those styles in culturally suitable ways.[53]

FIGURE 4.1

GLOBE Leadership Matrix

Source: Adapted from data in Peter W. Dorfman, Paul J. Hanges, and Felix C. Brodbeck, "Leadership and Cultural Variation: The Identification of Culturally Endorsed Leadership Profiles," in Robert J. House, Paul J. Hanges, Mansour Javidian, Peter W. Dorfman, and Vipin Gupta, *Culture, Leadership, and Organizations: The GLOBE Study of 62 Societies* (Thousand Oaks, Calif.: Sage, 2004), pp. 669–719; and Vipin Gupta and Paul J. Hanges, "Regional and Climate Clustering of Societal Cultures," in *Ibid.*, pp. 178–218.

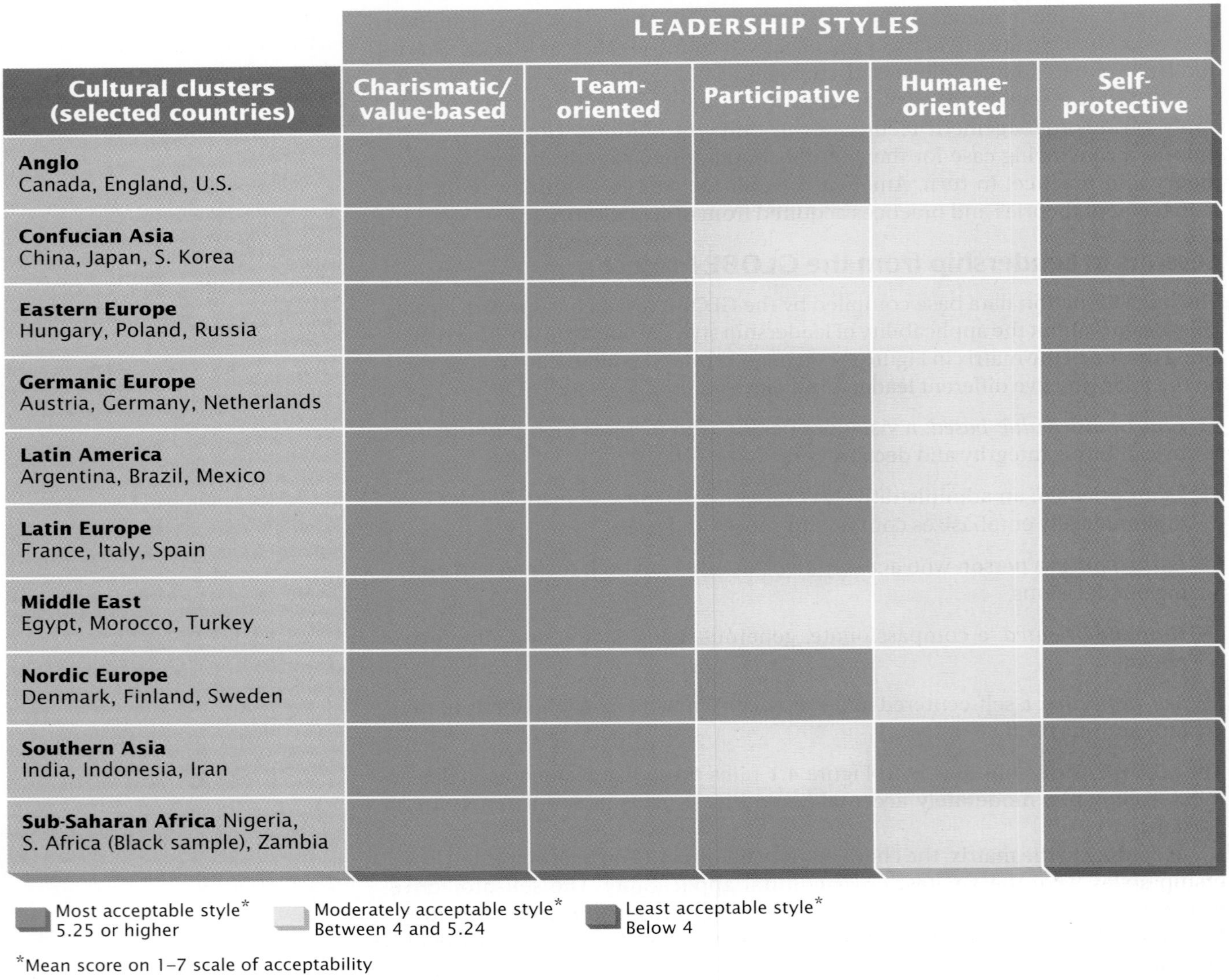

Cultural clusters (selected countries)	Charismatic/value-based	Team-oriented	Participative	Humane-oriented	Self-protective
Anglo Canada, England, U.S.					
Confucian Asia China, Japan, S. Korea					
Eastern Europe Hungary, Poland, Russia					
Germanic Europe Austria, Germany, Netherlands					
Latin America Argentina, Brazil, Mexico					
Latin Europe France, Italy, Spain					
Middle East Egypt, Morocco, Turkey					
Nordic Europe Denmark, Finland, Sweden					
Southern Asia India, Indonesia, Iran					
Sub-Saharan Africa Nigeria, S. Africa (Black sample), Zambia					

Most acceptable style* 5.25 or higher   Moderately acceptable style* Between 4 and 5.24   Least acceptable style* Below 4

*Mean score on 1–7 scale of acceptability

True or False?

_____ 1. Hofstede found American management theories to be universally applicable around the
world.

_____ 2. Humane-oriented leadership was found to be
the most widely applicable style by the GLOBE
project researchers.

_____ 3. A self-protective leadership style is the least
acceptable style, regardless of the culture,
according to the GLOBE project.

Multiple Choice

_____ 4. What is the practical conclusion from Hofstede's 40-country study?
   a. Japanese management practices will likely
       fail in North America.
   b. American management practice traces to
       Northern Europe.
   c. Management theory and practice need to
       be adapted to the local culture.
   d. American management theory and prac-
       tices are applicable worldwide.
   e. Japanese management is superior.

_____ 5. Katerina is viewed by coworkers as being compassionate, generous, considerate, and supportive. According to the GLOBE leadership
styles, what type of leader is she?
   a. Participative
   b. Team-oriented
   c. Charismatic/value-based
   d. Humane-oriented
   e. Self-protective

_____ 6. According to the GLOBE leadership matrix,
which two leadership styles have the greatest
cross-cultural applicability?
   a. Team-oriented and humane-oriented
   b. Charismatic/value-based and
       team-oriented
   c. Humane-oriented and self-protective
   d. Self-protective and
       charismatic/value-based
   e. Team-oriented and participative

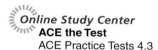

Online Study Center
ACE the Test
ACE Practice Tests 4.3

STAFFING FOREIGN POSITIONS

4 ► *Discuss why U.S. expatriates fail and what can be done about it, and
summarize the situation of North American women on foreign assignments.*

In our global economy, successful foreign experience is becoming a required
stepping-stone to top management.[54] *Fortune* magazine's Marshall Loeb observed,
"An assignment abroad, once thought to be a career dead end, has become a ticket
to speedy advance. And an increasingly necessary one."[55] Unfortunately, Americans
reportedly have a higher-than-average failure rate. Failure in this context means
foreign-posted employees perform so poorly that they are sent home early or they
voluntarily go home early. Estimates vary widely, from a modest 3.2 percent failure
rate to an alarming 25 percent.[56] Whatever the failure rate, *any* turnover among
employees on foreign assignments is expensive, considering that it costs an
average of $1 million to $2 million to send someone on a three-to-four-year foreign
assignment.[57] Predeparture training for the employee and education allowances
for children can drive the bill much higher. Managers are challenged not to waste
this sort of investment. They need to do a better job of preparing employees for
foreign assignments. Toward that end, let us examine why employees fail abroad
and what can be done about it.

Why Do U.S. Expatriates Fail?

Although historically a term for banishment or exile from one's native country, *expatriate* today refers to those who live and work in a foreign country. Living outside the comfort zone of one's native culture and surroundings can be immensely challenging—even overwhelming.[58] Expatriates typically experience some degree of **culture shock**, defined as feelings of anxiety, self-doubt, and isolation brought about by a mismatch between one's expectations and reality. Psychologist Elisabeth Marx offered these insights: "On average, managers in my study experienced culture shock symptoms for about seven weeks: 70 percent of managers reported these lasting up to five weeks and 30 percent had symptoms for up to ten weeks."[59] Those who view culture shock as a natural part of living and working in a foreign country are better equipped to deal with it. More precise knowledge of why U.S. expatriates fail also is helpful. Thanks to a recent survey of 74 large U.S. companies, encompassing a total of 3.6 million employees and 12,500 expatriates, we have a clearer picture[60] (see Table 4.4). Job performance—either so poor that it prompted recall (48.4%) or so good it attracted outside job offers (43.7%)—was the leading cause of expatriate failure. Also high on the list were factors relating to culture shock (36.6%) and homesickness (31%). Other factors trailed in relative importance. As with culture shock, it behooves candidates for foreign assignments to prepare accordingly.

Cross-Cultural Training

As we defined it earlier, culture is the unique system of values, beliefs, and symbols that fosters patterned behavior in a given population. It is difficult to distinguish the individual from his or her cultural context. Consequently, people tend to be very protective of their cultural identity. Careless defiance of cultural norms or traditions by outsiders can result in grave personal insult and put important business dealings at risk. Cultural sensitivity can be learned, fortunately, through cross-cultural training.

Specific Techniques

Cross-cultural training is defined as any form of guided experience aimed at helping people live and work comfortably in another culture. The following is a list of five basic cross-cultural training techniques, ranked in order of increasing complexity and cost.

> ▌ *Documentary programs.* Trainees read about a foreign country's history, culture, institutions, geography, and economics. Video presentations and Web searches and tutorials also are often used.

> ▌ *Culture assimilator.* Cultural familiarity is achieved through exposure to a series of simulated intercultural incidents or typical problem situations. This technique has been used to quickly train those who are given short notice of a foreign assignment.

> ▌ *Language instruction.* Conversational language skills are taught through a variety of methods. Months, sometimes years, of study are required to master difficult languages. A 2006 survey of 431 human resource specialists provided this window on the future:

> > *. . . knowledge of foreign languages, cultures and global markets will become increasingly important for graduates entering the U.S. workforce. When asked*

---

culture shock   Negative feelings triggered by an expectations-reality mismatch.

cross-cultural training   Guided experience that helps people live and work in foreign cultures.

to project the changing importance of several knowledge and skill needs over the next five years, 63 percent of survey respondents cited foreign languages as increasing in importance more than any other basic knowledge area or skill.[61]

Meanwhile, nearly 81 percent of Americans speak only English.[62]

▪ *Sensitivity training.* Experiential exercises teach awareness of the impact of one's actions on others.

▪ *Field experience.* Extensive firsthand exposure to ethnic subcultures in one's own country or to foreign cultures heightens awareness.[63]

Is One Technique Better than Another?

A study of 80 (63 male, 17 female) managers from a U.S. electronics company attempted to compare the relative effectiveness of different training techniques.[64] A documentary approach was compared with an interpersonal approach. The latter combined sensitivity training and local ethnic field experience. Both techniques were judged equally effective at promoting cultural adjustment, as measured during the managers' three-month stay in South Korea. The researchers recommended a *combination* of documentary and interpersonal training. The importance of language training was diminished in this study because the managers dealt primarily with English-speaking Koreans.

Considering that far too many U.S. companies have no formal expatriate training programs, the key issue is not which type of training is better, but whether companies have any systematic cross-cultural training at all. (*Note:* The cultural adjustment checklist in Best Practices on page 98 is useful for many major lifestyle dislocations, such as adjusting to a new college, city, or organization.)

An Integrated Expatriate Staffing System

Cross-cultural training, in whatever form, should not be an isolated experience. Rather, it should be part of an integrated, selection-orientation-repatriation process that is focused on a distinct career path.[65] The ultimate goal should be a positive and productive experience for the employee and his or her family and a smooth professional and cultural reentry back home.

▪ During the selection phase, the usual interview should be supplemented with an orientation session for the candidate's family. This session gives everyone an opportunity to "select themselves out" before a great deal of time and money has been invested. Experience has shown that, upon the expatriates' arrival at the foreign assignment, family sponsors or assigned mentors can effectively reduce culture shock.[66] Sponsors and mentors ease the expatriate family through the critical first six months by answering naive but important questions and by serving as cultural translators.

TABLE 4.4

Research Findings on Why U.S. Expatriates Go Home Early

Reason	Percentage in agreement
Not performing job effectively	48.4
Received other, more rewarding offers from other companies	43.7
Expatriate or family not adjusting to culture	36.6
Expatriate or family missing contact with family and friends at home	31.0
Received other, more rewarding offers from our company	12.2
Unable to adjust to deprived living standards in country of assignment	10.3
Concerned with problems of safety and/or health care in foreign location	10.3
Believed children's education was suffering	7.1
Feared that assignment would slow career advancement	7.1
Spouse wanted career	6.1
Compensation package was inadequate	0.0

Source: Reprinted from *Business Horizons,* Vol. 45, by Gary S. Insch and John D. Daniels, "Causes and Consequences of Declining Early Departures from Foreign Assignments," p. 41. Copyright © 2002, with permission from Elsevier.

■ Finally, repatriation should be a forethought rather than an afterthought.[67] Candidates for foreign assignments deserve a firm commitment from their organization that a successful tour of duty will lead to a step up the career ladder upon their return. Expatriates who spend their time worrying about being leapfrogged while they are absent from headquarters are less likely to succeed.

What About North American Women on Foreign Assignments?

Historically, companies in Canada and the United States have sent very few women on foreign assignments. Between the early 1980s and late 1990s, the representation of women among North American expatriates grew from 3 percent to a still small 14 percent.[68] Conventional wisdom—that women could not be effective because of foreign prejudice—has turned out to be a myth. Recent research and practical experience have given us these insights:

■ North American women have enjoyed above-average success on foreign assignments.

■ The greatest barriers to foreign assignments for North American women have been self-disqualification and prejudice among *home-country* managers. A recent survey led to this conclusion: "We found that American women in management and executive roles in foreign countries can do just as well as American men. Their biggest problem was convincing their companies to give them the assignments."[69]

■ Culture is a bigger hurdle than gender. In other words, North American women on foreign assignments are seen as North Americans first and women second.[70]

Testimonial evidence suggests that these last two factors are also true for African Americans, many of whom report smoother relations abroad than at home.[71] Thus, the best career advice for *anyone* seeking a foreign assignment is this: carefully prepare yourself, *go for it*, and don't take "no" for an answer![72]

Relying on Local Managerial Talent

In recent years, the expensive expatriate failure problem and globalization have led corporations to place a greater reliance on managers from host countries. Foreign nationals already know the language and culture and do not require huge relocation expenditures.[73] In addition, host-country governments tend to look favorably on a greater degree of local control. On the negative side, local managers may have an inadequate knowledge of home-office goals and procedures. The staffing of foreign positions is necessarily a case-by-case proposition.

REALITY CHECK 4.4

Michael Todman, President of Whirlpool International: "Traditionally, what many U.S. companies did was bring in many (Americans) to start the business. It's important to bring the corporate philosophy, but, at the end of the day, you need local talent, people who understand the market and the consumers, to drive your business in the marketplace."

Source: As quoted in Calum MacLeod, "Whirlpool Spins China Challenge into Turnaround," *USA Today* (April 5, 2007): 2B.

Question: What are the pros and cons of relying too heavily on local talent in a foreign business venture?

TEST PREPPER 4.4

ANSWERS CAN BE FOUND ON P. 101

True or False?

_____ 1. Mentors can help reduce culture shock for those on foreign assignments.

_____ 2. When selecting someone for a foreign assignment, it is a good idea to put the person's entire family through an orientation.

_____ 3. North American women have enjoyed above-average success on foreign assignments.

Multiple Choice

_____ 4. The leading reason for the comparatively high failure rate of U.S. managers on foreign assignments is
   a. poor job performance.
   b. excessive aggressiveness.
   c. emotional immaturity.
   d. poor language ability.
   e. inability of a spouse to adjust.

_____ 5. _____ can be defined as feelings of anxiety, self-doubt, and isolation brought on by an expectations-reality mismatch.
   a. Culture shock
   b. Culture drain
   c. Jet lag
   d. Travel weariness
   e. Travel trauma

_____ 6. Which technique is appropriate when managers have short notice of a foreign assignment and need to be trained quickly?
   a. Virtual transfer
   b. Culture assimilator
   c. Language instruction
   d. Sensitivity training
   e. Field experience

_____ 7. Which of these is true about North American women on foreign assignments?
   a. Most foreign executives simply refuse to work with women.
   b. Gender is a bigger hurdle than culture.
   c. The greatest barrier to foreign assignments for North American women has been self-disqualification and prejudice among home-country managers.
   d. North American women have suffered an above-average failure rate on foreign assignments.
   e. Canadian women have proven to be twice as successful as U.S. women.

Online Study Center
ACE the Test
ACE Practice Tests 4.4

Cultural Adjustment Checklist

▌ Are you continuing to make progress in the local language (if applicable)? Can you communicate with local people in everyday situations?

▌ Are you starting to be able to read the cultural signals of the local people that differ from yours and to understand what they mean in context?

▌ When you are with local people, are you learning to adapt your behavior to their cultural expectations?

▌ Do you have more positive than negative feelings about the local people and culture?

▌ Do you get regular exercise, and have you found other ways to reduce the stress of living overseas?

▌ Does your home feel like a comfortable oasis amidst the foreign environment?

▌ Do you maintain regular contact with people back home?

▌ Do you have a network of people you can turn to in an emergency or if you need support in other ways?

▌ Have you made friends outside the narrow circle of colleagues from your home country?

▌ Do you regularly get out and do things in your free time rather than isolating yourself at home?

▌ Do you feel that you know your way around and can find what you need?

▌ Do you feel as if you have a reason to get up in the morning? Is your work (whether paid or unpaid) meaningful and satisfying?

▌ Have you found enjoyable things to do in your free time, especially activities that were not possible back home?

▌ Do you view your overseas assignment as an opportunity for personal growth, rather than an unpleasant duty?

Source: Excerpt from Melissa Brayer Hess and Patricia Linderman, *The Expert Expatriate: Your Guide to Successful Relocation Abroad*, pp. 177–178, 2003. Reproduced with permission of Intercultural Press.

MTV's Passage to India

Seen from afar—say, from the executive suites atop Viacom's building in Times Square or NBC's Rockefeller Center headquarters or Disney's base camp in Burbank—India looks like a great place to be in the television business. More than one billion people live in India, and while most remain poor, the middle class is expanding rapidly. The economy grew by 8% last year; advertising grew faster. Consumers are getting their first credit cards and buying mobile phones, motor scooters, CD players, and of course TV sets. What's more, unlike China, where the central government tightly controls television and print, India enjoys a robust democracy, a boisterous press, and a vibrant film and music industry. So it's no surprise that every one of the global entertainment giants, whose businesses are maturing in the U.S. and in Western Europe, have journeyed to India—and to the rest of Asia—in search of growth.

What they have found upon arrival is a media landscape unlike any other—as noisy, chaotic, overcrowded, and impossible to navigate, at least for a stranger, as the streets of Mumbai, the nation's entertainment capital. Here the past, present, and future live side by side: Shiny new Mercedes swerve around the three-wheeled taxis powered by motorcycle engines and known as autorickshaws, whose drivers honk impatiently at men pulling ancient wooden carts piled high with mangoes and bananas. Roadside billboards advertise reality TV shows (*The Search for India's Smartest Kid*) and cable networks (cricket coverage on ESPN). You can almost see money being made. But each time my taxi stops at a traffic light, scrawny children cluster at the windows, tapping on the glass and pointing at their mouths, begging for money to buy something to eat.

I've come to Mumbai to see MTV India. Why MTV? Two reasons: first, because MTV has been doing business here since 1991, before most of its competitors arrived; second, because MTV has done better than any other global TV network—better than CNN or anything owned by Rupert Murdoch—at spreading its brand and programs into every nook and cranny of the globe. MTV Networks, a division of Viacom, operates 72 international channels, including versions of Nickelodeon and VH1, that reach 321 million homes in Europe, Asia, Latin America, Canada, and Australia, and generate nearly $1 billion in annual revenues from outside the U.S. If any global TV company could figure out how to build a business in India, MTV could.

And in fact, MTV India has built a business. It's just not a big business—not yet anyway—and therein lies a cautionary tale about operating in unfamiliar territory. Yes, the company figured out quickly that it couldn't simply blast its American programming at Indian teenagers, who don't like rock or rap music—and who were utterly mystified by *The Osbournes*. MTV knew it had to tailor operations to fit the market. But that has proven to be harder than it looks.

And it's not just a programming puzzle. India's freewheeling cable TV industry, it turns out, has too many channels chasing too few advertising dollars: The cable advertising market today amounts to about $600 million a year, which is divided among more than 100 channels. Prying revenue out of cable subscribers is hard, too—customers pay only about $3 a month for cable, leaving pennies, if that, for the networks. Finally, because most families own just one TV set, they tend to watch TV together, which means that MTV India has to compete with news, sports, and entertainment channels. India's top-rated TV show—a soap opera on Star Plus—generates ratings that dwarf anything on MTV.

Who would have thought that one of the world's strongest brands would get crushed by *Kyonki Saas Bhi Kabhi Bahu Thi*, which means "The Mother-in-Law Was the Daughter-in-Law Once"?

Alex Kuruvilla, MTV's top man in Mumbai, is not deterred by any of that. Doing business in the developing world requires enormous patience, he tells me. There's an art to refashioning products made in the U.S. to suit local tastes. . . .

"The mistake a lot of multinationals have made here is looking at the size of the middle class, multiplying by *x* number of boxes per person or whatever, and seeing a business that looks enormous—until they discover, to their horror, that you have to do things differently. You need to reflect the local culture," [Kuruvilla says].

Indeed, one country's MTV looks very little like another's. Bill Roedy, the globetrotting president of MTV Networks International, says, "MTV India is very colorful, self-effacing, full of humor, a lot of street culture. China's is about family values, nurturing, a lot of love songs. In Indonesia, with our largest Islamic population, there's a call to prayer five times a day on the channel. Brazil is very sexy. Italy is stylish, elegant, with food shows because of the love of food there. Japan's very techie, a lot of wireless product." Of the 2,500 or so people who work for MTV International, fewer than 10% are Americans.

What MTV exports is a global brand, a culture driven by creativity and a handful of big events, like its annual Video Music Awards, that cross boundaries. (The conventional wisdom among antiglobalists—that America is shoving Britney Spears and Big Macs down people's throats everywhere—is neither supported by evidence nor respectful of the fact that people in the developing world decide for themselves what they want to consume.) The trouble is, once you decide, as MTV has, to build dozens of original channels, each with local programs and staffs, the economies of scale enjoyed by the global media giants dwindle. Still, every big media company—News Corp., Disney, Sony, Time Warner, Discovery Communications, and NBC—has jumped into the global game.

Source: From Marc Gunther, "MTV's Passage to India," *Fortune*, August 9, 2004, pp. 116–125. Copyright © 2006 Time Inc. All rights reserved.

CLOSING CASE STUDY (CONTINUED)

Case Questions

1. What are your feelings about taking a foreign assignment in the global economy after reading both this chapter and this case? Explain.

2. How might an American (or someone from another country of your choosing) with an ethnocentric attitude interpret the facts of this case? Explain.

3. Which of the cross-cultural differences discussed in this chapter are evident in this case? Explain.

4. What was the most important international management lesson you learned from reading this case? Explain.

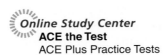

Online Study Center
ACE the Test
ACE Plus Practice Tests

Online Study Center
Improve Your Grade
Learning Objective Review
Audio Chapter Review
Audio Chapter Quiz
Study Guide to Go

LEARNING OBJECTIVE REVIEW

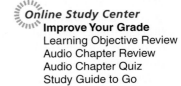

▶ *Describe the six-step internationalization process, and distinguish between a global company and a transnational company.*

- The study of international management is more important than ever as the huge global economy continues to grow.

- Doing business internationally typically involves much more than importing and/or exporting goods.

- The six stages of the internationalization process are:
  - Licensing
  - Exporting
  - Local warehousing and selling
  - Local assembly and packaging
  - Joint ventures
  - Direct foreign investments

- The main distinction between global companies and transnational companies is the difference between reality and a futuristic vision.
  - A global company does business simultaneously in many countries but pursues global strategies administered from a strong home-country headquarters.
  - A transnational company is envisioned as a decentralized global network of productive units with no distinct national identity. There is growing concern about the economic and political power of these stateless enterprises as they eclipse the power and scope of their host nations.

2 ▶ *Explain from a cross-cultural perspective the difference between high-context and low-context cultures, and identify at least four of the GLOBE cultural dimensions.*

- An ethnocentric attitude is home-country-oriented, and a serious roadblock in the global economy.

- Communication in high-context cultures such as Japan is based more on nonverbal and situational messages than it is in low-context cultures such as the United States.

- The nine cultural dimensions identified by the GLOBE project are:
  - Power distance
  - Uncertainty avoidance
  - Institutional collectivism
  - In-group collectivism
  - Assertiveness
  - Gender equality
  - Future orientation
  - Performance orientation
  - Humane orientation

3 ▶ *Explain what Hofstede's research has to say about the applicability of American management theories in foreign cultures, and summarize the leadership lessons from the GLOBE project.*

- Comparative management is a new field of study concerned with how organizational behavior and management practices differ across cultures. A unique study by Geert Hofstede of 116,000 IBM employees in 40 nations classified each country by its prevailing attitude toward four cultural variables. In view of significant international differences on these cultural dimensions, Hofstede suggests that American management theory and practice be adapted to local cultures rather than imposed on them.

- According to the GLOBE researchers, the two most widely accepted leadership styles around the world are the charismatic/value-based and team-oriented styles.

- The participative and humane-oriented styles have mixed applicability.

- The self-protective style is the least acceptable across the world's cultures.

- Global managers need a flexible repertoire of leadership styles that they use selectively.

---

4 *Discuss why U.S. expatriates fail and what can be done about it, and summarize the situation of North American women on foreign assignments.*

- Culture shock is a normal part of expatriate life.

- When U.S. expatriates go home early (a costly problem), it is normally due to:
  - Job performance issues
  - Family and/or individual culture shock
  - Homesickness

- Systematic cross-cultural training—ideally including comprehensive development of language skills—is needed to help reduce the expatriate failure rate.

- Use of local managerial talent is also a possible solution, depending on the situation.

- North American women fill a growing but still small share of foreign positions:
  - Women from the United States and Canada have been successful on foreign assignments but face two major hurdles at home: self-disqualification and prejudicial home-country managers.
  - Culture, not gender, is the primary challenge for women on foreign assignments.
  - The situation for African Americans parallels that of women.

TEST PREPPER ANSWERS

▶ **4.1**

1. F   2. F   3. T   4. F   5. b   6. d   7. c

▶ **4.2**

1. T   2. F   3. F   4. T   5. T   6. F   7. e
8. d   9. b   10. d   11. a

▶ **4.3**

1. F   2. F   3. T   4. c   5. d   6. b

▶ **4.4**

1. T   2. T   3. T   4. a   5. a   6. b   7. c

Online Study Center RESOURCES

Prepare for Class, Improve Your Grade, and ACE the Test. Student Achievement Series resources include:

ACE Practice Tests	Crossword Puzzles	Hangman
Audio Chapter Quizzes	Decision Case Questions	Key Issue Expansion
Audio Chapter Reviews	Ethical Hot Seat Exercises	Learning Objective Reviews
Career Snapshots	Flashcards	Study Guide to Go
Chapter Glossaries	Hands-on Exercises	Visual Glossaries
Chapter Outlines		

To access these learning and study tools, go to **college.hmco.com/pic/kreitnerSASfound**.

Anne Mulcahy's turnaround strategy and plans for Xerox hold promise because of her foresight, communication skills, and adaptability.

1. *Define the term* planning, *and identify four organizational responses to uncertainty.*

2. *Distinguish the three types of planning, write good objectives, and explain the 80/20 principle.*

3. *Explain the concept of synergy, describe Porter's model of competitive strategies, and identify at least three Internet business models.*

Chapter Outline

Online Study Center
Prepare for Class
Chapter Outline

4 ▶ *Identify and describe the four steps
in the strategic management process,
and explain the nature and purpose
of a SWOT analysis.*

Xerox CEO Anne Mulcahy: "We Saw the Opportunity"

*M*ulcahy: As we think about our future at Xerox, it's becoming less valuable to be able to predict it and more valuable to be able to adapt. That's not to say you don't develop multiple scenarios. You do. But the point is that the strategic choices you make can be roughly right. The real precision comes from your ability to adapt.

For example, in 2002 we decided to create a global services group. When I think back, those were not the most positive times for Xerox. But there's never a good time to take on strategic change. The key is to do it when the market is sending you signals instead of waiting until your back is against the wall.

Our customers told us what their problems were and what they needed. They wanted us to show them how they could cut costs—from which printers to buy to the most cost-effective way to service them. They also wanted a combination of software and

Online Study Center
Prepare for Class
Chapter Glossary

Improve Your Grade
Flashcards
Hangman
Crossword Puzzles

planning   Coping with uncertainty by formulating courses of action to achieve specified results.

hardware for document-intensive jobs, whether it was banks creating personalized client statements or law firms sorting and printing massive amounts of electronic documents for litigation. By listening, we saw the opportunity to focus on services.

We're four years into this shift to a services-led approach, and we're making good progress. You're at your best when you're changing from a position of strength—when you have viable core businesses that become, quite frankly, funding sources for new thrusts. But it's tough. This kind of change forces you to rethink a lot of the characteristics that made you successful in the first place. The hardware business is all about per-unit manufacturing cost and functionality. The services business is less asset-intensive and more dependent on people.

The skill is to stay connected to customers and to move quickly to capture the opportunity or avoid a risk.[2] ■

In the age of Internet speed, more and more managers are finding they have a lot in common with the strategists at Xerox. Small and large, public and private organizations are struggling to stay relevant and responsive. A standing joke among managers is that they are responsible for "doing the impossible by yesterday!" Indeed, virtually all of today's managers are asked to do a lot with limited budgets, resources, and time. All this takes thoughtful planning and a healthy dose of courage in the face of nerve-wracking uncertainty.

Planning is the process of coping with uncertainty by formulating future courses of action to achieve specified results. Planning enables humans to achieve great things by envisioning a pathway from concept to reality. The greater the mission, the longer and more challenging the pathway. For example, imagine the challenges awaiting Starbucks. In 2006, *Fortune* magazine reported Howard Schultz's ambitious growth plan: "the head of the world's largest coffee-shop chain said he plans to more than triple the number of stores, to 40,000, with half in the U.S. and half overseas."[3] Planning is a never-ending process because of constant change, uncertainty, new competition, unexpected problems, and emerging opportunities.[4]

Because planning affects all downstream management functions (see Figure 5.1), it has been called the primary management function. With this model in mind, in this chapter we shall discuss uncertainty, highlight five essential aspects of the planning function, discuss how to think strategically, and explore the strategic management process. In Appendix B at **college.hmco.com/pic/kreitnerSASfound**, we examine four practical planning tools (flow charts, Gantt charts, PERT networks, and break-even analysis).

COPING WITH UNCERTAINTY

1 ▶ Define the term planning, *and identify four organizational responses to uncertainty.*

Ben Franklin said that the only sure things in life are death and taxes. Although this is a gloomy prospect, it does capture a key theme of modern life, especially when global terrorism is added to the mix: We are faced with a great deal of

FIGURE 5.1

Planning: The Primary Management Function

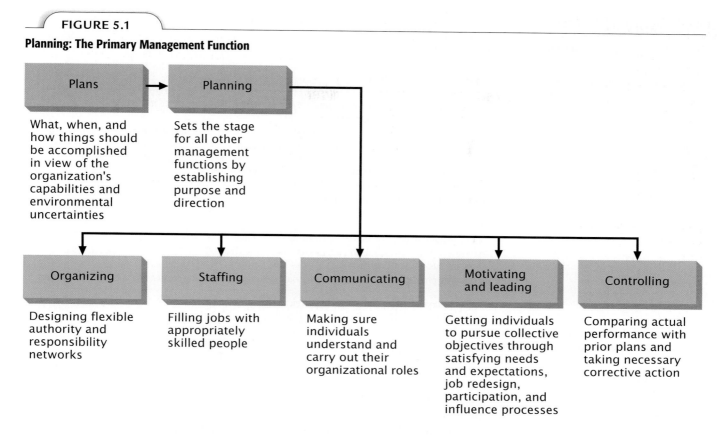

uncertainty.[5] Organizations, like individuals, are continually challenged to accomplish something in spite of general uncertainty. Organizations meet this challenge largely through planning. As a context for our discussion of planning, let us consider uncertainty from two perspectives: (1) organizational responses to environmental uncertainty and (2) the balance between planned action and spontaneity.

Organizational Responses to Uncertainty

Some organizations do a better job than others of planning amid various combinations of uncertainty. This is due in part to different ways in which they respond to the environmental factors beyond their immediate control. As outlined in Table 5.1 on page 106, organizations cope with environmental uncertainty by adopting one of four positions vis-à-vis the environment in which they operate. These positions are to act as defenders, prospectors, analyzers, or reactors.[6] Each position has its own characteristic impact on planning.

Defenders

A defender can be successful as long as its primary technology and narrow product line remain competitive. Defenders can become stranded on a dead-end road if their primary market seriously weakens. A prime example of a defender is Harley-Davidson, which sold its recreational vehicle division and other non-motorcycle businesses to get back to basics. Harley-Davidson enjoys such fierce brand loyalty among Hog riders that many sport a tattoo of the company's logo.

Online Study Center college.hmco.com/pic/kreitnerSASfound

TABLE 5.1

Different Organizational Responses to an Uncertain Environment

Type of organizational response	Characteristics of response
1. Defenders	Highly expert at producing and marketing a few products in a narrowly defined market Opportunities beyond present market not sought Few adjustments in technology, organization structure, and methods of operation because of narrow focus Primary attention devoted to efficiency of current operations
2. Prospectors	Primary attention devoted to searching for new market opportunities Frequent development and testing of new products and services Source of change and uncertainty for competitors Loss of efficiency because of continual product and market innovation
3. Analyzers	Simultaneous operations in stable and changing product market domains In relatively stable product/market domain, emphasis on formalized structures and processes to achieve routine and efficient operation In changing product/market domain, emphasis on detecting and copying competitors' most promising ideas
4. Reactors	Frequently unable to respond quickly to perceived changes in environment Make adjustments only when finally forced to do so by environmental pressures

Source: From Raymond E. Miles and Charles C. Snow, *Organizational Strategy, Structure, and Process,* 1978, Stanford University Press.

Can you imagine a Coca-Cola or Wal-Mart tattoo? But Harley-Davidson runs the risk of having its narrow focus miss the mark in an aging America. Specifically, the median age of Harley buyers rose from 35 in 1987 to 46 in 2002. Harley-Davidson is therefore seeking to lure younger riders who prefer sleek bikes away from Honda and other Japanese rivals.[7]

Prospectors

Prospector organizations are easy to spot because they have a reputation for aggressively making things happen rather than waiting for them to happen. But life can be challenging for prospectors such as Genentech, the fast-growing San Francisco biotech company:

> In an industry that sets its sights on the bet-the-farm blockbuster approach to drug development, it sometimes pays to step back and take aim before firing. "That can mean not going after the huge markets that everybody's going after, where all the science has been picked over," says consultant Michael Treachy, author of Double-Digit Growth. "Sometimes that involves going after market segments where perhaps there's been a lot less effort." . . . Genentech is doing just that: moving away from the mob-chasing, big-market, one-size-fits-all opportunities, and instead innovating through "targeted therapies"—that is, treatments for specific sets of patients, mostly in the areas of oncology and immunology.[8]

Prospectors (or pioneers) traditionally have been admired for their ability to gain what strategists call a *first-mover advantage.*[9] In other words, the first one to market wins. Following the Internet crash, when many dot-com pioneers were the first to go bankrupt, the first-mover advantage was given a second look. Two researchers, one from the United States and the other from France, recently offered

Talk about uncertainty! Pity the poor commercial airline business in recent years. First there were the 9/11 terrorist attacks in the United States that crippled travel and tourism. Then along came a recession, the war in Iraq, higher fuel prices, and SARS. This Thai Airways International flight attendant dealt with uncertainty by wearing a mask to avoid becoming a SARS victim. Unfortunately, public health officials said the masks provided more reassurance than actual protection. Facts and emotions need to be carefully sorted out when coping with uncertainty.

this finding about both industrial and consumer goods companies: "... we found that over the long haul, early movers are considerably *less* profitable than later entrants. Although pioneers do enjoy sustained revenue advantages, they also suffer from persistently *high* costs, which eventually overwhelm the sales gains."[10] Prospectors need to pick their opportunities very carefully, selecting those that offer the best combination of feasibility and profit potential. This is especially true for entrepreneurs starting small businesses.[11]

Analyzers

An essentially conservative strategy of following the leader marks an organization as an analyzer. It is a "me too" response to environmental uncertainty.[12] Analyzers let the market leader take expensive R&D risks and then imitate what works. This slower, more studied approach can pay off when the economy turns down and market leaders stumble. Verizon, the telephone company, is a good case in point:

> *Remember the tortoise and the hare? Sometimes slow and steady is better than fast and furious. A couple of years ago, industry observers cried that Verizon, weighed down by regulatory matters and merger pains, had missed the bandwidth wagon. But the Baby Bell's sluggishness turned out to be an asset: While other telecom companies are writing off billions, Verizon actually wins big as a result of the fiber glut.*
> *Instead of building its own system a couple of years ago, Verizon is now cobbling together an international network that it is buying in bits and pieces from other fiber carriers at enormous discounts.*[13]

Although analyzers may not get a lot of respect, they can perform the important economic function of breaking up monopolistic situations. Customers appreciate the resulting lower prices.

Reactors

The reactor is the exact opposite of the prospector. Reactors wait for adversity, such as declining sales, before taking corrective steps. They are slow to develop new products to supplement their tried-and-true ones. Their strategic responses to changes in the environment are often late. An interesting example of this is Joseph E. Seagram & Sons, Inc. The Canadian firm grew into the world's largest distiller by specializing in brown liquors such as Seagram's 7 Crown. But drinking habits changed over the years. Consequently, white liquors such as Bacardi rum and Smirnoff vodka pushed Seagram's 7 Crown from first place to third. Moreover, with more North Americans drinking wine, the public outcry against drunk driving, and higher excise taxes on liquor, Seagram's sales dropped. By the time Seagram reacted by bolstering its wine business in the 1980s, the wine market was glutted because of European imports and overplanted vineyards in California.[14]

According to one field study, reactors tended to be less profitable than defenders, prospectors, and analyzers.[15]

Balancing Planned Action and Spontaneity in the Twenty-First Century

In the obsolete command-and-control management model, plans were considered destiny. Top management formulated exacting plans for every aspect of operations and then kept everything under tight control to "meet the plan." All too often, however, plans were derailed by unanticipated events, and success was dampened by organizational inflexibility. Today's progressive managers:

▪ See plans as general guidelines for action, based on imperfect and incomplete information

▪ Believe planning is no longer the exclusive domain of top management; it now typically involves those who carry out the plans because they are closer to the customer

▪ Need to balance planned action with the flexibility to take advantage of surprise events and unexpected opportunities

A good analogy is to an improvisational comedy act. The stand-up comic has a plan for his or her introduction, the structure of the act, some tried-and-true jokes, and closing remarks. Within this planned framework, the comic will play off the audience's input and improvise as necessary. Harvard's Rosabeth Moss Kanter recently put the improvisational approach in a practical context by noting:

> *Because successful improvisation trusts the players to be unpredictable, it requires great discipline. Leaders must establish themes, set goals, identify priorities, and assess results. They must seed new projects and weed out others.*[16]

Accordingly, 3M Corporation had a plan for encouraging innovation that allowed it to capitalize on the spontaneous success of the Post-it Note. Planning should be a springboard to success, not a barrier to creativity.

TEST PREPPER 5.1

True or False?

_____ 1. Planning is the process of avoiding uncertainty.

_____ 2. Planning is the primary management function because it affects all other management functions such as organizing.

_____ 3. As long as a defender's primary technology remains competitive, it can be successful.

_____ 4. Analyzers represent a "me too" response to environmental uncertainty.

Multiple Choice

_____ 5. The process of coping with uncertainty by formulating future courses of action to achieve specified results refers to
    a. strategy.
    b. planning.
    c. pareto analysis.
    d. decision making.
    e. controlling.

Online Study Center
ACE the Test
ACE Practice Tests 5.1

_____ 6. Planning
    a. deals with what, why, and how much.
    b. eliminates uncertainty.
    c. is called the primary management function.
    d. helps managers avoid change.
    e. makes budgets obsolete.

_____ 7. A good example of a(n) _____ is motorcycle maker Harley-Davidson because it successfully produces and markets a few products in a narrowly defined market.
    a. reactor
    b. prospector
    c. analyzer
    d. opportunist
    e. defender

_____ 8. Which of these waits for adversity before taking corrective steps?
    a. Reactors
    b. Analyzers
    c. Creators
    d. Prospectors
    e. Defenders

THE ESSENTIALS OF PLANNING

2 Distinguish the three types of planning, write good objectives, and explain the 80/20 principle.

Planning is an ever-present feature of modern life, although there is no universal approach to it. Virtually everyone is a planner, at least in the informal sense. We plan leisure activities after school or work; we make career plans. Personal or informal plans give purpose and direction to our lives. In a similar fashion, more formalized plans enable managers to mobilize their intentions to accomplish organizational purposes. A **plan** is a specific, documented intention consisting of an objective and an action statement. The objective portion is the end, and the action statement represents the means to that end. Stated another way, objectives give management targets to shoot at, whereas action statements provide the arrows for hitting the targets. Properly conceived plans tell *what, when,* and *how* something is to be done.

In spite of the wide variety of formal planning systems that managers encounter on the job, we can identify some essentials of sound planning. Among these common denominators are organizational mission, types of planning, objectives, priorities, and the planning/control cycle.

Online Study Center
Improve Your Grade
Career Snapshot 5.1

plan An objective plus an action statement.

Online Study Center college.hmco.com/pic/kreitnerSASfound

Organizational Mission

To some, defining an organization's mission might seem an unnecessary exercise. But exactly the opposite is true. Some organizations drift along without a clear mission. Others lose sight of their original mission. Sometimes an organization, such as the U.S. Army Corps of Engineers, finds its original mission is no longer acceptable to key stakeholders. In fact, the Corps is stepping back from its tradition of building dams and levees, in favor of more environmentally sensitive projects. It has tackled "a 30-year, $7.8 billion restoration of the Florida Everglades"[17] that will involve tearing down levees to restore the natural flow of the Kissimmee River. Periodically redefining an organization's mission is both common and necessary in an era of rapid change.

A clear, formally written, and publicized statement of an organization's mission is the cornerstone of any planning system that will effectively guide the organization through uncertain times. The following satirical definition by Scott Adams, the *Dilbert* cartoonist, tells us how *not* to write an organizational mission statement: "A Mission Statement is defined as a long, awkward sentence that demonstrates management's inability to think clearly."[18] This sad state of affairs, too often true, can be avoided by a well-written mission statement that does the following things:

1. Defines your organization for its key stakeholders
2. Creates an inspiring vision of what the organization can be and can do
3. Outlines how the vision is to be accomplished
4. Establishes key priorities
5. States a common goal and fosters a sense of togetherness
6. Creates a philosophical anchor for all organizational activities
7. Generates enthusiasm and a "can do" attitude
8. Empowers present and future organization members to believe that every individual is the key to success[19]

A good mission statement generates a positive image for all the organization's stakeholders and provides a focal point for the entire planning process. A succinct example comes from Alan Brunacini, the long-time chief of the Phoenix, Arizona, Fire Department. He boiled his department's mission down to five words: "Prevent harm, survive, be nice."[20]

Jack Welch, the respected former CEO of General Electric, and his wife Suzy Welch, the former editor of the *Harvard Business Review*, offered this summation in their recent book *Winning*:

> At the end of the day, effective mission statements balance the possible and the impossible. They give people a clear sense of the direction to profitability and the inspiration to feel they are part of something big and important.[21]

Types of Planning

Ideally, planning begins at the top of the organizational pyramid and filters down. The rationale for beginning at the top is the need for coordination. It is top management's job to state the organization's mission, establish strategic priorities, and draw up major policies. After these statements are in place, successive rounds of strategic, intermediate, and operational planning can occur. Figure 5.2 presents an idealized picture of the three types of planning, as carried out by different levels of management.

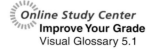

Online Study Center
Improve Your Grade
Visual Glossary 5.1

Strategic, Intermediate, and Operational Planning

Strategic planning is the process of determining how to pursue the organization's long-term goals with the resources expected to be available. A well-conceived strategic plan communicates much more than general intentions about profit and growth. It specifies how the organization will achieve a competitive advantage, with profit and growth as necessary by-products. **Intermediate planning** is the process of determining the contributions subunits can make with allocated resources. Finally, **operational planning** is the process of determining how specific tasks can best be accomplished on time with available resources. Each level of planning is vital to an organization's success and cannot effectively stand alone without the support of the other two levels.

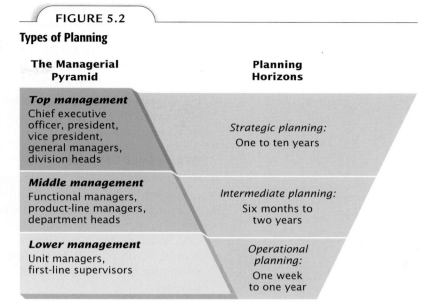

FIGURE 5.2

Types of Planning

The Managerial Pyramid	Planning Horizons
Top management Chief executive officer, president, vice president, general managers, division heads	*Strategic planning:* One to ten years
Middle management Functional managers, product-line managers, department heads	*Intermediate planning:* Six months to two years
Lower management Unit managers, first-line supervisors	*Operational planning:* One week to one year

Planning Horizons

As Figure 5.2 illustrates, planning horizons vary for the three types of planning. The term **planning horizon** refers to the time that elapses between the formulation and the execution of a planned activity. As the planning process evolves from strategic to operational, planning horizons shorten and plans become increasingly specific. Naturally, management can be more confident and hence more specific about the near future than it can about the distant future. For example, National Instruments, in Austin, Texas, reportedly has a 100-year plan that likely is written in very general terms.[22]

Notice, however, that the three planning horizons overlap, since their boundaries are elastic rather than rigid. The trend today is toward involving employees from all levels in the strategic planning process. Also, it is not uncommon for top- and lower-level managers to have a hand in formulating intermediate plans. Middle managers often help lower managers draw up operational plans as well. So, Figure 5.2 is an ideal instructional model with countless variations in the actual workplace.

strategic planning   Determining how to pursue long-term goals with available resources.

intermediate planning   Determining subunits' contributions using allocated resources.

operational planning   Determining how to accomplish specific tasks with available resources.

planning horizon   The elapsed time between planning and execution.

Objectives

Just as a distant port is the target or goal for a ship's crew, objectives are targets that organizational members steer toward. Although some theorists distinguish between goals and objectives, managers typically use the terms interchangeably. A goal or an **objective** is defined as a specific commitment to achieve a measurable result within a given time frame. Many experts view objectives as the single most important feature of the planning process. They help managers and entrepreneurs build a bridge between their dreams, aspirations, and visions and an achievable *reality*. Dan Sullivan, a consultant for entrepreneurs, explains:

> [Objectives and goals] should be achievable by definition. If you are setting functional goals, at useful increments, they should be both real and realizable.

objective   Commitment to achieve a measurable result within a specified period.

The distance between where you actually are now and your goal can be measured objectively, and when you achieve your goal, you know it. Think of the distinction this way: no matter how fast you run toward the horizon, you'll never get there, but if you run more quickly toward a goalpost, you will get there faster. Sounds simplistic, but I'm constantly amazed at how many people—and entrepreneurs in particular—confuse their goals with their ideals.[23]

It is important that present and future managers be able to write good objectives, be aware of their importance, and understand how objectives combine to form a means-ends chain.

Writing Good Objectives

An authority on objectives recommends that "as far as possible, objectives are expressed in quantitative, measurable, concrete terms, in the form of a written statement of desired results to be achieved within a given time period."[24] In other words, objectives represent a firm commitment to accomplish something specific. A well-written objective should state what is to be accomplished and when it is to be accomplished. In the following sample objectives, note that the desired results are expressed *quantitatively*, in units of output, dollars, or percentage of change.

▋ To increase subcompact car production by 240,000 units during the next production year

▋ To reduce bad-debt loss by $50,000 during the next six months

▋ To achieve an 18 percent increase in Brand X sales by December 31 of the current year

For skill practice, try writing some objectives and plans for everyday things such as eating right, exercising more, and getting better grades."

"...and although the tortoise was severely speed-challenged, he achieved his sales quota through a strict goal-specific program."

Source: Chris Wildt

The Importance of Objectives

From the standpoint of planning, carefully prepared objectives benefit managers by serving as targets and measuring sticks, which fosters commitment and enhances motivation.[25]

▋ *Targets.* As mentioned earlier, objectives provide managers with specific targets. Without objectives, managers at all levels would find it difficult to make coordinated decisions. People quite naturally tend to pursue their own ends in the absence of formal organizational objectives.

▋ *Measuring sticks.* An easily overlooked, after-the-fact feature of objectives is that they are useful for measuring how well an organizational subunit or individual has performed. When appraising performance, managers need an established standard against which they can measure performance. Concrete objectives enable managers to weigh performance objectively on the basis of accomplishment rather than subjectively on the basis of personality or prejudice.

▋ *Commitment.* The very process of getting an employee to agree to pursue a given objective gives that individual a personal stake in the success of the enterprise. Thus, objectives can be helpful

FIGURE 5.3

A Typical Means-Ends Chain of Objectives

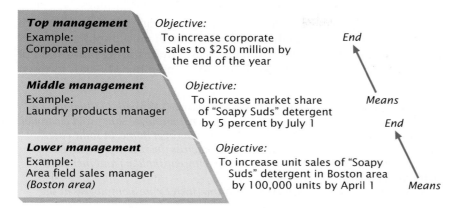

in encouraging personal commitment to collective ends. Without individual commitment, even well-intentioned and carefully conceived strategies are doomed to failure.

▌ *Motivation.* Good objectives represent a challenge—something to reach for. As such, they have a motivational aspect. People usually feel good about themselves and what they do when they successfully achieve a challenging objective. Moreover, objectives give managers a rational basis for rewarding performance. Employees who believe they will be equitably rewarded for achieving a given objective will be motivated to perform well.

Management by objectives (MBO) is a comprehensive and proven management system based on measurable and participatively set objectives that leverages the motivational power of objectives. MBO has been used effectively in profit and nonprofit organizations of all sizes.[26]

management by objectives (MBO)
Comprehensive management system based on measurable and participatively set objectives.

The Means-Ends Chain of Objectives

Like the overall planning process, objective setting is a top-to-bottom proposition. Top managers set broader objectives with longer time horizons than do successively lower levels of managers. In effect, this downward flow of objectives creates a means-ends chain. Working from bottom to top in Figure 5.3, supervisory-level objectives provide the means for achieving middle-level objectives (ends) that, in turn, provide the means for achieving top-level objectives (ends).

The organizational hierarchy shown in Figure 5.3 has, of course, been telescoped and narrowed at the middle and lower levels for illustrative purposes. Usually, two or three layers of management would separate the president and the product-line managers. Another layer or two would separate product-line managers from area sales managers. But the telescoping helps show that lower-level objectives provide the means for accomplishing higher-level ends or objectives.

Priorities

Defined as the ranking of goals, objectives, or activities in order of importance, **priorities** play a special role in planning. By listing long-range organizational

priorities Ranking goals, objectives, or activities in order of importance.

"[Canadian business professor Piers Steel] has concluded that about 95% of us procrastinate at times, with 15% to 20% being chronic offenders.

"Behind all the dilly-dallying is lack of confidence about finishing the job, boredom with the task, and a human tendency to go for immediate reward over long-term gain. . . .

"A common ploy for avoiding work at the office, he says—reading each e-mail as it comes in."

Source: Catherine Arnst, "We'll Get Around to It Later," *Business Week* (January 29, 2007): 10.

Questions: How much of a procrastinator are you? What is the link between priorities and procrastination?

objectives in order of their priority, top management prepares to make later decisions regarding the allocation of resources. Limited time, talent, and financial and material resources need to be channeled proportionately into more important endeavors and away from other areas. The establishment of priorities is a key factor in managerial and organizational effectiveness. Strategic priorities give both insiders and outsiders answers to the questions "What is most important to us?" and "How should we act and react during a crisis?" An inspiring illustration of the latter occurred for American Express after the September 11, 2001, terrorist attacks:

> The hundreds of ad hoc decisions made by [new CEO Kenneth I.] Chenault and his team were guided by two overriding concerns: employee safety and customer service. AmEx helped 560,000 stranded cardholders get home, in some cases chartering airplanes and buses to ferry them across the country. It waived millions of dollars in delinquent fees on late-paying cardholders and increased credit limits to cash-starved clients. . . .
>
> Most telling, Chenault gathered 5,000 American Express employees at the Paramount Theater in New York on Sept. 20 for a highly emotional "town hall meeting." During the session, Chenault demonstrated . . . poise, compassion, and decisiveness.[27]

Priorities also need to be established for day-to-day operations and activities.

The A-B-C Priority System

Despite time-management seminars, day planners, and computerized "personal digital assistants," establishing priorities remains a subjective process that is affected by organizational politics and value conflicts.[28] Although there is no universally acceptable formula for carrying out this important function, the following A-B-C priority system is helpful.

A: "Must do" objectives *critical* to successful performance. They may be the result of special demands from higher levels of management or other external sources.

B: "Should do" objectives *necessary* for improved performance. They are generally vital, but their achievement can be postponed if necessary.

C: "Nice to do" objectives *desirable* for improved performance, but not critical to survival or improved performance. They can be eliminated or postponed to achieve objectives of higher priority.[29]

The 80/20 Principle

80/20 principle   A minority of causes, inputs, or effort tends to produce a majority of results, outputs, or rewards.

Another proven priority-setting tool is the 80/20 principle (or Pareto analysis, as mentioned in Appendix A at **college.hmco.com/pic/kreitnerSASfound**). "The **80/20 principle** asserts that a minority of causes, inputs, or effort usually leads to a majority of the results, outputs, or rewards."[30] Care needs to be taken not to interpret the 80/20 formula too literally—it is approximate. Consider this situation, for example:

> Market Line Associates, an Atlanta financial consultancy, estimates that the top 20% of customers at a typical commercial bank generate up to six times as much revenue as they cost, while the bottom fifth cost three to four times more than they make for the company.[31]

For profit-minded banks and other businesses, all customers are not alike!

Avoiding the Busyness Trap

These two simple yet effective tools for establishing priorities can help managers avoid the so-called *busyness trap*.[32] In these fast-paced times, managers should not confuse being busy with being effective and efficient. *Results* are what really count. Activities and speed, without results, are an energy-sapping waste of time. By slowing down a bit, having clear priorities, and taking a strategic view of daily problems, busy managers can be successful *and* "get a life."

Finally, managers striving to establish priorities amid many competing demands would do well to heed management expert Peter Drucker's advice—that the most important skill for setting priorities and managing time is simply learning to say no.

The Planning/Control Cycle

To put the planning process in perspective, it is important to understand how it is connected with the control function. They are a package deal; one cannot succeed without the other. In fact, a recent seven-nation survey by a London-based company found inadequate planning and control to be the leading (43 percent) cause of lost productivity.[33] Figure 5.4 illustrates the cyclical relationship between planning and control. Planning gets things headed in the right direction, and control keeps them headed there. (Because of the importance of the control function, it is covered in detail in Chapter 8.) Basically, each of the three levels of planning is a two-step sequence followed by a two-step control sequence.

1. The initial planning/control cycle begins when top management establishes strategic plans. When those strategic plans are carried out, intermediate and operational plans are formulated, thus setting in motion two more planning/control cycles.

FIGURE 5.4

The Basic Planning/Control Cycle

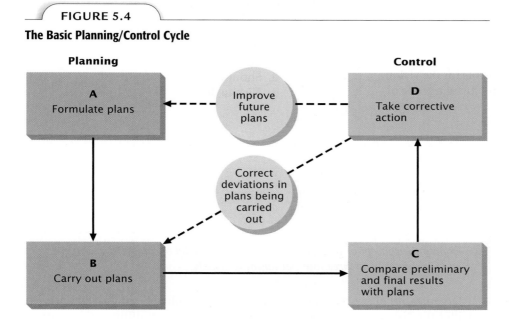

2. As strategic, intermediate, and operational plans are carried out, the control function begins. Corrective action is necessary when either the preliminary or the final results deviate from plans. For planned activities still in progress, the corrective action can get things back on track before it is too late. Deviations between final results and plans, on the other hand, are instructive feedback for the improvement of future plans.

The broken lines in Figure 5.4 on page 115 represent the important sort of feedback that makes the planning/control cycle a dynamic and evolving process. Our attention now turns to strategy.

TEST PREPPER 5.2   ANSWERS CAN BE FOUND ON P. 133

True or False?

____ 1. Well-written mission statements can generate enthusiasm and a "can-do" attitude.
____ 2. The planning horizon for operational planning is shorter than that for strategic planning.
____ 3. Objectives can serve as performance targets.
____ 4. A means-ends chain is created by the downward flow of objectives.
____ 5. Managers can use the 50/50 principle to establish priorities.
____ 6. The initial planning/control cycle begins when top management establishes strategic plans.

Multiple Choice

____ 7. A well-written mission statement should do all of the following *except*
   a. define the organization for key stakeholders.
   b. create an inspiring vision of what the organization can be and do.
   c. recognize who is responsible for the vision.
   d. state a common goal and foster a sense of togetherness.
   e. establish key priorities.

____ 8. The process of determining how to pursue the organization's long-term goals with the resources expected to be available refers to ____ planning.
   a. intermediate
   b. operational
   c. budgetary
   d. strategic
   e. contingency
____ 9. Objectives are both targets and
   a. barriers.
   b. measuring sticks.
   c. threats.
   d. priorities.
   e. flow charts.
____ 10. ____ is a term that best describes priority "C" objectives.
   a. Can't do
   b. Will do
   c. Must do
   d. Should do
   e. Nice to do

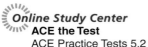

Online Study Center
  ACE the Test
  ACE Practice Tests 5.2

THINKING STRATEGICALLY (INCLUDING E-BUSINESS STRATEGIES)

 Explain the concept of synergy, describe Porter's model of competitive strategies, and identify at least three Internet business models.

Organizational success today requires *every* employee, on a daily basis, to consider the "big picture" and think strategically about gaining and keeping a competitive edge. ABB Power Technologies, based in Alamo, Tennessee, uses a team-building business simulation to get its employees to think strategically:

> ABB, along with its management consultancy, The Hayes Group, created "Learn or Burn: Making The Right Business Decisions," a one-day workshop required of all employees. Working in teams of four, employees participate in a simulation in which they must run a manufacturing business for three years. They purchase materials, move products through production, pay for overhead, complete profit and loss statements and analyze financial ratios. The idea is that employees will be able to more clearly see the direct impact that their decisions have on an organization.
>
> "It's everyone's responsibility to make decisions, not just management," says Eduardo Miller, ABB manager and workshop co-instructor. "If all of us are not learning to make the right decisions, we can burn the business."[34]

This section presents alternative perspectives for thinking strategically in today's fast-paced global economy: synergies, Porter's generic strategies, and e-business strategies. Strategic thinking is required for the strategic management process covered in the final section of this chapter.

Synergy

Although not necessarily a familiar term, *synergy* is a well-established and valuable concept. **Synergy** occurs when two or more variables (for example, chemicals, drugs, people, organizations) interact to produce an effect greater than the sum of the effects of any of the variables acting independently. Some call this the $1 + 1 = 3$ effect; others prefer to say that with synergy, the whole is greater than the sum of its parts. Either definition is acceptable as long as one appreciates the bonus effect in synergistic relationships. In strategic management, managers are urged to achieve as much *market, cost, technology,* and *management synergy*[35] as possible when making strategic decisions. Those decisions may involve mergers, acquisitions, new products, new technology or production processes, or executive replacement. When Procter & Gamble bought pet-food maker Iams, executives trumpeted the potential synergies. Five years later, unique synergies have materialized and the acquisition has proven to be a wise one.

> P&G, being P&G, flexed its marketplace muscle immediately: Using 3,000 trucks to move Iams into 25,000 mass retail outlets, it increased distribution nearly 50% overnight. Then, armed with research indicating that pet owners fear that their four-footed family members will die before they do, Iam's R&D folks began collaborating with Procter's scientists who study human hearts, bones, muscles, teeth, and gums. Iams unleashed a stream of new foods aimed at lengthening pets' lives—weight-control formulas, antioxidant blends, tartar-fighting "dental defense" ingredients.
>
> It paid off: Iams has moved from the nation's No. 5 pet-food brand to No. 1. Worldwide sales have doubled to $1.6 billion; profits have tripled.[36]

Because many promised synergies failed to materialize in recent years, especially during the dot-com bubble, the concept of synergy has become a hollow buzzword for some people.[37] But, as Jeffrey F. Rayport, founder and CEO of Marketspace LLC, recently noted: "Synergy isn't over; it isn't even passé. The era of synergy has just begun—and the wealth of the future will be created by heeding its inexorable logic."[38] Poor implementation does not render the concept of synergy invalid.[39]

synergy   The concept that the whole is greater than the sum of its parts.

REALITY CHECK 5.3

Some people think Reese's Peanut Butter Cups are a great example of synergy.

Questions: Why would they say that? Are they right?

Market Synergy

When one product or service fortifies the sales of one or more other products or services, market synergy has been achieved. Examples of market synergy are common in the business press. For example, consider this ironic example of marketing synergy:

> Swiss food giant Nestlé expanded its waistline by announcing . . . [in 2006] that it would buy weight-loss outfit Jenny Craig for $600 million. . . . Nestlé, best known for chocolate, already owns the Lean Cuisine line. Weight loss is an ever-richer business as the U.S. obesity epidemic worsens.[40]

Cost Synergy

Cost synergy can occur in almost every dimension of organized activity. When two or more products can be designed by the same engineers, produced in the same facilities, distributed through the same channels, or sold by the same salespeople, overall costs will be lower than if each product received separate treatment. In an interesting example of cost synergy, major hotels are trying to squeeze more value from their costly real estate: "At Miami Airport, Marriott has three hotels on the same plot of land. There's the Marriott Hotel, a full-service hotel. Behind the hotel are a Courtyard by Marriott, a midprice hotel, and a Fairfield Inn, an economy brand."[41]

Cost synergy also can be achieved by recycling by-products and hazardous wastes that would normally be thrown away. Human imagination is the only limit to creating cost synergies through recycling. For example, chicken farms in the Shenandoah Valley region of Virginia annually produce half a million tons of manure. Harmony Products, in Harrisonburg, Virginia, has found a way to make high-quality fertilizer pellets for golf courses from the chicken waste. Even better, Harmony burns some of the manure to produce heat for its drying process, thereby saving $500,000 a year on natural gas.[42] Cost synergy through waste recycling is good business ethics, too.

Technological Synergy

The third variety of synergy involves getting multiple benefits from a given technology investment. Consider this recent illustration:

> New York investment bank J.P. Morgan's computing muscle is scattered. Most divisions and some overseas offices have their own banks of computer servers—which other departments can't access. A trader in New York, for example, may not be able to access a financial program running on J.P. Morgan's London computers.
>
> That will soon change, thanks to J.P. Morgan's shared-computing program. When it's finished this year, bankers will have instant access to specialty computer programs used worldwide. That will make them more efficient, the company says, and let workers access computing power housed more places.[43]

This sort of synergy enables an investment in new technology to have multiple benefits and payoffs (see Best Practices on page 130).

Management Synergy

This fourth type of synergy occurs when a management team is more productive because its members have complementary rather than identical skills. Management synergy also is achieved when an individual with multiple skills or talents is hired for an administrative position. For example, Intel's top salesperson in its vitally important China operations is Jason Chen, someone who works comfortably across Chinese and North American cultures.[44]

You may find it difficult, if not impossible, to take advantage of all four types of synergy when developing new strategies. Nonetheless, your strategies are more likely to be realistic and effective if you give due consideration to all four types of synergy as early as possible.

Porter's Generic Competitive Strategies

In 1980, Michael Porter, a Harvard University economist, developed a model of competitive strategies. During a decade of research, Porter's model evolved to encompass these four generic strategies:

1. Cost leadership
2. Differentiation
3. Cost focus
4. Focused differentiation[45]

As shown in Figure 5.5, Porter's model combined two variables, *competitive advantage* and *competitive scope*.

On the horizontal axis is competitive advantage, which can be achieved via low costs or differentiation. A competitive advantage based on low costs, which means lower prices, is self-explanatory. **Differentiation**, according to Porter, "is the ability to provide unique and superior value to the buyer in terms of product quality, special features, or after-sale service."[46] Differentiation helps explain why consumers willingly pay more for branded products such as Sunkist oranges or Crest toothpaste.[47] On the vertical axis is competitive scope. Is the firm's target market broad or narrow? IBM, which sells many types of computers all around the world, serves a very broad market. A neighborhood pizza parlor offering one type of food in a small geographical area has a narrow target market.

differentiation Buyer perceives unique and superior value in a product.

Like the concept of synergy, Porter's model helps managers think strategically: it enables them to see the big picture as it affects the organization and its changing environment. Each of Porter's four generic strategies deserves a closer look.

Cost Leadership Strategy

Managers pursuing this strategy have an overriding concern for keeping costs, and therefore prices, lower than those of competitors. Normally, this means investing in extensive production or service facilities that offer efficient "economies of scale" (that is, low per-unit cost to make products or deliver services). Productivity improvement is a high priority for managers who follow the cost leadership strategy. Wal-Mart is a prime example of the cost leadership strategy.

How Wal-Mart thinks has never been a big mystery: Buy stuff at the lowest cost possible, pass the gains on to the

FIGURE 5.5

Porter's Generic Competitive Strategies

Source: Adapted with permission of The Free Press, a Division of Simon & Schuster Adult Publishing Group, from *Competitive Advantage: Creating and Sustaining Superior Performance* by Michael E. Porter. Copyright © 1985, 1998 by Michael E. Porter. All rights reserved.

	Competitive advantage	
	Lower cost	Differentiation
Broad target	Cost leadership	Differentiation
Narrow target	Cost focus	Focused differentiation

Competitive scope

consumer through superlow prices, watch stuff fly off the shelves at insane velocity. . . . As for a supplier raising prices, good luck: In some cases Wal-Mart has been known simply to keep sending payment for the old amount.[48]

Wal-Mart's world-class computerized warehouse network gives it an additional cost advantage over its less efficient competitors. When rival Kmart declared bankruptcy in 2002, a retail industry consultant bluntly observed: "Kmart is simply another piece of retail roadkill in Wal-Mart's march to dominance."[49]

In manufacturing firms, the preoccupation with minimizing costs flows beyond production into virtually all areas: purchasing, wages, overhead, R&D, advertising, and selling. A relatively large market share is required to accommodate this high-volume, low-profit margin strategy.[50]

Differentiation Strategy

For the differentiation strategy to succeed, a company's product or service must be considered unique by most of the customers in its industry. Advertising and promotion help the product to stand out from the crowd. Specialized design (BMW automobiles), a widely recognized brand (Diet Coke), leading-edge technology (Google), or reliable service (Caterpillar) also may serve to differentiate a product in the industry. Because customers with brand loyalty will usually spend more for what they perceive to be a superior product, the differentiation strategy can yield larger profit margins than the low-cost strategy.[51] But if a brand's image is not carefully nurtured and protected, brand loyalty and customers' willingness to pay a premium price can erode.[52] For businesses sticking to a differentiation strategy, it is important to note that cost reduction is not ignored; it simply is not the highest priority.

Cost Focus Strategy

Organizations with a cost focus strategy attempt to gain a competitive edge in a narrow (or regional) market by exerting strict control. For instance, Foot Locker has become a powerhouse in athletic footwear and apparel by selling off unrelated businesses, such as San Francisco Music Box, and focusing on what it does best.

> *With an 18% (and growing) share of the athletic retail market—nearly twice that of its nearest competitor—Foot Locker uses its weight to negotiate advantageous deals with manufacturers like Nike and Reebok. It gets the hottest products earlier and cheaper than its peers.*[53]

Foot Locker plans to increase its 2,000-store worldwide chain by 1,000 in the years ahead.

Focused Differentiation Strategy

This generic strategy involves achieving a competitive edge by delivering a superior product and/or service to a limited audience. The Mayo Clinic's world-class health care facilities—in Rochester, Minnesota; Jacksonville, Florida; and Scottsdale, Arizona—are an expression of this strategy.

Organizations must use a contingency management approach to determine which of Porter's generic strategies is appropriate. Research on Porter's model indicates that there is a positive relationship between long-term earnings growth and a good strategy/environment fit.[54]

E-Business Strategies for the Internet

The Internet is not a fixed thing. It is a complex bundle of emerging technologies at various stages of development.[55] Corporate strategists and entrepreneurs are challenged to build business models based on where they expect these technologies to be X years down the road. This exercise is akin to hitting a moving target from a moving platform—very difficult, at best. But Amazon.com's founder and CEO Jeff Bezos proved it can be done:

> . . . he was one of the few dot-com leaders to understand that sweating the details of Internet technologies would make all the difference. Amazon wasn't the first store on the Web. But Bezos beat rivals in inventing or rolling out new Internet technologies that made shopping online faster, easier, and more personal than traditional retail. He offered customized recommendations based on other buyers' purchases, let people buy an item with just one mouse click, and created personalized storefronts for each customer.[56]

E-business experts predict major changes ahead for several industries, including software development and distribution, real estate, bill payment, jewelry, wireless communication, and advertising.[57] Recall from our definition in Chapter 1 that e-business involves using the Internet to make *all* business functions—from sales to production to human resource management—more efficient, responsive, and speedier. The purpose of this section is to build a framework of strategic understanding for squeezing maximum value from the Internet.

Basic Internet Business Models

Relative to buying, selling, and trading things on the Internet, it is possible to fashion a strategy around one or a combination of seven basic business models (see Table 5.2 on page 122).[58] eBay, for example, has been hugely successful with the commission-based model.[59] Google, on the other hand, makes its money largely via an advertising-based model.[60] As indicated in Table 5.2, each of the Internet business models has its own unique set of opportunities for strategic competitive advantage. Our challenge is to take what we have learned about synergy and Porter's competitive strategies and develop a winning Internet strategy.

There Is No One-Size-Fits-All Internet Strategy

Harvard's Michael Porter, whose generic competitive strategies we just discussed, cautions us to avoid putting Internet strategies into one basket. Instead, he sees two major categories:

> At this critical juncture in the evolution of Internet technology, dot-coms and established companies face different strategic imperatives. Dot-coms must develop real strategies that create economic value. They must recognize that current ways of competing are destructive and futile and benefit neither themselves nor, in the end, customers. Established companies, in turn, must stop deploying the Internet on a stand-alone basis and instead use it to enhance the distinctiveness of their strategies.[61]

Janey Place, e-business manager at Mellon Financial Corp. in Pittsburgh, calls these two types of businesses "dot-coms" and "dot-corps."[62] Porter urges established "brick-and-mortar" businesses to weave the Internet into the very fabric of their operations—in short, to become true e-businesses.[63]

TABLE 5.2

Seven Basic Internet Business Models

Type	Features and content	Sources of competitive advantage
Commission-based	Commissions charged for brokerage or intermediary services. Adds value by providing expertise and/or access to a wide network of alternatives.	Search Evaluation Problem solving Transaction
Advertising-based	Web content paid for by advertisers. Adds value by providing free or low-cost content—including customer feedback, expertise, and entertainment programming—to audiences that range from very broad (general content) to highly targeted (specialized content).	Search Evaluation
Markup-based	Reselling marked-up merchandise. Adds value through selection, distribution efficiencies, and by leveraging brand image and reputation. May use entertainment programming to enhance sales.	Search Transaction
Production-based	Selling manufactured goods and custom services. Adds value by increasing production efficiencies, capturing customer preferences, and improving customer service.	Search Problem solving
Referral-based	Fees charged for referring customers. Adds value by enhancing a company's product or service offering, tracking referrals electronically, and generating demographic data. Expertise and customer feedback are often included with referral information.	Search Problem solving Transaction
Subscription-based	Fees charged for unlimited use of service or content. Adds value by leveraging strong brand name, providing high-quality information to specialized markets or access to essential services. May consist entirely of entertainment programming.	Evaluation Problem solving
Fee-for-service-based	Fees charged for metered services. Adds value by providing service efficiencies, expertise, and practical outsourcing solutions.	Problem solving Transaction

Source: Reprinted from *Organizational Dynamics,* 33, no. 2, G. T. Lumpkin and Gregory G. Dess, "E-Business Strategies and the Internet Business Models: How the Internet Adds Value," p. 169, Copyright 2004, with permission from Elsevier.

Customer Loyalty Is Built with Reliable Brand Names and "Sticky" Web Sites

Web surfers have proved to have very short attention spans. Seemingly attractive Web sites can have many visitors ("hits"), but few or no sales. When doing business at Internet speed, Web sites need to satisfy three criteria: (1) high-quality layout and graphics; (2) fast, responsive service; and (3) complete and up-to-date information.[64] A trusted brand name can further enhance what e-business people call the *stickiness* of a Web site, that is, the ability to draw the same customer back again and again. A great deal of work is needed in this area, considering the results of a recent study: two-thirds of the visitors to online stores did not return within a year.[65]

E-business strategy lesson: Even though e-retailing might appear to be a quick-and-easy and impersonal process, loyal customers still expect a personal touch and some "hand holding" when they have questions, problems, or suggestions.

TEST PREPPER 5.3

True or False?

_____ 1. Synergy has been called the "2 + 1 = 3 effect."

_____ 2. Market synergy occurs when a gas station sells food items and lottery tickets.

_____ 3. Wal-Mart is a prime example of Porter's cost leadership strategy.

_____ 4. Three types of Internet business models include advertising-based, markup-based, and referral-based.

Multiple Choice

_____ 5. When a lumber mill profitably recycles its scrap wood and sawdust, it is taking advantage of what type of synergy?
 a. Resource
 b. Material
 c. Technological
 d. Market
 e. Cost

_____ 6. _____ are the two key variables in Porter's generic competitive strategies model.
 a. Resources and markets
 b. Primary markets and secondary markets
 c. Time and cost
 d. Cost and volume
 e. Competitive advantage and competitive scope

_____ 7. When an upscale bakery competes on the basis of the high quality of its ingredients, it is relying on which of Porter's generic strategies?
 a. Market segmentation
 b. Economies of scale
 c. Cost leadership
 d. Differentiation
 e. Cost focus

_____ 8. All of the following are basic Internet business models except
 a. commission-based businesses.
 b. fee-for-service-based businesses.
 c. mark-up-based businesses.
 d. advertising-based businesses.
 e. word-of-mouth-based businesses.

_____ 9. _____ means that the Web site draws the same customer back again and again.
 a. Hits
 b. Clicks
 c. Stickiness
 d. Glue
 e. Cannibalism

Online Study Center
ACE the Test
ACE Practice Tests 5.3

THE STRATEGIC MANAGEMENT PROCESS

4 ▸ *Identify and describe the four steps in the strategic management process, and explain the nature and purpose of a SWOT analysis.*

Strategic management is the ongoing process of ensuring a competitively superior fit between an organization and its changing environment. Strategic plans are formulated during an evolutionary process that has identifiable steps. In line with the three-level planning pyramid discussed earlier, the strategic management process is broader and more general at the top and filters down to narrower and more specific terms. Figure 5.6 on page 124 outlines the four major steps of the strategic management process:

1. Formulation of a grand strategy
2. Formulation of strategic plans
3. Implementation of strategic plans
4. Strategic control

strategic management Seeking a competitively superior organization-environment fit.

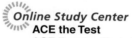

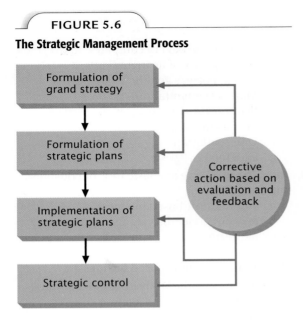

FIGURE 5.6

The Strategic Management Process

grand strategy How the organization's mission will be accomplished.

situational analysis Finding the organization's niche by performing a SWOT analysis.

Corrective action based on evaluation and feedback takes place throughout the entire strategic management process to keep things headed in the right direction.

It is important to note that this model represents an ideal approach for instructional purposes. Because of organizational politics, as discussed in Chapter 12, and different planning orientations among managers, a somewhat less systematic process typically results. Nevertheless, it is helpful to study the strategic management process as a systematic and rational sequence to better understand what it involves. Although noting that rational strategic planning models should not be taken literally, management scholar Henry Mintzberg acknowledged their profound instructional value. They teach necessary vocabulary, he states, and implant the notion "that strategy represents a fundamental congruence between external opportunity and internal capability."[66]

Formulation of a Grand Strategy

As pointed out earlier, a clear statement of organizational mission serves as a focal point for the entire planning process. Key stakeholders inside and outside the organization are given a general idea of why the organization exists and where it is headed. Working from the mission statement, top management formulates the organization's **grand strategy**, a general explanation of *how* the organization's mission is to be accomplished. Grand strategies are not drawn out of thin air. They are derived from a careful *situational analysis* of the organization and its environment. A clear vision of where the organization *is* headed and where it *should be* headed is the gateway to competitive advantage.[67]

Situational Analysis

A **situational analysis** is a technique for matching organizational strengths and weaknesses with environmental opportunities and threats to determine the organization's right niche (see Figure 5.7). Many strategists refer to this process as a SWOT analysis. SWOT stands for *Strengths, Weaknesses, Opportunities,* and *Threats.* Every organization should be able to identify the purpose for which it is best suited. But this matching process is more difficult than it may at first appear. Strategists are faced not with snapshots of the environment and the organization but with a movie of rapidly changing events. As one researcher said: "The task is to find a match between opportunities that are still unfolding and resources that are still being acquired."[68] For example, Citibank, whose headquarters are in New York City, has set its strategic sights on a greater share of emerging Asian markets:

> . . . *most foreign banks still shy away from developing countries such as India, Indonesia, and Thailand. Their rationale is that these markets are too small and that consumers lack experience in handling personal debt. . . .*
>
> *Citi, however, is gambling that such Asian economies won't remain backward. Consider India, with a population of [over 1 billion]. . . . The growing middle class still rides mopeds. But within a decade, Citi bets they'll be buying BMWs. To take advantage of that possibility, Citi has positioned itself as one of the country's leading moped-loan originators.*[69]

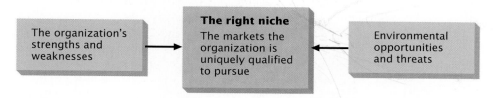

FIGURE 5.7

Determining Strategic Direction Through Situational (SWOT) Analysis

Strategic planners, whether top managers, key operating managers, or staff planning specialists, have many ways to scan the environment for opportunities and threats. They can study telltale shifts in the economy, recent innovations, growth and movement among competitors, market trends and forecasts, labor availability, and demographic shifts.

Unfortunately, according to a survey of executives at 100 U.S. corporations, not enough time is spent looking outside the organization: "Respondents said they spend less than half of their planning time (44 percent) evaluating external factors—competition and markets—compared with 48 percent on internal analysis—budget, organizational factors, human resources. 'That's the corporate equivalent of contemplating one's navel,'" [70] says the researcher.

Environmental opportunities and threats need to be sorted out carefully. A perceived threat may turn out to be an opportunity, or vice versa. Steps can be taken to turn negatives into positives.[71] This is how Reed Hastings, the co-founder and CEO of Netflix, handled just such a situation:

> Truly brilliant marketing happens when you take something most people think of as a weakness and reposition it so people think of it as a strength. . . . With Netflix, the big weakness is that it takes a day to get your movie. If we talked about that, that would be ineffective. So what we talk about is no late fees, no due dates, and being aggressive on price.[72]

Now Hastings needs to keep his eye on the looming threat of on-demand movies over broadband Internet, something that would make the present Netflix business model obsolete.

Capability Profile

After scanning the external environment for opportunities and threats, management's attention turns inward to identifying the organization's strengths and weaknesses.[73] This subprocess is called a **capability profile**. The following are key capabilities for today's companies:

capability profile Identifying the organization's strengths and weaknesses.

- Quick response to market trends
- Rapid product development
- Rapid production and delivery
- Continuous cost reduction
- Continuous improvement of processes, human resources, and products
- Greater flexibility of operations[74]

Since he started in the music business as a teenager, British businessman Richard Branson has had a flair for envisioning grand strategies and making them happen. Now the knighted billionaire wants to extend his Virgin empire beyond music and commercial air travel to include commercial space travel. If everything goes according to plan, Virgin spacecraft carrying five passengers per trip will be headed for space by 2007. Ticket price: $198,000 (round trip, of course).

Diversity initiatives are an important way to achieve continuous improvement of human resources. Also, notice the clear emphasis on *speed* in this list of key organizational capabilities.

Formulation of Strategic Plans

In the second major step in the strategic management process, general intentions are translated into more concrete and measurable strategic plans, policies, and budget allocations.[75] This translation is the responsibility of top management, though gaining input from staff planning specialists and middle managers is common. From our earlier discussion, recall that a well-written plan consists of both an objective and an action statement. Plans at all levels need to specify who, what, when, and how things are to be accomplished and for how much. Many managers prefer to call these specific plans "action plans" to emphasize the need to turn good intentions into action. Even though strategic plans may have a time horizon of one or more years, they must meet the same criteria as shorter-run intermediate and operational plans. They should do the following:

1. Develop clear, results-oriented objectives in measurable terms.
2. Identify the particular activities required to accomplish the objectives.
3. Assign specific responsibility and authority to the appropriate personnel.
4. Estimate times to accomplish activities and their appropriate sequencing.
5. Determine resources required to accomplish the activities.
6. Communicate and coordinate these elements or steps and complete the action plan.[76]

All of this does not happen in a single quick-and-easy session. Specific strategic plans usually evolve over a period of months as top management consults with key managers in all areas of the organization to gather their ideas and recommendations and, one hopes, to win their commitment.

Implementation of Strategic Plans

Because strategic plans are too often shelved without devoting adequate attention to implementation, top managers need to do a better job of facilitating the implementation process. Gary Loveman, CEO of Harrah's Entertainment Inc. and a former Harvard Business School professor, recently observed: "You spend a lot of time in the classroom talking about strategy—about what the company *ought* to do—and much less time talking about how the company can actually do it."[77] Another important consideration during implementation is building broad commitment.[78]

A Systematic Filtering-Down Process

Strategic plans require further translation into successively lower-level plans. Top-management strategists can do some groundwork to ensure that the filtering-down process occurs smoothly and efficiently. Planners need answers to four questions, each of which is tied to a different critical organizational factor:

1. *Organizational structure.* Is the organizational structure compatible with the planning process, with new managerial approaches, and with the strategy itself?
2. *People.* Are people with the right skills and abilities available for key assignments, or must attention be given to recruiting, training, management development, and similar programs?
3. *Culture.* Is the collective viewpoint on "the right way to do things" compatible with strategy, must it be modified to reflect a new perspective, or must top management learn to manage around it?
4. *Control systems.* Is the necessary apparatus in place to support the implementation of strategy and to permit top management to assess performance in meeting strategic objectives?[79]

Strategic plans that successfully address these four questions have a much greater chance of helping the organization achieve its intended purpose than those that do not. In addition, field research indicates the need to *sell* strategies to all affected parties. New strategies represent change, and people tend to resist change for a variety of reasons. "The strategist thus faces a major selling job; that is, trying to build and maintain support among key constituencies for a plan that is freshly emerging."[80] This brings us to the challenge of obtaining commitment among middle managers.

Building Middle-Manager Commitment

Resistance among middle managers can kill an otherwise excellent strategic management program. A study of 90 middle managers who wrote 330 reports about instances in which they had resisted strategic decisions documented the scope of this problem. It turned out that, to protect their own self-interests, the managers in the study frequently derailed strategies. This finding prompted the researchers to conclude as follows:

> *If general management decides to go ahead and impose its decisions in spite of lack of commitment, resistance by middle management can drastically lower the efficiency with which the decisions are implemented, if it does not completely stop them from being implemented. Particularly in dynamic,*

REALITY CHECK 5.4

James P. Hackett, CEO of office furniture maker Steelcase: "If you ask most people what it means to execute well, they usually say 'getting things done.' Boards tell CEOs that they want us to get things done. We tell our managers to get things done, and they make sure everyone who reports to them gets more things done. Companies celebrate their 'can-do' culture. Later on, after the errors show up, we all wish we had been more rigorous in scouting out the territory before we sprinted down the execution path."

Source: James P. Hackett, "Preparing for the Perfect Product Launch," *Harvard Business Review,* 85 (April 2007): 46.

Question: What is the take-away message here regarding the strategic planning process?

---

competitive environments, securing commitment to the strategy is crucial because rapid implementation is so important.[81]

Participative management (see Chapter 11) and influence tactics (see Chapter 13) can foster middle-management commitment.[82]

Strategic Control

Strategic plans, like our more informal daily plans, can go astray. But a formal control system helps keep strategic plans on track. Software programs that synchronize and track all contributors' goals in real time are indispensable today.[83] Importantly, strategic control systems need to be carefully designed ahead of time, not merely tacked on as an afterthought.[84] Before strategies are translated downward, planners should set up and test channels for providing information on progress, problems, and strategic assumptions about the environment or organization that have proved to be invalid. If a new strategy varies significantly from past ones, new production, financial, or marketing reports will probably have to be drafted and introduced.

The ultimate goal of a strategic control system is to detect and correct downstream problems in order to keep strategies updated and on target, without stifling creativity and innovation in the process. A survey of 207 planning executives found that in high-performing companies there was no tradeoff between strategic control and creativity. Both were delicately balanced.[85]

Corrective Action Based on Evaluation and Feedback

As illustrated in Figure 5.6 on page 124, corrective action makes the strategic management process a dynamic cycle. A rule of thumb is that negative feedback should prompt corrective action focused at the step immediately before. Should the problem turn out to be more deeply rooted, then the next earlier step also may require corrective action. The key is to detect problems and initiate corrective action, such as updating strategic assumptions, reformulating plans, rewriting policies, making personnel changes, or modifying budget allocations, as soon as possible. In the absence of prompt corrective action, problems can rapidly worsen.

True or False?

_____ 1. Formulation of a grand strategy, formulation of strategic plans, implementation of strategic plans, and strategic control are the four major steps in the strategic management process.

_____ 2. The "O" in a SWOT analysis stands for "outlook."

_____ 3. Strategic planning is a top-down process, as opposed to a bottom-up process.

_____ 4. Strategic control tends to stifle creativity, which causes poor results.

Multiple Choice

_____ 5. The first step of the strategic management process is
   a. a clear code of ethics.
   b. the formulation of strategic plans.
   c. a statement of corporate values.
   d. a staffing strategy.
   e. formulation of a grand strategy.

_____ 6. In a SWOT analysis, the "W" stands for
   a. weaknesses.
   b. workers.
   c. willingness.
   d. workability.
   e. window of opportunity.

_____ 7. _____ is the process of identifying an organization's strengths and weaknesses.
   a. Capability profile
   b. Scenario analysis
   c. Trend analysis
   d. Reengineering process
   e. Forecast

_____ 8. Research shows that middle managers resist or derail strategies for what reason?
   a. To protect co-workers
   b. Shortsightedness
   c. A lack of trust in top management
   d. To protect their self-interests
   e. An inability to think strategically

_____ 9. Researchers found what relationship between strategic control and creativity?
   a. No relationship at all
   b. No tradeoff
   c. The greater the control, the less the creativity
   d. Serious damage to top-management creativity
   e. Direct conflict at all levels

Online Study Center
ACE the Test
ACE Practice Tests 5.4

Want to Take Your New Toyota House for a Spin?

The Kasugai plant is one of three Toyota factories in Japan that make prefabricated houses. Just like Toyota's cars, these come with fancy, foreign-sounding names and plenty of options, such as solar roof panels and keyless entry.

. . . Toyota says it can find synergies in many activities that have nothing to do with cars. At Kasugai, Toyota's houses are 85% completed at the plant before being transported by road and built in just six hours. To improve efficiency, the company borrows knowhow from its fabled Toyota Production System with its prin-

ciples of just-in-time delivery and *kaizen*, or continuous improvement. Anticorrosive paint is applied evenly to houses' steel frames using methods adopted from car production. And just as in all Toyota's Japan auto factories, a banner proclaiming "good thinking, good products" hangs from the roof. "We follow the Toyota way in housing," says Senta Morioka, a managing officer at Toyota.

Source: Excerpted from Ian Rowley, "Way, Way Off-Road," *Business Week* (July 17, 2006): 36–37.

Lego: One Brick at a Time

Brick by plastic brick, the world of Lego is built on fantasy. Whether it's Viking ships and model houses for kids or high-tech toys for adults that can be plugged into a computer and designed via the Internet, following instructions has always been optional when it comes to arranging the 8,000 interlocking pieces that form the Lego universe. If, like Google co-founder Larry Page, you wanted to build an inkjet printer from scratch, well, you just built one out of Legos, as Page did in college. That same spirit prevailed for decades at Lego's headquarters in Billund, Denmark. Imagination and creativity, not structure and discipline, were what guided Lego from its founding by carpenter Ole Kirk Christiansen in 1932. Its very name comes from the Danish for "play well": *leg godt*.

Unfortunately, what makes for a great toy doesn't always make for a great toy company. And by the 1990s, with children turning away from traditional toys in favor of videogames and PCs, Lego had lost its way.

Privately held and still majority-controlled by Christiansen's heirs, Lego tried and failed to expand into everything from clothes and computer games to Lego theme parks in the U.S. and Europe. By 2004, Lego was losing hundreds of millions a year, and the company looked as if it might go the way of a once-beloved game now consigned to the attic.

Enter Jorgen Vig Knudstorp, a boyish 37-year-old Dane who combines Scandinavian modesty with very American bluntness about the importance of making money and surviving in a world dominated by PlayStations and iPods. Since taking over as CEO a year and a half ago, the former McKinsey consultant has done more than cut jobs (1,000 in Billund alone) and outsource manufacturing to cheaper locales like the Czech Republic.

Lego's first leader to come from outside the founding family, Knudstorp has also upended Lego's corporate culture, replacing "nurturing the child" as the top priority in Lego's employee mission statement with "I am here to make money for the company."

That might sound obvious to American ears, but in sleepy Billund, with a population of 6,500 who have long looked to Lego as both their chief employer and paterfamilias, it has been a shock. "The company was very focused on doing good—that's fine," says Knudstorp, sitting in a glass-enclosed office surrounded by Lego toys, from big block Duplos for the toddler set to Bionicles, futuristic creations that scarcely resemble the Legos most of us remember. "But the attitude was 'We're doing great stuff for kids—don't bother us with financial goals.' It was a culture where delivering what was promised wasn't critical."

Before the crisis of the past few years, says play expert and 22-year Lego veteran Niels Sandal Jakobsen, "money was not something people worried about or talked about." Similarly, toys that smacked of violence or fighting were frowned upon for decades, despite their obvious appeal to boys, who make up most of Lego's customer base.

When Lego decided in 1999 to launch a Star Wars series, recalls Jakobsen, "getting the license from Lucas was nothing compared to the internal struggle over having the word 'war' appear under the Lego brand."

Knudstorp's cultural revolution also reached into the cultlike quarters of Lego's design team. Development time for new toys has been sliced in half, with the goal of going from idea to box in 12 months. To save on manufacturing costs, Lego has cut the number of pieces, or "elements," as they are known—for example, eliminating different versions of a little chef, some with a mustache, some without.

"People had personal relationships with elements," says design director Dorthe Kjaerulff, describing how her staff fought to keep favorites alive but in the end created a memorial to the discontinued pieces, complete with little black crosses. (Only the chef with the mustache survives.)

More serious cuts were also made, like selling off Lego's theme parks division for nearly $500 million last summer and reducing Lego's worldwide employment from 7,300 in 2004 to 5,300 today. Lego still employs 1,000 blue-collar workers churning out elements in Billund, and while Knudstorp says he wants to preserve as many of those jobs as possible, the company is scouting out new factories in Eastern Europe.

Knudstorp says Lego still has a ways to go, but his efforts appear to be paying off. The company eked out an $87 million net profit last year [2005], after losing more than $300 million in 2004, while revenues rose 12 percent to $1.2 billion. And new games built around Batman comics, Star Wars movies, and Ferrari race cars seem to be connecting with the children of parents who grew up on simple red, white, and yellow Lego bricks.

Although there's more buzz coming from new releases like Mindstorms—featuring chip-enabled elements and downloadable software to build robots—Lego's more traditional games still generate roughly two-thirds of sales. And that's fine with Knudstorp. "Lego is a niche product, with 2 percent to 3 percent of the global toy market," he notes. "Our vision is to be based on the Lego brick—that's our heritage and our future."

Source: Nelson D. Schwartz, "One Brick at a Time," *Fortune,* June 12, 2006, pp. 45–46. Copyright © 2006 Time Inc. All rights reserved.

Case Questions

1. Would you call Lego a defender, prospector, analyzer, or reactor? Explain.
2. How would you rate the effectiveness of Lego's mission statement, given its new top priority? Explain.
3. What kinds of synergies can you detect in this case? Explain.
4. What does a SWOT analysis say about the strategic direction Lego should take? Explain.

6 Making Decisions and Solving Problems

Electronic Arts shows off its creativity for gamers at an entertainment convention in Germany.

1 Specify at least five sources of decision complexity, and explain the three decision traps: framing, escalation of commitment, and overconfidence.

2 Discuss why programmed and nonprogrammed decisions require different decision-making procedures, and distinguish between the two types of knowledge in knowledge management.

3 Summarize the advantages and disadvantages of group decision making.

4 Define creativity, and identify five of the ten "mental locks" that can inhibit creativity.

I got this crazy idea that I was going to download the entire web onto my computer. You should try to do things that most people would not."[1]

—Larry Page, Co-founder of Google

Chapter Outline

Online Study Center
Prepare for Class
Chapter Outline

5 ▶ *List and explain the four basic steps in the creative problem-solving process, and describe how causes of problems can be tracked down with fishbone diagrams.*

Creativity Rules at Electronic Arts

At Electronic Arts, creativity is built on a foundation of management discipline. EA even takes a disciplined approach to the challenge of developing creative leaders. A dozen or so producers and designers at each studio meet throughout the year for a series of workshops. A dancer came in to talk about how movement can be used to express physical and emotional states. A film expert talked about the use of music in silent films to enhance the action. The idea behind the program is simple yet effective, says Andy Billings, vice president of human resources and organizational development: Expose creative leaders to other art forms and new ideas, and see what rubs off.

This past September, the guest speaker was Henry Jenkins, a director of the comparative media-studies program at MIT and a passionate gamer. Imagine the motion-picture industry in its infancy, when it had been around for only 25 years, he told the

Online Study Center
Prepare for Class
Chapter Glossary

Improve Your Grade
Flashcards
Hangman
Crossword Puzzles

decision making   Identifying and choosing alternative courses of action.

group. "That's where you are now," said Jenkins. "Video games will be the most important American art form for the 21st century."

The challenge for EA's game creators is figuring out how to build an industry and how to create lasting art. In a previous workshop, Jenkins talked about narrative structure, character development, and memorable moments in Homer, Shakespeare, Dickens, and Poe. "What can you put in a game that will endure?" he asked.

Over two days at the Vancouver studio, EA's creative leaders pondered these and other issues. The nature of fandom. The propensity of rule breaking and how designers might encourage this to enhance a game. And the importance of leaving space in a game for imagination, or the "meta game." Meaning that the game continues in the player's mind even when the console is switched off.

That's how the creativity sessions are supposed to work as well. "We're taking a group of people who more or less grew up with 'fight or flight' video games and saying, We can't just have great graphics," says Rusty Rueff, senior VP of human resources at EA. "There has to be deep, nuanced storytelling."

Between presentations, producers and designers played video games. As they deconstructed competitors, there was gleeful criticism, along with something else: genuine admiration when they saw something unexpected. They couldn't help it. Deep down, they're gamers.[2] ■

Decision making is the process of identifying and choosing alternative courses of action in a manner appropriate to the demands of the situation. The act of choosing implies that alternative courses of action must be weighed and weeded out. Many choices face Electronic Arts's product development team members as they strive to turn ideas into profitable products amidst great change and uncertainty. They will need to make important decisions at a rapid pace, despite having incomplete information. Reason and judgment will need to be blended with creativity and unconventional thinking. This chapter focuses on major challenges facing decision makers, introduces a general decision-making model, considers group-aided decision making, and examines creativity and problem solving.

CHALLENGES FOR DECISION MAKERS

1 ▷ *Specify at least five sources of decision complexity, and explain the three decision traps: framing, escalation of commitment, and overconfidence.*

Though decision making has never been easy, it is especially challenging for managers today.[3] In an era of accelerating change, the pace of decision making also has accelerated. According to a recent survey of 479 managers, 77 percent reported making *more decisions* during the previous three years, and 43 percent said they had *less time* to make each of those decisions.[4] In addition to having to cope with this acceleration, today's decision makers face a host of tough challenges. Ones that we will discuss here include:

Scan the player rosters of Major League Basball teams and you'll find plenty of Latino names such as Gonzalez, Martinez, and Rodriguez. But when it comes to the front office, Hispanic names are as rare as a grand slam in the bottom of the ninth. One remarkable exception is Omar Minaya, general manager of the New York Mets. His cool-headed decision making during his time as G.M. of the troubled Montreal Expos helped him hit a career home run with the Mets.

1. Complex streams of decisions
2. Sources of decision complexity
3. Perceptual and behavioral decision traps

Dealing with Complex Streams of Decisions

Above all else, today's decision-making contexts are not neat and tidy. A pair of experts made the subject more realistic by using the analogy of a stream:

> If decisions can be viewed as streams—streams containing countless bits of information, events, and choices—then how should decision makers be viewed? . . . The streams flowing through the organization do not wait for them; they flow around them. The streams do not serve up problems neatly wrapped and ready for choice. Rather, they deliver the bits and pieces, the problems and choices, in no particular order. . . .
>
> In short, decision makers in an organization are floating in the stream, jostled capriciously by problems popping up, and finding anchors through action at a given time in a given place.[5]

In this stream, even *not* making a decision ends up being a decision. Importantly, the foregoing is a recognition of complexity, *not* an admission of hopelessness. A working knowledge of eight intertwined factors contributing to decision complexity can help decision makers successfully navigate the stream (see Figure 6.1 on page 138). They include the following:

1. *Multiple criteria.* Typically, a decision today must satisfy a number of often conflicting criteria that represent the interests of different groups. For example, the Denver International Airport was designed and built with much more than airplanes in mind:

> Denver's is the first airport to be built for maximum accessibility for the disabled. During construction, the city took blind people, deaf people and those who use wheelchairs and canes through the terminal and concourses to road-test the layout.

Sources of Complexity for Today's Managerial Decision Makers

"They wanted to make sure a sign wasn't too low or a drinking fountain sticking out too far," says Thom Walsh, project manager at Fentress Bradburn. "It's a completely accessible building and uses Braille and voice paging."[6]

Identifying stakeholders and balancing their conflicting interests is a major challenge for today's decision makers.

2. *Intangibles.* Factors such as customer goodwill, employee morale, increased bureaucracy, and aesthetic appeal (for example, a billboard on a scenic highway), although difficult to measure, often determine decision alternatives.

3. *Risk and uncertainty.* Along with every decision alternative goes the chance of some sort of failure (see Best Practices on page 158).[7] Poor choices can prove costly. Yet the right decision can open up whole new worlds of opportunity. For example, *Business Week* recently described toy-maker Mattel's precarious situation:

> *Selling toys can be a fickle business, in which the fortunes of the mightiest corporations can abruptly rise or fall on the whims of customers too young to use a credit card, or even cut their own food with a knife. It's a business constantly in search of the next hot thing. Find it, and not only will kids all over the world be happy but so will shareholders. Guess wrong, and you're left with a pile of unsellable knickknacks.*[8]

4. *Long-term implications.* Major decisions generally have a ripple effect, with today's decisions creating the need for later rounds of decisions. For example, consider the long-term implications for the world's largest commercial airplane now in production in Europe:

> *The [555-seat] Airbus A380 is so large that it cannot park at a terminal designed for a row of Boeing 747s. It is so long that it will handle some taxiways like a tractor-trailer truck turning into a suburban driveway. It is so heavy that it cannot taxi across some culverts and bridges.*
>
> *Its engines are spaced so far apart that their exhaust could fry a runway's guide lights. Its body is so wide and tall that tower controllers may have to ban aircraft from nearby runways and taxiways before the plane lands or takes off.*[9]

Airports will have to be significantly redesigned to accommodate super-sized jets such as the A380.

5. *Interdisciplinary input.* Decision complexity is greatly increased when technical specialists such as lawyers, consumer advocates, tax advisers, accountants, engineers, and production and marketing experts are consulted before making a decision. This also is a time-consuming process.

6. *Pooled decision making.* Rarely is a single manager totally responsible for the entire decision process. For example, consider the approach of Brian Ruder, the successful president of Heinz's U.S. unit:

> *[He] has collected a number of mentors and advisers over the course of his career. Ruder, in fact, has elected a group of people, including his father, to a*

personal board of directors. He canvasses them whenever he's faced with a major decision, such as introducing plastic ketchup bottles. . . . "I rely on them," he says, "for total frankness and objectivity." Obviously, it's helped.[10]

After pooled input, complex decisions wind their way through the organization, with individuals and groups interpreting, modifying, and sometimes resisting.[11] Minor decisions set the stage for major decisions, which in turn are translated back into local decisions. Typically, many people's fingerprints are on the final decisions made in the organizational world.

7. *Value judgments.* As long as decisions are made by people with differing backgrounds, perceptions, aspirations, and values, the decision-making process will be marked by disagreement over what is right or wrong, good or bad, and ethical or unethical.[12]

8. *Unintended consequences.* The **law of unintended consequences**, according to an expert on the subject, "states that you cannot always predict the results of purposeful action."[13] In other words, there can be a disconnect between intentions and actual results. Although unintended consequences can be positive, negative ones are most troublesome and have been called the "Frankenstein monster effect." For example, the tighter passenger-screening rules imposed at U.S. airports in 2006 produced both good and bad unintended consequences for the airlines and their customers:

> *In an unforeseen twist, new security rules for carry-on bags are enabling airline passengers to get on and off planes faster, helping flights leave on time. . . .*
> *But if more flights are operating on time, that isn't necessarily true for luggage operations. Many passengers report waits or other problems with checked bags.*[14]

And therein lies the crux of the problem of unintended consequences. Namely, *hurried or narrowly focused decision makers typically give little or no consideration to the broader consequences of their decisions.* Unintended consequences cannot be eliminated altogether in today's complex world. Still, they can be moderated to some extent by giving them creative and honest consideration when making important decisions.

Beware of Perceptual and Behavioral Decision Traps

Behavioral scientists have identified some common human tendencies that are capable of eroding the quality of decision making. Three well-documented ones are framing, escalation, and overconfidence. Awareness and conscious avoidance of these traps can give decision makers a competitive edge.

Framing Error

One's judgment can be altered and shaped by how information is presented or labeled. In other words, labels create frames of reference with the power to bias our interpretations. **Framing error** is the tendency to evaluate positively presented information favorably and negatively presented information unfavorably.[15] Those evaluations, in turn, influence one's behavior. A study involving 80 male and 80 female University of Iowa students documented the framing-interpretation-behavior linkage. Half of each gender group was told about a cancer treatment with a 50 percent success rate. The other two groups heard about the same cancer treatment but were told it had a 50 percent failure rate. The researchers summed up results of the study as follows:

law of unintended consequences The results of purposeful actions are often difficult to predict.

REALITY CHECK 6.1

Peter Bernstein, investment advisor: "Risk means more things can happen than will happen. That means you don't know the limits of what can happen, but you still have to make decisions. . . .

"Remember, just because more things can happen than will happen doesn't mean bad things will happen. The outcome can be better than you expect."

Source: As quoted in Christopher Farrell, "Philosopher of Risk," *Business Week* (April 9, 2007): 97.

Question: How do you perceive and handle risk when making important life decisions?

---

framing error How information is presented influences one's interpretation of it.

Describing a medical treatment as having a 50 percent success rate led to higher ratings of perceived effectiveness and higher likelihood of recommending the treatment to others, including family members, than describing the treatment as having a 50 percent failure rate.[16]

Framing thus influenced both interpretations and intended behavior. Given the importance of the information in this study (cancer treatment), ethical questions arise about the potential abuse of framing error.

In organizations, framing error can be used constructively or destructively. Advertisers, for instance, take full advantage of this perceptional tendency when attempting to sway consumers' purchasing decisions. A leading brand of cat litter boasts of being 99 percent dust free. Meanwhile, a shampoo claims to be fortified with 1 percent natural protein. Thanks to framing error, we tend to perceive very little dust in the cat litter and a lot of protein in the shampoo. Managers who couch their proposals in favorable terms hope to benefit from framing error. And who can blame them? On the negative side, prejudice and bigotry thrive on framing error. A male manager who believes women can't manage might frame interview results so that John looks good and Mary looks bad.

Escalation of Commitment

Why are people slow to write off bad investments? Why do companies stick to unprofitable strategies? And why has the U.S. government typically continued to fund over-budget and behind-schedule programs? Escalation of commitment is a possible explanation for these diverse situations.[17] **Escalation of commitment** is the tendency of individuals and organizations to get locked into losing courses of action because *quitting is personally and socially difficult.* This decision-making trap has been called the "throwing good money after bad" dilemma. Those victimized by escalation of commitment are often heard talking about "sunk costs" and "too much time and money invested to quit now." Within the context of management, psychological, social, and organizational factors conspire to encourage escalation of commitment[18] (see Figure 6.2).

The model in Figure 6.2 can be brought to life by using it to analyze a highly unusual decision by the Pentagon in 1991. Two giant defense contractors, McDonnell Douglas and General Dynamics, were under contract to design and build the A-12 attack plane. All told, 620 of the aircraft carrier–based bombers were to be built for the U.S. Navy at a cost of $60 billion. With the A-12 program 18 months behind schedule and $2.7 billion over budget, then–Secretary of Defense Dick Cheney terminated the contract. It was the Pentagon's biggest cancellation ever. An appreciation of the contributing factors shown in Figure 6.2 underscores how truly unusual Cheney's decision was. Psychologically, his termination decision flew in the face of three possible motives for throwing good money after bad. Cheney went against the social grain as well by publicly admitting the Defense Department's mistake and doing something culturally distasteful to Americans, giving up. (American folk heroes tend to be persistent to the bitter end.) Finally, Cheney had to overcome bureaucratic resistance in the defense establishment. He also had to withstand political opposition from the contractors about their having to lay off 8,000 A-12 project employees. Nevertheless, despite many pressures to continue the program, Cheney refused to let the forces of escalation carry the day.

Reality checks, that is, comparing actual progress with effectiveness and efficiency standards, are the best way to keep escalation in check.[19] In Cheney's case, he concluded: "No one can tell me exactly how much more it will cost to keep this

---

escalation of commitment   People get locked into losing courses of action to avoid the embarrassment of quitting or admitting error.

FIGURE 6.2

Why Escalation of Commitment Is So Common

Source: Adapted from discussion in Barry M. Staw and Jerry Ross, "Understanding Behavior in Escalation Situations," *Science,* 246 (October 13, 1989): 216–220.

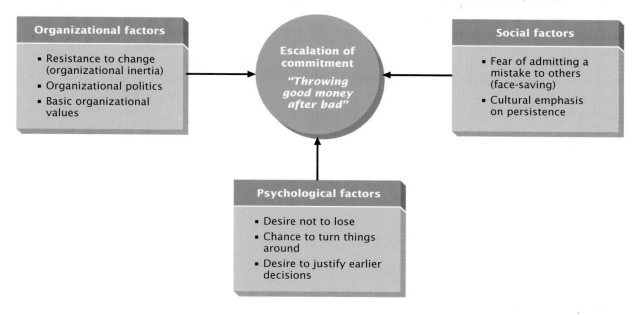

[A-12] program going. And I do not believe that a bailout is in the national interest. If we cannot spend the taxpayers' money wisely, we will not spend it."[20] This is an instructive lesson for all potential victims of escalation.

Overconfidence

The term *overconfidence* is commonplace and requires no formal definition. We need to comprehend the psychology of overconfidence because it can expose managers to unreasonable risks. For instance, overconfidence proved costly for Boeing in 1998. As *Business Week* reported at the time:

> Boeing's prized new Delta III rocket blew up on its maiden flight on Aug. 26, taking with it a $225 million PanAmSat Corp. satellite. Overconfidence lured Boeing into taking the risky step of carrying a live payload on the maiden voyage.[21]

Ironically, researchers have found a positive relationship between overconfidence and task difficulty. In other words, the more difficult the task, the greater the tendency for people to be overconfident.[22] Easier and more predictable situations foster confidence, but generally not unrealistic overconfidence. People may be overconfident about one or more of the following: accuracy of input data; individual, team, or organizational ability; and the probability of success. There are various theoretical explanations for this research evidence. One likely reason is that overconfidence is often necessary to generate the courage needed to tackle difficult situations.[23]

As with the other decision traps, managerial awareness of this problem is the important first step toward avoiding it. Careful analysis of situational factors, critical thinking about decision alternatives, and honest input from stakeholders can help managers avoid overconfidence.[24]

TEST PREPPER 6.1

ANSWERS CAN BE FOUND ON P. 161

True or False?

_____ 1. Along with every decision alternative goes the chance that it will fail in some way.

_____ 2. A single manager is typically responsible for a given decision from beginning to end.

_____ 3. According to the law of unintended consequences, you can predict the results of purposeful action.

_____ 4. In organizations, framing error is always destructive.

_____ 5. Escalation of commitment involves throwing good money after bad.

_____ 6. Overconfidence declines as the task becomes more difficult, according to research.

Multiple Choice

_____ 7. What is the meaning of the analogy of decision making as a stream?
   a. The decision maker as a swimmer going upstream
   b. A smooth and even flow of information
   c. Problems and choices flow by as random bits and pieces
   d. Solutions as boats
   e. Decisions as bridges

_____ 8. _____ is (are) not one of the contributors to decision complexity covered in the text.
   a. Long-term implications
   b. Risk and uncertainty
   c. Interdisciplinary input
   d. Multiple criteria
   e. Government regulation

_____ 9. Which one of the eight sources of decision complexity guarantees disagreement over ethical issues?
   a. Interdisciplinary input
   b. Risk and uncertainty
   c. Intangibles
   d. Value judgments
   e. Long-term implications

_____ 10. _____ is the tendency to evaluate positively presented information favorably and negatively presented information unfavorably.
   a. Escalation of commitment
   b. Overconfidence
   c. Framing error
   d. Short-term thinking
   e. Satisficing

_____ 11. Which of these is the tendency of individuals and organizations to get locked into losing courses of action because quitting is personally and socially difficult?
   a. Escalation of commitment
   b. Framing error
   c. Auction fever
   d. Satisficing
   e. Overconfidence

_____ 12. A psychological factor contributing to the decision trap of escalation of commitment is
   a. resistance to change.
   b. fear of admitting a mistake to others.
   c. cultural emphasis on persistence.
   d. desire to justify earlier decisions.
   e. organizational politics.

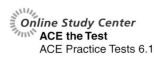

Online Study Center
ACE the Test
ACE Practice Tests 6.1

MAKING DECISIONS

> 2 ▸ *Discuss why programmed and nonprogrammed decisions require different decision-making procedures, and distinguish between the two types of knowledge in knowledge management.*

It stands to reason that if the degree of uncertainty varies from situation to situation, there can be no single way to make decisions.[25] A second variable with which decision makers must cope is the number of times a particular decision is made. Some decisions are made frequently, perhaps several times a day. Others are made infrequently or just once. Consequently, decision theorists have distinguished between programmed and nonprogrammed decisions.[26] Each of these types of decisions requires a different procedure.

Making Programmed Decisions

Programmed decisions are those that are repetitive and routine. Examples include hiring decisions, billing decisions in a hospital, supply reorder decisions in a purchasing department, consumer loan decisions in a bank, and pricing decisions in a university bookstore. Managers tend to devise fixed procedures for handling these everyday decisions. Most decisions made by the typical manager on a daily basis are of the programmed variety.

programmed decisions Repetitive and routine decisions.

At the heart of the programmed decision procedure are decision rules. A **decision rule** is a statement that identifies the situation in which a decision is required and specifies how the decision will be made. Behind decision rules is the idea that standard, recurring problems need to be solved only once. Decision rules permit busy managers to make routine decisions quickly without having to go through comprehensive problem-solving over and over again. Generally, decision rules should be stated in "if-then" terms. A decision rule for a consumer loan officer in a bank, for example, might be: "*If* the applicant is employed, has no record of loan default, and can put up 20 percent collateral, *then* a loan not to exceed $10,000 can be authorized." Carefully conceived decision rules can streamline the decision-making process by allowing lower-level managers to shoulder the responsibility for programmed decisions and freeing higher-level managers for relatively more important, nonprogrammed decisions.

decision rule Tells when and how programmed decisions should be made.

Making Nonprogrammed Decisions

Nonprogrammed decisions are those made in complex, important, and nonroutine situations, often under new and largely unfamiliar circumstances:

nonprogrammed decisions Decisions made in complex and nonroutine situations.

- This kind of decision is made much less frequently than are programmed decisions.

- Examples of nonprogrammed decisions include deciding whether to merge with another company, how to replace an executive who died unexpectedly, whether a foreign branch should be opened, and how to market an entirely new kind of product or service.

The following six questions need to be asked before making a nonprogrammed decision:

1. What decision needs to be made?
2. When does it have to be made?
3. Who will decide?
4. Who will need to be consulted prior to the making of the decision?
5. Who will ratify or veto the decision?
6. Who will need to be informed of the decision?[27]

The decision-making process becomes more sharply focused when managers take the time to answer these questions.

One respected decision theorist has described nonprogrammed decisions as follows: "There is no cut-and-dried method for handling the problem because it hasn't arisen before, or because its precise nature and structure are elusive

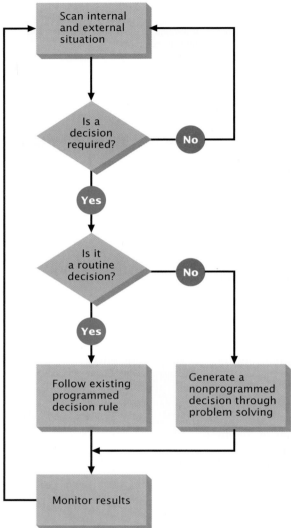

FIGURE 6.3

A General Decision-Making Model

or complex, or because it is so important that it deserves a custom-tailored treatment."[28]

Nonprogrammed decision making calls for creative problem solving. The four-step problem-solving process introduced later in this chapter helps managers make effective and efficient nonprogrammed decisions.

A General Decision-Making Model

Although different situations require different decision procedures, it is possible to construct a general decision-making model. Figure 6.3 shows an idealized, logical, and rational model of organizational decision making. Importantly, it describes how decisions can be made, but it does not portray how managers actually make decisions.[29] In fact, on-the-job research found managers did not follow a rational and logical series of steps when making decisions.[30] Why, then, should we even consider a rational, logical model? Once again, as in the case of the strategic management process in Chapter 5, a rational descriptive model has instructional value because it identifies key components of a complex process. It also suggests a better way of doing things.

The first step, a scan of the situation, is important, although it is often underemphasized or ignored altogether in discussions of managerial decision making. Scanning answers the question "How do I know a decision should be made?" More than 60 years ago, Chester I. Barnard gave one of the best answers to this question, stating that "the occasions for decision originate in three distinct fields: (a) from authoritative communications from superiors; (b) from cases referred for decision by subordinates; (c) from cases originating in the initiative of the [manager] concerned."[31]

In addition to signaling when a decision is required, scanning reveals the degree of uncertainty prevalent and provides necessary information for pending decisions.[32]

When the need for a decision has been established, the manager must determine whether the situation is routine. If it is routine and there is an appropriate decision rule, the rule is applied. But if it turns out to be a new situation that demands a nonprogrammed decision, comprehensive problem solving begins. In either case, the results of the final decision need to be monitored to see if any follow-up action is necessary.

Knowledge Management: A Tool for Improving the Quality of Decisions

An army of academics, consultants, and managers has rallied around the concept of knowledge management during the past decade. While some may dismiss it as a passing fad, knowledge management is a powerful and robust concept that deserves a permanent place in management theory and practice.[33] Authorities on the subject define **knowledge management** (KM) as "the development of tools, processes, systems, structures, and cultures explicitly to improve the creation,

knowledge management Developing a system to improve the creation and sharing of knowledge critical for decision making.

sharing, and use of knowledge critical for decision-making."[34] KM is at the heart of *learning organizations*. Our purpose here is to explore the basics of KM, with an eye toward improving organizational decisions. After all, decisions are only as good as the information on which they are based.

Two Types of Knowledge

KM specialists draw a fundamental distinction between two types of knowledge: tacit knowledge and explicit knowledge (see Figure 6.4). **Tacit knowledge** is personal, intuitive, and undocumented information about how to skillfully perform tasks, solve problems, and make decisions. People who are masters of their craft have tacit knowledge and more often than not have difficulty explaining how they actually do things. They simply "do" the task; they have a "feel" for the job; they know when they are in the "zone." For example, ask really good golfers how they achieve their "perfect" swing.[35] Meanwhile, **explicit knowledge** is readily sharable information because it is in verbal, textual, visual, or numerical form. It can be found in presentations and lectures, books and magazines (both hard copy and online), policy manuals, technical specifications, training programs, databases, and software programs. In short, explicit knowledge is public (to varying degrees), whereas tacit knowledge is private.

tacit knowledge Personal, intuitive, and undocumented information.

explicit knowledge Documented and readily sharable information.

Improving the Flow of Knowledge

As indicated in Figure 6.4, knowledge flows in two basic directions. Each is important in its own way; each needs to be carefully cultivated. But flow number one—the flow of constructive tacit knowledge between coworkers—is a top priority. Organizational support is needed to help individuals feel comfortable about giving and receiving useful task-related knowledge on demand.[36]

Sophisticated new KM software is proving very useful and cost-effective in large organizations for the second type of knowledge flow—sharing explicit knowledge.

FIGURE 6.4

Key Dimensions of Knowledge Management

Source: Adapted from discussion in Kiujiro Nonaka, "The Knowledge-Creating Company," *Harvard Business Review on Knowledge Management* (Boston: Harvard Business School Publishing, 1998), pp. 21–45; and Roy Lubit, "Tacit Knowledge and Knowledge Management: The Key to Sustainable Competitive Advantage," *Organizational Dynamics*, 29 (Winter 2001): 164–178.

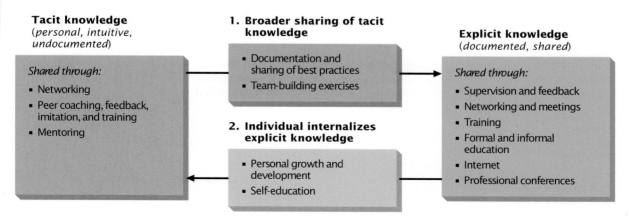

Tacit knowledge
(*personal, intuitive, undocumented*)

Shared through:
- Networking
- Peer coaching, feedback, imitation, and training
- Mentoring

1. Broader sharing of tacit knowledge
- Documentation and sharing of best practices
- Team-building exercises

2. Individual internalizes explicit knowledge
- Personal growth and development
- Self-education

Explicit knowledge
(*documented, shared*)

Shared through:
- Supervision and feedback
- Networking and meetings
- Training
- Formal and informal education
- Internet
- Professional conferences

For example, Deloitte Consulting uses a KM system based on a search engine from Verity, along with an Oracle database and content management software from BroadVision, to provide its nearly 20,000 employees with access to a repository of more than 250,000 documents. Deloitte chief information officer Larry Quinlan says the $2 million system provides an "essential" means of sharing information about consulting practices. "Deloitte is all over the world," he says. "Without [the KM system], we just wouldn't be able to function."[37]

According to KM advocates, it is important to know what you know, what you don't know, and how to find what you need to know. The result: better and more timely decisions.

You will encounter many topics in this text whose aim is to improve the flow of knowledge. Among them are organizational cultures, training, communication, empowerment, participative management, virtual teams, transformational leadership, and mentoring.

TEST PREPPER 6.2

ANSWERS CAN BE FOUND ON P. 161

True or False?

_____ 1. When making programmed decisions, "if-then" decision rules are used.

_____ 2. According to on-the-job research, managers do not necessarily follow a logical sequence of steps when making decisions.

_____ 3. There are two types of knowledge: personal knowledge and tactical knowledge.

_____ 4. The flow of constructive tacit knowledge between coworkers is a top priority of knowledge management.

Multiple Choice

_____ 5. Shelly works in the purchasing department of a theater chain and she is in charge of making routine supply reorder decisions. These decisions are considered _____ decisions.
- a. organizational
- b. passive
- c. spontaneous
- d. programmed
- e. nonprogrammed

_____ 6. Decisions that are made in complex, important, and nonroutine situations are called
- a. group decisions.
- b. nonprogrammed decisions.
- c. ethical decisions.
- d. programmed decisions.
- e. individual decisions.

_____ 7. Which of these is the first step in the general decision-making model?
- a. Forecasting
- b. Evaluating alternatives
- c. Making a decision
- d. Conducting a stakeholder audit
- e. Scanning the situation

_____ 8. Within the context of knowledge management (KM), what kind of knowledge is found in verbal, textual, visual, or numerical form?
- a. Implicit
- b. Tacit
- c. Explicit
- d. Nonverbal
- e. Contextual

Online Study Center
ACE the Test
ACE Practice Tests 6.2

GROUP-AIDED DECISION MAKING: A CONTINGENCY PERSPECTIVE

 Summarize the advantages and disadvantages of group decision making.

Decision making, like any other organizational activity, does not take place in a vacuum. Typically, decision making is a highly social activity in which committees, study groups, review panels, or project teams contribute in a variety of ways.

Group Involvement in Decisions

Whether the situation is a traditional face-to-face committee meeting or a global e-meeting, at least five aspects of the decision-making process can be assigned to groups:

1. Analyzing the problem
2. Identifying components of the decision situation
3. Estimating components of the decision situation (for example, determining probabilities, feasibilities, time estimates, and payoffs)
4. Designing alternatives
5. Choosing an alternative[38]

Maintaining Accountability

Assuming that two (or more) heads may be better than one and that managers can make better use of their time by delegating various decision-making chores, there is a strong case for turning to groups when making decisions. But before bringing

Nina Niu-Ok, employed by health-care provider Kaiser Permanente, appreciates the power of group-aided decision making. During this session in Palo Alto, California, she successfully tapped the creative energy of a mix of coworkers ranging from doctors to administrators. The idea was to map out scenarios to guide future strategy and decision making at Kaiser Permanente. Typically a six-month ordeal, this intense cooperative effort got the job done in three days. Cooperation and participation—just what the doctor ordered for these turbulent times in health care.

TABLE 6.1

Advantages and Disadvantages of Group Decision Making

Advantages	Disadvantages
1. **Greater pool of knowledge.** A group can bring much more information and experience to bear on a decision or problem than can an individual acting alone.	1. **Social pressure.** Unwillingness to "rock the boat" and pressure to conform may combine to stifle the creativity of individual contributors.
2. **Different perspectives.** Individuals with varied experience and interests help the group see decision situations and problems from different angles.	2. **Dispersed accountability.** It is difficult to hold individuals accountable for a decision made by everyone.
3. **Greater comprehension.** Those who personally experience the give-and-take of group discussion about alternative courses of action tend to understand the rationale behind the final decision.	3. **Domination by a vocal few.** Sometimes the quality of group action is reduced when the group gives in to those who talk the loudest and longest.
4. **Increased acceptance.** Those who play an active role in group decision making and problem solving tend to view the outcome as "ours" rather than "theirs."	4. **Logrolling.** Political wheeling and dealing can displace sound thinking when an individual's pet project or vested interest is at stake.
5. **Training ground.** Less experienced participants in group action learn how to cope with group dynamics by actually being involved.	5. **Goal displacement.** Sometimes secondary considerations such as winning an argument, making a point, or getting back at a rival displace the primary task of making a sound decision or solving a problem.
	6. **"Groupthink."** Sometimes cohesive "in groups" let the desire for unanimity override sound judgment when generating and evaluating alternative courses of action. (Groupthink is discussed in Chapter 12.)

others into the decision process, managers need to be aware of the tradeoffs between the advantages and disadvantages of group decision making (see Table 6.1). The disadvantage of dispersed accountability can be troublesome when "everyone" makes a decision. When this situation needs to be avoided—such as when the outcome has serious legal or ethical ramifications—a manager can tap group input for all aspects of the decision-making process, except making the final decision.

TEST PREPPER 6.3

ANSWERS CAN BE FOUND ON P. 161

True or False?

_____ 1. Choosing an alternative is the only aspect of the decision-making process that can be assigned to a group.

_____ 2. An advantage of group-aided decision making is "logrolling."

_____ 3. Groupthink is a potential disadvantage of group-aided decision making.

Multiple Choice

_____ 4. When groups make decisions, a major difficulty that managers face is
   a. increased uncertainty.
   b. loss of personal accountability.
   c. poor problem identification.
   d. choosing logical but impractical decisions.
   e. low job satisfaction.

_____ 5. _____ is an advantage of group-aided decision making.
   a. Domination by a vocal few
   b. Increased acceptance
   c. Groupthink
   d. Goal displacement
   e. Logrolling

_____ 6. _____ is not among the disadvantages of group-aided decision making.
   a. Social pressure
   b. Goal displacement
   c. Minority domination
   d. Groupthink
   e. Overconfidence

Online Study Center
ACE the Test
ACE Practice Tests 6.3

MANAGERIAL CREATIVITY

4 ▶ *Define* creativity, *and identify five of the ten "mental locks" that can inhibit creativity.*

Demands for creativity and innovation make the practice of management endlessly exciting (and often extremely difficult).[39] Nearly all managerial problem solving requires a healthy measure of creativity as managers mentally take things apart, rearrange the pieces in new and potentially productive configurations, and look beyond normal frameworks for new solutions. This process is like turning the kaleidoscope of one's mind. Thomas Edison used to retire to an old couch in his laboratory to do his creative thinking. Henry Ford reportedly sought creative insights by staring at a blank wall in his shop. Although the average manager's attempts at creativity may not be as dramatically fruitful as Edison's or Ford's, workplace creativity needs to be understood and nurtured.[40] As a stepping-stone for the next section on creative problem solving, this section defines *creativity*, discusses the management of creative people, and identifies barriers to creativity.

What Is Creativity?

Creativity is a rather mysterious process known chiefly by its results. It is therefore difficult to define. About as close as we can come is to say that **creativity** is the reorganization of experience into new configurations.[41] According to a management consultant who specializes in creativity:

> *Creativity is a function of knowledge, imagination, and evaluation. The greater our knowledge, the more ideas, patterns, or combinations we can achieve. But merely having the knowledge does not guarantee the formation of new patterns; the bits and pieces must be shaken up and interrelated in new ways. Then, the embryonic ideas must be evaluated and developed into usable ideas.*[42]

Creativity is often subtle and may not be readily apparent to the untrained eye. But the combination and extension of seemingly insignificant day-to-day breakthroughs lead to organizational progress.

Identifying general types of creativity is easier than explaining the basic process. One pioneering writer on the subject isolated three overlapping domains of creativity: art, discovery, and humor.[43] These have been called the "ah!" reaction, the "aha!" reaction, and the "haha!" reaction, respectively.[44]

The discovery ("aha!") variation is the most relevant to management. Entirely new products and businesses can spring from creative imagination and innovation. The iPod is a good example:

> *Its success was based on imagination as much as technology. MP3 players had been around for years and had never done much commercially. Apple's achievement was creating an appealing design and extraordinary software that yielded a superior, intuitive interface—plus the business innovation of iTunes online music store. The company then imbued the whole thing with an undeniable coolness. The result is an overwhelmingly dominant business, with about 75% of the MP3-player market and the online-music market—all based on existing basic technology plus a lot of ingenious creativity.*[45]

Online Study Center
Improve Your Grade
Career Snapshot 6.1

creativity The reorganization of experience into new configurations.

REALITY CHECK 6.3

"The next time you have a big . . . decision to make, have someone tell you a joke first. Cornell University psychology professor Alice M. Isen has found that positive affect—that is, being in a good mood—helps you make better decisions and solve problems more creatively."

Source: Janet Paskin, "Happily Ever After," *Money,* 35 (June 2006): 28.

Questions: How does humor stimulate creativity? What are the limits of humor in today's workplace?

Workplace Creativity: Myth and Modern Reality

Recent research has shattered a long-standing myth about creative employees. According to the myth, creative people are eccentric nonconformists. But Alan Robinson's field research paints a very different picture:

> *"We went to 450 companies in 13 countries and spoke to 600 people who'd done highly creative things, from big new innovations to tiny improvements,"* he explains. Only three out of the 600 were true nonconformists. The rest were more like your average corporate Joe, much more "plodding and cautious" than most managers would expect. Other creativity studies have had similar results, he says.
>
> One reason for the mismatch between popular perception and reality, he believes, is that so many steps are needed to bring most new ideas to fruition. Those who succeed must be able to build support for the idea among other team members, and they sometimes need a lot of patience as well. Corporate nonconformists may not have a great deal of either.[46]

Thus, creative self-expression through unconventional dress and strange behavior does not necessarily translate into creative work and marketable products.

Today's managers are challenged to create an organizational culture and climate that is capable of bringing to the surface the often hidden creative talents of *every* employee. In the Internet age, where intellectual capital is the number one resource, the emphasis is on having fun in high-energy work environments. For example, Theresa Garza, a vice president and general manager at Dell Computer, seeks to make the workplace "hum":

> Not the whirling white noise emanating from your computer, but the very tangible sense of fully engaged people, channeling unbounded energy into their work. "You know it as soon as you enter a building," says Garza, general manager of Dell's large corporate-accounts group. "You can tell when a company feels dead just by walking through its halls. We try to create the hum. It's people who have momentum, who are working hard, and who are excited to be here."
>
> To get hum, Garza has flung herself onto Velcro walls and had fellow employees dunk her in a water tank—all in the name of generating enthusiasm and encouraging accessibility.[47]

Learning to Be More Creative

Some people naturally seem to be more creative than others. But that does not mean that those who feel the need cannot develop their creative capacity. It does seem clear that creative ability can be learned, in the sense that our creative energies can be released from the bonds of convention, lack of self-confidence, and narrow thinking. We all have the potential to be more creative.

The best place to begin is by trying consciously to overcome what creativity specialist Roger von Oech calls *mental locks*. The following mental locks are attitudes that get us through our daily activities but tend to stifle our creativity:

1. *Looking for the "right" answer.* Depending on one's perspective, a given problem may have several right answers.
2. *Always trying to be logical.* Logic does not always prevail, given human emotions and organizational inconsistencies, ambiguity, and contradictions.
3. *Strictly following the rules.* If things are to be improved, arbitrary limits on thinking and behavior need to be questioned.
4. *Insisting on being practical.* Impractical answers to "what-if" questions can become stepping-stones to creative insights.

5. *Avoiding ambiguity.* Creativity can be stunted by too much objectivity and specificity.
6. *Fearing and avoiding failure.* Fear of failure can paralyze us into not acting on our good ideas. This is unfortunate because we learn many valuable and lasting lessons from our mistakes.[48]
7. *Forgetting how to play.* The playful experimentation of childhood too often disappears by adulthood.
8. *Becoming too specialized.* Cross-fertilization of specialized areas helps to define problems and generate solutions.
9. *Not wanting to look foolish.* Humor can release tensions and unlock creative energies. Seemingly foolish questions can enhance understanding.
10. *Saying "I'm not creative."* By nurturing small and apparently insignificant ideas we can convince ourselves that we are indeed creative.[49]

If these mental locks are conquered, the creative problem-solving process discussed in the next section can be used to its full potential.

TEST PREPPER 6.4   ANSWERS CAN BE FOUND ON P. 161

True or False?

_____ 1. "Discovery" is the most relevant domain of creativity to management.

_____ 2. Creative work is not necessarily the result of creative self-expression through unconventional dress and strange behavior.

_____ 3. Forgetting how to play can stifle creativity.

Multiple Choice

_____ 4. Creativity is said to be a function of
   a. knowledge, imagination, and evaluation.
   b. inspiration and persistence.
   c. skill, ability, and luck.
   d. motivation, insight, and luck.
   e. inspiration and perspiration.

_____ 5. The "aha!" reaction describes the _____ domain of creativity.
   a. technology
   b. enlightenment
   c. discovery
   d. surprise
   e. art

_____ 6. Which of the following is *not* among the ten mental locks on creativity?
   a. Strictly following the rules
   b. Not being logical or rational
   c. Insisting on being practical
   d. Avoiding ambiguity
   e. Not wanting to look foolish

Online Study Center
ACE the Test
ACE Practice Tests 6.4

CREATIVE PROBLEM SOLVING

5 ▶ *List and explain the four basic steps in the creative problem-solving process, and describe how causes of problems can be tracked down with fishbone diagrams.*

We are all problem solvers. But this does not mean that all of us are good problem solvers or even, for that matter, that we know how to solve problems systematically. Most daily problem solving is done on a haphazard, intuitive basis. A difficulty arises, we look around for an answer, jump at the first workable solution to come along, and move on to other things. In a primitive sense, this sequence of

problem solving   The conscious process of closing the gap between actual and desired situations.

events qualifies as a problem-solving process, and it works quite well for informal daily activities. But in the world of management, a more systematic problem-solving process is required to tackle difficult and unfamiliar nonprogrammed decision situations. In the context of management, **problem solving** is the conscious process of bringing the actual situation closer to the desired situation.[50] Managerial problem solving consists of a four-step sequence:

1. Identifying the problem
2. Generating alternative solutions
3. Selecting a solution
4. Implementing and evaluating the solution (see Figure 6.5)

FIGURE 6.5

The Problem-Solving Process

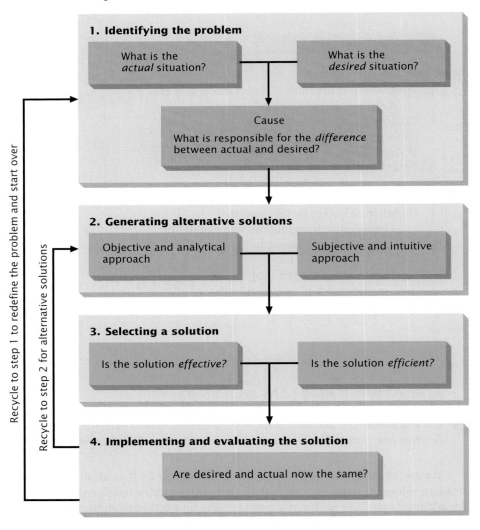

Identifying the Problem

As strange as it may seem, the most common problem-solving difficulty lies in identifying problems themselves. Busy managers have a tendency to rush into generating and selecting alternative solutions before they have actually isolated and understood the real problem. According to the late management scholar Peter Drucker, "the most common source of mistakes in management decisions is emphasis on finding the right answers rather than the right questions."[51] As problem finders, managers should probe for the right questions.[52] Only then can the right answers be found.

Problem finding can be a great career booster, too, as Michael Iem discovered. It all started with his love of tough challenges:

> This bricklayer's son has no formal job title and no office, but his career at Tandem Computers is on a tear. He personifies the advice that executive recruiter Robert Horton offers all who want to advance: "Find the biggest business problem your employer faces for which you and your skills are the solution." . . . [Iem's problem-solving ability] made him known throughout Tandem, bringing promotions and a doubling of his $32,000 starting salary. . . . The company lets him decide what projects to take on, making him the youngest of perhaps a dozen employees with the broad mandate.[53]

What Is a Problem?

Ask half a dozen people how they identify problems and you are likely to get as many answers. Consistent with our earlier definition of problem solving, a **problem** is defined as the difference between an actual state of affairs and a desired state of affairs. In other words, a problem is the gap between where one is and where one wants to be. Problem solving is meant to close this gap. For example, a person in New York who has to make a presentation in San Francisco in 24 hours has a problem. The problem is not being in New York (the actual state of affairs), nor is it presenting in San Francisco in 24 hours (the desired state of affairs). Instead, the problem is the distance between New York and San Francisco. Flying would be an obvious solution. But, thanks to modern communications technology such as videoconferencing, there are ways to overcome the 2,934-mile gap without having to travel.

problem   The difference between actual and desired states of affairs.

Managers need to define problems according to the gaps between the actual and the desired situations. A production manager, for example, would be wise to concentrate on the gap between the present level of weekly production and the desired level. This focus is much more fruitful than complaining about the current low production or wishfully thinking about high production. The challenge is discovering a workable alternative for closing the gap between actual and desired production.[54]

Stumbling Blocks for Problem Finders

There are three common stumbling blocks for those attempting to identify problems:

1. *Defining the problem according to a possible solution.* One should be careful not to rule out alternative solutions by the way one states a problem. For example, a manager in a unit plagued by high absenteeism who says, "We have a problem with low pay," may prevent management from discovering that

tedious and boring work is the real cause. By focusing on how to close the gap between actual and desired attendance, instead of simply on low pay, management stands a better chance of finding a workable solution.

2. *Focusing on narrow, low-priority areas.* Successful managers are those who can weed out relatively minor problems and reserve their attention for problems that really make a difference. Formal organizational goals and objectives provide a useful framework for determining the priority of various problems. Don't be concerned with waxing the floor when the roof is caving in.

3. *Diagnosing problems in terms of their symptoms.* As a short-run expedient, it may be appropriate to treat symptoms rather than underlying causes. Buying a bottle of aspirin is cheaper than trying to find a less stressful job, for example. In the longer run, however, symptoms tend to reappear and problems tend to get worse. There is a two-way test for discovering whether one has found the cause of a problem: "If I introduce this variable, will the problem (the gap) disappear?" or "If I remove this variable, will the problem (the gap) disappear?" **Causes** are variables that, because of their presence in or absence from the situation, are primarily responsible for the difference between the actual and the desired conditions. For example, the absence of a key can cause a problem with a locked door, and the presence of a nail can cause a problem with an inflated tire.[55]

causes Variables responsible for the difference between actual and desired conditions.

Pinpointing Causes with Fishbone Diagrams

Fishbone diagrams, discussed in Chapter 8 as a Total Quality Management process improvement tool, are a handy way to track down causes of problems. They work especially well in group problem-solving situations. Constructing a fishbone diagram begins with a statement of the problem (the head of the fish skeleton). "On the bones growing out of the spine one lists possible causes of . . . problems, in order of possible occurrence. The chart can help one see how various separate problem causes might interact. It also shows how possible causes occur with respect to one another, over time, helping start the problem-solving process."[56] (A sample fishbone diagram is illustrated in Figure 6.6.)

"THIS ENSURES THAT WE DON'T OVERANALYZE."

Source: Harvard Business Review, May 2006. Permission by Dave Carpenter.

Generating Alternative Solutions

After the problem and its most probable cause have been identified, attention turns to generating alternative solutions. This is the creative step in problem solving. Unfortunately, as the following statement points out, creativity is often shortchanged:

> *The natural response to a problem seems to be to try to get rid of it by finding an answer—often taking the first answer that occurs and pursuing it because of one's reluctance to spend the time and mental effort needed to conjure up a rich storehouse of alternatives from which to choose.*[57]

It takes time, patience, and practice to become a good generator of alternative solutions. A flexible combination of analysis and intuition is helpful. A good sense of

FIGURE 6.6

Sample Fishbone Diagram

Possible causes

Material

Exam

Too much
Too difficult
Boring

Ambiguous questions
Not enough time
No grading curve

Problem
Failed midterm exam

Stomachache on day of exam
Scribbled notes hard to read
Cut 20 percent of classes
No sleep night before exam

No review before exam
Talks too fast
Gets off subject
Standards too high

Student

Teacher

humor can aid the process as well. Several popular and useful techniques can stimulate individual and group creativity. Among them are the following approaches:

- *Brainstorming.* This is a group technique in which any and all ideas are recorded, in a nonjudgmental setting, for later critique and selection.[58] Computerized brainstorming on computer network systems is proving worthwhile now that sophisticated groupware is available.[59]

- *Free association.* Analogies and symbols are used to foster unconventional thinking. For example, think of your studies as a mountain that requires special climbing gear and skills.

- *Edisonian.* Named for Thomas Edison's tedious and persistent search for a durable light-bulb filament, this technique involves trial-and-error experimentation.

- *Attribute listing.* Ideal characteristics of a given object are collected and then screened for useful insights.

- *Scientific method.* Systematic hypothesis testing, manipulation of variables, situational controls, and careful measurement are the essence of this rigorous approach.

- *Creative leap.* This technique involves thinking up idealized solutions to a problem and then working back to a feasible solution.

Selecting a Solution

Simply stating that the best solution should be selected in step 3 (refer to Figure 6.5 on page 152) can be misleading. Because of time and financial constraints and political considerations, *best* is a relative term. Generally, alternative solutions should be screened to find the most appealing balance of effectiveness and efficiency in view of relevant constraints and intangibles. Russell Ackoff, a specialist in managerial problem solving, contends that three things can be done about problems: they can be resolved, solved, or dissolved.[60]

Resolving the Problem

satisfice To settle for a solution that is good enough.

When a problem is resolved, a course of action that is good enough to meet the minimum constraints is selected. The term **satisfice** has been applied to the practice of settling for solutions that are good enough rather than the best possible.[61] A badly worn spare tire may satisfice as a replacement for a flat tire for the balance of the trip, although getting the flat repaired is the best possible solution. According to Ackoff, most managers rely on problem resolving. This nonquantitative, subjective approach is popular because managers claim they do not have the necessary information or time for the other approaches. Satisficing, however, has been criticized as a shortsighted and passive technique that emphasizes expedient survival instead of improvement and growth.

Solving the Problem

optimize To systematically identify the solution offering the best combination of benefits.

A problem is solved when the best possible solution is selected. Managers are said to **optimize** when through scientific observation and quantitative measurement they systematically research alternative solutions and select the one with the best combination of benefits.

Dissolving the Problem

idealize To change the nature of a problem's situation.

A problem is dissolved when the situation in which it occurs is changed, so that the problem no longer exists. Problem dissolvers are said to **idealize** because they actually change the nature of the system in which a problem resides. Managers who dissolve problems rely on whatever combination of nonquantitative and quantitative tools is needed to get the job done. The replacement of automobile assembly-line welders with robots, for instance, has dissolved the problem of costly absenteeism among welders.

Whatever approach a manager chooses, the following advice from Ackoff should be kept in mind: "Few if any problems . . . are ever permanently resolved, solved, or dissolved; every treatment of a problem generates new problems."[62] A Japanese manager at the General Motors–Toyota joint venture auto plant in California put it this way: "No problem is a problem."[63] However, the cofounder of a successful import business pointed out that an administrative life made up of endless problems is a cause for optimism, not pessimism: "Spare yourself some grief. Understand that, in business, you will always have problems. They are where the opportunities lie."[64] Hence the need for continuous improvement.

Implementing and Evaluating the Solution

Time is the true test of any solution. Until a particular solution has had time to prove its worth, the manager can rely only on his or her judgment concerning its effectiveness and efficiency. Ideally, the solution selected will completely eliminate the difference between the actual and the desired in an efficient and timely manner. Should the gap fail to disappear, two options are open. If the manager remains convinced that the problem has been correctly identified, he or she can recycle to step 2 (see Figure 6.5 on page 152) to try another solution identified earlier. This recycling can continue until all feasible solutions have been given a fair chance or until the nature of the problem changes to the extent that the existing solutions are obsolete. If the gap between actual and desired persists in spite of repeated attempts to find a solution, then it is advisable to recycle to step 1: redefine the problem and engage in a new round of problem solving.

Of course, problem solving never ends for today's managers, as pointed out recently in *Industry Week*:

> Problems are a constant in business, whether economic times are good or bad. The best you can hope (and work) for is to constantly exchange one set of problems for a better set of problems.[65]

All the more reason to have polished problem-solving skills.

TEST PREPPER 6.5

ANSWERS CAN BE FOUND ON P. 161

True or False?

_____ 1. The beginning of the four-step problem-solving process is identifying the problem.
_____ 2. A problem is defined as any sort of deficiency.
_____ 3. The "head" of a fishbone diagram represents the main cause of the problem.
_____ 4. The creative leap approach to creativity involves listing of ideal characteristics of a given object.

Multiple Choice

_____ 5. Step 3 in the four-step problem-solving process calls for
    a. generating alternative solutions.
    b. selecting a solution.
    c. evaluating.
    d. implementing a solution.
    e. pinpointing the cause of the problem.

_____ 6. "Satisficing" means _____ relative to selecting a solution to a problem.
    a. finding the best cost-benefit relationship
    b. finding the least expensive solution
    c. finding the best possible solution
    d. making the most people happy
    e. settling for a solution that is good enough

_____ 7. When the situation in which a problem occurs is changed so that the problem no longer exists, it is
    a. resolved.
    b. created.
    c. optimized.
    d. dissolved.
    e. satisfied.

Online Study Center
ACE the Test
ACE Practice Tests 6.5

BEST PRACTICES

Google Thrives on Risk (and some mistakes along the way)

Take the case of Sheryl Sandberg, a 37-year-old vice president whose fiefdom includes the company's automated advertising system. Sandberg recently committed an error that cost Google several million dollars— "Bad decision, moved too quickly, no controls in place, wasted some money," is all she'll say about it—and when she realized the magnitude of her mistake, she walked across the street to inform Larry Page, Google's co-founder and unofficial thought leader. "God, I feel really bad about this," Sandberg told Page, who accepted her apology. But as she turned to leave, Page said something that surprised her. "I'm so glad you made this mistake," he said. "Because I want to run a company where we are moving too quickly and doing too much, not being too cautious and doing too little. If we don't have any of these mistakes, we're just not taking enough risk."

Source: Excerpted from Adam Lashinsky, "Chaos by Design," *Fortune* (October 2, 2006): 88.

CLOSING CASE STUDY

Texas Instruments' Lunatic Fringe

Gene Frantz has a big, impressive title: Texas Instruments principal fellow and business development manager, digital signal processing. Which tells you nothing about how he spends much of his time: searching for and encouraging all manner of lunatics and visionaries. Patient and relentless as a hunter, he stalks his quarry among TI's engineers as well as among academics, inventors and employees of small tech companies all over the world. "What I look for in these companies is the wild-eyed optimist who's going to tackle the market," Frantz says. . . .

Frantz is the dean of an informal and amorphous group of TI engineers (and their peers and contacts outside the company) who call themselves the Lunatic Fringe. They are senior people who have been given free rein to follow their curiosity wherever it goes. "There's this continuum between total chaos and total order," Frantz explains. "About 95% of the people in TI are total order, and I thank God for them every day, because they create the products that allow me to spend money. I'm down here in total chaos, that total chaos of innovation. As a company we recognize the difference between those two and encourage both to occur." The spirit of the Lunatics—look everywhere for good ideas first, worry about turning them into products later—has suffused TI for years, begotten some of the company's greatest hits, and largely explains the success it is currently enjoying.

What TI mainly makes are chips. Not the digital microprocessor computer-brain kind that Intel makes, but practically every other flavor. Key among them are analog- and digital-signal-processing (DSP) chips, which turn analog information into digital information. Both are essential for almost every electronic tool or toy. Open an Apple iPod, a Nokia cellphone, a Dell laptop, or a Samsung HDTV, and you'll see chips with the TI logo. . . .

CEO Richard Templeton, a 26-year veteran, says, "We have the ability to work with the biggest companies in the world and the smallest." As they say in

Texas, it ain't bragging if you can do it. TI has quietly become the world's third-largest semiconductor company, behind Intel and Samsung. . . . A key to that success is the Way of the Lunatic.

There isn't anything as formal as a Lunatic Fringe membership list. "There are more Lunatics within TI than show up and raise their hands," says Frantz, who somewhere in his 32 years at the company (he can't recall quite when) began bestowing the appellation admiringly on colleagues who were willing to explore crazy ideas. How many are there? "Within TI, maybe no more than 100," he says. The closest thing they have to regular gatherings is the weekly Sea of Ideas meeting, named after a call to action made by Templeton. ("There's a big sea of ideas out there in the world," he exhorted his engineers, "and I want you to cast a big net.") And there are plenty of people within TI who don't necessarily consider themselves card-carrying Lunatics but nonetheless partake of the Fringe's free-wheeling do-it-yourself ethos.

Dennis Buss, a TI fellow and vice president, recalls a group of engineers recognizing a looming problem a few years back. Next-generation mobile phones, they realized, would be used for receiving digital TV, taking digital photos, playing 3-D games, and other battery-draining tasks. So in 2003 they set a goal for themselves: a power-management chip that could cut consumption 1,000-fold. And a deadline: the end of 2004. "No marketing people, no businesspeople," Buss says. "For almost two years there were meetings at 7 A.M. Guys in Japan were giving up their Friday nights. People in India and Nice [France] were presenting data. This was not anybody's job. We were spending our own time to get

things going." They made their goal—with five hours to spare—and the resulting SmartReflex technology is now partly responsible for TI's success in the mobile-phone market. Buss says that at any time there may be a dozen or more such ad hoc groups working inside the company on under-the-radar projects.

What Buss is describing is Lunatic Lesson No. 1: Good things happen to the bottom line when engineers pursue projects because they are jazzed by a tough technical challenge, not by a mandate from the marketing department. . . .

There is always the chance that TI could lose touch with the Way of the Lunatic. It's happened before. Gene Frantz doesn't seem too worried. He points out that TI's current bets show no signs of busting anytime soon. And Frantz and his fellow Lunatics are still happily on the hunt for the next crazy idea. "The ones that excite me," he says, "are the ones we don't know about yet."

Source: Excerpted from Peter Lewis, "Texas Instruments' Lunatic Fringe," *Fortune*, September 4, 2006, pp. 120–128. Copyright © 2006 Time Inc. All rights reserved.

Case Questions

1. Which of the eight sources of decision complexity can you find in this case? Explain.
2. What role does knowledge management (KM) play in this case? Explain.
3. What are the pros and cons of this informal approach to organizational creativity? On balance, is it a good approach, in your opinion?
4. Which of the ten mental locks on creativity are apparently overcome by the Lunatic Fringe at TI? Explain.

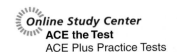

Online Study Center
ACE the Test
ACE Plus Practice Tests

Online Study Center
Improve Your Grade
Learning Objective Review
Audio Chapter Review
Audio Chapter Quiz
Study Guide to Go

LEARNING OBJECTIVE REVIEW

1 *Specify at least five sources of decision complexity, and explain the three decision traps: framing, escalation of commitment, and overconfidence.*

- Decision making is a fundamental part of management because it requires choosing among alternative courses of action.
- Eight factors that contribute to decision complexity are:
  - Multiple criteria
  - Intangibles
  - Risk and uncertainty
  - Long-term implications
  - Interdisciplinary input
  - Pooled decision making
  - Value judgments
  - Unintended consequences
- Researchers have identified three perceptual and behavioral decision traps that can hamper the quality of decisions:
  - Framing error occurs when people let labels and frames of reference sway their interpretations.
  - Escalation of commitment occurs when people get locked into losing propositions for fear of quitting and looking bad.
  - Overconfidence tends to grow with the difficulty of the task.

2 *Discuss why programmed and nonprogrammed decisions require different decision-making procedures, and distinguish between the two types of knowledge in knowledge management.*

- Decisions, generally, are either programmed or nonprogrammed:
  - Because programmed decisions are relatively clear-cut and routinely encountered, fixed decision rules can be formulated for them.
  - In contrast, nonprogrammed decisions require creative problem solving because they are novel and unfamiliar.

- Decision making can be improved by using a knowledge management (KM) program:
  - KM is a systematic approach to creating and sharing critical information throughout the organization.
  - Two types of knowledge are *tacit* (personal, intuitive, and undocumented) and *explicit* (documented and readily sharable).

3 *Summarize the advantages and disadvantages of group decision making.*

- Managers may choose to bring other people into virtually every aspect of the decision-making process. When a group rather than an individual is responsible for making the decision, personal accountability is lost.
- The advantages of group decision making include a greater pool of knowledge, different perspectives, greater comprehension, increased acceptance, and training ground.
- Among the disadvantages are social pressure, dispersed accountability, domination by a vocal few, logrolling, goal displacement, and groupthink.

4 *Define creativity, and identify five of the ten "mental locks" that can inhibit creativity.*

- Creativity is the reorganization of experience into new configurations. The domains of creativity may be divided into art, discovery (the most relevant to management), and humor.
- Ten mental locks on creativity are:
  - Looking for the "right" answer
  - Always trying to be logical
  - Strictly following the rules
  - Insisting on being practical
  - Avoiding ambiguity
  - Fearing and avoiding failure
  - Forgetting how to play
  - Becoming too specialized
  - Not wanting to look foolish
  - Saying "I'm not creative."

5 *List and explain the four basic steps in the creative problem-solving process, and describe how causes of problems can be tracked down with fishbone diagrams.*

- The creative problem-solving process consists of four steps:
    - Identifying the problem
    - Generating alternative solutions
    - Selecting a solution
    - Implementing and evaluating the solution
- Inadequately pinpointing the real problem is common among busy managers.

- Fishbone diagrams are a good problem-finding tool because they graphically trace a problem (the head of the fish) back to its primary and secondary causes (the fishbones connected to the skeleton).
- Problems can be:
    - Resolved ("satisficing" with a good enough solution)
    - Solved ("optimizing" with the best possible solution through research)
    - Dissolved ("idealizing" by changing the situation so the problem disappears)

TEST PREPPER ANSWERS

▶ **6.1**

1. T   2. F   3. F   4. F   5. T   6. F   7. c
8. e   9. d   10. c   11. a   12. d

▶ **6.2**

1. T   2. T   3. F   4. T   5. d   6. b   7. e
8. c

▶ **6.3**

1. F   2. F   3. T   4. b   5. b   6. e

▶ **6.4**

1. T   2. T   3. T   4. a   5. c   6. b

▶ **6.5**

1. T   2. F   3. F   4. F   5. b   6. e   7. d

Online Study Center RESOURCES

Prepare for Class, Improve Your Grade, and ACE the Test. Student Achievement Series resources include:

ACE Practice Tests	Crossword Puzzles	Hangman
Audio Chapter Quizzes	Decision Case Questions	Key Issue Expansion
Audio Chapter Reviews	Ethical Hot Seat Exercises	Learning Objective Reviews
Career Snapshots	Flashcards	Study Guide to Go
Chapter Glossaries	Hands-on Exercises	Visual Glossaries
Chapter Outlines		

To access these learning and study tools, go to **college.hmco.com/pic/kreitnerSASfound**.

Behind every Nokia cell phone is a global army of creative people with permission to make some mistakes.

1 ▶ *Identify and describe four characteristics common to all organizations, and explain the time dimension of organizational effectiveness.*

2 ▶ *Explain the concept of contingency organization design, distinguish between mechanistic and organic organizations, and identify the basic departmentalization formats.*

3 ▶ *Define the term* delegation, *and list at least five common barriers to delegation.*

4 ▶ *Explain how the traditional pyramid organization is being reshaped.*

162

> *"You have to think small to grow big."*[1]
>
> —Sam Walton, Founder of Wal-Mart

Chapter Outline

≡ *Online Study Center*
Prepare for Class
Chapter Outline

5 ▶ *Describe at least three characteristics of organizational cultures, and explain the cultural significance of stories.*

Finland's Nokia
Organizes for Innovation

Yrjö Neuvo's name is tricky to pronounce, even for fellow Finns, so let's just call him Mr. Advice. That's a literal translation of his surname, and slyly fitting for a former university professor. . . .

Neuvo is always trying to figure out how to get people to try something new, anything new; . . . it could be getting greenhorn engineers to ponder wild avenues of thought that lead to revolutionary cell-phone innovations—which, as it happens, Mr. Advice has done, repeatedly. Neuvo is the humble, if eccentric, technologist who heads research and development at Nokia, arguably the best product-driven R&D organization in the world.

Nokia's R&D apparatus is unlike anything in multinational corporate history. Most large-scale R&D operations are centralized, hierarchical, no-nonsense—science as brute force. Nokia's 18,000 engineers, designers, and sociologists are scattered across the globe and form a kind of federation of rule-breaking, risk-taking

≡ *Online Study Center* college.hmco.com/pic/kreitnerSASfound

"YOU KNOW, EVER SINCE I STARTED WORKING HERE, I'VE HAD THIS CRAVING FOR CHEESE."

Source: *Harvard Business Review,* September 2006. Permission by Dave Carpenter.

authority   The right to direct the actions of others.

The advantages of dividing labor have been known for a long time. One of its early proponents was the pioneering economist Adam Smith. While touring an eighteenth-century pin-manufacturing plant, Smith observed that a group of specialized laborers could produce 48,000 pins a day. This was an astounding figure, considering that each laborer could produce only 20 pins a day when working alone.[6]

Hierarchy of Authority

According to traditional organization theory, if anything is to be accomplished through formal collective effort, someone should be given the authority to see that the intended goals are carried out effectively and efficiently. Organization theorists have defined **authority** as the right to direct the actions of others. Without a clear hierarchy of authority, it is difficult, if not impossible, to coordinate effort. Accountability is also enhanced by having people serve in what is often called, in military language, the chain of command. For instance, a grocery store manager has authority over the assistant manager, who has authority over the produce department head, who in turn has authority over the employees in the produce department. Without such a chain of command, the store manager would have the impossible task of directly overseeing the work of every employee in the store.

The idea of hierarchy has many critics, particularly among those who advocate flatter organizations with fewer levels of management.[7] An organization theorist answered those critics as follows:

> At first glance, hierarchy may seem difficult to praise. Bureaucracy is a dirty word even among bureaucrats, and in business there is a widespread view that managerial hierarchy kills initiative, crushes creativity, and has therefore seen its day. Yet 35 years of research have convinced me that managerial hierarchy is the most efficient, the hardiest, and in fact the most natural structure ever devised for large organizations. Properly structured, hierarchy can release energy and creativity, rationalize productivity, and actually improve morale.[8]

Putting All the Pieces Together

All four of the foregoing characteristics are necessary before an organization can be said to exist. Many well-intentioned attempts to create organizations have failed because something was missing. In 1896, for example, Frederick Strauss, a boyhood friend of Henry Ford, helped Ford set up a machine shop, supposedly to produce gasoline-powered engines. But while Strauss was busy carrying out his end of the bargain by machining needed parts, Ford was secretly building a horseless carriage in a workshop behind his house.[9] Although Henry Ford eventually went on to become an automobile-industry giant, his first attempt at organization failed because not all of the pieces of an organization were in place. Ford's and his partner's efforts were not coordinated, they worked at cross-purposes, their labor was vaguely divided, and they had no hierarchy of authority. In short, they had organizational intentions, but no organization.

Organization Charts

An **organization chart** is a diagram of an organization's official positions and formal lines of authority. In effect, an organization chart is a visual display of an organization's structural skeleton. With their familiar pattern of boxes and connecting lines, these charts (called tables by some) are a useful management tool because they are an organizational blueprint for deploying human resources.[10] Organization charts are common in both profit and nonprofit organizations.

Every organization chart has two dimensions, one representing vertical hierarchy and one representing horizontal specialization. Vertical hierarchy establishes the chain of command, or who reports to whom. Horizontal specialization involves the division of labor. An appropriate balance needs to be struck between these two dimensions if the organization is to be effective.

organization chart Visual display of an organization's positions and lines of authority.

Organizational Effectiveness

According to one management scholar, "no single approach to the evaluation of effectiveness is appropriate in all circumstances or for all organizational types."[11] More and more, the effectiveness criteria for modern organizations are being prescribed by society in the form of explicit expectations, regulations, and laws. In the private sector, profitability is no longer the sole criterion of effectiveness.[12] Winslow Buxton, CEO of Pentair, Inc., a Minnesota manufacturing company with $2 billion in annual revenue and 10,000 employees, offered this perspective:

> One of the most challenging aspects of my job is balancing the differing expectations of employees, management, customers, financial analysts, and investors. The common denominator for all these groups is growth. But this seemingly simple term has different connotations for each constituency, and a successful company must satisfy all of those meanings.[13]

Moreover, today's managers are caught up in an enormous web of laws and regulations covering employment practices, working conditions, job safety, pensions, product safety, pollution, and competitive practices. To be truly effective, today's productive organizations need to strike a generally acceptable balance between organizational and societal goals. Direct conflicts, such as higher wages for employees versus lower prices for customers, are inevitable. Therefore, the process of determining the proper weighting of organizational effectiveness criteria is an endless one that requires frequent review and updating.[14]

Organizational effectiveness needs to be viewed in terms of a time dimension. As indicated in Figure 7.1 on page 168, the organization needs to be effective in the near, intermediate, and distant future. Consequently, **organizational effectiveness** can be defined as meeting organizational objectives and prevailing societal expectations in the near future, adapting and developing in the intermediate future, and surviving into the distant future.[15]

Most people think only of the near future. It is in the near future that the organization has to produce goods or render services, use resources efficiently, and satisfy both insiders and outsiders with its activity. But this is just the beginning, not the end. To grow and be effective, an organization must adapt to new environmental demands and mature and learn in the intermediate future (two to four years).[16]

REALITY CHECK 7.2

"... understanding that a company's greatest strength can become its greatest weakness when circumstances change can help build a mind-set of continuous learning and vigilance."

Source: Jeffrey Pfeffer, "The Agony of Victory," *Business 2.0,* 8 (January–February 2007): 62.

Questions: What specific organizational examples of the above quote have you observed? What adjustments should be made? Does this relate to you *personally* in any way?

organizational effectiveness Being effective, efficient, satisfying, adaptive and developing, and ultimately surviving.

FIGURE 7.1

The Time Dimension of Organizational Effectiveness

Source: Adapted from James L. Gibson, John M. Ivancevich, and James H. Donnelly Jr., *Organizations: Behavior, Structure, Processes,* 5th ed. (Homewood, Ill.: Richard D. Irwin, Inc.), p. 37. © 1991.

Time dimension	Near future (approximately 1 year)	Intermediate future	Distant future (approximately 5 years)
	The organization must be:	The organization must be:	The organization must be:
Effectiveness criteria	• *Effective* in accomplishing its purpose(s) • *Efficient* in the acquisition and use of limited resources • *A source of satisfaction* to its owners, employees, customers and clients, and society	• *Adaptive* to new opportunities and obstacles • *Capable of developing* the ability of its members and of itself	• *Capable of survival* in a world of uncertainties

---

TEST PREPPER 7.1

ANSWERS CAN BE FOUND ON P. 193

True or False?

_____ 1. By definition, it takes at least four people to make an organization.

_____ 2. Coordination of effort, common purpose, division of labor, and hierarchy of authority are all necessary before an organization is said to exist.

_____ 3. Horizontal specialization and vertical hierarchy are the two basic dimensions of an organization chart.

_____ 4. Profitability is the only acceptable criterion of organizational effectiveness.

Multiple Choice

_____ 5. As defined, how many people does it take to qualify as an "organization"?
  a. Two or more
  b. One or more
  c. More than fifty
  d. More than twenty
  e. At least six

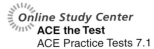
Online Study Center
ACE the Test
ACE Practice Tests 7.1

_____ 6. _____ permits each organization member to become more proficient by repeatedly doing the same specialized task.
  a. Division of labor
  b. Hierarchy of authority
  c. Span of control
  d. A common goal or purpose
  e. Coordination of effort

_____ 7. A diagram of an organization's official positions and formal lines of authority refers to a(n)
  a. fishbone diagram.
  b. organization chart.
  c. flow chart.
  d. position chart.
  e. pattern diagram.

_____ 8. If an organization is to be effective in the intermediate term, which of these criteria must be satisfied?
  a. Large and growing
  b. Efficient
  c. Satisfying for employees and customers
  d. Adaptive and developing
  e. Capable of survival

CONTINGENCY DESIGN

 2 ► *Explain the concept of contingency organization design, distinguish between mechanistic and organic organizations, and identify the basic departmentalization formats.*

Contingency thinking amounts to situational thinking (for further discussion, please refer to Appendix A at **college.hmco.com/pic/kreitnerSASfound**). Specifically, the contingency approach to organizing involves taking special steps to make sure that the organization fits the demands of the situation. In direct contrast to traditional bureaucratic thinking, contingency design is based on the assumption that there is no single best way to structure an organization. **Contingency design** is the process of determining the degree of environmental uncertainty and adapting the organization and its subunits to the situation. This does not necessarily mean that all contingency organizations will differ from each other. Instead, it means that managers who take a contingency approach select from a number of standard design alternatives to create the most situationally effective organization possible. Contingency managers typically start with the same basic collection of design alternatives but end up with unique combinations of them as dictated by the demands of their situations.[17]

The contingency approach to designing organizations boils down to two questions: (1) How much environmental uncertainty is there? (See Table 7.1 for a handy way to answer this question.) (2) What combination of structural characteristics is most appropriate? Let us examine a classic study to establish the validity of the contingency approach. It presents a rationale for systematically matching structural characteristics with environmental demands.

The Burns and Stalker Model

Tom Burns and G. M. Stalker, both British behavioral scientists, proposed a useful typology for categorizing organizations by structural design.[18] They distinguished

Online Study Center
Improve Your Grade
Career Snapshot 7.1

contingency design   Fitting the organization to its environment.

 TABLE 7.1

Determining Degree of Environmental Uncertainty

	Low	Moderate	High
1. How strong are social, political, and economic pressures on the organization?	Minimal	Moderate	Intense
2. How frequent are technological breakthroughs in the industry?	Infrequent	Occasional	Frequent
3. How reliable are resources and supplies?	Reliable	Occasional, predictable shortages	Unreliable
4. How stable is the demand for the organization's product or service?	Highly stable	Moderately stable	Unstable

TABLE 7.2

Mechanistic Versus Organic Organizations

Characteristic	Mechanistic organizations	Organic organizations
1. Task definition for individual contributors	Narrow and precise	Broad and general
2. Relationship between individual contribution and organization purpose	Vague	Clear
3. Task flexibility	Low	High
4. Definition of rights, obligations, and techniques	Clear	Vague
5. Reliance on hierarchical control	High	Low (reliance on self-control)
6. Primary direction of communication	Vertical (top to bottom)	Lateral (between peers)
7. Reliance on instructions and decisions from superior	High	Low (superior offers information and advice)
8. Emphasis on loyalty and obedience	High	Low
9. Type of knowledge required	Narrow, technical, and task-specific	Broad and professional

Source: Adapted from Tom Burns and G. M. Stalker, *The Management of Innovation,* 1961, pp. 119–125.

mechanistic organizations   Rigid bureaucracies.

organic organizations   Flexible, adaptive organizational structures.

between mechanistic and organic organizations. **Mechanistic organizations** tend to be rigid in design and have strong bureaucratic qualities. In contrast, **organic organizations** tend to be quite flexible in structure and adaptive to change. Actually, these two organizational types are the extreme ends of a single continuum. Pure types are difficult to find, but it is fairly easy to check off the characteristics listed in Table 7.2 to determine whether a particular organization (or subunit) is relatively mechanistic or relatively organic. It is notable that a field study found distinctly different communication patterns in mechanistic and organic organizations. Communication tended to be the formal command-and-control type in the mechanistic factory and participative in the organic factory.[19]

Telling the Difference

Here is a quick test of how well you understand the distinction between mechanistic and organic organizations. Read the following description of how an Emeryville, California, company maximizes the security of its clients' Web site data and attach a mechanistic or organic label.

> *SiteROCK employees . . . are required to read through several three-inch-thick binders of standard operating procedures before they can work in the command*

center. As each shift turns over, the staff must shuffle through 90 minutes of paperwork before handing over the keys. "Not everyone would be able to do this job. You have to be able to follow directions and follow the processes," says Lori Perrine, a customer-support specialist at siteROCK.[20]

If you said mechanistic, you're right. Using Table 7.2 as a guide, we see evidence of precise task definition, low task flexibility, clear definition of techniques, and high emphasis on obedience. Indeed, siteROCK is staffed mostly by former military personnel and is run with military precision. An organic organization would have exactly the opposite characteristics.

Situational Appropriateness

Burns and Stalker's research uncovered distinct organization-environment patterns that indicate the relative appropriateness of both mechanistic and organic organizations. They discovered that *successful organizations in relatively stable and certain environments tended to be mechanistic.* Conversely, they also discovered that *relatively organic organizations tended to be the successful ones when the environment was unstable and uncertain.*

In practical application, this means that mechanistic design is appropriate for environmental stability, and organic design is appropriate for high environmental uncertainty. Today, the trend necessarily is toward more organic organizations because uncertainty is the rule. *Management Review* summed up the situation this way:

> *Products, companies, and industries all have shorter life cycles, which means that product launches, corporate realignments, and other initiatives may take place in months rather than years. The global span of today's companies, which have employees, customers, and suppliers throughout the world, also multiplies the complexities of change. And let us not forget another complicator—technology. Companies must constantly upgrade systems, evaluate new technology, and adopt new ways of doing business.*[21]

This is not to say that organic is good and mechanistic is bad. Mechanistic organizations do have their appropriate places. SiteROCK's mechanistic structure, for example, makes it highly resistant to human error, technical failures, and attacks by hackers and terrorists.

The work of Burns and Stalker paved the way for two important conclusions about contingency design. First, research indicates that *there is no single best organization design.* Second, research supports the idea that the more uncertain the environment, the more flexible and adaptable the organization's structure must be.[22] With this contingency perspective in mind, we now consider some alternative ways of designing organizations.

Contingency Design Alternatives

Think of this section as a toolkit for the contingency design of organizations. Managers need to mix and match departmentalization formats, spans of control, and centralization/decentralization in an effective manner that is appropriate to the situation.

Basic Departmentalization Formats

As we noted earlier, one of the two basic dimensions of an organization chart is horizontal specialization (or division of labor). When labor is divided, complex

departmentalization Grouping related jobs or processes into major organizational subunits.

Online Study Center
Improve Your Grade
Visual Glossary 7.1

processes are reduced to distinct and less complex jobs. But because of the organizational fragmentation that results, something must be done to coordinate people who are going in many different specialized directions. Aside from the hierarchical chain of command, one of the most common ways to achieve greater coordination is via departmentalization. It is through **departmentalization** that related jobs, activities, or processes are grouped into major organizational subunits. For example, all jobs involving staffing activities such as recruitment, hiring, and training are often grouped into a human resources department. Grouping jobs through the formation of departments, according to management author James D. Thompson, "permits coordination to be handled in the least costly manner."[23] A degree of coordination is achieved through departmentalization because members of the department work on interrelated tasks, obey the same departmental rules, and report to the same department head. It is important to note that although the term *departmentalization* is used here, it does not always literally apply; managers commonly use labels such as *division, group,* or *unit* in large organizations.

Five basic types of departmentalization are:

▌ Functional departments

▌ Product-service departments

▌ Geographic location departments

▌ Customer classification departments

▌ Work-flow process departments in reengineered organizations

Each has its strengths and limitations.[24]

▌ *Functional Departments.* Functional departments categorize jobs according to the activity performed. Among profit-making businesses, variations of the functional production-finance-marketing arrangement shown in section A of Figure 7.2 are the most common forms of departmentalization. Functional departmentalization is popular because it permits those with similar technical expertise to work in a coordinated subunit. Of course, functional departmentalization is not restricted to profit-making businesses. The functional departments in a nonprofit hospital might be administration, nursing, housekeeping, food service, laboratory and x-ray, admission and records, and accounting and billing. A negative aspect of functional departmentalization is that it creates "technical ghettos," in which local departmental concerns and loyalties tend to override strategic organizational concerns.

▌ *Product-Service Departments.* This second, somewhat more organic, format is called product-service departmentalization because a product (or service), rather than a functional category of work, is the unifying theme. As diagrammed in section B of Figure 7.2, the product-service approach permits each of, say, two products to be managed as semiautonomous businesses. Organizations that render a service instead of turning out a tangible product might find it advantageous to organize around service categories. In reality, however, many of today's companies turn out bundles of products and services for customers. General Electric, for example, was reorganized around these major product/ service categories: energy (power generation equipment), transportation (aircraft engines and rail locomotives), NBC-Universal (television and films), health care (diagnostic equipment), and consumer and industrial products

FIGURE 7.2

Alternative Departmentalization Formats

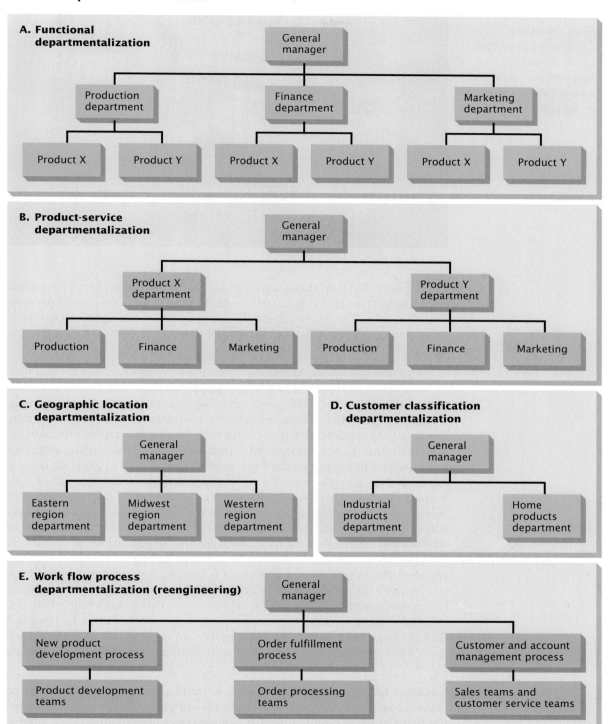

A. Functional departmentalization

B. Product-service departmentalization

C. Geographic location departmentalization

D. Customer classification departmentalization

E. Work flow process departmentalization (reengineering)

Sometimes, circumstances dictate a certain structural format for a business. In the case of online grocer Peapod, a geographic location structure is necessary. Customers in Boston, for example, don't want perishable grocery items such as milk and produce shipped in from Peapod's headquarters in Skokie, Illinois. So Peapod has regional distribution centers serving each of its six major markets around the United States.

and services.[25] Ideally, those working in this sort of product-service structure have a broad "business" orientation rather than a narrow functional perspective. As section B of Figure 7.2 shows, it is the general manager's job to ensure that these minibusinesses work in a complementary fashion, rather than competing with one another.

▍ *Geographic Location Departments.* Sometimes, as in organizations that have nationwide or worldwide markets, geography dictates structural format (see section C of Figure 7.2). The geographic dispersion of resources (for example, mining companies), facilities (for example, railroads), or customers (for example, chain supermarkets) may encourage the use of a geographic format to put administrators "closer to the action." One can imagine that drilling engineers in a Houston-based petroleum firm would be better able to get a job done in Alaska if they actually went there. Similarly, a department-store marketing manager would be in a better position to judge consumer tastes in Florida by working out of a regional office in Orlando than from a home office in Salt Lake City or Toronto. Long lines of communication among organizational units have traditionally been a limiting factor with geographically dispersed operations. But space-age telecommunications technology has created some interesting regional advantages. One case in point is Omaha, Nebraska. Its central location, along with the absence of a distinct regional accent among Nebraskans, has made Omaha the 1-800 capital of the country. Every major hotel chain and most of the big telemarketers have telephone service centers in Omaha.[26] Global competition is pressuring managers to organize along geographical lines. This structure allows multinational companies to serve local markets better.

▍ *Customer Classification Departments.* A fourth structural format centers on various customer categories (see section D of Figure 7.2). Aircraft maker Boeing, for example, was reorganized in 1998 into three units: commercial, defense, and space.[27] The rationale was to better serve the distinctly different needs of those three sets of customers. Customer classification departmentalization shares a weakness with the product-service and geographic location approaches: all three can create costly duplication of personnel and facilities. Functional design is the answer when duplication is a problem.

▪ *Work-flow Process Departments in Reengineered Organizations.* Reengineering involves starting with a clean sheet of paper and radically redesigning the organization into cross-functional teams that speed up the entire business process. The driving factors behind reengineering are lower costs, better quality, greater speed, better use of modern information technology, and improved customer satisfaction.[28] Organizations with work-flow process departments are called *horizontal organizations* because the emphasis is on the smooth and speedy horizontal flow of work between two key points: (1) identifying customer needs and (2) satisfying the customer.[29] This is a distinct *outward* focus, as opposed to the inward focus of functional departments. Here is what happens inside the type of organization depicted in section E of Figure 7.2:

> Rather than focusing single-mindedly on financial objectives or functional goals, the horizontal organization emphasizes customer satisfaction. Work is simplified and hierarchy flattened by combining related tasks—for example, an account-management process that subsumes the sales, billing, and service functions—and eliminating work that does not add value. Information zips along an internal superhighway. The knowledge worker analyzes it, and technology moves it quickly across the corporation instead of up and down, speeding up and improving decision making.[30]

Each of the preceding departmentalization formats is presented in its pure form, but in actual practice hybrid versions occur frequently. For example, Coca-Cola created a mix of three geographic location units and a functional unit in 2001 to make the global company more responsive to both customers and product trends. The four units are Americas, Asia, Europe/Africa, and New Business Ventures.[31]

Span of Control

The number of people who report directly to a manager represents that manager's **span of control**. (Some scholars and managers prefer the term *span of management*.) Managers with a narrow span of control oversee the work of a few people, whereas those with a wide span of control have many people reporting to them (see Figure 7.3). Generally, narrow spans of control foster tall organizations (many levels in the hierarchy). In contrast, flat organizations (few hierarchical levels) have wide spans of control. Everything else being equal, it stands to reason that an organization with narrow spans of control needs more managers than one with wide spans. Management theorists and practitioners have devoted a good deal of time and energy through the years attempting to answer the question "What is the ideal span of control?"[32] Today's emphasis on contingency organization design, combined with evidence that wide spans of control can be effective, has rendered obsolete the question of an ideal span. The relevant question is no longer how wide spans of control *should* be but instead,

Online Study Center
Improve Your Grade
Visual Glossary 7.2

span of control Number of people who report directly to a given manager.

FIGURE 7.3

Narrow and Wide Spans of Control

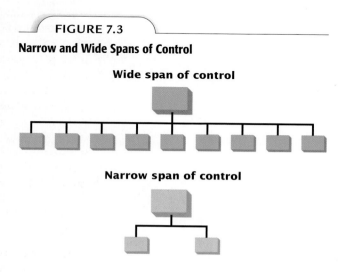

Wide span of control

Narrow span of control

"How wide *can* one's span of control be?" Wider spans of control mean less administrative expense and more self-management, both popular notions today. Ideally, the right span of control strikes an efficient balance between too little and too much supervision, important considerations in the era of lean organizations.

Both overly narrow and overly wide spans of control are counterproductive. Overly narrow spans create unnecessarily tall organizations that are plagued by such problems as:

▌ Oversupervision

▌ Long lines of communication

▌ Slow, multilevel decision making

▌ Limited initiative due to minimal delegation of authority

▌ Restricted development among managers who devote most of their time to direct supervision

▌ Increased administrative cost[33]

In contrast, overly wide spans can:

▌ Erode efficiency and inflate costs as a result of workers' lack of training

▌ Cause behavioral problems among inadequately supervised workers

▌ Result in a lack of coordination

Clearly, a rationale is needed for striking a workable balance.

Situational factors such as those listed in Figure 7.4 are a useful starting point. The narrow, moderate, and wide span of control ranges in Figure 7.4 are intended

---

FIGURE 7.4

Situational Determinants of Span of Control

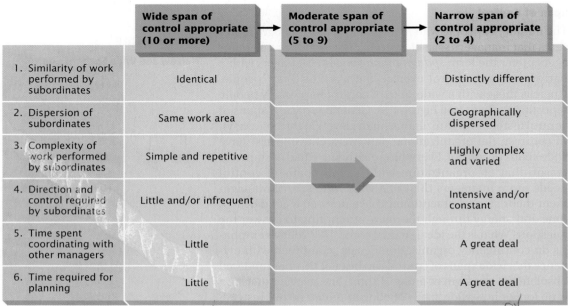

	Wide span of control appropriate (10 or more)	Moderate span of control appropriate (5 to 9)	Narrow span of control appropriate (2 to 4)
1. Similarity of work performed by subordinates	Identical		Distinctly different
2. Dispersion of subordinates	Same work area		Geographically dispersed
3. Complexity of work performed by subordinates	Simple and repetitive		Highly complex and varied
4. Direction and control required by subordinates	Little and/or infrequent		Intensive and/or constant
5. Time spent coordinating with other managers	Little		A great deal
6. Time required for planning	Little		A great deal

FIGURE 7.5

Factors in Relative Centralization/Decentralization

	Highly centralized organization	Highly decentralized organization
How many decisions are made at lower levels in the hierarchy?	Very few, if any	Many or most
How important are the decisions that are made at lower levels (i.e., do they impact organizational success or dollar values)?	Not very important	Very important
How many different functions (e.g., production, marketing, finance, human resources) rely on lower-level decision making?	Very few, if any	All or most
How much does top management monitor or check up on lower-level decision making?	A great deal	Very little or not at all

to be illustrative benchmarks rather than rigid limits. Each organization must do its own on-the-job experimentation. At FedEx, for example, the span of control varies with different areas of the company. Departments that employ many people doing the same or very similar jobs—such as customer service agents, handlers/sorters, and couriers—usually have a span of control of 15 to 20 employees per manager. Groups that perform multiple tasks, or tasks that require only a few people, are more likely to have spans of control of five or fewer.[34] No ideal span of control exists for all kinds of work.

Centralization and Decentralization

Where are the important decisions made in an organization? Are they made strictly by top management or by middle- and lower-level managers? These questions are at the heart of the decentralization design alternative. Centralization is at one end of a continuum, and at the other end is decentralization. **Centralization** is defined as the relative retention of decision-making authority by top management. Almost all decision-making authority is retained by top management in highly centralized organizations. In contrast, **decentralization** is the granting of decision-making authority by management to lower-level employees. Decentralization increases as the degree, importance, and range of lower-level decision making *increases* and the amount of checking up by top management *decreases* (see Figure 7.5).

When we speak of centralization or decentralization, we are describing a comparative degree, not an absolute. The challenge for managers, as one management consultant observed, is to strike a workable balance between two extremes.

> *The modern organization in transition will recognize the pull of two polarities: a need for greater centralization to create low-cost shared resources; and, a need*

centralization The retention of decision-making authority by top management.

decentralization Management shares decision-making authority with lower-level employees.

to improve market responsiveness with greater decentralization. Today's winning organizations are the ones that can handle the paradox and tensions of both pulls. These are the firms that analyze the optimum organizational solution in each particular circumstance, without prejudice for one type of organization over another. The result is, almost invariably, a messy mixture of decentralized units sharing cost-effective centralized resources.[35]

Support for greater decentralization in the corporate world has come and gone over the years in faddish waves. Today, the call is for the type of balance just discussed. The case against extreme decentralization can be summed up in three words: *lack of control.* Balance helps neutralize this concern. Again, the contingency approach dictates which end of the continuum needs to be emphasized.[36] Centralization, because of its mechanistic nature, generally works best for organizations that are in relatively stable situations.[37] A more organic, decentralized approach is appropriate for firms that are in complex and changing conditions.

TEST PREPPER 7.2

ANSWERS CAN BE FOUND ON P. 193

True or False?

_____ 1. Part of the contingency design process is determining the degree of environmental uncertainty.

_____ 2. Mechanistic organizations are quite rigid in structure.

_____ 3. According to Burns and Stalker's research, organic organizations tend to be more effective than mechanistic ones, whatever the situation.

_____ 4. Strategic departments are one of the five basic types of departmentalization.

_____ 5. Narrow spans of control generally create flat organizations.

_____ 6. An organization is centralized if top management makes all key decisions.

Multiple Choice

_____ 7. What is a key question in contingency design?
  a. How can we make our organization a closed system?
  b. Which structure will eliminate major uncertainties?
  c. What structural combination is situationally appropriate?
  d. Will our present structure help us formulate a good strategy?
  e. What is the single best organization design?

_____ 8. _____ organizations such as W.L. Gore tend to be quite flexible in structure and adaptive to change.
  a. Segmented
  b. Organic
  c. Centralized
  d. Mechanistic
  e. Matrix

_____ 9. "Horizontal organizations" have _____ departments.
  a. geographic location
  b. customer classification
  c. work-flow process
  d. product-service
  e. line and staff

_____ 10. Which statement about spans of control is true?
  a. Spans of control are irrelevant today.
  b. Today, narrower spans are better.
  c. Researchers say a span of no more than seven is best.
  d. It is difficult to directly manage more than three people.
  e. There is no ideal span of control.

_____ 11. _____ involves the granting of decision-making authority to lower-level employees.
  a. Centralization
  b. Differentiation
  c. Contingency design
  d. Decentralization
  e. Departmentalization

EFFECTIVE DELEGATION

 3 ► *Define the term* delegation, *and list at least five common barriers to delegation.*

Delegation is an important common denominator that runs through virtually all relatively organic design alternatives. It is vital to successful decentralization. Formally defined, **delegation** is the process of assigning various degrees of decision-making authority to lower-level employees.[38] As this definition implies, delegation is not an all-or-nothing proposition. There are at least five different degrees of delegation[39] (see Figure 7.6).

A word of caution about delegation is necessary because there is one thing it does *not* include. Former President Harry Truman is said to have had a little sign on his White House desk that read, "The Buck Stops Here!"[40] Managers who delegate should keep this idea in mind because, although authority may be passed along to people at lower levels, ultimate responsibility cannot be passed along. Thus, delegation is the sharing of authority, not the abdication of responsibility. Chrysler's former CEO Lee Iacocca admittedly fell victim to this particular lapse:

> When the company started to make money, it spent its cash on stock buybacks and acquisitions. For his part, Iacocca was distracted by nonautomotive concerns.
>
> [Iacocca] concedes that while he kept his finger on finance and marketing, he should have paid closer attention to new model planning. "If I made one mistake," he says now, "it was delegating all the product development and not going to one single meeting."[41]

Iacocca corrected this mistake before he retired, and customers liked Chrysler's bold new designs.

delegation Assigning various degrees of decision-making authority to lower-level employees.

Online Study Center
Improve Your Grade
Visual Glossary 7.3

The Advantages of Delegation

Managers stand to gain a great deal by adopting the habit of delegating. By passing along well-defined tasks to lower-level people, managers can free more of their time for important chores like planning, leading, and motivating. Regarding the question of exactly *what* should be delegated, Intel's chairman, Andy Grove, made the following recommendation: "Because it is easier to monitor something with which you are familiar, if you have a choice you should delegate those activities you know best."[42] Grove cautions that delegators who follow his advice will experience some psychological discomfort because they will quite naturally want to continue doing what they know best.

 FIGURE 7.6

The Delegation Continuum

Low		Moderate		High
Investigate and report back	Investigate and recommend action	Investigate and advise on action planned	Investigate and take action; advise on action taken	Investigate and take action

Online Study Center college.hmco.com/pic/kreitnerSASfound

REALITY CHECK 7.3

"There are two types of delegating that managers need to consider before passing the workload to their employees: delegating for results and delegating for employee development."

Source: Sharon Gazda, "The Art of Delegating," *HR Magazine,* 47 (January 2002): 75.

Questions: Why is this a useful distinction? How can a manager effectively blend the two types of delegation?

In addition to freeing valuable managerial time,[43] delegation is also a helpful management training and development tool. Moreover, lower-level managers who desire more challenge generally become more committed and satisfied when they are given the opportunity to tackle significant problems. Conversely, a lack of delegation can stifle initiative. Consider the situation of a California builder:

> [The founder and chairman] personally negotiates every land deal. Visiting every construction site repeatedly, he is critical even of details of cabinet construction. "The building business is an entrepreneurial business," he says. "Yes, you can send out people. But you better follow them. You have to manage your managers."
>
> Says one former . . . executive: "The turnover there's tremendous. He hires bright and talented people, but then he makes them eunuchs. He never lets them make any decisions."[44]

Perfectionist managers who avoid delegation have problems in the long run when they become overwhelmed by minute details.

Barriers to Delegation

There are several reasons why managers generally do not delegate as much as they should:

- Belief in the fallacy "If you want it done right, do it yourself"
- Lack of confidence and trust in lower-level employees
- Low self-confidence
- Fear of being called lazy
- Vague job definition
- Fear of competition from those below
- Reluctance to take the risks entailed in depending on others
- Lack of controls that provide early warning of problems with delegated duties
- Poor example set by bosses who do not delegate[45]

Managers can go a long way toward delegating effectively by recognizing and correcting these tendencies both in themselves and in their fellow managers.[46] Since successful delegation is habit forming, the first step usually is the hardest. Properly trained and motivated people who know how to take initiative in challenging situations often reward a delegator's trust with a job well done.[47]

Once managers have developed the habit of delegating, they need to remember this wise advice from Peter Drucker: "Delegation . . . requires that delegators follow up. They rarely do—they think they have delegated, and that's it. But they are still accountable for performance. And so they have to follow up, have to make sure that the task gets done—and done right."[48]

TEST PREPPER 7.3

ANSWERS CAN BE FOUND ON P. 193

True or False?

_____ 1. Delegation unavoidably is an all-or-nothing proposition.

_____ 2. Fear of being called lazy is a barrier to delegation.

_____ 3. Managerial follow-up is unnecessary if delegation is done right.

Multiple Choice

_____ 4. Delegation involves authority being
   a. replaced with responsibility.
   b. weakened.
   c. eliminated.
   d. shared with lower levels.
   e. greatly increased.

_____ 5. Which of these is helped by delegation?
   a. Integrating
   b. Departmentalization
   c. Training and development of managers
   d. Financial control
   e. Strategic planning

_____ 6. All of the following are typical barriers to delegation *except*
   a. lack of trust in subordinates.
   b. fear of being called lazy.
   c. fear of competition from subordinates.
   d. vague job definition.
   e. working for a manager who likes to delegate.

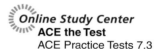

Online Study Center
ACE the Test
ACE Practice Tests 7.3

THE CHANGING SHAPE OF ORGANIZATIONS

4 ▶ *Explain how the traditional pyramid organization is being reshaped.*

Management scholars have been predicting the death of traditional pyramid-shaped bureaucracies for nearly 40 years.[49] Initial changes were slow in coming and barely noticeable. Observers tended to dismiss the predictions as naive and exaggerated. However, the pace and degree of change has picked up dramatically since the 1980s. All of the social, political-legal, economic, and technological changes discussed in Chapter 2 threaten to make traditional organizations obsolete. Why? Because they are too slow, unresponsive, uncreative, costly, and hard to manage. It is clear today that nothing less than a reorganization revolution is under way. Traditional pyramid organizations, though still very much in evidence, are being questioned as never before. General Electric's legendary CEO Jack Welch put it this way:

> The old organization was built on control, but the world has changed. The world is moving at such a pace that control has become a limitation. It slows you down. You've got to balance freedom with some control, but you've got to have more freedom than you ever dreamed of.[50]

Consequently, to be prepared for tomorrow's workplace, we need to take a look at how organizations are evolving. Figure 7.7 on page 182 illustrates three different ways in which the traditional pyramid organization is being reshaped. They are the hourglass organization, the cluster organization, and the virtual organization. To varying extents, these new configurations embody three current organizational trends:

FIGURE 7.7

Reshaping the Traditional Pyramid Organization

Traditional pyramid organization

Hourglass organization   Cluster organization   Virtual organization

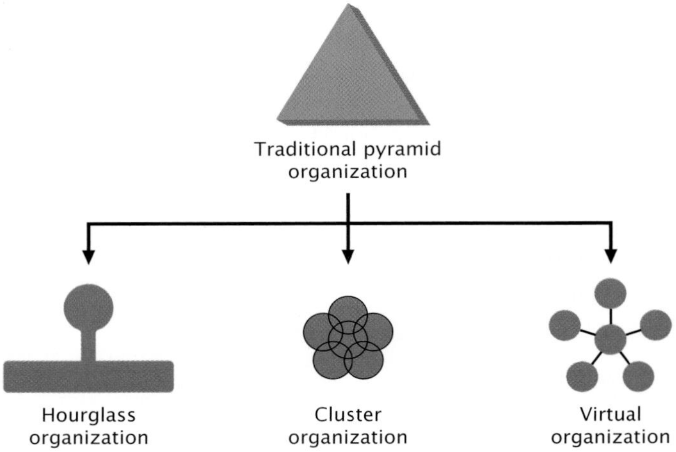

▌ Fewer layers (For example, CEO Andrea Jung recently streamlined Avon's hierarchy by 7 layers—from 15 layers down to 8—to enable the beauty products firm to respond more quickly to rapidly changing consumer tastes.[51])

▌ Greater emphasis on teams

▌ Smallness within bigness (For example, in 2002, "Nokia split its monolithic $21 billion mobile-phone unit into nine profit-and-loss centers, each charged with bolstering the company's position in a particular market."[52])

The new configurations may overlap, as when an hourglass organization relies extensively on teams. The new structures have important implications for both the practice of management and the quality of work life. Let us examine them and take an imaginary peek into the not-too-distant future of work organizations.

Hourglass Organizations

hourglass organization Three-layer structure with a constricted middle layer.

The **hourglass organization** consists of three layers, with the middle layer distinctly pinched. A strategic elite is responsible for formulating a vision for the organization and making sure it becomes reality. A significantly shrunken middle-management layer carries out a coordinating function for diverse lower-level activities. Thanks to computer networks that flash information directly from the factory floor or retail outlet to the executive suite and back again, middle managers are no longer simply conduits for warmed-over information. Also, unlike traditional middle managers, hourglass middle managers are generalists rather than narrow specialists. They are comfortable dealing with complex interfunctional problems. A given middle manager might deal with an accounting problem one day, a product design issue the next, and a marketing dilemma the next—all within crossfunctional team settings.

At the bottom of the hourglass is a broad layer of technical specialists who act as their own supervisors much of the time. Consequently, the distinction between supervisors and rank-and-file personnel is blurred. Employees at this operating level complain about a very real lack of promotion opportunities. Management tries to keep them motivated with challenging work assignments, lateral transfers, skill-training opportunities, and pay-for-performance schemes. Union organizers attempt to exploit complaints about employees "having to act like managers, but not being paid like managers."

Cluster Organizations

Another new configuration shown in Figure 7.7 is the **cluster organization**. This label is appropriate because teams are the primary structural unit.[53]

> For instance, Oticon Inc., a Danish hearing-aid manufacturer that also has operations in Somerset, NJ, abolished its formal organizational structure several years ago as part of a strategic turnaround. The old way of doing things has been replaced with a flexible work environment and project-based work processes. Self-directed teams have become the defining unit of work, disbanding and forming again as the work requires. Oticon typically has 100 projects running at any time, and most of its 1,500 employees work on several projects at once.[54]

Imagine we are working in a cluster organization. We see multiskilled people moving from team to team as projects dictate. Pay for knowledge is a common practice. Motivation seems to be high, but some complain about a lack of job security because things are constantly changing. Stress levels rise when the pace of change quickens. Special training efforts, involving team-building exercises (see Best Practices on page 189), are aimed at enhancing everyone's communication and group involvement skills.[55]

Virtual Organizations

From the time of the Industrial Revolution until the Internet age, the norm was to build an organization that was capable of designing, producing, and marketing products. Bigger was assumed to be better. And this approach worked as long as large batches of look-alike products were acceptable to consumers. But along came the Internet, e-business, and mass customization, discussed in Chapters 1 and 5. *Speed*—in the form of faster market research, faster product development, faster production, and faster delivery—became more important than size. Meanwhile, global competition kept a lid on prices. Suddenly, consumers realized they could get exactly what they wanted, at a good price, and fast. Many lumbering organizational giants of the past were not up to the task. Enter **virtual organizations**, flexible networks of value-adding subcontractors, linked by the Internet, e-mail, fax machines, and telephones.[56]

From a personal perspective, life in virtual organizations is *hectic*. Everything moves at Internet speed. Change and learning are constant. Cross-functional teams are the norm, and job reassignments are frequent. Project specialists rarely see a single project to completion because they are whisked off to other projects. Unavoidable by-products of constant change are stress and burnout. Unexpectedly, the need for face-to-face contact increases as geographically dispersed team members communicate via e-mail, instant messaging, groupware, and voice mail. Only face-to-face interaction, both on and off the job, can build the rapport and trust necessary to get something done quickly with people you rarely see. The growing gap between information haves and have-nots produces resentment and alienation among low-paid workers employed by factory, data-processing, and shipping subcontractors.

cluster organization Collaborative structure in which teams are the primary unit.

REALITY CHECK 7.4

"Underscoring the importance of establishing clear expectations in remote working relationships is the example of Best Buy, which recently implemented ROWE, for 'results only work environment,' an experiment designed to allow workers to get their work done wherever and whenever they want, as long as they meet agreed-to results. Initial data, reported in *Business Week,* indicate that this is a successful experiment: Productivity is up 35 percent, and turnover is down dramatically."

Source: Marjorie Derven, "The Remote Connection," *HR Magazine,* 52 (March 2007): 112.

Questions: What are the keys to being an effective manager in a virtual organization? Could you thrive in Best Buy's ROWE arrangement?

virtual organizations Internet-linked networks of value-adding subcontractors.

TEST PREPPER 7.4

ANSWERS CAN BE FOUND ON P. 193

True or False?

_____ 1. One of the three current organizational trends involves integrating small units into big units.

_____ 2. In hourglass organizations, there are no middle managers.

_____ 3. Internet-linked networks of value-adding sub-contractors qualify as virtual organizations.

Multiple Choice

_____ 4. A clear structural trend in modern organizations is
   a. more middle managers.
   b. more managers per employee.
   c. narrow spans of control.
   d. less teamwork.
   e. fewer layers.

_____ 5. You meet a business owner sitting next to you on a plane and she says her organization is structured around teams. Which label should you affix to her organization?
   a. Virtual
   b. Matrix
   c. Hourglass
   d. Cluster
   e. Lattice

_____ 6. In virtual organizations, what has become a factor of overriding importance?
   a. Quality
   b. Speed
   c. Organizational size
   d. Financial structure
   e. Culture

Online Study Center
ACE the Test
ACE Practice Tests 7.4

ORGANIZATIONAL CULTURES

5 ▸ *Describe at least three characteristics of organizational cultures, and explain the cultural significance of stories.*

No discussion of organizations, whatever their design and shape, would be complete without taking organizational cultures into consideration:

▌ The notion of organizational culture is rooted in cultural anthropology.[57]

▌ **Organizational culture** is the collection of shared (stated or implied) beliefs, values, rituals, stories, myths, and specialized language that foster a feeling of community among organization members.[58]

▌ Culture, although based largely on taken-for-granted or "invisible" factors, exerts a powerful influence on behavior. For example, a six-year study of more than 900 newly hired college graduates found significantly lower turnover among those who joined public accounting firms whose cultures emphasized respect for people and teamwork. New hires working for accounting firms whose cultures emphasized detail, stability, and innovation tended to quit 14 months sooner than their counterparts in the more people-friendly organizations. According to the researcher's estimate, the companies with people-friendly cultures saved $6 million in human resources expenses because of lower turnover rates.[59]

Some call organizational (or corporate) culture the "social glue" that binds an organization's members together. Accordingly, this final section binds together all

organizational culture Shared values, beliefs, and language that create a common identity and sense of community.

we have said about organizations in this chapter. Without an appreciation for the cultural aspect, an organization is just a meaningless collection of charts, tasks, and people. An anthropologist-turned-manager offered these cautionary words:

> *Corporate culture is not an ideological gimmick to be imposed from above by management or management consulting firms but a stubborn fact of human social organization that can scuttle the best of corporate plans if not taken into account.*[60]

Characteristics of Organizational Cultures

Because of the number of variables involved, organizational cultures can vary widely from one organization to the next. Even so, authorities on the subject have identified six common characteristics.[61] Let us briefly examine these common characteristics to gain a fuller understanding of organizational cultures.

1. *Collective.* Organizational cultures are *social* entities. While an individual may exert a cultural influence, it takes collective agreement and action for an organization's culture to take on a life of its own. Organizational cultures are truly synergistic ($1 + 1 = 3$). Jeffrey R. Immelt offered this companywide perspective soon after becoming the new head of General Electric: "We run a multibusiness company with common cultures, with common management . . . where the whole is always greater than the sum of its parts. Culture counts."[62]

2. *Emotionally charged.* People tend to find their organization's culture a comforting security blanket that enables them to deal with (or sometimes mask) their insecurities and uncertainties. Not surprisingly, people can develop a strong emotional attachment to their cultural security blanket. They will fight to protect it, often refusing to question its basic values. Corporate mergers often get bogged down in culture conflicts.[63]

3. *Historically based.* Shared experiences, over extended periods of time, bind groups of people together. We tend to identify with those who have had similar

Don't just sit there. Get up and dance! That's the scene once a week for employees at Mango's Tropical Café in Miami, Florida. Weekly dance classes are one way the organization gets its employees to embrace the look and feel of the company's culture, one of fun and multicultural celebration. It also builds friendship, trust, and a common bond. Okay, now—one, two, three, kick!

Online Study Center college.hmco.com/pic/kreitnerSASfound

life experiences. Trust and loyalty, two key components of culture, are earned by consistently demonstrating predictable patterns of words and actions.

4. *Inherently symbolic.* Actions often speak louder than words. Memorable symbolic actions are the lifeblood of organizational culture. For instance, consider what has been going on recently at Procter & Gamble:

> From the outside, Procter & Gamble Co.'s Cincinnati headquarters looks unchanged. But on the top floor—the haunt of P&G's top brass for 50 years—there's a major overhaul under way. Wood paneling and an executive cafeteria are making way for a training center that will bring employees from around the world within earshot of CEO Alan G. Lafley. "I have made a lot of symbolic, very physical changes so people understand we are in the business of leading change," says Lafley.[64]

The cultural message being communicated at P&G also tells top executives to focus less on power and privilege and more on employee development and open communication.

5. *Dynamic.* In the long term, organizational cultures promote predictability, conformity, and stability. Just beneath this apparently stable surface, however, change boils as people struggle to communicate and comprehend subtle cultural clues. A management trainee who calls the president by her first name after being invited to do so may be embarrassed to learn later that "no one actually calls the president by her first name, even if she asks you to."

6. *Inherently fuzzy.* Ambiguity, contradictions, and multiple meanings are fundamental to organizational cultures. Just as a photographer cannot capture your typical busy day in a single snapshot, it takes intense and prolonged observation to capture the essence of an organization's culture.

Forms and Consequences of Organizational Cultures

Figure 7.8 lists major forms and consequences of organizational cultures. To the extent that people in an organization share symbols, a common language, stories,

---

FIGURE 7.8

Forms and Consequences of Organizational Cultures

Source: Forms adapted from Harrison M. Trice and Janice M. Beyer, *The Cultures of Work Organizations* (Englewood Cliffs, N.J.: Prentice-Hall, 1993), pp. 77–128. Consequences adapted from Linda Smircich, "Concepts of Culture and Organizational Analysis," *Administrative Science Quarterly,* 28 (September 1983): 339–358.

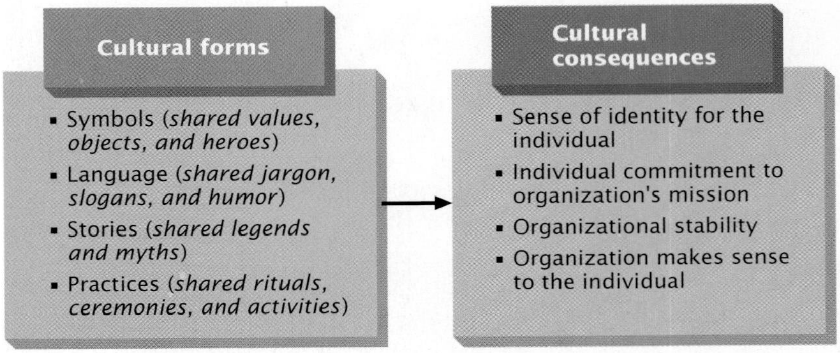

Cultural forms

- Symbols (*shared values, objects, and heroes*)
- Language (*shared jargon, slogans, and humor*)
- Stories (*shared legends and myths*)
- Practices (*shared rituals, ceremonies, and activities*)

Cultural consequences

- Sense of identity for the individual
- Individual commitment to organization's mission
- Organizational stability
- Organization makes sense to the individual

and practices, they will tend to experience the four consequences. The degree of sharing and intensity of the consequences determine whether the organization's culture is strong or weak.

Shared values stand out as a pivotal factor in Figure 7.8. **Organizational values** are *shared* beliefs about what the organization stands for.[65] For example, prior to its merger with EarthLink in 2000, Internet service provider MindSpring took great pride in providing superior customer service. MindSpring's founder, Charles Brewer, drove home his customer service ethic with strong corporate values. As reported at the time:

> MindSpring has nine "core values and beliefs" that govern how it operates. The principles are posted on office walls and on the backs of business cards. Mind-Springers even recite them before their weekly all-hands meeting. "Work is an important part of life," declares one principle, "and it should be fun. Being a good business person does not mean being stuffy and boring." Another declares, "We make commitments with care, and then live up to them."[66]

A recent visit to Earthlink's Web site found no sign of Brewer, but his corporate values (plus a new one) were definitely alive and well.

organizational values Shared beliefs about what the organization stands for.

The Organizational Socialization Process

Organizational socialization is the process through which outsiders are transformed into accepted insiders.[67] In effect, the socialization process shapes newcomers to fit the organizational culture.

organizational socialization The process of transforming outsiders into accepted insiders.

> The culture asserts itself when the taken-for-granted cultural assumptions are in some way violated by the uninitiated and provoke a response. As the uninitiated bump into one after another taken-for-granted assumption, more acculturated employees respond in a variety of ways (tell stories, offer advice, ridicule, lecture, shun, and so forth) that serve to mold the way in which the newcomer thinks about his or her role and about "how things are done around here."[68]

Orientations

Orientation programs—in which newly hired employees learn about their organization's history, culture, competitive realities, and compensation and benefits—are an important first step in the socialization process. Too often today, however, orientations are hurried or nonexistent, and new employees are left to "sink or swim." This is a big mistake, according to recent workplace research:

> One study at Corning Glass Works (in Corning, New York) found that new employees who went through a structured orientation program were 69 percent more likely to be with the company after three years than those who were left on their own to sort out the job. A similar two-year study at Texas Instruments concluded that employees who had been carefully oriented to both the company and their jobs reached full productivity two months sooner than those who weren't.[69]

Storytelling

Stories deserve special attention here because, as indicated in Figure 7.8, they are a central feature of organizational socialization and culture. Company stories about heroic or inspiring deeds let newcomers know what "really counts."[70] For example, 3M's eleventh commandment—"Thou shalt not kill a new product idea"—has been ingrained in new employees through one inspiring story about the employee who invented transparent cellophane tape.

> *According to the story, an employee accidentally discovered the tape but was unable to get his superiors to buy the idea. Marketing studies predicted a relatively small demand for the new material. Undaunted, the employee found a way to sneak into the board room and tape down the minutes of board members with his transparent tape. The board was impressed enough with the novelty to give it a try and experienced incredible success.[71]*

Upon hearing this story, a 3M newcomer has believable, concrete evidence that innovation and persistence pay off at 3M. It has been said that stories are "social roadmaps" for employees, telling them where to go and where not to go and what will happen when they get there. Moreover, stories are remembered longer than abstract facts or rules and regulations. How many times have you recalled a professor's colorful story but forgotten the rest of the lecture?

Strengthening Organizational Cultures

Given the inherent fuzziness of organizational cultures, how can managers identify the cultural weak spots needing improvement? Symptoms of a weak organizational culture include the following:

▌ *Inward focus.* Have internal politics become more important than real-world problems and the marketplace?

▌ *Morale problems.* Are there chronic unhappiness and high turnover?

▌ *Fragmentation/inconsistency.* Is there a lack of "fit" in the way people behave, communicate, and perceive problems and opportunities?

▌ *Ingrown subcultures.* Is there a lack of communication among subunits?

▌ *Warfare among subcultures.* Has constructive competition given way to destructive conflict?

▌ *Subculture elitism.* Have organizational units become exclusive "clubs" with restricted entry? Have subcultural values become more important than the organization's values?[72]

Evidence of these symptoms may encourage a potential recruit to look elsewhere. Each of these symptoms of a weak organizational culture can be a formidable barrier to organizational effectiveness. Organizations with strong cultures do a good job of avoiding these symptoms.[73]

REALITY CHECK 7.5

Recent survey: "Almost two-thirds of companies say they aren't great at integrating newly recruited managers and executives into their organizations."

Source: Margery Weinstein, "Outsider Longer," *Training,* 44 (March 2007): 6.

Question: What problems could this trigger and what sort of corrective action would you recommend?

TEST PREPPER 7.5

ANSWERS CAN BE FOUND ON P. 191

True or False?

_____ 1. Organizational culture is the "social glue" that binds an organization's members together.

_____ 2. Among the common characteristics of organizational cultures are being collective, emotionally charged, and future focused.

_____ 3. Actual behavior is what really counts in organizational culture, not stories of past situations.

_____ 4. Orientation is the first step in the socialization process.

Multiple Choice

_____ 5. The label that best matches the term organizational values is
   a. shared beliefs.
   b. hierarchy.
   c. instrumental values.
   d. informal authority.
   e. official policy.

_____ 6. According to a study of accounting firms, which type of organizational culture was associated with lower turnover rates?
   a. Professional
   b. Formally structured
   c. Ethical
   d. People-friendly
   e. Skill-oriented

_____ 7. Which process transforms organizational outsiders into accepted insiders?
   a. Recruitment
   b. Organizational socialization
   c. Self-management
   d. Behavior modification
   e. Staffing

_____ 8. _____ have been called "social roadmaps" in organizational socialization.
   a. Values
   b. Regulations
   c. Stories
   d. Policies
   e. Norms

_____ 9. Frank, the owner of a printing company, recently noticed a lack of communication between the graphic designers and the marketing people. This problem represents which symptom of a weak organizational culture?
   a. Ingrown subcultures
   b. Fragmentation/inconsistency
   c. Inward focus
   d. Morale problems
   e. Groupthink

Online Study Center
ACE the Test
ACE Practice Tests 7.5

BEST PRACTICES

Team Building = Community Building for This Las Vegas Company

The yuletide season isn't just about bonus checks and boozy office parties: It's also about giving back. At Las Vegas-based real estate developer Focus Property Group, CEO John Ritter wanted his staff to truly get into the holiday spirit, so he created Community 911, a charity competition that pits teams of employees against one another and blends in elements of reality TV shows like *American Idol* and *Survivor*. Last year the four employee teams raised $2.1 million and donated 4,100 hours to help fund projects for local charities. Today the groups are putting that money to good use. Team Mended Hearts . . . is renovating a 30-bed shelter for abused kids. "We really wanted to do something that all the employees could get behind," Ritter says.

Source: Excerpted from Mary Jane Irwin, "Spreading Holiday Cheer," *Business 2.0,* 7 (December 2006): 149.

CLOSING CASE STUDY

A Country Called Microsoft

. . . I spent several weeks trying to learn what it was like to work at Microsoft. I visited the company, and, at Microsoft's invitation, I spent time with the teams working on electronic books, or eBooks, and on the TabletPC, a flat pen-based computer that might be the Holy Grail of computer design and is a pet project of Bill Gates. I also spoke to researchers and programmers in other parts of the company, to so-called temporary workers, and to former employees as well. . . .

Over and over people there told me a story that I came to think of as the story of the secret garden: Once I was lost, they said; I did not fit in; then I found the key to the magical garden of Microsoft, where I had belonged in the first place.

"The reason I hated Florida," says Alex Loeb, general manager of the TabletPC group and a 12-year Microsoft employee, "was that I was seen as an upstart young woman who wasn't old enough or male enough to make decisions. Microsoft just took me as me." For a huge corporation, Microsoft is highly accepting of nonconformity, and there are a lot of people at Microsoft for whom being there is the key to being themselves. This is certainly true of the software tester I spoke with who comes to work every day dressed in extravagant Victorian outfits, and of the star programmer who keeps his given name a secret from colleagues and insists that he be called simply J. Microsoft's a tesseract; behind the door is a whole big world of similarly smart people, many of whom have made the decision that Being Microsoft trumps all. Says Bill Hill, a researcher who left Scotland six years ago to work at Microsoft: "Microsoft is a country. I moved here, and it is home to me."

Saying that Microsoft is a country might be going a little far, but only a little. It still lacks its own language, but it undoubtedly has its own mores and values, all of which stem from the conviction of its citizens that they are part of a new, very special secular elect. Behind the door to the secret garden is a place designed to constantly reinforce the belief in its employees—in a way in which few corporations bother to anymore—that they are different. Almost all of Microsoft's employees have their own office, and the company can feel hushed

in the way that one imagines the dusty hallways of the State Department must be hushed—only more so, because in this e-mail culture, the phones never ring. The public atriums are hung with contemporary paintings—not overly soothing "corporate" art or inspirational art, but real art that gets loaned to real museums. It is also, surprisingly, a place with a collegial (or, better, collegiate) sense of fun. When people go off on vacation, their colleagues take the trouble to welcome them back by filling their office with Styrofoam peanuts, covering it with spider webs, or even (as in one fairly recent Microsoft escapade) converting it into a miniature farm complete with potbellied pig.

All this emphasizes the distinction of working at Microsoft as opposed to working at either stodgy old-economy companies or the new-economy riffraff that happily pack their workers into "open offices," where they brush elbows as if at a crowded formal dinner. And yet strangely none of this veneer is central. It's just the icing on the cake of what anybody who spends much time at Microsoft, or talking in depth to people who work there, will recognize as the Microsoft way of thinking. . . .

"Bill" is famous for telling people that whatever they just told him is the stupidest thing he ever heard. This is pretty much the opposite of how the rest of Microsoft actually works. Microsoft managers do occasionally tell stories of pounding a table to get their way, but the intent of the tale is cautionary. More often—actually, incessantly—they talk of getting "buy-in," Microsoft slang for the cooperation of their colleagues. They argue and cajole. They publish white papers. They use sneaky tricks; when the eBooks team was getting started, the new managers set up a Website on the company intranet describing the project. By secretly tracking the e-mail addresses of visitors they compiled a list of Microsofters they could recruit. In these ways they do get buy-in, because if they don't, their projects just fall flat. . . .

It turns out that the more you talk to people at Microsoft, the more you find that these people who seem so spectacularly different on the surface all share a distinct ethos that transcends stock options or hours spent on their office couches or practical jokes. . . . And, yup, this ethos is even more important to Microsoft than the average IQ of its employees. It embodies a few very big concepts about work and life. It's this set of values that is the key to understanding life in the innermost sanctum of the Information Age. And it's the evolution of these values that will define what Microsoft will become in the future.

The cornerstone of the Microsoft ethos is the unwavering belief in *the moral value of zapping bugs and shipping products.* Like other Brahmin societies, Microsoft (certainly the Brahmin society of the Information Age) puts a premium on doing things that are hard, and doing them the hard way; this makes one a better person and justifies one's place in the privileged class. The American upper class used to send its youth on freezing swims and mountaineering expeditions to build moral character. At Microsoft, moral fiber is believed to grow out of interminable discussion of the smallest details of software features, painful rounds of compromise, and unbelievably tedious sessions of categorizing hundreds of software bugs. Going through this process strengthens the intellect, hones the passions, and fortifies character.

The primary currency of prestige at Microsoft is the SHIP-IT plaque, given to every member of a team that has successfully shipped a product to the market. Outsiders who notice this—and virtually everyone does, in part because Microsoft's PR machinery points it out—generally use it as evidence of Microsoftian drive, resolve, go-getterhood, and all that good stuff.

That's true, but there's more to it than that. The reality of software development in a huge corporation like Microsoft is that a substantial portion of the work involves days of boredom punctuated by hours of tedium. For instance, anybody who observes a "triage" session, in which developers and testers (the lowest rung in the Microsoft hierarchy) convene to enumerate and evaluate hundreds of bugs and potential bugs,

quickly sees that the level of gut-wrenching excitement falls as the lines of code rise. In the powerhouse applications group, whole teams are charged with missions like getting Microsoft Word to start three seconds faster. This is not the heady air of pure, research-driven science. Says Jim Gray, a Microsoft engineer who spent time at the University of California, Berkeley, "The attitude at Berkeley is primarily focused on creating ideas. Microsoft has some of that, but it's much more focused on the 99% perspiration."

That 99% perspiration isn't intuitively appealing, but in the world-view of the Microsoft Brahmin, perspiration is the vehicle of moral uplift. Even Bert Keely, the prime technical visionary behind the TabletPC, sitting in an office filled with ebony cubes engraved with the titles of patents he's applied for at Microsoft, pooh-poohs the significance of the creative spark that other organizations value so highly. "Creativity is highly regarded for a very short time, but that's not how people rank each other," says Keely. "The primary thing is to ship a product. Before you've done it, you're suspect. It involves taking this passion of yours and running it through a humiliating, exhausting process. You can't believe how many ego-deflating compromises people have to make to get it out. Some have quit. Others have made lifelong enemies." We can safely assume that the ones who quit are, in the Microsoft cosmology, *losers.*

Source: Mark Gimein, "Smart Is Not Enough," *Fortune,* January 8, 2001, pp. 124–136. Copyright © 2001 Time Inc. All rights reserved.

Case Questions

1. Is Microsoft mechanistic or organic? Explain. Is this an advantage or disadvantage for Microsoft? Explain.
2. How many of the six characteristics of organizational cultures are evident in the Microsoft case? Explain.
3. What organizational values are apparent in this case?
4. Would you like to work for Microsoft? Why or why not?

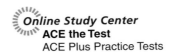

Online Study Center
ACE the Test
ACE Plus Practice Tests

Online Study Center
Improve Your Grade
Learning Objective Review
Audio Chapter Review
Audio Chapter Quiz
Study Guide to Go

LEARNING OBJECTIVE REVIEW

1 *Identify and describe four characteristics common to all organizations, and explain the time dimension of organizational effectiveness.*

- Whatever their purpose, all organizations must have four characteristics to exist:
  - Coordination of effort
  - Common goal or purpose
  - Division of labor
  - Hierarchy of authority
- As there is no one criterion for organizational effectiveness, both for-profit and nonprofit organizations must satisfy different effectiveness criteria in the near, intermediate, and distant future.
- An effective organization should:
  - Be effective, efficient, and satisfying in the near term
  - Be adaptive and developing in the intermediate term
  - Ultimately survive in the long term

2 *Explain the concept of contingency organization design, distinguish between mechanistic and organic organizations, and identify the basic departmentalization formats.*

- Contingency design structures the organization to fit situational demands.
- Contingency advocates contend that there is no one best organizational setup for all situations.
- Diagnosing the degree of environmental uncertainty is an important first step in contingency design.
- Burns and Stalker discovered that:
  - Mechanistic (rigid and bureaucratic) organizations are effective when the environment is relatively stable
  - Organic (flexible and adaptable) organizations are best when unstable conditions prevail

- There are five basic departmentalization formats, usually combined in various ways:
  - Functional (the most common approach)
  - Product-service
  - Geographic location
  - Customer classification
  - Work-flow process

3 *Define the term* delegation, *and list at least five common barriers to delegation.*

- Delegation of authority, although generally resisted for a variety of reasons, is crucial to decentralization.
- Effective delegation permits managers to tackle higher priority duties while helping to train and develop lower-level managers.
- Delegation varies in degree but never means abdicating primary responsibility.
- Successful delegation requires plenty of initiative from lower-level managers.
- Barriers to delegation include:
  - Doing everything yourself
  - Lack of confidence and trust in employees
  - Low self-confidence
  - Fear of being called lazy
  - Vague job definition
  - Fear of competition from those below
  - Not wanting to risk depending on others
  - Lack of early warning signs of problems with delegated duties
  - Poor role models who do not delegate

4 *Explain how the traditional pyramid organization is being reshaped.*

- Many factors, with global competition leading the way, are forcing management to reshape the traditional pyramid bureaucracy.
- These new organizations are characterized by fewer layers, extensive use of teams, and manageably small subunits.
- Three emerging organizational configurations are the hourglass organization, the cluster organization, and virtual organizations. Each has its own potentials and pitfalls.

5 *Describe at least three characteristics of organizational cultures, and explain the cultural significance of stories.*

- Organizational culture is the "social glue" that binds people together through shared symbols, language, stories, and practices.
- Organizational cultures can commonly be characterized as:
  - Collective
  - Emotionally charged
  - Historically based
  - Inherently symbolic
  - Dynamic
  - Inherently fuzzy (or ambiguous)
- Diverse outsiders are transformed into accepted insiders through the process of organizational socialization.
- Orientations and stories are powerful and lasting socialization techniques. Stories have been called social roadmaps that guide employees in certain directions.

TEST PREPPER ANSWERS

▶ **1.1**
1. F   2. T   3. T   4. F   5. a   6. a   7. b
8. d

▶ **1.2**
1. T   2. T   3. F   4. F   5. F   6. T   7. c
8. b   9. c   10. e   11. d

▶ **1.3**
1. F   2. T   3. F   4. d   5. c   6. e

▶ **1.4**
1. F   2. F   3. T   4. e   5. d   6. b

▶ **1.5**
1. T   2. F   3. F   4. T   5. a   6. d   7. b
8. c   9. a

Online Study Center RESOURCES

Prepare for Class, Improve Your Grade, and ACE the Test. Student Achievement Series resources include:

ACE Practice Tests
Audio Chapter Quizzes
Audio Chapter Reviews
Career Snapshots
Chapter Glossaries
Chapter Outlines

Crossword Puzzles
Decision Case Questions
Ethical Hot Seat Exercises
Flashcards
Hands-on Exercises

Hangman
Key Issue Expansion
Learning Objective Reviews
Study Guide to Go
Visual Glossaries

To access these learning and study tools, go to **college.hmco.com/pic/kreitnerSASfound**.

8 Maintaining Control and Improving Quality

These Costco shoppers in Los Angeles need big carts for the big savings they've come to expect from the admired retailer.

1 ▶ *Describe three types of control, and identify the components common to all control systems.*

2 ▶ *Identify five types of product quality, explain how providing a service differs from manufacturing a product, and list the five service-quality dimensions.*

3 ▶ *Define total quality management (TQM), discuss the basic TQM principles, and describe at least three of the seven TQM process improvement tools.*

> *"Our business is so dynamic, you have to get everyone to think, to be strategic, to create, to innovate, and to always think about what our customers and suppliers are looking for from us."*[1]
>
> —Cheryl Rosner, President, Hotels.com

Chapter Outline

Online Study Center
Prepare for Class
Chapter Outline

4 *Explain how Deming's PDCA cycle can improve the overall management process, and identify at least four of Deming's famous 14 points.*

Costco's Winning Formula: "Down in the Aisles"

If [CEO] Jim Sinegal is Costco's general, his 488 warehouse managers are field commanders. With the average warehouse generating $128 million in sales a year, they effectively run their own small companies. Humberto "Berto" Yniguez heads the 139,000-square-foot warehouse in Marina Del Rey, Calif., which employs about 500 people and moves $285 million of product a year—the highest-grossing store in the U.S. (Actually, it's No. 2, No. 1 is in Honolulu, where everything's so expensive you'd have to pay shoppers to stay away from Costco. So we're sticking with Berto.) "His store hums," says Sinegal.

That hum does not happen by chance. Yniguez is a model student of Sinegal's approach to retailing. Superstars at Costco have the usual skills recruiters look for: people skills, smarts. A yen for crisis management is a plus. Yniguez has that down: A brief stint as a police officer in his early 20s taught him how to settle disputes

Online Study Center college.hmco.com/pic/kreitnerSASfound

Online Study Center
Prepare for Class
Chapter Glossary

Improve Your Grade
Flashcards
Hangman
Crossword Puzzles

control Taking preventive or corrective actions to keep things on track.

quickly, which comes in handy when you're dealing with wild-eyed coupon clippers all day.

But Sinegal looks for something else in his employees too: that rare ability to know just what item will sell best in a given spot at a given time. It's more than just pushing candy near Halloween or air conditioners during a heat wave. "Berto's a great merchant," says Sinegal. "When you walk into his warehouse, you feel like you are enveloped in merchandise. It's all around you." And you have to know your customers: "A lot of our members are affluent, and they have higher expectations," Yniguez says. "I could sell a $45,000 diamond in this building, but it would not sell elsewhere."

Yniguez's merchandising ideas often take root elsewhere, like when he started selling large plants to local real estate developers at up to $350 a pop. To keep the plants from cluttering the sales floor, Yniguez leaves them in the parking lot for same-day pickup. Now a handful of other Costco's are doing the same—not surprising, given that seven of his former assistants are running their own warehouses. The student, in turn, becomes the teacher. "Without folks like Berto, we fail," Sinegal says. "It's that simple."[2] ■

As Costco's Berto Yniguez quickly learned, from his boss Jim Sinegal, a legendary discount retailer, great service organizations know how to get the little details right. No matter how well conceived, strategies and plans are no guarantee of organizational success in today's service economy. Those plans need to be carried out by skilled and motivated employees amid changing circumstances. Adjustments and corrective action are necessary. Thus, this chapter covers the fundamentals of organizational control and explores product and service quality.

FUNDAMENTALS OF ORGANIZATIONAL CONTROL

▶ 1 *Describe three types of control, and identify the components common to all control systems.*

The word *control* suggests the operations of checking, testing, regulating, verifying, or adjusting. As a management function, **control** is the process of taking the necessary preventive or corrective actions to ensure that the organization's mission and objectives are accomplished as effectively and efficiently as possible. Objectives are yardsticks against which actual performance can be measured. If actual performance is consistent with the appropriate objective, things will proceed as planned. If not, changes must be made. Successful managers detect (and even anticipate) deviations from desirable standards and make appropriate adjustments.[3] Those adjustments can range from ordering more raw materials to overhauling a production line; from discarding an unnecessary procedure to hiring additional personnel; from containing an unexpected crisis to firing a defrauder. Although the possible adjustments exercised as part of the control function are countless, the purpose of the control function is always the same: *get the job done despite environmental, organizational, and behavioral obstacles and uncertainties.*

Types of Control

Every open system processes inputs from the surrounding environment to produce a unique set of outputs. Natural open systems, such as the human body, are kept in life-sustaining balance through automatic feedback mechanisms. In contrast, artificial open systems, such as organizations, do not have automatic controls. Instead, they require constant monitoring and adjustment to control for deviations from standards. Figure 8.1 illustrates the control function. Notice the three different types of control: feedforward, concurrent, and feedback.

Feedforward Control

According to two early proponents of feedforward control, "the only way [managers] can exercise control effectively is to see the problems coming in time to do something about them."[4] **Feedforward control** is the active anticipation of problems and their timely prevention, rather than after-the-fact reaction. Carpenters have their own instructive version of feedforward control: "Measure twice, cut once." It is important to note that planning and feedforward control are two related but different processes. Planning answers the question "Where are we going and how will we get there?" Feedforward control addresses the issue "What can we do ahead of time to help our plan succeed?" *Preventive maintenance* on machinery and equipment and *due diligence* also qualify as feedforward control. In today's global economy, it is especially important to perform due diligence with far-flung suppliers and vendors. A prime example comes from Trieste, Italy, where Illycafé uses rigorous feedforward control to produce world-class espresso coffee beans:

> ... beans endure 114 quality tests, with samples eyeballed and scratched—and every bean put through a laser-driven sorting machine that rejects one bean before and after any defective ones just for good measure. Rooting out that one bad bean is essential because it can spoil an entire tin.[5]

On a more personal level, think of due diligence as refusing to go on a blind date until you have first researched the person's background and reputation.

Of the three types of control, managers tend to do the poorest job with feedforward control. For instance, poor feedforward control proved very costly—in terms of both money and reputation—for Sony when a suspected fire hazard forced the Japanese firm to recall 10 million laptop computer batteries at a cost of $429 million in 2006.[6]

feedforward control Active anticipation and prevention of problems, rather than passive reaction.

FIGURE 8.1

Three Types of Control

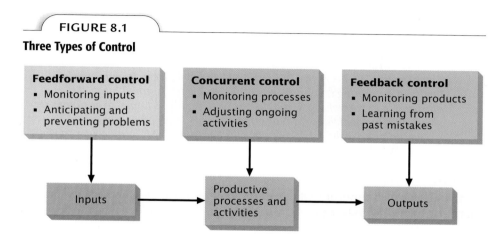

If ever there was a need for feedforward control, this is it! Malden Mill's giant circular knitting machine in Lawrence, Massachusetts, produces tubes of polyester fabric used to make Polartec garments for rugged outdoor wear. Feedforward control, the anticipation and prevention of problems, is required to make sure the automatic equipment is maintained and loaded properly. If not, costly batches of scrap material would pile up quickly.

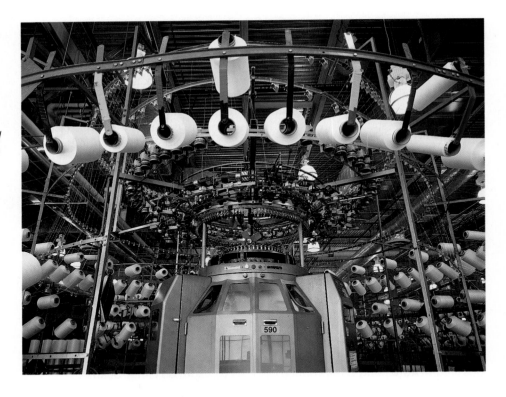

Concurrent Control

concurrent control   Monitoring and adjusting ongoing activities and processes.

This second type of control might well be called real-time control because it deals with the present rather than the future or past. **Concurrent control** involves monitoring and adjusting ongoing activities and processes to ensure that they comply with standards. You exercise a form of concurrent control in the shower when you try to adjust the water temperature as it pours over you. Of course, feedforward control (getting the water temperature just right *before* getting into the shower) reduces the chances of getting scalded or chilled. Surgeons exercise concurrent control when they help team members with difficult tasks in the operating room. As a sign of things to come, consider this high-tech example of concurrent control:

> EMC [a Massachusetts data storage company] likes to call it "service and support mind reading." Sensors that are built into its storage systems monitor things such as temperature, vibration, and tiny fluctuations in power, as well as unusual patterns in the way data is being stored and retrieved—over 1,000 diagnostics in all. Every two hours, an EMC system checks its own state of health. If everything is running smoothly, the log file is stored away. If the machine spots something that it doesn't like, it "phones home" to customer service over a line dedicated for that purpose.
>
> Every day, an average of 3,500 calls for help reach EMC's call center in Hopkinton. But it's not people who are calling in to ask for help—it's machines.[7]

Feedback Control

feedback control   Checking a completed activity and learning from mistakes.

Feedback control is gathering information about a completed activity, evaluating that information, and taking steps to improve similar activities in the future. Feedback control permits managers to use information on past performance to bring future performance in line with planned objectives and acceptable standards. For example, by monitoring complaints from discharged patients about billing errors, a hospital's comptroller learns about problems in the billing process.[8] Critics of feedback control say it is like closing the gate after the horse is gone. Because corrective action is taken after the fact, costs tend to pile up quickly, and problems and deviations persist.

On the positive side, feedback control tests the quality and validity of objectives and standards. Objectives that have been found to be impossible to attain should be made more reasonable. Those that prove too easy need to be toughened. A bank's loan officer, for example, may discover that too much potentially profitable business is being turned away because the criteria for granting credit are too strict. By exercising feedback control—loosening the credit standards loan applicants must meet—the bank's lending operation can be made more profitable. Of course, if this adjustment leads to a default rate that eats up the additional profits, the credit criteria may need yet another round of feedback control.

In summary, successful managers exercise all three types of control in today's complex organizations. Feedforward control helps managers avoid mistakes in the first place; concurrent control enables them to catch mistakes as they are being made; feedback control keeps them from repeating past mistakes. Interaction and a workable balance among the three types of control are desirable.

Components of Organizational Control Systems

The owner-manager of a small business such as a dry-cleaning establishment can keep things under control by personally overseeing operations and making necessary adjustments. An electrician can be called in to fix a broken pressing machine, poor workmanship can be improved through coaching, a customer's complaint can be handled immediately, or a shortage of change in the cash register can be remedied. A small organization directed by a single, highly motivated individual with expert knowledge of all aspects of the operation represents the ideal control situation.[9] Unfortunately, the size and complexity of most productive organizations have made the idea of firsthand control by a single person obsolete. Consequently, multilevel, multidimensional organizational control systems have evolved. Researchers have shed some needed light on the mechanics of complex organizational control systems by identifying seven distinct control subsystems:

1. *Strategic plans:* qualitative analyses of the company's position within the industry
2. *Long-range plans:* typically, five-year financial projections
3. *Annual operating budgets:* annual estimates of profit, expenses, and financial indicators
4. *Statistical reports:* quarterly, monthly, or weekly nonfinancial statistical summaries of key indicators such as orders received and personnel surpluses or shortages
5. *Performance appraisals:* evaluation of employees through the use of management by objectives (MBO) or rating scales
6. *Policies and procedures:* organizational and departmental standard operating procedures that are referred to on an as-needed basis
7. *Cultural control:* employees guided by company legends and stories and coworker peer pressure through glances, comments, or ridicule[10]

Online Study Center
Improve Your Grade
Visual Glossary 8.1

REALITY CHECK 8.1

"A month after one of the biggest pet-food recalls in history, a leading pet-food maker says it's taking steps to lessen the chance of it happening again.

"Procter & Gamble, owner of the Iams and Eukanuba brands, has set out its 'promise' to consumers that it will, in effect, exert more control over Menu Foods, the Canadian company that makes the Iams and Eukanuba wet foods for P&G."

Source: Julie Schmit, "P&G Vows More Control of Menu Foods," *USA Today* (April 19, 2007): 2B.

Question: What roles do feedforward and feedback control play in this case?

It's a hard life being a crash-test dummy. Thanks to the constant abuse they take, each of us is safer. Why? Feedback from the annual crash test motivated auto and truck manufacturers to design and build the safest and highest-quality motor vehicles ever. In fact, when the Insurance Institute for Highway Safety (IIHS) began its tests in 1995, many vehicles performed so poorly the dummies had to be cut out of the mangled wrecks. By 2002, every vehicle tested by IIHS achieved at least a "good" rating, for the first time ever. Now that's product quality we all can live with!

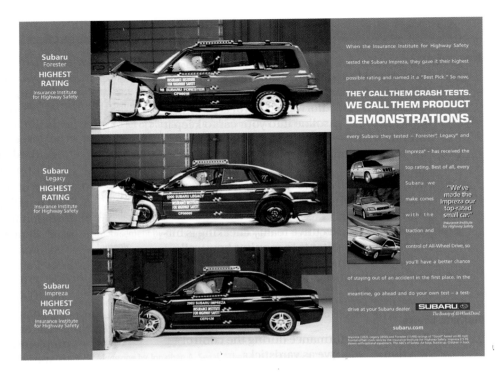

passing fad. Tom Peters, the well-known management writer and consultant, offered this instructive perspective in a recent question-and-answer session:

> *Q: Do you think the bloom is off the quality movement?*
>
> *A: I think it's in the genes. The quality movement has gone from hype to something people do. The average American manager, whether she or he is in accounting or purchasing or engineering, takes for granted that quality is a major thing you think about in life. You can't compete with shabby products.*[24]

On a more personal level, just ask anyone who has a surgically implanted medical device such as a heart pacemaker, arterial stent, or artificial joint what they think about the importance of product and service quality.[25] The balance of this chapter builds a foundation of understanding about quality. The following questions will be answered: How are product and service quality defined? What does total quality management (TQM) involve? What is Deming management?

Defining Quality

quality Conformance to requirements.

According to quality expert Philip Crosby, the basic definition of **quality** is "conformance to requirements."[26] But whose requirements? The sound quality of a CD player may seem flawless to its new owner, adequate to the engineer who helped design it, and terrible to an accomplished musician. In regard to *service* quality, being put on hold for 30 seconds when calling a computer company's hot line may be acceptable for one person but very irritating for another. Because quality is much more than a simple either/or proposition, both product and service quality need to be analyzed. To do this, we will explore five types of product quality, the unique challenges faced by service organizations, and the ways in which consumers judge service quality.

Five Types of Product Quality

Other specialists in the field have refined Crosby's general perspective by identifying at least five different types of product quality: transcendent, product-based, user-based, manufacturing-based, and value-based.[27] Each represents a unique and useful perspective on product quality.

Transcendent Quality

Inherent value or innate excellence is apparent to the individual. Observing people's varied reactions to pieces of art in a museum is a good way to appreciate the subjectiveness of this type of quality. Beauty, as they say, is in the eye of the beholder.

Product-Based Quality

The presence or absence of a given product attribute is the primary determinant of this type of quality. Soft tissues, rough sandpaper, flawless glass, sweet candy, and crunchy granola signify product-based quality in very different ways.

User-Based Quality

Here, the quality of a product is determined by its ability to meet the user's expectations. Does it get the job done? Is it reliable? Customer satisfaction surveys conducted by *Consumer Reports* magazine[28] give smart shoppers valuable input about user-based quality.

Manufacturing-Based Quality

How well does the product conform to its design specifications or blueprint? The closer the match between the intended product and the actual one, the higher the quality. Car doors designed to close easily, quietly, and snugly are high quality if they do so. This category corresponds to Crosby's "conformance to requirements" definition of quality.

Value-Based Quality

When you hear someone say, "I got a lot for my money," the speaker is describing value-based quality. Cost-benefit relationships are very subjective because they derive from human perception and personal preferences. About value, *Fortune* magazine observed: "The concept can be nebulous because each buyer assesses value individually. In the end, value is simply giving customers what they want at a price they consider fair."[29] Wal-Mart's "everyday low price" strategy successfully exploits this important type of product quality.

Unique Challenges for Service Providers

Services are a rapidly growing and increasingly important part of today's global economy. Startling evidence of this has appeared in recent *Fortune* 500 lists of the largest U.S. companies by sales revenue. In either the number one spot or number two spot has been Wal-Mart. A pure service business finally reached the top of a list long dominated by petroleum refiners and automobile companies. Wal-Mart, with annual revenues of over $315 billion, has more than 1.8 million employees.[30] (If Wal-Mart were a city, it would rank among the ten largest cities in the United States.) Indeed, the vast majority of the U.S. labor force now works in the service sector. *USA Today* offered this historical perspective:

REALITY CHECK 8.2

"Dell transformed buying computers over the Internet from a risky to a reliable experience. When it extended that set of procedures to the selection and purchase of expensive plasma HDTV sets, however, it disappointed. Dell did an effective job of creating positive customer expectations, but they turned out to be better fulfilled by the in-person sales force at Best Buy."

Source: Christopher Meyer and Andre Schwager, "Understanding Customer Experience," *Harvard Business Review,* 85 (February 2007): 120.

Questions: Best Buy did a better job with which type of product quality? Generally speaking, which type of quality ranks highest with you?

Fifty years ago, a third of U.S. employees worked in factories, making everything from clothing to lipstick to cars. Today, a little more than one-tenth of the nation's 131 million workers are employed by manufacturing firms. Four-fifths are in services.[31]

Because services are customer-driven, pleasing the customer is more important than ever.[32] Experts say it costs five times more to win a new customer than it does to keep an existing one.[33] Still, U.S. companies lose an average of about 20 percent of their customers each year.[34] Service-quality strategists emphasize that it is no longer enough simply to satisfy the customer. The strategic service challenge today is to *anticipate* and *exceed* the customer's expectations. Many managers of service operations regard service quality and customer satisfaction as an ethical responsibility. Indeed, "hospital errors kill as many as 100,000 people every year, according to the national Academy of Sciences Institute of Medicine"[35] (see the Closing Case Study on page 218).

To varying extents, virtually every organization is a service organization. Pure service organizations such as day-care centers and manufacturers providing delivery and installation services face similar challenges. Specifically, they need to understand and manage five distinctive service characteristics:[36]

1. *Customers participate directly in the production process.* Although people do not go to the factory to help build the cars and refrigerators they eventually buy, they do need to be present when their hair is styled or a broken bone is set.
2. *Services are consumed immediately and cannot be stored.* Hairstylists cannot store up a supply of haircuts in the same way electronics manufacturer Intel can amass an inventory of computer chips.
3. *Services are provided where and when the customer desires.* McDonald's does more business by building thousands of restaurants in convenient locations than it would if everyone had to travel to its Oakbrook, Illinois, headquarters to get a Big Mac and fries. Accommodating customers' sometimes odd schedules is a fact of life for service providers. Insurance salespersons generally work evenings and weekends during their clients' leisure periods.
4. *Services tend to be labor-intensive.* Although skilled labor has been replaced by machines such as automatic bank tellers in some service jobs, most services are provided by people to customers face to face. Consequently, the morale and social skills of service employees are vitally important. In fact, customer service has been called a *performing art* requiring a good deal of "emotional labor."[37] It isn't easy to look happy and work hard for an angry customer when you're having a bad day; but good customer service demands it.
5. *Services are intangible.* Objectively measuring an intangible service is more difficult than measuring a tangible good, but it is nonetheless necessary. For example, this is how a Pennsylvania electrical parts maker measures key services. During one observation period, the company reportedly shipped 93 percent of its orders on time and averaged a delay of 3.5 seconds in answering phone calls from customers.[38]

Because customers are more intimately involved in the service-delivery process than in the manufacturing process, we need to go directly to the customer for service-quality criteria. As service-quality experts tell us:

Quality control of a service entails watching a process unfold and evaluating it against the consumer's judgment. The only completely valid standard of comparison is the customer's level of satisfaction. That's a perception—something appreciably more slippery to measure than the physical dimensions of a product.[39]

So how do consumers judge service quality?

Defining Service Quality

Researchers at Texas A&M University uncovered valuable insights about customers' perceptions of service quality.[40] They surveyed hundreds of customers of various types of service organizations. The following five service-quality dimensions emerged (*Learning tip*: remember them with the acronym RATER).[41] Customers apparently judge the quality of each service transaction in terms of these five dimensions:

R *Reliability* (dependable, accurate, consistent)
A *Assurance* (courteous, able, trustworthy employees)
T *Tangibles* (appearance of facilities, equipment, personnel)
E *Empathy* (caring, individualized attention to customers)
R *Responsiveness* (prompt service and help for customers)

Which of the five RATER dimensions is most important to you? In the Texas A&M study, *reliability* was the most important dimension of service quality, regardless of the type of service involved. Anyone who has waited impatiently for an overdue airplane knows firsthand the central importance of service reliability.[42]

Specific ways to improve product and service quality are presented throughout the balance of this chapter (for example, see Best Practices on page 218).

TEST PREPPER 8.2

ANSWERS CAN BE FOUND ON P. 221

True or False?

_____ 1. According to Philip Crosby, "conformance to requirements" is the basic definition of quality.
_____ 2. Another name for value-based quality is manufacturing-based quality.
_____ 3. Because they are intangible, services cannot be measured.
_____ 4. "Assurance" was identified by Texas A&M researchers as one of the five service quality dimensions.

Multiple Choice

_____ 5. Which of the following is *not* a product quality type?
   a. Feature-based quality
   b. Transcendent quality
   c. Product-based quality
   d. User-based quality
   e. Value-based quality

_____ 6. When a textile manufacturing manager does a cost-benefit analysis on a new state-of-the-art stitching machine, the type of product quality at issue is
   a. value-based.
   b. product-based.
   c. user-based.
   d. manufacturing-based.
   e. transcendent.

_____ 7. The RATER service-quality dimension that relates to the provision of caring and individualized attention to customers is
   a. assurance.
   b. reliability.
   c. responsiveness.
   d. professionalism.
   e. empathy.

Online Study Center
ACE the Test
ACE Practice Tests 8.2

Online Study Center college.hmco.com/pic/kreitnerSASfound

AN INTRODUCTION TO
TOTAL QUALITY MANAGEMENT (TQM)

 Define total quality management (TQM), *discuss the basic TQM principles, and describe at least three of the seven TQM process improvement tools.*

Definitions of total quality management (TQM) are many and varied, which is not surprising for an area that has been subject to such intense discussion and debate in recent years.[43] For our present purposes, **total quality management (TQM)** is defined as creating an organizational culture that is committed to the continuous improvement of skills, teamwork, processes, product and service quality, and customer satisfaction.[44] Consultant Richard Schonberger's shorthand definition calls TQM "continuous, customer-centered, employee-driven improvement."[45]

Our definition of TQM is anchored to *organizational culture* because successful TQM is deeply embedded in virtually every aspect of organizational life. As discussed in detail in Chapter 7, an organization's culture encompasses all the assumptions that its employees take for granted about how people should think and act. In other words, personal commitment to systematic continuous improvement needs to become an everyday matter of "that's just the way we do things here." For example, Dr. Frank P. Carrubba, chief technical officer at Philips, the huge Dutch electronics firm, believes it is never too early to get people thinking about quality:

> *"It is not good enough to invent something new," he says. "An elegant result that is not strategic or reproducible in a reliable, high-quality way is not worth much to the customer. Quality has to begin in research. We have to invent in an environment that reflects the same quality we want to achieve throughout the company."*[46]

As might be expected with a topic that received so much attention so quickly, some unrealistic expectations were created. Unrealistic expectations inevitably lead to disappointment and the need for a new quick fix.[47] However, managers who have realistic expectations about the deep and long-term commitment necessary for successful TQM can make it work. TQM can have a positive impact if managers understand and enact these four principles of TQM:

1. Do it right the first time.
2. Be customer-centered.
3. Make continuous improvement a way of life.
4. Build teamwork and empowerment.[48]

Let us examine each of these TQM principles.

1. Do It Right the First Time

As mentioned in Chapter 1, the trend in quality has been toward designing and building quality into the product. This approach is much less costly than fixing or throwing away substandard parts and finished products. Ford Motor Company has learned the first lesson of TQM the hard way, not only in the Firestone tire debacle, but in the following more recent case as well: "Ford Motor must replace defective ignition devices on 2 million California vehicles prone to stalling, a judge ruled. . . . The order could cost Ford $300 million."[49] Schonberger, who has studied many

---

total quality management (TQM) Creating an organizational culture committed to continuous improvement in every regard.

Japanese and U.S. factories firsthand, contends that "errors, if any, should be caught and corrected at the source, i.e., where the work is performed."[50] At Dell, for example, "each PC or other product is built by one person, and it can be tracked back to that person if something goes wrong, making individuals accountable and keeping quality high."[51] Comprehensive training in TQM tools and statistical process control is essential if employees are to accept personal responsibility for quality improvement.

2. Be Customer-Centered

Everyone has one or more customers in a TQM organization. They may be internal or external customers. **Internal customers** are other members of the organization who rely on *your* work to get *their* job done.[52] For example, a corporate lawyer employed by Marriott does not directly serve the hotel chain's customers by changing beds, serving meals, or carrying luggage. But that lawyer has an *internal* customer when a Marriott manager needs to be defended in court. Boston Consulting Group, meanwhile, spares no expense in serving its *internal* customers:

> Knowledge really is power. Arrive at this management consultant firm with a B.A. degree, and the firm will send you to a top institution for an MBA, pick up the tuition bill, and double your salary if you agree to stay on.[53]

Regarding external customers, TQM requires all employees who deal directly with outsiders to be customer-centered (see Best Practices on page 218). Being **customer-centered** means:

1. Anticipating the customer's needs
2. Listening to the customer
3. Learning how to satisfy the customer
4. Responding appropriately to the customer

Listening to the customer is a major stumbling block for many companies. But at profitable Southwest Airlines, listening to the customer is practically a religion. "Frequent fliers sit in with personnel managers to interview and evaluate prospective flight attendants. They also participate in focus groups to help gauge response to new services or solicit ideas for improving old ones."[54] Appropriate responses depend upon the specific nature of the business.[55] For example, Table 8.2 lists good and bad customer service behaviors at a U.S. supermarket chain. Notice how service-quality training led to very different patterns of behavior for the different jobs.

internal customer   Anyone in your organization who cannot do a good job unless you do a good job.

customer-centered   Satisfying the customer's needs by anticipating, listening, and responding.

TABLE 8.2

Turning a Supermarket into a Customer-Centered Organization

Employees	Behaviors before the change	Behaviors after the change
Bag packers	Ignore customers Lack of packing standards	Greet customers Respond to customers Ask for customers' preference
Cashiers	Ignore customers Lack of eye contact	Greet customers Respond to customers Assist customers Speak clearly Call customers by name
Shelf stockers	Ignore customers Don't know store	Respond to customers Help customers with correct product location information Knowledgeable about product location
Department workers	Ignore customers Limited knowledge	Respond to customers Know products Know store
Department managers	Ignore customers Ignore workers	Respond to customers Reward employees for responding to customers
Store managers	Ignore customers Stay in booth	Respond to customers Reward employees for service Appraise employees on customer service

Source: Reprinted from *Organizational Dynamics*, Vol. 21, by Randall S. Schuler, "Strategic Human Resource Management: Linking the People with the Strategic Needs of the Business," Exhibit 4, Copyright © 1992, with permission from Elsevier.

Vague requests to "be nice to the customer" are useless in TQM organizations. *Behavior*, not good intentions, is what really matters. Desirable behavior needs to be strengthened with *positive reinforcement*. A good role model in this regard is Internet equipment giant Cisco Systems. CEO John T. Chambers sets the tone by giving his personal telephone number to *all* customers and taking calls in the middle of the night. As for the positive reinforcement, "all the company's top execs have their bonuses tied to customer-satisfaction ratings."[56] No surprise, then, that Cisco Systems gets high marks for customer service.

3. Make Continuous Improvement a Way of Life

kaizen   A Japanese word meaning "continuous improvement."

The Japanese word for "continuous improvement" is **kaizen**, which means improving the overall system by constantly improving the little details. TQM managers dedicated to *kaizen* are never totally happy with things. *Kaizen* practitioners view quality as an endless journey, not a final destination. They are always experimenting, measuring, adjusting, and improving. Rather than naively assuming that zero defects means perfection, they search for potential and actual trouble spots.

There are four general avenues for continuous improvement:

▮ Improved and more consistent product and service *quality*

▮ Faster *cycle times* (in cycles ranging from product development to order processing to payroll processing)

▮ Greater *flexibility* (for example, faster response to changing customer demands and new technology)

▮ Lower *costs* and less *waste* (for example, eliminating needless steps, scrap, rework, and non–value-adding activities)[57]

Significantly, these are not tradeoffs, as traditionally believed. In other words, TQM advocates reject the notion that a gain on one front necessitates a loss on another. Greater quality, speed, and flexibility have to be achieved at lower cost and with less waste. This is an "all things are possible" approach to management. It requires diligent effort and creativity.[58]

4. Build Teamwork and Empowerment

Earlier, we referred to TQM as employee-driven. In other words, it empowers employees at all levels in order to tap their full creativity, motivation, and commitment. *Empowerment*, as defined in Chapter 13, occurs when employees are adequately trained, provided with all relevant information and the best possible tools, fully involved in key decisions, and fairly rewarded for results.[59] TQM advocates prefer to reorganize the typical hierarchy into teams of people from different specialties.

In later chapters, you will encounter many ways to promote teamwork and employee involvement: suggestion systems (Chapter 10), open-book management and self-managed teams (Chapter 11), teamwork and trust (Chapter 12), and participative leadership (Chapter 13). Each can be a valuable component of TQM.

The Seven Basic TQM Process Improvement Tools

Continuous improvement of productive processes in factories, offices, stores, hospitals, hotels, and banks requires lots of measurement. Skilled TQM managers

---

REALITY CHECK 8.3

Howard Artrip, Manager at Toyota's Georgetown, Kentucky, assembly plant:
"Even at home, constant improvement is the rule: 'When I'm mowing the grass, I'm trying different turns to see if I can do it faster.'"

Source: As quoted in Charles Fishman, "No Satisfaction," *Fast Company*, No. 111 (January 2007): 86.

Questions: How does this exemplify TQM? How does this help explain why Toyota is growing and profitable while General Motors and Ford are laying off tens of thousands of employees and losing billions of dollars?

have a large repertoire of graphical and statistical tools at their disposal. The beginner's set consists of the seven tools displayed in Figure 8.2. A brief overview of each will help promote awareness and a foundation for further study.

Flow Chart

A **flow chart** is a graphic representation of a sequence of activities and decisions. Standard flow-charting symbols include boxes for events or activities, diamonds for key decisions, and ovals for start and stop points. Flow charts show, for instance, how a property damage claim moves through an insurance company. By knowing who does what to the claim, and in which sequence, management can streamline the process by eliminating unnecessary steps or delays. Appendix B at **college .hmco.com/pic/kreitnerSASfound** shows a sample flow chart as a planning and control tool. TQM teams have found flowcharting to be a valuable tool for increasing efficiency, reducing costs, and eliminating waste.

flow chart Graphic display of a sequence of activities and decisions.

Cause-and-Effect Analysis

The **fishbone diagram**, as introduced in Chapter 6, is named for its rough resemblance to a fish skeleton that visualizes important cause-and-effect relationships. (Some refer to fishbone diagrams as Ishikawa diagrams, in tribute to the Japanese quality pioneer mentioned in Appendix A at **college.hmco.com/pic/ kreitnerSASfound**.) For example, did a computer crash because of an operator error, an equipment failure, a power surge, or a software problem? A TQM team can systematically track down a likely cause by constructing a fishbone diagram.

fishbone diagram A cause-and-effect diagram.

Pareto Analysis

This technique, popularized by quality expert Joseph M. Juran and discussed in Chapter 5, is named for the Italian economist Vilfredo Pareto (1848–1923). Pareto

---

FIGURE 8.2

Seven Basic TQM Tools

Source: From Arthur R. Tenner and Irving J. DeToro, *Total Quality Management: Three Steps to Continuous Improvement*, p. 113, Figure 9.2. Copyright © 1992 by Addison-Wesley Publishing Company, Inc. Reproduced by permission of Pearson Education, Inc. All rights reserved.

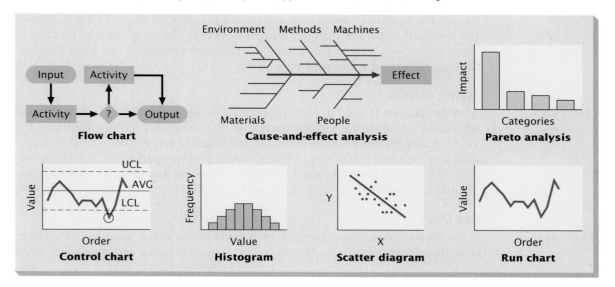

detected the so-called 80/20 pattern in many situations: relatively few people or events (about 20 percent) account for most of the results or impacts (about 80 percent). It is thus most efficient to focus on the few things (or people) that make the biggest difference. The next time you are in class, for example, notice how relatively few students offer the great majority of the comments in class. Likewise, a few students will account for most of the absenteeism during the semester. In TQM, a **Pareto analysis** involves constructing a bar chart by counting and tallying the number of times significant quality problems occur. The tallest bar on the chart, representing the most common problem, demands prompt attention. In a newspaper printing operation, for example, the most common cause of printing press stoppages for the week might turn out to be poor-quality paper. A quick glance at a Pareto chart would tell management to demand better quality from the paper supplier.

Pareto analysis Bar chart indicating which problem needs the most attention.

Control Chart

The use of *statistical process control* in repetitive operations helps employees keep key quality measurements within an acceptable range. A **control chart** is used to monitor actual-versus-desired quality measurements during repetitive operations. Consider the job of drilling a 2-centimeter hole in 1,000 pieces of metal. According to design specifications, the hole should have an inside diameter no larger than 2.1 centimeters and no smaller than 1.9 centimeters. These measurements are the upper control limit (UCL) and the lower control limit (LCL). Any hole diameters within these limits are of acceptable quality. Random measurements of the hole diameters need to be taken during the drilling operation to monitor quality. When these random measurements are plotted on a control chart, like the one in Figure 8.2, the operator has a handy visual aid that flags control limit violations and signals the need for corrective action. Perhaps the drill needs to be cleaned, sharpened, or replaced. This sort of statistical process control is less expensive than having to redrill or scrap 1,000 pieces of metal that have wrong-sized holes.

control chart Visual aid showing acceptable and unacceptable variations from the norm for repetitive operations.

Histogram

A **histogram** is a bar chart showing whether repeated measurements of a given quality characteristic conform to a standard bell-shaped curve. Deviations from the standard signal the need for corrective action. The controversial practice of teachers "curving" grades when there is an abnormally high or low grade distribution can be implemented with a histogram.

histogram Bar chart indicating deviations from a standard bell-shaped curve.

Scatter Diagram

A **scatter diagram** is used to plot the correlation between two variables. The one illustrated in Figure 8.2 indicates a negative correlation. In other words, as the value of variable X increases, the value of variable Y tends to decrease. A design engineer for a sporting goods company would find this particular type of correlation while testing the relationship between various thicknesses of fishing rods and flexibility. The thicker the rod, the lower the flexibility.

scatter diagram Diagram that plots relationships between two variables.

Run Chart

Also called a time series or trend chart, a **run chart** tracks the frequency or amount of a given variable over time. Significant deviations from the norm signal the need

run chart A trend chart for tracking a variable over time.

for corrective action. Hospitals monitor vital body signs such as temperature and blood pressure with daily logs that are actually run charts. TQM teams can use run charts to spot "bad days." For example, automobiles made in U.S. factories on a Friday or Monday historically have had more quality defects than those assembled on a Tuesday, Wednesday, or Thursday.

Before we move on to Deming management, an important point needs to be made. As experts on the subject remind us, "Tools are necessary but not sufficient for TQM."[60] Successful TQM requires a long-term, organizationwide drive for continuous improvement. The appropriate time frame is *years,* not days or months. Tools such as benchmarking and control charts are just one visible feature of that process. Invisible factors—such as values, learning, attitudes, motivation, and personal commitment—dictate the ultimate success of TQM.

TEST PREPPER 8.3

ANSWERS CAN BE FOUND ON P. 221

True or False?

_____ 1. TQM has no connection with the organization's culture (an internal factor) because it is customer-driven (an external force).

_____ 2. *Kaizen* is a Chinese word meaning "rise above."

_____ 3. Empowering employees at all levels is at the heart of TQM.

_____ 4. To reduce costs and eliminate unnecessary steps, managers should use flowcharts.

_____ 5. A data point between the upper and lower control limits indicates acceptable quality on a control chart.

Multiple Choice

_____ 6. What is at the core of the definition of *total quality management (TQM)*?
   a. Visionary leadership
   b. Employee satisfaction
   c. Pride
   d. Continuous improvement
   e. Motivation

_____ 7. One of the four principles of TQM is
   a. do it right the first time.
   b. inspecting everything twice.
   c. striving for zero defects.
   d. people are the biggest threat to quality improvement.
   e. technology is the key.

_____ 8. *Kaizen* practitioners view quality as
   a. a journey, not a destination.
   b. the only reality.
   c. perfection.
   d. spiritual fulfillment.
   e. the ultimate end.

_____ 9. A TQM tool that would be useful for identifying the roughly 20 percent of a supermarket's employees who are responsible for about 80 percent of the absenteeism is
   a. benchmarking.
   b. fishbone diagram.
   c. flowcharting.
   d. Pareto analysis.
   e. run chart.

_____ 10. Which of these would be most appropriate for graphically plotting the correlation between two product characteristics, such as the diameter and weight of tennis balls?
   a. A fishbone diagram
   b. A histogram
   c. A run chart
   d. A scatter diagram
   e. A control chart

Online Study Center
ACE the Test
ACE Practice Tests 8.3

DEMING MANAGEMENT

 Explain how Deming's PDCA cycle can improve the overall management process, and identify at least four of Deming's famous 14 points.

It is hard to overstate the worldwide impact of W. Edwards Deming's revolutionary ideas about management. His ideas have directly and indirectly created better and more productive work environments for countless millions of people. This section builds upon the historical sketch provided in Appendix A (at **college .hmco.com/pic/kreitnerSASfound**) by examining basic principles of Deming management as well as Deming's famous 14 points.

Principles of Deming Management

Deming management   Application of W. Edwards Deming's ideas for more responsive, more democratic, and less wasteful organizations.

Deming management is the application of W. Edwards Deming's ideas to revitalize productive systems by making them more responsive to the customer, more democratic, and more efficient. This approach qualifies as a revolution because, when first proposed by Deming in the 1950s, it directly challenged the legacy of Frederick Taylor's scientific management (for more on Taylor, see Appendix A at **college .hmco.com/pic/kreitnerSASfound**).[61] Scientific management led to rigid and autocratic organizations that were unresponsive to customers and employees alike. Deming management proposed essentially the opposite. Some of the principles we discuss here may not seem revolutionary today because Deming management has become ingrained in everyday *good* management.

Quality Improvement Drives the Entire Economy

Higher quality eventually means more jobs. Deming's simple yet convincing logic is presented in Figure 8.3. Quality improvement is a powerful engine that drives out waste and inefficiency. Quality also powers higher productivity, greater market share, and new business and employment opportunities. In short, everybody wins when quality improves.[62]

The Customer Always Comes First

In his influential 1986 text, *Out of the Crisis,* Deming wrote: "The consumer is the most important part of the production line. Quality should be aimed at the needs

---

FIGURE 8.3

Everyone Benefits from Improved Quality

Source: Adapted from W. Edwards Deming, *Out of the Crisis* (Cambridge, Mass.: MIT Press, 1986), p. 3.

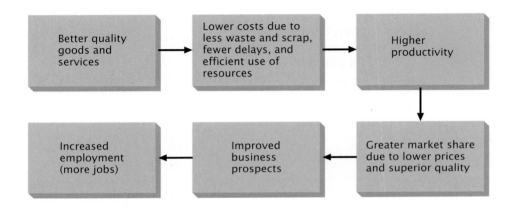

of the consumer, present and future."[63] Of course, these are just inspirational words until they are enacted faithfully by individuals on the job. Skip Tobey, who joined America West Airlines when it first started flying, embodies the Deming management spirit:

> "I'm not just an aircraft cleaner," the 36-year-old Phoenix native said. "That's my title, but that's not the end of my job."
>
> Tobey said he looks for ways to help passengers, lending a hand to young families maneuvering strollers through narrow aircraft aisles and assisting elderly travelers.
>
> "My satisfaction is tied into quality, helping the passengers," he said. "No matter what it takes, if it means going to the furthest extreme, I'll do it."[64]

Casual observers might dismiss the importance of Tobey's job, but his contribution was critical as America West fought its way out of bankruptcy in the mid-1990s.

Don't Blame the Person, Fix the System

Deming chided U.S. managers for their preoccupation with finding someone to blame rather than fixing problems. His research convinced him that "the system"—meaning management, work rules, technology, and the organization's structure and culture—typically is responsible for upwards of 85 percent of substandard quality. People can and will turn out superior quality, *if* the system is redesigned to permit them to do so. Deming's management philosophy urges managers to treat employees as internal customers, listening and responding to their ideas and suggestions for improvement. After all, who knows more about a particular job—the person who performs it for 2,000 hours a year or a manager who stops by now and again?

Plan-Do-Check-Act

Deming's approach calls for making informed decisions on the basis of hard data. His recommended tool for this process is what is popularly known as the **PDCA cycle** (plan-do-check-act). Deming preferred the term *Shewhart cycle*,[65] in recognition of the father of statistical quality control, Walter A. Shewhart. (Japanese managers call it the Deming cycle.) Whatever the label, the PDCA cycle reminds managers to focus on what is really important, use observed data, start small and build upon accumulated knowledge, and be research-oriented in observing changes and results (see Figure 8.4 on page 216). The influence of Deming management was obvious at Intel when CEO Craig Barrett met with division heads in 2000:

PDCA cycle Deming's plan-do-check-act cycle, which relies on observed data to continuously improve operations.

> He has told them to make sure they are following the fundamentals of decision-making: plan, do, check, act. And he has tied bonuses to performance in each group. "My job is to refresh in everyone's mind: This is how we do projects. These are the exact steps you go through. Don't take shortcuts," he says.[66]

Deming's 14 Points

Deming formulated his 14 points to transform U.S. industry from what he deemed its backward ways. Here is a summary of the 14 points, which constitute the heart and soul of Deming management:[67]

1. *Constant purpose.* Strive for continuous improvement in products and services to remain competitive.
2. *New philosophy.* Western management needs to awaken to the realities of a new economic age by demanding wiser use of all resources.

FIGURE 8.4

Deming's PDCA Cycle

Source: Adapted from Deming, *Out of the Crisis*, p. 88.

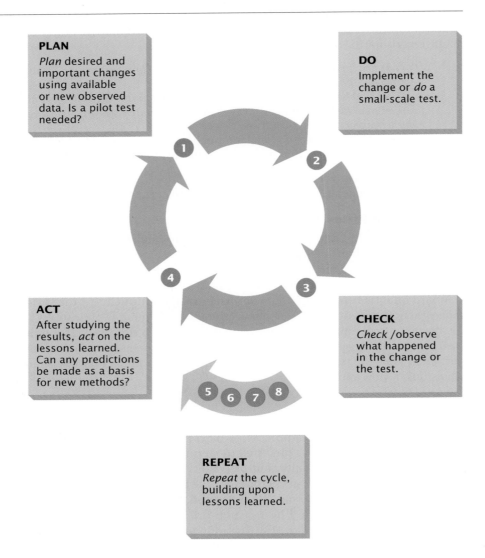

3. *Give up on quality by inspection.* Inspecting for faulty products is unnecessary if quality is built in from the very beginning.
4. *Avoid the constant search for lowest-cost suppliers.* Build long-term, loyal, and trusting relationships with single suppliers.
5. *Seek continuous improvement.* Constantly improve production processes for greater productivity and lower costs.
6. *Train everyone.* Make sure people have a clear idea of how to do their jobs. Informally learning a new job from coworkers entrenches bad work habits.
7. *Provide real leadership.* Leading is more than telling. It involves providing individualized help.
8. *Drive fear out of the workplace.* Employees continue to do things the wrong way when they are afraid to ask questions about why and how. According to Deming, "No one can put in his best performance unless he feels secure. *Se* comes from the Latin, meaning without, *cure* means fear or care. *Secure* means

without fear, not afraid to express ideas, not afraid to ask questions."[68] Lack of job security is a major stumbling block for quality improvement in America.

9. *Promote teamwork.* Bureaucratic barriers between departments and functional specialists need to be broken down. Customer satisfaction is the common goal.

10. *Avoid slogans and targets.* Because the *system* is largely responsible for product quality, putting pressure on individuals who feel they do not control the system breeds resentment. Posters with slogans such as "zero defects" and "take pride in quality" do nothing to help the individual measure and improve productive processes. Control charts and other process-control tools, in contrast, give employees direction and encouragement. Deming's approach tells managers that if they provide leadership and continually improve the system, the scoreboard will take care of itself.

11. *Get rid of numerical quotas.* When employees aggressively pursue numerical goals or quotas, they too often take their eyes off quality, continuous improvement, and costs. Hence, Deming management strongly rejects the practice of management by objectives (MBO),[69] mentioned in Chapter 5.

12. *Remove barriers that stifle pride in workmanship.* Poor management, inadequate instruction, faulty equipment, and pressure to achieve a numerical goal get in the way of continuous improvement.

13. *Education and self-improvement are key.* Greater knowledge means greater opportunity. Continuous improvement should be the number one career objective for everyone in the organization.

14. *"The transformation is everyone's job."*[70]

Virtually *everyone* in the organization plays a key role in implementing Deming management.

TEST PREPPER 8.4

ANSWERS CAN BE FOUND ON P. 221

True or False?

_____ 1. Deming's quality management philosophy is a direct outgrowth of Taylor's scientific management.

_____ 2. Deming believed quality improvement drives the entire economy.

_____ 3. In Deming's PDCA cycle, the "C" stands for "corrective action."

_____ 4. One of Deming's 14 points recommends getting rid of numerical quotas.

Multiple Choice

_____ 5. According to Deming, _____ is the most important part of the production line.
   a. the consumer
   b. the employee
   c. the supervisor
   d. engineering
   e. technology

_____ 6. Who or what did Deming blame up to 85 percent of substandard quality on?
   a. Lazy workers
   b. Substandard materials
   c. The system
   d. Careless management
   e. Poorly maintained machinery

_____ 7. What does "A" in Deming's PDCA cycle stand for?
   a. Alternatives
   b. Act
   c. Activities
   d. Attitudes
   e. Actual results

Online Study Center
ACE the Test
ACE Practice Tests 8.4

Online Study Center college.hmco.com/pic/kreitnerSASfound

How to Measure Customer Satisfaction with Just Two Simple Questions

"Many companies have forgotten that their customers are their most valuable assets," says Fred Reichheld, a veteran Bain & Co. consultant and author of the recent book *The Ultimate Question*. Reichheld has been studying customer loyalty for most of his 25-year career. . . .

With *The Ultimate Question*, he lays out the thinking behind his Net Promoter Score system, which Bain has been using for about three years. In essence, it's a customer survey that never has more than two questions: On a scale of 1 to 10, how likely are you to recommend us? If you would not recommend us, why not? Those who respond with nines and tens are considered "promoters"; sevens and eights are "passives"; and everyone else is a "detractor." Subtract the percentage of detractors from the promoters and you have what's called your Net Promoter Score. The number, according to Reichheld, is an almost perfect gauge of a company's reputation in the marketplace—and its ability

to land both repeat business and new customers. Most companies, says Reichheld, score between 10 and 20. The best achieve scores approaching 80 and 90.

The system has proved popular with many Bain clients, including General Electric and Microsoft. But the beauty of NPS is that virtually any company, of any size, can implement it, without the help of consultants. The surveys can be administered through the mail, over the phone, and by e-mail. And unlike traditional customer satisfaction surveys, which many people find time-consuming and annoying, this one takes only moments to complete.

Source: From *Inc.: The Magazine For Growing Companies* by Darren Dahl, "Would You Recommend Us?" September 2006. Copyright © 2006 by Mansueto Ventures LLC. Reproduced with permission of Mansueto Ventures LLC via Copyright Clearance Center.

Improving the Quality of Hospital Health Care: "Perfect Is Possible"

When defects are common, they can feel normal—inevitable. Instead of trying to fix them, people accept them. For a lot that is wrong with health care today, that is exactly the situation—even though the Institute of Medicine reports that as many as 100,000 people die each year in hospitals from avoidable errors. These errors aren't invisible. Many nurses, doctors, patients and families are all too familiar with what went wrong in care despite the best efforts of the clinicians. But if completely preventing errors seems a hopeless task, why even try? Recent experience—at first from just a

handful of hospitals, but now from hundreds—shows that this pessimism is unfounded. Many kinds of errors can be completely eliminated; "zero defects" is possible. Some hospitals are, for example, achieving once impossible success at eliminating certain kinds of infections and medication errors. There is no reason these successes can't be widely replicated, maybe everywhere.

In 2000, the Robert Wood Johnson Foundation, in cooperation with the Institute for Healthcare Improvement (IHI), challenged hospitals to apply for grants to help them "pursue perfection" in their safety, reliability, patient focus, waiting times and efficiency. More than 200 hospitals applied; seven were chosen as grantees in what became the Pursuing Perfection Project. After five years, each was still far from "perfect," but their achievements clearly raised the bar for all U.S. hospitals.

Two of the grantees—Hackensack University Hospital in New Jersey and McLeod Regional Medical Center in Florence, S.C.—used strict protocols and guidelines and automated systems to ensure that nearly 100 percent of all heart-attack patients received needed medications, driving heart-attack death rates down below 5 percent, compared with the U.S. average for Medicare patients of 10 percent. Cincinnati Children's Hospital Medical Center revolutionized its approach to children with cystic fibrosis and diabetes by giving patients and families much more power to make decisions about their own care, such as adjusting their own medications or creating their own schedules for therapy visits and treatments in the hospital. Complications dropped by 30 to 50 percent.

In Whatcom County, Wash., St. Joseph Hospital used "nurse navigator" coaches (to help coordinate information and plans among physicians and institutions) and a patient-controlled personal health record called the Shared Care Plan for chronically ill patients that defined specific goals and plans that every doctor and nurse involved would abide by. These measures reduced expenses for emergency visits and hospital admissions by an average of $3,000 per patient per year by keeping patients healthy at home. HealthPartners, an integrated-care system in Minneapolis, cut re-admission rates for congestive-heart-failure patients in half by making absolutely sure that medications were correctly prescribed and fully understood by patients every time. . . .

These projects are raising the bar for everyone. According to the Centers of Disease Control and Prevention, 2 million Americans get hospital infections each year. They do not need to. Rates in Norway and Sweden are nearly zero. Why should we accept as inevitable that patients have to die or suffer from hospital-acquired infections, wrong-site surgery, unreliable heart-attack treatment, medication errors—and myriad other forms of error and unreliability in care—when we can now name hospitals that have eliminated or drastically decreased each of these forms of harm? These hospitals have taken away the excuses. Every hospital—every board, executive and clinician—now has to ask, "If they can, why can't we?"

The old "benchmarks"—80 or 90 percent success at implementing guidelines and protocols—are no longer acceptable. No one would tolerate cars that started 90 percent of the time, or tax accountants that got 90 percent of the Form 1040 lines right. We consumers demand a whole different level of excellence in those cases. It's time to expect the same of health care.

Source: Excerpted from Donald M. Berwick and Lucian L. Leape, "Perfect Is Possible," *Newsweek,* October 16, 2006, pp. 70–71.

Case Questions

1. Why is feedforward control so important in the quest for higher-quality hospital care? Explain.
2. Which of the RATER service-quality dimensions are important at hospitals? Is one of them of overriding importance? Explain.
3. How could hospitals benefit from TQM programs? Explain.
4. What would Deming likely say about these hospital quality initiatives? Explain.

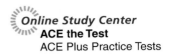*Online Study Center*
ACE the Test
ACE Plus Practice Tests

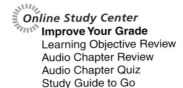*Online Study Center*
Improve Your Grade
Learning Objective Review
Audio Chapter Review
Audio Chapter Quiz
Study Guide to Go

LEARNING OBJECTIVE REVIEW

1 *Describe three types of control, and identify the components common to all control systems.*

- Feedforward control is preventive in nature.
- Feedback control is based on the evaluation of past performance.
- Concurrent control occurs when managers monitor and adjust ongoing operations to keep them performing to standard.
- The three basic components of organizational control systems are objectives, standards, and an evaluation-reward system.

2 *Identify five types of product quality, explain how providing a service differs from manufacturing a product, and list the five service-quality dimensions.*

- Product quality involves much more than the basic idea of "conformance to requirements."
- Five types of product quality are transcendent, product-based, user-based, manufacturing-based, and value-based.
- Service providers face a unique set of challenges that distinguish them from manufacturers:
  - Direct customer participation
  - Immediate consumption of services
  - Provision of services at customers' convenience

  - Tendency of services to be more labor-intensive than manufacturing
  - Intangibility of services, making them harder to measure
- Consumer research uncovered five service-quality dimensions: reliability, assurance, tangibles, empathy, and responsiveness (RATER). Consumers consistently rank reliability number one.

3 *Define total quality management (TQM), discuss the basic TQM principles, and describe at least three of the seven TQM process improvement tools.*

- Total quality management (TQM) involves creating a culture that is dedicated to customer-centered, employee-driven continuous improvement.
- The four TQM principles are:
  - Do it right the first time.
  - Be customer-centered.
  - Make continuous improvement a way of life.
  - Build teamwork and empowerment.
- Seven basic TQM process improvement tools are flow charts, fishbone diagrams, Pareto analysis, control charts, histograms, scatter diagrams, and run charts.

4▶ *Explain how Deming's PDCA cycle can improve the overall management process, and identify at least four of Deming's famous 14 points.*

- Deming's plan-do-check-act (PDCA) cycle forces managers to make decisions and take actions on the basis of observed and carefully measured data.
- PDCA work never ends because lessons learned from one cycle are incorporated into the next.

- Deming's famous 14 points seek to revolutionize Western management practices:
  - In general, they urge managers to seek continuous improvement through extensive training, leadership, teamwork, and self-improvement.
  - The points call for *doing away with* mass quality inspections, selecting suppliers only on the basis of low cost, fear, slogans and numerical quotas, and barriers to pride in workmanship.
- Transformation, according to Deming, is *everyone's* job.

TEST PREPPER ANSWERS

▶ **8.1**

1. T   2. T   3. T   4. F   5. F   6. T   7. e
8. b   9. c   10. a   11. e

▶ **8.2**

1. T   2. F   3. F   4. T   5. a   6. a   7. e

▶ **8.3**

1. F   2. F   3. T   4. T   5. T   6. d   7. a
8. a   9. d   10. d

▶ **8.4**

1. F   2. T   3. F   4. T   5. a   6. c   7. b

Online Study Center RESOURCES

Prepare for Class, Improve Your Grade, and ACE the Test. Student Achievement Series resources include:

ACE Practice Tests	Crossword Puzzles	Hangman
Audio Chapter Quizzes	Decision Case Questions	Key Issue Expansion
Audio Chapter Reviews	Ethical Hot Seat Exercises	Learning Objective Reviews
Career Snapshots	Flashcards	Study Guide to Go
Chapter Glossaries	Hands-on Exercises	Visual Glossaries
Chapter Outlines		

To access these learning and study tools, go to **college.hmco.com/pic/kreitnerSASfound**.

Human Resource Management

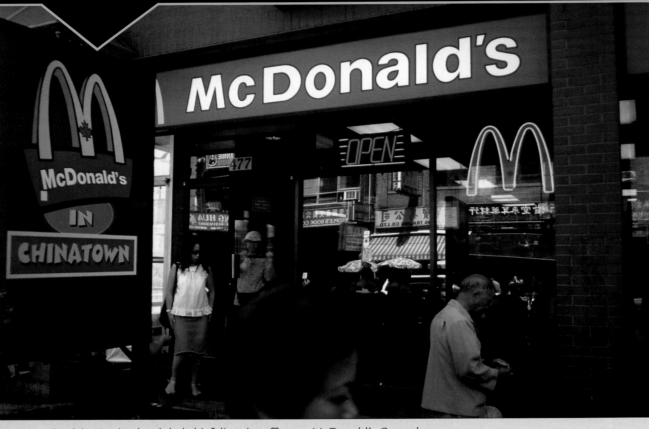

Patricia Harris, the global chief diversity officer at McDonald's Corp., has a passion for making diversity more than just a word at the fast-food giant.

1 ▸ *Define the term* human capital, *and identify at least four of Pfeffer's people-centered practices.*

2 ▸ *Identify and describe the seven steps in the PROCEED model of employee selection, explain the business case for diversity, and discuss how managers can be more effective interviewers.*

3 ▸ *Discuss how performance appraisals can be made legally defensible.*

Business is a game, and as with all games, the team that puts the best people on the field and gets them playing together wins. It's that simple."[1]

—Jack Welch, former CEO of General Electric, and
Suzy Welch, former editor of *Harvard Business Review*

Chapter Outline

Online Study Center
Prepare for Class
Chapter Outline

4 ▶ *Contrast the ingredients of good training programs for both skill and factual learning, and explain the role of training in preventing sexual harassment.*

Patricia Harris Champions Diversity at McDonald's

Patricia Harris, vice president of McDonald's USA and global chief diversity officer of McDonald's Corp., was still in college when she took a secretarial position at McDonald's. "I'll stay here until I finish school and get a real job," she told herself.

Thirty years later, she's still there. Far from being the exclusive province of short-term fast-food jobs, McDonald's offers "lots of 'real' jobs and lots of career paths," she says. "We have hamburger lawyers, hamburger accountants and hamburger HR people."

While Harris didn't start out behind the counter, many top managers did, she says—including McDonald's CEO Jim Skinner and the three U.S. division presidents. And many, like Harris, have long tenures with the company. "Things change so much at McDonald's," she says, "and I learn something new with every change."

Online Study Center
Prepare for Class
Chapter Glossary

Improve Your Grade
Flashcards
Hangman
Crossword Puzzles

The Road from McBee to McDonald's

The youngest of 11 children, Harris is "a proud South Carolinian" who grew up in the small town of McBee. After she graduated from high school at 16, however, the big city beckoned, and she was eager to follow her older sisters to New York.

In New York, Harris found a job as an administrative assistant and attended college classes part time, as she tried to "find myself," she says. After she met and married a man from Chicago, they moved there and she enrolled in classes at Roosevelt University.

In 1976, Harris heard about an opening in the legal department at McDonald's. Working there first in a secretarial position, she discovered her true calling when a job opened up in the HR [human resources] department and she was offered a compensation analyst position.

"It was just one of those wonderful things—being in the right place at the right time in the right company," she says. After three years in compensation, she moved into an HR generalist position and thoroughly enjoyed that as well. "I was an HR generalist for six or seven years, and I would have been happy to stay in that role. I knew by then that I wanted to be an HR professional."

Harris continued to attend school part time while she worked, completing a degree in public administration and personnel administration in 1979. "I was never a full-time student" but was determined to get a degree. "Today, I tell people, 'Yes, you can get that degree.'"

A Passion for Diversity

In 1985, Harris was offered the position of affirmative action manager, an opportunity that once again changed the course of her career.

She was apprehensive at first. Although interested, Harris wasn't sure she could do the job. In addition, "I knew affirmative action wasn't a popular topic." The affirmative action department was new, having been established in 1980, and it was seen as the "police," she says, coming in to enforce the rules. She wondered if this would be a wise career move.

Ultimately, however, she decided to "step out of my comfort zone" and take the risk, with the encouragement of her boss, Mel Hobson, McDonald's first director of affirmative action.

By the end of the 1980s, the work of the department had expanded. Partnerships were developed with external organizations, and affirmative action moved out of HR and became its own stand-alone unit. At the same time, the name was changed, from affirmative action to diversity.

Although the department was no longer part of HR, it continued to have a strong relationship with human resources. "I don't know how diversity people can do their job without HR's support," she says.

Looking back, Harris says that taking that risk in 1985 turned out to be the best decision she has ever made. "This job truly became my passion. It's who I am, both personally and professionally."

Nurturing Employee Networks

"When I joined the company in 1976, I think we had one female officer, one Asian officer and one African-American officer. There were no Hispanic officers," says Harris. Today, of McDonald's 200 U.S. officers, 26 percent are women and 23 percent are minorities.

Harris is particularly proud that McDonald's received an Equal Employment Opportunity Commission (EEOC) "Freedom to Compete Award" this year in recognition of the company's diversity and inclusion initiatives.

The EEOC specifically cited McDonald's employee networks, which include the African-American Council, the Hispanic Employee Network, the Asian Employee Network, the Women's Leadership Network (which is global now) and the Gays, Lesbians and Allies at McDonald's. Each group provides networking opportunities for its members and offers an avenue for sharing ideas with management....

One Foot Back in HR

Earlier this year, Harris was promoted to global chief diversity officer, and she has already begun to meet with HR leaders from McDonald's country areas around the world to enlist their help in ensuring that diversity reaches all levels of the organization across the globe. "Diversity has so many dimensions," she says. "It means different things to different countries." As she takes on this exciting new role, she says happily, "I feel like I'm starting over again, and I love it."[2] ■

Staffing has long been an integral part of the management process. Like other traditional management functions, such as planning and organizing, the domain of staffing has grown throughout the years. This growth reflects increasing environmental complexity and rising consumer expectations. Early definitions of staffing focused narrowly on hiring people for vacant positions. Today, the traditional staffing function is just one part of the more encompassing **human resource management** process, as illustrated by Patricia Harris's career at McDonald's. Human resource management involves the acquisition, retention, and development of human resources necessary for organizational success.[3] This broader definition underscores the point that people are valuable *resources* that require careful nurturing. In fact, what were once called personnel departments are now called human resource departments. In a more folksy manner, the top human resources executive at Wal-Mart is called the "senior vice president of people."[4]

human resource management The acquisition, retention, and development of human resources.

This people-centered approach to human resources emphasizes the serious moral and legal ramifications of viewing labor simply as a commodity to be bought, exploited to exhaustion, and discarded when convenient. Moreover, global opportunities and competitive pressures have made the skillful management of human resources more important than ever.[5] Progressive and successful organizations treat all their employees as valuable human resources. A prime example is Southwest Airlines. CEO Gary Kelly recently pointed out:

> Other airlines laid off a number of employees within days after Sept. 11. At Southwest Airlines after 35 years, we've never had a layoff. We've never had a pay

cut. So, there is a devotion to the people and a commitment to our people, once we hire them, that we have lived up to.[6]

The purpose of this chapter is to expand your knowledge of human resource management by taking a strategic perspective and exploring three important dimensions of human resource management: recruitment/selection, performance appraisal, and training.

HUMAN RESOURCE STRATEGY: A PEOPLE-CENTERED APPROACH

> **1** ▸ *Define the term* human capital, *and identify at least four of Pfeffer's people-centered practices.*

Online Study Center
Improve Your Grade
Career Snapshot 9.1

The conventional wisdom about how employees should be perceived and managed has evolved greatly over the past 50 years. The pendulum has swung from reactive to proactive. Following World War II, personnel departments filled the hiring requisitions and handled the disciplinary problems submitted by managers. During the 1970s and 1980s, human resource (HR) departments became the norm, and a more encompassing approach evolved. HR departments attempted to forecast labor supply and demand, recruit and hire, manage payrolls, and conduct training and development programs. Too often, however, HR was treated as a support-staff function with only an indirect link to corporate strategy. Today, in well-managed companies, HR is embedded in organizational strategy, and many traditional HR functions are being decentralized throughout the enterprise and selectively outsourced.[7] But the transition is far from complete, as indicated by this observation: "Some business pundits have likened the current status of HR to an awkward adolescent. The profession is just beginning to come of age but isn't quite sure where it's heading."[8] In fact, in a survey of senior HR managers, 37 percent said they "always" participated in corporate strategic planning. Another 42 percent said they "sometimes" had a hand in company strategy.[9] This section strives to improve those numbers by outlining a strategic agenda for human resource management.

The Age of Human Capital

The human capital perspective requires open-system thinking, as discussed in Appendix A at **college.hmco.com/pic/kreitnerSASfound**. It is a "big picture" approach to managing people and staying competitive. According to the authors of *The HR Scorecard: Linking People, Strategy, and Performance*:

> *We're living in a time when a new economic paradigm—characterized by speed, innovation, short cycle times, quality, and customer satisfaction—is highlighting the importance of intangible assets, such as brand recognition, knowledge, innovation, and particularly human capital.*[10]

human capital   The need to develop to their fullest potential all present and future employees.

The term **human capital** encompasses all present and future workforce participants and emphasizes the need to develop their fullest potential for the benefit of the global economy. Central to this perspective is the assumption that *every* employee is a valuable asset, not merely an expense item.[11] This broad concern for possible *future* employees is a marked departure from traditional "employees-only" perspectives.

Intel, the Santa Clara, California–based maker of computer microprocessors, is committed to developing human capital. The company adopts primary and secondary schools—providing computers, teaching talent, and money—and encourages its employees to help. "For every 20 hours workers volunteer at local schools, Intel donates $200."[12] As might be expected from a high-tech company, the emphasis is on math and science. Additionally, Intel matches employees' donations to their college alma maters up to $10,000 a year and awards $1,250,000 in school grants and scholarships each year to winners in a national science competition for high school seniors. Most of those who benefit from these initiatives will *not* end up working for Intel. That's what developing the *world's* human capital is all about—thinking big!

People-Centered Organizations Enjoy a Competitive Advantage

In an era of nonstop layoffs, the often-heard slogan "Employees are our most valuable asset" rings hollow. But cynicism can be put aside by noting how leading companies are building bridges between progressive human resource practices and market success. Once again, we turn to Southwest Airlines. Cofounder and chairman Herb Kelleher told *Fortune* magazine: "My mother taught me that your employees come first. If you treat them well, then they treat the customers well, and that means your customers come back and your shareholders are happy."[13] Well, Herb's mom was right! Solid research support for this approach comes from Stanford's Jeffrey Pfeffer, who reported a strong connection between *people-centered practices* and higher profits and lower employee turnover. Pfeffer identified these seven people-centered practices:

▌ Protection of job security (including a no-layoff policy)

▌ Rigorous hiring process

▌ Employee empowerment through decentralization and self-managed teams

▌ Compensation linked to performance

▌ Comprehensive training

▌ Reduction of status differences

▌ Sharing of key information

Pfeffer sees these practices as an integrated package and cautions against implementing them piecemeal. Unfortunately, according to Pfeffer's calculations, only about 12 percent of today's organizations qualify as being systematically people-centered.[14] Thus, we have a clear developmental agenda for human resource management. Significant payoffs await those who take up the challenge of truly putting employees first, as documented in a recent survey:

> The results of the survey of 370,378 employees showed that employees who do not feel their employers treat them with respect are more than three times likely (63 percent) to intend to leave their positions within a two-year time frame than those who feel their employers treat them like adults (19 percent).[15]

Ideas about how to enact people-centered practices can be found throughout the balance of this text.

TEST PREPPER 9.1

ANSWERS CAN BE FOUND ON P. 249

True or False?

_____ 1. The primary focus of human resource management is hiring people for vacant positions.

_____ 2. One of the current trends in HR is that its functions are being decentralized throughout the enterprise and being outsourced.

_____ 3. The human capital perspective focuses on keeping present employees happy.

_____ 4. According to Jeffrey Pfeffer, only about 12 percent of today's organizations qualify as being systematically people-centered.

Multiple Choice

_____ 5. In the past, HR was treated as a _____ function. Today, HR is being embedded in organizational strategy.
   a. line
   b. support-staff
   c. top-management
   d. training-only
   e. technical

_____ 6. A "big picture" approach to managing people and staying competitive is
   a. an open perspective.
   b. knowledge management.
   c. corporate leveraging.
   d. human capital.
   e. employee profiling.

_____ 7. Which of the following is *not* one of the seven people-centered practices identified by Pfeffer?
   a. Protection of job security
   b. Compensation linked to performance
   c. Sharing of key information
   d. Rigorous hiring process
   e. Emphasize status differences

Online Study Center
ACE the Test
ACE Practice Tests 9.1

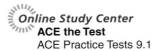

RECRUITMENT AND SELECTION

2 ▸ *Identify and describe the seven steps in the PROCEED model of employee selection, explain the business case for diversity, and discuss how managers can be more effective interviewers.*

Jim Collins, in his best-seller *Good to Great: Why Some Companies Make the Leap and Others Don't*, uses the metaphor of a bus when referring to the organization and its employees.[16] He believes that a busload of great people can go just about anywhere it wants. But a bus filled with confused and unruly passengers is destined for the ditch. A recent survey of 100 human resource managers underscores the importance of finding the right people for the organizational bus trip: *recruiting* was their number one concern both now (64 percent) and three years down the road (68 percent).[17] This section deals with that important challenge.

Recruiting for Diversity

The ultimate goal of recruiting is to generate a pool of qualified applicants for new and existing jobs. Everyday recruiting tactics include internal job postings, referrals by present and past employees, campus recruiters, newspaper ads, Web sites, public and private employment agencies, so-called headhunters, job fairs, temporary-help agencies, and union halls. Meanwhile, an underlying reality makes today's recruiting extremely challenging. Namely, applicant pools need to be demographically representative of the population at large if diversity is to be

Online Study Center
Improve Your Grade
Career Snapshot 9.1

Sonia Maria Green is a key person in General Motors' drive for a 2.7 percent increase in market share among Hispanics. She and two other directors of GM's new Center of Expertise on Diversity are responsible for minority outreach programs. Among the Hispanic marketing efforts will be Spanish-language television ads on Univision and Telemundo. Ms. Green believes cultural cues involving family, music, and colors are critical in Hispanic communities where some speak primarily English, some primarily Spanish, and some are bilingual. A successful Hispanic marketing program will enhance GM's minority recruitment and diversity efforts.

achieved.[18] A casual review of today's recruiting ads reveals abundant evidence of corporate diversity initiatives. Monica Reed, at Prudential in Newark, New Jersey, explains the rationale:

> Our corporate culture is diverse, because that brings a variety of new ideas and perspectives into the company. We also want to sell to a diverse audience, and someone who sees a recruitment ad that focuses on diversity may also become a customer.[19]

Research has revealed a major surprise about recruiting for diversity (see Table 9.1). Importantly, the study turned the tables and took a *job hunter's* perspective. Within the top five most frequently used search methods, corporate Web sites had the distinction of being the most frequently used but were the *least successful* job-hunting method. Referrals turned out to be the best way to land a job. So we have one word of advice for job hunters in all walks of life: *network*.

> Especially in a tough economy, networking is the key. Resume-deluged employers are posting job openings only as a last resort, says Kirsten Watson, president of HireTopTalent. Rather, job leads come from "a friend who had a friend who had an uncle." . . .
>   To network effectively, start with friends, family, and others who know you well and can help present your case, says Bob Critchley, executive VP for global relationships at outplacement firm Drake Beam Morin.[20]

TABLE 9.1

How Diverse Candidates Search for and Find Jobs

Top 5 Search Methods	
1. Corporate web sites	70%
2. General job-listing sites	67
3. Classified ads	53
4. Referrals	52
5. Headhunters/agencies	35
Top 5 Ways Candidates Found Jobs	
1. Referrals	25%
2. General job-listing sites	17
3. Headhunters/agencies	17
4. Classified ads	15
5. Corporate web sites	6

Source: From *HR Magazine* by Ruth E. Thaler-Carter, "Diversify Your Recruitment Advertising," June 2001. Copyright © 2001 by Society for Human Resource Management (SHRM). Reproduced with permission of Society for Human Resource Management (SHRM) via Copyright Clearance Center.

Indeed, in a recent survey of 703 people, 61 percent said they had found their most recent job via "Networking/word of mouth."[21]

The Selection Process: An Overview

HR experts commonly compare the screening and selection process to a hurdle race. Equal employment opportunity (EEO) legislation in the United States and elsewhere attempts to ensure a fair and unprejudiced race for all job applicants.[22] The first two hurdles are résumé screening and reference checking; both are very important because "57 percent of hiring managers have found fabrications on a résumé, and, of that group, 93 percent opted not to hire the candidate."[23] Background checks for criminal records and citizenship/immigration status are more essential than ever in an age of workplace violence and international terrorism. Consider this: "Between January 1998 and October 2000, American Background Information Services Inc. (ABI), based in Winchester, Va., found undisclosed criminal backgrounds on 12.6 percent of the people it screened."[24] Other hurdles may include psychological tests, physical examinations, interviews, work-sampling tests, and drug tests.

Del J. Still, a respected author and trainer, summarizes the employee selection process with the acronym PROCEED, in which each letter represents one of the seven steps involved (see Table 9.2). This model encourages managers to take a systems perspective, all the way from preparing to hire to the final hiring decision. Before examining the key elements of the PROCEED model in depth, we need to clarify the first three action items for step 1 of PROCEED. This is where job analysis and job descriptions come into play. **Job analysis** is the process of identifying basic task and skill requirements for specific jobs by studying superior performers. A **job description** is a concise document that outlines the role expectations and skill requirements for a specific job. Although some say they have become obsolete in today's fast-paced world, up-to-date job descriptions foster discipline in selection and performance appraisal by offering a formal measuring stick.[25]

Equal Employment Opportunity

Although earlier legislation still applies selectively, the landmark EEO law in the United States is Title VII of the Civil Rights Act of 1964. Subsequent amendments, presidential executive orders, and related laws have expanded EEO's coverage. EEO law now provides a broad umbrella of employment protection for certain categories of disadvantaged individuals:

> The result of this legislation has been that in virtually all aspects of employment, it is unlawful to discriminate on the basis of race, color, sex, religion, age, national origin, . . . [disabilities], being a disabled veteran, or being a veteran of the Vietnam Era.[26]

What all this means is that managers cannot refuse to hire, promote, train, or transfer employees simply on the basis of the characteristics just mentioned. Nor can they lay off or discharge employees on these grounds. Sexual preference has been added to the list in some local jurisdictions.[27] Selection and all other personnel decisions must be made solely on the basis of objective criteria such as ability to perform or seniority. Lawsuits and fines by agencies such as the Equal Employment Opportunity Commission (EEOC) are powerful incentives to comply with

job analysis Identifying task and skill requirements for specific jobs by studying superior performers.

job description Document that outlines role expectations and skill requirements for a specific job.

EEO laws. In fact, racial discrimination settlements cost Texaco $176 million in 1996 and Coca-Cola $192.5 million in 2000.[28]

Affirmative Action

A more rigorous refinement of EEO legislation is affirmative action. An **affirmative action program (AAP)** is a plan for actively seeking out, employing, and developing the talents of those groups traditionally discriminated against in employment.[29] Affirmative action amounts to a concerted effort to make up for *past* discrimination. EEO, in contrast, is aimed at preventing *future* discrimination. Typical AAPs attack employment discrimination with the following four methods:

1. Active recruitment of women and minorities
2. Elimination of prejudicial questions on employment application forms
3. Establishment of specific goals and timetables for minority hiring
4. Statistical validation of employment testing procedures

Like any public policy that has legal ramifications, the EEO/AAP area is fraught with complexity. Varying political and legal interpretations and inconsistent court decisions have sometimes frustrated and confused managers.[30] Researchers have uncovered both negative and positive findings about affirmative action. On the negative side, "people believed to be hired through affirmative action programs carry a stigma of incompetence no matter how qualified they are for the job."[31] On the positive side, a study based on nationwide U.S. Census Bureau data found that affirmative action had helped the promotion opportunities of black workers in both government and business organizations. In fact, according to the researcher, "with the exception of women in the public sector, women and blacks enjoyed better promotion opportunities than equally qualified and situated white male workers."[32] These findings disturb some white males, who claim to be the victims of "reverse discrimination."[33] At the same time, some minority employees complain of swapping one injustice for another when they take advantage of affirmative action. Legislated social change, however necessary or laudable, is not without pain. Much remains to be accomplished to eliminate the legacy of unfair discrimination in the workplace.

From Affirmative Action to Managing Diversity

As discussed in Chapter 2, the "managing-diversity" movement promises to raise the discussion of equal employment opportunity and affirmative action to a higher plane. One authority on the subject, R. Roosevelt Thomas Jr., put it this way:

> Managers usually see affirmative action and equal employment opportunity as centering on minorities and women, with very little to offer white males. The diversity I'm talking about includes not only race, gender, creed, and ethnicity but also age, background, education, function, and personality differences. The

TABLE 9.2

The Employee Selection Process: Still's PROCEED Model

Step 1: **PREPARE**	▪ Identify existing superior performers ▪ Create a job description for the position ▪ Identify the competencies or skills needed to do the job ▪ Draft interview questions
Step 2: **REVIEW**	▪ Review questions for legality and fairness
Step 3: **ORGANIZE**	▪ Select your interview team and your method of interviewing ▪ Assign roles to your team and divide the questions
Step 4: **CONDUCT**	▪ Gather data from the job candidate
Step 5: **EVALUATE**	▪ Determine the match between the candidate and the job
Step 6: **EXCHANGE**	▪ Share data in a discussion meeting
Step 7: **DECIDE**	▪ Make the final decision

Source: From Del J. Still, *High Impact Hiring: How to Interview and Select Outstanding Employees*, 3rd edition revised, 2006, pp. 43–44. Reproduced with permission of Del J. Still, Management Development Systems, www.HireUp.com.

affirmative action program (AAP) Making up for past discrimination by actively seeking and employing minorities.

objective is not to assimilate minorities and women into a dominant white male culture but to create a dominant heterogeneous culture.[34]

In short, diversity advocates want to replace all forms of bigotry, prejudice, and intolerance with tolerance and, ideally, *appreciation* of interpersonal differences.[35] They also want to broaden the focus to include recruitment and retention of a diverse collection of people. Joe Watson, the African-American founder and CEO of Virginia-based StrategicHire.com, an executive search firm, recently stated the business case for diversity:

> *... it's smart business strategy. If you want to satisfy clients and customers from diverse backgrounds, Watson says, you need a diverse mix of employees who are more likely to understand them. Diversity can also stimulate creativity: People from various cultural and ethnic backgrounds offer different perspectives that can spur innovation.*[36]

Periodically, as in the cases of Texaco and Coca-Cola, we are reminded of just how much remains to be done (See Best Practices on page 246).

Accommodating the Needs of People with Disabilities

From the perspective of someone in a wheelchair, the world can be a very unfriendly place. Curbs, stairways, and inward-swinging doors in small public toilet stalls all symbolically say, "You're not welcome here; you don't fit in." Human disabilities vary widely, but historically, disabled people have had one thing in common— unemployment. Consider these telling statistics:

> *Today, more than 54 million Americans are disabled, nearly 20 percent of the U.S. population. One in five disabled adults has not graduated from high school, and more than 70 percent of disabled people between ages 18 and 55 are unemployed.*[37]

Reducing the unemployment rate for people with disabilities is not just about jobs and money. It is about self-sufficiency, hopes, and dreams.[38] With the enactment of the Americans with Disabilities Act of 1990 (ADA), disabled Americans hoped to get a real chance to take their rightful place in the workforce.[39] But according to recent data, this hope remains unfulfilled. In fact, added government regulation reportedly has discouraged some employers from hiring disabled people. The disappointing findings: "analysis of Census Bureau survey data from 1987 to 1996 indicates that the act's impact on employment of the disabled was negative."[40]

The ADA, enforced by the EEOC, requires employers to make *reasonable* accommodations to the needs of present and future employees with physical and mental disabilities. As the ADA was being phased in to cover nearly all employers, many feared their businesses would be saddled with burdensome expenses and many lawsuits. But a 1998 White House–sponsored survey "determined that the mean cost of helping disabled workers to overcome their impairments was a mere $935 per person."[41]

New technology is also making accommodation easier.[42] Large-print computer screens for the partially blind, braille keyboards and talking computers for the blind, and telephones with visual readouts for the deaf are among today's helpful technologies. Here are some general policy guidelines for employers:

▌ Audit all facilities, policies, work rules, hiring procedures, and labor union contracts to eliminate barriers and bias.

The world changed for Carmen Jones when a car accident during her junior year at Virginia's Hampton University left her in a wheelchair for life. After months of painful rehabilitation, an inspiring boost from the university's president helped her eliminate deep self-doubts and earn a marketing degree with honors. It's been onward and upward ever since. Now she's the founding president of Solutions Marketing Group in Arlington, Virginia. The company helps businesses reach and better serve disabled people—a group Jones believes is seriously underserved. For Jones, the key word in disability is "ability."

▌ Train all managers in ADA compliance and all employees in how to be sensitive to coworkers and customers with disabilities.

▌ Do not hire anyone who cannot safely perform the basic duties of a particular job with reasonable accommodation.

With lots of low-tech ingenuity, a touch of high tech, and support from coworkers, millions of disabled people can make meaningful contributions in the workplace.

Employment Selection Tests

EEO guidelines in the United States have broadened the definition of an **employment selection test** to include any procedure used as a basis for an employment decision. This means that, in addition to traditional pencil-and-paper tests, numerous other procedures qualify as tests, such as unscored application forms; informal and formal interviews; performance tests; and physical, educational, or experience requirements.[43] This definition of an employment test takes on added significance when you realize that in the United States the federal government requires that all employment tests be statistically valid and reliable predictors of job success.[44] Historically, women and minorities have been victimized by invalid, unreliable, and prejudicial employment selection procedures. Similar complaints have been voiced about the use of personality tests, polygraphs, drug tests, and AIDS and DNA screening during the hiring process[45] (see Table 9.3 on page 234).

employment selection test   Any procedure used in the employment decision process.

Effective Interviewing

Interviewing warrants special attention here because it is the most common tool for selecting employees. Line managers at all levels are often asked to interview candidates for job openings and promotions and should be aware of the

TABLE 9.3

Employment Testing Techniques: An Overview

Type of test	Purpose	Comments
Pencil-and-paper psychological and personality tests	Measure attitudes and personality characteristics such as emotional stability, intelligence, and ability to deal with stress.	Renewed interest based on claims of improved validity. Can be expensive when scoring and interpretations are done by professionals. Validity varies widely from test to test.
Pencil-and-paper honesty tests (integrity testing)	Assess candidate's degree of risk for engaging in dishonest behavior.	Inexpensive to administer. Promising evidence of validity. Growing in popularity since recent curtailment of polygraph testing. Women tend to do better than men.
Job skills tests (clerical and manual dexterity tests, math and language tests, assessment centers, and simulations)	Assess competence in actual "hands-on" situations.	Generally good validity if carefully designed and administered. Assessment centers and simulations can be very expensive.
Polygraph (lie detector) tests	Measure physical signs of stress, such as rapid pulse and perspiration.	Growing use in recent years severely restricted by federal (Employee Polygraph Protection Act of 1988), state, and local laws. Questionable validity.
Drug tests	Check for controlled substances through urine, blood, or hair samples submitted to chemical analysis.	Rapidly growing in use despite strong employee resistance and potentially inaccurate procedures.
Handwriting analysis (graphoanalysis)	Infer personality characteristics and styles from samples of handwriting.	Popular in Europe and growing in popularity in United States. Sweeping claims by proponents leave validity in doubt.
AIDS/HIV antibody tests	Find evidence of AIDS virus through blood samples.	An emerging area with undetermined legal and ethical boundaries. Major confidentiality issue.
Genetic/DNA screening	Use tissue or blood samples and family history data to identify those at risk of costly diseases.	Limited but growing use strongly opposed on legal and moral grounds. Major confidentiality issue.

weaknesses of the traditional unstructured interview. The traditional unstructured or informal interview, which has no fixed question format or systematic scoring procedure, has been criticized on grounds such as the following:

▌ It is highly susceptible to distortion and bias.

▌ It is highly susceptible to legal attack.

▌ It is usually indefensible if legally contested.

▌ It may have apparent validity, but no real validity.

▌ It is rarely totally job-related and may incorporate personal items that infringe on privacy.

▌ It is the most flexible selection technique, and thereby highly inconsistent.

- There is a tendency for the interviewer to look for qualities he or she prefers and then to justify the hiring decision based on these qualities.

- Often the interviewer does not hear about the selection mistakes.

- There is an unsubstantiated confidence in the traditional interview.[46]

The Problem of Cultural Bias

Traditional unstructured interviews are notorious for being culturally insensitive. Evidence of this problem surfaced in a study of the interviewing practices of 38 general managers employed by nine different fast-food chains. According to the researcher:

> *Considering the well-known demographics of today's workforce, it's amazing that 9 percent of those receiving a negative hiring decision are turned down for inappropriate eye contact. To give a firm handshake and look someone straight in the eyes is a very important lesson taught by Dad to every middle-class male at a tender age. Not only do nonmainstream groups miss the lesson from Dad, some are taught that direct eye contact is rude or worse. Girls are frequently taught that direct eye contact is unbecoming in a female. In reality, having averted or shifty eyes may indicate mostly that the job applicant is not a middle-class male.[47]*

Managers can be taught, however, to be aware of and to overcome cultural biases when interviewing. This is particularly important in today's era of managing diversity and showing greater sensitivity to disabled people.

Structured Interviews

Structured interviews are the recommended alternative to traditional unstructured or informal interviews.[48] A **structured interview** is defined as a set of job-related questions with standardized answers that are applied consistently across all interviews for a specific job.[49] Structured interviews are constructed, conducted, and scored by a committee of three to six members with the goal of eliminating individual bias. The systematic format and scoring of structured interviews eliminate the weaknesses inherent in unstructured interviews. Four types of questions typically characterize structured interviews:

1. Situational
2. Job knowledge
3. Job sample simulation
4. Worker requirements (see Table 9.4 on page 236)

Behavioral Interviewing

Behavioral scientists tell us that past behavior is the best predictor of future behavior. We are, after all, creatures of habit. Situational-type interview questions can be greatly strengthened by anchoring them to actual past behavior (as opposed to hypothetical situations).[50] Structured, job-related, behaviorally specific interview questions keep managers from running afoul of the problems associated with unstructured interviews, as previously listed.

> *In a **behavior-based interview**, candidates are asked to recall specific actions they have taken in past job-related situations and describe them in detail. . . . Behavior-based interviews are rich with verifiable data. Candidates are required to include details such as names, dates, times, locations, and numbers.*

structured interview A set of job-related questions that have standardized answers.

behavior-based interview Detailed questions about specific behavior in past job-related situations.

TABLE 9.4

Types of Structured Interview Questions

Type of question	Method	Information sought	Sample question
Situational	Oral	Can the applicant handle difficult situations likely to be encountered on the job?	"What would you do if you saw two of your people arguing loudly in the work area?"
Job knowledge	Oral or written	Does the applicant possess the knowledge required for successful job performance?	"Do you know how to do an Internet search?"
Job sample simulation	Observation of actual or simulated performance	Can the applicant actually do essential aspects of the job?	"Can you show us how to compose and send an e-mail message?"
Worker requirements	Oral	Is the applicant willing to cope with job demands such as travel, relocation, or hard physical labor?	"Are you willing to spend 25 percent of your time on the road?"

Source: Updated from "Structured Interviewing: Avoiding Selection Problems," by Elliott D. Pursell, Michael A. Campion, and Sarah R. Gaylord, *Personnel Journal*, November 1980. Reprinted with permission of the authors.

> *Candidates are reminded to use the word "I" rather than using "we" or "they" as they describe past experiences. This helps the candidate remain focused on their role in each situation and helps the interviewer evaluate the presence or absence of specific competencies.*[51]

If the questions are worded appropriately, the net result should provide a good grasp of the individual's relevant skills, initiative, problem-solving ability, and ability to recover from setbacks and learn from mistakes.

For example, this is what a job applicant at Google can expect:

> *Google loves people who are highly analytical and quantitative—people who prefer to wrestle with huge amounts of data rather than be presented with three or four neatly laid out bullets on PowerPoint. If you're a computer scientist, you should be prepared to write code on the spot on a whiteboard during your interview, according to Google engineer Nelson Minar. He adds that interviewers frequently ask job candidates to talk about something they did in the past—and why it was interesting. They're looking not for abstractly brilliant types but rather for "smart people who can build things that work that people will use."*[52]

Business Week recently explained the growing popularity of behavior-based situational interviewing:

> *Whereas the conventional interview has been found to be only 7% accurate in predicting job performance, situational interviews deliver a rating of 54%—the most of any interviewing tool.*[53]

TEST PREPPER 9.2

ANSWERS CAN BE FOUND ON P. 249

True or False?

_____ 1. Networking is critical to job finding, especially in a tough economy.

_____ 2. Job analysis is the process of identifying basic task and skill requirements for specific jobs by studying superior performers.

_____ 3. Determining the match between the candidate and the job involves the "organize" step in the PROCEED model.

_____ 4. The aim of affirmative action programs is preventing future discrimination.

_____ 5. The ultimate goal of managing diversity programs is appreciation of interpersonal differences.

_____ 6. The ADA's impact on employment of the disabled has been negative, according to a Census Bureau survey.

_____ 7. Only pencil-and-paper tests legally qualify as employment selection tests.

_____ 8. Unstructured interviews are preferable because they give the interviewer room for adjusting to the interviewee's personality.

Multiple Choice

_____ 9. In the PROCEED model of the employee selection process, the P and C stand for
   a. Preliminary interview and Credit check.
   b. Plan and Contract.
   c. Preview of job and Candidate selection.
   d. Prepare and Conduct.
   e. Preparation and Commitment.

Online Study Center
ACE the Test
ACE Practice Tests 9.2

_____ 10. The landmark equal employment opportunity (EEO) law in the United States is the
   a. Americans with Disabilities Act of 1990.
   b. Civil Rights Act of 1964.
   c. Bell Act of 1949.
   d. Sherman Act of 1895.
   e. Fair Employment Act of 1982.

_____ 11. _____ is aimed at preventing future discrimination, while _____ amounts to a concerted effort to make up for past discrimination.
   a. ADA; affirmative action
   b. Affirmative action; EEO
   c. EEO; reverse discrimination
   d. Reverse discrimination; ADA
   e. EEO; affirmative action

_____ 12. According to the Americans with Disabilities Act (ADA) of 1990, for people with physical and mental disabilities, what is required of employers?
   a. To provide on-the-job therapists
   b. To eliminate unemployment among the disabled
   c. To make reasonable accommodations
   d. To offer guaranteed employment
   e. To pay all medical benefits

_____ 13. What type of structured interview question has been used if a Walgreens drug store manager asks a job applicant to demonstrate his or her ability to run a cash register?
   a. Job sample simulation
   b. Skill set
   c. Situational
   d. Job knowledge
   e. Worker requirements

PERFORMANCE APPRAISAL

3 ▶ *Discuss how performance appraisals can be made legally defensible.*

Annual performance appraisals are such a common part of modern organizational life that they qualify as a ritual. As with many rituals, the participants repeat the historical pattern without really asking the important questions—"Why?" and "Is there a better way?" Both appraisers and subjects tend to express general dissatisfaction with performance appraisals. In fact, nearly 75 percent of

Online Study Center college.hmco.com/pic/kreitnerSASfound

the companies responding to a survey expressed major dissatisfaction with their performance appraisal system.[54] This is not surprising, in view of the following observation:

> The annual performance review process, touted by some as the gateway to future prosperity, is, in reality for many companies, nothing more than a fill-in-the-blank, form-completing task that plots an individual's performance against a sanitized list of often generic corporate expectations and required competencies.[55]

Considering that experts estimate the average cost of a *single* performance appraisal to be $1,500, the waste associated with poorly administered appraisals is mind boggling![56] Performance appraisal can be effective and satisfying if systematically developed and implemented techniques replace haphazard methods. For our purposes, **performance appraisal** is the process of evaluating individual job performance as a basis for making objective personnel decisions.[57] This definition intentionally excludes occasional coaching, in which a supervisor simply checks an employee's work and gives immediate feedback. Although personal coaching is fundamental to good management, formally documented appraisals are needed both to ensure that opportunities and rewards are equitably distributed and to avoid prejudicial treatment of protected minorities.[58]

performance appraisal Evaluating job performance as a basis for personnel decisions.

In this section, we will examine two important aspects of performance appraisal: (1) legal defensibility and (2) alternative techniques.

Making Performance Appraisals Legally Defensible

Lawsuits that challenge the legality of specific performance appraisal systems and the personnel actions that result from them have left scores of human resource managers asking themselves, "Will my organization's performance appraisal system stand up in court?" From the standpoint of limiting legal exposure, it is better to ask this question while you are developing a formal appraisal system rather than after it has been implemented. Managers need specific criteria to develop legally defensible performance appraisal systems. Fortunately, researchers have discerned some instructive patterns in court decisions.

After studying the verdicts in 66 employment discrimination cases in the United States, one pair of researchers found that employers could successfully defend their appraisal systems if they satisfied four criteria:

1. A *job analysis* was used to develop the performance appraisal system.
2. The appraisal system was *behavior-oriented*, not trait-oriented.
3. Performance evaluators followed *specific written instructions* when conducting appraisals.
4. Evaluators *reviewed the results* of the appraisals with the ratees.[59]

Each of these conditions has a clear legal rationale. Job analysis, which we discussed earlier relative to employee selection, anchors the appraisal process to specific job duties, not to personalities. Behavior-oriented appraisals properly focus management's attention on *how* the individual actually performed his or her job.[60] Performance appraisers who follow specific written instructions are less likely to be plagued by vague performance standards and/or personal bias. Finally, by reviewing employees' performance appraisal results with them personally, managers provide the feedback to help them learn and improve. Managers who keep in mind these criteria for legal defensibility as well as the elements of a good appraisal shown in

Table 9.5 are better equipped to select a sound appraisal system from alternative approaches and techniques.

Alternative Performance Appraisal Techniques

The list of alternative performance appraisal techniques is long and growing. Appraisal software programs also are proliferating. Unfortunately, many are simplistic, invalid, and unreliable. In general terms, an *invalid* appraisal instrument does not accurately measure what it is supposed to measure. *Unreliable* instruments do not measure criteria in a consistent manner. Many other performance appraisal techniques are so complex that they are impractical and burdensome to use. But armed with a working knowledge of the most popular appraisal techniques, a good manager can distinguish the strong from the weak. Once again, the strength of an appraisal technique is gauged by its conformity to the criteria for legal defensibility discussed previously. The following are some of the techniques that have been used through the years:

TABLE 9.5

Elements of a Good Performance Appraisal

Appraisals can be used to justify merit increases, document performance problems, or simply "touch base" with employees. Experts say HR first must decide what it wants the appraisal to accomplish, then customize the form and the process to meet that goal. Elements to consider include:

1. Objectives set by the employee and manager at the last appraisal.
2. List of specific competencies or skills being measured, with examples of successful behaviors.
3. Ratings scale appropriate to the organization.
4. Space for employee's self-appraisal.
5. Space for supervisor's appraisal.
6. Space for specific comments from the supervisor about the employee's performance.
7. Suggestions for employee development.
8. Objectives to meet by the next appraisal date.

Source: From *HR Magazine* by Carla Joinson, "Making Sure Employees Measure Up," March 2001. Copyright © 2001 by Society for Human Resource Management (SHRM). Reproduced with permission of Society for Human Resource Management (SHRM) via Copyright Clearance Center.

- *Goal setting.* Within a management-by-objectives (MBO) framework, performance is typically evaluated in terms of formal objectives set at an earlier date. This is a comparatively strong technique if desired outcomes are clearly linked to specific behavior. For example, a product design engineer's "output" could be measured in terms of the number of product specifications submitted per month.

- *Written essays.* Managers describe the performance of employees in narrative form, sometimes in response to predetermined questions. Evaluators often criticize this technique for consuming too much time. This method is also limited by the fact that some managers have difficulty expressing themselves in writing.

- *Critical incidents.* Specific instances of inferior and superior performance are documented by the supervisor when they occur. Accumulated incidents then provide an objective basis for evaluations at appraisal time. The strength of the critical incidents technique is enhanced when evaluators document specific behavior in specific situations and ignore personality traits.[61]

- *Graphic rating scales.* Various traits or behavior are rated on incremental scales. For example, "initiative" could be rated on a 1 (= low)—2—3—4—5 (= high) scale. This technique is among the weakest when personality traits are employed. However, **behaviorally anchored rating scales (BARS)**, which are performance rating scales that are divided into increments of observable job behavior determined through job analysis, are considered to be one of the

behaviorally anchored rating scales (BARS) Performance appraisal scales with notations about observable behavior.

strongest performance appraisal techniques. For example, managers at credit-card issuer Capital One use performance rating scales with behavioral anchors such as: "Do you get things done well through other people? Do you play well as a team member?"[62]

▌ *Weighted checklists.* In weighted checklists, evaluators check appropriate adjectives or behavioral descriptions that have predetermined weights. The weights, which gauge the relative importance of the randomly mixed items on the checklist, are usually unknown to the evaluator. Following the evaluation, the weights of the checked items are added or averaged to permit interpersonal comparisons. As with the other techniques, the degree of behavioral specificity largely determines the strength of weighted checklists.

▌ *Rankings/comparisons.* Coworkers in a subunit are ranked or compared in head-to-head fashion according to specified accomplishments or job behavior. A major shortcoming of this technique is that the absolute distance between ratees is unknown. For example, the employee ranked number one may be five times as effective as number two, who in turn is only slightly more effective than number three. Rankings/comparisons are also criticized for causing resentment among lower-ranked, but adequately performing, coworkers. *Fortune* recently offered this update:

> In companies across the country, from General Electric to Hewlett-Packard, such grading systems—in which all employees are ranked against one another and grades are distributed along some sort of bell curve—are creating a firestorm of controversy. In the past 15 months employees have filed class-action suits against Microsoft and Conoco as well as Ford, claiming that the companies discriminate in assigning grades. In each case, a different group of disaffected employees is bringing the charges: older workers at Ford, blacks and women at Microsoft, U.S. citizens at Conoco.[63]

Ford has since dropped its forced ranking system.[64] This technique can be strengthened by combining it with a more behavioral technique, such as critical incidents or BARS.

▌ *Multirater appraisals.* This is a general label for a diverse array of nontraditional appraisal techniques involving more than one rater of the evaluated person's performance. The rationale for multirater appraisals is that "two or more heads are less biased than one." One approach that has enjoyed faddish popularity in recent years is "360-degree feedback." In a **360-degree review**, a manager is evaluated by his or her boss, peers, and subordinates. The results may or may not be statistically pooled and are generally fed back anonymously.[65] Although 360-degree feedback is best suited for use in management development programs, some companies have turned it into a performance appraisal tool, with predictably mixed results.[66] If 360-degree appraisals are to be successful, they need to be carefully designed and skillfully implemented.

360-degree review Pooled, anonymous evaluation by one's boss, peers, and subordinates.

"I work best when someone is looking over my shoulder and telling me that I'm a screw-up."

Source: Cartoon by VOJTKO

True or False?

_____ 1. General dissatisfaction with performance appraisals is expressed by both appraisers and subjects.

_____ 2. Trait-oriented performance appraisals, from a legal viewpoint, are more defensible than behavior-oriented ones.

_____ 3. Behaviorally anchored rating scales (BARS) are a strong performance appraisal technique.

_____ 4. Only the immediate supervisor should perform 360-degree appraisals if they are to be successful.

Multiple Choice

_____ 5. Which of the following is *not* a criterion for legally defensible performance appraisals in the United States?
   a. Results linked with compensation decisions
   b. Results reviewed with ratees
   c. Based on job analysis
   d. Specific written instructions for evaluators
   e. Behavior-oriented

_____ 6. If Abdula writes down specific examples of his employees' good and bad performance as they occur, and later he uses that evidence during performance appraisals, he is relying on which performance appraisal technique?
   a. Rankings/comparisons
   b. Weighted checklists
   c. Graphic rating scales
   d. Critical incidents
   e. Checklists

_____ 7. Which performance appraisal technique involves input from one's boss, peers, and subordinates?
   a. Ranking/comparisons
   b. An inverted appraisal
   c. A 360-degree review
   d. Goal setting
   e. A sunset review

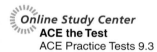
Online Study Center
ACE the Test
ACE Practice Tests 9.3

TRAINING

4 ► *Contrast the ingredients of good training programs for both skill and factual learning, and explain the role of training in preventing sexual harassment*

No matter how carefully job applicants are screened and selected, typically a gap remains between what employees *do* know and what they *should* know. Training is needed to fill in this knowledge gap. In 2006, U.S. companies with 100 or more employees spent $55.8 billion on training, according to *Training* magazine's annual industry survey.[67] Huge as this number sounds, it still is not nearly enough. How the $55.8 billion was spent is also a problem. Most of it was spent by big companies training already well-educated managers and professionals.

Clearly, American managers need to rethink the country's training priorities. Remedial education and basic-skills training for nonmanagement personnel are good for both the employer and the employee.

> *At Borden Foodservice, 71 percent of those who received basic-skills certification remained employed five years later, despite downsizing and the sale of the company. Of those who received other training, but not basic skills, only 54 percent are still with the company. In the same period and among the same groups of employees, 21 percent of basic-skills trainees were promoted, while not a single promotion was made from among those who had not received the training.[68]*

FIGURE 9.1

The Content and Delivery of Today's Training

Source: Data from top portion and graphic in bottom portion from Tammy Galvin "2006 Industry Report," *Training,* 43, December 2006, pp. 25–26. Copyright © 2006 Nielsen Business Media, Inc. Reprinted with permission from *Training.*

Which program areas will receive the most funding resources in the coming year?

- Sales training — 33%
- Management/Supervisory training — 29%
- IT/Systems training — 24%
- Mandatory/Compliance training — 19%
- Customer service training — 19%
- Profession/Industry-specific training — 17%
- Interpersonal skills — 13%
- Desktop application training — 10%
- Executive development — 7%

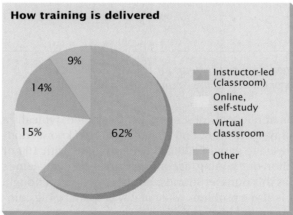

How training is delivered

- Instructor-led (classroom) — 62%
- Online, self-study — 15%
- Virtual classsroom — 14%
- Other — 9%

The need for more extensive worker skill training is inescapable in view of a "perfect storm" of demographic and technological trends. Demographically, the huge post–World War II baby-boom generation is hitting retirement age. Jeff Taylor, founder of Monster.com, the Internet job-search leader, recently framed the demographic dilemma this way: "About 70 million baby boomers, some highly skilled, will exit the workforce over the next 18 years with only 40 million workers coming in."[69] Meanwhile, technological change will continue to increase the need for so-called knowledge workers, people who are comfortable with math, science, and technology.

Formally defined, **training** is the process of changing employee behavior and/or attitudes through some type of guided experience. In this section we focus on the content and delivery of modern training, the ingredients of a good training program, the important distinction between skill and factual learning, and a contemporary training challenge (discouraging sexual harassment).

Today's Training: Content and Delivery

Training magazine's annual survey of companies with at least 100 employees gives us a revealing snapshot of current training practices.[70] The top portion of Figure 9.1 lists the nine most common types of training. How that training was delivered in 2006 is displayed in the bottom portion of the figure. Surprisingly, despite all we read and hear about computer-based training and e-learning over the Internet, the majority of today's training is remarkably low tech.[71] We anticipate growth of e-learning and other nontraditional methods as the technology becomes more user-friendly and more affordable.[72] Meanwhile, the old standbys—classroom presentations, workbooks/manuals, videotapes/DVDs, and seminars—are still the norm. For better or for worse, the typical college classroom is still a realistic preview of what awaits you in the world of workplace training.

Which instructional method is best? There are probably as many answers to this question as there are trainers. Given variables such as different learning styles, budget limitations, and instructors'capabilities, it is safe to say that there is no one best training technique. For example, the lecture method, though widely criticized for being dull and encouraging learner passivity, is still on top in the study just discussed. Whatever method is used, trainers need to do their absolute best because they are key facilitators for people's achievement of their hopes and dreams.

The Ingredients of a Good Training Program

Although training needs and approaches vary, managers can get the most out of their training budgets by following a few guidelines. According to two training specialists, every training program should be designed along the following lines to maximize retention and transfer learning to the job:

1. Maximize the similarity between the training situation and the job situation.
2. Provide as much experience as possible in the task being taught.
3. Provide a variety of examples when teaching concepts or skills.
4. Label or identify the important features of a task.
5. Make sure that general principles are understood before expecting much transfer.
6. Make sure that the trained behaviors and ideas are rewarded in the job situation.
7. Design the training content so that the trainees can see its applicability.
8. Use adjunct questions to guide the trainee's attention.[73]

Skill Versus Factual Learning

The ingredients of a good training program vary according to whether skill learning or factual learning is the goal.

> *Effective skill learning should incorporate four essential ingredients: (1) goal setting, (2) modeling, (3) practice, and (4) feedback. Let's take as an example the*

training   Using guided experience to change employee behavior/attitudes.

REALITY CHECK 9.4

"... the decline in American education threatens U.S. competitiveness. If the gap continues to grow, our standard of living will fall relative to those countries that are doing a better job educating their workforces. Reversing this trend, and preparing Americans for 21st century work, will require the collaboration efforts of government, business, and the academic community."

Source: Susan Meisinger, "Education Gap Threatens U.S. Competitiveness," *HR Magazine,* 52 (March 2007): 10.

Question: As a life-long "consumer" of the educational process, what are your recommendations for schools and corporate trainers to improve the quality of the nation's workforce?

task of training someone to ride horseback. How would you do it? You must tell the person specifically what you want him or her to do (goal setting), show the person how you want him or her to do it (modeling), give the person the opportunity to try out what you have told and shown him or her (practice), and then tell the person what they are doing correctly (feedback).[74]

When factual learning is the goal, the same sequence is used, except that in step 2, "meaningful presentation of the materials" is substituted for modeling. Keep in mind that the object of training is *learning*. Learning requires thoughtful preparation, carefully guided exposure to new ideas or behavior, and motivational support.[75]

Needed: Training to Discourage Sexual Harassment

A great deal of misunderstanding surrounds the topic of sexual harassment because of sexist attitudes, vague definitions, and inconsistent court findings. **Sexual harassment**, defined generally as unwanted sexual attention or conduct, has both behavioral and legal dimensions (see Table 9.6). Important among these are the following:

sexual harassment Unwanted sexual attention that creates an offensive or intimidating work environment.

▮ Although typically it is female employees who are the victims of sexual harassment, both women and men (in the United States) are protected under Title VII of the Civil Rights Act of 1964.

▮ Sexual harassment includes, but is not limited to, unwanted physical contact. Gestures, displays, joking, and language also may create a sexually offensive or intimidating work environment.

▮ It is the manager's job to be aware of and correct cases of sexual harassment. Ignorance of such activity is not a valid legal defense.

▮ A proactive approach, including sexual harassment training, is strongly recommended.[76]

Research evidence indicates that sexual harassment is commonplace and persistent in the United States. A telephone survey of 612 employees from across the

---

TABLE 9.6

Behavioral and Legal Dimensions of Sexual Harassment

What exactly is sexual harassment? According to the Equal Employment Opportunity Commission (EEOC) sexual harassment is:

▮ Unwelcome sexual advances

▮ Requests for sexual favors, and other verbal or physical conduct of a sexual nature constitute sexual harassment when submission to such conduct is made a condition of employment

▮ When submission to or rejection of sexual advances is used as a basis for employment decisions

▮ When such conduct creates an intimidating, hostile, or offensive work environment

These EEOC guidelines interpreting Title VII of the Civil Rights Act of 1964 further state that employers are responsible for the actions of their supervisors and agents and that employers are responsible for the actions of other employees if the employer knows or should have known about the sexual harassment.

Source: From *Personnel* by Terry Thornton, "Sexual Harassment, 1: Discouraging It in the Work Place," April 1986. Copyright © 1986 by American Management Association. Reproduced with permission of American Management Association via Copyright Clearance Center.

country yielded this finding: "Following a pattern seen for the last three years, the most frequent offensive remarks were sexually related, with remarks rising by 4 percentage points, from 31 percent in 2004 to 35 percent [in 2005]."[77] Employees using e-mail systems must also contend with problems of sexual harassment in the form of rape threats and obscene words and graphics. In 2000, "Dow Chemical fired 50 employees and disciplined 200 others after an e-mail investigation turned up hard-core pornography and violent subject matter. . . . 'This sort of activity creates a harassment environment that we can't tolerate,' [said a company official]."[78] Sexual harassment begins early, with 83 percent of high school girls and 60 percent of high school boys reportedly experiencing it.[79] According to research, people generally agree that unwanted sexual propositions, promises, or threats tied to sexual favors; lewd comments, gestures, or jokes; and touching, grabbing, or brushing qualify as sexual harassment. Beyond that, opinions differ.[80] Personal tastes and sensibilities vary widely from individual to individual. Employees need to take proactive steps to respond to harassment.

What Can the Victim Do?

Employees who believe they are victims of sexual harassment can try to live with it, fight back, complain to higher-ups, find another job, or sue their employer. Those who choose to file a lawsuit need to know how to arrange the odds in their favor. An analysis of sexual harassment cases revealed that the following five factors are likely to lead to success. Victims of sexual harassment tended to win their lawsuits when the following applied:

▌ The harassment was severe.

▌ There were witnesses.

▌ Management had been notified.

▌ There was supporting documentation.

▌ Management had failed to take action.[81]

The more of these five factors that apply, the greater the chances of success for a sexual harassment lawsuit. Courtrooms are the last line of defense for victims of sexual harassment. Preventive and remedial actions are also needed. Harassers need to be told by their victims, coworkers, and supervisors that their actions are illegal, unethical, and against company policy. As more organizations develop and enforce sexual harassment policies and conduct training programs, the problem can be greatly reduced without costly court battles and the loss of valued employees.

What Can the Organization Do?

Starting with top management, an organizationwide commitment to eliminating sexual harassment should be established. A clear policy statement, with behavioral definitions of sexual harassment and associated penalties, is essential. As with all policies, sexual harassment policies need to be disseminated and uniformly enforced if they are to have the desired impact. Appropriate training, particularly for new employees, can alert people to the problem and consequences of sexual harassment.[82] Finally, in accordance with EEOC guidelines, management can remain adequately informed of any sexual harassment in the organization by establishing a grievance procedure. Harassed employees should be able to get a fair hearing of their case without fear of retaliation.

TEST PREPPER 9.4

ANSWERS CAN BE FOUND ON P. 249

True or False?

_____ 1. The U.S. labor force faces a shortage of skilled workers in the next 10 to 20 years.

_____ 2. The vast bulk of today's training is remarkably low-tech, despite what is published about computer-based training and e-learning via the Internet.

_____ 3. For both skill and factual learning, the ingredients of a good training program are identical.

_____ 4. Verbal misconduct cannot be considered sexual harassment.

Multiple Choice

_____ 5. According to *Training* magazine's recent survey of training practices in the United States, _____ is (are) the most common instructional method.
   a. traditional classroom programs
   b. virtual reality
   c. internships
   d. e-learning
   e. role-playing

_____ 6. What advice should you give to a hotel manager who wants to create a good training program for service trainees?
   a. Don't waste your time with training; simply hire qualified people.
   b. Make the training situation as realistic as possible.
   c. Don't distract trainees with questions.
   d. Minimize examples to avoid confusion.
   e. Have the trainees themselves act as instructors.

_____ 7. _____ is *not* an essential ingredient of an effective skill-learning program.
   a. Showing trainees how to do it with modeling
   b. Letting trainees practice
   c. Setting goals
   d. Using lecture/discussion to present the materials
   e. Giving feedback

_____ 8. Individuals who believe they are being sexually harassed at work and would like to file a lawsuit should follow which advice?
   a. Find witnesses
   b. Threaten the harasser with dire consequences
   c. Wait until you're physically assaulted
   d. Just ignore it
   e. Make sure a manager is the aggressor

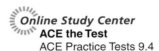

Online Study Center
ACE the Test
ACE Practice Tests 9.4

BEST PRACTICES

Dick Kovacevich, CEO of Wells Fargo Bank, Tells Why Diversity Is Good for Business

Question:

I know firsthand that in California you have a very diverse workforce. In some branches, I'd guess one in three workers is foreign-born. Have you thought about why you employ so many immigrants?

Answer:

Well, first of all, our customer base is that way too. So we need a diverse workforce to better serve our customer base. There's certainly a lot of cultural familiarity that is important, as well as language skills.

And unfortunately, there are corporations that aren't as welcoming to diversity. There's accidental and not-so-accidental discrimination. We will go out of our way to help with issues related to diversity—for example, we'll give people language classes, and we'll make sure our supervisors know that they may ask more questions and have some problems for a while.

Question:

How does that pay off for Wells Fargo?

Answer:

We think it's the right thing to do, but also these people, if they become loyal to Wells Fargo, are going to tell a lot of people about their positive experience working here. Once you have people saying "Hey, this is a great place to work, I love it"—well, word of mouth in these communities is much more effective than advertising.

One of our fastest-growing areas is mortgages for first-time homeowners, and more than half of first-time homeowners come from minority groups. Almost all of that is done by word of mouth. That's going to do nothing but grow. We may make a little more money or lose a little money in that today, but it's definitely going to pay off in the future.

Source: Excerpted from G. Pascal Zachary, "Bank Different," *Business 2.0*, 7, June 2006, pp. 101–103. Copyright © 2006 Time Inc. All rights reserved.

CLOSING CASE STUDY

American Airlines Trains New Hires How to Soar

At 72, there's nothing new about Fort Worth, Texas-based American Airlines. However, the company, which is enough of an industry stalwart to brag that it partly got its start by acquiring a company that Charles Lindbergh was chief pilot of, tries to keep its recruiting and training methods as up-to-date as possible.

The process of flight attendant recruitment begins with a telephone screening followed by two in-person interviews, one by a panel of three or four flight attendants, and another that is one-on-one, says Gary Cordray, manager of flight attendant training. Questions usually focus on gauging the potential employee's grasp of good customer service, he observes, "to try to drill down to see how that person will treat other people." Another characteristic the panel evaluates is the recruit's ability to work on a team.

To get a sense of how applicants would handle themselves on board, they are also given hypothetical scenarios to work through and are asked to explain how they would handle various situations that might happen in the air.

Recruiters also are eager to see how well the applicant is able to work in a diverse environment, Cordray says. He says a potential employee might be asked if she were a waitress in a restaurant, whether or not there would be any group she would not want to wait on, such as table of senior citizens, teenagers or individuals from another country.

American tries its best to replicate on the ground the conditions flight attendants will experience up in the air, Cordray says, through the use of two types of simulators, one that is used to train new hires in the art of food service, and another that is used to train them how to handle emergencies. "They look exactly like a real aircraft, real seats, real galleys," he says. Adjacent to the simulator there's a viewing area that allows instructors to keep an eye on new hires as they go through their exercises. Here, students practice "serving" each other to get a feel for the real-world demands of catering to passengers. The simulator isn't an operable airplane, but Cordray says it was built with aircraft parts. "It's the actual parts re-built into a classroom setting," he says. Students' performances also can be videotaped for further review.

Approximately six-and-a-half weeks long, initial training, like all of the training provided to the company's flight attendants, is conducted in Dallas, home to the American Airlines Training and Conference Center and the American Airlines Flight Academy.

"The major components of [initial] training are the customer-service aspect, the service they provide on the airplane, food service, making sure passengers are comfortable, the safety and security and being able to handle any kind of emergency situation, all the way from medical to evacuating the aircraft," Cordray says. In addition to the use of simulators, in-flight crisis training is also facilitated in a separate room at the training center that has a mock-up of every door and window exit flight attendants need to know how to open.

American currently has close to 19,000 flight attendants, with about 100 receiving federally required recurrent training most days of the year at one of its Dallas facilities, Cordray says. To accommodate this volume, American holds three classes a day at three start times, with approximately 40 flight attendants in each class. . . .

For new hires, all testing at American is done online, and there are modules containing reviews of course material that can be accessed during training.

American also hosts a flight service Web site to reference procedural changes and other training-related concerns, says curriculum program developer Pete Zografos. "When we first embarked on e-learning, we evaluated where our instructor-led curriculum was currently, and through several sets of evaluations, or tests on what type of audience we had, and the way it was presently conducted, we determined which [classes] would be good candidates for e-learning and which should remain instructor-led," says Zografos, adding the company also consulted about this with the Federal Aviation Administration (FAA). "There are some classes that are practical, that require some sort of practical,

accomplished task, and would not be a good candidate for e-learning," he says.

Source: Excerpted from Margery Weinstein, "The American Way," *Training*, 43, May 2006, pp. 54–55. Copyright © 2006 Nielsen Business Media, Inc. Reprinted with permission from *Training*.

Case Questions

1. Is the concept of "human capital" evident in this case? Explain.
2. Which, if any, of Pfeffer's seven people-centered practices are evident in this case? Explain.
3. If you were an American Airlines recruiter, what specific behavioral interview questions would you ask job applicants for flight attendant positions? Explain.
4. Why not just put the entire flight attendant curriculum online to eliminate all the travel expense and classroom time? Explain.
5. Overall, how do you rate American Airlines's flight attendant program? How could it be improved? Explain.

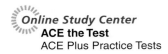

Online Study Center
ACE the Test
ACE Plus Practice Tests

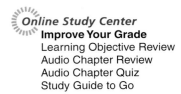

Online Study Center
Improve Your Grade
Learning Objective Review
Audio Chapter Review
Audio Chapter Quiz
Study Guide to Go

LEARNING OBJECTIVE REVIEW

1   *Define the term* human capital, *and identify at least four of Pfeffer's people-centered practices.*

- A systems approach to human resource strategy views both present and future employees as human capital that needs to be developed to its fullest potential.

- Pfeffer's seven people-centered practices can serve as a strategic agenda for human resource management. The seven practices are:
  - Provision of job security
  - Rigorous hiring practices
  - Employee empowerment
  - Performance-based compensation
  - Comprehensive training
  - Reduction of status differences
  - Sharing of key information

2   *Identify and describe the seven steps in the PROCEED model of employee selection, explain the business case for diversity, and explain how managers can be more effective interviewers.*

- The employee selection process can be summed up in the seven-step PROCEED model:
  1. Prepare (job analysis, job descriptions, and interview questions)
  2. Review (legality and fairness of questions)
  3. Organize (assign questions to interview team)
  4. Conduct (collect information from the candidate)
  5. Evaluate (judge candidate's qualifications)
  6. Exchange (meet and discuss information about candidate)
  7. Decide (extend job offer or not)

- Managers need to recruit for diversity to increase their companies' appeal to job applicants and customers alike.

- Federal equal employment opportunity laws require managers to make hiring and other personnel decisions on the basis of the individual's ability to perform rather than personal prejudice.

- Affirmative action—making up for past discrimination—is evolving into managing diversity.
- Appreciation of interpersonal differences within a heterogeneous organizational culture is the goal of managing-diversity programs.
- The Americans with Disabilities Act of 1990 (ADA) requires employers to make reasonable accommodations so that disabled people can succeed in the workforce.
- Because interviews are the most popular employee-screening device, experts recommend structured rather than traditional, informal interviews. Behavioral interviews, with situation-specific questions, are the best structured-interview technique for predicting job performance.

3 *Discuss how performance appraisals can be made legally defensible.*

- Legally defensible performance appraisals enable managers to make objective personnel decisions.
- Four key legal criteria are:
  - Job analysis

  - Behavior-oriented appraisals
  - Specific written instructions
  - Evaluation of results with ratees
- Seven common performance appraisal techniques are:
  - Goal setting
  - Written essays
  - Critical incidents
  - Graphic rating scales
  - Weighted checklists
  - Rankings/comparisons
  - 360-degree reviews

4 *Contrast the ingredients of good training programs for both skill and factual learning, and explain the role of training in preventing sexual harassment.*

- Training programs should be designed with an eye toward maximizing the retention of learning and its transfer to the job.
- Successful skill learning and factual learning both depend on goal setting, practice, and feedback.
- Factual information should be presented in a logical and meaningful manner.
- A sexual harassment policy needs to define the problem of sexual harrassment behaviorally, specify penalties, be disseminated through training, and be enforced.

TEST PREPPER ANSWERS

9.1
1. F 2. T 3. F 4. T 5. b 6. d 7. e

9.2
1. T 2. T 3. F 4. F 5. T 6. T 7. F
8. F 9. d 10. b 11. e 12. c 13. a

9.3
1. T 2. F 3. T 4. F 5. a 6. d 7. c

9.4
1. T 2. T 3. F 4. F 5. a 6. b 7. d
8. a

Online Study Center RESOURCES

Prepare for Class, Improve Your Grade, and ACE the Test. Student Achievement Series resources include:

ACE Practice Tests
Audio Chapter Quizzes
Audio Chapter Reviews
Career Snapshots
Chapter Glossaries
Chapter Outlines

Crossword Puzzles
Decision Case Questions
Ethical Hot Seat Exercises
Flashcards
Hands-on Exercises

Hangman
Key Issue Expansion
Learning Objective Reviews
Study Guide to Go
Visual Glossaries

To access these learning and study tools, go to **college.hmco.com/pic/kreitnerSASfound**.

This transaction at a Starbucks symbolizes the essence of CEO Jim Donald's management style—effective communication.

1 ▸ *Identify each major link to the communication process, explain the concept of media richness, and specify guidelines for using the five communication strategies.*

2 ▸ *Discuss the managerial importance of the grapevine and nonverbal communication, and explain how to encourage upward communication.*

3 ▸ *List two practical tips for each of the major communication technologies (e-mail, cell phones, and videoconferences) and summarize the pros and cons of telecommuting.*

Chapter Outline

Online Study Center
Prepare for Class
Chapter Outline

4 ▶ *Specify at least three practical tips for improving each of the following communication skills: listening, writing, and running a meeting.*

Jim Donald, CEO of Starbucks: "A Double Shot of Productivity"

I'm kind of a simple guy—brewed coffee, straight black. And I do my own e-mails. If anyone in our company e-mails me or leaves me a voicemail, they get a response, quickly. I'm fanatical about communicating. We have to operate like a store. Nobody likes to wait in line. My Treo is a godsend. I get 200 to 250 e-mails a day, and I respond to 75 percent of them. I'm brief, but that's better than not responding.

I also carry a hardback black binder with me. If someone says something particularly smart or not smart, I write it down so I have actual facts to use when I coach people or give reviews.

Return Calls at Dawn

My day in the office starts around 6 A.M. for one reason only: It's the perfect time to reach out to people. This morning I left a voice-mail for 100 regional managers. I also wrote personal thank-you notes to 25 partners—that's what we call our employees. I also

Online Study Center college.hmco.com/pic/kreitnerSASfound

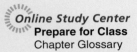

Online Study Center
Prepare for Class
Chapter Glossary

Improve Your Grade
Flashcards
Hangman
Crossword Puzzles

signed 500 birthday cards. Everybody at headquarters gets one from me. My assistant Janet keeps track of birthdays on her computer, and I sign the cards a month ahead. I'll sign more than 3,500 this year.

Limit Meetings to 45 Minutes

I have gotten smarter about meetings. I now book hourlong meetings and insist we do them in 45 minutes. That leaves me 15 minutes to download ideas and check messages. By paring back my meetings, I have saved eight hours a week. Rob Grady, our vice president of the beverage category, told me we could save $12 million in productivity costs if all our senior people did it. I told my SVPs [senior vice presidents], "I want you to take your extra 15 minutes to call someone you usually do not contact every day."

Don't Manage Time: Chart It

Every month Janet catalogs my schedule and gives me a pie chart. My ideal is 40 to 45 percent travel, 20 to 25 percent time with staff, about 8 percent walking around and sticking my head into meetings, 8 percent talking with other CEOs and business partners. I started doing this pie chart because my direct reports said to me, "Hey, where the hell are you?" I wanted to prove to them that I'm here.

Stay Close to Customers

Store visits are my favorite thing. When I'm in Seattle, I visit about 20 stores a week. When I'm traveling, I visit about ten a day. Whenever I go into a Starbucks, I walk right to the back of the counter, put on an apron and start talking to our partners.

You can tell how a store is doing by smelling it, so I stick my nose in the pastry display. I check out the restrooms. I did this in my previous job, as CEO of Pathmark, but I really learned it from Sam Walton, who hired me to run Wal-Mart's Supercenters six months before he died. Sam used to say, "If you want to know what's wrong with the business, ask the front line."[2] ■

One of the most difficult challenges for management is getting individuals to understand and voluntarily pursue organizational objectives. Effective communication, of the sort Starbucks's Jim Donald is striving to achieve, is vital to meeting this challenge. Organizational communication takes in a great deal of territory—virtually every management function and activity can be considered communication in one way or another. Planning and controlling require a lot of communicating, as do organization design and development, decision making and problem solving, leadership, and staffing. Organizational cultures would not exist without communication. Studies have shown that both organizational and individual performance improve when managerial communication is effective.[3] Given today's team-oriented organizations where things need to be accomplished with and through people over whom a manager all too often has no direct authority, communication skills are more important than ever. In fact, a recent survey of 133 executives yielded this evidence:

The most-desired management skill is good communication, followed by a sense of vision, honesty, decisiveness, and ability to build good relationships with employees.[4]

Thanks to modern technology, we can communicate more quickly and less expensively. But the ensuing torrent of messages has proved to be a mixed blessing for managers and nonmanagers alike. Complaints of information overload are common today. Marketing executive Hilary Billings has observed:

There's a growing realization that we're all becoming victims of the technological devices that were supposed to make our lives simpler. The proliferation of laptops, PDAs, and pagers means that we're working harder and harder to keep up with our own inventions. The price of being available 24-7 is the loss of time for reflection, creative thinking, and connections with our loved ones— the things that are really important for our emotional and spiritual lives.[5]

Worse yet, managers have a growing suspicion that more communication is not necessarily better. Research validates this suspicion: "Executives say 14 percent of each 40-hour workweek is wasted because of poor communication between staff and managers. . . . That amounts to a staggering seven workweeks of squandered productivity a year."[6] The challenge to improve this situation is both immense and immediate. But before managers, or anyone else for that matter, can become more effective communicators, they need to appreciate that communication is a complex process subject to much perceptual distortion and many problems. This is especially true for the apparently simple activity of communicating face to face.

THE COMMUNICATION PROCESS AND COMMUNICATION STRATEGIES

1 ► *Identify each major link to the communication process, explain the concept of media richness, and specify guidelines for using the five communication strategies.*

Management scholar Keith Davis defined **communication** as "the transfer of information and understanding from one person to another person."[7] Communication is inherently a social process. Whether one communicates face to face with a single person or with a group of people via television, it is still a social activity involving two or more people. By analyzing the communication process, one discovers that it is a chain made up of identifiable links (see Figure 10.1 on page 254). Links in this process include sender, encoding, medium, decoding, receiver, and feedback.[8] The essential purpose of this chainlike process is to send an idea from one person to another in a way that will be understood by the receiver. Like any other chain, the communication chain is only as strong as its weakest link.[9]

communication Interpersonal transfer of information and understanding.

Encoding

Thinking takes place within the privacy of your brain and is greatly affected by how you perceive your environment. But when you want to pass along a thought to someone else, an entirely different process begins. This second process, communication, requires that you, the sender, package the idea for understandable transmission. Encoding starts at this point. The purpose of encoding is to translate

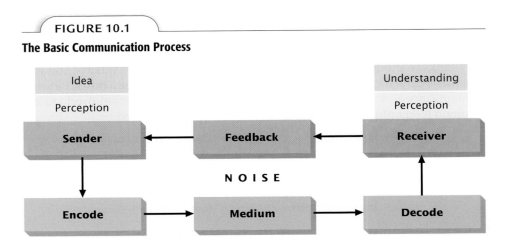

FIGURE 10.1

The Basic Communication Process

internal thought patterns into a language or code that the intended receiver of the message will probably understand.

Managers usually rely on words, gestures, or other symbols for encoding. Their choice of symbols depends on several factors, one of which is the nature of the message itself. Is it technical or nontechnical, emotional or factual? Perhaps it could be expressed better with colorful PowerPoint slides than with words, as in the case of a budget report. To express skepticism, merely a shrug might be enough. More fundamentally, will the encoding help get the attention of busy and distracted people?[10]

Greater cultural diversity in the workplace also necessitates careful message encoding. Trudy Milburn, an American Management Association program coordinator, offers this perspective:

> *Communication becomes problematic when organizations adopt a narrow perspective of communication that focuses on a single normative standard. Some African-American employees, for example, may be discouraged from speaking in a dialect defined as "black English" and may be mandated to adopt proper business grammar. When companies deem their standard to be the only acceptable one, they will not be able to appreciate different ways of interacting.[11]*

In the global marketplace, where language barriers hamper communication, e-mail translation programs promise to make the encoding process a bit easier.

Selecting a Medium

Managers can choose among a number of media: face-to-face conversations, telephone calls, e-mails, memos, letters, computer reports and networks, photographs, bulletin boards, meetings, organizational publications, and others. Communicating with those outside the organization opens up further possibilities, such as news releases, press conferences, and advertising on television and radio or in magazines, in newspapers, and on the Internet.

Media Selection in Cross-Cultural Settings

The importance of selecting an appropriate medium is magnified in both internal and external cross-cultural dealings (see the Closing Case Study on page 277).

Recalling the distinction we made in Chapter 4, managers moving from low-context cultures to high-context cultures need to select communication media with care.

> *The United States, Canada, and northern European nations are defined as low-context cultures, meaning that the verbal content of a message is more important than the medium—the setting through which the message is delivered. In such cultures, a videoconference or an e-mail is usually accepted as an efficient substitute for an in-person meeting.*
>
> *But in other countries—including many in Asia and the Middle East—context, or setting, with its myriad nonverbal cues, can convey far more meaning than the literal words of a given message. In such high-context cultures, business transactions are ritualized, and the style in which the rituals are carried out matters more than the words. A high value is placed on face-to-face interaction, and after-hours socialization with customers and colleagues is almost a daily occurrence.*[12]

A Contingency Approach

A contingency model for media selection has been proposed by Robert Lengel and Richard Daft.[13] It pivots on the concept of media richness. **Media richness** describes the capacity of a given medium to convey information and promote learning. Media vary in richness from high (or rich) to low (or lean). Face-to-face conversation is a rich medium because it:

media richness A medium's capacity to convey information and promote learning.

1. Simultaneously provides *multiple information cues,* such as message content, tone of voice, facial expressions, and so on
2. Facilitates immediate *feedback*
3. Is *personal* in focus. A personal phone call is a relatively rich medium (but a voice-mail message is not as rich). In contrast, posted bulletins and general computer reports are lean media—that is, they convey limited information and foster limited learning. Lean media—such as general e-mails—provide a single cue, do not facilitate immediate face-to-face feedback, and are impersonal.

Management's challenge is to match media richness with the situation. Non-routine problems are best handled with rich media such as face-to-face, telephone, or video interactions. Lean media are appropriate for routine problems. Examples of mismatched media include reading a corporate annual report at a stockholders' meeting (data glut) or announcing a layoff through an impersonal e-mail (data starvation). The latter situation has major ethical implications, as these examples illustrate:

> *In August [2006], RadioShack Corp. notified about 400 employees at its Texas headquarters by e-mail that their positions had been eliminated. And just a few weeks earlier, a London-based body-piercing and jewelry shop reportedly fired one of its sales assistants via a text message.*[14]

Imagine being on the receiving end of these poor media-selection decisions.

Decoding

Even the most expertly fashioned message will not accomplish its purpose unless it is understood. After physically receiving the message, the receiver needs to comprehend it. If the message has been properly encoded, decoding will take place rather routinely. But perfect encoding is nearly impossible to achieve in our world of many languages and cultures. Jerry Adriano, an official with the Hispanic Contractors of America, says the language barrier is a major reason why workplace deaths among Hispanic workers jumped 53 percent between 1992 and 2000:

> *Many Hispanic laborers are Mexican immigrants who don't speak English. Their supervisors often don't speak Spanish. That makes safety training harder. Translating training materials into Spanish doesn't always help, because many immigrants don't read Spanish, Adriano says.*[15]

Also, the receiver's willingness to receive the message is a principal prerequisite for successful decoding. Successful decoding is more likely if the receiver knows the language and terminology used in the message. It helps, too, if the receiver understands the sender's purpose and background situation. Effective listening is given special attention later in this chapter.

Feedback

Some sort of verbal or nonverbal feedback from the receiver to the sender is required to complete the communication process. Appropriate forms of feedback are determined by the same factors that govern the sender's encoding decision. Without feedback, senders have no way of knowing whether their ideas have been accurately understood. Knowing whether others understand us significantly affects both the form and content of our follow-up communication.

Employee surveys consistently underscore the importance of receiving timely and personal feedback from management. For example, one survey of 500,000 employees from more than 300 firms contrasted satisfaction with "coaching and feedback from boss" between two groups of employees: (1) committed employees who planned to stay with their employer for at least five years and (2) those who intended to quit within a year. Satisfaction with coaching and feedback among the committed employees averaged 64 percent, while it dropped to 34 percent among those ready to quit.[16]

Noise

noise Any interference with the normal flow of communication.

Noise is not an integral part of the chainlike communication process, but it may influence the process at any or all points. As the term is used here, **noise** is any interference with the normal flow of understanding from one person to another. This is a very broad definition. Thus, the following also qualify as noise:[17]

▌ A speech impairment

▌ Garbled technical transmission

▌ Negative attitudes

▌ Lies[18]

▌ Misperception

▌ Illegible print or pictures

▌ Telephone static

▌ Partial loss of hearing

▌ Poor eyesight

Nowhere is precise communications more important than in health care. Medical histories, medications, and current symptoms all need to be kept straight. UnitedHealth Group, the largest health-care provider in the United States, relies on high-tech communications to get the job done. Here, an employee at a UnitedHealth nursing home updates a patient's records with a laptop computer. Because nurses and doctors now review all relevant information from an Internet database prior to visiting patients, UnitedHealth has cut down on unnecessary and costly hospitalizations.

Understanding tends to diminish as noise increases. In general, the effectiveness of organizational communication can be improved in two ways. Steps can be taken to make verbal and written messages more understandable. At the same time, noise can be minimized by foreseeing and neutralizing sources of interference.

Communication Strategies

A good deal of effort goes into plotting product development, information technology, financial, and marketing strategies these days. Much less, if any, attention is devoted to organizational communication strategies. Hence, organizational communication tends to be haphazard and often ineffective. A more systematic approach is needed.[19] This section introduces five basic communication strategies, with an eye toward improving the overall quality of communication.

A Communication Continuum with Five Strategies

A team of authors led by communication expert Phillip G. Clampitt created the useful communication strategy continuum shown in Figure 10.2 on page 258. Communication effectiveness is the vertical dimension of the model and ranges from low to high. A message that is communicated via any of the media discussed earlier is effective if the sender's intended meaning is conveyed fully and accurately to the receiver. The horizontal dimension of Clampitt's model is the amount of information transmitted, ranging from great to little. Plotted on this quadrant are five common communication strategies. Let us examine each one more closely.

▌ *Spray & Pray.* This is the organizational equivalent of a large lecture section in which passive receivers are showered with information in the hopes that some of it will stick. Managers employing the Spray & Pray strategy assume "more is better." Unfortunately, as employees swamped every day by corporate e-mail

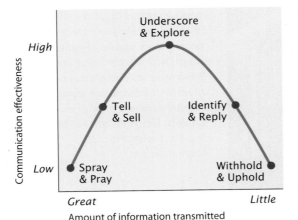

directives and announcements will attest, more is *not* necessarily better. This strategy suffers from being one-way, impersonal, and unhelpful because it leaves receivers to sort out what is actually important or relevant.

■ *Tell & Sell.* This strategy involves communicating a more restricted set of messages and taking time to explain their importance and relevance. Top executives often rely on Tell & Sell when introducing new strategies, merger plans, and reorganizations. A potentially fatal flaw arises when more time is spent polishing the presentation than assessing the receivers' actual needs.

■ *Underscore & Explore.* With this give-and-take strategy, key information and issues closely tied to the organization's success are communicated. Priorities are included and justifications are offered. Unlike the first two strategies, this one is two-way. Receivers are treated as active rather than passive participants in the process. Feedback is generated by "allowing employees the creative freedom to explore the implications of those ideas in a disciplined way."[20] Listening, resolving misunderstandings, building consensus and commitment, and addressing actual or potential obstacles are fundamental to success in the Underscore & Explore strategy.

■ *Identify & Reply.* This is a reactive and sometimes defensive strategy. Employee concerns about prior communications are the central focus here. Employees are not only viewed as active participants; they essentially drive the process because they are assumed to know the key issues. According to Clampitt and his colleagues, "Employees set the agenda, while executives respond to rumors, innuendoes, and leaks."[21] Those using the Identify & Reply strategy need to be good listeners.

■ *Withhold & Uphold.* With this communication strategy, you tell people what you think they need to know only when you believe they need to know it. Secrecy and control are paramount. Because information is viewed as power, it is rationed and restricted. In this command-and-control management style, those in charge uphold their rigid and narrow view of things when challenged or questioned. The Withhold & Uphold communication strategy virtually guarantees rumors and resentment.

In organizational life, one can find hybrid combinations of these five strategies. But usually there is a dominant underlying strategy that may or may not be effective.

Seeking a Middle Ground

Both ends of the continuum in Figure 10.2 are problematic.

> *On one extreme, employees receive all the information they could possibly desire, while at the other, they are provided with little or no communication. Strategies at the extremes have a similar quality: employees have difficulty framing and making sense out of organizational events. Discovering salient information, focusing on core issues, and creating the proper memories are left to employees' personal whims.*[22]

Accordingly, managers need to adhere to the following set of guidelines when selecting a communication strategy appropriate to the situation:

▮ Avoid Spray & Pray and Withhold & Uphold.

▮ Use sparingly Tell & Sell and Identify & Reply.

▮ Use Underscore & Explore as much as possible.

Merging Communication Strategies and Media Richness

Present and future managers who effectively blend lessons from media richness (discussed earlier) and communication strategies (Figure 10.2) are on the path toward improved organizational communication. The trick is to select the richest medium possible (given resource constraints) when employing the Tell & Sell, Identify & Reply, and Underscore & Explore strategies.[23]

TEST PREPPER 10.1

ANSWERS CAN BE FOUND ON P. 279

True or False?

_____ 1. One of the links in the basic communication process is feedback.

_____ 2. The basic communication process begins with decoding.

_____ 3. Face-to-face communication ranks high on media richness, according to the Lengel-Daft model.

_____ 4. For routine problems, lean media are most appropriate.

_____ 5. Two examples of "noise" are lies and a speech impairment.

_____ 6. Managers who employ the Tell & Sell communication strategy apply the "more is better" strategy.

_____ 7. The Withhold & Uphold communication strategy should be used as much as possible.

Multiple Choice

_____ 8. According to research, _____ percent of each 40-hour workweek is wasted because of poor communication between staff and managers.
    a. 14   c. 29   e. 58
    b. 4   d. 96

_____ 9. Communication involves the interpersonal transfer of _____ and _____.
    a. authority; responsibility
    b. sender; receiver
    c. social; political activities
    d. encoding; decoding
    e. information; understanding

_____ 10. Which of these is *not* part of the basic communication process?
    a. Medium   d. Receiver
    b. Encoding   e. Technology
    c. Sender

_____ 11. According to the Lengel-Daft model of media richness, what can happen when a rich medium is used to communicate a routine message?
    a. Maximum understanding
    b. Speedier action
    c. Data glut
    d. Communication success
    e. Creative feedback

_____ 12. Users of Clampitt's Spray & Pray communication strategy would likely say
    a. "More is better."
    b. "Be quiet."
    c. "Help."
    d. "Let's talk."
    e. "Less is more."

_____ 13. When selecting a communication strategy appropriate to the situation, managers need to follow all of these guidelines *except*
    a. use Identify & Reply sparingly.
    b. avoid Spray & Pray.
    c. avoid Underscore & Explore.
    d. use Underscore & Explore as much as possible.
    e. use Tell & Sell sparingly.

Online Study Center
ACE the Test
ACE Practice Tests 10.1

DYNAMICS OF ORGANIZATIONAL COMMUNICATION

 Discuss the managerial importance of the grapevine and nonverbal communication, and explain how to encourage upward communication.

As a writer on the subject pointed out, "civilization is based on human cooperation and without communication, no effective cooperation can develop."[24] Accordingly, effective communication is essential for cooperation within productive organizations. At least three dynamics of organizational communication—the grapevine, nonverbal communication, and upward communication—largely determine the difference between effectiveness and ineffectiveness in this important area.

The Grapevine

In every organization, large or small, there are actually two communication systems, one formal and the other informal. Sometimes these systems complement and reinforce each other; at other times they come into direct conflict. Although theorists have found it convenient to separate the two, distinguishing one from the other in real life can be difficult. Information required to accomplish official objectives is channeled throughout the organization via the formal system. Official or formal communication by definition flows in accordance with established lines of authority and structural boundaries. Media for official communication include all of those discussed earlier in this chapter. But superimposed on this formal network is the **grapevine**, the unofficial and informal communication system. The term *grapevine* can be traced back to Civil War days, when vinelike telegraph wires were strung from tree to tree across battlefields. *Inc.* magazine recently offered this comment about the grapevine.

grapevine Unofficial and informal communication system.

> *Good news travels fast, bad news travels faster, and embarrassing news travels at warp speed. So long as people have mouths to speak and fingers to type they will gossip.*[25]

All the more reason to learn more about the grapevine and how to deal with it.

Words of Caution About the E-Grapevine and "Blogs"

Modern Internet and communication technologies—including e-mail, cell phones, and instant and text messaging—have been a boon for the grapevine, vastly and instantly extending its reach. But this new communication landscape holds some nasty surprises for the unwary. As a pair of business writers recently pointed out,

> *E-mail allows workplace tales to spread faster than ever. But without the opportunity for nonverbal cues and interactivity, e-mail makes it even harder for employees to accurately interpret the message. Because in many if not most work environments e-mail messages are stored and subject to inspection (by people for whom the message was not intended), the savviest employees will not engage in e-gossip. Indeed, companies have pursued legal action to deal with some of the more harmful aspects of their e-grapevine.*[26]

So a bit of gossip shared by the water cooler is not the same as a bit of gossip shared online, because the latter leaves an electronic trail that could be read by anyone. The same goes for *blogs* (short for Web logs) that amount to online diaries. The number of blogs worldwide reportedly mushroomed from 20 million in 2005 to 57 million in 2006.[27] The e-grapevine and blogs are just two more areas where lawmakers, ethics specialists, and company policy makers are racing to catch up with new technology. In the meantime,

> *If you're creating a company blog policy, law firm Greenberg Traurig recommends addressing the following issues:*
>
> ▌ *How much blogging is acceptable during work hours?*
>
> ▌ *All company-posted blogs should clearly state that the employee's opinions are not necessarily shared by the company.*
>
> ▌ *Protect confidentiality. Ensure that employees know what corporate or personal information is not to be disclosed.*[28]

Managerial Attitudes Toward the Grapevine

One survey of 341 participants in a management development seminar uncovered predominantly negative feelings among managers toward the grapevine. Moreover, first-line supervisors perceived the grapevine to be more influential than did middle managers. This second finding led the researchers to conclude that "apparently the grapevine is more prevalent, or at least more visible, at lower levels of the managerial hierarchy where supervisors can readily feel its impact."[29] Finally, the survey found that employees of relatively small organizations (fewer than 50 people) viewed the grapevine as being less influential than did those from larger organizations (more than 100 people). A logical explanation for this last finding is that smaller organizations are usually more informal.

In spite of the negative attitude that many managers have toward it, the grapevine does have a positive side. In fact, experts estimate that grapevine communication is about 75 percent accurate.[30] Though the grapevine has a reputation among managers as a bothersome source of inaccurate information and gossip, it helps satisfy a natural desire to know what is really going on and gives employees a sense of belonging. The grapevine also serves as an emotional outlet for employee fears and apprehensions.[31] Consider, for example, what happened when investor Laurence A. Tisch became chairman of CBS:

> *Tisch's reputation as a ferocious cost cutter, which he despises, forces him to watch every word and gesture. Simple questions—such as why a department needs so many people—are sometimes interpreted as orders to slash. One day Tisch and [the CBS News department head] were talking outside CBS's broadcast center on Manhattan's West 57th Street when Tisch pointed to a tower atop the building, asking what it was. Apparently staffers at a window saw him pointing in their general direction, and the next day newspaper reporters called CBS checking out a rumor that Tisch planned to sell the building.*[32]

Nevertheless, grapevine communication can carry useful information through the organization with amazing speed. Moreover, grapevine communication can help management learn how employees truly feel about policies and programs.[33]

Coping with the Grapevine

Considering how the grapevine can be an influential and sometimes negative force, what can management do about it? First and foremost, the grapevine *cannot be extinguished.* In fact, attempts to stifle grapevine communication may serve instead to stimulate it. Subtly monitoring the grapevine and officially correcting or countering any potentially damaging misinformation is about all any management team can do.[34] "Management by walking around" is an excellent way to monitor the grapevine in a nonthreatening manner. Some managers selectively feed information into the grapevine. For example, a health care administrator has admitted: "Sure, I use the grapevine. Why not? The employees sure use it. It's fast, reaches everyone, and employees believe it—no matter how preposterous. I limit its use, though."[35] Rumor-control hotlines and Web sites have proved useful for neutralizing disruptive and inaccurate rumors and grapevine communication.[36]

Nonverbal Communication

In today's hurried world, our words often have unintended meanings. The facial expressions and body movements that accompany our words can send negative signals. This nonverbal communication, sometimes referred to as **body language**, is an important part of the communication process.[37] In fact, one expert contends that only 7 percent of the impact of our face-to-face communication comes from the words we utter. The other 93 percent comes from our vocal intonations, facial expressions, posture, and appearance.[38] Even periods of silence can carry meaning. Consider this recent advice:

> Your job as a manager is to learn to hear not only what people are saying, but also what they may not be saying in a conversation. So the next time you encounter someone's silence during an interview or a meeting, don't interrupt unless the person is clearly anxious or having a hard time responding.[39]

Silence may indicate doubt, lack of understanding, or polite disagreement. Even the whole idea of "dressing for success" is an attempt to send a desired nonverbal message about oneself. Image consultants have developed a thriving business helping aspiring executives look the part:

> Vanda Sachs had a problem. The 35-year-old senior marketing executive for a well-known fashion magazine had her sights set on the publisher's office. Her trouble? Projecting enough authority to be considered for the job. "I'm petite and blonde and I'm baby-faced," she says, "none of which goes over very well in a world of 45-year-old men who are 6-foot-2." Being short, in particular, is a "major liability," she adds, "more so than being a woman."
>
> Beyond wearing high heels, Sachs (a pseudonym) couldn't do much about her height, but she decided she could improve on her appearance. The first step was to hire a personal image consultant. Her choice: Emily Cho, founder of New Image, a respected New York City personal-image shopping service that for 19 years has been helping women choose clothes compatible with their private and professional aspirations. Four days and $3,000 later, Sachs had a knockout wardrobe and a newly acquired savvy that would help her look the part of a publisher. "Like it or not," she explains, "we're a society that's built on first impressions."[40]

Types of Body Language

There are three kinds of body language: facial, gestural, and postural.[41] Without the speaker or listener consciously thinking about it, seemingly insignificant changes in facial expressions, gestures, and posture send various messages. A speaker can tell whether a listener is interested by monitoring a combination of nonverbal cues, including an attentive gaze, an upright posture, and confirming or agreeing gestures. Unfortunately, many people in positions of authority—parents, teachers, and managers—ignore or misread nonverbal feedback. When this happens, they become ineffective communicators.

body language   Nonverbal communication based on facial expressions, posture, and appearance.

REALITY CHECK 10.2

"E-mail messages brim with the potential for misinterpretation because recipients rely solely on the typewritten word without visual or auditory cues to provide context for the message....

"'In other communication channels, there are barriers to going overboard that do not exist when someone sends an e-mail,' [psychologist Gail] Gooden says. 'If I write you an e-mail saying that you are a complete and total jerk, I don't have to see what your expression is or hear your voice when you read my e-mail.'"

Source: Eric Krell, "Do Not Hit Send," *HR Magazine,* 51 (August 2006): 53.

Question: In what situations does a manager need the exchange of nonverbal communication that is not possible in an e-mail message?

TABLE 10.1

Reading Body Language

Unspoken message	Behavior
"I want to be helpful."	Uncrossing legs Unbuttoning coat or jacket Unclasping hands Moving closer to other person Smiling face Removing hands from pockets Unfolding arms from across chest
"I'm confident."	Avoiding hand-to-face gestures and head scratching Maintaining an erect stance Keeping steady eye contact Steepling fingertips below chin
"I'm nervous."	Clearing throat Expelling air (such as "Whew!") Placing hand over mouth while speaking Hurried cigarette smoking
"I'm superior to you."	Peering over tops of eyeglasses Pointing a finger Standing behind a desk and leaning palms down on it Holding jacket lapels while speaking

Source: Adapted from William Friend, "Reading Between the Lines," *Association Management,* Vol. 36, June 1984, pp. 94–100. Reprinted with permission of ASAE & the Center for Association Leadership.

Receiving Nonverbal Communication

Like any other interpersonal skill, sensitivity to nonverbal cues can be learned (see Table 10.1). Listeners need to be especially aware of subtleties, such as the fine distinctions between an attentive gaze and a glaring stare and between an upright posture and a stiff one. Knowing how to interpret a nod, a grimace, or a grin can be invaluable to managers.[42] If at any time the response seems inappropriate to what one is saying, it is time to back off and reassess one's approach. It may be necessary to explain things more clearly, adopt a more patient manner, or make other adjustments.

Nonverbal behavior can also give managers a window on deep-seated emotions. For example, consider the situation Michael C. Ruettgers encountered shortly after joining EMC Corp., a leading manufacturer of computer data storage equipment:

> *Four months into Ruettgers' new job as head of operations and customer service, EMC's product quality program erupted into a full-blown crisis. Every piece of equipment the company sold was crashing because EMC engineers [had] failed to detect faulty disk drives supplied by NEC Corp. Ruettgers made a series of marathon swings across the country to meet personally with customers. In Denver and Salt Lake City, he came face to face with the scope of the catastrophe*

Online Study Center college.hmco.com/pic/kreitnerSASfound

when managers broke down in tears because their computer operations were in shambles. "Nothing can really prepare you for that," Ruettgers says.[43]

After his promotion to CEO, Ruettgers helped make EMC a leader in product quality. No doubt his face-to-face interaction with frustrated customers, who conveyed powerful nonverbal emotional messages, drove home the need for improvement.

Giving Nonverbal Feedback

What about the nonverbal feedback that managers give rather than receive?

▌ A research study carried out in Great Britain suggests that nonverbal feedback from authority figures significantly affects employee behavior.

▌ Among the people who were interviewed, those who received nonverbal approval from the interviewers in the form of smiles, positive head nods, and eye contact behaved quite differently from those who received nonverbal disapproval through frowns, head shaking, and avoidance of eye contact.

▌ Those receiving positive nonverbal feedback were judged by neutral observers to be significantly more relaxed, more friendly, more talkative, and more successful in creating a good impression.[44]

Positive nonverbal feedback to and from managers is a basic building block of good interpersonal relations:

▌ A smile or nod of the head in the appropriate situation tells the individual that he or she is on the right track and to keep up the good work. Such feedback is especially important for managers, who must avoid participating in the subtle but powerful nonverbal discrimination experienced by women in leadership positions.[45]

▌ When men and women leaders in one study presented the same arguments and suggestions in a controlled setting, the women leaders received more negative and less positive nonverbal feedback than did the men.[46]

▌ Managing-diversity workshops target this sort of "invisible barrier" that faces women and minorities. Similarly, cross-cultural training alerts employees bound for foreign assignments to monitor their nonverbal gestures carefully.

▌ For example, the familiar thumbs-up sign tells American employees to keep up the good work. Much to the embarrassment of poorly informed expatriates, that particular nonverbal message does not travel well. The same gesture would be a vulgar sign in Australia, would say "I'm winning" in Saudi Arabia, and would signify the number one in Germany and the number five in Japan. Malaysians use the thumb, instead of their forefinger, for pointing.[47]

Two other trends in nonverbal communication are etiquette classes for students and management trainees and teaching sign language to coworkers of deaf employees.[48]

Upward Communication

upward communication Encouraging employees to share their feelings and ideas with management.

As used here, the term **upward communication** refers to a process of systematically encouraging employees to share their feelings and ideas with management. Although upward communication is more important than ever, a survey of 25,000 employees at 17 companies in the United States found it lacking: "Less than half of workers, 45 percent, said their senior managers both talk and listen. And almost half said there was no procedure to raise questions and answers with upper management."[49] A refreshing exception is IBM's CEO, Sam Palmisano:

> [His lofty position as the head of a $91 billion-a-year company with nearly 330,000 employees] doesn't stop him from reading every single e-mail message sent to him by IBM employees, aides say, or from calling midlevel managers just to ask them what they think.[50]

At least seven different options are open to managers who want to improve upward communication.

Formal Grievance Procedures

When unions represent rank-and-file employees, provisions for upward communication are usually spelled out in the collective bargaining agreement. Typically, unionized employees utilize a formal grievance procedure for contesting managerial actions and oversights. Grievance procedures usually consist of a series of progressively more rigorous steps. For example, union members who have been fired may talk with their supervisor in the presence of the union steward. If the issue is not resolved at that level, the next step may be a meeting with the department head. Sometimes the formal grievance process includes as many as five or six steps, with a third-party arbitrator as the last resort. Formal grievance procedures are also found in nonunion situations.

Employee Attitude and Opinion Surveys

Both in-house and commercially prepared surveys can bring employee attitudes and feelings to the surface. Thanks to commercial software packages, time-saving paperless electronic surveys are popular in today's workplaces.[51] Employees will usually complete surveys if they are convinced meaningful changes will result. Du Pont, for example, took the right approach:

> Du Pont surveyed 6,600 of its people, including some at Towanda, [Pennsylvania,] and found that flexible work hours were a top priority. Working mothers and single parents said it was hard to cope with the kids while keeping to a rigid plant schedule. A team at Towanda got together and devised a novel solution: Take vacation time by the hour. During slack times when three of the four [task] team members could easily handle the job, one could take off a few hours in the afternoon to go to a school play or bring a sick kid to the doctor. Today other Du Pont workers and managers visit Towanda to learn about flextime. A few have already borrowed it for their own plants.[52]

Surveys with no feedback or follow-up action tend to alienate employees, who feel they are just wasting their time.[53] On the other hand, a researcher found unionized companies conducting regular attitude surveys were less likely to experience a labor strike than companies that failed to survey their employees.[54]

Suggestion Systems

Who knows more about a job than someone who performs that job day in and day out? This rhetorical question is the primary argument for suggestion systems. Fairness and prompt feedback are keys to successful suggestion systems. Monetary incentives can help, too. For example, consider this success story at Winnebago Industries, the recreational vehicle maker in Forest City, Iowa:

> The program works because employees take it seriously. All reasonable suggestions submitted—an impressive 10,355 since the program began in 1991—are

*investigated by two full-time employees. The company has ended up imple-
menting fully a third of these ideas, and employees have won more than
$500,000 (they receive 10 percent of what the company saves in the first year).
Winnebago says the program's first-year savings have added up to $5.8
million.*[55]

Nice return on investment! A study of U.S. government employees found a positive
correlation between suggestions and productivity.[56]

Open-Door Policy

The open-door approach to upward communication has been both praised and
criticized. Proponents say that problems can be nipped in the bud when managers
keep their doors open and employees feel free to walk in at any time and talk with
them. For Jeff Potter, CEO of Frontier Airlines, an open-door policy is a key part of
a comprehensive upward communication program. As he noted in a recent interview with *Business 2.0* magazine:

> *When you ask employees what they want, yeah, everybody wants more money.
> But they also want to feel like they have a voice. It's often a cliché, but here it's
> real—I have an open-door policy. I sat with four or five employees yesterday, one
> this morning, and a few more will probably show up at my door later today.
> Over the holidays, all of our officers did a few shifts to support our people at the
> airport. I worked the ticket counter in Denver. If you take care of employees, they
> take care of the customers, who improve shareholder value.*[57]

Critics, meanwhile, say an open-door policy encourages employees to leapfrog the
formal chain of command (something that happens a lot these days because of
e-mail). They further argue that it is an open invitation to annoying interruptions
when managers can least afford them. A limited open-door policy—afternoons
only, for example—can effectively remedy this last objection.

Informal Meetings

Employees may feel free to air their opinions and suggestions if they are confident
that management will not criticize or penalize them for being frank. Organizational "town hall meetings" and "employee roundtables" have proven useful for
generating upward communication[58] (see Best Practices on page 276).

Internet Chat Rooms

In the Internet age, a convenient way for management to get candid feedback is to
host a meeting place on the Web. These so-called virtual water coolers give employees unprecedented freedom of speech. Dave Barram, head of the huge General Services Administration (GSA) in Washington, D.C., offered this assessment:

> *. . . GSA has set up a Web-based "chat line," in which employees exchange uncen-
> sored thoughts and ideas. "If we have honest conversations about what's work-
> ing and what isn't, we can become really good," Barram says. "If we don't, we'll
> never help each other."*[59]

This approach takes lots of managerial courage, if the rough-and-tumble "cyber-
venting" on unauthorized Web sites and blogs aimed at specific companies is any
indication.[60]

Exit Interviews

An employee leaving the organization, for whatever reason, no longer fears possible recrimination from superiors and so can offer unusually frank and honest

feedback, obtained in a brief, structured **exit interview**.[61] On the other hand, exit interviews have been criticized for eliciting artificially negative feedback because the employee may have a sour-grapes attitude toward the organization. Research finds the use of exit interviews to be spotty and haphazard, although many employers claim to use them. "If done well, managers and consultants said, exit interviews can show trends and point to potential problems that need to be addressed."[62] Systematic use of exit interviews is recommended.

In general, attempts to promote upward communication will be successful only if employees truly believe that their contributions will have a favorable impact on their employment. Halfhearted or insincere attempts to get employees to open up and become involved will do more harm than good.

exit interview   Brief structured interview with a departing employee.

TEST PREPPER 10.2

ANSWERS CAN BE FOUND ON P. 279

True or False?

_____ 1. Based on research, employees of relatively small organizations viewed the grapevine as less influential than did those from larger organizations.

_____ 2. The three kinds of body language are facial, gestural, and vocal.

_____ 3. Examples of upward communication include attitude and opinion surveys.

_____ 4. With an open-door policy, employees are free to leave work whenever they choose.

Multiple Choice

_____ 5. The term *grapevine* best matches which description?
  a. Dangerous
  b. Sociotechnical
  c. Legitimate
  d. Informal
  e. Official

_____ 6. The term _____ refers to an online diary.
  a. blog
  b. grapevine
  c. spam
  d. IM
  e. e-mail

_____ 7. Which statement about grapevine accuracy is correct?
  a. Nearly 30 percent accurate
  b. About 75 percent accurate
  c. Never accurate
  d. The lower the organizational level, the more accurate
  e. The higher the organizational level, the more accurate

_____ 8. During a job interview, Lucinda places her hand over her mouth while speaking, thus indicating that she
  a. feels superior to the interviewer.
  b. is confident.
  c. wants to be helpful.
  d. is nervous.
  e. is shy.

_____ 9. In unionized organizations, which description most accurately portrays the formal grievance process?
  a. Ineffective thing of the past
  b. Third party mediation
  c. Too little, too late
  d. One strike and you're out
  e. Multistep appeal process

_____ 10. One of your friends, the owner of a dry cleaning chain, is thinking about starting a suggestion system. You should recommend which of these?
  a. Verbal suggestions only
  b. Only managers eligible
  c. No monetary incentives
  d. Prompt feedback
  e. Part-timers not eligible

_____ 11. Which of these is a useful method for getting feedback from departing employees?
  a. Third-party mediation
  b. Suggestion systems
  c. Arbitration
  d. Outplacement
  e. Exit interviews

Online Study Center
ACE the Test
ACE Practice Tests 10.2

Sleep just may be the number one casualty of nonstop communication in today's 24/7 global economy. Just ask Park City, Utah, business coach Ernest Oriente. He bends his sleep patterns around phone calls to international clients. Typically, he works from 3:30 A.M. to 10 A.M., takes an hour or so refreshment nap, and eventually calls it a day at 9:30 P.M. For more, go to www.powerhour.com.

COMMUNICATING IN THE ONLINE AND WIRELESS WORKPLACE

 List two practical tips for each of the major communication technologies (e-mail, cell phones, and videoconferences) and summarize the pros and cons of telecommuting.

Online Study Center
Improve Your Grade
Career Snapshot 10.1

Computers speak a simple digital language of 1s and 0s. Today, every imaginable sort of information is being converted into a digital format, including text, numbers, still and moving pictures, and sound. This process represents nothing short of a revolution for the computer, telecommunications, consumer electronics, publishing, and entertainment industries. Organizational communication, already significantly reshaped by computer technology, is undergoing its own revolutionary change. This section does *not* attempt the impossible task of describing all the emerging communication technologies, which range from speech recognition computers to online full-motion video to virtual reality.[63] Rather, it explores the impact of some established Internet-age technologies on workplace communications. Our goal is to more effectively use the technologies we have and prepare for those to come.

Getting E-Mail Under Control

E-mail via the Internet has precipitated a communication revolution akin to those brought about by the printing press, telephone, radio, and television. If you are on the Internet, you are ultimately linked to hundreds of millions of people on Earth capable of sending and receiving e-mail. Both on and off the job, e-mail is more than a way of communication—it's a lifestyle! Jim Keyes, CEO of the 7-Eleven convenience store chain, "burns three to four hours of his day on 200 e-mails and is such a heavy user that if a top field executive or licensee were to phone him, he might not recognize the voice."[64] Shifting the focus from individual to organization, we run into astonishing numbers. After discovering that many of its 88,000 employees worldwide were spending about two and a half hours each day exchanging three million e-mails, Intel decided to act:

> *The chipmaker recently started classes on how to manage e-mail. Some tips: Put short messages in the subject line so recipients don't have to open it to read the note. Intel also is asking workers to sparingly use graphics and attachments and get off unnecessary distribution lists.*
> *"We're not discouraging e-mail use, just better use," spokesman Chuck Mulloy says.*[65]

Meanwhile, PBD Worldwide Fulfillment Services—an Alpharetta, Georgia, call center firm—recently instituted a "no e-mail" on Fridays policy:

> *[CEO Scott A. Dockter] instructed his 275 employees to pick up the phone or meet in person each Friday, and reduce e-mail use the rest of the time.*
> *That was tough to digest, especially for younger staffers and some senior managers. . . . But in less than four months, the simple directive has resulted in quicker problem-solving, better teamwork, and, best of all, happier customers.*[66]

E-mail is a two-headed beast: easy and efficient, while at the same time grossly abused and mismanaged. By properly managing e-mail, the organization can take a big step toward properly using the Internet. An organizational e-mail policy that embraces these recommendations from experts can help:

▮ The e-mail system belongs to the company, which has the legal right to monitor its use. (*Never* assume privacy when using company e-mail.)[67]

▮ Workplace e-mail is for business purposes only.

▮ Harassing and offensive e-mail will not be tolerated.

▮ E-mail messages should be concise (see Table 10.2). As in all correspondence, grammar and spelling count because they reflect on your diligence and credibility. Typing in all capital letters makes the message hard to read and amounts to SHOUTING in cyberspace. (All-capital letters can be appropriate, for contrast purposes, when adding comments to an existing document.)

▮ Lists of bullet items (similar to the format you are reading now) are acceptable because they tend to be more concise than paragraphs.

▮ Long attachments defeat the quick-and-easy nature of e-mail.

▮ Recipients should be told when a reply is *unnecessary.*

▮ An organization-specific priority system should be used for sending and receiving all e-mail. *Example:* "At Libit, a company in Palo Alto, Calif., that makes silicon products for the cable industry, e-mail is labeled as either informational or action items to avoid time wasting."[68]

TABLE 10.2

How to Compose a CLEAR E-Mail Message

Concise. A brief message in simple conversational language is faster for you to write and more pleasant for your readers to read.

Logical. A message in logical steps, remembering to include any context your readers need, will be more easily understood.

Empathetic. When you identify with your readers, your message will be written in the right tone and in words they will readily understand.

Action-oriented. When you remember to explain to your readers what you want them to do next, they are more likely to do it.

Right. A complete message, with no important facts missing, all the facts right, and correct spelling, will save your readers having to return to you to clarify details.

Source: From Joan Tunstall, *Better, Faster Email: Getting the Most Out of Email,* 1999, Allen & Unwin Book Publishers, www.allenandunwin.com.au. Reproduced with permission of the publisher.

TABLE 10.3

Five Commandments of Cell Phone Etiquette

> 1. Thou shalt not subject defenseless others to cell phone conversations. [Cell phone etiquette, like all forms of etiquette, centers on having respect for others.]
> 2. Thou shalt not set thy ringer to play La Cucaracha every time thy phone rings. [It's a phone, not a public address system.]
> 3. Thou shalt turn thy cell phone off during public performances. [Set your phone on vibrate when in meetings or in the company of others and, if necessary, take or return the call at a polite distance.]
> 4. Thou shalt not dial while driving. [If you must engage in cell phone conversations while driving, use a hands-off device.]
> 5. Thou shalt not speak louder on thy cell phone than thou would on any other phone. [It's called "cell yell" and it's very annoying to others.]

Source: Five basic commandments excerpted from Dan Briody, "The Ten Commandments of Cell Phone Etiquette," *InfoWorld,* February 5, 2005, www.infoworld.com.

- "Spam" (unsolicited and unwanted e-mail) that gets past filters should be deleted without being read. Despite passage of a federal anti-spam law in the United States, spam is still a significant problem. So-called spyware and adware should be blocked and should be uninstalled when a system has been infected.[69]

- To avoid file clutter, messages that are unlikely to be referred to again should not be saved.[70]

Hello! Can We Talk About Cell Phone Etiquette?

Cell phones are in wide use in the United States, with a market penetration rate of 70 percent (210 million subscribers) in 2006. Other countries, including the United Kingdom, the Netherlands, and Sweden, have nearly 100 percent subscriber rates.[71] Like e-mail, cell phones have proved to be both a blessing and a curse. Offsetting the mobility and convenience are concerns about distracted drivers and loud, obnoxious phone conversations in public places.[72] Managers need to be particularly sensitive to the risk of inadvertently broadcasting proprietary company information, names, and numbers. Competitors could be standing in the same airport line or sitting in the next restaurant booth. Table 10.3 offers some practical tips to help make cell phone use more effective, secure, and courteous.

Videoconferences

videoconference Live television or broadband Internet video exchange between people in different locations.

A **videoconference** is a live television or broadband Internet video exchange between people in different locations. The decreasing cost of steadily improving videoconferencing technologies and the desire to reduce costly travel time have fostered wider use of this approach to organizational communication.[73]

As a sample of what is available, it now is possible to go to one of 150 Kinko's stores and rent a videoconferencing room for either a meeting or a "virtual interview."[74] Moreover, "companies turned off by the $30,000 bulky systems of a decade ago can outfit a broadband-connected conference room for $5,000."[75]

Communication pointers for videoconference participants include the following:

- Test the system before the meeting convenes.

- Dress for the occasion. The video image is distorted by movement of wild patterns and flashy jewelry. Solid white clothing tends to "glow" on camera.

- Make sure everyone is introduced.

- Check to make sure everyone can see and hear the content of the meeting.

- Do not feel compelled to direct your entire presentation to the camera or monitor. Directly address those in the same room.

- Speak loudly and clearly. Avoid slang and jargon in cross-cultural meetings where translations are occurring.

- Avoid exaggerated physical movements that tend to blur on camera.

- Adjust your delivery to any transmission delay, pausing longer than usual when waiting for replies.

- Avoid side conversations, which are disruptive.

- Do not nervously tap the table or microphone or shuffle papers.[76]

Telecommuting

Futurist Alvin Toffler used the term *electronic cottage* to refer to the practice of working at home on a personal computer connected—typically by telephone—to an employer's place of business. More recently, this practice has been labeled **telecommuting** because work, rather than the employee, travels between a central office and the employee's home, reaching the computer via telephone or cable modem. The advent of overnight delivery services, low-cost facsimile (fax) machines, e-mail, and high-speed modems, combined with traditional telephone

Online Study Center
Improve Your Grade
Visual Glossary 10.1

telecommuting   Sending work to and from one's office via computer modem while working at home.

TABLE 10.4

Telecommuting: Promises and Problems

Promises	Potential problems
1. Significantly boosts individual productivity.	1. Can cause fear of stagnating at home.
2. Saves commuting time and travel expenses (lessens traffic congestion).	2. Can foster sense of isolation, due to lack of social contact with coworkers.
3. Taps broader labor pool (such as mothers with young children, disabled and retired persons, and prison inmates).	3. Can result in competition or interference with family duties, thus causing family conflict.
4. Eliminates office distractions and politics.	4. Can disrupt traditional manager-employee relationship.
5. Reduces employer's cost of office space.	5. Can cause fear of being "out of sight, out of mind" at promotion time.

communication, has broadened the technical potential for telecommuting. The growth of telecommuting has stalled, according to a recent study by the Society for Human Resource Management: "About 19 percent of companies permit telecommuting by full-time employees, down from the peak of 23 percent three years ago."[77] Despite some compelling advantages, telecommuting has enough drawbacks to make it unsuitable for many employees as well as employers (see Table 10.4 on page 271). Telecommuting seriously disrupts the normal social and communication patterns in the workplace. Telecommuting will not become the prevailing work mode anytime soon, but it certainly is more than a passing fad.[78]

TEST PREPPER 10.3

ANSWERS CAN BE FOUND ON P. 279

True or False?

_____ 1. Workplace e-mail systems can be used for personal purposes without being monitored, according to the recent privacy laws in the United States.

_____ 2. Because of the growing use of cell phones, managers need to be particularly sensitive to the risk of inadvertently broadcasting proprietary company information.

_____ 3. Videoconference participants should avoid wearing solid white clothing because it tends to glow on camera.

_____ 4. A potential problem with telecommuting is the fear of being overlooked at promotion time.

Multiple Choice

_____ 5. When using organizational e-mail systems, what assumption should managers make?
   a. Use of capital letters required to get attention
   b. No privacy
   c. Increased productivity
   d. Immediate response required
   e. The longer the message, the better

_____ 6. Which of these is *not* a suggestion by Joan Tunstall for composing a CLEAR e-mail message?
   a. Action-oriented
   b. Copies to all relevant parties
   c. Logical
   d. Empathetic
   e. Concise

_____ 7. A live television exchange between people in different locations is called a(n)
   a. videoconference.
   b. closed-system e-mail.
   c. teleconference.
   d. telemetric display.
   e. off-network television system.

_____ 8. The text sums up the future of telecommuting as
   a. a serious threat to productivity.
   b. just a passing fad.
   c. more than a passing fad.
   d. already obsolete.
   e. the standard work routine in twenty years.

Online Study Center
ACE the Test
ACE Practice Tests 10.3

Granted, this is a rather tall order to fill. It has been pointed out that "a truly self-actualized individual is more of an exception than the rule in the organizational context."[11] Take Bill Gates, for example. The co-founder of Microsoft and the world's richest man made this statement when he announced he would devote most of his time to philanthropy by 2008:

> . . . there's a pretty big piece that I'll continue to handle in my part-time role, which is brainstorming with research and product groups. I love that part of my work. Whatever time I do spend, it will be with research guys, or with the tablet [PC] guys, or search technology, or other special projects. It's pretty neat, because it's kind of a pure thing.[12]

Whether productive organizations need more self-actualized individuals is subject to debate. On the positive side, self-actualized employees might help break down barriers to creativity and steer the organization in new directions. On the negative side, too many unconventional nonconformists could wreak havoc with the typical administrative setup dedicated to predictability.

Relevance of Maslow's Theory for Managers

Behavioral scientists who have attempted to test Maslow's theory in real life claim it has some deficiencies. Even Maslow's hierarchical arrangement has been questioned. Practical evidence points toward a two-level rather than a five-level hierarchy. In this competing view, physiological and safety needs are arranged in hierarchical fashion, as Maslow contends. But beyond that point, any one of a number of needs may emerge as the single most important need, depending on the individual. Edward Lawler, a leading motivation researcher, observed, "Which higher-order needs come into play after the lower ones are satisfied and in which order they come into play cannot be predicted. If anything, it seems that most people are simultaneously motivated by several of the same-level needs."[13]

Although Maslow's theory has not stood up well under actual testing, it teaches managers one important lesson: a *fulfilled* need does not motivate an individual. For example, the promise of unemployment benefits may partially fulfill an employee's need for economic security (the safety need). But the added security of additional unemployment benefits will probably not motivate fully employed individuals to work any harder. Effective managers anticipate each employee's personal need profile and provide opportunities to fulfill *emerging* needs. Because challenging and worthwhile jobs and meaningful recognition tend to enhance self-esteem, the esteem level presents managers with the greatest opportunity to motivate better performance.

Now here's someone who can tell school children a thing or two about self-actualization needs. Grammy Award-winning singer and song writer Alicia Keys fires up a classroom of eighth—graders at the Betty Shabazz International Charter School in Chicago. If Ms. Keys ever tires of entertaining, she obviously would make a great teacher!

Herzberg's Two-Factor Theory

During the 1950s, Frederick Herzberg proposed a theory of employee motivation based on satisfaction.[14] His theory implied that a satisfied employee is motivated from within to work harder and that a dissatisfied

TABLE 11.1

Herzberg's Two-Factor Theory of Motivation

Dissatisfiers: Factors mentioned most often by dissatisfied employees	Satisfiers: Factors mentioned most often by satisfied employees
1. Company policy and administration	1. Achievement
2. Supervision	2. Recognition
3. Relationship with supervisor	3. Work itself
4. Work conditions	4. Responsibility
5. Salary	5. Advancement
6. Relationship with peers	6. Growth
7. Personal life	
8. Relationship with subordinates	
9. Status	
10. Security	

Source: Reprinted by permission of *Harvard Business Review.* From "One More Time: How Do You Motivate Employees?" by Frederick Herzberg, January–February 1968. Copyright © 1968 by the Harvard Business School Publishing Corporation; all rights reserved.

Percentage of surveyed workers in the United States who say they are satisfied with their jobs:

1987	61 percent
2000	51 percent
2006	46 percent

Source: Data from "U.S. Job Satisfaction Declines," *USA Today* (April 9, 2007): 1B.

Questions: Do you have much faith in general surveys like this? If, in fact, job satisfaction has been declining in the U.S., what do you believe are the major causes?

employee is not self-motivated. Herzberg's research uncovered two classes of factors associated with employee satisfaction and dissatisfaction (see Table 11.1). As a result, his concept has come to be called Herzberg's two-factor theory.

Dissatisfiers and Satisfiers

Herzberg compiled his list of dissatisfiers by asking a sample of about 200 accountants and engineers to describe job situations in which they felt exceptionally bad about their jobs. An analysis of their responses revealed a consistent pattern. Dissatisfaction tended to be associated with complaints about the job context or factors in the immediate work environment.

Herzberg then drew up his list of satisfiers, factors responsible for self-motivation, by asking the same accountants and engineers to describe job situations in which they had felt exceptionally good about their jobs. Again, a patterned response emerged, but this time different factors were described: the opportunity to experience achievement, receive recognition, work on an interesting job, take responsibility, and experience advancement and growth. Herzberg observed that these satisfiers centered on the nature of the task itself. Employees appeared to be motivated by *job content*—that is, by what they actually did all day long. Consequently, Herzberg concluded that enriched jobs were the key to self-motivation. The work itself—not pay, supervision, or some other environmental factor—was the key to satisfaction and motivation.

Implications of Herzberg's Theory

By insisting that satisfaction is not the opposite of dissatisfaction, Herzberg encouraged managers to think carefully about what actually motivates employees. According to Herzberg, "the opposite of job satisfaction is not job dissatisfaction, but rather *no* job satisfaction; and similarly, the opposite of job dissatisfaction is not job satisfaction, but *no* dissatisfaction."[15] Rather, the dissatisfaction–satisfaction continuum contains a zero midpoint at which both dissatisfaction and satisfaction are absent. An employee stuck on this midpoint, though not dissatisfied with pay and working conditions, is not particularly motivated to work hard because the job itself lacks challenge. Herzberg believes that the most managers can hope for when attempting to motivate employees with pay, status, working conditions, and other contextual factors is to reach the zero midpoint. But the elimination of dissatisfaction is not the same as truly motivating an employee. To satisfy and motivate employees, an additional element is required: meaningful, interesting, and challenging work. Herzberg believed that money is a weak motivational tool because, at best, it can only eliminate dissatisfaction.

Like Maslow, Herzberg triggered lively debate among motivation theorists. His assumption that job performance improves as satisfaction increases has been criticized for its weak empirical basis. For example, one researcher, after reviewing 20 studies that tested this notion, concluded that the relationship, though positive, was too weak to have any theoretical or practical significance.[16] Others have found that one person's dissatisfier may be another's satisfier (for example, money).[17] Nonetheless, Herzberg made a useful contribution to motivation theory by emphasizing the motivating potential of meaningful work and paving the way for job enrichment theory.

TEST PREPPER 11.1

ANSWERS CAN BE FOUND ON P. 311

True or False?

_____ 1. From bottom to top, Maslow's needs hierarchy includes physiological, safety, love, esteem, and self-actualization needs.

_____ 2. According to Maslow, becoming everything one is capable of becoming refers to esteem.

_____ 3. Maslow's theory suggests that a fulfilled need always motivates an individual.

_____ 4. Satisfiers involve job content in Herzberg's two-factor theory.

_____ 5. According to Herzberg's two-factor theory of motivation, an employee can reach a point of being neither dissatisfied nor satisfied.

Multiple Choice

_____ 6. In the general motivation model, _____ affects the relationship between motivational factors (such as needs and expectations) and job performance.
   a. educational level
   b. formal authority
   c. ability
   d. value system
   e. work attitude

_____ 7. Which of these best sums up Maslow's ideas about human needs?
   a. They form a three-level hierarchy.
   b. They are consciously selected.
   c. They emerge according to a predictable hierarchy.
   d. They have no predictable form.
   e. They come in two types.

Online Study Center
ACE the Test
ACE Practice Tests 11.1

_____ 8. People in war-torn areas of the world, such as Afghanistan, who struggle for basic survival every day, exist on the _____ level(s) in Maslow's needs hierarchy.
   a. love and esteem
   b. esteem
   c. self-actualization
   d. physiological and safety
   e. love

_____ 9. Why are the self-actualization needs on Maslow's hierarchy "open-ended"?
   a. People deny they have these needs.
   b. People can never be fully satisfied.
   c. People don't know they exist.
   d. They recycle people to the bottom of the needs hierarchy.
   e. They cannot be even partially satisfied.

_____ 10. Frederick Herzberg equated _____ with employee motivation in his two-factor theory of motivation.
   a. satisfaction
   b. challenging goals
   c. self-actualization
   d. leadership
   e. self-control

_____ 11. _____ is a satisfier, according to Herzberg's two-factor theory.
   a. Responsibility
   b. Work conditions
   c. Personal life
   d. Company policy and administration
   e. Status

_____ 12. _____ is a dissatisfier, according to Herzberg's two-factor theory.
   a. Growth
   b. Salary
   c. Recognition
   d. Work itself
   e. Responsibility

Online Study Center college.hmco.com/pic/kreitnerSASfound

ADVANCED THEORIES OF WORK MOTIVATION

 Explain how job enrichment can enhance the motivating potential of jobs, and describe the motivational processes in expectancy and goal-setting theory.

Other researchers followed in the footsteps of Maslow and Herzberg to more fully explain what motivates people in the workplace. Job enrichment focuses on the nature of the work itself, expectancy theory probes underlying mental processes, and goal-setting theory demonstrates the power of intention and purpose. Each perspective helps us better understand both ourselves and others.

Job Enrichment Theory

job enrichment   Redesigning jobs to increase their motivational potential.

In general terms, **job enrichment** is redesigning a job to increase its motivating potential. Two job-design experts have proposed that managers address the question, "How can we achieve a fit between persons and their jobs that fosters *both* high work productivity and a high-quality organizational experience for the people who do the work?"[18] Job enrichment increases the challenge of one's work by reversing the trend toward greater specialization. Unlike job enlargement, which merely combines equally simple tasks, job enrichment builds more complexity and depth into jobs by introducing the planning and decision-making responsibility normally carried out at higher levels. Thus, enriched jobs are said to be *vertically loaded,* whereas enlarged jobs are *horizontally loaded.* Managing an entire project can be immensely challenging and motivating due to vertical job loading. Scott Nichols, a home construction foreman, had this to say about his job:

> *I find it very rewarding. Just building something, creating something, and actually seeing your work. . . . You start with a bare, empty lot with grass growing up and then you build a house. A lot of times you'll build a house for a family, and you see them move in, that's pretty gratifying. . . . I'm proud of that.*[19]

Jobs can be enriched by upgrading five core dimensions of work: (1) skill variety, (2) task identity, (3) task significance, (4) autonomy, and (5) job feedback. Each of these core dimensions deserves a closer look.

- *Skill variety.* The degree to which the job requires a variety of different activities in carrying out the work, involving the use of a number of different skills and talents of the person

- *Task identity.* The degree to which the job requires completion of a "whole" and identifiable piece of work; that is, doing a job from beginning to end with a visible outcome

- *Task significance.* The degree to which the job has a substantial impact on the lives of other people, whether those people are in the immediate organization or in the world at large

- *Autonomy.* The degree to which the job provides substantial freedom, independence, and discretion to the individual in scheduling the work and in determining the procedures to be used in carrying it out

- *Job feedback.* The degree to which carrying out the work activities required by the job provides the individual with direct and clear information about the effectiveness of his or her performance[20]

FIGURE 11.3

How Job Enrichment Works

Source: From J. Richard Hackman and Greg R. Oldham, *Work Redesign*, © 1980, p. 90. Reprinted by permission of Pearson Education, Inc., Upper Saddle River, New Jersey.

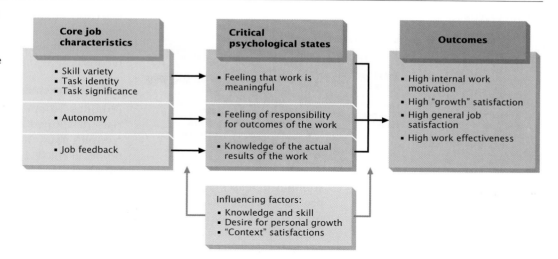

Figure 11.3 shows the theoretical connection between enriched core job characteristics and high motivation and satisfaction. At the heart of this job-enrichment model are three psychological states that highly specialized jobs usually do not satisfy: meaningfulness, responsibility, and knowledge of results.

It is important to note that not all employees will respond favorably to enriched jobs. Personal traits and motives influence the connection between core job characteristics and desired outcomes. Only those with the necessary knowledge and skills plus a desire for personal growth will be motivated by enriched work. Furthermore, in keeping with Herzberg's two-factor theory, dissatisfaction with factors such as pay, physical working conditions, or supervision can neutralize enrichment efforts. Researchers have reported that fear of failure, lack of confidence, and lack of trust in management's intentions can stand in the way of effective job enrichment. But job enrichment can and does work when it is carefully thought out, when management is committed to its long-term success, and when employees desire additional challenge. "Indeed, one recent study by two University of British Columbia researchers suggests that workers would be happy to forgo as much as a 20% raise if it meant a job with more variety or one that required more skill."[21] How about you?

Expectancy Theory

Both Maslow's and Herzberg's theories have been criticized for making unsubstantiated generalizations about what motivates people. Practical experience shows that people are motivated by lots of different things. Fortunately, expectancy theory, based largely on Victor H. Vroom's 1964 classic *Work and Motivation*, effectively deals with the highly personalized rational choices that individuals make when faced with the prospect of having to work to achieve rewards. Individual perception, though secondary in the Maslow and Herzberg models, is central to expectancy theory. Accordingly, **expectancy theory** is a motivation model based on the assumption that motivational strength is determined by perceived probabilities of success. The term **expectancy** refers to the subjective probability (or expectation) that one thing will lead to another. Work-related expectations, like all

expectancy theory Model that assumes motivational strength is determined by perceived probabilities of success.

expectancy One's belief or expectation that one thing will lead to another.

A Basic Expectancy Model

Motivational strength   "How much effort should I put forth?"

Perceived effort-performance probability	Perceived value of rewards	Perceived performance-reward probability
"What are my chances of getting the job done if I put forth the necessary effort?"	"What rewards do I value?"	"What are my chances of getting the rewards I value if I satisfactorily complete the job?"

other expectations, are shaped by ongoing personal experience. For instance, an employee's expectation of a raise, though diminished after the raise is turned down, later rebounds when the supervisor indicates a willingness to reconsider the matter.

A Basic Expectancy Model

Although Vroom and other expectancy theorists developed their models in somewhat complex mathematical terms, the descriptive model in Figure 11.4 is helpful for basic understanding. In this model, one's motivational strength increases as one's perceived effort-performance and performance-reward probabilities increase. All this is not as complicated as it sounds. For example, estimate your motivation to study if you expect to do poorly on a quiz no matter how hard you study (low effort-performance probability) and you know the quiz will not be graded (low performance-reward probability). Now contrast that estimate with your motivation to study if you believe that you can do well on the quiz with minimal study (high effort-performance probability) and that by doing well on the quiz your course grade will significantly improve (high performance-reward probability). Like students, employees are motivated to expend effort when they believe it will ultimately lead to rewards they themselves value. This expectancy approach not only appeals strongly to common sense; it also has received encouraging empirical support from researchers.[22]

Relevance of Expectancy Theory for Managers

According to expectancy theory, effort → performance → reward expectations determine whether motivation will be high or low. Although these expectations are in the mind of the employee, they can be influenced by managerial action and organizational experience. Training, combined with challenging but realistic objectives, helps give people the idea that they can get the job done if they put forth the necessary effort. But perceived effort-performance probabilities are only half the battle. Listening skills enable managers to discover each individual's perceived performance-reward probabilities. Employees tend to work harder when they believe they have *a good chance* of getting *personally meaningful* rewards. Both sets of expectations require managerial attention. Each is a potential barrier to work motivation.

Goal-Setting Theory

Think of the three or four most successful people you know personally. Their success may have come via business or professional achievement, politics, athletics, or community service. Chances are they got where they are today by being goal-oriented. In other words, they committed themselves to (and achieved) progressively more challenging goals in their professional and personal affairs.[23] A prime example is Martina Navratilova, the Hall of Fame tennis star and champion of 18 Grand Slam singles tournaments:

Now that I am playing doubles, I want to be the best doubles player I can be.... And that means doing everything I can to get to that point. You set your goals and then break it down and try to figure out how to get there. Then it becomes a palatable, doable daily routine. You say, "OK, how was my serve?" This is where I can make it better. "How is my level of fitness?" Well, I am in shape, but I could have better endurance. And then you get into the solution. Maybe I need to start running more long distance or I need to practice more of my backhand down the line or I need to think more about strategy. You break it down and you are into solutions. You figure it out. And all of the sudden you realize you are not such a bad tennis player.[24]

Biographies and autobiographies of successful people in all walks of life generally attest to the virtues of goal setting. Accordingly, goal setting is acknowledged today as a respected and useful motivation theory.

Within an organizational context, **goal setting** is the process of improving individual or group job performance with formally stated objectives, deadlines, or quality standards.[25] Management by objectives (MBO), mentioned in Chapter 5, is a specific application of goal setting that advocates participative and measurable objectives. Also, recall from Chapter 5 how managers tend to use the terms *goal* and *objective* interchangeably.

goal setting Process of improving performance with objectives, deadlines, or quality standards.

A General Goal-Setting Model

Thanks to motivation researchers such as Edwin A. Locke, there is a comprehensive body of knowledge about goal setting.[26] Goal setting has been researched more rigorously than the four motivation theories just discussed.[27] Important lessons from goal-setting theory and research are incorporated in the general model in Figure 11.5. This model shows how properly conceived goals trigger a motivational process that improves performance. Let us explore the key components of this goal-setting model.

Personal Ownership of Challenging Goals

In Chapter 5, the discussion about MBO and writing good objectives stressed how goal effectiveness is enhanced by *specificity, difficulty,* and *participation*. Measurable and challenging goals encourage an individual or group to stretch while striving to attain progressively more difficult levels of achievement. For instance, parents who are paying a college student's tuition and expenses are advised to specify a challenging grade-point goal rather than to simply tell their son or daughter, "Just do your best." Otherwise, the student could show up at the end of the semester with two Cs and three Ds, saying, "Well, I did my best!" It is important to note that goals need to be difficult enough to be challenging but not impossible. Impossible goals hamper performance; they are a handy excuse for not even trying.[28]

Participating in the goal-setting process gives the individual *personal ownership*. From the employee's viewpoint, it is "something I helped develop, not just my boss's wild idea." Feedback on performance operates in concert with well-conceived goals. Feedback lets the person or group know if things are on track or if corrective action is required to reach the goal. An otherwise excellent goal-setting program can be compromised by a lack of timely

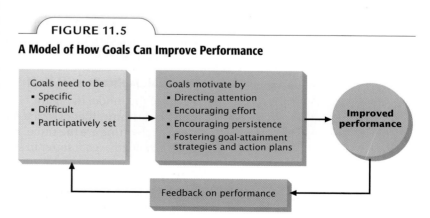

FIGURE 11.5

A Model of How Goals Can Improve Performance

Goals need to be
- Specific
- Difficult
- Participatively set

Goals motivate by
- Directing attention
- Encouraging effort
- Encouraging persistence
- Fostering goal-attainment strategies and action plans

Improved performance

Feedback on performance

and relevant feedback from managers. Researchers have documented the motivational value of matching *specific goals* with *equally specific feedback*.[29] Sam Walton, the founder of Wal-Mart, was a master of blending goals and feedback. For example, consider this exchange between Sam Walton and an employee during one of his regular visits:

> *A manager rushes up with an associate in tow.*
> *"Mr. Walton, I want you to meet Renee. She runs one of the top ten pet departments in the country."*
> *"Well, Renee, bless your heart. What percentage of the store [sales] are you doing?"*
> *"Last year it was 3.1 percent," Renee says, "but this year I'm trying for 3.3 percent."*
> *"Well, Renee, that's amazing," says Sam. "You know our average pet department only does about 2.4 percent. Keep up the great work."*[30]

How Do Goals Actually Motivate?

Goal-setting researchers say goals perform a motivational function by doing the four things listed in the center of Figure 11.5:

1. A goal is an exercise in selective perception because it directs one's *attention* to a specific target.
2. A goal encourages one to exert *effort* toward achieving something specific.
3. Because a challenging goal requires sustained or repeated effort, it encourages *persistence*.
4. Because a goal creates the problem of bridging the gap between actual and desired, it fosters the creation of *strategies and action plans*.

Consider, for example, how all these motivational components were activated by the following program at Marriott's hotel chain:

> *For years, Marriott's room-service business didn't live up to its potential. But after initiating a 15-minute-delivery guarantee for breakfast in 1985, Marriott's breakfast business—the biggest portion of its room-service revenue—jumped 25 percent. [Hotel guests got their breakfast free if it was delivered late.] Marriott got employees to devise ways to deliver the meals on time, including having deliverers carry walkie-talkies so they [could] receive instructions more quickly.*[31]

Marriott's goal, increased room-service revenue, was the focal point for this program. In effect, the service-guarantee program told Marriott employees that prompt room service was important, and they rose to the challenge with persistent and creative effort. Clear, reasonable, and challenging goals, reinforced by specific feedback and meaningful rewards, are indeed a powerful motivational tool.[32]

Practical Implications of Goal-Setting Theory

Because the model in Figure 11.5 is a generic one, the performance environment may range from athletics to academics to the workplace. The motivational mechanics of goal setting are the same, regardless of the targeted performance. If you learn to be an effective goal setter in school, that ability will serve you faithfully throughout life.

Anyone tempted to go through life without goals should remember the smiling Cheshire Cat's good advice to Alice when she asked him to help her find her way through Wonderland:

"Would you tell me, please, which way I ought to walk from here?"
    "That depends a good deal on where you want to get to," replied the Cat.
    "I don't much care where—" said Alice.
    "Then it doesn't matter which way you walk," said the Cat.
    "—so long as I get somewhere," Alice added as an explanation.
    "Oh, you're sure to do that," said the Cat, "if you only walk long enough."[33]

TEST PREPPER 11.2

ANSWERS CAN BE FOUND ON P. 311

True of False?

_____ 1. For motivation purposes, job enlargement and job enrichment involve the same process.

_____ 2. One of the five core job characteristics in job enrichment is skill-based pay.

_____ 3. Task significance is the degree to which the job has a substantial impact on the lives of other people.

_____ 4. In Vroom's expectancy theory of employee motivation, perception plays a central role.

_____ 5. Rewards have equal value to people in the expectancy theory of motivation.

_____ 6. Managers have little or no influence over employee expectations, according to expectancy motivation theory.

_____ 7. Goals tend to be more effective if they are stated in general terms and are relatively easy to understand.

_____ 8. According to goal-setting theory, employee participation is important.

Multiple Choice

_____ 9. What advice would you give a Disneyland manager if she wants to enrich the jobs of her food-service employees?
   a. Move your people from job to job.
   b. Give everyone clearer and more detailed instructions.
   c. Give each employee more tasks at the same level.
   d. Vertically load the jobs with more decision-making responsibility.
   e. Let your people go home when they choose.

Online Study Center
ACE the Test
ACE Practice Tests 11.2

_____ 10. Doing a "whole" piece of work from beginning to end refers to which of the following?
   a. Job feedback
   b. Task identity
   c. Autonomy
   d. Skill variety
   e. Task significance

_____ 11. Which of these best describes the word *expectancy*?
   a. Subjective probability
   b. Self-doubt
   c. Social needs
   d. Personal values
   e. Achievement needs

_____ 12. In the expectancy model, how do rewards influence motivational strength?
   a. Intrinsic versus extrinsic
   b. Immediate versus delayed
   c. Negative impact only
   d. No impact
   e. Perceived value

_____ 13. Based on what you have learned about goal-setting theory, what type of goals should you recommend to a friend who has taken a supervisory job?
   a. Specific and difficult
   b. General
   c. Ones determined by management
   d. Easy
   e. Impossible

_____ 14. _____ is the key to creating a sense of personal ownership of goals.
   a. Feedback
   b. Time-based pay
   c. Clear policies and procedures
   d. Employee participation
   e. Incentive compensation

MOTIVATION THROUGH REWARDS

3 ▶ *Distinguish extrinsic rewards from intrinsic rewards, and list four rules for administering extrinsic rewards effectively.*

rewards Material and psychological payoffs for working.

All workers, including volunteers who donate their time to worthy causes, expect to be rewarded in some way for their contributions. **Rewards** may be defined broadly as the material and psychological payoffs for performing tasks in the workplace. Managers have found that job performance and satisfaction can be improved with properly administered rewards. Rewards today vary greatly in both type and scope, depending on one's employer and geographical location. In fact, a review of comments about the companies listed in *Fortune* magazine's most recent "100 Best Companies to Work For" list reveals dozens of creative reward programs. For example, consider the situation at No. 20 Kimley-Horn & Assoc., in Cary, North Carolina:

> *Rewards are plentiful at the employee-owned engineering firm. It still pays the entire health insurance premium (for employees and dependents), hands out annual bonuses up to 12% of pay, and funds 401(k) retirement plans generously.*[34]

In this section, we distinguish between extrinsic and intrinsic rewards, review alternative employee compensation plans, and discuss the effective management of extrinsic rewards.

Extrinsic Versus Intrinsic Rewards

extrinsic rewards Payoffs, such as money, that are granted by others.

intrinsic rewards Self-granted and internally experienced payoffs, such as a feeling of accomplishment.

There are two different categories of rewards. **Extrinsic rewards** are payoffs granted to the individual by other people. Examples include money, employee benefits, promotions, recognition, status symbols, and praise. The second category is called **intrinsic rewards**, which are self-granted and internally experienced payoffs. Among intrinsic rewards are a sense of accomplishment, self-esteem, and self-actualization. Usually, on-the-job extrinsic and intrinsic rewards are intermingled. For instance, employees at Campbell Soup Co. typically experience a psychological boost when they receive a handwritten note from the firm's CEO, Douglas R. Conant:

> *In his . . . [six years] at Campbell, he has sent out more than 16,000 hand-written thank-you notes to staffers, from the chief investment officer to the receptionist at headquarters—notes often found hanging in people's offices or above their desks.*[35]

Harvard Business School's Abraham Zaleznik offers this perspective:

> *I think a paycheck buys you a baseline level of performance. But one thing that makes a good leader is the ability to offer people intrinsic rewards, the tremendous lift that comes from being aware of one's own talents and wanting to maximize them.*[36]

Employee Compensation

Compensation deserves special attention because money is the universal extrinsic reward.[37] Moreover, since "labor costs are about two-thirds of total business expenses,"[38] compensation practices need to be effective and efficient. Employee

TABLE 11.2

Guide to Employee Compensation Plans

Pay plan	Description/calculation	Main advantage	Main disadvantage
Nonincentive			
Hourly wage	Fixed amount per hour worked	Time is easier to measure than performance	Little or no incentive to work hard
Annual salary	Contractual amount per year	Easy to administer	Little or no incentive to work hard
Incentive			
Piece rate	Fixed amount per unit of output	Pay tied directly to personal output	Negative association with sweatshops and rate-cutting abuses
Sales commission	Fixed percentage of sales revenue	Pay tied directly to personal volume of business	Morale problem when sales personnel earn more than other employees
Merit pay	Bonus granted for outstanding performance	Gives salaried employees incentive to work harder	Fairness issue raised when tied to subjective appraisals
Profit sharing	Distribution of specified percentage of bottom-line profits	Individual has a personal stake in firm's profitability	Profits affected by more than just performance (for example, by prices and competition)
Gain sharing	Distribution of specified percentage of productivity gains and/or cost savings	Encourages employees to work harder and smarter	Calculations can get cumbersome
Pay-for-knowledge	Salary or wage rates tied to degrees earned or skills mastered	Encourages lifelong learning	Tends to inflate training and labor costs
Stock options	Selected employees earn right to acquire firm's stock free or at a discount	Gives individual a personal stake in firm's financial performance	Can be resented by ineligible personnel; morale tied to stock price; regulators concerned about abuses among top executives
Other			
Cafeteria compensation (life-cycle benefits)	Employee selects personal mix of benefits from an array of options	Tailored benefits package fits individual needs	Can be costly to administer

compensation is a complex area fraught with legal and tax implications. Although an exhaustive treatment of employee compensation plans is beyond our present purpose, we can identify major types. Table 11.2 lists and briefly describes ten different pay plans. Two are nonincentive plans, seven qualify as incentive plans, and one plan is in a category of its own. Each type of pay plan has advantages and disadvantages. Therefore, there is no single best plan suitable for all employees.

Indeed, two experts at the U.S. Bureau of Labor Statistics say the key words in compensation for the next 25 years will be *flexible* and *varied*.[39] A diverse work-force will demand an equally diverse array of compensation plans.

Improving Performance with Extrinsic Rewards

Extrinsic rewards, if they are to motivate job performance effectively, need to be administered in ways that (1) satisfy operative needs, (2) foster positive expecta-tions, (3) ensure equitable distribution, and (4) reward results. Let us see how these four criteria can be met relative to the ten different pay plans in Table 11.2.

Rewards Must Satisfy Individual Needs

Whether it is a pay raise or a pat on the back, a reward has no motivational impact unless it satisfies an operative need. Not all people need the same things, and one person may need different things at different times. Money is a powerful motivator for those who seek security through material wealth. But the promise of more money may mean little to a financially secure person who seeks ego gratification from challenging work. People's needs concerning when and how they want to be paid also vary.

cafeteria compensation Plan that allows employees to select their own mix of benefits.

Because cafeteria compensation is rather special and particularly promising, we will examine it more closely. **Cafeteria compensation** (also called life-cycle bene-fits) is a plan that allows each employee to determine the makeup of his or her benefit package.[40] Because today's nonwage benefits are a significant portion of total compensation, the motivating potential of such a privilege can be sizable.

> Under these plans, employers provide minimal "core" coverage in life and health insurance, vacations, and pensions. The employee buys additional benefits to suit [his or her] own needs, using credit based on salary, service, and age.
>
> The elderly bachelor, for instance, may pass up the maternity coverage he would receive, willy-nilly, under conventional plans and "buy" additional pen-sion contributions instead. The mother whose children are covered by her hus-band's employee health insurance policy may choose legal and dental care insurance instead.[41]

Although some organizations have balked at installing cafeteria compensation because of the added administrative expense, the number of programs in effect in the United States has grown steadily. Cafeteria compensation enhances employee satisfaction, according to at least one study,[42] and represents a revolutionary step toward fitting rewards to people, rather than vice versa.

Employees Must Believe Effort Will Lead to Reward

According to expectancy theory, an employee will not strive for an attractive reward unless it is perceived as being attainable. For example, the promise of an expenses-paid trip to Hawaii for the leading salesperson will prompt additional efforts at sales only among those who feel they have a decent chance of winning. Those who believe they have little chance of winning will not be moti-vated to try any harder than usual. Incentive pay plans, especially merit pay, profit sharing, gain sharing, and stock options, need to be designed and communicated in a way that will foster believable effort-reward linkages.[43]

"HIGGINS, BOTH YOU AND FERGUSON WILL BE GOING AFTER THE SAME CARROT."

Source: Harvard Business Review, September 2006. Permission by Dave Carpenter.

FIGURE 11.6

Personal and Social Equity

Personal equity

"I am underpaid. That's unfair. I'm going to take it easy from now on."

"I am paid what I deserve. That's fair."

"I am overpaid. I feel guilty about getting more than I deserve."

Social equity

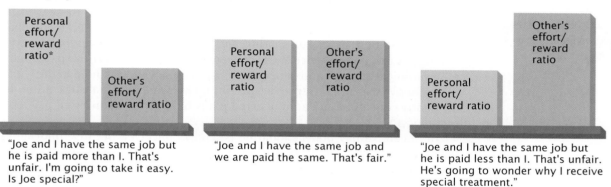

"Joe and I have the same job but he is paid more than I. That's unfair. I'm going to take it easy. Is Joe special?"

"Joe and I have the same job and we are paid the same. That's fair."

"Joe and I have the same job but he is paid less than I. That's unfair. He's going to wonder why I receive special treatment."

* The lower the effort/reward ratio, the greater the motivation.

Rewards Must Be Equitable

Something is equitable if people perceive it to be fair and just. Each of us carries in our head a pair of scales upon which we weigh equity.[44] Figure 11.6 shows one scale for *personal equity* and another for *social equity.* The personal equity scale tests the relationship between effort expended and rewards received. The social equity scale, in contrast, compares our own effort-reward ratio with that of someone else in the same situation. We are motivated to seek personal and social equity and to avoid inequity.[45] Interestingly, research on this topic has demonstrated that inequity is perceived by those who are *overpaid* as well as by those who are underpaid.[46]

Since perceived inequity is associated with feelings of dissatisfaction, anger, and jealousy or guilt, inequitable reward schemes tend to be counterproductive and are ethically questionable. Record-setting executive pay in recent years of painful downsizing, pay cuts, and sharp stock market declines has been roundly criticized as inequitable and unfair.[47] For example, consider the following lopsided situation.

"The protest from unions representing 30,000 United [Airlines] employees came one day after the Chicago-based carrier reported 2006 executive compensation, . . . and 14 months after it exited Chapter 11 bankruptcy reorganization. United said its top five executives received $25.7 million in the form of cash, stock or exercisable stock options. Of that, CEO Glenn Tilton received $9.3 million. . . .

"'Throughout United's bankruptcy, 'shared sacrifice' was the mantra employees heard from upper management,' the unions' statement said."

Source: Marilyn Adams, "United Unions Protest Exec Pay," *USA Today* (March 28, 2007): 3B.

Questions: How does equity theory explain the unions' reaction? How does this sort of news report affect worker motivation and job satisfaction, in general?

Michael Armstrong earned $4.01 million in salary and bonus as chairman and CEO of AT&T in 2001, an increase of 70.8 percent over the previous year. Meanwhile, AT&T said 5,100 employees had left its payroll by the end of 2001, and 5,000 more positions would be cut.[48]

In stark contrast was the CEO of Xilinx, a semiconductor company in San Jose, California, who took a 20 percent pay cut to help maintain the firm's no-layoff policy during the recent tech downturn.[49] From a motivational standpoint, which company would you like to work for? L. M. Baker, Jr., chairman of Wachovia, the Charlotte, North Carolina–based bank, recently summed up the motivational importance of reward equity:

Most people think motivating people is about pushing others to do what you want them to do, but I've found that the secret to motivating others has really been to adhere to simple values, things like honesty, fairness, and generosity.[50]

Rewards Must Be Linked to Performance

Ideally, there should be an if-then relationship between task performance and extrinsic rewards. Traditional hourly wage and annual salary pay plans are weak in this regard. They do little more than reward the person for showing up at work. Managers can strengthen motivation to work by making sure that those who give a little extra get a little extra. In addition to piece-rate and sales-commission plans, merit pay, profit sharing, gain sharing, and stock option plans are popular ways of linking pay and performance.[51] The concept of team-based incentive pay as a way of rewarding teamwork and cooperation has been slow to take hold in the United States for two reasons: (1) it goes against the grain of an individualistic culture, and (2) poorly conceived and administered plans have given team-based pay a bad reputation.[52]

All incentive pay plans should be carefully conceived because undesirable behavior may inadvertently be encouraged. Consider, for example, what the head of Nucor Corporation, a successful minimill steel company, had to say about his firm's bonus system:

[Nucor's] bonus system . . . is very tough. If you're late even five minutes, you lose your bonus for the day. If you're late more than 30 minutes, or you're absent because of sickness or anything else, you lose your bonus for the week. Now, we do have what we call four "forgiveness" days during the year when you can be sick or you have to close on a house or your wife is having a baby. But only four. We have a melter, Phil Johnson, down in Darlington, and one of the workers came in one day and said that Phil had been in an automobile accident and was sitting beside his car off of Route 52, holding his head. So the foreman asked, "Why didn't you stop and help him?" And the guy said, "And lose my bonus?"[53]

Like goals, incentive plans foster selective perception.[54] Consequently, managers need to make sure goals and incentives point people in ethical directions.

TEST PREPPER 11.3

ANSWERS CAN BE FOUND ON P. 311

True or False?

_____ 1. Examples of extrinsic rewards include praise from a parent and a pat on the back from a coach.

_____ 2. Intrinsic rewards are those granted by the organization, such as a cash bonus.

_____ 3. An example of incentive compensation is an annual salary.

_____ 4. Employees receive free meals and treats in cafeteria compensation plans.

_____ 5. Perceived inequity can be experienced by employees who are either underpaid or overpaid.

Multiple Choice

_____ 6. _____ is an extrinsic reward.
a. A feeling of accomplishment
b. Self-actualization
c. Praise from an executive
d. Self-esteem
e. A feeling of doubt

_____ 7. According to the experts at the U.S. Bureau of Labor Statistics, the term(s) _____ will apply to future compensation plans.
a. time-based
b. uniform and standardized
c. flexible and varied
d. lean and uniform
e. skill-based

_____ 8. At E-Designs Inc., salary and wages are tied to degrees earned and skills mastered. This is an example of
a. gain sharing.
b. pay-for-knowledge.
c. piece rate.
d. cafeteria compensation.
e. profit sharing.

_____ 9. All of these are ways to increase the motivational impact of extrinsic rewards *except*
a. reward effort, not results.
b. make employees believe effort will lead to reward.
c. link rewards to performance.
d. make rewards equitable.
e. satisfy individual needs.

_____ 10. Which ratio relates to the perception of reward equity?
a. Effort-reward
b. Task-results
c. Effort-results
d. Pay-performance
e. Task difficulty-results

Online Study Center
ACE the Test
ACE Practice Tests 11.3

MOTIVATION THROUGH EMPLOYEE PARTICIPATION

4 ▶ *Explain how open-book management and self-managed teams promote employee participation.*

While noting that the term *participation* has become a "stewpot" into which every conceivable kind of management fad has been tossed, one management scholar has helpfully identified four key areas of participative management. Employees may participate in (1) setting goals, (2) making decisions, (3) solving problems, and (4) designing and implementing organizational changes.[55] Thus, **participative management** is defined as the process of empowering employees to assume greater control of the workplace.[56] When employees are personally and meaningfully involved, above and beyond just doing assigned tasks, they are likely to be more motivated and productive. In fact, a recent study of 164 New Zealand companies with at least 100 employees found lower employee

Online Study Center
Improve Your Grade
Career Snapshot 11.1

participative management Empowering employees to assume greater control of the workplace.

turnover and higher organizational productivity among firms using participative management practices.[57]

This section focuses on two approaches to participation: open-book management and self-managed teams. After taking a closer look at each, we consider four keys to successful employee participation programs.

Open-Book Management

open-book management Sharing key financial data and profits with employees who are trained and empowered.

Open-book management (OBM) involves "opening a company's financial statements to all employees and providing the education that will enable them to understand how the company makes money and how their actions affect its success and bottom line."[58] Clearly, this is a bold break from traditional management practice. Many companies claim to practice OBM, but few actually do.[59] Why? OBM asks managers to correct three typical shortcomings by:

1. Displaying a high degree of trust in employees
2. Having a deep and unwavering commitment to employee training
3. Being patient when waiting for results[60]

A four-step approach to OBM is displayed in Figure 11.7. The S.T.E.P. acronym stands for *share, teach, empower,* and *pay.* Skipping or inadequately performing a step virtually guarantees failure. Experts tell us that it takes at least two complete budget cycles (typically two years) to see positive results:

1. In step 1, employees are exposed to eye-catching public displays of key financial data. Sales, expense, and profit data for both the organization and relevant business units are shared in hallways, cafeterias, and on internal Web sites.

FIGURE 11.7

The Four S.T.E.P. Approach to Open-Book Management

Source: Based on discussion in Raj Aggarwal and Betty J. Simkins, "Open Book Management—Optimizing Human Capital," *Business Horizons,* 44 (September–October 2001): 5–13.

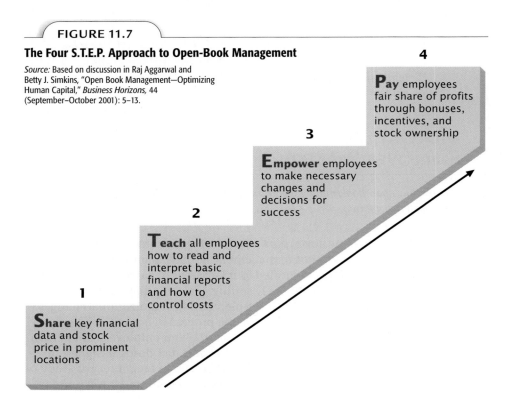

1. **S**hare key financial data and stock price in prominent locations

2. **T**each all employees how to read and interpret basic financial reports and how to control costs

3. **E**mpower employees to make necessary changes and decisions for success

4. **P**ay employees fair share of profits through bonuses, incentives, and stock ownership

2. Of course, without step 2, step 1 would be meaningless. Comprehensive, ongoing training gives *all* employees a working knowledge of the firm's business model. Here is what Jelly Belly Candy Co. does:

> *Through Jelly Belly University, employees from the upper-most management level to administrative support personnel learn the art of candy-making, evaluate the results and conduct product evaluations, production scheduling and inventory control.*[61]

Thus, Jelly Belly's employees not only learn how to make great jelly beans; they also learn what it takes to make a profit in the process. In OBM companies, finance specialists teach other employees how to read and interpret basic financial documents such as profit-loss statements. Entertaining and instructive business board games and computer simulations have proved effective. Remedial education is provided when needed. Armed with knowledge about the company's workings and financial health, employees are ready for step 3.

3. Managers find it easier to trust empowered employees to make important decisions when the employees are adequately prepared. (More on empowerment in Chapter 13.)

4. In step 4, employees enjoy the fruits of their efforts by sharing profits and/or receiving bonuses and incentive compensation. There is no magic to OBM. It simply involves doing *important* things in the *right* way.[62]

Self-Managed Teams

According to the logic of this comprehensive approach to participation, self-management is the best management because it taps people's full potential. Advocates say self-management fosters creativity, motivation, and productivity. **Self-managed teams**, also known as *autonomous work groups* or *high-performance work teams,* take on traditional managerial tasks as part of their normal work routine.[63] They can have anywhere from 5 to more than 30 members, depending on the job. Employees are assigned to self-managed teams, as opposed to voluntary membership in quality improvement programs such as *quality circles.* Cross-trained team members typically rotate jobs as they turn out a complete product or service. Any supervision tends to be minimal, with managers acting more as *facilitators* than as order givers.

self-managed teams High-performance teams that assume traditional managerial duties such as staffing and planning.

Vertically Loaded Jobs

In the language of job enrichment, team members' jobs are vertically loaded. This means nonmanagerial team members assume duties traditionally performed by managers. But specifically which duties? A survey of industry practices in *Training* magazine gave us some answers. Over 60 percent of the companies using self-managed teams let team members determine work schedules, deal directly with customers, and conduct training. Between 30 and 40 percent of the teams were allowed to manage budgets, conduct performance appraisals, and hire people. Only 15 percent of the teams were permitted to fire coworkers. The researchers concluded that *true* self-managed teams are in the early growth stage.[64] Still, Google Inc., creator of the popular Internet search engine, shows how far the concept can go:

> *When [chief engineer Wayne] Rosing started at Google in 2001, "we had management in engineering. And the structure was tending to tell people, No, you can't do that." So Google got rid of the managers. Now most engineers work in*

teams of three, with project leadership rotating among team members. If some-thing isn't right, even if it's in a product that has already gone public, teams fix it without asking anyone.

"For a while," Rosing says, "I had 160 direct reports. No managers. It worked because the teams knew what they had to do. That set a cultural bit in people's heads: You are the boss. Don't wait to take the hill. Don't wait to be managed."

And if you fail, fine. On to the next idea. "There's faith here in the ability of smart, well-motivated people to do the right thing," Rosing says. "Anything that gets in the way of that is evil."[65]

Consequently, Google hires very carefully, putting applicants through a rigorous screening process. *Fortune* quoted the head of Texas Instruments as saying, "No matter what your business, these teams are the wave of the future."[66]

Managerial Resistance

Not surprisingly, managerial resistance is the number one barrier to self-managed teams. More than anything else, self-managed teams represent *change*, and lots of it.

Adopting the team approach is no small matter; it means wiping out tiers of managers and tearing down bureaucratic barriers between departments. Yet companies are willing to undertake such radical changes to gain workers' knowledge and commitment—along with productivity gains that exceed 30 percent in some cases.[67]

Traditional authoritarian supervisors view autonomous teams as a threat to their authority and job security. For this reason, *new* facilities built around the concept of self-managed teams, so-called greenfield sites, tend to fare better than reworked existing operations.

Managers who take the long view and switch to self-managed teams are find-ing it well worth the investment of time and money. Self-managed teams even show early promise of boosting productivity in the huge service sector.[68] (Team-work is discussed in the next chapter.)

Keys to Successful Employee Participation Programs

According to researchers, four factors build the *employee* support necessary for any sort of participation program to work:

1. A profit-sharing or gain-sharing plan
2. A long-term employment relationship with good job security
3. A concerted effort to build and maintain group cohesiveness
4. Protection of the individual employee's rights[69]

Working in combination, these factors can be a powerful motivational force.

It should be clear by now that participative management involves more than simply announcing a new program, such as open-book management. To make sure a supportive climate exists, a good deal of background work often needs to be done.[70] This is particularly important in view of the conclusion drawn by research-ers who analyzed 41 participative management studies:

Participation has ... [a positive] effect on both satisfaction and productivity, and its effect on satisfaction is somewhat stronger than its effect on productiv-ity.... Our analysis indicates specific organizational factors that may enhance or constrain the effect of participation. For example, there is evidence that a participative climate has a more substantial effect on workers' satisfaction than participation in specific decisions.[71]

In the end, effective participative management is as much a managerial attitude about sharing power as it is a specific set of practices. In some European countries, such as Germany, the supportive climate is reinforced by government-mandated participative management.[72]

TEST PREPPER 11.4

ANSWERS CAN BE FOUND ON P. 311

True or False?

_____ 1. In open-book management, the S.T.E.P. acronym stands for share, teach, empower, and perform.

_____ 2. The final step of the S.T.E.P. approach to open-book management involves paying employees a fair share of profits through bonuses, incentives, and stock ownership.

_____ 3. Self-managed teams are a form of job enrichment.

_____ 4. According to researchers, profit sharing can help an employee participation program succeed.

Multiple Choice

_____ 5. _____ is a key word in the definition of participative management.
   a. Empowerment   d. Authority
   b. Independence   e. Goals
   c. Equality

_____ 6. The *S* in the S.T.E.P. approach to OBM stands for
   a. Success.   d. Strength.
   b. Separate.   e. Share.
   c. Sales.

_____ 7. The main barrier to self-managed teams is
   a. self-confidence.
   b. blue-collar personnel.
   c. organized labor.
   d. managerial resistance.
   e. use of part-time employees.

_____ 8. Which of these was *not* found by researchers to be a success factor for employee participation programs?
   a. Job security
   b. Protection of employee rights
   c. Flexible work schedules
   d. Profit-sharing or gain-sharing plan
   e. An effort to build group cohesiveness

Online Study Center
ACE the Test
ACE Practice Tests 11.4

MOTIVATION THROUGH QUALITY-OF-WORKLIFE PROGRAMS

5 ► *Discuss how companies are striving to motivate employees with quality-of-worklife programs.*

Workforce diversity has made "flexibility" a must for managers today. This chapter concludes with a look at ways of accommodating previously unmet and emerging employee needs. For example, a big concern these days involves helping employees strike a proper life balance between work, family, and leisure through

Through four generations of the Smucker family and 105 years of making great jams, jellies, and other goodies, J. M. Smucker knows a few things about how to motivate and retain good employees. For instance, the Orrville, Ohio, company grants unlimited paid time off to employees who want to volunteer. Here Brenda Dempsey, Smucker's corporate communications director, instructs an economics class at Orrville High School. This sort of community-building program has a broad range of direct and indirect benefits.

quality-of-worklife programs.[73] By meeting these needs in creative ways, such as flexible work schedules, family support services, wellness programs, and sabbaticals, managers hope to enhance motivation and job performance.

Flexible Work Schedules

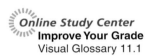

Online Study Center
Improve Your Grade
Visual Glossary 11.1

flextime   Allows employees to choose their own arrival and departure times within specified limits.

The standard 8 A.M. to 5 P.M., 40-hour workweek has come under fire as dual-income families, single parents, and others attempt to juggle hectic schedules. Taking its place is **flextime**, a work-scheduling plan that allows employees to determine their own arrival and departure times within specific limits.[74] All employees must be present during a fixed core time (see the center portion of Figure 11.8). If an eight-hour day is required, as in Figure 11.8, an early bird can put in the required eight hours by arriving at 7:00 A.M., taking half an hour for lunch, and departing at 3:30 P.M. Alternatively, a late starter can come in at 9:00 A.M. and leave at 5:30 P.M. When given the choice of "flexible work hours" versus an "opportunity to advance" in a survey, 58 percent of the women opted for flexible hours. Forty-three percent of the men chose that option.[75] The growing use of flextime and other alternative work arrangements, such as telecommuting, is partly due to employer self-interest. Employers want to cut the cost of unscheduled absenteeism. A 2001 survey found the average annual cost for each employee's unscheduled absenteeism (68 percent of which was *not* for illness) to be $775.[76] Flextime can also be used to accommodate the special needs of disabled employees.[77]

Benefits

In addition to many anecdotal reports citing the benefits of flextime, research studies have uncovered promising evidence. Flextime has several documented benefits:

▌ Better employee-supervisor relations

▌ Reduced absenteeism

▌ Selective positive impact on job performance (e.g., a 24 percent improvement for computer programmers over a two-year period but no effect on the performance of data-entry workers)[78]

Flextime, though very popular among employees because of the degree of freedom it brings, is not appropriate for all situations. Problems reported by adopters include greater administrative expense, supervisory resistance, and inadequate coverage of jobs.

Alternatives

Other work-scheduling innovations include *compressed workweeks* (40 or more hours in fewer than five days)[79] and *permanent part-time* (workweeks with fewer than 40 hours). *Job sharing* (complementary scheduling that allows two or more part-timers to share a single full-time job), yet another work-scheduling innovation, is growing in popularity among employers of working parents and semi-retired employees.[80] (See Best Practices on page 308 for the most radical approach to work scheduling of all.)

A European study suggests that employees may be paying a price for the freedom of flexible and nonstandard work scheduling. Compared with a control group of employees on fixed schedules, employees with compressed workweeks, rotating shifts, irregular schedules, and part-time jobs experienced significantly more health, psychological, and sleeping problems.[81]

Family Support Services

With dual-income families and single parents caught between obligations to family and the job, both the U.S. government and companies are coming to the rescue. On the federal government front, the Family and Medical Leave Act (FMLA) took effect in the United States in 1993 after years of political debate.[82] Unfortunately, FMLA has significant holes and limitations. First, only companies with 50 or more employees are required to comply with the law, which mandates up to 12 weeks of unpaid leave per year for family events such as births, adoptions, or sickness. Because the vast majority of U.S. businesses (95 percent) employ fewer than 50 people, millions of working Americans (43 percent) are left unprotected by FMLA. Second, employees can be required by their employer to exhaust their sick leave and vacation allotments before taking FMLA leave. Fortunately, states and businesses can plug some of the holes in FMLA.

At least 35 states have equivalent or more generous parental and family leave laws. Eligible employees can choose the more generous option when both federal

_/ **FIGURE 11.8**

Flextime in Action

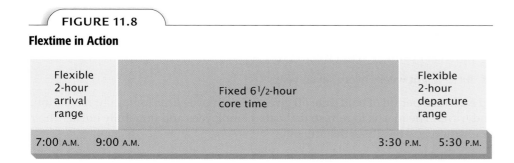

Online Study Center college.hmco.com/pic/kreitnerSASfound

and state laws apply.[83] Meanwhile, on the business front, a few companies go so far as to grant *paid* parental and family sickness leaves. Many other exciting corporate family support service initiatives are cropping up. A growing but still very small number of companies in the United States (11 percent in 1999) provide on-site day-care facilities. About 15 percent provide emergency child-care services.[84] Elder-care centers, for employees' elderly relatives who cannot be left home alone, are starting to appear.[85] Some companies have banded together to form reduced-rate day-care cooperatives for their employees. Emergency child care is a welcome corporate benefit for working parents.

Wellness Programs

Stress and burnout are all-too-common consequences of modern work life.[86] Family-versus-work conflict, long hours, overload, hectic schedules, deadlines, frequent business travel, and accumulated workplace irritations are taking their toll. According to Anne Stevens, an executive at Ford Motor Co., modern business life is like an athletic event that requires a well-trained mind and body:

> You have to be physically, emotionally and intellectually durable. You have to take care of yourself. I wake up at 4:30 and I work out. People come into my office and have cookies for lunch. I go get them a piece of fruit. I say, "Eat right. Take care of yourself. Get some sleep." Because we're a human body. If we're not in tiptop shape, how can we possibly have top performance?[87]

Progressive companies are coming to the rescue with *wellness programs* featuring a wide range of offerings. Among them are stress reduction, healthy eating and living clinics, quit-smoking and weight-loss programs, exercise facilities, massage breaks, behavioral health counseling, and health screenings. The ultimate objective is to help employees achieve a sustainable balance between their personal lives and work lives, with win-win benefits all around.

> For example, Citibank experienced decreases in health risks and savings of between $4.56 and $4.73 for each dollar spent on its health education and awareness program. In another example, Glaxo Wellcome's health promotion program saved the company an estimated $1 million in 1998, and has reduced medical leaves of absence by 20,000 workdays since 1996.[88]

Sabbaticals

Some progressive companies give selected employees paid sabbaticals after a certain number of years of service. Here is a sampling to illustrate the variations:

- *Adobe Systems:* Three weeks every five years

- *Silicon Graphics:* Six weeks every four years

- *Genentech:* Six weeks every six years

- *American Century:* Four weeks every seven years

- *Intel:* Eight weeks every seven years[89]

An extended period of paid time off gives the employee time for family, recreation, and travel. The idea is to refresh dedicated employees and hopefully bolster their motivation and loyalty in the process.

ANSWERS CAN BE FOUND ON P. 311

True or False?

_____ 1. In a flextime program, hourly employees can arrive at work whenever they choose.

_____ 2. Two part-timers share the same job when the job-sharing concept is in effect.

_____ 3. Every employer in the United States must comply with the Family and Medical Leave Act.

_____ 4. The ultimate objective of wellness programs is to reduce turnover.

Multiple Choice

_____ 5. Flextime can be most accurately described by which of these?
   a. Arrive at a fixed time, but depart when the job is done
   b. Arrive and depart within specified limits
   c. Arrive on time, but depart as desired
   d. Arrive and depart when you choose
   e. Arrive when you like, but depart at a fixed time

Online Study Center
ACE the Test
ACE Practice Tests 11.5

_____ 6. Shawn works ten-hour shifts four days every week so that he can pursue a college degree. What flexible work schedule is he using?
   a. Rolling time
   b. Compressed workweek
   c. Job sharing
   d. Permanent part-time
   e. Flextime

_____ 7. How does the text characterize the United States Family and Medical Leave Act that took effect in 1993?
   a. Long overdue universal coverage
   b. More generous than state laws
   c. The first law to require paid leave for everyone
   d. Probably unconstitutional
   e. Has significant holes and limitations

_____ 8. When companies such as Wells Fargo and McDonald's grant employees paid time off after a specified number of years of service, this refers to
   a. job rotation.
   b. cafeteria compensation.
   c. flextime.
   d. a sabbatical.
   e. mental health time.

BEST PRACTICES

Are You Getting Enough Sleep?

Your mother was right—to perform at your best, you need sleep. Discoveries about sleep cycles have given researchers new insights into the specific roles sleep plays in overall health and performance. For example, there is growing evidence that sleep aids in immune function, memory consolidation, learning, and organ function. "Some researchers now think sleep may be the missing link when it comes to overall health, safety, and productivity," says Darrel Drobnich, the senior director of government and transportation affairs for the National Sleep Foundation. One new field of study is looking at a specific correlation between sleep and productivity, and the benefits of what sleep researchers call a "power nap"—a 20-minute period of sleep in the afternoon that heads off problems associated with cumulative sleep deficit.

Source: Excerpted from Bronwyn Fryer, "What's New in Sleep?" *Harvard Business Review*, 84 (October 2006): 58.

Best Buy Reinvents the Work-a-Day Routine

The nation's leading electronics retailer has embarked on a radical—if risky—experiment to transform a culture once known for killer hours and herd-riding bosses. The endeavor, called ROWE, for "results-only work environment," seeks to demolish decades-old business dogma that equates physical presence with productivity. The goal at Best Buy is to judge performance on output instead of hours.

Hence workers pulling into the company's amenity-packed headquarters at 2 P.M. aren't considered late.

Nor are those pulling out at 2 P.M. seen as leaving early. There are no schedules. No mandatory meetings. No impression-management hustles. Work is no longer a place where you go, but something you do. It's O.K. to take conference calls while you hunt, collaborate from your lakeside cabin, or log on after dinner so you can spend the afternoon with your kid.

Source: Excerpted from Michelle Conlin, "Smashing the Clock," *Business Week,* December 11, 2006, pp. 60–68. Reprinted with permission.

Hey, Big Spender!

Rick Sapio keeps a sign on the wall of his office. Its message: Profit equals revenues divided by expenses. There's an upward-pointing arrow next to revenues and a downward-pointing arrow next to expenses. "One of these two things has to happen in every decision you make in order for there to be a profit. Either revenue is going up or expenses are going down," Sapio says.

The chart is a gimmick but nevertheless is important to Sapio, the CEO of Dallas-based Mutuals.com, which provides mutual-fund advisory services and account management to its customers for a flat fee. Sapio didn't always have that sign on the wall, and he didn't believe he needed it—or anything else—as a manifesto. Back in 1994, when he started Mutuals.com, Sapio never really thought about keeping an eye on expenses. He didn't have to. "I found it very easy to raise money," he says, and as the boom of the 1990s wore on and the marketplace was flush with investment capital,

raising money got even simpler. Over the course of the decade, Sapio was able to raise an enviable $14 million, mostly from angels and institutional investors.

All that cash was not necessarily a good thing, Sapio admits now. "We were not accountable to being a profitable company at the beginning and hence our energies weren't focused on looking at expenses. We were looking only at the revenue," he says. Indeed, during his first six years, revenues increased by an average of 113% a year, but Mutuals.com consistently ran in the red.

Since then, Sapio and his company have done some growing up. By 1999, Sapio was finding it difficult to raise money. Then in March 2000 came the Nasdaq crash, which hammered the mutual-fund industry.

During the past few years, Sapio has made small changes in the company and himself that add up to a big difference. These days, despite a wobbly stock market, the 10-employee company has a 15% profit margin. Revenues are up 190% since 1999, and expenses have leveled off and are projected to drop by nearly 4% this year.

Sapio's first step was learning to keep an eye on the numbers. After reading that Cisco Systems Inc. closes its books every day, Sapio took up the practice at Mutuals.com in July 2000. Now all financial transactions are entered the same day they occur, to create a real-time picture of the company's revenues and expenses. It's good discipline and surprisingly easy with today's accounting software, says Regina Lian, president of New York City's Financial Comfort, who advises small businesses on financial management.

Now Sapio gathers his top managers in a daily huddle at 4:37 P.M., just after the stock market closes, to go over the figures. Each person is responsible for updating at least one revenue item and one expense. "Every line item on our financial statement has a name next to it," Sapio says. "So if travel's out of whack, I'll say, 'Ernie, give us a report on how we can lower travel next week.'"

Sapio also practices open-book management, showing a current profit-and-loss statement and balance sheet to the 10 employees at a weekly meeting. All those eyes help spot potential savings. Last year one employee noticed that revenues were up but so were the processing charges for trades. Sapio negotiated a 25% reduction in fees with the outside processor.

Reviewing the numbers daily forced Sapio to get serious about sticking to a budget. "If something is not on the budget, we say no to it," he says. "If we absolutely have to spend the money, then we have a line

item on our P&L statement that says 'unbudgeted expense' and we track that number."

Employees who overspend without getting prior approval can wind up paying out of their own packets. Just ask president Eric McDonald, who ended up covering a $300 bill for an in-house dinner that went over budget. Or Sapio himself, who hired a consultant last year in order to get some leadership coaching, even though he didn't have an OK from his executive team. Sapio figured the managers would approve the expense retroactively. Unfortunately for Sapio, they never came around. So when the $6,000 invoice arrived, it was Sapio's to pay.

Source: From *Inc.: The Magazine For Growing Companies* by Emily Barker, "Cheap Executive Officer," April 2002. Copyright © 2002 by Mansueto Ventures LLC. Reproduced with permission of Mansueto Ventures LLC via Copyright Clearance Center.

Case Questions

1. Referring back to Figure 11.3 on page 289 as a guide, what evidence of job enrichment can you detect in this case? How is motivation enhanced?
2. What role, if any, does equity play in this case? Explain the likely motivational impact.
3. In terms of the S.T.E.P. approach in Figure 11.7 on page 300, does Sapio have a good open-book management program? Explain.
4. From a general standpoint, is Sapio a good manager? Explain.
5. Would you like to be on Rick Sapio's executive team? Why or why not?

Managing Groups and Teams

12

Want more teamwork in the office? Then start by tearing down some walls to create "communal space."

1 ▸ *Define the term* group, *and explain the significance of roles, norms, and ostracism in regard to the behavior of group members.*

2 ▸ *Characterize a mature group, and identify and briefly describe the six stages of group development.*

3 ▸ *Summarize the research insights about organizational politics, and explain how groupthink can lead to blind conformity.*

4 ▸ *Define cross-functional teams, discuss the management of virtual teams, and explain what makes a team effective.*

When I'm working with a group now, I can honestly say that I think about the team first. The 'I first' approach has been drilled out of me."[1]

—Jim Vesterman, U.S. Marine combat veteran and M.B.A. student

Chapter Outline

Online Study Center
Prepare for Class
Chapter Outline

5 ▶ *Explain why trust is a key ingredient of teamwork, and discuss what management can do to build trust.*

Another Space Race

There may be no "I" in "team," but there is one smack in the middle of the word "office." The most heated discussions over office design center around individual, not communal, workspace. But that's starting to change.

When A.G. Lafley took over as CEO of Procter & Gamble in 2000, he wanted to create an environment that encouraged teamwork and collaboration. So in 2002 he gutted the stodgy executive floor, opened it up, and added a "living room" for casual gatherings. Throughout the building the company added "huddle rooms" with laptop connections and phones. There are espresso areas with cushy sofas, CNN on flat screens, and in one a faux fireplace. The Cincinnati headquarters still looks professional, but also open and egalitarian. "Knowing that people are different, we provide different settings," says Serge Bruylants, P&G's global architect. "We shouldn't put too many boundaries in place."

Online Study Center college.hmco.com/pic/kreitnerSASfound

Online Study Center
Prepare for Class
Chapter Glossary

Improve Your Grade
Flashcards
Hangman
Crossword Puzzles

social capital   Productive potential of strong relationships, goodwill, trust, and cooperation.

Online Study Center
Improve Your Grade
Career Snapshot 12.1

That kind of thinking is making inroads across corporate America. Right now, according to office furniture maker Knoll, offices are 80% individual and 20% collaborative space, but communal space is closing the gap. The reason: Group time is more important, and therefore so is group space, says Christine Barber, Knoll's director of workplace research. Gathering around a table in a windowless conference room is not the answer. "Employees need more spaces for impromptu meetings," says Herman Miller's Betty Hase, a workplace strategist, for those off-the-cuff chats where ideas start to froth. So designers are creating offices to replicate dense, urban environments, with areas built to look like piazzas, "intersections" where groups can form spontaneously, and homier spots like coffee bars. "It is much more conducive to conversation," says Jennifer Becker, who works for P&G's global snack division, about the seventh-floor coffee lounge.[2] ■

Relationships rule in daily life. For example, when youngsters between the ages of 8 and 18 were surveyed about the causes of a "bad day at school," the number one reason was "Not getting along with friends" (35%).[3] The same goes for modern work organizations. Relationships do matter. The more managers know about building and sustaining good working relationships, the better. A management consultant put it this way:

> At the end of the day, a company's only sustainable competitive advantage is its relationships with customers, business partners, and employees. After all, we provide products and services to people, not to companies. A commitment to developing effective relationships strengthens the fabric of the organization in the long run.[4]

What is involved here is the concept of **social capital**, "productive potential resulting from strong relationships, goodwill, trust, and cooperative effort."[5] In line with our discussion of human capital in Chapter 9, managers need to build social capital by working on strong, constructive, and mutually beneficial relationships. The purpose of this chapter is to build a foundation of understanding about how groups and teams function in today's organizations.

FUNDAMENTAL GROUP DYNAMICS

> **1** ▶ Define the term group, *and explain the significance of roles, norms, and ostracism in regard to the behavior of group members.*

According to one organization theorist, "All groups may be collections of individuals, but all collections of individuals are not groups."[6] This observation is more than a play on words; mere togetherness does not automatically create a group. Consider, for example, this situation. Half a dozen people who worked for different companies in the same building often shared the same elevator in the morning. As time passed, they introduced themselves and exchanged pleasantries. Eventually, four of the elevator riders discovered that they all lived in the same suburb. Arrangements for a car pool were made, and they began to take turns picking up and delivering one another. A group technically came into existence only when

FIGURE 12.1

What Does It Take to Make a Group?

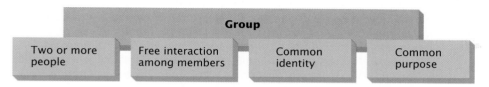

the car pool was formed. To understand why this is so, we need to examine the definition of the term *group*.

What Is a Group?

From a sociological perspective, a **group** can be defined as two or more freely interacting individuals who share a common identity and purpose.[7] Careful analysis of this definition reveals four important dimensions (see Figure 12.1). First, a group must be made up of two or more people if it is to be considered a social unit. Second, the individuals must freely interact in some manner. An organization may qualify as a sociological group if it is small and personal enough to permit all its members to interact regularly with each other. Generally, however, larger organizations with bureaucratic tendencies are made up of many overlapping groups. Third, the interacting individuals must share a common identity. Each must recognize himself or herself as a member of the group. Fourth, interacting individuals who have a common identity must also have a common purpose. That is, there must be at least a rough consensus on why the group exists.

group   Two or more freely interacting individuals with a common identity and purpose.

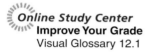
Online Study Center
Improve Your Grade
Visual Glossary 12.1

Types of Groups

Human beings belong to groups for many different reasons. Some people join a group as an end in itself. For example, an accountant may enjoy the socializing that is part of belonging to a group at a local health club. That same accountant's membership in a work group is a means to a professional end. Both the exercise group and the work group satisfy the sociological definition of a group, but they fulfill very different needs. The former is an informal group, and the latter is a formal group.

Informal Groups

As Abraham Maslow pointed out, a feeling of belonging is a powerful motivator. People generally have a great need to fit in, to be liked, to be one of the gang. Whether the group meets at work or during leisure time, it is still an **informal group** if the principal reason for belonging is friendship.[8] Informal groups usually evolve spontaneously. They serve to satisfy esteem needs because one develops a better self-image when accepted, recognized, and liked by others. Sometimes, as in the case of a group of friends forming an investment club, an informal group may evolve into a formal one.

informal group   Collection of people seeking friendship.

Managers cannot afford to ignore informal groups because grassroots social networks can either advance or threaten the organization's mission.[9] As experts on the subject explained:

> These informal networks can cut through formal reporting procedures to jump-start stalled initiatives and meet extraordinary deadlines. But informal

networks can just as easily sabotage companies' best-laid plans by blocking communication and fomenting opposition to change unless managers know how to identify and direct them. . . .

If the formal organization is the skeleton of a company, the informal is the central nervous system driving the collective thought processes, actions, and reactions of its business units. Designed to facilitate standard modes of production, the formal organization is set up to handle easily anticipated problems. But when unexpected problems arise, the informal organization kicks in. Its complex web of social ties form[s] every time colleagues communicate and solidif[ies] over time into surprisingly stable networks. Highly adaptive, informal networks move diagonally and elliptically, skipping entire functions to get work done.[10]

Formal Groups

A **formal group** is a group created for the purpose of doing productive work. It may be called a *team*, a *committee*, or simply a *work group*. Whatever its name, a formal group is usually formed for the purpose of contributing to the success of a larger organization. Formal groups tend to be more rationally structured and less fluid than informal groups. Rather than joining formal task groups, people are assigned to them according to their talents and the organization's needs. One person normally is granted formal leadership responsibility to ensure that the members carry out their assigned duties. Informal friendship groups, in contrast, generally do not have officially appointed leaders, although informal leaders often emerge by popular demand. For the individual, the formal group and an informal group at the place of employment may or may not overlap. In other words, one may or may not be friends with one's coworkers. According to a recent survey of 1,385 office workers, 88 percent said they had attended a wedding, funeral, or other social event with coworkers.[11]

Attraction to Groups

What attracts a person to one group but not to another? And why do some group members stay while others leave? Managers who can answer these questions can take steps to motivate others to join and remain members of a formal work group. Individual commitment to either an informal or formal group hinges on two factors. The first is *attractiveness*, the outside-looking-in view.[12] A nonmember will want to join a group that is attractive and will shy away from a group that is unattractive. The second factor is **cohesiveness**, the tendency of group members to follow the group and resist outside influences. This is the inside-looking-out view. In a highly cohesive group, individual members tend to see themselves as "we" rather than "I." Cohesive group members stick together.[13]

Factors that either enhance or destroy group attractiveness and cohesiveness are listed in Table 12.1. It is important to note that each factor is a matter of degree. For example, a group may offer the individual little, moderate, or great opportunity for prestige and status. Similarly, group demands on the individual may range from somewhat disagreeable to highly disagreeable. What all this means is that both the decision to join a group and the decision to continue being a member depend on a net balance of the factors in Table 12.1. Naturally, the resulting balance is colored by one's perception and frame of reference, as it was in the case of Richard Dale, a former manager of distribution at Commodore International, during his first meeting with the company's founder, Jack Tramiel:

formal group Collection of people created to do something productive.

Can you be friends with the people you manage? "Working with people you really like for 8 to 10 hours a day adds fun to everything.

"That said, remember that boss-subordinate friendships live or die because of one thing: complete, unrelenting candor. . . . You don't want your liking someone's personality to automatically communicate that you like his or her performance."

Source: The second Q&A in Jack Welch and Suzy Welch, "From the Old, Something New," *Business Week* (November 20, 2006): 124.

Question: What is your experience with such friendships and are you generally for or against them? Explain.

cohesiveness The tendency of a group to stick together.

TABLE 12.1

Factors That Enhance or Detract from Group Attractiveness and Cohesiveness

Factors that enhance	Factors that detract
1. Prestige and status	1. Unreasonable or disagreeable demands on the individual
2. Cooperative relationship	2. Disagreement over procedures, activities, rules, and the like
3. High degree of interaction	3. Unpleasant experience with the group
4. Relatively small size	4. Competition between the group's demands and preferred outside activities
5. Similarity of members	5. Unfavorable public image of the group
6. Superior public image of the group	6. Competition for membership by other groups
7. A common threat in the environment	

Source: Table adapted from *Group Dynamics: Research and Theory* 2d ed., by Dorwin Cartwright and Alvin Zander. New York: HarperCollins Publishers, Inc.

> *Dale's first meeting with Tramiel began with a summons to appear at Tramiel's office. Dale flew from his office in Los Angeles to Santa Clara . . . , only to find that Tramiel had decided to visit him instead.*
>
> *Terrified, Dale caught a plane back to find his secretary shaking in her shoes and the burly Tramiel sitting at his desk. For an hour Tramiel grilled Dale on his philosophy of business, pronounced it all wrong, and suggested a tour of the warehouse. When they passed boxes of . . . [computers] waiting for shipment, recalls Dale, Tramiel seemed to "go crazy," pounding the boxes with his fists and yelling, "Do you think this is bourbon? Do you think it gets better with age?"[14]*

Dale's departure within a few months of this episode is not surprising in view of the fact that Tramiel's conduct destroyed work group attractiveness and cohesiveness.

Roles

According to Shakespeare, "All the world's a stage, and all the men and women merely players." In fact, Shakespeare's analogy between life and play-acting can be carried a step further—to organizations and their component formal work groups. Although employees do not have scripts, they do have formal positions in the organizational hierarchy, and they are expected to adhere to company policies and rules. Furthermore, job descriptions and procedure manuals spell out how jobs are to be done. In short, every employee has one or more organizational roles to play. An organization that is appropriately structured, in which everyone plays his or her role(s) effectively and efficiently, will have a greater chance for organizational success.

A social psychologist has described the concept of *role* as follows:

> *The term role is used to refer to (1) a set of expectations concerning what a person in a given position must, must not, or may do, and (2) the actual behavior of the person who occupies the position. A central idea is that any person occupying a position and filling a role behaves similarly to anyone else who could be in that position.[15]*

A **role**, then, is a socially determined prescription for behavior in a specific position. Roles evolve out of the tendency for social units to perpetuate themselves,

role Socially determined way of behaving in a specific position.

and roles are socially enforced. Role models are a powerful influence. Roles cannot be ignored by those trying to resolve the inherent conflicts between work and family.[16]

Norms

norms General standards of conduct for various social settings.

Norms define "degrees of acceptability and unacceptability."[17] More precisely, **norms** are general standards of conduct that help individuals judge what is right or wrong or good or bad in a given social setting (such as work, home, play, or religious organization). Because norms are culturally derived, they vary from one culture to another. For example, public disagreement and debate, which are normal in Western societies, are often considered rude in Eastern countries such as Japan.

Norms have a broader influence than do roles, which focus on a specific position. Although usually unwritten, norms influence behavior enormously.[18]

Every mature group, whether informal or formal, generates its own pattern of norms that constrains and directs the behavior of its members. Norms are enforced for at least four different reasons:

1. To facilitate survival of the group
2. To simplify or clarify role expectations
3. To help group members avoid embarrassing situations (protect self-images)
4. To express key group values and enhance the group's unique identity[19]

As illustrated in Figure 12.2, norms tend to go above and beyond formal rules and written policies. Compliance is shaped with social reinforcement in the form of attention, recognition, and acceptance.[20] Those who fail to comply with the norm may be criticized or ridiculed. For example, consider the pressure Gwendolyn Kelly experienced in medical school:

> The word among students is that if you've got any brains, "tertiary" medicine— which involves complex diagnostic procedures and comprehensive care—is

REALITY CHECK 12.2

"Ultimately it is a company's culture that sustains high performance with high integrity. Leaders and employees compete ferociously and meet tough economic goals lawfully and ethically not only because they are afraid of being caught and punished but because the company's norms and values are so widely shared and its reputation for integrity is so strong that most leaders and employees want to win the right way."

Source: Ben W. Heineman, Jr., "Avoiding Integrity Land Mines," *Harvard Business Review,* 85 (April 2007): 182.

Questions: What general ethical norms should managers follow? How should they be enforced?

FIGURE 12.2

Norms Are Enforced for Different Reasons

Sample norms	Why these norms would be enforced
"Don't criticize the work of our Celebrating Diversity Task Force in front of the director of finance, a person who thinks we're wasting time and money."	Helps the group survive
"Make sure you've done your homework before meeting with the division head."	Clarifies role expectations
"Don't discuss religion in the company cafeteria."	Avoids embarrassment and protects self-images
"Listen carefully to complaints from minority employees because, unlike the other shifts, the second-shift supervisors have never had a discrimination complaint filed against them."	Emphasizes key values and enhances group's identity

where it's at. Instructors often refer to the best students as "future surgeons" and belittle the family-practice specialty. These attitudes trickle down. I've heard my peers say the reason so many women choose pediatrics is that "they want to be mommies." And students who take a family-practice residency may be maligned by colleagues who say the choice is a sign of subpar academic credentials.[21]

Reformers of the U.S. health care system, who want to increase the number of primary care (family practice) doctors from one-third to one-half, need to begin by altering medical school norms.

Worse than ridicule is the threat of being ostracized. **Ostracism**, or rejection from the group, is figuratively the capital punishment of group dynamics. Informal groups derive much of their power over individuals through the ever-present threat of ostracism. Thus, informal norms play a pivotal role in on-the-job ethics.[22] Police officers, for example, who honor the traditional "code of silence" norm that demands *total* loyalty to one's fellow officers, face a tough moral dilemma when they witness policy violations.

ostracism Rejection from a group.

TEST PREPPER 12.1

ANSWERS CAN BE FOUND ON P. 339

True or False?

_____ 1. By definition, a group is any gathering of people.

_____ 2. An informal group can also be called a team, a committee, or simply a work group.

_____ 3. Members of a cohesive group tend to see themselves as "we" rather than "I."

_____ 4. Both expectations for behavior and actual behavior are involved in the concept of role.

_____ 5. Norms clarify role expectations.

Multiple Choice

_____ 6. According to the definition of a group, the members must
  a. have the same boss.
  b. like one another.
  c. have the same technical skills.
  d. be freely interacting.
  e. work in the same area.

_____ 7. If friendship is the principal reason for belonging, it is referred to as a(n)
  a. informal group.   d. formal group.
  b. task group.   e. committee.
  c. team.

_____ 8. The tendency of group members to follow the group and resist outside influences is called
  a. attractiveness.   d. conformity.
  b. groupthink.   e. cohesiveness.
  c. ostracism.

_____ 9. A socially determined prescription for behavior in a specific position refers to
  a. roles.
  b. norms.
  c. ostracism.
  d. organizational politics.
  e. groupthink.

_____ 10. Which of these is the best description of norms?
  a. Prescriptions for behavior in specific positions
  b. General standards of conduct
  c. Individually determined
  d. Universal
  e. Culturally neutral

_____ 11. What does ostracism involve?
  a. Voluntarily leaving a group
  b. Starting an ostrich ranch
  c. Rejection by group members
  d. Praise from group members
  e. Management-labor role reversals

Online Study Center
ACE the Test
ACE Practice Tests 12.1

GROUP DEVELOPMENT

 Characterize a mature group, and identify and briefly describe the six stages of group development.

Like inept youngsters who mature into talented adults, groups undergo a maturation process before becoming effective. We have all experienced the uneasiness associated with the first meeting of a new group, be it a class, club, or committee. Initially, there is little mutual understanding, trust, and commitment among the new group members, and their uncertainty about objectives, roles, and leadership doesn't help. The prospect of cooperative action seems unlikely in view of defensive behavior and differences of opinion about who should do what. Someone steps forward to assume a leadership role, and the group is off and running toward eventual maturity (or perhaps premature demise). A working knowledge of the characteristics of a mature group can help managers envision a goal for the group development process.

Characteristics of a Mature Group

If and when a group takes on the following characteristics, it can be called a *mature group:*

1. Members are aware of their own and each other's assets and liabilities vis-à-vis the group's task.

For Procter & Gamble's Tide brand laundry detergent, a seemingly small one percentage point gain in market share in the United States alone translates into an additional $60 million in sales. So Craig Bahner (left) assembled a team to broaden the brand's exposure. Here, they pose with a Tide-sponsored race car. Just as the car's pit crew had to do, Bahner had to develop his task group into a winning team. And it's Tide, by a car length!

2. These individual differences are accepted without being labeled as good or bad.
3. The group has developed authority and interpersonal relationships that are recognized and accepted by the members.
4. Group decisions are made through rational discussion. Minority opinions and dissension are recognized and encouraged. Attempts are not made to force decisions or a false unanimity.
5. Conflict is over substantive group issues such as group goals and the effectiveness and efficiency of various means for achieving those goals. Conflict over emotional issues regarding group structure, processes, or interpersonal relationships is minimal.
6. Members are aware of the group's processes and their own roles in them.[23]

Effectiveness and productivity should increase as the group matures. Research with groups of school teachers found positive evidence in this regard. The researchers concluded: "Faculty groups functioning at higher levels of development have students who perform better on standard achievement measures."[24] This finding could be fruitful for those seeking to reform and improve the American education system.

A hidden but nonetheless significant benefit of group maturity is that individuality is strengthened, not extinguished.[25] Protecting the individual's right to dissent is particularly important in regard to the problem of blind conformity. Also, as the fifth item in the preceding list indicates, members of mature groups tend to be emotionally mature.[26] This paves the way for building much-needed social capital.

Six Stages of Group Development

Experts have identified six distinct stages in the group development process[27] (see Figure 12.3 on page 322). During stages 1 through 3, attempts are made to overcome the obstacle of uncertainty about power and authority. Once this first obstacle has been surmounted, uncertainty over interpersonal relations becomes the challenge. This second obstacle must be cleared during stages 4 through 6 if the group is to achieve maturity. Each stage confronts the group's leader and contributing members with a unique combination of problems and opportunities.

Stage 1: Orientation

Attempts are made to "break the ice." Uncertainty about goals, power, and interpersonal relationships is high. Members generally want and accept any leadership at this point. Emergent leaders often misinterpret this "honeymoon period" as a mandate for permanent control.

Stage 2: Conflict and Challenge

As the emergent leader's philosophy, objectives, and policies become apparent, individuals or subgroups advocating alternative courses of action struggle for control. This second stage may be prolonged while members strive to clarify and reconcile their roles as part of a complete redistribution of power and authority. Many groups never continue past stage 2 because they get bogged down due to emotionalism and political infighting. Committees within the organization often bear the brunt of jokes because their frequent failure to mature beyond stage 2 prevents them from accomplishing their goals. (As one joke goes, a camel is a horse designed by a committee.)

FIGURE 12.3

Group Development from Formation to Maturity

Source: Group Effectiveness in Organizations, by Linda N. Jewell and H. Joseph Reitz, p. 20. Used with permission of the authors.

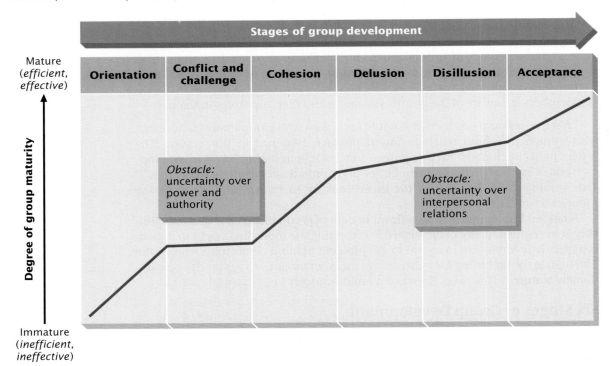

Stage 3: Cohesion

The shifts in power started in stage 2 are completed, under a new leader or the original leader, with a new consensus on authority, structure, and procedures. A "we" feeling becomes apparent as everyone becomes truly involved. Any lingering differences over power and authority are resolved quickly. Stage 3 is usually relatively short. If not, the group is likely to stall.

Stage 4: Delusion

A feeling of "having been through the worst of it" prevails after the rather rapid transition through stage 3. Issues and problems that threaten to break this spell of relief are dismissed or treated lightly. Members seem committed to fostering harmony at all costs. Participation and camaraderie run high as members believe that all the difficult emotional problems have been solved.

Stage 5: Disillusion

Subgroups tend to form as the delusion of unlimited goodwill wears off, and there is a growing disenchantment with the way things are turning out. Those with unrealized expectations challenge the group to perform better and are prepared to reveal their personal strengths and weaknesses if necessary. Others hold back. Tardiness and absenteeism are symptomatic of diminishing cohesiveness and commitment.

Stage 6: Acceptance

It usually takes a trusted and influential group member who is concerned about the group to step forward and help it move from conflict to cohesion. This individual, acting as the group catalyst, is usually someone other than the leader. Members are encouraged to test their self-perceptions against the reality of others' perceptions of them. Greater personal and mutual understanding helps members adapt to situations without causing problems. Members' expectations are more realistic than ever before. Since the authority structure is generally accepted, subgroups can pursue different matters without threatening group cohesiveness. Consequently, stage 6 groups tend to be highly effective and efficient.

Time-wasting problems and inefficiencies can be minimized if group members are consciously aware of this developmental process. Just as it is impossible for a child to skip being a teenager on the way to adulthood, committees and other work groups will find there are no short cuts to group maturity. Some emotional stresses and strains are inevitable along the way.[28]

TEST PREPPER 12.2
ANSWERS CAN BE FOUND ON P. 339

True or False?

_____ 1. Individual differences are eliminated as groups mature.

_____ 2. A "we" feeling becomes apparent as everyone becomes truly involved in the cohesion stage of the group development process.

_____ 3. According to the group development model, problems usually end for groups once they achieve cohesiveness.

_____ 4. The proper order of the six stages of the group development process is orientation, conflict and challenge, cohesion, delusion, disillusion, and acceptance.

Multiple Choice

_____ 5. In mature groups, the status of minority opinions is
    a. strongly discouraged.
    b. punished.
    c. not expressed.
    d. considered irrelevant.
    e. recognized and encouraged.

_____ 6. During the first three stages of the group development process, conflict tends to be over
    a. power and authority.
    b. personalities.
    c. interpersonal relations.
    d. lack of cohesion.
    e. finances.

_____ 7. What is the first stage of the group development process?
    a. Acceptance
    b. Orientation
    c. Cohesion
    d. Alignment
    e. Conflict and challenge

_____ 8. _____ is *not* one of the stages in the six-stage group development process.
    a. Cohesion
    b. Orientation
    c. Acceptance
    d. Social bonding
    e. Conflict and challenge

Online Study Center
ACE the Test
ACE Practice Tests 12.2

ORGANIZATIONAL POLITICS AND GROUPTHINK

 Summarize the research insights about organizational politics, and explain how groupthink can lead to blind conformity.

Group dynamics, like any area of human endeavor, can get out of control. In this section, we focus on organizational politics and groupthink, with an eye toward avoiding the dysfunctional side of groups and teams.[29]

What Does Organizational Politics Involve?

As we all know from practical experience, organizational life is often highly charged with political wheeling-and-dealing. For example, consider this complaint:

> *I've been working at my current job as a marketing manager for about a year now, and one thing is bugging me. Every time I propose a strategy or a solution in a meeting, someone else at the table repeats it, in somewhat altered form— and ends up getting the credit for having thought of it. This is no trivial problem, since in my department, year-end bonuses are based on how many of each person's ideas have been put into (profitable) practice.[30]*

Workplace surveys reveal that organizational politics and *impression management* (trying to influence how others perceive you)[31] can hinder effectiveness and be an irritant to coworkers. A three-year study of 46 companies attempting to establish themselves on the Internet "found that poor communication and political infighting were the No. 1 and No. 2 causes, respectively, for slowing down change."[32] Meanwhile, 44 percent of full-time employees and 60 percent of independent contractors listed "freedom from office politics" as extremely important to their job satisfaction.[33]

Whether politically motivated or not, managers need to be knowledgeable about organizational politics because their careers will be affected by it.[34] Certain political maneuvers also have significant ethical implications (especially when they involve misrepresentations or pressure tactics).

As the term implies, *self-interest* is central to organizational politics. In fact, **organizational politics** has been defined as "the pursuit of self-interest at work in the face of real or imagined opposition."[35] Political maneuvering is said to encompass all self-serving behavior above and beyond competence, hard work, and luck.[36] Although the term *organizational politics* has a negative connotation, researchers have identified both positive and negative aspects:

> *Political behaviors widely accepted as legitimate would certainly include exchanging favors, "touching bases," forming coalitions, and seeking sponsors at upper levels. Less legitimate behaviors would include whistle-blowing, revolutionary coalitions, threats, and sabotage.[37]*

Recall our discussion of whistle-blowing in Chapter 3.

Employees resort to political behavior when they are unwilling to trust their career solely to competence, hard work, or luck. One might say that organizational politicians help luck along by relying on political tactics. Whether employees will fall back on political tactics has a lot to do with an organization's climate or culture. A culture that presents employees with unreasonable barriers to individual and group success tends to foster political maneuvering. Consider this situation, for

organizational politics   The pursuit of self-interest in response to real or imagined opposition.

example: "A cadre of Corvette lovers inside General Motors lied, cheated, and stole to keep the legendary sports car from being eliminated during GM's management turmoil and near-bankruptcy in the late 1980s and early 1990s."[38] The redesigned Corvette finally made it to market in 1997, thanks in part to the Corvette team giving high-level GM executives thrilling unauthorized test rides in the hot new model.

Research on Organizational Politics

Researchers in one widely cited study of organizational politics conducted structured interviews with 87 managers employed by 30 electronics firms in southern California. Included in the sample were 30 chief executive officers, 28 middle managers, and 29 supervisors. Significant results included the following:

- The higher the level of management, the greater the perceived amount of political activity.

- The larger the organization, the greater the perceived amount of political activity.

- Personnel in staff positions were viewed as more political than those in line positions.

- People in marketing were the most political; those in production were the least political.

- "Reorganization changes" reportedly prompted more political activity than any other type of change.

- A majority (61 percent) of those interviewed believed organizational politics helps advance one's career.

- Forty-five percent believed that organizational politics distracts from organizational goals.[39]

Regarding the last two findings, it was clear that political activities were seen as helpful to the individual. On the other hand, the interviewed managers were split on the question of the value of politics to the organization. Managers who believed political behavior had a positive impact on the organization cited the following reasons: "gaining visibility for ideas, improving coordination and communication, developing teams and groups, and increasing *esprit de corps*. . . ."[40] As the preceding list indicated, the most-often-cited negative effect of politics was its distraction of managers from organizational goals. Misuse of resources and conflict were also mentioned as typical problems.

Political Tactics

As defined earlier, organizational politics encompasses a lot of behavioral territory. The following six political tactics are common expressions of politics in the workplace:

- *Posturing.* Those who use this tactic look for situations in which they can make a good impression. "One-upmanship" and taking credit for other people's work are included in this category.

- *Empire building.* Gaining and keeping control over human and material resources is the principal motivation behind this tactic. Those with large budgets usually feel more safely entrenched in their positions and believe they have more influence over peers and superiors.

▮ *Making the supervisor look good.* Traditionally referred to as "apple polishing," this political strategy is prompted by a desire to favorably influence those who control one's career ascent. Anyone with an oversized ego is an easy target for this tactic.

▮ *Collecting and using social IOUs.* Reciprocal exchange of political favors can be done in two ways: (1) by helping someone look good or (2) by preventing someone from looking bad by ignoring or covering up a mistake. Those who rely on this tactic feel that all favors are coins of exchange rather than expressions of altruism or unselfishness.

▮ *Creating power and loyalty cliques.* Because there is power in numbers, the idea here is to face superiors and competitors as a cohesive group rather than alone.

▮ *Engaging in destructive competition.* As a last-ditch effort, some people will resort to character assassination through suggestive remarks, vindictive gossip, or outright lies. This tactic also includes sabotaging the work of a competitor.[41]

Obvious illegalities notwithstanding, one's own values and ethics as well as organizational sanctions are the final arbiters of whether or not these tactics are acceptable. (See Table 12.2 for a practicing manager's advice on how to win at office politics.)

Antidotes to Political Behavior

Each of the foregoing political tactics varies in degree. The average person will probably acknowledge using at least one of these strategies. But excessive political maneuvering can become a serious threat to productivity when self-interests clearly override the interests of the group or organization. Organizational politics can be kept within reasonable bounds by applying the following five tips:

▮ Strive for a climate of openness and trust.

▮ Measure performance results rather than personalities.

▮ Encourage top management to refrain from exhibiting political behavior that will be imitated by employees.

▮ Strive to integrate individual and organizational goals through meaningful work and career planning.[42]

▮ Practice job rotation to encourage broader perspectives and understanding of the problems of others.[43]

Groupthink

After studying the records of several successful and unsuccessful American foreign policy decisions, psychologist Irving Janis uncovered an undesirable by-product of group cohesiveness. He labeled this problem **groupthink** and defined it as a "mode of thinking that people engage in when they are deeply involved in a

groupthink   Janis's term for blind conformity in cohesive in-groups.

TABLE 12.2

One Manager's Rules for Winning at Office Politics

1. Find out what the boss expects.

2. Build an information network. Knowledge is power. Identify the people who have power and the extent and direction of it. Title doesn't necessarily reflect actual influence. Find out how the grapevine works. Develop good internal public relations for yourself.

3. Find a mentor. This is a trusted counselor who can be honest with you and help train and guide you to improve your ability and effectiveness as a manager.

4. Don't make enemies without a very good reason.

5. Avoid cliques. Keep circulating in the office.

6. If you must fight, fight over something that is really worth it. Don't lose ground over minor matters or petty differences.

7. Gain power through allies. Build ties that bind. Create IOUs, obligations, and loyalties. Do not be afraid to enlist help from above.

8. Maintain control. Don't misuse your cohorts. Maintain the status and integrity of your allies.

9. Mobilize your forces when necessary. Don't commit your friends without their approval. Be a gracious winner when you do win.

10. Never hire a family member or a close friend.

Source: Reprinted with permission from the National Association of Credit Management's *Credit & Financial Management* (Vol. 86, No. 4), "Winning at Office Politics," by David E. Hall.

cohesive in-group, when the members' strivings for unanimity override their motivation to realistically appraise alternative courses of action."[44] Groupthink helps explain how intelligent policymakers, in both government and business, can sometimes make incredibly unwise decisions.

One dramatic result of groupthink in action was the Vietnam War. Strategic advisers in three successive administrations unwittingly rubber-stamped battle plans laced with false assumptions. Critical thinking, reality testing, and moral judgment were temporarily shelved as decisions to escalate the war were enthusiastically railroaded through. Although Janis acknowledges that cohesive groups are not inevitably victimized by groupthink, he warns group decision makers to be alert for the signs of groupthink—the risk is always there.

Symptoms of Groupthink

According to Janis, the onset of groupthink is foreshadowed by a definite pattern of symptoms. Among these are:

▌ Excessive optimism

▌ An assumption of inherent morality

▌ Suppression of dissent

▌ Almost desperate quest for unanimity[45]

Given such a decision-making climate, the probability of a poor decision is high. Managers face a curious dilemma here. While a group is still in stage 1 or stage 2 of development, its cohesiveness is too low to get much accomplished because of emotional and time-consuming power struggles. But by the time the group achieves enough cohesiveness in stage 3 to make decisions promptly, the risk of groupthink is high. The trick is to achieve needed cohesiveness without going to the extreme of groupthink.

Preventing Groupthink

According to Janis, one of the group members should periodically ask, "Are we allowing ourselves to become victims of groupthink?"[46] More fundamental preventive measures include the following:

- Avoiding the use of groups to rubber-stamp decisions that have already been made by higher management[47]

- Urging each group member to be a critical evaluator

- Bringing in outside experts for fresh perspectives

- Assigning someone the role of devil's advocate to challenge assumptions and alternatives[48]

- Taking time to consider possible side effects and consequences of alternative courses of action[49]

Ideally, decision quality improves when these steps become second nature in cohesive groups. But groupthink remains a constant threat in management circles. One major area ripe for abuse is corporate governance.[50] Corporate boards of directors are supposed to represent the interests of stockholders and hold top executives accountable for results. Too often, however, domineering CEOs and pliable boards and employees create the perfect environment for groupthink. For instance, consider the situation at Enron when now-imprisoned Jeffrey Skilling was in charge as CEO:

> *Paula Rieker, who worked in Enron investor relations and pleaded guilty to a count of inside trading, testified that Skilling made false statements about the source of Enron's earnings during a 2000 conference call. When Skilling attorney Dan Petrocelli asked why she didn't correct him after he gave false information to analysts, Rieker said that her experience with Skilling "had conditioned me that he didn't want to be corrected."*[51]

Disturbing? Yes. Unusual? Not really, especially when groupthink prevails.

Managers who cannot imagine themselves being victimized by this sort of unthinking conformity are prime candidates for groupthink.[52] "Cooperative conflict," as discussed in Chapter 14, is a potent weapon against groupthink.

True or False?

_____ 1. Workplace surveys reveal that organizational politics can hinder effectiveness and can be an irritant to employees.

_____ 2. Organizational politics is defined as the pursuit of self-interest at work in the face of real or imagined opposition.

_____ 3. Political activity tends to decrease as one moves into higher levels of management.

_____ 4. In organizational politics, empire building is traditionally referred to as "apple polishing."

_____ 5. A desperate quest for unanimity is a sure symptom of groupthink.

_____ 6. Groupthink occurs when someone plays the devil's advocate role.

Multiple Choice

_____ 7. Everyone in Penelope's sales office accuses her of organizational politics. If they are correct, what is her primary interest?
    a. Power
    b. Getting the job done
    c. Vindication
    d. Herself
    e. Money

_____ 8. People in _____ were the most political, according to research.
    a. line positions
    b. finance
    c. marketing
    d. legal affairs
    e. production

_____ 9. Which of these was *not* among the rules for winning at office politics?
    a. Avoid cliques.
    b. Gain power through allies and create IOUs.
    c. Don't make enemies without a very good reason.
    d. Whenever possible, hire family and friends who can be trusted.
    e. Find a mentor.

_____ 10. Which of these best describes a group likely to be victimized by groupthink?
    a. Very cohesive
    b. Made up of independent thinkers
    c. Very large
    d. Open to outside "expert" opinions
    e. A participative and open-minded leader

_____ 11. Groupthink tends to occur when a group has all of these characteristics *except*
    a. strong desire for unanimity.
    b. excessive optimism.
    c. assumption of inherent morality.
    d. extensive use of outside experts.
    e. suppression of dissent.

Online Study Center
ACE the Test
ACE Practice Tests 12.3

TEAMS AND TEAMWORK

4 ▶ *Define* cross-functional teams, *discuss the management of virtual teams, and explain what makes a team effective.*

Teams of specialists from different areas are the organizational unit of choice today. For instance, IBM's CEO, Samuel J. Palmisano, has staked the future of his giant corporation on teams, starting at the top:

> *For generations, . . . [the] 12-person body presiding over IBM's strategy and initiatives represented the inner sanctum for every aspiring Big Blue executive. . . . [In 2003], the CEO hit the send button on an e-mail to 300 senior managers announcing that this venerable committee was finito, kaput. Palmisano*

instead would work directly with three teams he had put in place the year before—they comprised people from all over the company who could bring the best ideas to the table. The old committee, with its monthly meetings, just slowed things down.[53]

Thus, teams and teamwork are vital group dynamics in the modern workplace.[54] Unfortunately, team skills in today's typical organization tend to lag far behind technical skills.[55] It is one thing to be a creative software engineer, for example. It is quite another for that software specialist to be able to team up with other specialists in accounting, finance, and marketing to beat the competition to market with a profitable new product. In this section, we explore teams and teamwork by discussing cross-functional teams, virtual teams, and a model of team effectiveness.

Cross-Functional Teams

cross-functional team   Task group staffed with a mix of specialists pursuing a common objective.

A **cross-functional team** is a task group staffed with a mix of specialists who are focused on a common objective. This structural device deserves special attention here because cross-functional teams are becoming commonplace,[56] although they are hardly a new idea (see, for example, Best Practices on page 336). They may or may not be self-managed, although self-managed teams generally are cross-functional. Cross-functional teams are based on assigned rather than voluntary membership. Cross-functional teams stand in sharp contrast to the tradition of lumping specialists into functional departments, thereby creating the problem of integrating and coordinating those departments. Boeing, for example, relies on cross-functional teams to integrate its various departments to achieve important strategic goals. The giant aircraft manufacturer thus accelerated its product development process for the Boeing 777 jetliner. Also, Boeing engineer Grace Robertson turned to cross-functional teams for faster delivery of a big order of customized jetliners to United Parcel Service:

When UPS ordered 30 aircraft, Boeing guaranteed that it could design and build a new, all-cargo version of the 767 jet in a mere 33 months—far faster than the usual cycle time of 42 months. The price it quoted meant slashing development costs dramatically.

Robertson's strategy has been to gather all 400 employees working on the new freighter into one location and organize them into "cross-functional" teams. By combining people from the design, planning, manufacturing, and tooling sectors, the teams speed up development and cut costs by enhancing communication and avoiding rework.[57]

This teamwork approach helped Robertson's group stay on schedule and within budget, both vitally important achievements in Boeing's battle with Europe's Airbus to be the world's leading aircraft maker.

Cross-functional teams have exciting potential. But they present management with the immense challenge of getting technical specialists to be effective boundary spanners.

Virtual Teams

virtual team   Task group members from dispersed locations who are electronically linked.

Along with the move toward virtual organizations, discussed in Chapter 7, have come virtual teams. A **virtual team** is a physically dispersed task group that interacts primarily by electronic means.[58] In a recent study of virtual teams, the researchers applied these definitional parameters: "We considered a team to be virtual if members met face-to-face less than once per month, and used some form of communication technology as the primary medium for conducting group meetings."[59] Telephones and voice mail, e-mail, videoconferencing, Web-based project software, and other forms of electronic interchange allow members of virtual teams from anywhere on the planet to pursue a common goal.[60] It is commonplace today for virtual teams to have members from different organizations, different time zones, and different cultures.[61] Because virtual organizations and teams are so new, paced as they are by emerging technologies, managers are having to learn from the school of hard knocks rather than from established practice.

TABLE 12.3

The Basics of Managing a Virtual Team

Forming the Team

▮ Develop a team mission statement along with teamwork expectations and norms, project goals, and deadlines

▮ Recruit team members with complementary skills and diverse backgrounds who have the ability and willingness to contribute

▮ Get a high-level sponsor to champion the project

▮ Post a skill, biographical sketch, contact information, and "local time" matrix to familiarize members with each other and their geographic dispersion

Preparing the Team

▮ Make sure everyone has a broadband connection and is comfortable with virtual teamwork technologies (e.g., e-mail, instant messaging, conference calls, online meeting and collaboration programs such as WebEx, and videoconferencing)

▮ Establish hardware and software compatibility

▮ Make sure everyone is comfortable with *synchronous* (interacting at the same time) and *asynchronous* (interacting at different times) teamwork

▮ Get individuals to buy-in on team goals, deadlines, and individual tasks

Building Teamwork and Trust

▮ Make sure everyone is involved (during meetings and overall)

▮ Arrange periodic face-to-face work meetings, team-building exercises, and leisure activities

▮ Encourage collaboration between and among team members on sub-tasks

▮ Establish an early-warning system for conflicts (e.g., gripe sessions)

Motivating and Leading the Team

▮ Post a scoreboard to mark team progress toward goals

▮ Celebrate team accomplishments both virtually and face-to-face

▮ Begin each virtual meeting with praise and recognition for outstanding individual contributions

▮ Keep team members' line managers informed of their accomplishments and progress

Sources: Based on discussions in Jack Gordon, "Do Your Virtual Teams Deliver Only Virtual Performance?" *Training,* 42 (June 2005): 20–26; Deborah L. Duarte and Nancy Tennant Snyder, *Mastering Virtual Teams,* 3rd edition (San Francisco: Jossey-Bass, 2006); and Arvind Malhotra, Ann Majchrzak, and Benson Rosen, "Leading Virtual Teams," *Academy of Management Perspectives,* 21 (February 2007): 60–70.

As discussed in Chapter 7 with respect to virtual organizations, one reality of managing virtual teams is clear. *Periodic face-to-face interaction, trust building, and team building are more important than ever when team members are widely dispersed in time and space.* While faceless interaction may work in Internet chat rooms, it can doom a virtual team with a crucial task and pressing deadline. Additionally, special steps need to be taken to clearly communicate role expectations, performance norms, goals, and deadlines (see Table 12.3 on page 331). Virtual teamwork may be faster than the traditional face-to-face kind, but it is by no means easier[62] (see the Closing Case Study on page 336).

What Makes Workplace Teams Effective?

The widespread use of team formats—self-managed teams, cross-functional teams, and virtual teams—necessitates greater knowledge of team effectiveness.[63] A model of team effectiveness criteria and determinants is presented in Figure 12.4. This model is the product of two field studies involving 360 new product-development managers employed by 52 high-tech companies.[64] Importantly, it is a generic model that applies equally well to all workplace teams.[65]

The five criteria for effective team performance listed on the right in Figure 12.4 parallel the criteria for organizational effectiveness discussed in Chapter 7. Thus, team effectiveness feeds organizational effectiveness.

Determinants of team effectiveness, shown in Figure 12.4, are grouped into people-, organization-, and task-related factors. Considered separately, these factors involve rather routine aspects of good management. But the collective picture reveals each factor to be part of a complex and interdependent whole. Managers cannot maximize just a few of them, ignore the rest, and hope to have an effective team. In the spirit of the Japanese concept of *kaizen*, managers and team leaders need to strive for "continuous improvement" on all fronts. Because gains on one front will inevitably be offset by losses in another, the pursuit of team effectiveness and teamwork is an endless battle with no guarantees of success.[66]

In the next section, let us focus on trust, one of the people-related factors in Figure 12.4 that can make or break work teams.

FIGURE 12.4

A Model of Team Effectiveness

Source: From Hans J. Thamhain, "Managing Technologically Innovative Team Efforts Toward New Product Success," *Journal of Product Innovation Management,* Vol. 7, pp. 5–18, 1990. Reprinted with permission of Blackwell Publishing Ltd.

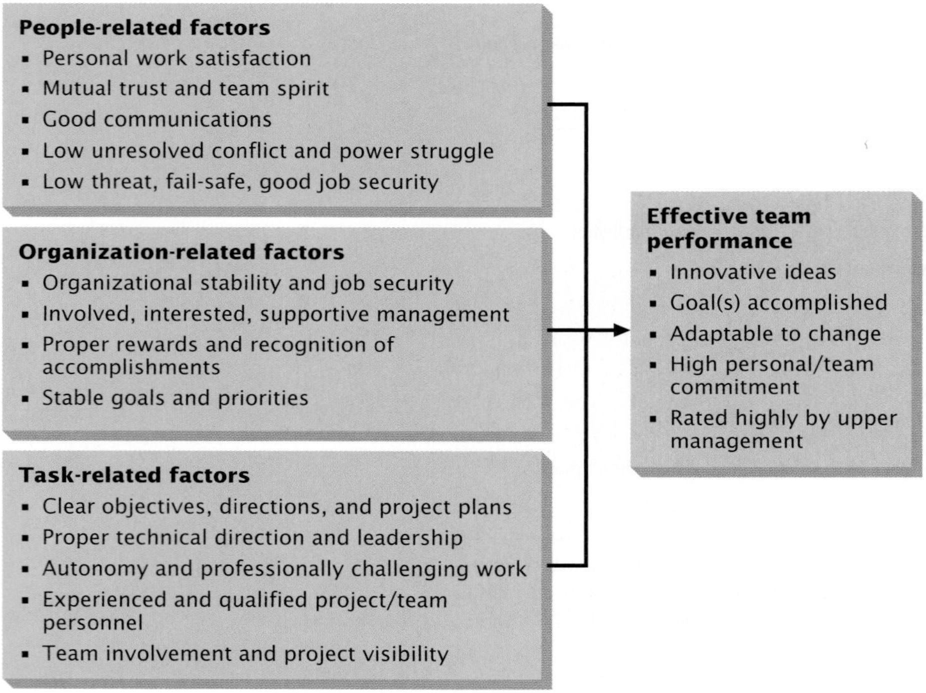

People-related factors
- Personal work satisfaction
- Mutual trust and team spirit
- Good communications
- Low unresolved conflict and power struggle
- Low threat, fail-safe, good job security

Organization-related factors
- Organizational stability and job security
- Involved, interested, supportive management
- Proper rewards and recognition of accomplishments
- Stable goals and priorities

Task-related factors
- Clear objectives, directions, and project plans
- Proper technical direction and leadership
- Autonomy and professionally challenging work
- Experienced and qualified project/team personnel
- Team involvement and project visibility

Effective team performance
- Innovative ideas
- Goal(s) accomplished
- Adaptable to change
- High personal/team commitment
- Rated highly by upper management

TEST PREPPER 12.4

ANSWERS CAN BE FOUND ON P. 339

True or False?

_____ 1. Cross-functional teams are made up of specialists from the same function, such as marketing.

_____ 2. A virtual team's members must be from the same organization and the same national culture for it to succeed.

_____ 3. In the model of team effectiveness, much more than goal accomplishment is involved.

_____ 4. Team effectiveness can be enhanced through clear objectives, good communication, and job security.

Multiple Choice

_____ 5. A cross-functional team can be best described as
   a. a mix of employees and outside consultants.
   b. someone assigned devil's advocate role.
   c. no more than three members.
   d. both managers and nonmanagers from the same department.
   e. a mix of specialists.

_____ 6. A(n) _____ is a physically dispersed task group that is linked electronically.
   a. informal group
   b. line position group
   c. virtual team
   d. IT quality control team
   e. executive team

_____ 7. According to the team effectiveness model, the criteria for an effective team include all of these *except*
   a. goal accomplishment.
   b. aligned roles and norms.
   c. adaptability to change.
   d. high personal/team commitment.
   e. innovative ideas.

_____ 8. The three groups of determinants in the team effectiveness model involve
   a. strategy, structure, and task.
   b. time, space, and money.
   c. who, what, and where.
   d. people, places, and things.
   e. people, organization, and task.

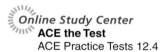

Online Study Center
ACE the Test
ACE Practice Tests 12.4

TRUST: A KEY TO TEAM EFFECTIVENESS

5 ▶ *Explain why trust is a key ingredient of teamwork, and discuss what management can do to build trust.*

Trust, a belief in the integrity, character, or ability of others, is essential if people are to achieve anything together in the long run.[67] Participative management programs are very dependent on trust.[68] Sadly, trust is not one of the hallmarks of the current U.S. business scene. "The distrust is widespread. Only 10% of adults surveyed think corporations can be trusted a great deal to look out for the interests of their employees, according to a *USA Today*/CNN/Gallup poll."[69] To a greater extent than they may initially suspect, managers determine the level of trust in the organization and its component work groups and teams. Experts in the area of social capital tell us:

> No one can manufacture trust or mandate it into existence. When someone says, "You can trust me," we usually don't, and rightly so. But leaders can make deliberate investments in trust. They can give people reasons to trust one another instead of reasons to watch their backs. They can refuse to reward successes that are built on untrusting behavior. And they can display trust and trustworthiness in their own actions, both personally and on behalf of the company.[70]

trust   Belief in the integrity, character, or ability of others.

Online Study Center   college.hmco.com/pic/kreitnerSASfound

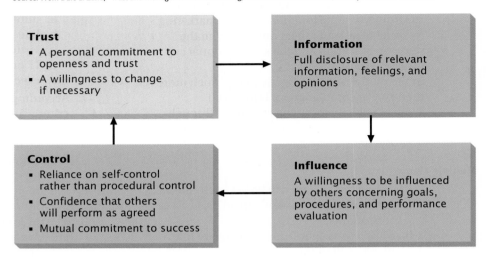

FIGURE 12.5

Trust and Effective Group Interaction

Source: From Dale E. Zand, "Trust and Managerial Problem Solving," *Administrative Science Quarterly,* 17, No. 2, June 1972.

Trust
- A personal commitment to openness and trust
- A willingness to change if necessary

Information
Full disclosure of relevant information, feelings, and opinions

Control
- Reliance on self-control rather than procedural control
- Confidence that others will perform as agreed
- Mutual commitment to success

Influence
A willingness to be influenced by others concerning goals, procedures, and performance evaluation

Zand's Model of Trust

REALITY CHECK 12.4

"Employees say Lane wants them to give bad news early, and he wants it straight. By the same token, Lane believes in leveling with employees when the news is bad."

Source: "Company Is a Team, Not a Family," *HR Magazine,* 52 (April 2007): 18.

Question: Why is this a good way to build trust in the workplace?

Trust is not a free-floating variable. It affects, and in turn is affected by, other group processes. Dale E. Zand's model of work group interaction puts trust into proper perspective (see Figure 12.5). Zand believes that trust is the key to establishing productive interpersonal relationships.[71]

Primary responsibility for creating a climate of trust falls on the manager. Team members usually look to the manager, who enjoys hierarchical advantage and greater access to key information, to set the tone for interpersonal dealings. Threatening or intimidating actions by the manager will probably encourage the group to bind together in cohesive resistance. Therefore, trust needs to be developed right from the beginning, when team members are still receptive to positive managerial influence.

Trust is initially encouraged by a manager's openness and honesty. Trusting managers talk *with* their people rather than *at* them. A trusting manager, according to Zand's model, demonstrates a willingness to be influenced by others and to change if the facts indicate a change is appropriate. Mutual trust between a manager and team members encourages *self-control*, as opposed to control through direct supervision.

Paradoxically, managerial control actually expands when committed group or team members enjoy greater freedom in pursuing consensual goals. Those who trust each other generally avoid taking advantage of others' weaknesses or shortcomings.[72]

Six Ways to Build Trust

Trust is a fragile thing. As most of us know from personal experience, trust grows at a painfully slow pace yet can be destroyed in an instant with a thoughtless remark. Mistrust can erode the long-term effectiveness of work teams and organizations.

According to management professor and consultant Fernando Bartolomé, managers need to concentrate on six areas: communication, support, respect, fairness, predictability, and competence.

▌ *Communication.* Keep your people informed by providing accurate and timely feedback and by explaining policies and decisions. Be open and honest about your own problems. Do not hoard information or use it as a political device or reward.

▌ *Support.* Be an approachable person who is available to help, encourage, and coach your people. Show an active interest in their lives and be willing to come to their defense.

▌ *Respect.* Delegating important duties is the sincerest form of respect, followed closely by being a good listener.

▌ *Fairness.* Evaluate your people fairly and objectively and be liberal in giving credit and praise.

▌ *Predictability.* Be dependable and consistent in your behavior and keep all your promises.

▌ *Competence.* Be a good role model by exercising good business judgment and being technically and professionally competent.[73]

Managers find that trust begets trust. In other words, those who feel they are trusted tend to trust others in return.

TEST PREPPER 12.5   ANSWERS CAN BE FOUND ON P. 339

True or False?

_____ 1. In Zand's model of trust, mentors play an important role.

_____ 2. According to Zand's model, leaders who want to be trusted must be influenced by their followers with respect to goals and procedures.

_____ 3. According to the six ways to build trust, managers should use information as a political device or reward.

_____ 4. Managers must keep their promises if they want to be trusted.

Multiple Choice

_____ 5. What is central to the definition of trust?
   a. Participation
   b. Cohesiveness
   c. Power
   d. Integrity
   e. Informal leadership

_____ 6. According to Zand's model of trust, managers need to switch from procedural control to
   a. intrinsic rewards.
   b. managerial control.
   c. joint control.
   d. financial control.
   e. self-control.

_____ 7. What advice would you give a fashion magazine editor who desires to build more trusting relationships with her employees by demonstrating her respect for them?
   a. Get rid of outside consultants.
   b. Centralize decision making.
   c. Delegate more.
   d. Communicate more clearly.
   e. Form quality circles.

_____ 8. _____ is *not* recommended in the six ways to build trust.
   a. Competence
   b. Friendship
   c. Fairness
   d. Communication
   e. Predictability

Online Study Center
ACE the Test
ACE Practice Tests 12.5

The Invention Factory

Charles Batcheldor was an English machinist. John Kruesi was a Swiss clockmaker. Ludwig Boehm was a German glassblower. Francis Upton was a Princeton-trained mathematician. They were drawn to the then-isolated New Jersey hamlet of Menlo Park by the magnetic force of Thomas Edison's genius. But it was Edison's unique ability to tap into their skills that turned his half-formed visions into an astonishing stream of workable products. "He was never the lone inventor," says Bill Pretzer, a curator of the Edison collection at the Henry Ford Museum.

"Edison himself flits about, first to one bench, then to another, examining here, instructing there," wrote the *New York Herald*. A sketch handed to Kruesi unexpectedly yielded the phonograph. The work was "strenuous but joyous," one lab hand wrote. The boss got as dirty as his workmen. And there was the day when the team rode Edison's miniature locomotive to a nearby fishing hole. "The strangest thing to me is the $12 that I get each Saturday," Upton wrote his father, "for my labor does not seem like work but like study."

It was Upton who bought the instruments that led to a breakthrough insight on electric lighting. It was Batcheldor's nimble hands that threaded a carbon filament into a bulb that Boehm evacuated to a millionth of an atmosphere. And on Oct. 22, 1879, when the bulb finished a 14-hour burn, the darkness filled with the cheers of five men and four nationalities.

Source: Jerry Useem, "The Invention Factory, Secrets of Greatness—Six Teams That Made Business History," *Fortune,* June 12, 2006, p. 3. Copyright © 2006 Time Inc. All rights reserved.

Thirteen Time Zones Can't Keep Lucent's Virtual Team from Succeeding

Note: After this case study was written, Lucent merged with France's Alcatel to form Alcatel-Lucent, a global company with 79,000 employees in 130 countries. The executive offices are in Paris and the CEO is an American, Patricia Russo.[73]

Imagine designing the most complex product in your company's history. You need 500 engineers for the job. They will assemble the world's most delicate hardware and write more than a million lines of code. In communicating, the margin for error is minuscule.

Now, scatter those 500 engineers over 13 time zones. Over three continents. Over five states in the United States alone. The Germans schedule to perfection. The Americans work on the fly. In Massachusetts, they go to work early. In New Jersey, they stay late.

Now you have some idea of what Bill Klinger and Frank Polito have been through in the past 18 months.

As top software-development managers in Lucent Technologies' Bell Labs division, they played critical roles in creating a new fiber-optic phone switch called the Bandwidth Manager, which sells for about $1 million. . . . The high-stakes development was Lucent's most complex undertaking by far since its spin-off from AT&T in 1996.

Managing such a far-flung staff ("distributed development," it's called) is possible only because of technology. But as the two Lucent leaders painfully learned, distance still magnifies differences, even in a high-tech age. "You lose informal interaction—going to lunch, the water cooler," Mr. Klinger says. "You can never discount how many issues get solved that way."

The product grew as a hybrid of exotic, widely dispersed technologies: "lightwave" science from Lucent's Merrimack Valley plant, north of Boston, where Mr. Polito works; "cross-connect" products here in New

Jersey, where Mr. Klinger works; timing devices from the Netherlands; and optics from Germany.

Development also demanded multiple locations because Lucent wanted a core model as a platform for special versions for foreign and other niche markets. Involving overseas engineers in the flagship product would speed the later development of spin-offs and impress foreign customers.

And rushing to market meant tapping software talent wherever it was available—ultimately at Lucent facilities in Colorado, Illinois, North Carolina, and India. "The scary thing, scary but exciting, was that no one had really pulled this off on this scale before," says Mr. Polito.

Communication technology was the easy part. Lashing together big computers in different cities assured everyone was working on the same up-to-date software version. New project data from one city were instantly available on Web pages everywhere else. Test engineers in India could tweak prototypes in New Jersey. The project never went to sleep.

Technology, however, couldn't conquer cultural problems, especially acute between Messrs. Klinger's and Polito's respective staffs in New Jersey and Massachusetts. Each had its own programming traditions and product histories. Such basic words as "test" could mean different things. A programming chore requiring days in one context might take weeks in another. Differing work schedules and physical distance made each location suspect the other of slacking off. "We had such clashes," says Mr. Klinger.

Personality tests revealed deep geographic differences. Supervisors from the sleek, glass-covered New Jersey office, principally a research facility abounding in academics, scored as "thinking" people who used cause-and-effect analysis. Those from the old, brick facility in Massachusetts, mainly a manufacturing plant, scored as "feeling" types who based decisions on subjective, human values. Sheer awareness of the differences ("Now I know why you get on my nerves!") began to create common ground.

Amid much cynicism, the two directors hauled their technical managers into team exercises—working in small groups to scale a 14-foot wall and solve puzzles. It's corny, but such methods can accelerate trust building when time is short and the stakes are high. At one point Mr. Klinger asked managers to show up with the product manuals from their previous projects—then, in a ritualistic break from technical parochialism, instructed everyone to tear the covers to pieces.

More than anything else, it was sheer physical presence—face time—that began solidifying the group. Dozens of managers began meeting fortnightly in rotating cities, socializing as much time as their technical discussions permitted. (How better to grow familiar than over hot dogs, beer, and nine innings with the minor league Durham Bulls?) Foreign locations found the direct interaction especially valuable. "Going into the other culture is the only way to understand it," says Sigrid Hauenstein, a Lucent executive in Nuremberg, Germany. "If you don't have a common understanding, it's much more expensive to correct it later."

Eventually the project found its pace. People began wearing beepers to eliminate time wasted on voice-mail tag. Conference calls at varying levels kept everyone in the loop. Staffers posted their photos in the project's Web directory. Many created personal pages. "It's the ultimate democracy of the Web," Mr. Klinger says.

The product is now shipping—on schedule, within budget, and with more technical versatility than Lucent expected. Distributed development "paid off in spades," says Gerry Butters, Lucent optical-networking chief.

Even as it helps build the infrastructure of a digitally connected planet, Lucent is rediscovering the importance of face-to-face interaction. All the bandwidth in the world can convey only a fraction of what we are.

Source: From *Wall Street Journal* by Thomas Petzinger, Jr., "With the Stakes High, a Lucent Duo Conquers Distance and Culture," April 23,1999. Copyright © 1999 by Dow Jones & Company, Inc. Reproduced with permission of Dow Jones & Company, Inc. via Copyright Clearance Center.

Case Questions

1. Which team effectiveness criteria in Figure 12.4 on page 332 are apparent in this case?
2. How big a problem do you suppose organizational politics was during this project? Explain.
3. What practical lessons does this case teach managers about managing a virtual team?
4. Would you be comfortable working on this sort of global virtual team? Explain.

Online Study Center
ACE the Test
ACE Plus Practice Tests

Online Study Center
Improve Your Grade
Learning Objective Review
Audio Chapter Review
Audio Chapter Quiz
Study Guide to Go

LEARNING OBJECTIVE REVIEW

1 *Define the term* group, *and explain the significance of roles, norms, and ostracism in regard to the behavior of group members.*

- Both informal (friendship) and formal (work) groups are made up of two or more freely interacting individuals who have a common identity and purpose.

- After someone has been attracted to a group, cohesiveness—a "we" feeling—encourages continued membership.

- Roles are social expectations for behavior in a specific position, whereas norms are more general standards for conduct in a given social setting.

- Norms are enforced because they help the group survive, clarify role expectations, protect self-images, and enhance the group's identity by emphasizing key values.

- Compliance with role expectations and norms is rewarded with social reinforcement; noncompliance is punished by criticism, ridicule, and ostracism.

2 *Characterize a mature group, and identify and briefly describe the six stages of group development.*

- Mature groups are characterized by mutual acceptance, encouragement of minority opinion, and minimal emotional conflict. They are the product of a developmental process with identifiable stages.

- The six stages in the group development process are:
  - Stage 1: Orientation—Uncertainty is high, members generally accept any leadership at this point.
  - Stage 2: Conflict and Challenge—As a leader emerges, individuals or subgroups in favor of alternative courses of action struggle for control. Many groups never continue past this stage.

  - Stage 3: Cohesion—A "we" feeling emerges as everyone becomes truly involved and remaining differences are resolved quickly.
  - Stage 4: Delusion—Issues or problems are treated lightly and members are committed to harmony at all costs.
  - Stage 5: Disillusion—Subgroups tend to form and disenchantment grows. Tardiness and absenteeism occur.
  - Stage 6: Acceptance—Greater personal and mutual understanding exists as well as more realistic expectations. This stage tends to be highly effective and efficient.

3 *Summarize the research insights about organizational politics, and explain how groupthink can lead to blind conformity.*

- Organizational politics centers on the pursuit of self-interest. Research shows greater political activity to be associated with:
  - Higher levels of management
  - Larger organizations
  - Staff and marketing personnel
  - Reorganizations

- Political tactics such as posturing, empire building, making the boss look good, collecting and using social IOUs, creating power and loyalty cliques, and engaging in destructive competition need to be kept in check if the organization is to be effective.

- Cohesive decision-making groups can be victimized by groupthink when unanimity becomes more important than critical evaluation of alternative courses of action.

▶ *Define* cross-functional teams, *discuss the management of virtual teams, and explain what makes a team effective.*

- A cross-functional team is a collection of people with different specialties pursuing a common objective.
- Although members of virtual teams, by definition, collaborate via electronic media, there is still a need for periodic face-to-face interaction and team building.
- Five criteria of team effectiveness are:
  - Innovative ideas
  - Goals accomplished
  - Adaptable to change
  - High personal/team commitment
  - Rated highly by upper management

- Three sets of factors—relating to people, organization, and task—combine to determine the effectiveness of a work team.

▶ *Explain why trust is a key ingredient of teamwork, and discuss what management can do to build trust.*

- Trust is a key ingredient of effective teamwork because, when work group members trust one another, a more active exchange of information, more interpersonal influence, and hence greater self-control result.
- Managers can build trust through communication, support, respect (primarily in the form of delegation), fairness, predictability, and competence.

TEST PREPPER ANSWERS

▶ **12.1**
1. F   2. F   3. T   4. T   5. T   6. d   7. a
8. e   9. a   10. b   11. c

▶ **12.2**
1. F   2. T   3. F   4. T   5. e   6. a   7. b
8. d

▶ **12.3**
1. T   2. T   3. F   4. F   5. T   6. F   7. d
8. c   9. d   10. a   11. d

▶ **12.4**
1. F   2. F   3. T   4. T   5. e   6. c   7. b
8. e

▶ **12.5**
1. F   2. T   3. F   4. T   5. d   6. e   7. c
8. b

Online Study Center RESOURCES

Prepare for Class, Improve Your Grade, and ACE the Test. Student Achievement Series resources include:

ACE Practice Tests
Audio Chapter Quizzes
Audio Chapter Reviews
Career Snapshots
Chapter Glossaries
Chapter Outlines

Crossword Puzzles
Decision Case Questions
Ethical Hot Seat Exercises
Flashcards
Hands-on Exercises

Hangman
Key Issue Expansion
Learning Objective Reviews
Study Guide to Go
Visual Glossaries

To access these learning and study tools, go to **college.hmco.com/pic/kreitnerSASfound**.

15 Influencing and Leading

Personal success is not enough for Janet Hanson. She is now committed to helping girls and women around the world network their way to success.

1 ▶ Identify and describe eight generic influence tactics used in modern organizations.

2 ▶ Identify the five bases of power, and explain what it takes to make empowerment work.

3 ▶ Explain the concept of emotional intelligence in terms of Goleman's four leadership traits, and summarize what the Ohio State model and the Leadership Grid® have taught managers about leadership.

4 ▶ Contrast the assumptions behind Fiedler's contingency theory and path-goal leadership theory, and describe transformational and servant leaders.

"A good set of values is part of successful leadership and great organizations."[1]

—John Wooden, legendary U.C.L.A. basketball coach

Chapter Outline

▶ **INFLUENCE TACTICS IN THE WORKPLACE**

▶ **POWER**
What is Power?
The Five Bases of Power
Empowerment

▶ **LEADERSHIP: FOUNDATION CONCEPTS**
Leadership Defined
Formal Versus Informal Leaders
Trait Theory
Behavioral Styles Theory

▶ **LEADERSHIP: ADVANCED CONCEPTS**
Situational Theory
Transformational Leadership Theory
Servant Leaders: Putting to Work What You've Learned

▶ **MENTORING**
Learning from a Mentor
Dynamics of Mentoring

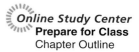
Online Study Center
Prepare for Class
Chapter Outline

5 ▶ *Identify the two key functions that mentors perform, and explain how a mentor can help develop a junior manager's leadership skills.*

The Millionaire Mentor: Janet Hanson

For two decades Janet Hanson was a typical Wall Street workaholic. She started her career at Goldman Sachs in 1977 straight out of Columbia Business School, quickly mastered the 18-hour day, and became the first woman promoted to sales management. Then, after 14 years, she struck out on her own, forming a money-management firm called Milestone Capital. While she loved running her own show, Hanson realized that she deeply missed all the accomplished women and mentors she'd had at Goldman. So she dreamed up 85 Broads—a play on Goldman's Manhattan street address—as an old-girls' network for current and former Goldman bankers. Once the group started meeting, however, it found a bigger mission: helping young women pursue careers in business. "I wanted to see whether women could help each other and support each other's careers the way men do," she says. "And it's clear that, given the right framework, they can." That framework involves hosting networking seminars on college campuses, introducing people she thinks might pair up nicely as mentor

Online Study Center
Prepare for Class
Chapter Glossary

Improve Your Grade
Flashcards
Hangman
Crossword Puzzles

influence   Any attempt to change another's behavior.

and protégé, and putting together special events like a recent fundraiser for a clinic in Lwala, Kenya. The group has evolved beyond Goldman alums to include college undergrads and B-school students, with more than 15,000 members in all. Hanson, who is still chairman of the board at Milestone Capital and a part-time advisor to the president of Lehman Brothers, finances the group's $1.8 million operating budget (including a staff of 12) out of her own pocket. "For me, the thrill is seeing girls who are still in school see their opportunities as limitless. Just gun the engine and go for it."[2] ■

What do the following situations have in common?

▌ A magazine editor praises her supervisor's new outfit shortly before asking for the afternoon off.

▌ A milling-machine operator tells a friend that he will return the favor if his friend will watch out for the supervisor while he takes an unauthorized cigarette break.

▌ An office manager attempts to head off opposition to a new Internet-use policy by carefully explaining how it will be fair and will increase productivity.

Aside from the fact that all of these situations take place on the job, the common denominator is "influence." In each case, someone is trying to get his or her own way or get something accomplished by influencing someone else's behavior. Janet Hanson is an inspiring role model for the skillful and responsible use of influence, power, and leadership.

Influence is any attempt by a person to change the behavior of superiors, peers, or lower-level employees. Influence is not inherently good or bad. As the foregoing situations illustrate, influence can be used for purely selfish reasons, to subvert organizational objectives, or to enhance organizational effectiveness. Managerial success is firmly linked to the ability to exercise the right sort of influence at the right time. But, according to a recent survey of 1,845 workers in the United States, managers may not be as influential as they think (or wish):

Nearly all managers—a whopping 92 percent—would rate themselves as an "excellent" or "good" boss. And maybe they are. The problem is this—only 67 percent of the employees who report to them would agree. In fact, 10 percent of workers say their bosses do a poor job.[3]

The purpose of this chapter is to examine different approaches to influencing others in the workplace. We focus specifically on influence tactics, power, leadership, and mentoring.

INFLUENCE TACTICS IN THE WORKPLACE

▶ 1 *Identify and describe eight generic influence tactics used in modern organizations.*

A replication and refinement of an earlier groundbreaking study provides useful insights about on-the-job influence.[4] Both studies asked employees basically

TABLE 13.1

Use of Generic Organizational Influence Tactics

Tactic	Rank order (by direction of influence)		
	Downward	Lateral	Upward
Consultation	1	1	2
Rational persuasion	2	2	1
Inspirational appeals	3	3	3
Ingratiating tactics	4	4	5
Coalition tactics	5	5	4
Pressure tactics	6	7	7
Upward appeals	7	6	6
Exchange tactics	8	8	8

Source: Adapted from discussion in Gary Yukl and Cecilia M. Falbe, "Influence Tactics and Objectives in Upward, Downward, and Lateral Influence Attempts," *Journal of Applied Psychology*, 75 (April 1990): 132–140.

the same question: "How do you get your boss, coworker, or subordinate to do something you want?" The following eight generic influence tactics emerged:

1. *Consultation.* Seeking someone's participation in a decision or change
2. *Rational persuasion.* Trying to convince someone by relying on a detailed plan, supporting information, reasoning, or logic
3. *Inspirational appeals.* Appealing to someone's emotions, values, or ideals to generate enthusiasm and confidence
4. *Ingratiating tactics.* Making someone feel important or good before making a request; acting humble or friendly before making a request
5. *Coalition tactics.* Seeking the aid of others to persuade someone to agree
6. *Pressure tactics.* Relying on intimidation, demands, or threats to gain compliance or support
7. *Upward appeals.* Obtaining formal or informal support of higher management
8. *Exchange tactics.* Offering an exchange of favors; reminding someone of a past favor; offering to make a personal sacrifice[5]

These influence tactics are *generic* because they are used by various organizational members to influence lower-level employees (downward influence), peers (lateral influence), or superiors (upward influence). Table 13.1 indicates what the researchers found out about patterns of use for the three different directions of influence. Notice how consultation, rational persuasion, and inspirational appeals were the three most popular tactics, regardless of the direction of influence. Meanwhile, pressure tactics, upward appeals, and exchange tactics consistently were the least used influence tactics. Ingratiating and coalition tactics fell in the midrange of use. This is an encouraging pattern from the standpoint of getting things done through problem solving rather than through intimidation and conflict.

REALITY CHECK 13.1

Margaret G. McGlynn, President of Merck Vaccines: "An ability to argue her case in a 'relentlessly logical and wonderfully intense way,' as ex-boss David Anstice puts it, helped McGlynn rise rapidly."

Source: Arlene Weintraub, "Making Her Mark at Merck," *Business Week* (January 8, 2007): 65.

Questions: Which influence tactic does this illustrate? What are the pros and cons of this tactic?

Do women and men tend to rely on different influence tactics? Available research evidence reveals no systematic gender-based differences relative to influencing others.[6] In contrast, influence tactics used by employees to influence their bosses were found to vary with different leadership styles. Employees influencing authoritarian managers tended to rely on ingratiating tactics and upward appeals. Rational persuasion was used most often to influence participative managers.[7]

TEST PREPPER 13.1

ANSWERS CAN BE FOUND ON P. 365

True or False?

_____ 1. An "exchange tactic" is one of the generic influence tactics.

_____ 2. The eight generic influence tactics involve downward, but not upward, influence.

_____ 3. According to researchers, there are no systematic gender-based differences in influencing others.

Multiple Choice

_____ 4. Which of these is *not* among the generic influence tactics described in the text?
   a. Upward appeals
   b. Exchange tactics
   c. Consultation
   d. Participative tactics
   e. Coalition tactics

_____ 5. _____ refers to making someone feel important or good before making a request.
   a. The coalition tactic
   b. Consultation
   c. The ingratiating tactic
   d. An upward appeal
   e. An inspirational appeal

_____ 6. Employees tend to use which of these with participative managers?
   a. Coalition tactics
   b. Rational persuasion
   c. Consultation
   d. Ingratiating tactics
   e. Exchange tactics

Online Study Center
ACE the Test
ACE Practice Tests 13.1

POWER

2 ▸ *Identify the five bases of power, and explain what it takes to make empowerment work.*

Power is inevitable in modern organizations. According to one advocate of the positive and constructive use of power:

> *Power must be used because managers must influence those they depend on. Power also is crucial in the development of managers' self-confidence and willingness to support subordinates. From this perspective, power should be accepted as a natural part of any organization. Managers should recognize and develop their own power to coordinate and support the work of subordinates; it is powerlessness, not power, that undermines organizational effectiveness.*[8]

As a manager, if you understand power, its bases, and empowerment, you will have an advantage when it comes to getting things accomplished with and through others.[9]

formal authority. Beyond that, both types rely on expedient combinations of reward, coercive, referent, and expert power. Informal leaders who identify with the job to be done are a valuable asset to an organization. Conversely, an organization can be brought to its knees by informal leaders who turn cohesive work groups against the organization.

Like the study of management, the study of leadership has evolved as theories were developed and refined by successive generations of researchers.[26] Something useful has been learned at each stage of development. In the next two major sections, we discuss four different models in the evolution of leadership theory. (see Figure 13.1).

Trait Theory

During most of recorded history the prevailing assumption was that leaders are born and not made. Leaders such as Alexander the Great, Napoleon Bonaparte, and George Washington were said to have been blessed with an inborn ability to lead. This so-called great-man approach to leadership[27] eventually gave way to trait theory. According to one observer, "under the influence of the behavioristic school of psychological thought, the fact was accepted that leadership traits are not completely inborn but can also be acquired through learning and experience. Attention turned to the search for universal traits possessed by leaders."[28]

As the popularity of the trait approach mushroomed during the second quarter of the twentieth century, literally hundreds of physical, mental, and personality traits were said to be the key determinants of successful leadership. Unfortunately, few theorists agreed on the most important traits of a good leader. The predictive value of trait theory was severely limited because traits tend to be a chicken-and-egg proposition: Was George Washington a good leader because he had self-confidence, or did he have self-confidence because he was thrust into a leadership role at a young age? In spite of inherent problems, trait profiles provide a useful framework for examining what it takes to be a good leader.

An Early Trait Profile

Not until 1948 was a comprehensive review of competing trait theories conducted. After comparing more than 100 studies of leader traits and characteristics, the reviewer uncovered moderate agreement on only five traits. In the reviewer's

---

FIGURE 13.1

The Evolution of Leadership Theory

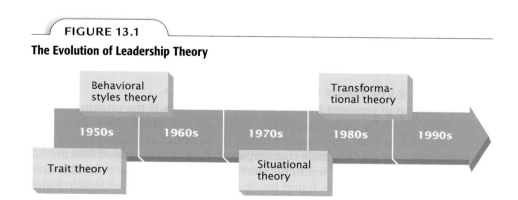

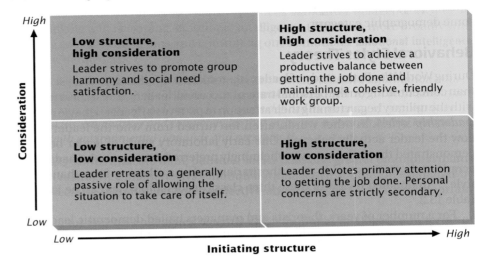

FIGURE 13.2

Basic Leadership Styles from the Ohio State Study

Low structure, high consideration
Leader strives to promote group harmony and social need satisfaction.

High structure, high consideration
Leader strives to achieve a productive balance between getting the job done and maintaining a cohesive, friendly work group.

Low structure, low consideration
Leader retreats to a generally passive role of allowing the situation to take care of itself.

High structure, low consideration
Leader devotes primary attention to getting the job done. Personal concerns are strictly secondary.

Consideration — High / Low

Initiating structure — Low / High

The Ohio State Model

While the democratic style of leadership was receiving attention, a slightly different behavioral approach to leadership emerged. This second approach began in the late 1940s when a team of Ohio State University researchers defined two independent dimensions of leader behavior.[38] One dimension, called "initiating structure," was the leader's efforts to get things organized and get the job done. The second dimension, labeled "consideration," was the degree of trust, friendship, respect, and warmth that the leader extended to subordinates. By making a matrix out of these two independent dimensions of leader behavior, the Ohio State researchers identified four styles of leadership (see Figure 13.2).

This particular scheme proved to be fertile ground for leadership theorists, and variations of the original Ohio State approach soon appeared.[39] Leadership theorists began a search for the "one best style" of leadership. The high-structure, high-consideration style was generally hailed as the best all-around style. This "high-high" style has intuitive appeal because it embraces the best of both categories of leader behavior. But one researcher cautioned in 1966 that, although there seemed to be a positive relationship between consideration and employee satisfaction, a positive link between the high-high style and work group performance had not been proved conclusively.[40]

The Leadership Grid®

Developed by Robert R. Blake and Jane S. Mouton, and originally called the Managerial Grid®, the Leadership Grid® is a trademarked and widely recognized typology of leadership styles.[41] Today, amid the growing popularity of situational and transformational leadership theories, Blake's followers remain convinced that there is one best style of leadership.[42] As we will see, they support this claim with research evidence.

As illustrated in Figure 13.3, the Leadership Grid® has "concern for production" on the horizontal axis and "concern for people" on the vertical axis. Concern for production involves a desire to achieve greater output, cost-effectiveness, and profits in profit-seeking organizations. Concern for people involves promoting friendship, helping coworkers get the job done, and attending to things that matter to people, like pay and working conditions. By scaling each axis from 1 to 9, the grid is highlighted by five major styles:

9,1 style: primary concern for production; people secondary

1,9 style: primary concern for people; production secondary

1,1 style: minimal concern for either production or people

5,5 style: moderate concern for both production and people to maintain the status quo

9,9 style: high concern for both production and people as evidenced by personal commitment, mutual trust, and teamwork

Although they stress that managers and leaders need to be versatile enough to select the courses of action appropriate to the situation, Blake and his colleagues contend that a 9,9 style correlates positively with better results, better mental and

---

FIGURE 13.3

Blake and McCanse's Leadership Grid®

Source: From *Leadership Dilemmas—Grid Solutions,* by Robert R. Blake and Anne Adams McCanse, 1991. Reprinted with permission of Grid International®.

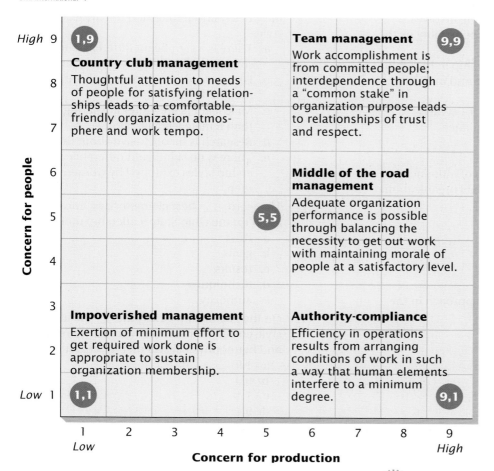

physical health, and effective conflict resolution. They believe there is one best leadership style. As they see it, the true 9,9 style has never been adequately tested by the situationalists. In a study by Blake and Mouton, 100 experienced managers overwhelmingly preferred the 9,9 style, regardless of how the situation varied.[43] Consequently, Blake's management training and organization development programs were designed to help individuals and entire organizations move into the 9,9 portion of the Leadership Grid®.

TEST PREPPER 13.3

ANSWERS CAN BE FOUND ON P. 365

True or False?

_____ 1. As defined, informal leaders are a serious threat to the organization's mission.

_____ 2. Leaders who rely on kindness and humor to build strong relationships possess Goleman's "relationship management" trait.

_____ 3. According to Judy B. Rosener's survey, male leaders were found to be worse at sharing power and information than were their female counterparts.

_____ 4. The laissez-faire leadership style involves retention of authority and responsibility by the leader.

_____ 5. The two dimensions of leadership in the Ohio State model are consideration and initiating structure.

_____ 6. On the Leadership Grid®, the 9,1 style is referred to as authority-compliance.

Multiple Choice

_____ 7. _____ leadership is the process of influencing relevant others to pursue official organizational objectives.
   a. Informal
   b. Ad hoc
   c. Decentralized
   d. Intermittent
   e. Formal

_____ 8. Which of these is the newest approach in the evolution of leadership theory?
   a. Transformational
   b. Behavioral styles
   c. Virtual
   d. Trait
   e. Situational

_____ 9. An array of noncognitive skills, capabilities, and competencies that influence a person's ability to cope with environmental demands and pressures refers to
   a. self-management.
   b. emotional intelligence.
   c. behavior modification.
   d. empowerment.
   e. IQ.

_____ 10. What did a comprehensive review of research have to say about male and female leadership styles?
   a. There is a significant difference in leadership styles exhibited by women and men.
   b. Female leaders are more authoritarian than male leaders.
   c. Male leaders are better at sharing power than female leaders.
   d. Research is inconclusive about this issue.
   e. There is no significant difference in leadership styles exhibited by women and men.

_____ 11. The word _____ best characterizes "consideration" in the Ohio State leadership model.
   a. trust
   b. goals
   c. results
   d. techniques
   e. authority

_____ 12. On the Leadership Grid®, the _____ leadership style correlates positively with better results and better physical and mental health.
   a. 1,9
   b. 9,9
   c. 1,1
   d. 9,1
   e. 5,5

Online Study Center
ACE the Test
ACE Practice Tests 13.3

LEADERSHIP: ADVANCED CONCEPTS

 Contrast the assumptions behind Fiedler's contingency theory and path-goal leadership theory, and describe transformational and servant leaders.

Now that we have built a foundation of understanding in the previous section by defining the term *leadership*, contrasting formal and informal leaders, and deriving basic lessons from trait and behavioral styles theories, we turn to more advanced and more recent models. The overriding challenge remains the same: achieving organizational objectives with and through others.

Situational Theory

Convinced that no one best style of leadership exists, some management scholars have advocated situational or contingency thinking. Although a number of different situational-leadership theories have been developed, they all share one fundamental assumption: successful leadership occurs when the leader's style matches the situation. Situational-leadership theorists stress the need for flexibility. They reject the notion of a universally applicable style. Research is under way to determine precisely when and where various styles of leadership are appropriate. Fiedler's contingency theory and the path-goal theory are introduced and discussed here because they represent distinctly different approaches to situational leadership.

Fiedler's Contingency Theory

Among the various leadership theories proposed so far, Fiedler's is the most thoroughly tested. It is the product of more than 30 years of research by Fred E. Fiedler and his associates. Fiedler's contingency theory gets its name from the following assumption:

> *The performance of a leader depends on two interrelated factors: (1) the degree to which the situation gives the leader control and influence—that is, the likelihood that [the leader] can successfully accomplish the job; and (2) the leader's basic motivation—that is, whether [the leader's] self-esteem depends primarily on accomplishing the task or on having close supportive relations with others.*[44]

Regarding the second factor, the leader's basic motivation, Fiedler believes leaders are either task-motivated or relationship-motivated. These two motivational profiles are roughly equivalent to initiating structure (or concern for production) and consideration (or concern for people).

A consistent pattern has emerged from the many studies of effective leaders carried out by Fiedler and others.[45] As illustrated in Figure 13.4 on page 356, task-motivated leaders seem to be effective in extreme situations when they have either very little control or a great deal of control over situational variables. In moderately favorable situations, however, relationship-motivated leaders tend to be more effective. Consequently, Fiedler and one of his colleagues summed up their findings by noting that "everything points to the conclusion that there is no such thing as an ideal leader."[46] Instead, there are leaders, and there are situations. The challenge, according to Fiedler, is to analyze a leader's basic motivation and then match that leader with a suitable situation to form a productive combination. He believes it is more efficient to move leaders to a suitable situation than to tamper with their personalities by trying to get task-motivated leaders to become relationship-motivated, or vice versa.

FIGURE 13.4

Fiedler's Contingency Theory of Leadership

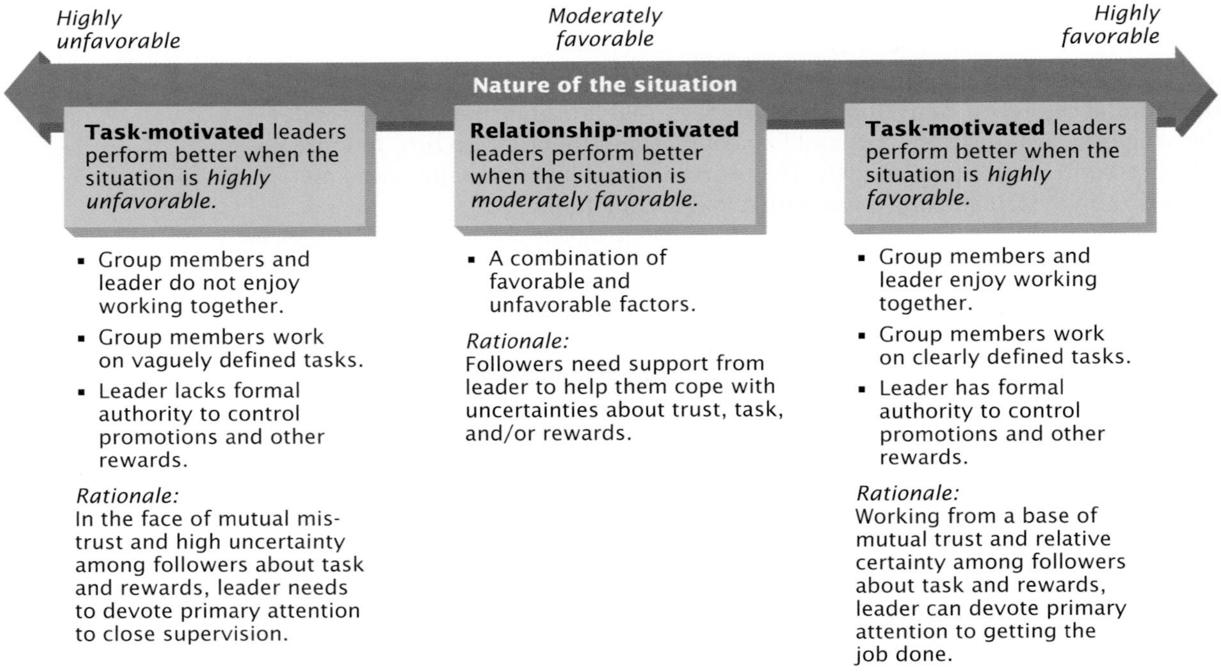

Highly unfavorable

Moderately favorable

Highly favorable

Nature of the situation

Task-motivated leaders perform better when the situation is *highly unfavorable.*

Relationship-motivated leaders perform better when the situation is *moderately favorable.*

Task-motivated leaders perform better when the situation is *highly favorable.*

- Group members and leader do not enjoy working together.
- Group members work on vaguely defined tasks.
- Leader lacks formal authority to control promotions and other rewards.

Rationale:
In the face of mutual mistrust and high uncertainty among followers about task and rewards, leader needs to devote primary attention to close supervision.

- A combination of favorable and unfavorable factors.

Rationale:
Followers need support from leader to help them cope with uncertainties about trust, task, and/or rewards.

- Group members and leader enjoy working together.
- Group members work on clearly defined tasks.
- Leader has formal authority to control promotions and other rewards.

Rationale:
Working from a base of mutual trust and relative certainty among followers about task and rewards, leader can devote primary attention to getting the job done.

Path-Goal Theory

Another situational leadership theory is the path-goal theory, a derivative of expectancy motivation theory (see Chapter 11). Path-goal theory gets its name from the assumption that effective leaders can enhance employee motivation by:

1. Clarifying the individual's perception of work goals
2. Linking meaningful rewards with goal attainment
3. Explaining how goals and desired rewards can be achieved

In short, leaders should motivate their followers by providing clear goals and meaningful incentives for reaching them. Path-goal theorists believe that motivation is essential to effective leadership.

According to path-goal theorists Robert J. House and Terence R. Mitchell, leaders can enhance motivation by "increasing the number and kinds of personal payoffs to subordinates for work-goal attainment and making paths to these payoffs easier to travel by clarifying the paths, reducing road blocks and pitfalls, and increasing the opportunities for personal satisfaction en route."[47] Personal characteristics of employees, environmental pressures, and demands on employees will all vary from situation to situation. Thus, path-goal proponents believe managers need to rely contingently on eight categories of leader behavior:

▌ *Path-goal clarifying behaviors:* Make it clear how goal attainment is linked with meaningful rewards.

- *Achievement-oriented behaviors:* Set challenging goals,[48] emphasize excellence, and seek continuous improvement while maintaining a high degree of confidence that employees will meet difficult challenges in a responsible manner.

- *Work-facilitation behaviors:* Plan and coordinate work, make decisions, provide feedback and coaching, provide resources, remove roadblocks, and empower employees.

- *Supportive behaviors:* Be friendly and approachable, and show concern for employees' well-being.

- *Interaction-facilitation behaviors:* Resolve disputes and encourage collaboration, diverse opinions, and teamwork.

- *Group-decision behaviors:* Encourage group input, problem solving, and participation.

- *Networking behaviors:* Build bridges to influential people and represent the group's best interests to others.

- *Value-based behaviors:* Self-confidently formulate and passionately support a vision.[49]

The assumption that managers can and do shift situationally from style to style clearly sets path-goal theory apart from Fiedler's model. Recall that Fiedler claims that managers cannot and do not change their basic leadership styles.

Although research on the path-goal model has produced mixed results,[50] the experience of Leonard D. Schaeffer, CEO of Wellpoint Health Networks, based in Thousand Oaks, California, validates the path-goal contention that leaders do in fact change leadership styles:

> As the company has changed, I've gone through my own transformation as chief executive. The top-down, autocratic style I had to adopt to turn around the business gave way to a more hands-off style that focused on motivating others to act rather than managing them directly. And more recently, I've been going through yet another shift—away from the participative mode and toward what I call a reformer style of leadership in which the chief executive's role is to represent the company's interests on a broader stage.[51]

Another valuable contribution of path-goal theory is its identification of the achievement-oriented leadership behavior. As managers deal with an increasing number of highly educated and self-motivated employees in advanced-technology industries, they will need to become skilled facilitators rather than just order givers or hand holders.

Transformational Leadership Theory

In his 1978 book, *Leadership,* James McGregor Burns drew a distinction between transactional and transformational leadership. Burns characterized **transformational leaders** as visionaries who challenge people to achieve exceptionally high levels of morality, motivation, and performance.[52] Only transformational leaders, Burns argued, are capable of charting necessary new courses for modern organizations. Why? Because they are masters of change.[53] They can envision a better future, effectively communicate that vision, and get others to willingly make it a reality.

REALITY CHECK 13.3

"Situations differ, often wildly, in the extent to which one individual can make a difference and in the set of attributes required to be successful."

Source: Jeffrey Pfeffer, "In Defense of the Boss From Hell," *Business 2.0,* 8 (March 2007): 70.

Question: So who (or what) is *really* in charge when it comes to leadership, the person or the situation?

---

transformational leaders Visionaries who challenge people to do exceptional things.

Transactional Versus Transformational Leaders

Extending the work of Burns, Bernard Bass more recently emphasized the importance of charisma in transformational leadership. Transformational leaders rely heavily on referent power. Wendy's Dave Thomas, Wal-Mart's Sam Walton, and Southwest Airline's Herb Kelleher exemplify charismatic leaders who engineered great success at their respective companies.[54] While acknowledging how transformational leaders exhibit widely different styles and tend to stir their fair share of controversy, Bass rounded out Burns's distinction between transactional and transformational leaders (see Table 13.3). Transactional leaders monitor people so they do the expected, according to plan. In contrast, transformational leaders inspire people to do the unexpected, above and beyond the plan. This distinction can mean the difference between maintaining the status quo and fostering creative and productive growth.

Positive Evidence

It is important to note that the distinction in Table 13.3 is not between bad and good leaders—both types are needed today. This is where transformational leadership theory effectively combines the behavioral styles and situational approaches just discussed. To the traditional behavioral patterns of initiating structure and consideration have been added charismatic and other behaviors.[55] Transformational leadership also needs to be situationally appropriate. Specifically, transformational leadership is needed in rapidly changing situations; transactional leaders can best handle stable situations.[56]

Available laboratory and field research evidence generally supports the transformational leadership pattern. Followers of transformational leaders tend to perform better and to report greater satisfaction than do those of transactional leaders.[57]

TABLE 13.3

Transactional Versus Transformational Leaders

Transactional leader		Transformational leader	
Contingent reward	Contracts exchange of rewards for effort, promises rewards for good performance, recognizes accomplishments.	**Charisma**	Provides vision and sense of mission, instills pride, gains respect and trust.
Management by exception (active)	Watches and searches for deviations from rules and standards, takes corrective action.	**Inspiration**	Communicates high expectations, uses symbols to focus efforts, expresses important purposes in simple ways.
Management by exception (passive)	Intervenes only if standards are not met.	**Intellectual stimulation**	Promotes intelligence, rationality, and careful problem solving.
Laissez-faire	Abdicates responsibilities, avoids making decisions.	**Individualized consideration**	Gives personal attention, treats each employee individually, coaches, advises.

Source: Reprinted from *Organizational Dynamics,* Vol. 18, by Bernard M. Bass et al., "From Transactional to Transformational Leadership: Learning to Share the Vision," Coypright © 1990, with permission from Elsevier.

TABLE 13.4

Characteristics of the Servant Leader

▪ **They are servants first.** . . . servant leaders are motivated by a natural desire to serve, not to lead. They must make a conscious choice to *aspire* to lead. People who are leaders first are responding to an innate drive to acquire power or material possessions.

▪ **They articulate goals.** A servant leader gives certainty and purpose to others by clearly articulating a goal or, in today's leadership parlance, a vision.

▪ **They inspire trust.** Followers are confident of the leader's values, competence, and judgment. He has a sustaining spirit (*entheos*) that supports the tenacious pursuit of a goal.

▪ **They know how to listen.** The true, natural servant leader responds to any problem by listening first. You can discipline yourself to learn to listen first, and thus become a natural servant. Here, Greenleaf draws on the prayer of St. Francis, "Lord, grant that I may not seek so much to be understood as to understand."

▪ **They are masters of positive feedback.** The servant leader always offers unqualified acceptance of the person, although she doesn't necessarily accept the person's effort or performance.

▪ **They rely on foresight.** No leader ever has all the information necessary to make major decisions. But servant leaders have an intuitive sense that they use to bridge information gaps. Their ability to detach from day-to-day events allows their conscious and unconscious to work together to "better foresee the unforeseeable."

▪ **They emphasize personal development.** A servant leader views every problem as originating inside, rather than outside, himself. To remedy any "flaw in the world," the process of change starts in the servant, not "out there." Notes Greenleaf, "This is a difficult concept for that busybody, modern man."

Source: From "The Servant Leader" by Chris Lee, *Training,* 1993. Copyright © 1993 Nielsen Business Media, Inc. Reprinted with permission from *Training.*

Servant Leaders: Putting to Work What You've Learned

Finding ways to practice leadership both on and off the job can help present and future managers develop their abilities. Serving in campus, community, or religious organizations, for example, will give you an opportunity to experiment with different leadership styles in a variety of situations. Leading effectively, like riding a bike, is learned only by doing.

In addition to a working knowledge of the various leadership theories we have just discussed, aspiring leaders need an integrative model to tie everything together.[58] This is where Robert K. Greenleaf's philosophy of the *servant leader* enters the picture as an instructive and inspiring springboard. The servant leader is an ethical person who puts others—not herself or himself—in the foreground (see Table 13.4). As a devout Quaker, Greenleaf wove humility and a genuine concern for the whole person into the philosophy of leadership he developed during his career at AT&T.[59] One person who embodies the servant leader philosophy is Ralph Cruz, a retired U.S. Army officer who is the co-owner of Technology Providers Inc., an Arizona firm that makes high-tech teaching tools for college classrooms:

> "As a business owner . . . you take a pledge to honor and respect the lives of your employees," he said. "It's not about you and not about the money. . . .
>
> "We do have a tremendously high focus on our employees, and, ultimately, I am a servant to them. I come in every day and ask them what they need me to do."[60]

REALITY CHECK 13.4

"People trust you when you are genuine and authentic, not a replica of someone else."

Source: Bill George, Peter Sims, Andrew N. McLean, and Diana Mayer, "Discovering Your Authentic Leadership," *Harvard Business Review,* 85 (February 2007): 129.

Questions: How well does this describe a servant leader? How does this affect having a role model?

True or False?

_____ 1. According to Fiedler's contingency theory of leadership, a leader's effectiveness depends on both the situation and his or her motivation.

_____ 2. Relationship-motivated leaders tend to be effective when the situation is highly favorable, according to Fiedler's theory.

_____ 3. According to path-goal theory, there is one best style of leadership that applies in all situations.

_____ 4. Management by exception is a favorite technique for transactional leaders.

_____ 5. Servant leaders put the company's survival ahead of people.

Multiple Choice

_____ 6. According to Fiedler's contingency theory, _____ leaders tend to perform better when the situation is _____ favorable.
   a. relationship-motivated; moderately
   b. visionary; highly
   c. achievement-oriented; moderately
   d. social; highly
   e. task-motivated; moderately

_____ 7. The path-goal theory of leadership is based on
   a. Goleman's EQ theory.
   b. goal-setting theory.
   c. McGregor's Theory Y.
   d. expectancy theory.
   e. Herzberg's two-factor theory.

Online Study Center
ACE the Test
ACE Practice Tests 13.4

_____ 8. Which leader behavior, according to the path-goal theory, involves being approachable while showing concern for employees' well-being?
   a. Achievement-oriented
   b. Directive
   c. Participative
   d. Supportive
   e. Transformational

_____ 9. What do transformational leaders such as Southwest Airline's former CEO Herb Kelleher rely heavily on?
   a. Transactional power
   b. Legitimate power
   c. Reward power
   d. Expert power
   e. Referent power

_____ 10. Which of the following is a characteristic of a transactional leader?
   a. Individualized consideration
   b. Intellectual stimulation
   c. Inspiration
   d. Laissez-faire
   e. Charisma

_____ 11. In Greenleaf's servant-leadership theory, the center of attention is on
   a. others.
   b. God.
   c. the customer.
   d. top management.
   e. the mission.

MENTORING

5 ▶ *Identify the two key functions that mentors perform, and explain how a mentor can help develop a junior manager's leadership skills.*

In spite of mountains of leadership research, much remains to be learned about why some people are good leaders whereas many others are not.[61] One thing is clear, though: mentors can make an important difference. Let us explore this interesting process whereby leadership skills are acquired by exposure to role models.

Learning from a Mentor

The many obstacles and barriers blocking the way to successful leadership make it easy to understand why there is no simple formula for developing leaders.

Abraham Zaleznik, a respected sociologist, insists that leaders must be nurtured under the wise tutelage of a mentor. A **mentor** is an individual who systematically develops another person's abilities through intensive tutoring, coaching, and guidance.[62] Zaleznik explains the nature of this special relationship:

> Mentors take risks with people. They bet initially on talent they perceive in [junior] people. Mentors also risk emotional involvement in working closely with their juniors. The risks do not always pay off, but the willingness to take them appears crucial in developing leaders.[63]

A survey of 246 health care industry managers found that among managers with mentors there was:

- Higher satisfaction
- Greater recognition
- More promotion opportunities[64]

Other research suggests that *informal* relationships that arise naturally work better than formally structured pairings.[65] Still, KLA-Tencor, the 6,400-employee semiconductor maker, prefers the structured approach (see Best Practices on page 362).

Dynamics of Mentoring

According to Kathy Kram, who conducted intensive biographical interviews with both members in 18 different senior manager–junior manager mentor relationships, mentoring fulfills two important functions:

1. A career enhancement function
2. A psychological support function (see Table 13.5)

Mentor relationships were found to average about five years in length.[66] Thus, a manager might have a series of mentors during the course of an organizational career.

Interestingly, the junior member of a mentor relationship is not the only one to benefit. Mentors often derive great intrinsic pleasure from seeing their protégés move up through the ranks and conquer difficult challenges. Renetta McCann, CEO of Starcom MediaVest Group, a leading advertising and marketing firm, sees another benefit for mentors who coach others to make tough decisions:

> I have taken on that task by mentoring women and young African-Americans who want to go into business. Being a mentor helps overcome those feelings of loneliness and isolation [at the top], and it also helps you maintain contact with the next generation or even the next couple of generations. It keeps you connected.[67]

mentor Someone who develops another person through tutoring, coaching, and guidance.

"One of the most common problems, especially with formal programs, is simply that the mentor and apprentice are incompatible. As we all know, there's no accounting for chemistry. . . . Respect isn't enough, though. Ideally, both people know what they want out of the arrangement."

Source: Excerpted from Susan Berfield, "Mentoring Can Be Messy," *Business Week* (January 29, 2007): 80.

Question: What makes a mentoring relationship a win-win proposition?

TABLE 13.5

Mentors Serve Two Important Functions

Career functions*	Psychosocial functions**
Sponsorship	Role modeling
Exposure and visibility	Acceptance and confirmation
Coaching	Counseling
Protection	Friendship
Challenging assignments	

* Career functions are those aspects of the relationship that primarily enhance career advancement.

** Psychosocial functions are those aspects of the relationship that primarily enhance a sense of competence, clarity of identity, and effectiveness in the managerial role.

Source: From *Academy of Management Journal* by Kathy E. Kram, "Phases of the Mentor Relationship," December 1983. Copyright © 1983 by Academy of Management (NY). Reproduced with permission of Academy of Management (NY) via Copyright Clearance Center.

Online Study Center college.hmco.com/pic/kreitnerSASfound

Moreover, by passing along their values and technical and leadership skills to promising junior managers, mentors can wield considerable power. Mentor relationships do sometimes turn sour. A mentor can become threatened by a protégé who surpasses him or her. Also, cross-gender[68] and cross-race mentor relationships can be the victim of bias and social pressures.[69]

TEST PREPPER 13.5

ANSWERS CAN BE FOUND ON P. 365

True or False?

_____ 1. Mentors develop another person's abilities through tutoring, coaching, and guidance.

_____ 2. According to research, the practice of formally assigning mentors tends to be the most effective approach.

_____ 3. Role modeling is one of the psychosocial functions of mentoring.

_____ 4. One way a mentor can serve a career function is to provide challenging assignments.

Multiple Choice

_____ 5. Which role parallels the concept of a mentor?
   a. Master   d. Servant
   b. Confessor   e. Coach
   c. Student

Online Study Center
ACE the Test
ACE Practice Tests 13.5

_____ 6. According to researchers, mentor relationships average about which length of time?
   a. No identifiable time frame
   b. Five years
   c. Six months
   d. One year
   e. Lifetime

_____ 7. _____ is a career function of mentors.
   a. Indoctrination   d. Friend
   b. Sponsorship   e. Socialization
   c. Role modeling

_____ 8. Which of the following is a psychosocial function of mentoring?
   a. Protection
   b. Sponsorship
   c. Exposure
   d. Counseling
   e. Challenging assignments

BEST PRACTICES

Mentoring with IMPAKT at KLA-Tencor

As part of the company's Internal Mentoring Program at KLA-Tencor (IMPAKT), senior-level managers receive mentoring from board members as well as retired company executives. Each year between 10 and 20 executives, selected from a talent list to participate, focus on improving a specific skill set during the mentorship. Participants are expected to broaden their functional experience, clarify performance goals and develop strategies to address concrete job-related issues while increasing their understanding of the company's culture, political structure and vision.

In addition to the senior-level manager mentoring program, KLA-Tencor . . . has also developed an online peer-mentoring program for identified top talent. Key features include an automated relationship pairing function, a 360-degree review process to apply mentoring relationships to address skills gaps, formal mentoring goals and financial incentives for achieving knowledge transfer, among others. Plans call for the program to be developed for all employees.

Source: From "Best Practice: Mentoring (KLA-Tencor)" *Training,* March 2003. Copyright © 2003 Nielsen Business Media, Inc. Reprinted with permission from *Training.*

Leadership Development GE-Style

As companies evolve, so do their leadership philosophies. And General Electric's John F. Welch Leadership Center at Crotonville has had more time to evolve than any other corporate university, as . . . [2006] marks its 50th anniversary. In that half century, the center, in Ossining, N.Y., 30 miles outside of Manhattan, has turned out internal and external leaders ready to take on global-scale business challenges—and there's no sign of a slowdown.

"Crotonville is embedded in the GE culture and the GE values," GE Chief Learning Officer Bob Corcoran says. "All of our major change initiatives—cultural change and business change processes—have either originated at Crotonville as a result of best practice assessments and evaluations or executive leadership summits, or they have been broadcast, trained, amplified or rolled out with Crotonville as the change agent."

Corcoran himself is a 27-year GE veteran in human resources and executive leadership, and holds the distinction of being the first CLO and head of Crotonville who is a graduate of all of the executive development programs. . . .

Nominated executives stay in the Residence Building, a 190-bed facility where each room is a carbon copy of the next, reinforcing the level playing field Corcoran says he wants all attendees to be playing on. "Every person who comes here wears a little nametag; it doesn't say you're the [head] of health care, it doesn't say you're a junior finance accountant. It says your name and your business." He says employees are there to discuss values, processes and change initiatives, regardless of position. "It really is a place that fundamentally reinforces the concepts and principles of a meritocracy."

And while students are there, they'll be treated to lectures from not only leadership experts in the academic world (the late Peter Drucker taught there), but also GE leaders. In 25 years, [former CEO Jack] Welch and current Chairman and CEO Jeffrey Immelt have spoken at 329 of the last 330 executive-level courses at the facility, which is 60 miles from the GE headquarters in Fairfield, Conn. Welch, who missed one when he had heart bypass surgery, was known to speak up to six hours to students.

But lest one think taking leadership courses at Crotonville is a cushy reward for good behavior or a golf-centric retreat, Corcoran stresses that students, who represent each GE business, are there to work. "Our classes don't just go 8 to 5," he says, explaining project work, evening lectures and roundtable discussions take up participants' time.

In the first of the three progressive courses, Manager Development Course (MDC), 75 to 80 students compete in an artificial intelligence marketplace via computer simulation following lectures that teach them business management basics. Instructors, who Corcoran says are two-thirds internal, one-third external, stress both theory and practical application. The format of the course, given eight times a year, Corcoran explains, is "concept, application, practice." And although it's the first of the top three courses, a GE executive won't be eligible for the program until 10 to 20 years into his or her career.

In the second and third courses, Business Manager Course (BMC) and Executive Development Course (EDC), respectively, not only do participants get assigned a real problem GE is facing, but also must present their findings to Immelt, who hand selects the problem. In BMC, given three times a year to 50 to 60 participants who are eligible about three to four years after MDC, the focus is on assessing and evaluating change with action-learning techniques, Corcoran says. The program typically involves a week of world travel, as many of the problems students are given hinge on staying competitive in a global market. The students conduct interviews and merge that into a recommendation for Immelt and his team.

EDC, meanwhile, focuses on changing GE's culture. The annual course is given to 35 individuals who are among the top 300 in the company and could potentially become one of the 170 GE corporate officers. "They get big issues to deal with," Corcoran says. There are guest lecturers, and students wrestle with broad-based solutions. Lectures are given in "The Pit" at Crotonville, which is a 100-seat amphitheater that Corcoran says truly puts the speaker in the spotlight. "When lecturers are there at the bottom, our classes don't sit quietly and say, 'Thank you very much,' and then talk badly about them when they leave. They smack them around live, and it doesn't matter if it's a vice president or not of GE." Participants also present their findings to Immelt and corporate officers.

While all this learning is happening under Immelt's scrutiny, Corcoran stresses that participants' experiences, successes and failures are not reported to supervisors.

CLOSING CASE STUDY (CONTINUED)

"We create a very, very safe learning environment. We fundamentally said Crotonville is a safe haven," Corcoran says. "You have to be free to make mistakes. The reality is that in the real world, in real life when you're not in the classroom, people learn most when they make mistakes. We encourage people to take risks; we encourage them to try."

There is no grading process during the courses, Corcoran says, stressing that it's more important that students take the lessons learned and apply it and create value in their jobs. "Potential's good, but results are better."

Source: Excerpted from Jacqueline Durett, "GE Hones Its Leaders at Crotonville," *Training,* May 2006, Vol. 42, pp. 25–27.

Copyright © 2006 Nielsen Business Media, Inc. Reprinted with permission from *Training.*

Case Questions

1. Is this an effective way to teach leadership? Explain.
2. Is GE's Crotonville a better learning environment than the typical college classroom? Why or why not?
3. If you were a GE employee and nominated to attend Crotonville, what would you look forward to the most (and fear the most) about the experience? Explain.
4. How would you integrate a formal mentoring program with the Crotonville course work?

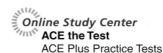

Online Study Center
ACE the Test
ACE Plus Practice Tests

Online Study Center
Improve Your Grade
Learning Objective Review
Audio Chapter Review
Audio Chapter Quiz
Study Guide to Go

LEARNING OBJECTIVE REVIEW

1 *Identify and describe eight generic influence tactics used in modern organizations.*

- Recent research has identified eight generic influence tactics that people use on the job:
  - Consultation (Seeking someone's participation in a decision or change)
  - Rational persuasion (Trying to convince someone by relying on a plan, reasoning, or logic)
  - Inspirational appeals (Appealing to someone's emotions, values, or ideals to generate enthusiasm and confidence)
  - Ingratiating tactics (Making someone feel important or good before making a request)
  - Coalition tactics (Seeking the aid of others to persuade someone to agree)
  - Pressure tactics (Relying on intimidation, demands, or threats to gain compliance or support)
  - Upwards appeals (Obtaining support of higher management)
  - Exchange tactics (Offering an exchange of favors or a personal sacrifice)

2 *Identify the five bases of power, and explain what it takes to make empowerment work.*

- The five bases of power are:
  - Reward (Gaining compliance through rewards)

  - Coercive (Gaining compliance through threats or punishment)
  - Legitimate (Compliance based on one's formal position)
  - Referent (Compliance based on charisma or personal identification)
  - Expert (Compliance based on ability to dispense valued information)

- Empowerment cannot work without a supporting situation such as a skilled individual; an organizational culture of empowerment; an emotionally mature individual with a well-developed character; and empowerment opportunities such as delegation, participation, and self-managed teams.

3 *Explain the concept of emotional intelligence in terms of Goleman's four leadership traits, and summarize what the Ohio State model and the Leadership Grid® have taught managers about leadership.*

- Goleman's trait approach identifies four dimensions of emotional intelligence: self-awareness, self-management, social awareness, and relationship management. Managers with emotional intelligence (the ability to cope with pressures and demands in a mature fashion) can build needed social capital in today's workplaces.

- Leadership studies at Ohio State University isolated four styles of leadership based on two categories of leader behavior: initiating structure and consideration. Despite the claim that the high-structure, high-consideration leadership style is the single best style, convincing research evidence is lacking.

- The Leadership Grid® has taught managers that a high concern for both production and people achieves better results.

---

4 *Contrast the assumptions behind Fiedler's contingency theory and path-goal leadership theory, and describe transformational and servant leaders.*

- Many years of study led Fiedler to conclude that task-motivated leaders are more effective in either very favorable or very unfavorable situations, whereas relationship-motivated leaders are better suited to moderately favorable situations. The favorableness of a situation is dictated by the degree of the leader's control and influence in getting the job done.

- Path-goal leadership theory, an expectancy perspective, assumes that leaders are effective to the extent that they can motivate followers by clarifying goals and clearing the paths to achieving those goals and valued rewards. Unlike Fiedler, path-goal theorists believe that managers can and should adapt their leadership style to the situation.

- Transformational leaders are visionaries who challenge people to do exceptional things and servant leaders are ethical people who put others first.

---

5 *Identify the two key functions that mentors perform, and explain how a mentor can help develop a junior manager's leadership skills.*

- Mentors help develop less experienced people by fulfilling five career functions (sponsorship, exposure and visibility, coaching, protection, and challenging assignments) and four psychosocial functions (role modeling, acceptance and confirmation, counseling, and friendship).

- Mentors serve as role models and engage in intensive tutoring, coaching, and guidance of junior managers.

TEST PREPPER ANSWERS

▶ **13.1**

1. T   2. F   3. T   4. d   5. c   6. b

▶ **13.2**

1. F   2. T   3. F   4. c   5. b   6. a   7. e
8. e

▶ **13.3**

1. F   2. T   3. T   4. F   5. T   6. T   7. e
8. a   9. b   10. e   11. a   12. b

▶ **13.4**

1. T   2. F   3. F   4. T   5. F   6. a   7. d
8. d   9. e   10. d   11. a

▶ **13.5**

1. T   2. F   3. T   4. T   5. e   6. b   7. b
8. d

Online Study Center RESOURCES

Prepare for Class, Improve Your Grade, and ACE the Test. Student Achievement Series resources include:

ACE Practice Tests
Audio Chapter Quizzes
Audio Chapter Reviews
Career Snapshots
Chapter Glossaries
Chapter Outlines

Crossword Puzzles
Decision Case Questions
Ethical Hot Seat Exercises
Flashcards
Hands-on Exercises

Hangman
Key Issue Expansion
Learning Objective Reviews
Study Guide to Go
Visual Glossaries

To access these learning and study tools, go to **college.hmco.com/pic/kreitnerSASfound**.

14 Managing Change and Conflict

At 160 years old, British Telecom is building a single Internet protocol network to handle all of its customers' needs. Will BT's classic red telephone booths be relegated to its corporate museum?

1 ▶ *Describe four types of organizational change according to the Nadler-Tushman model, and explain how people tend to respond differently to changes they like and those they dislike.*

2 ▶ *List at least six reasons why employees resist change, and discuss what management can do about resistance to change.*

3 ▶ *Explain the unfreezing-change-refreezing analogy in OD, describe a tempered radical, and identify the 5Ps in the checklist for grassroots change agents.*

"Change begets conflict, conflict begets change."[1]

—Dean Tjosvold, Management Professor, Lingnan University, Hong Kong

Chapter Outline

Online Study Center
Prepare for Class
Chapter Outline

4 *Contrast the competitive and cooperative conflict styles, and identify five conflict resolution techniques.*

British Telecom: The 160-Year-Old Startup

Ben Verwaayen and Matt Bross agreed to meet in a New Jersey cafe in 2002 to talk turkey. They were both telecom veterans, but they made an unlikely duo: Verwaayen was a Dutchman, Bross an Oklahoman. Verwaayen had recently been named chief executive of British Telecom, the venerable but doddering phone company, and he wanted Bross, a retired networking wiz, to come to London to help him fix BT. Bross wasn't interested—until Verwaayen grabbed a napkin and started scribbling.

That napkin is now being prepared for preservation in the 160-year-old BT's corporate museum, as befits a document that will likely prove a historic turning point for BT and possibly for the telecom industry as a whole. Soon after that New Jersey meeting, Bross did indeed move to London and join BT, and Verwaayen's team is now well into a startling transformation of the company.

Online Study Center *college.hmco.com/pic/kreitnerSASfound*

Online Study Center
Prepare for Class
Chapter Glossary

Improve Your Grade
Flashcards
Hangman
Crossword Puzzles

BT, burdened by massive debt and persistent legacies from its past as a government-owned monopoly, lost $4.3 billion in 2001 and seemed hopelessly in retreat. But Verwaayen's napkin plan put the company back on the offensive. BT would remake itself based on the latest evolution in Web technologies, building a single Internet protocol network to handle all of a customer's needs: voice, data, e-mail, movies, everything. It would create—and let customers, from a single individual to giant corporations, create—a menu of services and capabilities tailored to the Web 2.0 era of mashups, remixes, and user-generated content. It would operate not like a bloated bureaucracy but like a hungry startup fighting for survival.

Other big telecoms, from AT&T to Verizon to [Japan's] NTT DoCoMo, have talked of a similar need for user-centric networks and startup-like zeal. But implausibly, it's BT that now appears to be closest to achieving both.[2] ∎

Change is constant today, even for old and well-established companies such as British Telecom. *Business Week* recently quoted Kaoru Tosaka, president of Japan's NEC Electronics, as saying, "The choice is simple. . . . We change or go out of business."[3] Indeed, change-resistant managers and organizations risk becoming irrelevant in a world of constant demographic, technological, political/legal, and economic changes. They need to be adept at managing both revolutionary and evolutionary change, as circumstances dictate.[4]

According to the U.S. Federal Aviation Administration, Lanny McAndrew (pictured here in a flight simulator) was fully qualified to pilot a commercial airliner for JetBlue Airways on January 24, 2003. The following day the FAA said he was no longer qualified. Why? Because he had reached his 60th birthday. The FAA's Age 60 rule, in force since 1959, supposedly prevents age-related safety problems. Despite evidence that older pilots are as safe as younger ones and an age limit of 65 in Europe, resistance to change rules at the FAA.

The purpose of this chapter is to explore the dynamics of organizational change and its natural by-product, conflict. We discuss change from organizational and individual perspectives, address resistance to change, and examine how to make change happen. We then consider the nature and management of conflict.

CHANGE: ORGANIZATIONAL AND INDIVIDUAL PERSPECTIVES

 Describe four types of organizational change according to the Nadler-Tushman model, and explain how people tend to respond differently to changes they like and those they dislike.

Researchers report that there is a constant tension between opposing forces for stability and change in today's work organizations.[5] A productive balance is required. If there is too much stability, organizational decline begins. Too much change and the mission blurs and employees burn out. Today's managers need a robust set of concepts and skills to juggle stability and change. Let us tackle this major challenge for managers by looking at four types of organizational change and at how individuals tend to respond to significant changes. These twin perspectives are important because organizational changes unavoidably have personal impacts.

Types of Organizational Change

Consultant David A. Nadler and management professor Michael L. Tushman together developed an instructive typology of organizational change (see Figure 14.1). On the vertical axis of their model, change is characterized as either anticipatory or reactive. **Anticipatory changes** are any systematically planned changes intended to take advantage of expected situations. Oppositely, **reactive changes** are those necessitated by unexpected environmental events or pressures. The horizontal axis deals with the scope of a particular change, either incremental or strategic. **Incremental changes** involve subsystem adjustments that are needed to keep the organization on its chosen path. **Strategic changes** alter the overall shape or direction of the organization. For instance, adding a night shift to meet unexpectedly high demand for the company's product is an incremental change. Switching from building houses to building high-rise apartment complexes would be a strategic change. Four resulting types of organizational change in the Nadler-Tushman model are tuning, adaptation, re-orientation, and re-creation.[6] These types of organizational changes— listed in order of increasing complexity, intensity, and risk—require a closer look.

Tuning

This is the most common, least intense, and least risky type of change. Other names for it include preventive maintenance and the Japanese concept of *kaizen* (continuous improvement). The key to effective tuning is to actively

anticipatory changes Planned changes based on expected situations.

reactive changes Changes made in response to unexpected situations.

incremental changes Subsystem adjustments required to keep the organization on course.

strategic changes Altering the overall shape or direction of the organization.

FIGURE 14.1

Four Types of Organizational Change

Source: Copyright © 1990, by The Regents of the University of California. Reprinted from David A. Nadler and Michael L. Tushman, "Beyond the Charismatic Leader: Leadership and Organizational Change," *California Management Review*, Vol. 32, No. 2. By permission of The Regents.

	Incremental	Strategic
Anticipatory	Tuning	Re-orientation
Reactive	Adaptation	Re-creation

anticipate and avoid problems rather than passively waiting for things to go wrong before taking action. Notice how *kaizen* is at the heart of Michael Dell's philosophy of management:

> *Always find ways to improve. Never stop innovating or taking risks, and keep your whole team engaged and moving in the same direction. Remember the fundamentals and maintain a solid business plan. Keep raising the bar, not just for the industry but for yourself.*[7]

No wonder Dell was able to turn his college dorm room business into an industrial giant in record time.

Adaptation

Like tuning, adaptation involves incremental changes.[8] But this time, the changes are in reaction to external problems, events, or pressures. For example, after Ford had great success with its aerodynamic styling, General Motors and Chrysler followed suit. In turn, Ford and GM broadened their product lines to compete with Chrysler's trend-setting minivans.

Re-orientation

This type of change is anticipatory and strategic in scope. Nadler and Tushman call re-orientation "frame bending" because the organization is significantly redirected. Importantly, there is not a complete break with the organization's past. Consider this example of frame bending at Cisco Systems, the leading maker of Internet gear, after it had reported a 21 percent jump in sales in 2006:

> *Much of the jump came from Cisco's $6.9 billion acquisition of Scientific-Atlanta, a company that makes cable TV set-top boxes for Time Warner, Comcast and others. The deal . . . was a major strategic shift.*
>
> *Cisco's core business is pricey networking gear used by big businesses. But the company hopes that the growth of digital movies, music, television and telephony will give it an entry into consumer sales. Cisco's ultimate goal is a complete line of networking products, from back-end systems used by telephone companies to consumer gear used at home.*[9]

Cisco's frame bending is motivated by a desire to broaden its customer base to avoid getting hurt as badly as it was when the Internet bubble burst in 2001.

Re-creation

REALITY CHECK 14.1

"You will succeed in the face of change when you make the difficult decisions first."

Source: Seth Godin, "If It's Urgent, Ignore It," *Fast Company,* No. 81 (April 2004): 101.

Questions: How does this relate to Re-creation? Why do we too often fail to heed this good advice?

Competitive pressures normally trigger this most intense and risky type of organizational change. Nadler and Tushman say it amounts to "frame breaking." A stunning example of frame breaking is the software giant Microsoft. Cofounder Bill Gates tied his company's future to the Internet in the mid-1990s after initially dismissing it as a passing fad. According to observers at the time:

> *Indeed, in just six months, Gates has done what few executives have dared. He has taken a thriving, $8 billion, 20,000-employee company and done a massive about-face. "I can't think of one corporation that has had this kind of success and after 20 years, just stopped and decided to reinvent itself from the ground up," says Jeffrey Katzenberg, a principal of DreamWorks SKG, which has a joint venture with Microsoft. "What they're doing is decisive, quick, breathtaking."*[10]

FIGURE 14.2

How People Tend to Respond to Changes They *Like*

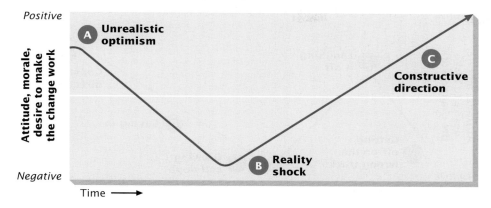

Frame breaking helped Bill Gates to re-create Microsoft's strategy and products around the Internet.

Individual Reactions to Change

Ultimately, workplace changes of all types become a *personal* matter for employees. A merger, for example, means a new job assignment for one person and a new boss for another. The first person may look forward to the challenge of a new assignment, while the second may dread the prospect of adjusting to a new boss. Researchers tell us these two people will tend to exhibit distinctly different response patterns.[11] Specifically, people tend to respond to changes they *like* differently than they do to changes they *dislike*. Let us explore these two response patterns with the goal of developing a contingency model for managers. Importantly, both models are generic—that is, they apply equally to on- and off-the-job changes.

How People Respond to Changes They Like

According to Figure 14.2, a three-stage adjustment is typical when people encounter a change they like. New college graduates, for instance, often see their unrealistic optimism (stage A) give way to the reality shock (stage B) of earning a living before getting their life and career on track (stage C). Key personal factors—including attitude, morale, and desire to make the change work—dip during stage B. Sometimes the dip is so severe or prolonged the person gives up as, say, when newlyweds head for the divorce court. Stage B is thus a critical juncture where leadership can make a difference.[12]

How People Respond to Changes They Fear and Dislike

Although exact statistics are not available, the situation in Figure 14.3 on page 372 is probably more common in the workplace than the one in Figure 14.2. In other words, on-the-job change generally is more feared than welcomed. Changes, particularly sudden ones, represent the unknown. Most of us fear the unknown. We

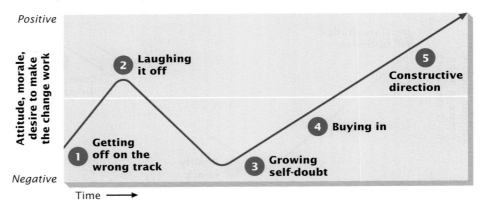

FIGURE 14.3

How People Tend to Respond to Changes They *Fear* and *Dislike*

can bring the model in Figure 14.3 to life by walking through it with Maria, a production supervisor at a dairy products cooperative. She and her coworkers face a major reorganization involving a switch to team-based production:

1. In stage 1, Maria feels a bit unsure and somewhat overwhelmed by the sudden switch to teams. She needs a lot more information to decide whether she really likes the idea. She feels twinges of fear.
2. Stage 2 finds Maria joking with the other supervisors about how upper management's enthusiasm for teams will blow over in a few days, so there's no need to worry. Her attitude, mood, and desire for change improve a bit. After an initial training session on team-based management and participation, Maria begins to worry about her job security. Even if she keeps her job, she wonders if she is up to the new way of doing things.
3. Her morale drops sharply in stage 3.
4. In stage 4, after a stern but supportive lecture from her boss about being a team player, Maria comes to grips with her resistance to the team approach. She resolves to stop criticizing management's "fad of the week" and help make the switch to teams a success.
5. Her attitude turns positive, and her morale takes an upswing in stage 5, as she tries participative management techniques and gets positive results. Additional training and some personal research and reading on team-based management convince Maria that this approach is the wave of the future.

Ten months after the switch to teams was announced, Maria has become an outspoken advocate for teams and participative management. Her job security is strengthened by a pending promotion to the training department, where she will coordinate all team training for supervisors. Unknown to upper management, Maria has even toyed with the idea of starting her own consulting business, specializing in team management. Maria's transition from fear to full adaptation has taken months and has not been easy. But the experience has been normal and positive, including a timely nudge from her manager between stages 3 and 4.

TABLE 14.1

How to Help Individuals Deal with Change: A Contingency Approach

Situation: The person *likes* the change.	
Stage	**Managerial action steps**
A. Unrealistic optimism "What a great idea! It will solve all our problems."	Encourage enthusiasm while directing attention to potential problems and the cooperation and work necessary to get the job done.
B. Reality shock "This is going to be a lot harder than it seemed."	Listen supportively to negative feelings and neutralize unreasonable fears. Set realistic short-term goals. Build self-confidence. Recognize and reward positive comments and progress.
C. Constructive direction "This won't be easy, but we can do it."	Set broader and longer-term goals. Encourage involvement. Emphasize group problem solving and learning. Celebrate individual and group achievements. Prepare for bigger and better things.

Situation: The person *fears* and *dislikes* the change.	
Stage	**Managerial action steps**
1. Getting off on the wrong track "What a dumb idea!"	Be an advocate and a positive role model for the vision of a better way. Be a supportive listener and correct any misunderstanding.
2. Laughing it off "Just another wild idea that won't go anywhere. Don't worry about it."	Same as action step A above.
3. Growing self-doubt "I don't think I have what it takes."	Same as action step B above.
4. Buying in "Okay, I'll give this thing a try."	Encourage the person to let go of the past and look forward to a better future. Build personal commitment. Recognize and reward positive words and actions.
5. Constructive direction "This won't be easy, but we can do it."	Same as action step C above.

A Contingency Model for Getting Employees Through Changes

Contingency managers, once again, adapt their techniques to the situation. The response patterns in Figures 14.2 and 14.3 call for different managerial actions. Managerial action steps for both situations are listed in Table 14.1. When employees understand that stages B and 3 are normal and expected responses, they will be less apt to panic and more likely to respond favorably to managerial guidance through action steps C and 4 and 5.[13]

True or False?

_____ 1. According to the Nadler-Tushman model, anticipatory changes are planned changes for expected situations.

_____ 2. One type of change—tuning—involves *kaizen*, or continuous improvement.

_____ 3. Nadler and Tushman call re-creation "frame breaking" because it is the most risky type.

_____ 4. Response patterns tend to be similar when people either like changes or when they fear and dislike them.

_____ 5. When people like a proposed change, they typically begin with constructive direction.

Multiple Choice

_____ 6. What type of changes are planned and based on expected situations?

     a. Exponential   d. Incremental
     b. Anticipatory   e. Reactive
     c. Strategic

_____ 7. _____ change is not represented on either the vertical axis or horizontal axis of the Nadler-Tushman model.

     a. Incremental   d. Segmented
     b. Reactive   e. Anticipatory
     c. Strategic

Online Study Center
ACE the Test
ACE Practice Tests 14.1

_____ 8. According to the Nadler-Tushman model, what is the most common and least risky type of change?

     a. Re-creation   d. Adaptation
     b. Strategic   e. Tuning
     c. Reactive

_____ 9. Nadler and Tushman call re-orientation _____ because the organization is significantly redirected.

     a. adaptation   d. unfreezing
     b. frame bending   e. tuning
     c. frame breaking

_____ 10. _____ is typically an employee's first response when coping with a change he or she dislikes or fears.

     a. Low self-esteem
     b. Unrealistic optimism
     c. Getting off on the wrong track
     d. Laughing it off
     e. Self-doubt

_____ 11. If Ivana is given an assignment that she has dreaded and feared for weeks, she must reach the _____ step in the change-response cycle before successfully adjusting.

     a. laughing it off
     b. buying in
     c. understanding
     d. peer acceptance
     e. personal satisfaction

OVERCOMING RESISTANCE TO CHANGE

2   *List at least six reasons why employees resist change, and discuss what management can do about resistance to change.*

Dealing with change is an integral part of modern management.[14] Change expert Ichak Adizes puts it this way:

> *Living means solving problems, and growing up means being able to solve bigger problems.*
> *The purpose of management, leadership, parenting, or governing is exactly that: to solve today's problems and get ready to deal with tomorrow's problems. This is necessary because there is change. No management is needed when there are no problems, and there are no problems only when we are dead. To manage is to be alive, and to be alive means to experience change with the accompanying problems it brings.*[15]

Within the change typology just discussed, organizational change comes in all sizes and shapes. Often it's new and unfamiliar technology, such as the Internet. It could be a reorganization, a merger, a new pay plan, or perhaps a new performance appraisal program. Whatever its form, change is like a stone tossed into a still pond. The initial impact causes ripples to radiate in all directions, often with unpredictable consequences. A common consequence of change in organizations is resistance from those whose jobs are directly affected. Both rational and irrational resistance can bring the wheels of progress to a halt. Management faces the challenge of foreseeing and neutralizing resistance to change. The question is, how? To answer that question, we need to examine why employees resist change.

Why Do Employees Resist Change?

Employees resist change for many reasons.[16] The most common reasons are outlined in the following sections:

Surprise

Significant changes that are introduced on the spur of the moment or with no warning can create a threatening sense of imbalance in the workplace. Regarding this problem, an executive task force at J.C. Penney Co., the well-known retailer, recommended: "Schedule changes in measurable, comfortable stages. Too much, too soon can be counterproductive."[17]

Inertia

Many members of the typical organization desire to maintain a safe, secure, and predictable status quo. The bywords of this group are, "But we don't do things that way here." Technological inertia also is a common problem. Consider, for example, the history of the standard typewriter keyboard (referred to as the Qwerty keyboard because *Q, W, E, R, T,* and *Y* are the first six letters in the upper-left-hand corner).

> The ungainly layout of the Qwerty keyboard was introduced in 1873 to slow down typists so they wouldn't jam keys. That design imperative quickly disappeared, yet Qwerty has turned back all attempts—including one by its own inventor—to replace it with something faster. The productive cost? Undoubtedly billions of dollars.[18]

Thanks to resistance to change, the latest high-tech marvels in personal computing come out of the box today complete with an 1873-style keyboard! Supervisors and middle managers who fall victim to unthinking inertia can effectively kill change programs.

Misunderstanding/Ignorance/Lack of Skills

Without adequate introductory or remedial training, an otherwise positive change may be perceived in a negative light.

Emotional Side Effects

Those who are forced to accept on-the-job changes can experience a sense of powerlessness and even anger. The subsequent backlash can be passive (stalling, pretending to not understand) or active (vocal opposition, sabotage, or aggression).

Lack of Trust

Promises of improvement are likely to fall on deaf ears when employees do not trust management. Conversely, managers are unlikely to permit necessary participation if they do not trust their people.

REALITY CHECK 14.2

"The notion that workers resist change is just . . . silly. Employees will always change when the change makes them and their companies more successful and is consistent with a more enjoyable work experience."

Source: Jeffrey Pfeffer, "Tech Answers No Prayers," *Business 2.0,* 5 (January–February 2004): 58.

Questions: Do you agree or disagree? What is the take-away lesson for managers?

Fear of Failure

Just as most college freshmen have doubts about their chances of ever graduating, challenges presented by significant on-the-job changes can also be intimidating.

Personality Conflicts

Managers who are disliked by their people are poor conduits for change.

Poor Timing

In every work setting, internal and/or external events can conspire to create resentment about a particular change. For example, an otherwise desirable out-of-state transfer would only make things worse for an employee with an ailing elderly parent.

Lack of Tact

As we all know, it is not necessarily what is said that shapes our attitude toward people and events. *How* it is said is often more important. Tactful and sensitive handling of change is essential.

Threat to Job Status/Security

Because employment fulfills basic needs, employees can be expected to resist changes with real or imaginary impacts on job status or job security.

Breakup of Work Group

Significant changes can tear the fabric of on-the-job social relationships. Accordingly, members of cohesive work groups often exert peer pressure on one another to resist changes that threaten to break up the group.[19]

Competing Commitments

Employees may not have a problem with the change itself, but rather with how it disrupts their pursuit of other goals. Such competing commitments are often unconscious and need to be skillfully brought to the surface to make progress. "For example, overloaded employees may cooperate with a change if their managers lighten their load a bit or adjust their project deadlines."[20]

These reasons for resisting change help demonstrate that participation is not a panacea. For example, imagine the futility of trying to gain the enthusiastic support of a team of assembly-line welders for a robot that will eventually take over their jobs. In extreme form, each reason for resisting change can become an insurmountable barrier to genuine participation. Therefore, managers need a broad array of methods for dealing with resistance to change.

Strategies for Overcoming Resistance to Change

Only in recent years have management theorists begun to give serious attention to alternative ways of overcoming resistance to change.[21] At least six options, including participation, are available in this area:

1. *Education and communication.* This strategy is appealing because it advocates prevention rather than cure. The idea here is to help employees understand the true need for a change as well as the logic behind it. Various media

may be used, including face-to-face discussions, formal group presentations, or special reports or publications.

2. *Participation and involvement.* Once again, personal involvement through participation tends to defuse both rational and irrational fears about a workplace change. By participating in both the design and implementation of a change, one acquires a personal stake in its success.

3. *Facilitation and support.* When fear and anxiety are responsible for resistance to doing things in a new and different way, support from management in the form of special training, job stress counseling, and compensatory time off can be helpful. According to the CEO of Medtronic, this is how the heart pacemaker company facilitates employees' acceptance of a constant stream of product innovations:

> We set up venture teams of people who aren't emotionally invested in the old product. Once the new one has enough strength to stand on its own, we reintegrate the doubters. That's key. If you just tell them that "here's the new product," it demoralizes people. You have to go from the venture team to integrating it into the mainstream business.[22]

TABLE 14.2

Dealing with Resistance to Change

Approach	Commonly used in situations	Advantages	Drawbacks
1. **Education + communication**	Where there is a lack of information or inaccurate information and analysis	Once persuaded, people will often help with the implementation of the change	Can be very time-consuming if lots of people are involved
2. **Participation + involvement**	Where the initiators do not have all the information they need to design the change, and where others have considerable power to resist	People who participate will be committed to implementing change, and any relevant information they have will be integrated into the change plan	Can be very time-consuming if participators design an inappropriate change
3. **Facilitation + support**	Where people are resisting because of adjustment problems	No other approach works as well with adjustment problems	Can be time-consuming, expensive, and still fail
4. **Negotiation + agreement**	Where someone or some group will clearly lose out in a change, and where that group has considerable power to resist	Sometimes it is a relatively easy way to avoid major resistance	Can be too expensive in many cases if it alerts others to negotiate for compliance
5. **Manipulation + co-optation**	Where other tactics will not work or are too expensive	It can be a relatively quick and inexpensive solution to resistance problems	Can lead to future problems if people feel manipulated
6. **Explicit + implicit coercion**	Where speed is essential, and the change initiators possess considerable power	It is speedy, and can overcome any kind of resistance	Can be risky if it leaves people mad at the initiators

Source: Reprinted by permission of *Harvard Business Review.* From "Choosing Strategies for Change," by John P. Kotter and Leonard A. Schlesinger, March–April 1979. Copyright © 1979 by the Harvard Business School Publishing Corporation; all rights reserved.

4. *Negotiation and agreement.* Sometimes management can neutralize potential or actual resistance by exchanging something of value for cooperation. An hourly clerical employee may, for instance, be put on a salary in return for learning how to operate a new Internet workstation.

5. *Manipulation and co-optation.* Manipulation occurs when managers selectively withhold or dispense information and consciously arrange events to increase the chance that a change will be successful. Co-optation normally involves token participation. Those who are co-opted with token participation cannot claim they have not been consulted, yet the ultimate impact of their input is negligible.

6. *Explicit and implicit coercion.* Managers who cannot or will not invest the time required for the other strategies can try to force employees to go along with a change by threatening them with termination, loss of pay raises or promotions, transfer, and the like.

As shown in Table 14.2 on page 377, each of these strategies for overcoming resistance to change has advantages and drawbacks. Situational appropriateness is the key to success.

TEST PREPPER 14.2 ANSWERS CAN BE FOUND ON P. 393

True or False?

_____ 1. Surprise and inertia are among the most common reasons employees resist change.

_____ 2. In the facilitation-and-support strategy for overcoming resistance to change, negotiating for cooperation is involved.

_____ 3. When trying to get employees to overcome their resistance to change, it is never appropriate to rely on manipulation such as withholding information.

_____ 4. A major drawback of explicit and implicit coercion is that it can be risky if it leaves people mad at the initiators.

Multiple Choice

_____ 5. According to the text, which of the following is *not* a reason that employees resist change?
   a. Breakup of a work group
   b. Fear of failure
   c. Technophobia
   d. Emotional side effects
   e. Misunderstanding, ignorance, or lack of skills

_____ 6. What strategy should managers use for overcoming resistance to change if the concern is prevention rather than cure?
   a. Education and communication
   b. Explicit and implicit coercion
   c. Negotiation and agreement
   d. Manipulation and co-optation
   e. Participation and involvement

_____ 7. The _____ strategy for overcoming resistance to change would be most appropriate if an inventory specialist faced resistance to a new record-keeping technology because of fear and anxiety among employees.
   a. explicit and implicit coercion
   b. manipulation and co-optation
   c. negotiation and agreement
   d. education and involvement
   e. facilitation and support

_____ 8. When a speedy change is necessary, management should use which strategy for overcoming resistance to change?
   a. Education and communication
   b. Manipulation and co-optation
   c. Participation and involvement
   d. Explicit and implicit coercion
   e. Facilitation and support

Online Study Center
ACE the Test
ACE Practice Tests 14.2

MAKING CHANGE HAPPEN

 Explain the unfreezing-change-refreezing analogy in OD, describe a tempered radical, and identify the 5Ps in the checklist for grassroots change agents.

In these fast-paced times, managers need to be active agents of change rather than passive observers or, worse, victims of circumstances beyond their control. This active role requires foresight, responsiveness, flexibility, and adaptability.[23] In this section, we focus on two approaches to making change happen: (1) organization development, a formal top-down approach, and (2) grassroots change, an unofficial and informal bottom-up approach.

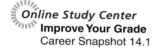

Online Study Center
Improve Your Grade
Career Snapshot 14.1

Planned Change Through Organization Development (OD)

Organization development has become a convenient label for a host of techniques and processes aimed at making sick organizations healthy and healthy organizations healthier.[24] According to experts in the field:

> **Organization development (OD)** *consists of planned efforts to help persons work and live together more effectively, over time, in their organizations. These goals are achieved by applying behavioral science principles, methods, and theories adapted from the fields of psychology, sociology, education, and management.*[25]

organization development (OD) Planned change programs intended to help people and organizations function more effectively.

Others simply call OD *planned change*. Regarding the degree of change involved, OD consultant and writer Warner Burke contends:

> *Organization development is a process of fundamental change in an organization's culture. By fundamental change, as opposed to fixing a problem or improving a procedure, I mean that some significant aspect of the organization's culture will never be the same.*[26]

OD programs generally are facilitated by hired consultants,[27] although inside OD specialists can also be found.[28]

The Objectives of OD

OD programs vary because they are tailored to unique situations. What is appropriate for one organization may be totally out of place in another. In spite of this variation, certain objectives are common to most OD programs. In general, OD programs develop social processes such as trust, problem solving, communication, and cooperation to facilitate organizational change and enhance personal and organizational effectiveness. More specifically, the typical OD program tries to achieve the following seven objectives:

1. Deepen the sense of organizational purpose (or vision) and align individuals with that purpose.
2. Strengthen interpersonal trust, communication, cooperation, and support.
3. Encourage a problem-solving rather than problem-avoiding approach to organizational problems.
4. Develop a satisfying work experience capable of building enthusiasm.
5. Supplement formal authority with authority based on personal knowledge and skill.
6. Increase personal responsibility for planning and implementing.
7. Encourage personal willingness to change.[29]

Critics of OD point out that there is nothing really new in this list of objectives. Directly or indirectly, each of these objectives is addressed by one or another general management technique. OD advocates respond by saying general management lacks a systematic approach. They claim the usual practice of teaching managers how to plan, solve problems, make decisions, organize, motivate, lead, and control leads to a haphazard, bits-and-pieces management style. According to OD thinking, organization development gives managers a vehicle for systematically introducing change by applying a broad selection of management techniques as a unified and consistent package. This, they claim, leads to greater personal, group, and organizational effectiveness.

The OD Process

A simple metaphor helps introduce the three major components of OD.[30] Suppose someone hands you a coffee cup filled with clear, solid ice. You look down through the ice and see a penny lying tails up on the bottom of the cup. Now suppose for some reason you want the penny to be frozen in place in a heads-up position. What can you do? There is really only one practical solution. You let the ice in the cup thaw, reach in and flip the penny over, and then refreeze the cup of water. This is precisely how social psychologist Kurt Lewin recommended that change be handled in social systems. Specifically, Lewin told change agents to unfreeze, change, and then refreeze social systems.[31]

Unfreezing prepares the members of a social system for change and then helps neutralize initial resistance. Sudden, unexpected change, according to Lewin, is socially disruptive. Patricia A. Woertz was mindful of the need for some unfreezing in 2006 when she gave up her position as the head of a 30,000-person, $100-billion-a-year unit at Chevron Corp. for a huge new challenge. As *Business Week* reported at the time:

> Now, Woertz, 53, is the new president and CEO of Archer Daniels Midland Co., the alpha male of agribusiness. No woman runs a bigger public company....
> Her first day at ADM..., Woertz held a town hall meeting. "I told them I'm not interested in making changes quickly," she says. "I'll be asking what people are afraid I'll do and what people are hoping I'll do."[32]

When the change has been introduced, **refreezing** is necessary to follow up on problems, complaints, unanticipated side effects, and any lingering resistance. This seemingly simple approach to change spells the difference between systematic and haphazard change.

The OD model introduced here is based on Lewin's approach to handling change (see Figure 14.4). Diagnosis is carried out during the unfreezing phase. Change is then carefully introduced through tailor-made intervention. Finally, a systematic follow-up refreezes the situation. Each phase is critical to successful organizational change and development. Still, it takes continual recycling through this three-phase sequence to make OD an ongoing system of planned change.

Unofficial and Informal Grassroots Change

OD is rationally planned, formal, systematic, and initiated by top management. As a sign of the times, many of today's organizations cannot be described in those terms. They tend to be spontaneous, informal, experimental, and driven from

unfreezing Neutralizing resistance by preparing people for change.

refreezing Systematically following up a change program for lasting results.

FIGURE 14.4

A General Model of OD

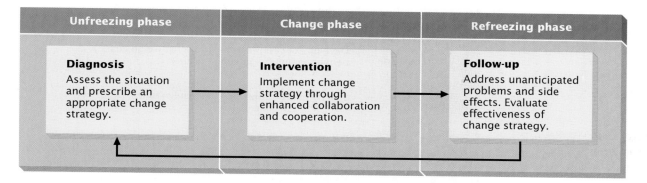

Unfreezing phase	Change phase	Refreezing phase
Diagnosis Assess the situation and prescribe an appropriate change strategy.	**Intervention** Implement change strategy through enhanced collaboration and cooperation.	**Follow-up** Address unanticipated problems and side effects. Evaluate effectiveness of change strategy.

within. (Interestingly, employees in some of these modern organizations were empowered by earlier OD programs.)[33] Unusual things can happen when empowered employees start to take the initiative. Consider the unconventional language in this recent description of change:

> *Change starts with finding a backer—someone who can sell your plan to the senior team. Change dies without a fighter—someone smart enough and skilled enough to win over the opposition. Change kicks in when people start to trust—in the plan and in one another. Trust is the glue that invariably holds a change effort together. Change just might work when people are focused—on the goal, and on each step that's necessary to achieve it.*
>
> *Getting the buy-in. Overcoming resistance. Building trust. Zeroing in on the objective. These are the critical skills that every change team must leverage if it is to have any hope of succeeding.*[34]

This is not top-down change in the tradition of OD. Rather, it involves change from inside the organization. Let us explore two perspectives of unofficial and informal grassroots change: tempered radicals and the 5P model.

Tempered Radicals

This intriguing term and the concept it embraces come from Stanford professor Debra E. Meyerson. She defines **tempered radicals** as

> *people who want to succeed in their organizations yet want to live by their values or identities, even if they are somehow at odds with the dominant culture of their organizations. Tempered radicals want to fit in and they want to retain what makes them different. They want to rock the boat, and they want to stay in it.*[35]

tempered radicals People who quietly try to change the dominant organizational culture in line with their convictions.

Meyerson's research has found many "square pegs in round holes" who identify powerfully with her concept of the tempered radical. They tend to work quietly yet relentlessly to advance their vision of a better organization and a better world. If progressive managers are to do a good job of managing diversity, then they need to handle their tempered radicals in win-win fashion. Too often those with different ideas are marginalized and/or trivialized. When this happens, the organization's intellectual and social capital suffer greatly.

FIGURE 14.5

The 5P Checklist for Change Agents

Key action steps	
✓ **P**reparation	Develop concept; test assumptions; weigh costs and benefits; identify champion or driver.
✓ **P**urpose	Specify measurable objectives, milestones, deadlines.
✓ **P**articipation	Refine concept while building broad and powerful support.
✓ **P**rogress	Keep things moving forward despite roadblocks.
✓ **P**ersistence	Foster realistic expectations and a sense of urgency while avoiding impatience.

Four practical guidelines for tempered radicals stem from Meyerson's research:

1. *Think small for big results.* Don't try to change the organization's culture all at once. Start small and build a string of steadily larger victories. Learn as you go. Encourage small, nonthreatening experiments. Trust and confidence in you and your ideas will grow with the victories.
2. *Be authentic.* Base your actions on your convictions and thoughtful preparation, not on rash emotionalism. Anger, aggression, and arrogance give people an easy excuse to dismiss you and your ideas.
3. *Translate.* Build managerial support by explaining the business case for your ideas.
4. *Don't go it alone.* Build a strong support network of family, friends, and coworkers to provide moral support and help advance your cause.[36]

The 5P Checklist for Grassroots Change Agents (Turning Ideas into Action)

The 5P model consists of an easy-to-remember list for anyone interested in organizational change: *preparation, purpose, participation, progress,* and *persistence* (see Figure 14.5). The model is generic, meaning it applies to all levels in profit and nonprofit organizations of all sizes. Let us examine each item more closely.

▎ *Preparation.* Is the concept or problem clearly defined? Has adequate problem *finding* taken place? Are underlying assumptions sound? Will the end result be worth the collective time, effort, and expense? Can the change initiative be harnessed to another change effort with a high probability of success, or should it stand alone? Does the proposed change have a *champion* or a *driver* who has the passion and persistence to see the process through to completion?

▎ *Purpose.* Can the objective or goal of the change initiative be expressed in clear, measurable terms? Can it be described quickly to busy people? What are the specific progress milestones and critical deadlines?

▌ *Participation.* Have key people been involved in refining the change initiative to the extent of having personal ownership and willingness to fight for it? Have potential or actual opponents been offered a chance to participate? Have powerful people in the organization been recruited as advocates and defenders?

▌ *Progress.* Are performance milestones and intermediate deadlines being met? If not, why? Is support for the initiative weakening? Why? Have unexpected roadblocks been encountered? How can they be removed or avoided?

▌ *Persistence.* Has a reasonable sense of urgency been communicated to all involved? (*Note:* Extreme impatience can fray relationships and be stressful.) Has the change team drifted away from the original objective as time passed? Does everyone on the team have realistic expectations about how long the change process will take?

With situational adjustments for unique personalities and circumstances, the 5P approach can help ordinary employees create extraordinary change.[37] So sharpen your concept and take your best shot!

TEST PREPPER 14.3

ANSWERS CAN BE FOUND ON P. 393

True or False?

_____ 1. According to the OD process, refreezing is necessary before the change has been introduced.

_____ 2. Grassroots change occurs from the top down, rather than from inside the organization.

_____ 3. "Think big for small results" is a practical guideline for tempered radicals.

_____ 4. Top-level managers are the only ones who use the 5P checklist for change agents.

_____ 5. "Planning" is one of the five Ps in the 5P checklist for change agents.

Multiple Choice

_____ 6. _____ is a good description of organization development (OD).
a. Frame bending
b. Employee renewal
c. Expectation shaping
d. Planned change
e. Organizational modification

_____ 7. To _____ is not one of the seven objectives of OD.
a. build trust and cooperation
b. encourage willingness to change
c. mentor young talent
d. increase personal responsibility for planning and implementing
e. encourage problem solving

_____ 8. In OD, _____ prepares the members of a social system for change and then helps neutralize initial resistance.
a. unfreezing
b. implementation
c. refreezing
d. intervention
e. adjustment

_____ 9. Which guideline for tempered radicals involves building managerial support by explaining the business case for ideas?
a. Be authentic.
b. Think small for big results.
c. Don't go it alone.
d. Translate.
e. Be exploitative.

_____ 10. Relative to the 5P checklist for change agents, measurable objectives, milestones, and deadlines are specified in which P?
a. Purpose
b. Persistence
c. Participation
d. Publication
e. Preparation

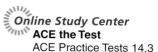

Online Study Center
ACE the Test
ACE Practice Tests 14.3

MANAGING CONFLICT

 Contrast the competitive and cooperative conflict styles, and identify five conflict resolution techniques.

Conflict is intimately related to change and interpersonal dealings. Harvard's Abraham Zaleznik offered this perspective:

> *Because people come together to satisfy a wide array of psychological needs, social relations in general are awash with conflict. In the course of their interactions, people must deal with differences as well as similarities, with aversions as well as affinities. Indeed, in social relations, Sigmund Freud's parallel of humans and porcupines is apt: like porcupines, people prick and injure one another if they get too close; they will feel cold if they get too far apart.[38]*

The term *conflict* has a strong negative connotation, evoking words such as *opposition, anger, aggression,* and *violence.*[39] But conflict does not have to be a negative experience. For example, this is how Chris Lofgren, CEO of the trucking firm Schneider National, views conflict:

> *Conflict between people or between groups of people is not positive. Conflict around business issues is the most wonderful, healthy thing. . . . Any business without tension will fall to its lowest level of performance.[40]*

Students who want to argue for a higher grade may not want to tackle this particular professor. He's Bruce Patton, who teaches conflict management seminars in Harvard Law School's Program on Negotiation. For better or for worse, he calls conflict "a growth industry." He advises managers not to waste their time minimizing conflict, but rather to harness it in creative and constructive ways. Now, about that grade.

FIGURE 14.6

Competitive Versus Cooperative Conflict

Source: (right figure): From *Learning to Manage Conflict: Getting People to Work Together Productively* by Dean Tjosvold, 1993. Reprinted with permission of Rowman & Littlefield Publishing Group.

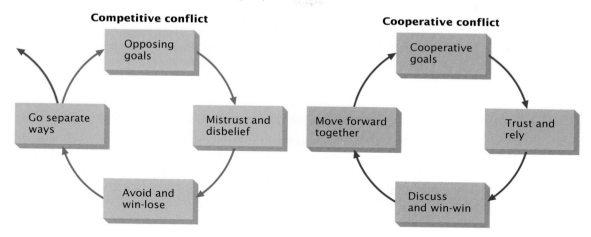

Based on research evidence that most organizational conflict occurs within a cooperative context, Dean Tjosvold offered this more positive definition: "**Conflict** involves incompatible behaviors; one person interfering, disrupting, or in some other way making another's actions less effective."[41] This definition paves the way for an important distinction between *competitive* (or destructive) conflict and *cooperative* (or constructive) conflict. Cooperative conflict is based on a win-win attitude. Also, recall our mention of cooperative conflict in Chapter 12 as a tool for avoiding groupthink.

conflict Incompatible behaviors that make another person less effective.

Dealing with the Two Faces of Conflict

Tjosvold contrasts competitive and cooperative conflict as follows:

> The assumption that conflict is based on opposing interests leads to viewing conflict as a struggle to see whose strength and interests will dominate and whose will be subordinated. We must fight to win, or at least not lose. The assumption that you have largely cooperative goals leads to viewing the conflict as a common problem to be solved for mutual benefit, which in turn makes it more likely that the conflict will be constructive and that people will improve their abilities to deal with conflict.[42]

Figure 14.6 graphically illustrates the difference between competitive and cooperative conflict. In the competitive mode, the parties pursue directly opposite goals. Each mistrusts the other's intentions and disbelieves what the other party says. Both parties actively avoid constructive dialogue and have a win-lose attitude. Unavoidably, the disagreement persists and they go their separate ways.[43] Does this self-defeating cycle sound familiar? Probably, because most of us at one time or another have suffered through a broken relationship or destructive conflict with someone else.

"You have to get people upset. When things get disruptive, people really get work done, and learning takes place."

Source: Fiona Haley, "Tough-Love Leadership," *Fast Company*, no. 86 (September 2004): 110.

Questions: Do you agree or disagree? How can managers stimulate healthy conflict without going too far?

In sharp contrast, the *cooperative* conflict cycle in Figure 14.6 is a mutually reinforcing experience that serves the best interests of both parties. Cooperative conflict is standard practice at Anheuser-Busch, brewer of Budweiser beer:

> When the policy committee of that company considers a major move—getting into or out of a business, or making a big capital expenditure—it sometimes assigns teams to make the case for each side of the question. There may be two teams or even three. Each is knowledgeable about the subject; each has access to the same information. Occasionally someone in favor of the project is chosen to lead the dissent, and an opponent to argue for it. Pat Stokes, who heads the company's beer empire, describes the result: "We end up with decisions and alternatives we hadn't thought of previously," sometimes representing a synthesis of the opposing views. "You become a lot more anticipatory, better able to see what might happen, because you have thought through the process."[44]

As a skill-building exercise, you might want to use the cooperative conflict model in Figure 14.6 to salvage a personal relationship mired in competitive conflict. Show the cooperative model to the other party and suggest starting over with a new set of ground rules. Cooperative goals are the necessary starting point. This process can be difficult, yet very rewarding. Win-win conflict is not just a good idea; it is one of the keys to career success and a better world (see Best Practices on page 390).

There are two sets of tools available for managing conflict.[45] The first we call *conflict triggers*, for stimulating conflict; the second involves *conflict resolution techniques*, used when conflict becomes destructive.

Conflict Triggers

conflict trigger Any factor that increases the chances of conflict.

A **conflict trigger** is a circumstance that increases the chances of intergroup or interpersonal conflict. As long as a conflict trigger appears to stimulate constructive conflict, it can be allowed to continue. But as soon as the symptoms of destructive conflict[46] become apparent, steps need to be taken to remove or correct the offending conflict trigger. Major conflict triggers include the following:

▌ *Ambiguous or overlapping jurisdictions.* Unclear job boundaries often create competition for resources and control. Reorganization can help to clarify job boundaries if destructive conflict becomes a problem (refer to the organization design alternatives discussed in Chapter 7).

▌ *Competition for scarce resources.* As the term is used here, *resources* include funds, personnel, authority, power, and valuable information. In other words, anything of value in an organizational setting can become a competitively sought-after scarce resource. Sometimes, as in the case of money and people, destructive competition for scarce resources can be avoided by enlarging the resource base (such as increasing competing managers' budgets or hiring additional personnel).[47]

▌ *Communication breakdowns.* Because communication is a complex process beset by many barriers, these barriers often provoke conflict. It is easy to misunderstand another person or group of people if two-way communication is hampered in some way. The battle for clear communication never ends, especially in the world of e-business where there is less direct person-to-person communication.[48]

■ *Time pressure.* Deadlines and other forms of time pressure can stimulate prompt performance or trigger destructive emotional reactions. When imposing deadlines, managers should consider individuals' ability to cope.

■ *Unreasonable standards, rules, policies, or procedures.* These triggers generally lead to dysfunctional conflict between managers and the people they manage. The best remedy is for the manager to tune into employees' perceptions of fair play and correct extremely unpopular situations before they mushroom.

■ *Personality clashes.* It is very difficult to change one's personality on the job. Therefore the practical remedy for serious personality clashes is to separate the antagonistic parties by reassigning one or both to a new job.[49]

■ *Status differentials.* As long as productive organizations continue to be arranged hierarchically, this trigger is unavoidable. But managers can minimize dysfunctional conflict by showing a genuine concern for the ideas, feelings, and values of lower-level employees.

■ *Unrealized expectations.* Dissatisfaction grows when expectations are not met. Conflict is another by-product of unrealized expectations. Destructive conflict can be avoided in this area by taking time to discover, through frank discussion, what people expect from their employment. Unrealistic expectations can be countered before they become a trigger for dysfunctional conflict.

Managers who understand these conflict triggers will be in a much better position to manage conflict in a systematic and rational fashion. Those who passively wait for things to explode before reacting will find conflict managing them.

Resolving Conflict

Even the best managers sometimes find themselves in the middle of destructive conflict, whether it is due to inattention or to circumstances beyond their control. In such situations, they may choose to do nothing, called an *avoidance* strategy by some, or try one or more of the following conflict resolution techniques.[50]

Problem Solving

When conflicting parties take the time to identify and correct the source of their conflict, they are engaging in problem solving. This approach is based on the assumption that causes must be rooted out and attacked if anything is really to change. Problem solving (refer to our discussion of creative problem solving in Chapter 6) encourages managers to focus their attention on causes, factual information, and promising alternatives rather than on personalities or scapegoats. The major shortcoming of the problem-solving approach is that it takes time, but the investment of extra time can pay off handsomely when the problem is corrected instead of ignored and allowed to worsen.

Superordinate Goals

"Superordinate goals are highly valued, unattainable by any one group [or individual] alone, and commonly sought."[51] When a manager relies on superordinate goals to resolve destructive conflict, he or she brings the conflicting parties together and, in effect, says, "Look, we're all in this together. Let's forget our differences so we can get the job done." For example, a company president might remind the

REALITY CHECK 14.5

"Couples who routinely trade nasty or controlling remarks during marital spats might be harming their hearts—and not just emotionally, a study suggests.

"The findings fit in with a body of research suggesting that hostile and domineering men and women are at risk of developing heart disease, the No. 1 killer in the USA."

Source: Kathleen Fackelmann, "Arguing Hurts the Heart in More Ways Than One," *USA Today* (March 6, 2006): 10D.

Question: What is the general life lesson here about how to deal more effectively with conflict?

production and marketing department heads who have been arguing about product design that the competition is breathing down their necks. Although this technique often works in the short run, the underlying problem tends to crop up later to cause friction once again.

Compromise

This technique generally appeals to those living in a democracy. Advocates of compromise say everyone wins because it is based on negotiation, on give and take.[52] However, most people do not have good negotiating skills. They approach compromise situations with a win-lose attitude. So compromises tend to be disappointing, leaving one or both parties feeling cheated. Conflict is only temporarily suppressed when people feel cheated. Successful compromise requires skillful negotiation.

Forcing

Sometimes, especially when time is important or a safety issue is involved, management must simply step into a conflict and order the conflicting parties to handle the situation in a certain manner. Reliance on formal authority and the power of a superior position is at the heart of forcing. As one might suspect, forcing does not resolve the conflict and, in fact, may serve to compound it by hurting feelings and/or fostering resentment and mistrust.

Smoothing

A manager who relies on smoothing says to the conflicting parties something like, "Settle down. Don't rock the boat. Things will work out by themselves." This approach may tone down conflict in the short run, but it does not solve the underlying problem. As with each of the other conflict resolution techniques, smoothing has its place. It can be useful when management is attempting to hold things together until a critical project is completed or when there is no time for problem solving or compromise and forcing is deemed inappropriate.

Problem solving and skillfully negotiated compromises are the only approaches that remove the actual sources of conflict. They are the only resolution techniques capable of improving things in the long run. The other approaches amount to short-run, stopgap measures. And managers who fall back on an avoidance strategy are simply running away from the problem. Nonetheless, as mentioned, problem solving and full negotiation sessions can take up valuable time, time that managers may not be willing or able to spend at the moment. When this is the case, management may choose to fall back on superordinate goals, forcing, or smoothing, whichever seems most suitable.[53]

TEST PREPPER 14.4

True or False?

_____ 1. Conflict, by definition, is a negative and destructive aspect of organizational life.

_____ 2. The competitive conflict mode is associated with a win-lose attitude.

_____ 3. In the cooperative conflict cycle, cooperative goals are essential.

_____ 4. A conflict trigger is a circumstance that increases the chances of intergroup or interpersonal conflict.

_____ 5. Common conflict triggers are personality clashes and time pressure.

_____ 6. Smoothing and superordinate goals are the only approaches that remove the actual sources of conflict.

Multiple Choice

_____ 7. The two faces of conflict are
   a. social and economic.
   b. short-term and long-term.
   c. competitive and cooperative.
   d. personal and social.
   e. static and dynamic.

Online Study Center
ACE the Test
ACE Practice Tests 14.4

_____ 8. Individuals involved in a cycle of competitive conflict typically have a(n) _____ attitude.
   a. win-win
   b. collective
   c. greedy
   d. win-lose
   e. altruistic

_____ 9. Personality clashes, communication breakdowns, and time pressure are
   a. superordinate goals.
   b. OD trouble spots.
   c. OD failure factors.
   d. constructive conflict.
   e. conflict triggers.

_____ 10. Which conflict resolution technique involves a time-consuming search for causes?
   a. Problem solving
   b. Superordinate goals
   c. Compromise
   d. Smoothing
   e. Forcing

_____ 11. Which conflict resolution strategy relies on formal authority and power?
   a. Problem solving
   b. Avoidance
   c. Compromise
   d. Smoothing
   e. Forcing

BEST PRACTICES

How to Express Anger

Although not every angry feeling should be expressed to the person held accountable, this approach is direct and has the most potential to initiate a productive conflict. There are several rules to keep in mind when expressing anger.

▮ *Check assumptions.* No matter how convinced employees are that someone has deliberately interfered and tried to harm them, they may be mistaken. People can ask questions and probe. It may be that the other person had no intention and was unaware that others were frustrated. The incident may just dissolve into a misunderstanding.

▮ *Be specific.* People find being the target of anger stressful and anxiety provoking. They fear insults and rejection. The more specific the angry person can be, the less threatening and less of an attack on self-esteem the anger is. Knowing what angered the other can give the target of the anger concrete ways to make amends.

▮ *Be consistent.* Verbal and nonverbal messages should both express anger. Smiling and verbally expressing anger confuses the issue.

▮ *Take responsibility for anger.* Persons expressing anger should let the target know that they are angry and . . . [why they] feel unjustly frustrated.

▮ *Avoid provoking anger.* Expressing anger through unfair, insinuating remarks ("I can't believe someone can be as stupid as you!") can make the target of the anger angry too. Such situations can quickly deteriorate.

▮ *Watch for impulsivity.* Anger agitates and people say things they later regret.

▮ *Be wary of self-righteousness.* People can feel powerful, superior, and right; angry people can play "Now I got 'ya and you will pay." But anger should be used to get to the heart of the matter and solve problems, not for flouting moral superiority.

▮ *Be sensitive.* People typically underestimate the impact their anger has on others. Targets of anger often feel defensive, anxious, and worried. It is not usually necessary to repeat one's anger to get people's attention.

▮ *Make the expression cathartic.* Anger generates energy. Telling people releases that energy rather than submerges it. Anger is a feeling to get over, not to hang on to.

▮ *Express positive feelings.* Angry people depend upon and usually like people they are angry with. People expect help from people who have proved trustworthy, and are angry when it is not forthcoming.

▮ *Move to constructive conflict management.* Feeling affronted, personally attacked, and self-righteous should not side-track you from solving the underlying problems. Use the anger to create positive conflict.

▮ *Celebrate joint success.* Anger tests people's skills and their relationship. Be sure to celebrate the mutual achievement of expressing and responding to anger successfully.

Source: Dean Tjosvold, *The Conflict-Positive Organization* (pp. 133–134). © 1991. Reprinted by permission of Pearson Education, Inc., Upper Saddle River, New Jersey.

The Unstoppable Entrepreneur

"We've never done it that way before." In these hyper-competitive times, it's hard to believe people utter such words. Yet Bob Schmonsees hears that excuse with maddening frequency.

His small software firm, WisdomWare Inc., has developed a slick tool that makes salespeople better informed and more efficient. But it requires them—and their bosses—to do things just a little bit differently, and the wall of resistance looms high. "The good news is we've got something that's truly visionary," he says. "That's also the bad news."

But Mr. Schmonsees, 51 years old, as you'll soon see, has plenty of experience scaling huge obstacles. And although his story is intensely personal, it holds lessons for anyone facing an uphill climb in business.

As a high-tech sales manager in the 1970s, Mr. Schmonsees made a priority of protecting salespeople from the endless white papers, binders, and other epistles churned out by marketing types. Each quarter, he condensed a mountain of documents into a pocket-sized booklet that crisply summarized what a sales rep needed to know about the product, the market, and the competition.

Then came disaster. A contender in mixed-doubles tennis and a former football star, Mr. Schmonsees was standing near a ski lift when an out-of-control skier rammed him. His legs were paralyzed. He would spend the rest of his life in a wheelchair.

Fortunately, he discovered a formula for his different world: figure out the new rules for any activity, then take as many small steps as necessary to master those rules. After learning the physics of a tennis swing on wheels and the geometry of playing a second bounce (standard rules), he became the world's top wheelchair player over age 40.

No number of steps, however, could change the behavior of others. The sudden wariness of his former colleagues drove him from the company he loved. Then came many crushing job rejections. But after landing in a junior supervisory position in software sales, he climbed to top marketing management. Later, switching to software vendor Legent Corp., he became global sales chief. "Finally, I was back to where I should have been," he says, though once again it had taken many small steps.

As always, he worked to keep his sales staff informed but not inundated. This was a losing battle by the 1990s, with electronic libraries of marketing material growing like digital kudzu. Pondering this problem one day in the shower, he thought back to those little leatherbound digests he used to hand out.

Why not put something like that online? Even more important, why not enable every piece of information to link with any other piece? That way, salespeople could assemble just the right combination of facts necessary for the task of the moment.

Moving forward with an engineering team, Mr. Schmonsees created the interactive equivalent of Cliffs Notes. While planning a call, a sales rep makes a few menu choices to identify the customer, the product, and the like. One click creates the most up-to-date qualifying questions, another reveals how the competition stacks up, another reports the most common objections, still another suggests an "elevator speech" for precisely those circumstances. Though only a few concise sentences pop on the screen, detailed reports are just a click away.

Mr. Schmonsees left Legent in late 1995. But in his own effort at selling the new product, he ran smack into a powerful objection.

The issue wasn't training; that takes five minutes. Nor was it compatibility; WisdomWare works seamlessly with other front-office software. Neither has any customer winced at the price of $500 and up per user.

The problem was culture. WisdomWare requires marketing managers to write snappy summaries in addition to (or instead of) their beloved white papers. "We've never done it that way!" came the reply.

"When this becomes part of your culture, it's a real competitive advantage," says Dan Gillis, president of SAGA Software, which embraces WisdomWare. "But it takes a real commitment."

The culture of the field force is another hurdle. Users love the encapsulated, up-to-date information that comes to the screen. But WisdomWare depends on those same users to provide intelligence from the field: what the competition is up to, for instance, and which pitches are getting the best and worst results. Sharing information? "We've never had to do *that* before!" came the cry.

Platinum Technology, for one, equipped its sales force of 1,000 with WisdomWare in January [1999]. And

CLOSING CASE STUDY (CONTINUED)

although efficiencies are already evident, too few sales-people are giving back information. Platinum's Glenn Shimkus is now searching for ways to reward contributors. "We have to change the culture so that power and rewards come from sharing information, not from hoarding it," he says.

With 20 employees, Mr. Schmonsees is grinding out orders one at a time, counting 10 customers to date. And despite the slow takeoff, the company's venture-capital backers are about to step up for another round. Eventually, the product will run on a hand-held, wireless device that sales reps will consult on their way into sales calls—then use to submit feedback on their way out.

Mr. Schmonsees concedes that the business, for now, is behind his expectations. "It's going to take some time to change the world," he says. But as a metaphor for business, his personal life encourages him. "I take pride in taking a lot of little steps toward a long-term vision," he says.

Source: From *Wall Street Journal* by Thomas Petzinger, Jr., "Bob Schmonsees Has a Tool for Better Sales, and It Ignores Excuses," March 26, 1999. Copyright © 1999 by Dow Jones & Company, Inc. Reproduced with permission of Dow Jones & Company, Inc. via Copyright Clearance Center.

Case Questions

1. Why is Schmonsees uniquely qualified to fight resistance to change?
2. Which of the reasons discussed in this chapter that account for employees' resistance to change are evident in this case? Explain.
3. Using Table 14.2 on page 377 as a guide, which strategy (or strategies) should Schmonsees use to overcome resistance to WisdomWare? Explain.
4. What lessons from OD apply to this case? Explain.
5. What lessons from the 5P checklist for change agents apply to this case? Explain.

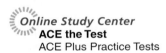

Online Study Center
ACE the Test
ACE Plus Practice Tests

Online Study Center
Improve Your Grade
Learning Objective Review
Audio Chapter Review
Audio Chapter Quiz
Study Guide to Go

LEARNING OBJECTIVE REVIEW

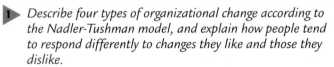 *Describe four types of organizational change according to the Nadler-Tushman model, and explain how people tend to respond differently to changes they like and those they dislike.*

- Nadler and Tushman's model identifies four types of organizational change that result from the interaction of anticipatory and reactive change with incremental and strategic change. Four resulting types of change are:
  - Tuning; *kaizen* (preventive maintenance, continuous improvement)
  - Adaptation (changes in reaction to external problems)
  - Re-orientation (frame bending, redirection of an organization)
  - Re-creation (frame breaking, intense and risky change)

- People who like a change tend to go through three stages: unrealistic optimism, reality shock, and constructive direction.

- When someone fears or dislikes a change, a more complex process involving five stages tends to occur:
  - Getting off on the wrong track
  - Laughing it off
  - Growing self-doubt
  - Buying in
  - Constructive direction

- Managers are challenged to help employees deal effectively with reality shock and self-doubt.

 List at least six reasons why employees resist change, and discuss what management can do about resistance to change.

- Employees resist change for many different reasons, including (but not limited to):
  - Surprise
  - Inertia
  - Misunderstanding/ Ignorance/ Lack of-skills
  - Emotional side effects
  - Lack of trust
  - Fear of failure
  - Personality conflicts
  - Poor timing
  - Lack of tact
  - Threat to job status/ Security
  - Breakup of work group
  - Competing commitments

- Modern managers facing resistance to change can select from several strategies, including education and communication, participation and involvement, facilitation and support, negotiation and agreement, manipulation and co-optation, and explicit and implicit coercion.

3 ▶ *Explain the unfreezing-change-refreezing analogy in OD, describe a tempered radical, and identify the 5Ps in the checklist for grassroots change agents.*

- Organization development (OD) is a systematic approach to planned organizational change.

- The principal objectives of OD are increased trust, better problem solving, more effective communication, improved cooperation, and greater willingness to change.

- The typical OD program is a three-phase process of unfreezing, change, and refreezing.
  - During unfreezing, the situation is diagnosed and a change strategy is prescribed.
  - In the next phase, the change is introduced.
  - The refreezing phase involves dealing with unanticipated problems and evaluating the effectiveness of the change strategy.

- Unofficial and informal grassroots change can be initiated by tempered radicals, who quietly follow their convictions when trying to change the dominant organizational culture.

- Four guidelines for tempered radicals are (1) think small for big results, (2) be authentic, (3) translate, and (4) don't go it alone.

- The 5P checklist for grassroots change include:
  - Preparation (develop concept, test assumptions, weigh costs and benefits)
  - Purpose (specify measurable objectives, milestones, deadlines)
  - Participation (refine concept while building support)
  - Progress (keep things moving forward despite roadblocks)
  - Persistence (foster realistic expectations and a sense of urgency)

4 ▶ *Contrast the competitive and cooperative conflict styles, and identify five conflict resolution techniques.*

- Competitive conflict is characterized by a destructive cycle of opposing goals, mistrust and disbelief, and avoidance and a win-lose attitude. On the other hand, cooperative conflict involves a constructive cycle of cooperative goals, trust and reliance, and discussion and a win-win attitude.

- Conflict triggers can cause either constructive or destructive conflict.

- Destructive conflict can be resolved through problem solving, superordinate goals, compromise, forcing, or smoothing.

TEST PREPPER ANSWERS

▶ **14.1**

1. T   2. T   3. T   4. F   5. F   6. b   7. d
8. e   9. b   10. c   11. b

▶ **14.2**

1. T   2. F   3. F   4. T   5. c   6. a   7. e
8. d

▶ **14.3**

1. F   2. F   3. F   4. F   5. F   6. d   7. c
8. a   9. d   10. a

▶ **14.4**

1. F   2. T   3. T   4. T   5. T   6. F   7. c
8. d   9. e   10. a   11. e

Online Study Center RESOURCES

Prepare for Class, Improve Your Grade, and ACE the Test. Student Achievement Series resources include:

ACE Practice Tests	Crossword Puzzles	Hangman
Audio Chapter Quizzes	Decision Case Questions	Key Issue Expansion
Audio Chapter Reviews	Ethical Hot Seat Exercises	Learning Objective Reviews
Career Snapshots	Flashcards	Study Guide to Go
Chapter Glossaries	Hands-on Exercises	Visual Glossaries
Chapter Outlines		

To access these learning and study tools, go to **college.hmco.com/pic/kreitnerSASfound**.

REFERENCES

Chapter 1

1. Excerpted from "Leadership for the 21st Century: Leading the Way," *Newsweek*, September 25, 2006, p. 60.
2. Joan Magretta, *What Management Is: How It Works and Why It's Everyone's Business* (New York: The Free Press, 2002), p. 7.
3. See Andrew Molinsky and Joshua Margolis, "The Emotional Tightrope of Downsizing: Hidden Challenges for Leaders and Their Organizations," *Organizational Dynamics*, 35, no. 2 (2006): 145–159; Bill Nichols, "Hard Lesson Learned at Red Cross," *USA Today* (June 6, 2006): 3A; and Harry Maurer, "Brother, Can You Spare $18 Billion?" *Business Week* (December 11, 2006): 34.
4. Ellen Van Velsor and Jean Brittain Leslie, "Why Executives Derail: Perspectives Across Time and Cultures," *Academy of Management Executive*, 9 (November 1995): 63. For a related study, see Frank Shipper and John E. Dillard Jr., "A Study of Impending Derailment and Recovery of Middle Managers Across Career Stages," *Human Resource Management*, 39 (Winter 2000): 331–345. Also see Joel Schettler, "It's What You Don't Know," *Training*, 40 (January 2003): 19.
5. Linda Grant, "Rambos in Pinstripes: Why So Many CEOs Are Lousy Leaders," *Fortune* (June 24, 1996): 147.
6. See Roderick M. Kramer, "The Great Intimidators," *Harvard Business Review*, 84 (February 2006): 88–96; and Jack and Suzy Welch, "Send the Jerks Packing," *Business Week* (November 13, 2006): 136.
7. Data from Jay Greene, "The Soul of a New Microsoft," *Business Week* (December 4, 2006): 58.
8. See, for example, Mara Der Hovanesian, "The Bank of Technology," *Business Week* (June 19, 2006): 54; and Kenji Hall, "No One Does Lean Like the Japanese," *Business Week* (July 10, 2006): 40–41.
9. Peter Greenberg, as quoted in Kitty Bean Yancey, "Peek Under the Wing at Airline Secrets," *USA Today* (October 13, 2006): 6D. Also see Roger Yu, "Get Used to Seeing Turned-Up Wing Tips," *USA Today* (June 6, 2006): 10B.
10. Data from Victoria Markham, "America's Supersized Footprint," *Business Week* (October 30, 2006): 132. Also see James E. Ellis, "No Sacrifices, Please," *Business Week* (May 22, 2006): 63; and Saheli S.R. Datta, "Spinning Straw into Black Gold," *Business 2.0*, 7 (November 2006): 108–110.
11. Data from "How Much the Global Population Grows," *USA Today* (April 14, 2004): 1A.
12. Data from Margie Mason, "World Populace Will Max Out, Study Finds," *USA Today* (August 2, 2001): 8D.
13. For example, see Elizabeth Weise, "Food Scientists Warn of Looming Fish Shortage," *USA Today* (November 4, 2002): 7D.
14. Diane Brady, "Wanted: Eclectic Visionary with a Sense of Humor," *Business Week* (August 28, 2000): 143. Also see Harry G. Barkema, Joel A. C. Baum, and Elizabeth A. Mannix, "Management Challenges in a New Time," *Academy of Management Journal*, 45 (October 2002): 916–930; and Geoffrey Colvin, "Managing in Chaos," *Fortune* (October 2, 2006): 76–82.
15. Quoted from "About McDonald's," www.mcdonalds.com, December 10, 2006.
16. Data from Robert Barker, "Why Things May Go Better with Coke," *Business Week* (February 10, 2003): 89.
17. Data from Robert J. Samuelson, "The Oil Factor," *Newsweek* (May 8, 2006): 37. Also see Stanley Reed, "Why You Should Worry About Big Oil," *Business Week* (May 15, 2006): 66–78; Peter Coy, "Can't Stop Guzzling," *Business Week* (July 31, 2006): 26–29; Erica S. Downs, "How Oil Fuels Sino-U.S. Fires," *Business Week* (September 4, 2006): 102; and Mark Morrison, "Plenty of Oil—Just Drill Deeper," *Business Week* (September 18, 2006): 38.
18. Data from Monica Gagnier, "3M's Sticky Situation," *Business Week* (November 1, 2004): 48.
19. Diane E. Lewis, "Jobs Offshoring Here to Stay," *Arizona Republic* (October 17, 2004): D1. Also see Peronet Despeignes, "Offshoring: A Reality Check," *Fortune* (June 27, 2005): 29; Jack and Suzy Welch, "Outsourcing is Forever," *Business Week* (July 31, 2006): 88; Manjeet Kripalani, "Call Center? That's So 2004," *Business Week* (August 7, 2006): 40–41; and Steve Hamm and Dawn Kopecki, "Rethinking the Safety of Software Coded Over There," *Business Week* (November 13, 2006): 14.
20. For more, see Kee Young Kim, Jeffrey G. Miller, and Janelle Heineke, "Mastering the Quality Staircase, Step by Step," *Business Horizons*, 40 (January–February 1997): 17–21; Lin Grensing-Pophal, "Building Service with a Smile," *HR Magazine*, 51 (November 2006): 84–89; Frances X. Frei, "Breaking the Trade-Off Between Efficiency and Service," *Harvard Business Review*, 84 (November 2006): 92–101; and Charles Fishman, "No Satisfaction," *Fast Company*, no. 111 (January 2007): 82–92.
21. See Jerry Adler, Going Green," *Newsweek* (July 17, 2006): 42–52; John Carey, "Business on a Warmer Planet," *Business Week* (July 17, 2006): 26–29; Stanley Holmes, "Nike Goes for the Green," *Business Week* (September 25, 2006): 106, 108; and Kathryn Tyler, "Going Green," *HR Magazine*, 51 (October 2006): 99–104.
22. William McDonough and Michael Braungart, *Cradle to Cradle: Remaking the Way We Make Things* (New York: North Point Press, 2002), pp. 15–16. For a brief overview, see Brian Dumaine, "Mr. Natural," *Fortune* (October 29, 2002): 184, 186.
23. Data from Gene Koretz, "On Wall Street, Green Is Golden," *Business Week* (January 8, 2001): 30.
24. Keith Naughton, "The CEO Party Is Over," *Newsweek* (January 6, 2003): 55. Also see Lynn Paine, Rohit Deshpande, Joshua D. Margolis, and Kim Bettcher, "Up to Code: Does Your Company's Conduct Meet World-Class Standards?" *Harvard Business Review*, 83 (December 2005): 122–133; Edwin A. Locke, "Business Ethics: A Way Out of the Morass," *Academy of Management Learning and Education*, 5 (September 2006): 324–332; and Ann Pomeroy, "Ethics and Compliance Field is Booming," *HR Magazine*, 51 (December 2006): 14, 16.
25. Julie Amparano, "As Ethics Crisis Grows, Businesses Take Action," *The Arizona Republic* (November 24, 1996): D9. Also see Scott Westcott, "Are Your Staffers Stealing? How to Prevent Employee Theft and Protect Your Bottom Line," *Inc.*, 28 (October 2006): 33–35; and Emily Thornton, "Gluttons at the Gate," *Business Week* (October 30, 2006): 58–66.
26. See Janet Kornblum, "First U.S. Web Page Went Up 10 Years Ago," *USA Today* (December 11, 2001): 3D.
27. "Worldwide Internet Users Top 1 Billion in 2005," *Computer Industry Almanac Press Release* (January 4, 2006), www.c-i-a.com.
28. For updates about Web technology and issues, see Erick Schonfeld, "Web 2.0 Around the World," *Business 2.0*, 7 (August 2006): 105–106; Patricia Sellers, "Myspace Cowboys," *Fortune* (September 4, 2006): 66–74; Oliver Ryan, "Don't Touch That Dial," *Fortune* (September 4, 2006): 76–77; Sarah Lacy, "Web Numbers: What's Real?" *Business Week* (October 23, 2006): 98–103; Jeffrey M. O'Brien, "You're Soooooooooo Predictable," *Fortune* (November 27, 2006): 224–234; and David H. Freedman, "Everyone is Chasing Internet Buzz. But Be Careful. Online Hype Doesn't Always Deliver," *Inc.*, 28 (December 2006): 81–82.
29. Dot-com wreckage is discussed in Eric Hellweg, "Excite.com—99.85% Off!!!" *Business 2.0*, 3 (January 2002): 18; and Jon Swartz, "Dot-Commers Buy Back Start-Ups at Bargain Prices," *USA Today* (January 22, 2002): 1B.
30. See Brian Caulfield, "Toward a More Perfect (and Realistic) EBusiness," *Business 2.0*, 3 (January 2002): 77–84; Paul Hemp, "Are You Ready for E-tailing 2.0?" *Harvard Business Review*, 84 (October 2006): 28; and Robert D. Hof, "Jeff Bezos' Risky Bet," *Business Week* (November 13, 2006): 52–58.
31. As quoted in Cheryl Dahle, "Putting Its Chips on the Net," *Fast Company*, no. 48 (July 2001): 154.

32. See Henri Fayol, *General and Industrial Management,* trans. Constance Storrs (London: Isaac Pitman & Sons, 1949).

33. See Scott Adams, *The Dilbert Principle* (New York: Harper-Business, 1996); and Lisa A. Burke and Jo Ellen Moore, "Contemporary Satire of Corporate Managers: Time to Cut the Boss Some Slack?" *Business Horizons,* 42 (July–August 1999): 63–67.

34. "AMA Research," *Management Review,* 85 (July 1996): 10. Also see Ann Pomeroy, "Middle Managers Unhappy," HR Magazine, 51 (July 2006): 16.

35. Henry Mintzberg, "The Manager's Job: Folklore and Fact," *Harvard Business Review,* 53 (July–August 1975): 54. Also see William B. Werther, "From Manager to Executive," *Organizational Dynamics,* 35, no. 2 (2006): 196–204.

36. Trends in higher education are discussed in Michael Schrage, "Brave New World for Higher Education," *Technology Review,* 104 (October 2001): 90–91; William C. Symonds, "Giving It the Old Online Try," *Business Week* (December 3, 2001): 76–80; Warren G. Bennis and James O'Toole, "How Business Schools Lost Their Way," *Harvard Business Review,* 83 (May 2005): 96–104; and Scott D. Julian and Joseph C. Ofori-Dankwa, "Is Accreditation Good for the Strategic Decision Making of Traditional Business Schools?" *Academy of Management Learning and Education,* 5 (June 2006): 225–233.

37. See Stanley Bing, "Ego," *Fortune* (February 17, 2003): 164; and Christopher Palmeri, "Putting Managers to the Test," *Business Week* (November 20, 2006): 82.

38. See Ron Zemke, "The Honeywell Studies: How Managers Learn to Manage," *Training,* 22 (August 1985): 46–51.

39. Adapted from Robin Snell, "Graduating from the School of Hard Knocks?" *Journal of Management Development,* 8, no. 5 (1989): 23–30. For a look at one manager's experiences in the school of hard knocks, see Paula Lehman, "A Clear Road to the Top," *Business Week* (September 18, 2006): 72.

40. See Charles R. Stoner and John F. Gilligan, "Leader Rebound: How Successful Managers Bounce Back from the Tests of Adversity," *Business Horizons,* 45 (November–December 2002): 17–24; Milton R. Blood, "Only *You* Can Create Actionable Knowledge," *Academy of Management Learning and Education,* 5 (June 2006): 209–212; Kathy Chu, "Discover CEO Nelms Seeks Opportunities for Growth," *USA Today* (August 28, 2006): 3B; and James Michael Brodie, "Getting Managers on Board," *HR Magazine,* 51 (November 2006): 105–108.

41. Jim Hopkins, "PCs, Immigrants Help Launch Millions of Little Firms," *USA Today* (October 30, 2002): 1B.

42. Data from Jim Hopkins, "Small Businesses Not Making Full Use of the Web," *USA Today* (August 28, 2001): 1B.

43. Data from Jim Hopkins, "Small Businesses Hold Off on Big Purchases," *USA Today* (October 16, 2001): 1B. Also see Renuka Rayasam, "Credit: Entrepreneurs Find It's in the Cards," *U.S. News and World Report,* 141 (October 2, 2006): 62.

44. Data from Jim Hopkins, "New Bosses Should Develop Management Skills," *USA Today* (September 12, 2001): 9B; and Jim Hopkins, "Micro-Businesses Targeted as Source of Sales Revenue," *USA Today* (April 3, 2001): 1B. Also see Stephen Covey, "Small Business, Big Opportunities," *Training,* 43 (November 2006): 40.

45. See George Gendron, "The Failure Myth," *Inc.,* (January 2001): 13; and Ryan D'Agostino, "Road Trip to Riches," *Money,* 35 (September 2006): 85–91.

46. See David R. Francis, "Spiking Stereotypes About Small Firms," *The Christian Science Monitor* (May 7, 1993): 9; Gene Koretz, "A Surprising Finding on New-Business Mortality Rates," *Business Week* (June 14, 1993): 22; and James Aley, "Debunking the Failure Fallacy," *Fortune* (September 6, 1993): 21. For related reading, see Sydney Finkelstein, "The Myth of Managerial Superiority in Internet Startups: An Autopsy," *Organizational Dynamics,* 30 (Fall 2001): 172–185.

47. Data from Larry Light, "Small Business: The Job Engine Needs Fuel," *Business Week* (March 1, 1993): 78.

48. Data from Charles Burck, "Where Good Jobs Grow," *Fortune* (June 14, 1993): 22. Also see Gene Koretz, "Where the New Jobs Are," *Business Week* (March 20, 1995): 24.

49. For more on Birch's research, see Alan Webber, "Business Race Isn't Always to the Swift, but Bet That Way," *USA Today* (February 3, 1998): 15A. Also see "The Gazelle Theory," *Inc.,* 23 (May 29, 2001): 28–29.

50. For data on pay in big companies versus small companies, see Michael Mandel, "Big Players Offer Better Pay," *Business Week* (August 30, 1999): 30.

51. See "You Incorporated," *Business 2.0,* 3 (January 2003): 141–142; Mary Kwak, "The Advantages of Family Ownership," MIT Sloan Management Review, 44 (Winter 2003): 12; and Erin Ryan, "Little Initials for Firm's Name Can Make a Big Difference," *Arizona Republic* (July 30, 2006): D5.

52. See Surinder Tikoo, "Assessing the Franchise Option," *Business Horizons,* 39 (May–June 1996): 78–82; and Carleen Hawn, "Blessed Are the Sandwich Makers," *Business 2.0,* 6 (September 2005): 124.

53. Jim Hopkins, "Minority Businesses Boom," *USA Today* (July 29, 2005): 5B. See Anna Kuchment, "Moms Mean Business," *Newsweek* (September 25, 2006): 66. See recent issues of *Inc., Fast Company,* and *Business 2.0* magazines for inspiring small-business success stories. For example, see Robert Levine, "How to Build a Startup Out of Nothing," *Business 2.0,* 7 (August 2006): 66; Michael Fitzgerald, "Losing Your Lunch and Finding Your Vision: How We Did It," *Inc.,* 28 (December 2006): 116, 118; and Linda Tischler, "Fast Talk: Karen Walker, Fashion Designer," *Fast Company,* no. 111 (January 2007): 38–39.

54. Howard H. Stevenson and J. Carlos Jarillo, "A Paradigm of Entrepreneurship: Entrepreneurial Management," *Strategic Management Journal,* 11 (Summer 1990): 23 (emphasis added). For practical advice, see Michael V. Copeland, "How to Make Your Business Plan the Perfect Pitch," *Business 2.0,* 6 (September 2005): 88; Michael V. Copeland and Om Malik, "How to Build a Bulletproof Startup," *Business 2.0,* 7 (June 2006): 76–92; and Dirk De Clercq, Vance H. Fried, Oskari Lehtonen, and Harry J. Sapienza, "An Entrepreneur's Guide to the Venture Capital Galaxy," *Academy of Management Perspectives,* 19 (August 2006): 90–111.

55. See Hao Zhao and Scott E. Seibert, "The Big Five Personality Dimensions and Entrepreneurial Status: A Meta-Analytical Review," *Journal of Applied Psychology,* 91 (March 2006): 259–271; S. Trevis Certo, Samuel C. Certo, and Christopher R. Reutzel, "Spotlight on Entrepreneurship," *Business Horizons,* 49 (July–August 2006): 265–268; Catherine M. Dalton, "Recipe for Success: An Interview with Marla Gottschalk, President and Chief Executive Officer of the Pampered Chef," *Business Horizons,* 49 (September–October 2006): 353–357; and Jim Melloan, "The Big Picture," *Inc.,* 28 (September 2006): 138–139.

56. Norm Brodsky, "The X Factor," *Inc.,* 23 (September 2001): 84.

57. Stephanie Armour, "UBUBU Boldly Launches Start-Up in Cyberspace," *USA Today* (June 19, 2000): 3B. Also see Mark Morrison, "For Small-Biz Owners, It's Tough to Let Go," *Business Week* (July 24, 2006): 65; and Thea Singer, "Our Companies, Ourselves: Can You Separate Yourself from Your Business?" *Inc.,* 28 (November 2006): 38–40.

58. Steven Berglas, "*G* is for *Guts,*" *Inc.,* 22 (May 2000): 45.

59. See Warren Boeker and Rush Karichalil, "Entrepreneurial Transitions: Factors Influencing Founder Departure," *Academy of Management Journal,* 45 (August 2002): 818–826; and John Hamm, "Why Entrepreneurs Don't Scale," *Harvard Business Review,* 80 (December 2002): 110–115.

Chapter 2

1. As quoted in Betsy Morris, "The New Rules," *Fortune* (July 24, 2006): 84. Also see Geoff Colvin, "Lafley and Immelt: In Search of Billions," *Fortune* (December 11, 2006): 70–72.

2. Excerpted from Jacqueline Durett, "Oldest? Youngest? Who Cares?" *Training,* 43 (November 2006): 15.

3. Based on Kenji Hall, "Better Than Robots," *Business Week* (December 26, 2005): 46–47; Paul Wiseman, "Wave of Retiring Workers Could Force Big Changes," *USA Today* (May 3, 2006): 1B–2B; and Robert J. Samuelson, "The End of Motherhood?" *Newsweek* (May 29, 2006): 39.

4. Stephen Baker, "The Coming Battle for Immigrants," *Business Week* (August 26, 2002): 138, 140. Also see Haya El Nasser, "A Nation of 300 Million," *USA Today* (July 5, 2006): 1A, 6A.

5. Stephanie Armour, "Cupid Finds Work As Office Romance No Longer Taboo," *USA Today* (February 11, 2003): 1B.

6. For a good overview of U.S. populations changes, see Silla Brush, "A Nation in Full," *U.S. News and World Report,* 141 (October 2, 2006): 46–57.

7. Janet Kornblum, "A Nation of Caregivers," *USA Today* (April 6, 2004): 6D. Also see Grace A. Odums, "A New Year's Resolution: Optimize Older Workers," *Training + Development*, 60 (January 2006): 34–36; Jonathan A. Segal, "Time Is on Their Side," *HR Magazine*, 51 (February 2006): 129–133; Stephen Covey, "Asking the Age-Old Question," *Training*, 43 (June 2006): 56; and Sandra Block and Stephanie Armour, "Many Americans Retire Before They Want To," *USA Today* (July 10, 2006): 1A–2A.

8. Mark Yost, "GE Focuses on Fridges from Bottom Freezer Up," *USA Today* (November 29, 2002): 10B.

9. Data from Edward Iwata, "Immigrants Courted as Good Customers," *USA Today* (May 11, 2006): 3B. Also see Erica Sagon, "Fry's Launches Market Tailored to Hispanics," *Arizona Republic* (July 4, 2006): D1, D3.

10. Barbara Hagenbaugh, "Women's Pay Suffers Setback vs. Men's," *USA Today* (August 27, 2004): 4B.

11. Data from Aaron Bernstein, "Women's Pay: Why the Gap Remains a Chasm," *Business Week* (June 14, 2004): 58–59.

12. Data from "Female Managers Still Earn Less, GAO Says," *USA Today* (January 24, 2002): 1B. Also see Margery Weinstein, "Sex and Money," *Training*, 43 (November 2006): 26–27.

13. See Jonathan A. Segal, "Shatter the Glass Ceiling, Dodge the Shards," HR Magazine, 50 (April 2005): 121–126; and Sylvia Ann Hewlett, Carolyn Buck Luce, and Cornel West, "Leadership in Your Midst: Tapping the Strength of Minority Executives," *Harvard Business Review*, 83 (November 2005): 74–82.

14. Ann M. Morrison and Mary Ann Von Glinow, "Women and Minorities in Management," *American Psychologist*, 45 (February 1990): 200 (emphasis added).

15. Data from Elizabeth Woyke, "Glass Ceilings: Corner Office Crawl," *Business Week* (December 4, 2006): 14. Also see Susan Berfield, "From One Male Bastion to Another," *Business Week* (May 15, 2006): 38; Theresa Howard, "Pepsico Names Nooyi its First Female CEO," *USA Today* (August 15, 2006): 1B; Eugenia Levenson, Christopher Tkaczyk, and Jia Lynn Yang, "50 Most Powerful Women," *Fortune* (October 16, 2006): 145–154; Andrea Stone, "Pelosi to be First Woman to Lead Congress," *USA Today* (November 9, 2006): 6A; and Constance E. Helfat, Dawn Harris, and Paul J. Wolfson, "The Pipeline to the Top: Women and Men in the Top Executive Ranks of U.S. Corporations," *Academy of Management Perspectives*, 20 (November 2006): 42–64.

16. Alison M. Konrad and Vicki W. Kramer, "How Many Women Do Boards Need?" *Harvard Business Review*, 84 (December 2006): 22. Also see Barbara Kantrowitz, Holly Peterson, and Karen Breslau, "Leading the Way," *Newsweek* (September 25, 2006): 44–60.

17. As quoted in Rhonda Richards, "More Women Poised for Role As CEO," *USA Today* (March 26, 1996): 2B. Also see Dawn S. Carlson, K. Michele Kacmar, and Dwayne Whitten, "What Men Think They Know About Women Executives," *Harvard Business Review*, 84 (September 2006): 28.

18. Data from Robert Levering and Milton Moskowitz, "100 Best Companies to Work For," *Fortune* (January 20, 2003): 152.

19. Ying Lowrey, "Women in Business, 2006: A Demographic Review of Women's Business Ownership," *Small Business Research Summary*, no. 280 (August 2006), www.sba.gov/advo. Also see Jim Hopkins, "African-American Women Step Up in Business World," *USA Today* (August 24, 2006): 3B.

20. Stephanie Armour, "Job Hunt Gets Harder for African-Americans," *USA Today* (December 9, 2002): 1B.

21. "Nearly 1 in 7 Workers Foreign Born," *USA Today* (April 17, 2006): 1B.

22. Tamara Henry, "Societal Shifts Could Alter Education by Midcentury," *USA Today* (February 26, 2001): 6D.

23. Dave Patel, "Minority Rules," *HR Magazine*, 46 (July 2001): 168.

24. As quoted in Stephanie Armour, "Welcome Mat Rolls Out for Hispanic Workers," *USA Today* (April 12, 2001): 2B.

25. Data from Del Jones, "Setting Diversity's Foundation in the Bottom Line," *USA Today* (October 15, 1996): 4B.

26. See Jon Birger and Jenny Mero, "Shaking the Foundation," *Fortune* (June 12, 2006): 30.

27. See Mike Hofman, "It Takes All Kinds," *Inc.*, 23 (July 2001): 70–75.

28. For example, see Jonathan Hickman, "America's 50 Best Companies for Minorities," *Fortune* (July 8, 2002): 110–120.

29. Jack McDevitt, "Are We Becoming a Country of Haters?" *USA Today* (September 2, 1992): 9A. Also see Robin J. Ely, Debra E. Meyerson, and Martin N. Davidson, "Rethinking Political Correctness," *Harvard Business Review*, 84 (September 2006): 78–87.

30. Adapted from Sheryl Hilliard Tucker and Kevin D. Thompson, "Will Diversity = Opportunity + Advancement for Blacks?" *Black Enterprise*, 21 (November 1990): 50–60; and Lee Gardenswartz and Anita Rowe, "Important Steps for Implementing Diversity Training," *Mosaics*, 8 (July–August 2002): 5. Also see Kathryn Tyler, "Financial Fluency," *HR Magazine*, 51 (July 2006): 76–81.

31. Research support can be found in Joseph J. Martocchio, "Age-Related Differences in Employee Absenteeism: A Meta-Analysis," *Psychology and Aging*, 4 (December 1989): 409–414.

32. Douglas T. Hall and Victoria A. Parker, "The Role of Workplace Flexibility in Managing Diversity," *Organizational Dynamics*, 22 (Summer 1993): 8.

33. Megan Rooney, "Freshmen Show Rising Political Awareness and Changing Social Views," *Chronicle of Higher Education* (January 31, 2003): A35.

34. See Michael D. Eisner, "Critics of Disney's America on Wrong Track," *USA Today* (July 12, 1994): 10A; and Steve Marshall and Carrie Dowling, "Disney Abandons Va. Site," *USA Today* (September 29, 1994): 1A.

35. Julie Schmit, "Baptists Threaten to Boycott Disney," *USA Today* (June 13, 1996): 1A.

36. Ibid.

37. For example, see Allan Sloan, "Laying Enron to Rest," *Newsweek* (June 5, 2006): 224–30; Bethany McLean and Peter Elkind, "The Guiltiest Guys in the Room," *Fortune* (June 12, 2006): 26–28; Bethany McLean and Peter Elkind, "Death of a Disgraced Salesman," *Fortune* (July 24, 2006): 30–32; and Harry Maurer, "Hoosegow Watch," *Business Week* (October 9, 2006): 34.

38. David B. Yoffie and Mary Kwak, "Playing by the Rules," *Harvard Business Review*, 79 (June 2001): 119–120. Also see George Parloff, "Intel's Worst Nightmare," *Fortune* (August 21, 2006): 60–70.

39. Drawn from S. Prakash Sethi, "Serving the Public Interest: Corporate Political Action for the 1980s," *Management Review*, 70 (March 1981): 8–11. Also see Michael D.Watkins, "Government Games," *MIT Sloan Management Review*, 44 (Winter 2003): 91–95.

40. See Eamon Javers, "When Pork-Barrel Pols Aren't Enough," *Business Week* (June 12, 2006): 68, 71.

41. Data from Evan Thomas, "Decline and Fall," *Newsweek* (November 20, 2006): 60–65.

42. Sandra Sobiera, "Bush Signs Corporate Fraud Crackdown Bill," www.azcentral.com (July 31, 2002): 1. For updates, see David Henry, "A SarbOx Surprise," *Business Week* (June 12, 2006): 38; Paul Falcone, "Reporting for SOX Duty," *HR Magazine*, 51 (June 2006): 161–168; David Henry, "Slipping Past the SEC," *Business Week* (June 19, 2006): 52; Andy Serwer, "Stop Whining About SarbOx!" *Fortune* (August 7, 2006): 39; and Annette L. Nazareth, "Keeping SarbOx is Crucial," *Business Week* (November 13, 2006): 134.

43. Data from Nicholas Varchaver, "Long Island Confidential," *Fortune* (November 27, 2006): 172–186; and Christopher Palmeri, "One of Them Is Still Laughing," *Business Week* (October 30, 2006): 13.

44. Roger Parloff, "Is Fat the Next Tobacco?" *Fortune* (February 3, 2003): 52. Also see "Edict of the Week," *Business Week* (December 18, 2006): 37.

45. Marianne M. Jennings and Frank Shipper, *Avoiding and Surviving Lawsuits* (San Francisco: Jossey-Bass, 1989), p. 118 (emphasis added). Also see Jathan Janove, "In Defense of Litigation," *HR Magazine*, 51 (May 2006): 125–129; Deborah Stead, "The Big Picture," *Business Week* (November 27, 2006): 13; and Ann Pomeroy, "Corporate Lawsuits Part of Doing Business," *HR Magazine*, 51 (December 2006): 14.

46. See Jeff Rasley, "The Revolution You Won't See on TV," *Newsweek* (November 25, 2002): 13.

47. John R. Allison, "Easing the Pain of Legal Disputes: The Evolution and Future of Reform," *Business Horizons*, 33 (September–October 1990): 15. For more, see F. Peter Phillips, "Ten Ways to Sabotage Dispute Management," *HR Magazine*, 49 (September 2004): 163–168; and John Parauda and Jathan Janove, "Settle for Less," *HR Magazine*, 49

(November 2004): 135–139. Also see Alison Stein Wellner, "Making Amends," *Inc.*, 28 (June 2006): 41–42.

48. Dave Patel, "Location, Location, Location," *HR Magazine*, 46 (November 2001): 168.

49. Data from 1998–1999 *Occupational Outlook Handbook*, September 1999 (stats.bls.gov/oco/oco2003.htm). Also see "Education and Earnings," *USA Today* (December 10, 2002): 1B.

50. Data from Gene Koretz, "A D+ for Dismal Scientists," *Business Week* (September 25, 1995): 25. Also see Roben Farzad, "A Frank Look at the Economy," *Business Week* (August 28, 2006): 14.

51. See Robert J. Samuelson, "Optimists—Or Just Dreamers?" *Newsweek* (January 14, 2002): 39.

52. For an informative discussion of the value of economic forecasting, see Peter L. Bernstein and Theodore H. Silbert, "Are Economic Forecasters Worth Listening To?" *Harvard Business Review*, 62 (September–October 1984): 32–40. Also see Margaret Popper, "No Confidence in These Indexes," *Business Week* (January 28, 2002): 26.

53. Lawrence S. Davidson, "Knowing the Unknowable," *Business Horizons*, 32 (September–October 1989): 7.

54. Michael Mandel, "Can Anyone Steer This Economy?" *Business Week* (November 20, 2006): 58.

55. John Naisbitt and Patricia Aburdene, *Megatrends 2000* (New York: William Morrow, 1990), p. 21. Also see Patricia Aburdene, *Megatrends 2010: The Rise of Conscious Capitalism* (Charlottesville, Va.: Hampton Roads, 2005).

56. Thomas A. Stewart, "Welcome to the Revolution," *Fortune* (December 13, 1993): 67. Also see Janet Guyon, "The American Way," *Fortune* (November 26, 2001): 114–120; and Margaret Popper, "The Payoff from Free Trade," *Business Week* (June 24, 2002): 26.

57. Michael J. Mandel, "From America: Boom—and Bust," *Business Week* (January 28, 2002): 26. Also see Robert J. Samuelson, "Terror's Economics," *Newsweek* (August 28, 2006): 57.

58. Data from "What is CHIPS?" www.chips.org, December 12, 2006.

59. Data from "World's Largest Corporations," *Fortune* (July 24, 2006): 113–126; Toyota advertisement, *Business Week* (August 30, 2004): 144; and www.toyota.com. Also see Charles Fishman, "No Satisfaction," *Fast Company*, no. 111 (January 2007): 82–92.

60. Del Jones, "Foreign Firms Snap Up U.S. Rivals," *USA Today* (March 7, 2001): 6B.

61. Pete Engardio, Aaron Bernstein, and Manjeet Kripalani, "Is Your Job Next?" *Business Week* (February 3, 2003): 53. Also see Michael G. Harvey and Milorad M. Novicevic, "The World is Flat: A Perfect Storm for Global Business?" *Organizational Dynamics*, 35, no. 3 (2006): 207–219; Pankaj Ghemawat, "Globalization: Apocalypse Now?" *Harvard Business Review*, 84 (October 2006): 32; and Ann E. Harrison and Margaret S. McMillan, "Dispelling Some Myths about Offshoring," *Academy of Management Perspectives*, 20 (November 2006): 6–22.

62. Jerome B. Wiesner, "Technology and Innovation," in *Technological Innovation and Society*, ed. Dean Morse and Aaron W. Warner (New York: Columbia University Press, 1966), p. 11.

63. Walter Kiechel III, "How We Will Work in the Year 2000," *Fortune* (May 17, 1993): 39. Also see Willem F. G. Mastenbroek, "Organizational Innovation in Historical Perspective: Change As Duality Management," *Business Horizons*, 39 (July–August 1996): 5–14.

64. For good reading on innovation, see Tom Kelley, *The Ten Faces of Innovation* (N.Y.: Currency Doubleday, 2005); Scott D. Anthony, Matt Eyring, and Lib Gibson, "Mapping Your Innovation Strategy," *Harvard Business Review*, 84 (May 2006): 104–113; Charles Dhanaraj and Arvind Parkhe, "Orchestrating Innovation Networks," *Academy of Management Review*, 31 (July 2006): 659–669; C. Brooke Dobni, "The Innovation Blueprint," *Business Horizons*, 49 (July–August 2006): 329–339; Timothy J. Hargrave and Andrew H. Van de Ven, "A Collective Action Model of Institutional Innovation," *Academy of Management Review*, 31 (October 2006): 864–888; and Rosabeth Moss Kanter, "Innovation: The Classic Traps," *Harvard Business Review*, 84 (November 2006): 72–83.

65. Brian Dumaine, "Closing the Innovation Gap," *Fortune* (December 2, 1991): 57.

66. Craig Barrett, "Good Times and Bad, Innovation Is Key," *Information Week* (January 27, 2003): 21.

67. Based on Stratford Sherman, "When Laws of Physics Meet Laws of the Jungle," *Fortune* (May 15, 1995): 193–194.

68. Joseph Weber, "Quick, Save the Ozone," *Business Week* (May 17, 1993): 78. For a graphic snapshot of how long it takes consumers to adopt new electronic technologies, see "New Technologies Take Time," *Business Week* (April 19, 1999): 8.

69. David Whitford, "A Human Place to Work," *Fortune* (January 8, 2001): 110. Medtronic's employee data from "Fortune 500 Largest U.S. Corporations," *Fortune* (April 17, 2006): F-57.

70. Robert J. Herbold, "Inside Microsoft: Balancing Creativity and Discipline," *Harvard Business Review*, 80 (January 2002): 73–74.

71. See Morgan L. Swink, J. Christopher Sandvig, and Vincent A. Mabert, "Adding 'Zip' to Product Development: Concurrent Engineering Methods and Tools," *Business Horizons*, 39 (March–April 1996): 41–49; and Bob Filipczak, "Concurrent Engineering: A Team by Any Other Name?" *Training*, 33 (August 1996): 54–59.

72. See Timothy D. Schellhardt, "David and Goliath," *Wall Street Journal* (May 23, 1996): R14; and Saj-Nicole A. Joni, C. Gordon Bell, and Heidi Mason, "Innovations from the Inside," *Management Review*, 86 (September 1997): 49–53.

73. See Gifford Pinchot III, *Intrapreneuring* (New York: Harper & Row, 1985), p. xvii.

74. Tim Smart, "Kathleen Synnott: Shaping the Mailrooms of Tomorrow," *Business Week* (November 16, 1992): 66.

75. Vince Luchsinger and D. Ray Bagby, "Entrepreneurship and Intrapreneurship: Behaviors, Comparisons, and Contrasts," *SAM Advanced Management Journal*, 52 (Summer 1987): 12. For related reading, see David A. Garvin and Lynne C. Levesque, "Meeting the Challenge of Corporate Entrepreneurship," *Harvard Business Review*, 84 (October 2006): 102–112.

Chapter 3

1. Muhammad Yunus, "Seek Big Rewards in Small Ideas," *Business 2.0*, 7 (December 2006): 100.

2. "15 People Who Make America Great," *Newsweek*, July 3–10, 2006, p. 56.

3. "The Big Picture," *Business Week* (November 6, 2006): 13. Also see Lindsey Gerdes, "Get Ready for a Pickier Workforce," *Business Week* (September 18, 2006): 82; and "College Students Take Lead in Volunteering," *USA Today* (October 17, 2006): 9D.

4. Susie Gharib, "Last Word," *Nightly Business Report* (September 22, 2006), www.pbs.org/nbr/site/onair/transcripts/060922d/.

5. Thomas A. Stewart, "Corporate Social Responsibility: Getting the Logic Right," *Harvard Business Review*, 84 (December 2006): 14. Also see Patricia Aburdene, *Megatrends 2010: The Rise of Conscious Capitalism* (Charlottesville, Va.: Hampton Roads, 2005): Naomi A. Gardberg and Charles J. Fombrun, "Corporate Citizenship: Creating Intangible Assets Across Institutional Environments," *Academy of Management Review*, 31 (April 2006): 329–346; and Christia Gibbons, "Doing Well by Doing Good," *Arizona Republic* (June 11, 2006): D1, D7.

6. Thomas M. Jones, "Corporate Social Responsibility Revisited, Redefined," *California Management Review*, 22 (Spring 1980): 59–60. Also see Michael E. Porter and Mark R. Kramer, "Strategy and Society," *Harvard Business Review*, 84 (December 2006): 78–92; and Clayton M. Christensen, Heiner Baumann, Rudy Ruggles, and Thomas M. Sadtler, "Disruptive Innovation for Social Change," *Harvard Business Review*, 84 (December 2006): 94–101.

7. Sir Richard Branson, "Making the Skies Green," *Newsweek* (December 18, 2006): 48. Also see Steve Hamm, "A Passion for the Planet," *Business Week* (August 21–28, 2006): 92–94; and Jenny Barchfield, "Denim Showing Its Do-Good Side," *Arizona Republic* (December 8, 2006): D5.

8. Jones, "Corporate Social Responsibility Revisited," p. 65.

9. These arguments have been adapted in part from Jones, "Corporate Social Responsibility Revisited," p. 61; and Keith Davis and William C. Frederick, *Business and Society: Management, Public Policy, and Ethics*, 5th ed. (New York: McGraw-Hill, 1984), pp. 28–41. Also see Betsy Morris, "The New Rules," *Fortune* (July 24, 2006): 70–87; Jack and Suzy Welch, "Whose Company Is It Anyway?" *Business Week* (October

9, 2006): 122; and Pete Engardio, "Karma Capitalism," *Business Week* (October 30, 2006): 84–91.

10. See I. A. Jawahar and Gary L. McLaughlin, "Toward a Descriptive Stakeholder Theory: An Organizational Life Cycle Approach," *Academy of Management Review,* 26 (July 2001): 397–414; Alfred Rappaport, "10 Ways to Create Shareholder Value," *Harvard Business Review,* 84 (September 2006): 66–77; and Angelo Fanelli and Vilmos F. Misangyi, "Bringing Out Charisma: CEO Charisma and External Stakeholders," *Academy of Management Review,* 31 (October 2006): 1049–1061.

11. Davis and Frederick, *Business and Society,* p. 34.

12. As quoted in Aaron Bernstein, "Bracing for a Backlash," *Business Week* (February 4, 2002): 34. Also see Geoff Colvin, "Lafley and Immelt: In Search of Billions," *Fortune* (December 11, 2006): 70–72; and Geoff Lafley, "On the Hot Seat," *Fortune* (December 11, 2006): 75–82.

13. Drawn from Ian Wilson, "What One Company Is Doing About Today's Demands on Business," in *Changing Business-Society Interrelationships,* ed. George A. Steiner (Los Angeles: UCLA Graduate School of Management, 1975).

14. Gary Boulard, "Combating Environmental Racism," *Christian Science Monitor* (March 17, 1993): 8. For updates, see Dennis Cauchon, "Racial, Economic Divide in La.," *USA Today* (September 9, 1997): 3A; Paul Hoversten, "EPA Puts Plant on Hold in Racism Case," *USA Today* (September 11, 1997): 3A; Traci Watson, "La. Town Successful in Stopping Plastics Plant," *USA Today* (September 18, 1998): 7A; and Lorraine Woellert, "Dumping on the Poor?" *Business Week* (November 19, 2001): 120–121.

15. Mike France, "The World War on Tobacco," *Business Week* (November 11, 1996): 100. Also see John Carey, "Big Tobacco Blows Some Smoke," *Business Week* (August 14, 2000): 8; and Paul Raeburn, "Blowing Smoke over Ventilation," *Business Week* (May 7, 2001): 72–73.

16. Bruce Horovitz, "Wendy's Will Be 1st Fast Foodie with Healthier Oil," *USA Today* (June 8, 2006): 2B. Also see Harry Maurer, "Sic Transit Trans Fat?" *Business Week* (June 26, 2006): 32; Michael Arndt, "Out, Damned Trans Fats!" *Business Week* (July 31, 2006): 12; Bruce Horovitz and Laura Petrecca, "Disney to Make Food Healthier for Kids," *USA Today* (October 17, 2006): 1B; and "Healthier Chicken?" *Business Week* (November 13, 2006): 33.

17. Geoff Colvin, "The 100 Best Companies to Work For," *Fortune* (January 23, 2006): 102.

18. See Robert Berner, "Cheap Chic," *Business Week* (August 21–28, 2006): 14; Scott Boeck, "Sneaker Attack," *USA Today* (November 1, 2006): 8C; and "Work in Progress: The *Fast Company*/Monitor Group Social Capitalist Awards," *Fast Company,* no. 111 (January 2007): 67–81.

19. See Vincent Jeffries, "Virtue and the Altruistic Personality," *Sociological Perspectives,* 41, no. 1 (1998): 151–166.

20. Based on Joseph Weber, "3M's Big Cleanup," *Business Week* (June 5, 2000): 96–98.

21. Data from Michael V. Russo and Paul A. Fouts, "A Resource- Based Perspective on Corporate Environmental Performance and Profitability," *Academy of Management Journal,* 40 (June 1997): 534–559. Also see Douglas A. Schuler and Margaret Cording, "A Corporate Social Performance-Corporate Financial Performance Behavioral Model for Consumers," *Academy of Management Review,* 31 (July 2006): 540–558.

22. Based on Daniel B. Turban and Daniel W. Greening, "Corporate Social Performance and Organizational Attractiveness to Prospective Employees," *Academy of Management Journal,* 40 (June 1996): 658–672.

23. Data from Marc Bain, "Donating Our Dollars and Hours," Newsweek (July 3–10, 2006): 65. Also see Elliot Blair Smith, "Buffett Pledges $37.1B to Charity," *USA Today* (June 26, 2006): 1A; Michelle Conlin, "Philanthropy: Shop (In the Name of Love)," *Business Week* (October 2, 2006): 9; Russ Juskalian, "878-Page Tome Offers New Insights on Carnegie," *USA Today* (October 23, 2006): 8B; and Suzanne Woolley and Bremen Leak, "The Top Givers," *Business Week* (November 27, 2006): 72–80.

24. Louis W. Fry, Gerald D. Keim, and Roger E. Meiners, "Corporate Contributions: Altruistic or For-Profit?" *Academy of Management Journal,* 25 (March 1982): 105. Also see David Bright, "Virtuousness Is

25. Necessary for Genuineness in Corporate Philanthropy," *Academy of Management Review,* 31 (July 2006): 752–754.

26. For complete details, see Richard E. Wokutch and Barbara A. Spencer, "Corporate Saints and Sinners: The Effects of Philanthropic and Illegal Activity on Organizational Performance," *California Management Review,* 29 (Winter 1987): 62–77. Also see Kimberly D. Elsbach and Robert I. Sutton, "Acquiring Organizational Legitimacy Through Illegitimate Actions: A Marriage of Institutional and Impression Management Theories," *Academy of Management Journal,* 35 (October 1992): 699–738.

26. Data from Michael E. Porter and Mark R. Kramer, "The Competitive Advantage of Corporate Philanthropy," *Harvard Business Review,* 80 (December 2002): 56–68. See Susan Orenstein, "The Selling of Breast Cancer," *Business 2.0,* 4 (February 2003): 88–94.

27. Thomas A. Fogarty, "Corporations Use Causes for Effect," *USA Today* (November 10, 1997): 7B. More examples of enlightened self-interest can be found in Bruce Einhorn, "In Search of a PC for the People," *Business Week* (June 12, 2006): 40–41; and Jeff Nachtigal, "It's Easy and Cheap Being Green," *Fortune* (October 16, 2006): 53.

28. For examples, see Peter Burrows, "Stalking High-Tech Sweatshops," *Business Week* (June 19, 2006): 62–63; Stephanie Armour, "More Companies Offer Benefits to Domestic Partners," *USA Today* (June 29, 2006): 1B; Rajiv Kashyap, Raza Mir, and Easwar Iyer, "Toward a Responsive Pedagogy: Linking Social Responsibility to Firm Performance Issues in the Classroom," *Academy of Management Learning and Education,* 5 (September 2006): 366–376; and Jeanette Borzo, "From Lands' End to Fair Trade," *Business 2.0,* 7 (December 2006): 31.

29. See Ronald W. Clement, "Just How Unethical is American Business?" *Business Horizons,* 49 (July–August 2006): 313–327

30. See Harry R. Weber, "Three Charged with Stealing Trade Secrets from Coke," *USA Today* (July 6, 2006): 6B; Michael Orey, "Corporate Snoops," *Business Week* (October 9, 2006): 46–49; Harry Maurer, "Options Watch," *Business Week* (October 30, 2006): 32; Emily Thornton, "Gluttons at the Gate," *Business Week* (October 30, 2006): 58–66; and Peter Burrows, "In the Valley, Scars that Could Last a Long Time," *Business Week* (October 30, 2006): 82.

31. Shoshana Zoboff, "From Subject to Citizen," *Fast Company,* no. 82 (May 2004): 104.

32. Data from Karen Colteryahn and Patty Davis, "8 Trends You Need to Know Now," *Training and Development,* 58 (January 2004): 28–36. Also see Deborah Stead, "The Big Picture," *Business Week* (June 19, 2006): 13.

33. An excellent resource book is LaRue Tone Hosmer, *Moral Leadership in Business* (Burr Ridge, Ill.: Irwin, 1994). Also see Edwin A. Locke, "Business Ethics: A Way Out of the Morass," *Academy of Management Learning and Education,* 5 (September 2006): 324–332.

34. See Rushworth M. Kidder, "Tough Choices: Why It's Getting Harder to Be Ethical," *The Futurist,* 29 (September–October 1995): 29–32.

35. See W. Edward Stead, Dan L. Worrell, and Jean Garner Stead, "An Integrative Model for Understanding and Managing Ethical Behavior in Business Organizations," *Journal of Business Ethics,* 9 (March 1990): 233–242; Robert Elliott Allinson, "A Call for Ethically-Centered Management," *Academy of Management Executive,* 9 (February 1995): 73–76; and Dawn-Marie Driscoll, "Don't Confuse Legal and Ethical Standards," *Business Ethics,* 10 (July–August 1996): 44.

36. O. C. Ferrell and John Fraedrich, *Business Ethics: Ethical Decision Making and Cases* (Boston: Houghton Mifflin, 1991), pp. 10–11. Also see Barbara Ettorre, "Temptation of Big Money," *Management Review,* 85 (February 1996): 13–17; and "The Ethical Dilemma," *Selling Power* (March 1996): 32, 34.

37. Business ethics research findings are reviewed in Phillip V. Lewis, "Defining 'Business Ethics': Like Nailing Jell-O to a Wall," *Journal of Business Ethics,* 4 (October 1985): 377–383. Also see William A. Kahn, "Toward an Agenda for Business Ethics Research," *Academy of Management Review,* 15 (April 1990): 311–328; Gene R. Laczniak, Marvin W. Berkowitz, Russell G. Brooker, and James P. Hale, "The Ethics of Business: Improving or Deteriorating?" *Business Horizons,* 38 (January–February 1995): 39–47; and J (Hans) Van Oosterhout, Pursey P.M.A.R. Heugens, and Muel Kaptein, "The Internal Morality

of Contracting: Advancing the Contractualist Endeavor in Business Ethics," *Academy of Management Review,* 31 (July 2006): 521–539.

38. Del Jones, "48% of Workers Admit to Unethical or Illegal Acts," *USA Today* (April 4, 1997): 1A. Also see Jacqueline Durett, "Will That Fax Machine Fit in Your Briefcase?" *Training,* 43 (August 2006): 12; Jacqueline Durett, "And Just Where Do You Think You're Going with That Stapler?" *Training,* 43 (October 2006): 17; and Scott Westcott, "Are Your Staffers Stealing? How to Prevent Employee Theft and Protect Your Bottom Line," *Inc.,* 28 (October 2006): 33–35.

39. Jones, "48% of Workers Admit to Unethical or Illegal Acts," p. 2A. Also see Sharon Jones, "Teens Face Up to Ethics Choices—If You Can Believe Them," *USA Today* (December 6, 2006): 6D.

40. As quoted in Julia Flynn, "Did Sears Take Other Customers for a Ride?" *Business Week* (August 3, 1992): 24.

41. Based on Kelley Holland, "Sears Settles Up with the Feds," *Business Week* (February 22, 1999): 45; and John McCormick, "The Sorry Side of Sears," *Newsweek* (February 22, 1999): 36–39.

42. For more recent cases, see Ian Mount, "Out of Control," *Business 2.0,* 3 (August 2002): 38–44; and "Sandy Weill: Citigroup," *Business Week* (January 13, 2003): 78. Also see Christine A. Henle, "Bad Apples or Bad Barrels? A Former CEO Discusses the Interplay of Person and Situation With Implications for Business Education," *Academy of Management Learning and Education,* 5 (September 2006): 346–355.

43. William Rudelius and Rogene A. Buchholz, "Ethical Problems of Purchasing Managers," *Harvard Business Review,* 57 (March–April 1979): 12. Also see Alan J. Dubinsky, Eric N. Berkowitz, and William Rudelius, "Ethical Problems of Field Sales Personnel," *MSU Business Topics,* 28 (Summer 1980): 11–16; James R. Davis, "Ambiguity, Ethics, and the Bottom Line," *Business Horizons,* 32 (May–June 1989): 65–70; and "Cheating Hearts," *USA Today* (February 15, 2001): 1B.

44. Thomas R. Horton, "The Ethics Crisis Continues: What to Do?" *Management Review,* 75 (November 1986): 3. Derek Bok, former president of Harvard University, calls for greater civic mindedness in "A Great Need of the 90s," *Christian Science Monitor* (May 22, 1992): 18.

45. See Kerry Hannon, "How to Build in Values in Building a Business," *USA Today* (July 31, 2006): 6B; Catherine M. Dalton, "When Organizational Values Are Mere Rhetoric," *Business Horizons,* 49 (September–October 2006): 345–348; and Alan Wolfe, "Bringing Religion Into Your Company Can Be a Test of Faith—But Not in the Way You Might Expect," *Inc.,* 28 (December 2006): 63–64.

46. Marc Gunther, "God & Business," *Fortune* (July 9, 2001): 58–80; and Gary R. Weaver and Bradley R. Agle, "Religiosity and Ethical Behavior in Organizations: A Symbolic Interactionist Perspective," *Academy of Management Review,* 27 (January 2002): 77–97.

47. See Edward Soule, "Managerial Moral Strategies—In Search of a Few Good Principles," *Academy of Management Review,* 27 (January 2002): 114–124.

48. See Archie B. Carroll, "In Search of the Moral Manager," *Business Horizons,* 30 (March–April 1987): 7–15. Also see Archie B. Carroll, "Managing Ethically with Global Stakeholders: A Present and Future Challenge," *Academy of Management Executive,* 18 (May 2004): 114–120.

49. Data from "Ethics Training a Low Priority," *USA Today* (January 29, 2004): 1B.

50. See Tom Vanden Brook, "Troops Will Get 'Values' Training," *USA Today* (June 2, 2006): 1A; Greg Farrell, "Bad Harvard Grads Are Poster Boys for Ethics Classes," *USA Today* (September 28, 2006): 4B; and the series of articles about ethics education in the September 2006 issue of *Academy of Management Learning and Education.*

51. For details, see John A. Byrne, "The Best-Laid Ethics Programs . . ." *Business Week* (March 9, 1992): 67–69.

52. Based on Robert Levering and Milton Moskowitz, "100 Best Companies to Work For," *Fortune* (January 20, 2003): 140.

53. Based on Thompson, "Ethics Training Enters the Real World." Also see Greg Farrell and Jayne O'Donnell, "Ethics Training as Taught By Ex-cons: Crime Doesn't Pay," *USA Today* (November 16, 2005): 1B–2B; and Margery Weinstein, "Survey Says: Ethics Training Works," *Training,* 42 (November 2005): 15.

54. See Alynda Wheat, "Keeping an Eye on Corporate America," *Fortune* (November 25, 2002): 44, 46; and Gary R. Weaver, Linda Klebe Trevino, and Bradley Agle, " 'Somebody I Look Up To:' Ethical Role

Models in Organizations," *Organizational Dynamics,* 34, no. 4 (2005): 313–330.

55. See Bruce Horovitz, "Scandals Grow Out of CEO's Warped Mind-Set," *USA Today* (October 11, 2002): 1B–2B.

56. "Business' Big Morality Play," *Dun's Review* (August 1980): 56.

57. See Lynn Paine, Rohit Deshpande, Joshua D. Margolis, and Kim Eric Bettcher, "Up to Code: Does Your Company's Conduct Meet World-Class Standards?" *Harvard Business Review,* 83 (December 2005): 122–133; and Ann Pomeroy, "Ethics and Compliance Field Is Booming," *HR Magazine,* 51 (December 2006): 14, 16.

58. See Richard P. Nielsen, "Changing Unethical Organizational Behavior," *Academy of Management Executive,* 3 (May 1989): 123–130. Relative to the Enron case, see Wendy Zellner, "A Hero—And a Smoking-Gun Letter," *Business Week* (January 28, 2002): 34–35; and Greg Farrell and Jayne O'Donnell, "Watkins Testifies Skilling, Fastow Duped Lay, Board," *USA Today* (February 15, 2002): 1B–2B.

59. See Michael J. Gundlach, Scott C. Douglas, and Mark J. Martinko, "The Decision to Blow the Whistle: A Social Information Processing Framework," *Academy of Management Review,* 28 (January 2003): 107–123; and Kathy Gurchiek, "U.S. Workers Unlikely To Report Office Misconduct," *HR Magazine,* 51 (May 2006): 29, 38.

60. See Jodie Morse and Amanda Bower, "The Party Crasher," *Time* (January 6, 2003): 52–56; Maria Bartiromo, "The Ones Who Got Away," *Business Week* (June 12, 2006): 98; and Amanda Ripley and Maggie Sieger, "The Special Agent," *Time* (January 6, 2003): 34–40.

61. Ralph Nader, "An Anatomy of Whistle Blowing," in *Whistle Blowing,* ed. Ralph Nader, Peter Petkas, and Kate Blackwell (New York: Bantam, 1972), p. 7. For interesting case studies of whistle-blowers, see William McGowan, "The Whistleblowers Hall of Fame," *Business and Society Review,* 52 (Winter 1985): 31–36.

62. The federal Whistleblowers Protection Act of 1989 is discussed in David Israel and Anita Lechner, "Protection for Whistleblowers," *Personnel Administrator,* 34 (July 1989): 106. Also see Neil Weinberg, "The Dark Side of Whistleblowing," *Forbes,* 175 (March 14, 2005): 90–98; and Catherine Rampell, "Whistle-Blowers Tell of Cost of Conscience," *USA Today* (November 24, 2006): 13A.

63. Adapted from Kenneth D. Walters, "Your Employees' Right to Blow the Whistle," *Harvard Business Review,* 53 (July–August 1975): 26–34, 161–162. Also see Janet P. Near and Marcia P. Miceli, "Effective Whistle-Blowing," *Academy of Management Review,* 20 (July 1995): 679–708; and Kate Walter, "Ethics Hot Lines Tap into More than Wrongdoing," *HR Magazine,* 40 (September 1995): 79–85.

Chapter 4

1. As quoted in Saren Starbridge, "Anita Roddick: Fair Trade," *Living Planet,* 3 (Spring 2001): 92.

2. Excerpted from Michael V. Copeland, "The Mighty Micro-Multinational," *Business 2.0,* 7, July 2006, pp. 106–114. Copyright © 2006 Time Inc. All rights reserved.

3. Excerpted from Marcus W. Brauchli, "Echoes of the Past," *Wall Street Journal* (September 26, 1996): R24. Republished with permission of *Wall Street Journal*; permission conveyed through Copyright Clearance Center, Inc. Also see Geoffrey G. Jones, "The Rise of Corporate Nationality," *Harvard Business Review,* 84 (October 2006): 20–22; and Brian Bremner, "The Dragon's Way or the Tiger's," *Business Week* (November 20, 2006): 55.

4. Data from "Snapshots of the Next Century," *Business Week:* "21st Century Capitalism" (special issue, 1994): 194.

5. Nancy J. Adler, *International Dimensions of Organizational Behavior,* 4th ed. (Cincinnati: Thomson Learning, 2002), p. 3. For examples, see David Welch and Dean Foust, "The Good News About America's Auto Industry," *Business Week* (February 13, 2006): 32–35; Frederik Balfour, "One Foot in China," *Business Week* (May 1, 2006): 44–45; and Tarun Khanna and Krishna G. Palepu, "Emerging Giants: Building World-Class Companies in Developing Countries," *Harvard Business Review,* 84 (October 2006): 60–69.

6. See Sandra Mottner and James P. Johnson, "Motivations and Risks in International Licensing: A Review and Implications for Licensing to Transitional and Emerging Economies," *Journal of World Business,* 35 (Summer 2000): 171–188. For good overviews of the internationalization process, see Pankaj Ghemawat, "Regional Strategies for Global

Leadership," *Harvard Business Review,* 83 (December 2005): 98–108; Harry J. Sapienza, Erkko Autio, Gerard George, and Shaker A. Zahra, "A Capabilities Perspective on the Effects of Early Internationalization on Firm Survival and Growth," *Academy of Management Review,* 31 (October 2006): 914–933; and Jack and Suzy Welch, "From the Old, Something New," *Business Week* (November 20, 2006): 124.

7. Data from "Chip Licensing Deal," *USA Today* (November 27, 1996): 1B. *Note:* This six-step sequence is based on Alan M. Rugman, "A New Theory of the Multinational Enterprise: Internationalization Versus Internalization," *Columbia Journal of World Business,* 15 (Spring 1980): 23–29. Also see Roland Calori, Leif Melin, Tugrul Atamer, and Peter Gustavsson, "Innovative International Strategies," *Journal of World Business,* 35 (Winter 2000): 333–354; Anil K. Gupta and Vijay Govindarajan, "Managing Global Expansion: A Conceptual Framework," *Business Horizons,* 43 (March–April 2000): 45–54; Joseph A. Monti and George S. Yip, "Taking the High Road When Going International," *Business Horizons,* 43 (July–August 2000): 65–72; and Walter Kuemmerle, "Go Global—or No?" *Harvard Business Review,* 79 (June 2001): 37–49.

8. See Jeff Bailey, "The Exporting Advantage," *Inc.,* 27 (August 2005): 40, 42; and James C. Cooper, "Exports Are Giving the Economy a Surprise Lift," *Business Week* (November 27, 2006): 27–28.

9. For related discussion, see Anthony Goerzen, "Managing Alliance Networks: Emerging Practices of Multinational Corporations," *Academy of Management Executive,* 19 (May 2005): 94–107.

10. David P. Hamilton, "United It Stands," *Wall Street Journal* (September 26, 1996): R19.

11. Data from "About Xerox: Online Fact Book," at www.xerox.com.

12. Jeremy Main, "Making Global Alliances Work," *Fortune* (December 17, 1990): 121–126.

13. Adapted from ibid. and David Lei and John W. Slocum Jr., "Global Strategic Alliances: Payoffs and Pitfalls," *Organizational Dynamics,* 19 (Winter 1991): 44–62. Also see John B. Cullen, Jean L. Johnson, and Tomoaki Sakano, "Success Through Commitment and Trust: The Soft Side of Strategic Alliance Management," *Journal of World Business,* 35 (Fall 2000): 223–240; John Child, "Trust—The Fundamental Bond in Global Collaboration," *Organizational Dynamics,* 29 (Spring 2001): 274–288; and Rekha Krishnan, Xavier Martin, and Niels G. Noorderhaven, "When Does Trust Matter to Alliance Performance," *Academy of Management Journal,* 49 (October 2006): 894–917.

14. See David A. Andelman, "Merging Across Borders," *Management Review,* 87 (June 1998): 44–46. Also see Cristiano Busco, "Growing by Acquisitions: The Role of Measurement as GE Met Italy," *Business Horizons,* 46 (January–February 2003): 37–45.

15. Joan Warner, "The World Is Not Always Your Oyster," *Business Week* (October 30, 1995): 132. Also see John Elliott, "Wal-Mart Must Wait," *Fortune* (May 29, 2006): 37–40; and Alex Taylor III, "The World According to Ghosn," *Fortune* (December 11, 2006): 114–121.

16. For example, see Thomas M. Begley and David P. Boyd, "The Need for a Corporate Global Mind-Set," *MIT Sloan Management Review,* 44 (Winter 2003): 25–32.

17. See Peter Gwynne, "The Myth of Globalization?" *MIT Sloan Management Review,* 44 (Winter 2003): 11.

18. Based on Fons Trompenaars and Charles Hampden-Turner, *Riding the Waves of Culture: Understanding Cultural Diversity in Global Business,* 2d ed. (New York: McGraw-Hill, 1998), pp. 191–192; Marie-Claude Boudreau, Karen D. Loch, Daniel Robey, and Detmar Straud, "Going Global: Using Information Technology to Advance the Competitiveness of the Virtual Transnational Organization," *Academy of Management Executive,* 12 (November 1998): 120–128; and Anil K. Gupta and Vijay Govindarajan, "Converting Global Presence into Global Competitive Advantage," *Academy of Management Executive,* 15 (May 2001): 45–56.

19. Stanley Reed, "Busting Up Sweden Inc.," *Business Week* (February 22, 1999): 52, 54.

20. For example, see Dexter Roberts and Pete Engardio, "Secrets, Lies, and Sweatshops," *Business Week* (November 27, 2006): 50–58.

21. "Amidst Stiffer International Competition, U.S. Managers Need a Broader Perspective," *Management Review,* 69 (March 1980): 34.

22. For example, see "Leading the Way: Joyce Chang, Managing Director, JPMorgan," *Newsweek* (September 25, 2006): 59–60; and Ed Cohen,

"Practicing Diversity—Multi-Dimensionally," *Training,* 43 (October 2006): 48.

23. Based on David A. Heenan and Howard V. Perlmutter, *Multinational Organization Development* (Reading, Mass.: Addison-Wesley, 1979).

24. Drawn from Brian Dumaine, "The New Turnaround Champs," *Fortune* (July 16, 1990): 36–44. Also see Douglas McGray, "Translating Sony into English," *Fast Company,* no. 66 (January 2003): 38.

25. See Amy Borrus, "Can Japan's Giants Cut the Apron Strings?" *Business Week* (May 14, 1990): 105–106.

26. Data from Kitty Bean Yancey, "Learning Like There's No *Mañana,*" *USA Today* (June 22, 2001): 1D–2D.

27. Adrienne Carter, "It's Norman Time," *Business Week* (May 29, 2006): 68. Also see Wendy Koch, "Ads Are Yanked as Offensive to Arabs, Muslims," *USA Today* (September 26, 2006): 3A.

28. See Silla Brush, "A Nation in Full," *U.S. News and World Report,* 141 (October 2, 2006): 46–57; and "Diverse Landscape of the Newest Americans," *USA Today* (December 4, 2006): 8A.

29. See Nandani Lynton and Kirsten Hogh Thogersen, "How China Transforms an Executive's Mind," *Organizational Dynamics,* 35, no. 2 (2006): 170–181; Diane Coutu, "Leveraging the Psychology of the Salesperson: A Conversation with Psychologist and Anthropologist G. Clotaire Rapaille," *Harvard Business Review,* 84 (July–August 2006): 42–47; Paula Lehman, "The Evolution of a Diplomat," *Business Week* (September 18, 2006): 74; and Keith Naughton, "The Great Wal-Mart of China," *Newsweek* (October 30, 2006): 50–52.

30. Arvind V. Phatak and Mohammed M. Habib, "The Dynamics of International Business Negotiations," *Business Horizons,* 39 (May–June 1996): 34.

31. Data from Stacy Lawrence, "Greetings from Planet Vagabond," *Business 2.0,* 4 (February 2003): 32.

32. For more, see Adler, *International Dimensions of Organizational Behavior,* pp. 16–34.

33. As quoted in "How Cultures Collide," *Psychology Today,* 10 (July 1976): 69.

34. Trompenaars and Hampden-Turner, *Riding the Waves of Culture,* p. 3.

35. Ronald Inglehart and Wayne E. Baker, "Modernization's Challenge to Traditional Values: Who's Afraid of Ronald McDonald?" *The Futurist,* 35 (March–April 2001): 18, 21.

36. See "How Cultures Collide," pp. 66–74, 97; Edward T. Hall, *The Hidden Dimension* (Garden City, N.Y.: Doubleday, 1966); and Mary Munter, "Cross-Cultural Communication for Managers," *Business Horizons,* 36 (May–June 1993): 69–78.

37. Ronald E. Dulek, John S. Fielden, and John S. Hill, "International Communication: An Executive Primer," *Business Horizons,* 34 (January–February 1991): 21.

38. For example, see Robert House, Mansour Javidan, Paul Hanges, and Peter Dorfman, "Understanding Cultures and Implicit Leadership Theories Across the Globe: An Introduction to Project GLOBE," *Journal of World Business,* 37 (Spring 2002): 3–10; Felix C. Brodbeck, Michael Frese, and Mansour Javidan, "Leadership Made in Germany: Low on Compassion, High on Performance," *Academy of Management Executive,* 16 (February 2002): 16–29; Jeffery C. Kennedy, "Leadership in Malaysia: Traditional Values, International Outlook," *Academy of Management Executive,* 16 (August 2002): 15–26; Robert J. House, Paul J. Hanges, Mansour Javidan, Peter W. Dorfman, and Vipin Gupta, eds. *Culture Leadership, and Organizations: The GLOBE Study of 62 Societies* (Thousand Oaks, Calif.: Sage, 2004); and Mansour Javidan and Nandani Lynton, "The Changing Face of the Chinese Executive," *Harvard Business Review,* 83 (December 2005): 28, 30. Also see George B. Graen, "In the Eye of the Beholder: Cross-Cultural Lessons in Leadership from Project GLOBE: A Response Viewed from the Third Culture Bonding (TCB) Model of Cross-Cultural Leadership," *Academy of Management Perspectives,* 20 (November 2006): 95–101; and Robert J. House, Mansour Javidan, Peter W. Dorfman, and Mary Sully de Luque, "A Failure of Scholarship: Response to George Graen's Critique of GLOBE," *Academy of Management Perspectives,* 20 (November 2006): 102–114.

39. For more, see Mansour Javidan and Robert J. House, "Cultural Acumen for the Global Manager: Lessons from Project GLOBE," *Organizational Dynamics,* 29 (Spring 2001): 289–305.

40. This list is based on Edward T. Hall, "The Silent Language in Overseas Business," *Harvard Business Review*, 38 (May–June 1960): 87–96; Rose Knotts, "Cross-Cultural Management: Transformations and Adaptations," *Business Horizons*, 32 (January–February 1989): 29–33; and Adler, *International Dimensions of Organizational Behavior*, pp. 27–28.

41. For related research, see John Schaubroeck and Simon S. K. Lam, "How Similarity to Peers and Supervisor Influences Organizational Advancement in Different Cultures," *Academy of Management Journal*, 45 (December 2002): 1120–1136.

40. For detailed discussion, see Allen C. Bluedorn, Carol Felker Kaufman, and Paul M. Lane, "How Many Things Do You Like to Do at Once? An Introduction to Monochronic and Polychronic Time," *Academy of Management Executive*, 6 (November 1992): 17–26. Also see Allen C. Bluedorn and Rhetta L. Standifer, "Time and the Temporal Imagination," *Academy of Management Learning and Education*, 5 (June 2006): 196–206.

43. Multitasking is discussed in Alison Overholt, "The Art of Multitasking," *Fast Company*, no. 63 (October 2002): 118–125.

44. See Gregory K. Stephens and Charles R. Greer, "Doing Business in Mexico: Understanding Cultural Differences," *Organizational Dynamics*, 24 (Summer 1995): 39–55; Mike Johnson, "Untapped Latin America," *Management Review*, 85 (July 1996): 31–34; and Yongsun Paik and J. H. Derick Sohn, "Confucius in Mexico: Korean MNCs and the Maquiladoras," *Business Horizons*, 41 (November–December 1998): 25–33. For an account of monochromic time in action, see Laura Petrecca, "Stores, Banks Go Speedy to Win Harried Customers," *USA Today* (December 1, 2006): 1B.

45. See Karl Albrecht, "Lost in the Translation," *Training*, 33 (June 1996): 66–70; Daniel Pianko, "Smooth Translations," *Management Review*, 85 (July 1996): 10; and Rebecca Ganzel, "Universal Translator? Not Quite," *Training*, 36 (April 1999): 22, 24.

46. Jerry Shine, "More U.S. Students Tackle Japanese," *Christian Science Monitor* (November 25, 1991): 14.

47. Based on Kathryn Tyler, "Targeted Language Training Is Best Bargain," *HR Magazine*, 43 (January 1998): 61–64; and "When in Rio . . . ," *Training*, 35 (December 1998): 25.

48. Based on Figure 2 in Gary Bonvillian and William A. Nowlin, "Cultural Awareness: An Essential Element of Doing Business Abroad," *Business Horizons*, 37 (November–December 1994):44–50.

49. "Burger Boost," *USA Today* (October 11, 1995): 1B. Also see Michael Arndt, "A Misguided Beef with McDonald's," *Business Week* (May 21, 2001): 14.

50. See Geert Hofstede, *Culture's Consequences: Comparing Values, Behaviors, Institutions, and Organizations Across Nations*, 2d ed. (Thousand Oaks, Calif.: Sage, 2001).

51. Based on discussion in Peter W. Dorfman, Paul J. Hanges, and Felix C. Brodbeck, "Leadership and Cultural Variation: The Identification of Culturally Endorsed Leadership Profiles," in Robert J. House, Paul J. Hanges, Mansour Javidan, Peter W. Dorfman, and Vipin Gupta, eds. *Culture Leadership, and Organizations: The GLOBE Study of 62 Societies* (Thousand Oaks, Calif.: Sage, 2004), pp. 669–719.

52. See Dianne H. B. Welsh, Fred Luthans, and Steven M. Sommer, "Managing Russian Factory Workers: The Impact of U.S.-Based Behavioral and Participative Techniques," *Academy of Management Journal*, 36 (February 1993): 58–79. For related reading, see Dong I. Jung and Bruce J. Avolio, "Effects of Leadership Style and Followers' Cultural Orientation on Performance in Group and Individual Task Conditions," *Academy of Management Journal*, 42 (April 1999): 208–218.

53. See Baruch Shimoni and Harriet Bergmann, "Managing in a Changing World: From Multiculturalism to Hybridization—The Production of Hybrid Management Cultures in Israel, Thailand, and Mexico," *Academy of Management Perspectives*, 20 (August 2006): 76–89; and Jeanne Brett, Kristin Behfar, and Mary C. Kern, "Managing Multicultural Teams," *Harvard Business Review*, 84 (November 2006): 83–91.

54. For example, see Dean Foust, "Queen of Pop," *Business Week* (August 7, 2006): 44–51.

55. Marshall Loeb, "The Real Fast Track Is Overseas," *Fortune* (August 21, 1995): 129. For more, see Mason A. Carpenter, Wm. Gerard Sanders, and Hal B. Gregersen, "Building Human Capital with Organizational Content: The Impact of International Assignment Experience on Multicultural Firm Performance and CEO Pay," *Academy of Management Journal*, 44 (June 2001): 493–511; and "International Experience Aids Career," *USA Today* (January 28, 2002): 1B.

56. Data from J. Stewart Black and Hal B. Gregersen, "The Right Way to Manage Expats," *Harvard Business Review*, 77 (March–April 1999): 52–63; and Gary S. Insch and John D. Daniels, "Causes and Consequences of Declining Early Departures from Foreign Assignments," *Business Horizons*, 45 (November–December 2002): 39–48.

57. Data from Robert O'Connor, "Plug the Expat Knowledge Drain," *HR Magazine*, 47 (October 2002): 101–107; and Carla Joinson, "No Returns," *HR Magazine*, 47 (November 2002): 70–77.

58. See Susan Ladika, "Working Together," *HR Magazine*, 50 (June 2005): 86–91; G. Pascal Zachary, "As Easy as ABC? Not Exactly," *Business 2.0*, 6 (August 2005): 66; Sidra Durst, "Risky Business," *Business 2.0*, 7 (August 2006): 114–115; and Barney Gimbel, "A Master Traveler Tells All," *Fortune* (October 16, 2006): 218, 220.

59. Elisabeth Marx, *Breaking Through Culture Shock: What You Need to Succeed in International Business* (London: Nicholas Brealey Publishing, 2001), p. 7.

60. Based on Insch and Daniels, "Causes and Consequences of Declining Early Departures from Foreign Assignments."

61. Theresa Minton-Eversole and Kathy Gurchiek, "New Workers Not Ready for Prime Time," *HR Magazine*, 51 (December 2006): 34. Also see Kathryn Tyler, "Clear Language/*Lenguaje Claro*," *HR Magazine*, 50 (December 2005): 66–70; and Jonathan Alter, "Trouble From the Top Down," *Newsweek* (December 18, 2006): 44.

62. Data from "Diverse Landscape of the Newest Americans," *USA Today* (December 4, 2006): 8A.

63. Adapted from Rosalie L. Tung, "Selection and Training of Personnel for Overseas Assignments," *Columbia Journal of World Business*, 16 (Spring 1981): 68–78. Also see Lyn Glanz, Roger Williams, and Ludwig Hoeksema, "Sensemaking in Expatriation—A Theoretical Basis," *Thunderbird International Business Review*, 43 (January–February 2001): 101–119; and "Cross-Cultural Training Helps Offshore Issues," *USA Today* (October 5, 2006): 1B.

64. See P. Christopher Earley, "Intercultural Training for Managers: A Comparison of Documentary and Interpersonal Methods," *Academy of Management Journal*, 30 (December 1987): 685–698. Also see J. Stewart Black and Mark Mendenhall, "Cross-Cultural Training Effectiveness: A Review and a Theoretical Framework for Future Research," *Academy of Management Review*, 15 (January 1990): 113–136.

65. See Steven Shepard, *Managing Cross-Cultural Transition: A Handbook for Corporations, Employees, and Their Families* (Bayside, N.Y.: Aletheia Publications, 1998).

66. See Barbara A. Anderson, "Expatriate Management: An Australian Tri-Sector Comparative Study," *Thunderbird International Business Review*, 43 (January–February 2001): 33–51; and Eric Krell, "Budding Relationships," *HR Magazine*, 50 (June 2005): 114–118.

67. See Andrea C. Poe, "Welcome Back," *HR Magazine*, 45 (March 2000): 94–105; and Jeff Barbian, "Return to Sender," *Training*, 39 (January 2002): 40–43.

68. Data from Rosalie L. Tung, "American Expatriates Abroad: From Neophytes to Cosmopolitans," *Journal of World Business*, 33 (Summer 1998): 125–144. For updated statistics, see Ann Pomeroy, "Outdated Policies Hinder Female Expats," *HR Magazine*, 51 (December 2006): 16.

69. David Stauffer, "No Need for Inter-American Culture Clash," *Management Review*, 87 (January 1998): 8. Also see Arup Varma, Linda K. Stroh, and Lisa B. Schmitt, "Women and International Assignments: The Impact of Supervisor-Subordinate Relationships," *Journal of World Business*, 36 (Winter 2001): 380–388.

70. See Louisa Wah, "Surfing the Rough Sea," *Management Review*, 87 (September 1998): 25–29; and Paula M. Caligiuri and Wayne F. Cascio, "Can We Send Her There? Maximizing the Success of Western Women on Global Assignments," *Journal of World Business*, 33 (Winter 1998): 394–416.

71. See Lynette Clemetson, "Soul and Sushi," *Newsweek* (May 4, 1998): 38–41.

72. For helpful tips, see Linda K. Stroh, Arup Varma, and Stacey J. Valy-Durbin, "Why Are Women Left Home: Are They Unwilling to Go on

International Assignments?" *Journal of World Business*, 35 (Fall 2000): 241–255.

73. For more, see Frank Jossi, "Successful Handoff," *HR Magazine*, 47 (October 2002): 48–52.

Chapter 5

1. As quoted in Eugenia Levenson, Christopher Tkaczyk, and Jia Lynn Yang, "50 Most Powerful Women: Indra Rising," *Fortune* (October 16, 2006): 145.
2. Eugenia Levenson, "'We Saw the Opportunity:' How Xerox is Preparing for Tomorrow," *Fortune*, October 16, 2006, p. 136. Copyright © 2006 Time Inc. All rights reserved.
3. David Stires, "A Darker View of Starbucks," *Fortune* (November 13, 2006): 197.
4. See Andrew Campbell, "Tailored, Not Benchmarked: A Fresh Look at Corporate Planning," *Harvard Business Review*, 77 (March–April 1999): 41–50. The importance of planning for college students is covered in George Mannes, "Earning a Degree in Debt," *Money*, 35 (September 2006): 98–102.
5. See Geoffrey Colvin, "Anxious? Get Used to It," *Fortune* (March 3, 2003): 39–40.
6. See Raymond E. Miles and Charles C. Snow, *Organizational Strategy, Structure, and Process* (New York: McGraw-Hill, 1978), p. 29. A validation of the Miles and Snow model can be found in Stephen M. Shortell and Edward J. Zajak, "Perceptual and Archival Measures of Miles and Snow's Strategic Types: A Comprehensive Assessment of Reliability and Validity," *Academy of Management Journal*, 33 (December 1990): 817–832.
7. Data from Joseph Weber, "Harley Investors May Get a Wobbly Ride," *Business Week* (February 11, 2002): 65. For updates, see John Teresko, "Fueled by Innovation," *Industry Week* (December 2002): 52–57; and Gene G. Marcial, "Going Whole Hog at Harley," *Business Week* (January 20, 2003): 86.
8. Ellen Florian, "Six Lessons from the Fast Lane," *Fortune* (September 6, 2004): 150. For related reading, see Gary P. Pisano, "Can Science Be a Business? Lessons from Biotech," *Harvard Business Review*, 84 (October 2006): 114–125.
9. Another prospector, Intel, is discussed in David Kirkpatrick, "See This Chip?" *Fortune* (February 17, 2003): 78–88. Also see Max Chafkin, "Need a High-Tech Infusion?" *Inc.*, 28 (July 2006): 39–40.
10. William Boulding and Markus Christen, "First-Mover Disadvantage," *Harvard Business Review*, 79 (October 2001): 20–21 (emphasis added). Also see Jim Collins, "Best Beats First," *Inc.*, 22 (August 2000): 48–52; and Kevin Maney, "Impregnable 'First Mover Advantage' Philosophy Suddenly Isn't," *USA Today* (July 18, 2001): 3B.
11. For inspiring examples, see Bo Burlingham, "The Young and the Restless: Entrepreneurship Keeps Getting Cooler, and the Entrepreneurs Keep Getting Younger," *Inc.*, 28 (July 2006): 86–91; Bo Burlingham, "The Coolest Little Start-up in America," *Inc.*, 28 (July 2006): 78–85; and Patrick J. Sauer, "An Athlete Scores Again: How I Did It," *Inc.*, 28 (August 2006): 122–124.
12. See Pete Engardio and Faith Keenan, "The Copycat Economy," *Business Week* (August 26, 2002): 94, 96; and Georgia Flight, "Grinding Out Success Next to Starbucks," *Business 2.0*. 7 (October 2006): 62–63.
13. Christine Y. Chen, "The Last-Mover Advantage," *Fortune* (July 9, 2001): 84. Another "analyzer" is profiled in Edward O. Welles, "The Next Starbucks," *Inc.*, 23 (January 2001): 48–53.
14. See "How Seagram Is Scrambling to Survive 'The Sobering of America,'" *Business Week* (September 3, 1984): 94–95; Andrea Rothman, "The Maverick Boss at Seagram," *Business Week* (December 18, 1989): 90–98; Laura Zinn, "Edgar Jr.'s Not So Excellent Ventures," *Business Week* (January 16, 1995): 78–79; and David Jones and Caroline Brothers, "Diageo, Pernod Buy Seagram Division," *USA Today* (December 20, 2000): 3B.
15. For details, see Jeffrey S. Conant, Michael P. Mokwa, and P. Rajan Varadarajan, "Strategic Types, Distinctive Marketing Competencies and Organizational Performance: A Multiple Measures Based Study," *Strategic Management Journal*, 11 (September 1990): 365–383. Also see Shaker A. Zahra and John A. Pearce II, "Research Evidence on the Miles-Snow Typology," *Journal of Management*, 16 (December 1990): 751–768.

16. Rosabeth Moss Kanter, "Obstacles in Your Way? Don't Freeze—Improvise," *Business 2.0*, 3 (September 2002): 64. Also see Mary M. Crossan, Henry W. Lane, Roderick E. White, and Leo Klus, "The Improvising Organization: Where Planning Meets Opportunity," *Organizational Dynamics*, 24 (Spring 1996): 20–35.
17. "$1.4B Authorized to Restore Everglades," *USA Today* (December 12, 2000): 15A.
18. Scott Adams, "Dilbert's Management Handbook," *Fortune* (May 13, 1996): 104.
19. Based on R. Duane Ireland and Michael A. Hitt, "Mission Statements: Importance, Challenge, and Recommendations for Development," *Business Horizons*, 35 (May–June 1992): 34–42. Also see Barbara Bartkus, Myron Glassman, and R. Bruce McAfee, "Mission Statements: Are They Smoke and Mirrors?" *Business Horizons*, 43 (November–December 2000): 23–28.
20. As quoted in Jon Talton, "What in Blazes Has the Chief Done? Create a Model for Managers," *Arizona Republic* (January 27, 2002): D1.
21. Jack Welch, with Suzy Welch, *Winning* (New York: HarperBusiness, 2005), p. 15. Also see Jack and Suzy Welch, "Growing Up but Staying Young," *Business Week* (December 11, 2006): 112.
22. Data from Robert Levering and Milton Moskowitz, "100 Best Companies to Work For," *Fortune* (January 20, 2003): 138.
23. Dan Sullivan, "The Reality Gap," *Inc.*, 21 (March 1999): 119.
24. Anthony P. Raia, *Managing by Objectives* (Glenview, Ill.: Scott, Foresman, 1974), p. 24.
25. For an excellent and comprehensive treatment of goal setting, see Edwin A. Locke and Gary P. Latham, *Goal Setting: A Motivational Technique That Works!* (Englewood Cliffs, N.J.: Prentice-Hall, 1984). Also see Robert D. Pritchard, Philip L. Roth, Steven D. Jones, Patricia J. Galgay, and Margaret D. Watson, "Designing a Goal-Setting System to Enhance Performance: A Practical Guide," *Organizational Dynamics*, 17 (Summer 1988): 69–78.
26. See Richard S. Handscombe, "Managing by Individual Objectives," in *Business: The Ultimate Resource* (Cambridge, Mass.: Perseus Publishing, 2002), pp. 171–172; and Harry Levinson, "Management by Whose Objectives?" *Harvard Business Review*, 81 (January 2003): 107–116.
27. John A. Byrne and Heather Timmons, "Tough Times for a New CEO," *Business Week* (October 29, 2001): 66.
28. For example, see Martin Delahoussaye, "Houston, Problem Solved," *Training*, 39 (June 2002): 24; and Ann Pomeroy, "Time Management Challenges CFOs," *HR Magazine*, 51 (December 2006): 16.
29. Raia, *Managing by Objectives*, p. 54.
30. Richard Koch, *The 80/20 Principle: The Secret of Achieving More with Less* (New York: Currency Doubleday, 1998), p. 4.
31. Diane Brady, "Why Service Stinks," *Business Week* (October 23, 2000): 126.
32. See Barbara Moses, "The Busyness Trap," *Training*, 35 (November 1998): 38–42; David H. Freedman, "Go Ahead, Make a Mess," *Inc.*, 28 (December 2006): 120–125; Richard Branson, "Learn How to Say No (Even if You're Known as 'Dr. Yes')," *Business 2.0*, 7 (December 2006): 92; and "A Perfect Mess," *Fast Company*, no. 111 (January 2007): 56.
33. Data from Adrienne Fox, "Companies Worldwide Fail to Hit Full Capacity," *HR Magazine*, 47 (December 2002): 25.
34. Heather Johnson, Learn or Burn," *Training*, 41 (April 2004): 19. Also see Ann Pomeroy, "Train Leaders With Corporate Strategy in Mind," *HR Magazine*, 51 (June 2006): 24; "Most Employers Don't Share Company Strategy," *USA Today* (November 15, 2006): 1B; Wendy R. Boswell, John B. Bingham, and Alexander J. S. Colvin, "Aligning Employees Through "Line of Sight," *Business Horizons*, 49 (November–December 2006): 499–509; and Chip Heath and Dan Heath, "The Curse of Knowledge," *Harvard Business Review*, 84 (December 2006): 20–22.
35. See William R. King and David I. Cleland, *Strategic Planning and Policy* (New York: Van Nostrand Reinhold, 1978), pp. 180–183; Laura Landro, "Giants Talk Synergy but Few Make It Work," *Wall Street Journal* (September 25, 1995): B1–B2; and Thomas Osegowitsch, "The Art and Science of Synergy: The Case of the Auto Industry," *Business Horizons*, 44 (March–April 2001): 17–24.
36. Patricia Sellers, "P&G: Teaching an Old Dog New Tricks," *Fortune* (May 31, 2004): 168.

37. For example, see Anne Kreamer and Kurt Andersen, "Culture," *Fast Company*, no. 63 (October 2002): 78.

38. Jeffrey F. Rayport, "Idea Fest," *Fast Company*, no. 66 (January 2003): 103.

39. See Dominic Dodd and Ken Favaro, "Managing the Right Tension," *Harvard Business Review*, 84 (December 2006): 62–74.

40. "Swallowing Jenny Craig," *Business Week* (July 3, 2006): 33. For more, see Matt Krantz, "Chocolate Diet? Nestle to Buy Jenny Craig," *USA Today* (June 20, 2006): 1B.

41. "Hotels Developing Multiple Personalities," *USA Today* (September 10, 1996): 4B.

42. Based on Ian Mount, "Ashes to Ashes, Poop to Power," *Business 2.0*, 2 (December 2001): 42.

43. Michelle Kessler, "High Tech's Latest Bright Idea: Shared Computing," *USA Today* (January 9, 2003): 2B. Technological synergies are reported in Cliff Edwards, "To See Where Tech Is Headed, Watch TI," *Business Week* (November 6, 2006): 74; and Adrienne Carter, "Harvesting Green Power," *Business Week* (November 13, 2006): 60–70.

44. Drawn from Fred Vogelstein, "How Intel Got Inside," *Fortune* (October 4, 2004): 127–136.

45. See Michael E. Porter, *Competitive Strategy* (New York: Free Press, 1980), p. 35; Michael E. Porter, *The Competitive Advantage of Nations* (New York: Free Press, 1990), p. 39; and the five-article collection beginning with Nicholas Argyres and Anita M. McGahan, "Introduction: Michael Porter's *Competitive Strategy*," *Academy of Management Executive*, 16 (May 2002): 41–42.

46. Porter, *The Competitive Advantage of Nations*, p. 37. Also see Keith H. Hammonds, "Michael Porter's Big Ideas," *Fast Company*, no. 44 (March 2001): 150–156.

47. See Kevin Lane Keller, Brian Sternthal, and Alice Tybout, "Three Questions to Ask about Your Brand," *Harvard Business Review*, 80 (September 2002): 80–86; and Pierre Berthon, Morris B. Holbrook, and James M. Hulbert, "Understanding and Managing the Brand Space," *MIT Sloan Management Review*, 44 (Winter 2003): 49–54.

48. Jerry Useem, "One Nation Under Wal-Mart," *Fortune* (March 3, 2003): 68.

49. As quoted in Bruce Horovitz and Theresa Howard, "With Image Crumbling, Kmart Files Chapter 11," *USA Today* (January 23, 2002): 1B.

50. For other implications of the low-cost strategy, see Wayne F. Cascio, "The High Cost of Low Wages," *Harvard Business Review*, 84 (December 2006): 23; and Nirmalya Kumar, "Strategies to Fight Low-Cost Rivals," *Harvard Business Review*, 84 (December 2006): 104–112.

51. See Chris Lederer and Sam Hill, "See Your Brands Through Your Customer's Eyes," *Harvard Business Review*, 79 (June 2001): 125–133.

52. For example, see Alex Taylor III, The Ultimate Fairly Inexpensive Driving Machine," *Fortune* (November 1, 2004): 131–132.

53. Adrienne Carter, "Foot Locker," *Money*, 31 (January 2002): 69.

54. For details, see Luis Ma. R. Calingo, "Environmental Determinants of Generic Competitive Strategies: Preliminary Evidence from Structured Content Analysis of *Fortune* and *Business Week* Articles (1983–1984)," *Human Relations*, 42 (April 1989): 353–369. For related research, see Praveen R. Nayyar, "Performance Effects of Three Foci in Service Firms," *Academy of Management Journal*, 35 (December 1992): 985–1009.

55. See good overviews, see Stephen Baker, "Wiser about the Web," *Business Week* (March 27, 2006): 54–58; Steven Levy and Brad Stone, "The New Wisdom of the Web," *Newsweek* (April 3, 2006): 46–53; Adam Lashinsky, "The Boom is Back," *Fortune* (May 1, 2006): 70–87; Robert D. Hof, "Web 2.0: The New Guy at Work," *Business Week* (June 19, 2006): 58–59; Erick Schonfeld, "Web 2.0 Around the World," *Business 2.0*, 7 (August 2006): 105–109.

56. Robert D. Hof, "The Wizard of Web Retailing," *Business Week* (December 20, 2004): 1B. Also see Paul Hemp, "Are You Ready for E-tailing 2.0?" *Harvard Business Review*, 84 (October 2006): 28; and Robert D. Hof, "Jeff Bezos' Risky Bet," *Business Week* (November 13, 2006): 52–58.

57. For more, see Anya Kamenetz, "The Network Unbound," *Fast Company*, no. 106 (June 2006): 68–73; David Kirkpatrick, "Life in a Connected World," *Fortune* (July 10, 2006): 98–100; Patricia Sellers, "Myspace Cowboys," *Fortune* (September 4, 2006): 66–74; Oliver Ryan, "Don't Touch That Dial," *Fortune* (September 4, 2006): 76–77; Amy Feldman, "Fast, Cheap, and Ready for Move-in," *Inc.*, 28 (November 2006): 23–24; and Jeffrey M. O'Brien, "You're Soooooooooo Predictable," *Fortune* (November 27, 2006): 224–234.

58. Based on G.T. Lumpkin and Gregory G. Dess, "E-Business Strategies and Internet Business Models: How the Internet Adds Value," *Organizational Dynamics*, 33, no. 2 (2004): 161–173.

59. See Erick Schonfeld, "How to Manage Growth: Meg Whitman, CEO, eBay," *Business 2.0*, 5 (December 2004): 99.

60. See Jefferson Graham, "Google Profit Rockets on 'Very, Very Good' Business," *Business Week* (October 20, 2006): 1B; Jefferson Graham, "Google to Experiment with Newspaper Ad Sales Online," *USA Today* (November 6, 2006): 1B; and Jon Fine, "The Google/YouTube Come-On," *Business Week* (December 11, 2006): 28.

61. Michael E. Porter, "Strategy and the Internet," *Harvard Business Review*, 79 (March 2001): 76. Also see Glenn Rifkin and Joel Kurtzman, "Is Your E-Business Plan Radical Enough?" *MIT Sloan Management Review*, 43 (Spring 2002): 91–95; and G. T. Lumpkin, Scott B. Droege, and Gregory G. Dess, "Ecommerce Strategies: Achieving Sustainable Competitive Advantage and Avoiding Pitfalls," *Organizational Dynamics*, 30 (Spring 2002): 325–340.

62. As quoted in Bill Breen, "Banker's Hours," *Fast Company*, no. 52 (November 2001): 200, 202.

63. See Jack Ewing, "Otto the Modest," *Business Week* (June 5, 2006): 42, 44.

64. Based on Leyland Pitt, Pierre Berthon, and Richard T. Watson, "Cyberservice: Taming Service Marketing Problems with the World Wide Web," *Business Horizons*, 42 (January–February 1999): 11–18; Stephen H. Wildstrom, "You, Too, Can Be a Webmaster," *Business Week* (February 3, 2003): 29; Jeremy Anwyl, "Build a Better Website," *Business 2.0*, 3 (January 2003): 95; and Michael Fitzgerald, "Put Some Wow in Your Website: New Graphics, Sounds, and More," *Inc.*, 28 (September 2006): 44–45.

65. Data from Jon Swartz, "E-Tailers Ring Up a Record Holiday Week," *USA Today* (December 27, 2001): 3B. Also see Jayne O'Donnell and Mindy Fetterman, "Point & Click Holidays," *USA Today* (November 24, 2006): 1A–2A.

66. Henry Mintzberg, "The Design School: Reconsidering the Basic Premises of Strategic Management," *Strategic Management Journal*, 11 (March–April 1990): 192. Also see Michael A. Hitt, "Spotlight on Strategic Management," *Business Horizons*, 49 (September–October 2006): 349–352; and Dodo zu Knyphausen-Aufsess, Nils Bickhoff, and Thomas Bieger, "Understanding and Breaking the Rules of Business: Toward a Systematic Four-Step Process," *Business Horizons*, 49 (September–October 2006): 369–377.

67. See Donald N. Sull, "Strategy as Active Waiting," *Harvard Business Review*, 83 (September 2005): 120–129; Geoffrey A. Moore, "Strategy and Your Stronger Hand," *Harvard Business Review*, 83 (December 2005): 62–72; and Thomas A. Stewart, "Growth as a Process," *Harvard Business Review*, 84 (June 2006): 60–70.

68. Richard F. Vancil, "Strategy Formulation in Complex Organizations," *Sloan Management Review*, 17 (Winter 1976): 18. Also see Robert E. Linneman and John L. Stanton Jr., "Mining for Niches," *Business Horizons*, 35 (May–June 1992): 43–51.

69. Pete Engardio, "For Citibank, There's No Place Like Asia," *Business Week* (March 30, 1992): 66. (Winter)

70. "Is Your Company an Extrovert?" *Management Review*, 85 (March 1996): 7. Also see Ruth C. May Wayne, H. Stewart Jr., and Robert Sweo, "Environmental Scanning Behavior in a Transnational Economy: Evidence from Russia," *Academy of Management Journal*, 43 (June 2000): 403–427; and M. Carl Drott, "Personal Knowledge, Corporate Information: The Challenges for Competitive Intelligence," *Business Horizons*, 44 (March–April 2001): 31–37.

71. See Thea Singer, "Comeback Markets," *Inc.*, 23 (May 2001): 53–54; Prithviraj Chattopadhyay, William H. Glick, and George P. Huber, "Organizational Actions in Response to Threats and Opportunities," *Academy of Management Journal*, 44 (October 2001): 937–955; and Krysten Crawford, "The BIG Opportunity," *Business 2.0*, 7 (June 2006): 94–99.

72. As quoted in Carleen Hawn, Susanna Hamner, and Erick Schonfeld, "How to Succeed in 2007," *Business 2.0*, 7 (December 2006): 102.

73. See Jay B. Barney, "Looking Inside for Competitive Advantage," *Academy of Management Executive*, 9 (November 1995): 49–61;W. Jack Duncan, Peter M. Ginter, and Linda E. Swayne, "Competitive Advantage and Internal Organizational Assessment," *Academy of Management Executive*, 12 (August 1998): 6–16; and Leyland F. Pitt, Michael T. Ewing, and Pierre Berthon, "Turning Competitive Advantage into Customer Equity," *Business Horizons*, 43 (September–October 2000): 11–18; and Bernard L. Rosenbaum, "Seven Emerging Sales Competencies," *Business Horizons*, 44 (January–February 2001): 33–36.

74. Adapted from Andrew Bartmess and Keith Cerny, "Building Competitive Advantage Through a Global Network of Capabilities," *California Management Review*, 35 (Winter 1993): 78–103. Also see Robert L. Cardy and T.T. Selvarajan, "Competencies: Alternative Frameworks for Competitive Advantage," *Business Horizons*, 49 (May–June 2006): 235–245; and Karen S. Cravens and Elizabeth Goad Oliver, "Employees: The Key Link to Corporate Reputation Management," *Business Horizons*, 49 (July–August 2006): 293–302.

75. According to Henry Mintzberg, there are four reasons why organizations need strategies: (1) to set direction, (2) to focus the effort of contributors, (3) to define the organization, and (4) to provide consistency. For more, see Henry Mintzberg, "The Strategy Concept II: Another Look at Why Organizations Need Strategies," *California Management Review*, 30 (Fall 1987): 25–32.

76. Waldron Berry, "Beyond Strategic Planning," *Managerial Planning*, 29 (March–April 1981): 14.

77. Ryan Underwood, "In the Hot Seat," *Fast Company*, no. 67 (February 2003): 44. Also see Larry Bossidy and Ram Charan, *Execution: The Discipline of Getting Things Done* (New York: Crown Business, 2002).

78. See Julie I. Siciliano, "Governance and Strategy Implementation: Expanding the Board's Involvement," *Business Horizons*, 45 (November–December 2002): 33–38.

79. Charles H. Roush Jr. and Ben C. Ball Jr., "Controlling the Implementation of Strategy," *Managerial Planning*, 29 (November–December 1980): 4.

80. Donald C. Hambrick and Albert A. Cannella Jr., "Strategy Implementation As Substance and Selling," *Academy of Management Executive*, 3 (November 1989): 282–283. Another good discussion of strategic implementation may be found in Orit Gadiesh and James L. Gilbert, "Transforming Corner-Office Strategy into Frontline Action," *Harvard Business Review*, 79 (May 2001): 72–79.

81. William D. Guth and Ian C. Macmillian, "Strategy Implementation Versus Middle Management Self-Interest," *Strategic Management Journal*, 7 (July–August 1986): 321.

82. See Christopher McDermott and Kenneth K. Boyer, "Strategic Consensus: Marching to the Beat of a Different Drummer?" *Business Horizons*, 42 (July–August 1999): 21–28; and Adelaide Wilcox King, Sally W. Fowler, and Carl P. Zeithaml, "Managing Organizational Competencies for Competitive Advantage: The Middle-Management Edge," *Academy of Management Executive*, 15 (May 2001): 95–106.

83. See Gary Meyer, "eWorkbench: Real-Time Tracking of Synchronized Goals," *HR Magazine* (April 2001): 115–118. For details, see www .workscape.com.

84. See Michael Goold and John J. Quinn, "The Paradox of Strategic Controls," *Strategic Management Journal*, 11 (January 1990): 43–57; and Georg Kellinghusen and Klaus Wubbenhorst, "Strategic Control for Improved Performance," *Long Range Planning*, 23 (June 1990): 30–40.

85. See Vasudevan Ramanujan and N. Venkatraman, "Planning and Performance: A New Look at an Old Question," *Business Horizons*, 30 (May–June 1987): 19–25.

Chapter 6

1. As quoted in Harvey Mackay, "Google Teaches Us a Lesson in Can-Do Attitude," *Arizona Republic* (September 4, 2006): D2. Also see Ben Elgin, "Google: So Much Fanfare, So Few Hits," *Business Week* (July 10, 2006): 26–29.

2. From *Fast Company* by Chuck Salter, "The Discipline of Creativity," December 2002. Copyright © 2002 by Mansueto Ventures LLC. Reproduced with permission of Mansueto Ventures LLC via Copyright Clearance Center.

3. See George T. Doran and Jack Gunn, "Decision Making in High-Tech Firms: Perspectives of Three Executives," *Business Horizons*, 45 (November–December 2002): 7–16; Peter Drucker, "The Right and Wrong Compromise," *Harvard Business Review*, 81 (February 2003): 128; and R. Duane Ireland and C. Chet Miller, "Decision Making and Firm Success," *Academy of Management Executive*, 18 (November 2004): 8–12.

4. Data from "Hurry Up and Decide!" *Business Week* (May 14, 2001): 16.

5. Morgan W. McCall Jr. and Robert E. Kaplan, *Whatever It Takes: The Realities of Managerial Decision Making*, 2d ed. (Englewood Cliffs, N.J.: Prentice-Hall, 1990), p. 5.

6. Paul Hoversten, "Backers Hope Amenities Will Quiet Critics," *USA Today* (February 22, 1995): 2A.

7. See Craig R. Davis, "Calculated Risk: A Framework for Evaluating Product Development," *MIT Sloan Management Review*, 43 (Summer 2002): 71–77; David Ropeik and George Gray, *Risk: A Practical Guide for Deciding What's Really Safe and What's Really Dangerous in the World Around You* (Boston: Houghton Mifflin, 2002); and "Denis Boyles's Five-Minute Guide to Risk," *AARP: The Magazine*, 49 (July–August 2006): 88, 90.

8. Christopher Palmeri, "Mattel's New Toy Story," *Business Week* (November 18, 2002): 72. The risks of drilling for oil five miles deep beneath a mile of ocean depth is discussed in Mark Morrison, "Plenty of Oil—Just Drill Deeper," *Business Week* (September 18, 2006): 38.

9. Matthew L. Ward, "Airports Must Make Way for Airbus' Gigantic A380," *Arizona Republic* (February 11, 2001): D1. See Carol Matlock, "Airbus Has a Weight Problem," *Business Week* (June 28, 2004): 63; and "Airbus Sees End to A380 Cancellations," *USA Today* (November 24, 2006): 5B.

10. Justin Martin, "Tomorrow's CEOs," *Fortune* (June 24, 1996): 90.

11. For example, see George Anders, "The Carly Chronicles," *Fast Company*, no. 67 (February 2003): 66–73.

12. See, for example, Kay M. Nicols and Amy J. Hillman, "Blending Personal Values and Organizational Decision-Making: An Interview with Randall Grahm, President-for-Life, Bonny Doon Vineyards," *Business Horizons*, 49 (November–December 2006): 437–442.

13. Steven M. Gillon, "Unintended Consequences: Why Our Plans Don't Go According to Plan," *The Futurist*, 35 (March–April 2001): 49. See Edward Tenner, *Why Things Bite Back: Technology and the Revenge of Unintended Consequences* (New York: Vintage Books, 1996), chapter 1.

14. Marilyn Adams, "Fliers Board Faster as Fewer Carry on Bags," *USA Today* (August 29, 2006): 2B. Also see Jena McGregor, "Check Those Impulses," *Business Week* (August 21–28, 2006): 16; and Mitchell Lee Marks, "Workplace Recovery after Mergers, Acquisitions, and Downsizings: Facilitating Individual Adaptation to Major Organizational Transitions," *Organizational Dynamics*, 35, no. 4 (2006): 384–399.

15. See Bevery Geber, "A Quick Course in Decision Science," *Training*, 25 (April 1988): 54–55; Alan E. Singer, Steven Lysonski, Ming Singer, and David Hayes, "Ethical Myopia: The Case of 'Framing' by Framing," *Journal of Business Ethics*, 10 (January 1991): 29–36; and Glen Whyte, "Decision Failures: Why They Occur and How to Prevent Them," *Academy of Management Executive*, 5 (August 1991): 23–31.

16. Irwin P. Levin, Sara K. Schnittjer, and Shannon L. Thee, "Information Framing Effects in Social and Personal Decisions," *Journal of Experimental Social Psychology*, 24 (November 1988): 527. For additional research evidence, see Michael J. Zickar and Scott Highhouse, "Looking Closer at the Effects of Framing on Risky Choice: An Item Response Theory Analysis," *Organizational Behavior and Human Decision Processes*, 75 (July 1998): 75–91; and Vikas Mittal and William T. Ross Jr., "The Impact of Positive and Negative Affect and Issue Framing on Issue Interpretation and Risk Taking," *Organizational Behavior and Human Decision Processes*, 76 (December 1998): 298–324.

17. For good background reading, see Barry M. Staw and Jerry Ross, "Knowing When to Pull the Plug," *Harvard Business Review*, 65 (March–April 1987): 68–74; and Barry M. Staw and Jerry Ross, "Understanding Behavior in Escalation Situations," *Science*, 246 (October 13, 1989): 216–220. Also see William S. Silver and Terence R. Mitchell, "The Status Quo Tendency in Decision Making," *Organizational Dynamics*, 18 (Spring 1990): 34–46; and Kin Fai Ellick Wong, Michelle

Yik, and Jessica Y.Y. Kwong, "Understanding the Emotional Aspects of Escalation of Commitment: The Role of Negative Affect," *Journal of Applied Psychology,* 91 (March 2006): 282–297.

18. See Joel Brockner, "The Escalation of Commitment to a Failing Course of Action: Toward Theoretical Progress," *Academy of Management Review,* 17 (January 1992): 39–61; Beth Dietz-Uhler, "The Escalation of Commitment in Political Decision-Making Groups: A Social Identity Approach," *European Journal of Social Psychology,* 26 (July–August 1996): 611–629; Jennifer L. DeNicolis and Donald A. Hantula, "Sinking Shots and Sinking Costs? Or, How Long Can I Play in the NBA?" *Academy of Management Executive,* 10 (August 1996): 66–67; and Marc D. Street and William P. Anthony, "A Conceptual Framework Establishing the Relationship Between Groupthink and Escalating Commitment Behavior," *Small Group Research,* 28 (May 1997): 267–293.

19. For related research evidence, see Itamar Simonson and Barry M. Staw, "Deescalation Strategies: A Comparison of Techniques for Reducing Commitment to Losing Courses of Action," *Journal of Applied Psychology,* 77 (August 1992): 419–426.

20. As quoted in "Navy Cancels Contract for Attack Planes," *Christian Science Monitor* (January 9, 1991): 3. Also see Russell Mitchell, "Desperately Seeking an Attack Bomber," *Business Week* (January 21, 1991): 35; and James Carney, "7 Clues to Understanding Dick Cheney," *Time* (January 6, 2003): 98–104. Another good case study of escalation can be found in Jerry Ross and Barry M. Staw, "Organizational Escalation and Exit: Lessons from the Shoreham Nuclear Power Plant," *Academy of Management Journal,* 36 (August 1993): 701–732.

21. Andy Reinhardt, "A Space Venture That's Sputtering," *Business Week* (November, 9, 1998): 156. Also see Kerry Sulkowicz, "CEO Pay: The Prestige, the Peril," *Business Week* (November 20, 2006): 18.

22. For an interesting exercise, see J. Edward Russo and Paul J. H. Schoemaker, "The Overconfidence Quiz," *Harvard Business Review,* 68 (September–October 1990): 236–237.

23. See Mark Simon, "Man, I'm Smart About How Stupid I Am!" *Business Horizons,* 44 (July–August 2001): 21–24; and Leigh Buchanan, "The New Face of Confidence," *Inc.,* 25 (February 2003): 58–65.

24. Decision traps and personal investing are instructively covered in Jason Zweig, "Do You Sabotage Yourself?" *Money,* 30 (May 2001): 74–78. Neutralizing overconfidence is discussed in Paul J.H. Schoemaker and Robert E. Gunther, "The Wisdom of Deliberate Mistakes," *Harvard Business Review,* 84 (June 2006): 108–115.

25. An excellent resource book is James G. March, *A Primer on Decision Making: How Decisions Happen* (New York: Free Press, 1994). Also see Catherine A. Maritan, "Capital Investment As Investing in Organizational Capabilities: An Empirically Grounded Process Model," *Academy of Management Journal,* 44 (June 2001): 513–531.

26. For example, see Herbert A. Simon, *The New Science of Management Decision,* rev. ed. (Englewood Cliffs, N.J.: Prentice-Hall, 1977), p. 40. Also see James W. Dean Jr. and Mark P. Sharfman, "Does Decision Process Matter? A Study of Strategic Decision-Making Effectiveness," *Academy of Management Journal,* 39 (April 1996): 368–396; Jerre L. Stead, "Whose Decision Is It, Anyway?" *Management Review,* 88 (January 1999): 13; Anna Muoio, "All the Right Moves," *Fast Company,* no. 24 (May 1999): 192–200; and Brian Palmer, "Click Here for Decisions," *Fortune* (May 10, 1999): 153–156.

27. Andrew S. Grove, *High Output Management* (New York: Random House, 1983), p. 98.

28. Simon, *The New Science of Management Decision,* p. 46.

29. See David R. A. Skidd, "Revisiting Bounded Rationality," *Journal of Management Inquiry,* 1 (December 1992): 343–347; March, *A Primer on Decision Making,* pp. 8–9; and Larry Yu, "The Principles of Decision Making," *MIT Sloan Management Review,* 43 (Spring 2002): 15.

30. See Charles R. Schwenk, "The Use of Participant Recollection in the Modeling of Organizational Decision Processes," *Academy of Management Review,* 10 (July 1985): 496–503. Also see Justin Fox, "Is the Market Rational?" *Fortune* (December 9, 2002): 117–126.

31. Chester I. Barnard, *The Functions of the Executive* (Cambridge, Mass.: Harvard University Press, 1938), p. 190. Also see Susan S. Kirschenbaum, "Influence of Experience on Information-Gathering Strategies," *Journal of Applied Psychology,* 77 (June 1992): 343–352.

32. See Stuart F. Brown, "Making Decisions in a Flood of Data," *Fortune* (August 13, 2001): 148[B]–148[H].

33. For good background reading, see *Harvard Business Review on Knowledge Management* (Boston: Harvard Business School Publishing, 1998); Thomas A. Stewart, "The Case Against Knowledge Management," *Business 2.0,* 3 (February 2002): 80–83; Julian Birkinshaw and Tony Sheehan, "Managing the Knowledge Life Cycle," *MIT Sloan Management Review,* 44 (Fall 2002): 75–83; and Syed H. Akhter, "Strategic Planning, Hypercompetition, and Knowledge Management," *Business Horizons,* 46 (January–February 2003): 19–24.

34. David W. De Long and Patricia Seemann, "Confronting Conceptual Confusion and Conflict in Knowledge Management," *Organizational Dynamics,* 29 (Summer 2000): 33. Also see Al Jacobson and Laurence Prusak, "The Cost of Knowledge," *Harvard Business Review,* 84 (November 2006): 34; and Don Cohen, "What's Your Return on Knowledge?" *Harvard Business Review,* 84 (December 2006): 28.

35. For more on tacit knowledge, see Roy Lubit, "Tacit Knowledge and Knowledge Management: The Keys to Sustainable Competitive Advantage," *Organizational Dynamics,* 29 (Winter 2001): 164–178; and Kent D. Miller, Meng Zhao, and Roger J. Calantone, "Adding Interpersonal Learning and Tacit Knowledge to March's Exploration-Exploitation Model," *Academy of Management Journal,* 49 (August 2006): 709–722. Intuition is discussed in Lisa A. Burke and Eugene Sadler-Smith, "Instructor Intuition in the Educational Setting," *Academy of Management Learning and Education,* 5 (June 2006): 169–181; Jack and Suzy Welch, "When to Go with Your Gut," *Business Week* (September 4, 2006): 104; and Margery Weinstein, "Leadership: It's Not All In Their Heads, But It Can Be," *Training,* 43 (November 2006): 11.

36. See David W. De Long and Liam Fahey, "Diagnosing Cultural Barriers to Knowledge Management," *Academy of Management Executive,* 14 (November 2000): 113–127; and Rob Cross, Andrew Parker, Laurence Prusak, and Stephen P. Borgatti, "Knowing What We Know: Supporting Knowledge Creation and Sharing in Social Networks," *Organizational Dynamics,* 30 (Fall 2001): 100–120.

37. Dylan Tweney, "How to Beat Corporate Alzheimer's," *Business 2.0,* 2 (October 2001): 114.

38. George P. Huber, *Managerial Decision Making* (Glenview, Ill.: Scott, Foresman, 1980), pp. 141–142. Also see David H. Freedman, "Collaboration Is the Hottest Buzzword in Business Today. Too Bad it Doesn't Work," *Inc.,* 28 (September 2006): 61–62; and Michael Useem, "How Well-Run Boards Make Decisions," *Harvard Business Review,* 84 (November 2006): 130–138.

39. See William L. Shanklin, "Creatively Managing for Creative Destruction," *Business Horizons,* 43 (November–December 2000): 29–35; Stefan Thomke, "Enlightened Experimentation: The New Imperative for Innovation," *Harvard Business Review,* 79 (February 2001): 66–75; George Anders, "Roche's New Scientific Method," *Fast Company,* no. 54 (January 2002): 60–67; and George Anders, "How Intel Puts Innovation Inside," *Fast Company,* no. 56 (March 2002): 122, 124.

40. A good historical perspective on creativity can be found in Michael Michalko, "Thinking Like a Genius," *The Futurist,* 32 (May 1998): 21–25. Also see Kerrie Unsworth, "Unpacking Creativity," *Academy of Management Review,* 26 (April 2001): 289–297.

41. Based on discussion in N. R. F. Maier, Mara Julius, and James Thurber, "Studies in Creativity: Individual Differences in the Storing and Utilization of Information," *American Journal of Psychology,* 80 (December 1967): 492–519.

42. Sidney J. Parnes, "Learning Creative Behavior," *The Futurist,* 18 (August 1984): 30–31. Also see Liz Simpson, "Fostering Creativity," *Training,* 38 (December 2001): 54–57; and Polly LaBarre, "Weird Ideas That Work," *Fast Company,* no. 54 (January 2002): 68–73.

43. See Arthur Koestler, *The Act of Creation* (London: Hutchinson, 1969), p. 27.

44. See James L. Adams, *Conceptual Blockbusting* (San Francisco: Freeman, 1974), p. 35; Dean Foust, "Getting to 'Aha!'" *Business Week* (September 4, 2006): 100; and Siri Schubert, "A Duffer's Dream," *Business 2.0,* 7 (November 2006): 56.

45. Geoffrey Colvin, "The Imagination Economy," *Fortune* (July 10, 2006): 53.

46. Minda Zetlin, "Nurturing Nonconformists," *Management Review*, 88 (October 1999): 30. Also see Diane L. Coutu, "Genius at Work," *Harvard Business Review*, 79 (October 2001): 63–68; Ryan Mathews and Watts Wacker, "Deviants, Inc.," *Fast Company*, no. 56 (March 2002): 70–80; and Robin Hanson, "The Myth of Creativity," *Business Week* (July 3, 2006): 134.

47. John Byrne, "The Search for the Young and Gifted," *Business Week* (October 4, 1999): 108. Also see Thomas H. Davenport, Laurence Prusak, and H. James Wilson, "Who's Bringing You Hot Ideas, and How Are You Responding?" *Harvard Business Review*, 81 (February 2003): 58–64.

48. See Ian Wylie, "Failure Is Glorious," *Fast Company*, no. 51 (October 2001): 35–38; and Jena McGregor, "How Failure Breeds Success," *Business Week* (July 10, 2006): 42–52.

49. List adapted from Roger von Oech, *A Whack on the Side of the Head* (N. Y.: Warner Books, 1983). Reprinted by permission. For more on creativity, see Alyssa Danigelis, "Freak Control: Channeling Blue Man Group's Creative Fire Isn't Easy—Unless You're Jennie Willink," *Fast Company*, no. 107 (July–August 2006): 103; Nancy K. Napier, Nancy H. Leonard, and Zorina Sendler, "Facilitating Management and Marketing Creativity in Global Markets," *Organizational Dynamics*, 35, no. 3 (2006): 220–236; Christina Ting Fong, "The Effects of Emotional Ambivalence on Creativity," *Academy of Management Journal*, 49 (October 2006): 1016–1030; Diane Coutu, "Ideas as Art," *Harvard Business Review*, 84 (October 2006): 82–89.

50. Huber, *Managerial Decision Making*, p. 12. Also see Brent Roper, "Sizing Up Business Problems," *HR Magazine*, 46 (November 2001): 50–56.

51. Peter F. Drucker, *The Practice of Management* (New York: Harper & Row, 1954), p. 531.

52. See Margery Weinstein, "Program Aims to Solve Your Biggest Problems," *Training*, 43 (June 2006): 14.

53. Louis S. Richman, "How to Get Ahead in America," *Fortune* (May 16, 1994): 48.

54. For an empirical classification of organizational problems, see David A. Cowan, "Developing a Classification Structure of Organizational Problems: An Empirical Investigation," *Academy of Management Journal*, 33 (June 1990): 366–390.

55. Adapted from Huber, *Managerial Decision Making*, pp. 13–15.

56. Marshall Sashkin and Kenneth J. Kiser, *Total Quality Management* (Seabrook, Md.: Ducochon Press, 1991), p. 153.

57. Adams, *Conceptual Blockbusting*, p. 7.

58. See Margery Weinstein, "Innovate or Die Trying," *Training*, 43 (May 2006): 40–44; Jessi Hempel, "Big Blue Brainstorm," *Business Week* (August 7, 2006): 70; and Michael Myser, "When Brainstorming Goes Bad," *Business 2.0*, 7 (October 2006): 76.

59. For related research, see John J. Sosik, Bruce J. Avolio, and Surinder S. Kahai, "Inspiring Group Creativity: Comparing Anonymous and Identified Electronic Brainstorming," *Small Group Research*, 29 (February 1998): 3–31.

60. See Russell L. Ackoff, "The Art and Science of Mess Management," *Interfaces*, 11 (February 1981): 20–26. Also see Russell L. Ackoff, *Management in Small Doses* (New York: Wiley, 1986), pp. 102–103; and Glenn Detrick, "Russell L. Ackoff," *Academy of Management Learning and Education*, 1 (September 2002): 56–63.

61. See March, *A Primer on Decision Making*, p. 18; and Gina Imperato, "When Is 'Good Enough' Good Enough?" *Fast Company*, no. 26 (July–August 1999): 52.

62. Ackoff, "The Art and Science of Mess Management," p. 22.

63. As quoted in James B. Treece, "Shaking Up Detroit," *Business Week* (August 14, 1989): 78.

64. Paul Hawken, "Problems, Problems," *Inc.*, 9 (September 1987): 24.

65. John R. Brandt, "What's Your Problem?" *Industry Week*, 251 (December 2002): 23. Also see Geoffrey Colvin, "How One CEO Learned to Fly," *Fortune* (October 30, 2006): 98.

Chapter 7

1. "Sam Walton in His Own Words," *Fortune* (June 29, 1992): 104.

2. From Paul Kaihla, "Nokia's Hit Factory," *Business 2.0*, 3 (August 2002): 66–70. Copyright 2002 Time Inc. All rights reserved. Reprinted with permission.

3. Nokia's employment data from www.nokia.com, March 30, 2007.

4. See B. J. Hodge, William P. Anthony, and Lawrence M. Gales, *Organization Theory: A Strategic Approach*, 5th ed. (Upper Saddle River, N.J.: Prentice-Hall, 1996), p. 10.

5. Adapted from Edgar H. Schein, *Organizational Psychology*, 3d ed. (Englewood Cliffs, N.J.: Prentice-Hall, 1980), pp. 12–15.

6. See Adam Smith, *The Wealth of Nations* (New York: Modern Library, 1937), p. 7.

7. For example, see Jay R. Galbraith and Edward E. Lawler III, "Effective Organizations: Using the New Logic of Organizing," in *Organizing for the Future: The New Logic for Managing Complex Organizations*, eds. Jay R. Galbraith, Edward E. Lawler III, and Associates (San Francisco: Jossey-Bass, 1993), pp. 293–294. Related research is reported in Kees van den Bos, Henk A. M. Wilke, and E. Allan Lind, "When Do We Need Procedural Fairness? The Role of Trust in Authority," *Journal of Personality and Social Psychology*, 75 (December 1998): 1449–1458.

8. Elliot Jaques, "In Praise of Hierarchy," *Harvard Business Review*, 68 (January–February 1990): 127. Also see Jack and Suzy Welch, "Are You a Boss-Hater?" *Business Week* (July 3, 2006): 136; Jack and Suzy Welch, "A Twisted Chain of Command," *Business Week* (September 18, 2006): 116; and Jack and Suzy Welch, "A Dangerous Division of Labor," *Business Week* (November 6, 2006): 122.

9. For an interesting biography of Henry Ford, see Ann Jardim, *The First Henry Ford: A Study in Personality and Business Leadership* (Cambridge, Mass.: MIT Press, 1970), p. 40.

10. See Marc Cecere, "Drawing the Lines," *Harvard Business Review*, 79 (November 2001): 24.

11. Kim Cameron, "Critical Questions in Assessing Organizational Effectiveness," *Organizational Dynamics*, 9 (Autumn 1980): 70.

12. See Raj Aggarwal, "Using Economic Profit to Assess Performance: A Metric for Modern Firms," *Business Horizons*, 44 (January–February 2001): 55–60.

13. Winslow Buxton, "Growth from Top to Bottom," *Management Review*, 88 (July–August 1999): 11.

14. See Frits K. Pil and Matthias Holweg, "Exploring Scale: The Advantages of Thinking Small," *MIT Sloan Management Review*, 44 (Winter 2003): 33–39; and Karina Funk, "Sustainability and Performance," *MIT Sloan Management Review*, 44 (Winter 2003): 65–70.

15. See Jeffrey Pfeffer, "When It Comes to 'Best Practices'—Why Do Smart Organizations Occasionally Do Dumb Things?" *Organizational Dynamics*, 25 (Summer 1996): 33–44; and Michael Beer, "How to Develop an Organization Capable of Sustained High Performance: Embrace the Drive for Results-Capability Development Paradox," *Organizational Dynamics*, 29 (Spring 2001): 233–247.

16. It is instructive to ponder why companies fall from grace over the years. One tracking device is *Fortune* magazine's annual list of "America's Most Admired Corporations." For example, see Anne Fisher, "America's Most Admired Companies," *Fortune* (March 6, 2006): 65–76. Also see Jack and Suzy Welch, "How Healthy Is Your Company?" *Business Week* (May 8, 2006): 126; and Edward E. Lawler III and Christopher G. Worley, *Built to Change: How to Achieve Sustained Organizational Effectiveness* (San Francisco: Jossey-Bass, 2006).

17. See Michael Goold and Andrew Campbell, "Do You Have a Well-Designed Organization?" *Harvard Business Review*, 80 (March 2002): 117–124; and Jay R. Galbraith, "Organizing to Deliver Solutions," *Organizational Dynamics*, 31 (Autumn 2002): 194–207.

18. See Tom Burns and G. M. Stalker, *The Management of Innovation* (London: Tavistock, 1961), chapter 5.

19. See John A. Courtright, Gail T. Fairhurst, and L. Edna Rogers, "Interaction Patterns in Organic and Mechanistic Systems," *Academy of Management Journal*, 32 (December 1989): 773–802.

20. Ben Elgin, "Running the Tightest Ship on the Net," *Business Week* (January 29, 2001): 126.

21. Jenny C. McCune, "The Change Makers," *Management Review*, 88 (May 1999): 17. Also see David Lei and John W. Slocum Jr., "Organization Designs to Renew Competitive Advantage," *Organizational Dynamics*, 31 (August 2002): 1–18.

22. See Marco Iansiti, "Shooting the Rapids: Managing Product Development in Turbulent Environments," *California Management Review*,

38 (Fall 1995): 37–58; and David A. Morand, "The Role of Behavioral Formality and Informality in the Enactment of Bureaucratic Versus Organic Organizations," *Academy of Management Review,* 20 (October 1995): 831–872.

23. James D. Thompson, *Organizations in Action* (New York: McGraw-Hill, 1967), p. 59.

24. Based in part on Jay R. Galbraith, *Designing Organizations: An Executive Briefing on Strategy, Structure, and Process* (San Francisco: Jossey-Bass, 1995): pp. 24–37.

25. Based on "General Electric Reorganizes Some Businesses for Growth," *East Valley/Scottsdale Tribune* (December 5, 2003): B3.

26. Adapted from "Dial 800, Talk to Omaha," *Fortune* (January 29, 1990): 16; Rhonda Richards, "Technology Makes Omaha Hotel-Booking Capital," *USA Today* (April 7, 1994): 4B; and Robert D. Kaplan, *An Empire Wilderness: Travels into America's Future* (New York: Random House, 1998), p. 59.

27. Based on Andy Reinhardt and Seanna Browder, "Fly, Damn It, Fly," *Business Week* (November 9, 1998): 150–156. Also see Wim G. Biemans, "Marketing in the Twilight Zone," *Business Horizons,* 41 (November–December 1998): 69–76.

28. For more, see Michael Hammer and James Champy, *Reengineering the Corporation: A Manifesto for Business Revolution* (New York: HarperCollins, 1993); James Champy, *Reengineering Management: The Mandate for New Leadership* (New York: HarperBusiness, 1995); Dutch Holland and Sanjiv Kumar, "Getting Past the Obstacles to Successful Reengineering," *Business Horizons,* 38 (May–June 1995): 79–85; and Rob Duboff and Craig Carter, "Reengineering from the Outside In," *Management Review,* 84 (November 1995): 42–46.

29. See John A. Byrne, "The Horizontal Corporation," *Business Week* (December 20, 1993): 76–81; and Susan Sonnesyn Brooks, "Managing a Horizontal Revolution," *HR Magazine,* 40 (June 1995): 52–58.

30. Rahul Jacob, "The Struggle to Create an Organization for the 21st Century," *Fortune* (April 3, 1995): 91. For related reading, see Michael H. Martin, "Smart Managing," *Fortune* (February 2, 1998): 149–151; and David Stamps, "Enterprise Training: This Changes *Everything,*" *Training,* 36 (January 1999): 40–48.

31. David Kiley, "Coke Reorganizes; President Resigns," *USA Today* (March 5, 2001): 2B. Another example can be found in "GE to Merge Appliance, Lighting Units," *USA Today* (August 30, 2000): 1B.

32. For an extensive bibliography on this subject, see David D. Van Fleet and Arthur G. Bedeian, "A History of the Span of Management," *Academy of Management Review,* 2 (July 1977): 356–372.

33. Drawn from C. W. Barkdull, "Span of Control—A Method of Evaluation," *Michigan Business Review,* 15 (May 1963): 25–32.

34. William H. Wagel, "Keeping the Organization Lean at Federal Express," *Personnel,* 64 (March 1987): 4–12.

35. Paul Kaestle, "A New Rationale for Organizational Structure," *Planning Review,* 18 (July–August 1990): 22. Also see Robert W. Keidel, "Triangular Design: A New Organizational Geometry," *Academy of Management Executive,* 4 (November 1990): 21–37.

36. For example, see Jeffrey Schmidt, "Breaking Down Fiefdoms," *Management Review,* 86 (January 1997): 45–49; and Michael E. Raynor and Joseph L. Bower, "Lead from the Center: How to Manage Divisions Dynamically," *Harvard Business Review,* 79 (May 2001): 92–100.

37. For a comprehensive research summary on centralization and organizational effectiveness, see George P. Huber, C. Chet Miller, and William H. Glick, "Developing More Encompassing Theories About Organizations: The Centralization-Effectiveness Relationship As an Example," *Organization Science,* 1 (1990): 11–40.

38. See Larry Bossidy, "The Job No CEO Should Delegate," *Harvard Business Review,* 79 (March 2001): 46–49; and Sharon Gazda, "The Art of Delegating," *HR Magazine,* 47 (January 2002): 75–78.

39. Adapted from Marion E. Haynes, "Delegation: There's More to It Than Letting Someone Else Do It!" *Supervisory Management,* 25 (January 1980): 9–15. Three types of delegation—incremental, sequential, and functional—are discussed in William R. Tracey, "Deft Delegation: Multiplying Your Effectiveness," *Personnel,* 65 (February 1988): 36–42.

40. The delegation styles of selected U.S. presidents are examined in Edward J. Mayo and Lance P. Jarvis, "Delegation 101: Lessons from the White House," *Business Horizons,* 31 (September–October 1988): 2–12.

41. Alex Taylor III, "Iacocca's Time of Trouble," *Fortune* (March 14, 1988): 79, 81.

42. Andrew S. Grove, *High Output Management* (New York: Random House, 1983), p. 60. Also see Wilson Harrell, "Your Biggest Mistake," *Success,* 43 (March 1996): 88.

43. For interesting facts about delegating, see "Top Dogs," *Fortune* (September 30, 1996): 189; and Bill Leonard, "Good Assistants Make Managers More Efficient," *HR Magazine,* 44 (February 1999): 12.

44. "How Conservatism Wins in the Hottest Market," *Business Week* (January 17, 1977): 43.

45. Adapted from William H. Newman, "Overcoming Obstacles to Effective Delegation," *Management Review,* 45 (January 1956): 36–41; and from Eugene Raudsepp, "Why Supervisors Don't Delegate," *Supervision,* 41 (May 1979): 12–15. Also see Gary Yukl and Ping Ping Fu, "Determinants of Delegation and Consultation by Managers," *Journal of Organizational Behavior,* 20 (March 1999): 219–232.

46. Practical tips on delegation can be found in Douglas Anderson, "Supervisors and the Hesitate to Delegate Syndrome," *Supervision,* 53 (November 1992): 9–11; and Michael C. Dennis, "Only Superman Didn't Delegate," *Business Credit,* 95 (February 1993): 41.

47. For more on initiative, see Michael Frese, Wolfgang Kring, Andrea Soose, and Jeanette Zempel, "Personal Initiative at Work: Differences between East and West Germany," *Academy of Management Journal,* 39 (February 1996): 37–63; and Alan L. Frohman, "Igniting Organizational Change from Below: The Power of Personal Initiative," *Organizational Dynamics,* 25 (Winter 1997): 39–53.

48. Peter F. Drucker, *Managing the Non-Profit Organization* (New York: HarperCollins, 1990), p. 117. Also see Jim Holt, "Management Master," *Management Review,* 88 (November 1999): 15.

49. See, for example, Warren G. Bennis, *Changing Organizations* (New York: McGraw-Hill, 1966).

50. As quoted in Noel M. Tichy and Stratford Sherman, *Control Your Destiny or Someone Else Will: How Jack Welch Is Making General Electric the World's Most Competitive Corporation* (New York: Doubleday, 1993), p. 21. Also see Peter Coy, "The 21st Century Corporation: The Creative Economy," *Business Week* (August 28, 2000): 76–82.

51. Data from Patricia Sellers, "'Now Is the Time to Invest," *Fortune* (October 16, 2006): 142.

52. Andy Reinhardt, "Nokia's Next Act," *Business Week* (July 1, 2002): 56.

53. See Deborah Ancona, Henrik Bresman, and Katrin Kaeufer, "The Comparative Advantage of X-Teams," *MIT Sloan Management Review,* 43 (Spring 2002): 33–39.

54. Toby Tetenbaum and Hilary Tetenbaum, "Office 2000: Tear Down the Walls," *Training,* 37 (February 2000): 60.

55. For some good ideas on team building, see Margery Weinstein, "Getting Your Employees' Act Together," *Training,* 43 (September 2006): 10; Jacqueline Durett, "Make Music, Build Teams," *Training,* 43 (September 2006): 42–43; and Nanette Byrnes, "In the Trenches at VF Boot Camp," *Business Week* (November 20, 2006): 93–94.

56. See Melissa A. Schilling and H. Kevin Steensma, "The Use of Modular Organizational Forms: An Industry-Level Analysis," *Academy of Management Journal,* 44 (December 2001): 1149–1168; and Stephen J. Zaccaro and Paige Bader, "E-Leadership and the Challenges of Leading E-Teams: Minimizing the Bad and Maximizing the Good," *Organizational Dynamics,* 31, no. 4 (2003): 377–387.

57. See David M. Slipy, "Anthropologist Uncovers Real Workplace Attitudes," *HR Magazine,* 35 (October 1990): 76–79; David A. Kaplan, "Studying the Gearheads," *Newsweek* (August 3, 1998): 62; and Paul J. Kampas, "Shifting Cultural Gears in Technology-Driven Industries," *MIT Sloan Management Review,* 44 (Winter 2003): 41–48.

58. This definition is based in part on Linda Smircich, "Concepts of Culture and Organizational Analysis," *Administrative Science Quarterly,* 28 (September 1983): 339–358. Also see Patrick M. Lencioni, "Make Your Values Mean Something," *Harvard Business Review,* 80 (July 2002): 113–117; and James M. Higgins and Craig McAllaster, "Want Innovation? Then Use Cultural Artifacts that Support It," *Organizational Dynamics,* 31 (August 2002): 74–84.

59. Data from John E. Sheridan, "Organizational Culture and Employee Retention," *Academy of Management Journal,* 35 (December 1992): 1036–1056. For parallel findings, see Shelly Branch, "The 100 Best Companies to Work for in America," *Fortune* (January 11, 1999): 118–144.

60. Peter C. Reynolds, "Imposing a Corporate Culture," *Psychology Today,* 21 (March 1987): 38.

61. Based on Harrison M. Trice and Janice M. Beyer, *The Cultures of Work Organizations* (Englewood Cliffs, N.J.: Prentice-Hall, 1993), pp. 5–8. For related research, see Davide Ravasi and Majken Schultz, "Responding to Organizational Identity Threats: Exploring the Role of Organizational Culture," *Academy of Management Journal,* 49 (June 2006): 433–458.

62. As quoted in Stephen B. Shepard, "A Talk with Jeff Immelt," *Business Week* (January 28, 2002): 103.

63. See, for example, Beverly Geber, "100 Days of Training," *Training,* 36 (January 1999): 62–66; Peter Troiano, "Post-Merger Challenges," *Management Review,* 88 (January 1999): 6; and Robert J. Grossman, "Irreconcilable Differences," *HR Magazine,* 44 (April 1999): 42–48.

64. "A.G. Lafley: Procter & Gamble," *Business Week* (January 13, 2003): 67.

65. See Amy C. Edmondson and Sandra E. Cha, "When Company Values Backfire," *Harvard Business Review,* 80 (November 2002): 18–19; and Anne Mulcahy, "Stay True to Your Values," *Business 2.0,* 7 (December 2006): 98.

66. Gina Imperato, "MindSpring Does a Mind-Flip," *Fast Company,* no. 22 (February–March 1999): 40.

67. See Elizabeth Wolfe Morrison, "Newcomers' Relationships: The Role of Social Network Ties During Socialization," *Academy of Management Journal,* 45 (December 2002): 1149–1160.

68. Alan L. Wilkins, "The Culture Audit: A Tool for Understanding Organizations," *Organizational Dynamics,* 12 (Autumn 1983): 34–35.

69. Rebecca Ganzel, "Putting Out the Welcome Mat," *Training,* 35 (March 1998): 54. Also see Joseph Kornik, "Dial 1 for New-Employee Orientation," *Training,* 43 (July 2006): 11; and Margery Weinstein, "Hello, My Name Is . . . Is Your Employee Orientation Lacking?" *Training,* 43 (August 2006): 11.

70. For the full story, see Douglas A. Ready, "How Storytelling Builds Next-Generation Leaders," *MIT Sloan Management Review,* 43 (Summer 2002): 63–69.

71. Alan L. Wilkins, "The Creation of Company Cultures: The Role of Stories and Human Resource Systems," *Human Resource Management,* 23 (Spring 1984): 43.

72. Adapted from Terrence E. Deal and Allan A. Kennedy, *Corporate Cultures: The Rites and Rituals of Corporate Life* (Reading, Mass.: Addison-Wesley, 1982), pp. 136–139. Also see Haidee E. Allerton, "Dysfunctional Checklist," *Training & Development,* 53 (June 1999): 10; and Jenny C. McCune, "Sorry, Wrong Executive," *Management Review,* 88 (October 1999): 16–21.

73. Eight tips for maintaining the strength of an organization's culture are presented in Trice and Beyer, *Cultures of Work Organizations,* pp. 378–391. Also see Carol Lavin Bernick, "When Your Culture Needs a Makeover," *Harvard Business Review,* 79 (June 2001): 53–61; Ram Charan, "Home Depot's Blueprint for Culture Change," *Harvard Business Review,* 84 (April 2006): 60–70; and Matt Bolch, "Bidding Adieu," *HR Magazine,* 51 (June 2006): 122–126.

Chapter 8

1. As quoted in David Lidsky, "Fast Talk: Share Best Practices," *Fast Company,* no. 91 (February 2005): 42.

2. Matthew Boyle, "Down in the Aisles," *Fortune,* October 30, 2006. Boxed article accompanying Matthew Boyle, "Why Costco Is So Damn Addictive," *Fortune* (October 30, 2006): 126–132. Copyright © 2006 Time Inc. All rights reserved.

3. For related reading, see Carol Hymowitz, "How CEOs Can Keep Informed Even As Work Stretches Across Globe," *Wall Street Journal* (March 12, 2002): B1; Bin Zhao and Fernando Olivera, "Error Reporting in Organizations," *Academy of Management Review,* 31 (October 2006): 1012–1030; Andrew McAfee, "Mastering the Three Worlds of Information Technology," *Harvard Business Review,* 84 (November 2006): 141–149; and Mimi Hall, "Katrina Aid is Still Being Abused, U.S. Investigators Say," *USA Today* (December 7, 2006): 7A.

4. For example, see Harold Koontz and Robert W. Bradspies, "Managing Through Feedforward Control," *Business Horizons,* 15 (June 1972): 27.

5. Gail Edmondson, "*Basta* with the Venti Frappuccinos," *Business Week* (August 7, 2006): 42–43.

6. Data from Michelle Kessler and Jayne O'Donnell, "3.5 Million More Sony Batteries Under Recall," *USA Today* (October 24, 2006): 2B. Also see Michelle Kessler, "Recall May Speed Safer Battery Push," *USA Today* (November 6, 2006): 1B. For another example of the need for feedforward control, see Chris Woodyard, Paul Davidson, and Brad Heath, "BP Spill Highlights Aging Oil Field's Increasing Problems," *USA Today* (August 14, 2006): 1B–2B.

7. Paul C. Judge, "EMC Corporation," *Fast Company,* no. 47 (June 2001): 144. Also see Michael Behar, "Computer Heal Thyself," *Business 2.0,* 3 (July 2002): 100–101.

8. For more on monitoring customer complaints, see Robert Johnston and Sandy Mehra, "Best-Practice Complaint Management," *Academy of Management Executive,* 16 (November 2002): 145–154.

9. For discussion of a small business that got out of control, see D. M. Osborne, "Fast-Paced Rivals Silence Talking-Beeper Service," *Inc.,* 21 (December 1999): 40. Also see Anne Stuart, "The Pita Principle," *Inc.,* 23 (August 2001): 58–64.

10. See Richard L. Daft and Norman B. Macintosh, "The Nature and Use of Formal Control Systems for Management Control and Strategy Implementation," *Journal of Management,* 10 (Spring 1984): 43–66; and Harrison M. Trice and Janice M. Beyer, *The Cultures of Work Organizations* (Englewood Cliffs, N.J.: Prentice-Hall, 1993).

11. Based on Eric Flamholtz, "Organizational Control Systems As a Managerial Tool," *California Management Review,* 22 (Winter 1979): 50–59.

12. Chris Woodyard, "'Slow and Steady' Drives Toyota's Growth," *USA Today* (December 21, 2005): 2B. Also see Chris Woodyard, "Toyota Delays Some New Models as Quality Control Scrutinized," *USA Today* (August 28, 2006): 6B.

13. See Stanley F. Slater, Eric M. Olson, and Venkateshwar K. Reddy, "Strategy-Based Performance Measurement," *Business Horizons,* 40 (July–August 1997): 37–44.

14. For more, see Gabriel Szulanski and Sidney Winter, "Getting It Right the Second Time," *Harvard Business Review,* 80 (January 2002): 62–69; Marc Abrahams, "Business Lessons from Leeches," *Harvard Business Review,* 84 (October 2006): 21; and Jack and Suzy Welch, "Dialing for Growth," *Business Week* (October 30, 2006): 134.

15. "Tying Up Loose Change," *Money,* 32 (January 2003): 40. Also see Faith Keenan, "The Marines Learn New Tactics—From Wal-Mart," *Business Week* (December 24, 2001): 74; and Frank Jossi, "Take a Peek Inside," *HR Magazine,* 47 (June 2002): 46–52.

16. For a brief case study of financial control problems in the Catholic Church, see William C. Symonds, "The Economic Strain on the Church," *Business Week* (April 15, 2002): 34–40.

17. Ian Wylie, "Down the Up Staircase," *Fast Company,* no. 56 (March 2002): 34.

18. See Max H. Bazerman, George Loewenstein, and Don A. Moore, "Why Good Accountants Do Bad Audits," *Harvard Business Review,* 80 (November 2002): 96–102; Paul Falcone, "Reporting for SOX Duty," *HR Magazine,* 51 (June 2006): 161–168; David Henry, "A SarbOx Surprise," *Business Week* (June 12, 2006): 38; Andy Serwer, "Stop Whining About SarbOx!" *Fortune* (August 7, 2006): 39; Annette L. Nazareth, "Keeping SarbOx Is Crucial," *Business Week* (November 13, 2006): 134; and "Question of the Week: What do you make of recent efforts to scale back Sarbanes-Oxley corporate reform legislation?" *Business Week* (December 18, 2006): 18.

19. Data from Justin Fox, "What's So Great About GE?" *Fortune* (March 4, 2002): 64–67.

20. Lawrence B. Sawyer, "Internal Auditing: Yesterday, Today, and Tomorrow," *The Internal Auditor,* 36 (December 1979): 26 (emphasis added). Also see Joseph F. Berardino and Gregory J. Jonas, "Power to the Audit Committee People," *Financial Executive,* 15 (November–December 1999): 36–38.

21. See Scott Herhold, "The Blunt Bean Counter," *Business 2.0,* 3 (April 2002): 91–92; and Thomas Mucha, "The Fraud Cop," *Business 2.0,* 3 (April 2002): 90–91.

22. This list is based in part on Donald W. Murr, Harry B. Bracey Jr., and William K. Hill, "How to Improve Your Organization's Management Controls," *Management Review,* 69 (October 1980): 56–63. Also see Jeremy Hope and Robin Fraser, "Who Needs Budgets?" *Harvard Business Review,* 81 (February 2003): 108–115; Mara Der Hovanesian,

"Eagle Eye on Your T&E," *Business Week* (May 8, 2006): 40; and Fataneh Taghaboni-Dutta and Betty Velthouse, "RFID Technology Is Revolutionary: Who Should Be Involved in this Game of Tag?" *Academy of Management Perspectives*, 20 (November 2006): 65–78.

23. See David A. Garvin, "How the Baldrige Award Really Works," *Harvard Business Review*, 69 (November–December 1991): 80–93; Robert Bell and Bernard Keys, "A Conversation with Curt W. Reimann on the Background and Future of the Baldrige Award," *Organizational Dynamics*, 26 (Spring 1998): 51–61; John R. Dew, "Learning from Baldrige Winners at the University of Alabama," *Journal of Organizational Excellence*, 20 (Spring 2001): 49–56; and Del Jones, "History of Baldrige Award Winner Angers Some," *USA Today* (November 30, 2006): 4B.

24. Chris Woodyard, Bruce Horovitz, Gary Strauss, and Anne Willette, "Quality Guru Now Plugs Innovation," *USA Today* (February 27, 1998): 8B.

25. See William C. Symonds, "Boston Scientific's Bypass," *Business Week* (October 9, 2006): 90–91.

26. Philip B. Crosby, *Quality Without Tears: The Art of Hassle-Free Management* (New York: Plume, 1984), p. 64. Also see Philip B. Crosby, *Completeness: Quality for the 21st Century* (New York: Dutton, 1992), p. 116.

27. Adapted in part from Ron Zemke, "A Bluffer's Guide to TQM," *Training*, 30 (April 1993): 48–55.

28. For subscription information, see www.consumerreports.org.

29. Stratford Sherman, "How to Prosper in the Value Decade," *Fortune* (November 30, 1992): 91. Also see Gerald E. Smith and Thomas T. Nagle, "Frames of Reference and Buyers' Perception of Price and Value," *California Management Review*, 38 (Fall 1995): 98–116.

30. Data from "Fortune 500 Largest U.S. Corporations," *Fortune* (April 17, 2006): F1, F52; and Jerry Useem, "One Nation Under Wal-Mart," *Fortune* (March 3, 2002): 64–78.

31. Barbara Hagenbaugh, "U.S. Manufacturing Jobs Fading Away Fast," *USA Today* (December 13, 2002): 1B.

32. See the series of interesting stories about customer service award winners in the September 2006 issue of *Fast Company* magazine, pp. 47–68.

33. Data from Patricia Sellers, "Getting Customers to Love You," *Fortune* (March 13, 1989): 38–49.

34. Data from Patricia Sellers, "What Customers Really Want," *Fortune* (June 4, 1990): 58–68.

35. Howard Gleckman, "Welcome to the Health-Care Economy," *Business Week* (August 26, 2002): 148.

36. Based on discussions in M. Jill Austin, "Planning in Service Organizations," *SAM Advanced Management Journal*, 55 (Summer 1990): 7–12; Everett E. Adam Jr. and Paul M. Swamidass, "Assessing Operations Management from a Strategic Perspective," *Journal of Management*, 15 (June 1989): 181–203; and Ron Zemke, "The Emerging Art of Service Management," *Training*, 29 (January 1992): 37–42.

37. See, for example, Richard B. Chase and Sriram Dasu, "Want to Perfect Your Company's Service? Use Behavioral Science," *Harvard Business Review*, 79 (June 2001): 79–84; and Alicia A. Grandey, "When 'The Show Must Go On': Surface Acting and Deep Acting as Determinants of Emotional Exhaustion and Peer-Related Service Delivery," *Academy of Management Journal*, 46 (February 2003): 86–96.

38. Data from Andrew Erdman, "Staying Ahead of 800 Competitors," *Fortune* (June 1, 1992): 111–112.

39. Ron Zemke and Dick Schaaf, *The Service Edge: 101 Companies That Profit from Customer Care* (New York: New American Library, 1989), p. 14. Also see Mohanbir Sawhney, "Don't Homogenize, Synchronize," *Harvard Business Review*, 79 (July–August 2001): 101–108; and Chun Hui, Simon S. K. Lam, and John Schaubroeck, "Can Good Citizens Lead the Way in Providing Quality Service? A Field Quasi Experiment," *Academy of Management Journal*, 44 (October 2001): 988–995.

40. See Leonard L. Berry, A. Parasuraman, and Valarie A. Zeithaml, "The Service-Quality Puzzle," *Business Horizons*, 31 (September–October 1988): 35–43; Leonard L. Berry, A. Parasuraman, and Valarie A. Zeithaml, "Improving Service Quality in America: Lessons Learned," *Academy of Management Executive*, 8 (May 1994): 32–45; Leonard L.

Berry, Kathleen Seiders, and Larry G. Gresham, "For Love and Money: The Common Traits of Successful Retailers," *Organizational Dynamics*, 26 (Autumn 1997): 7–23; Kathleen Seiders and Leonard L. Berry, "Service Fairness: What It Is and Why It Matters," *Academy of Management Executive*, 12 (May 1998): 8–20; and Leonard L. Berry, Eileen A. Wall, and Lewis P. Carbone, "Service Clues and Customer Assessment of the Service Experience," *Academy of Management Perspectives*, 20 (May 2006): 43–57.

41. Based on Paul Hellman, "Rating Your Dentist," *Management Review*, 87 (July–August 1998): 64.

42. See Leonard L. Berry and Neeli Bendapudi, "Clueing In Customers," *Harvard Business Review*, 81 (February 2003): 100–106; Brian Hindo, "Satisfaction Not Guaranteed," *Business Week* (June 19, 2006): 32–36; Margery Weinstein, "How May I Train You? Customer Service Training Programs Put the Focus on Buyer Bliss," *Training*, 43 (August 2006): 28–32; Frances X. Frei, "Breaking the Trade-Off Between Efficiency and Service," *Harvard Business Review*, 84 (November 2006): 92–101; Lin Grensing-Pophal, "Building Service with a Smile," *HR Magazine*, 51 (November 2006): 84–89; and James G. Combs, David J. Ketchen Jr., and R. Duane Ireland, "Effectively Managing Service Chain Organizations," *Organizational Dynamics*, 35, no. 4 (2006): 357–371.

43. For example, see Steven N. Silverman and Lori L. Silverman, "TOM: The Story of How the Q Lost Its Tail," *Nonprofit World*, 18 (November–December 2000): 25–26; Thomas J. Douglas and William Q. Judge Jr., "Total Quality Management Implementation and Competitive Advantage: The Role of Structural Control and Exploration," *Academy of Management Journal*, 44 (February 2001): 158–169; William Roth and Terry Capuano, "Systemic Versus Nonsystemic Approaches to Quality Improvement," *Journal of Organizational Excellence*, 20 (Spring 2001): 57–64; and Richard S. Allen and Ralph H. Kilmann, "Aligning Reward Practices in Support of Total Quality Management," *Business Horizons*, 44 (May–June 2001): 77–84.

44. Inspired by a more lengthy definition in Marshall Sashkin and Kenneth J. Kiser, *Total Quality Management* (Seabrook, Md.: Ducochon Press, 1991), p. 25. Another good introduction to TQM is Arthur R. Tenner and Irving J. DeToro, *Total Quality Management: Three Steps to Continuous Improvement* (Reading, Mass.: Addison-Wesley, 1992). Also see the entire July 1994 issue of *Academy of Management Review*.

45. Richard J. Schonberger, "Total Quality Management Cuts a Broad Swath—Through Manufacturing and Beyond," *Organizational Dynamics*, 20 (Spring 1992): 18.

46. "Aiming for the Stars at Philips," special advertising section, Quality '92: Leading the World-Class Company, *Time* (September 21, 1992): 26.

47. See John Shea and David Gobeli, "TQM: The Experiences of Ten Small Businesses," *Business Horizons*, 38 (January–February 1995): 71–77; Loyd Eskildson, "TQM's Role in Corporate Success: Analyzing the Evidence," *National Productivity Review*, 14 (Autumn 1995): 25–38; Richard Reed, David J. Lemak, and Joseph C. Montgomery, "Beyond Process: TQM Content and Firm Performance," *Academy of Management Review*, 21 (January 1996): 173–202; and William A. Hubiak and Susan Jones O'Donnell, "Do Americans Have Their Minds Set Against TQM?" *National Productivity Review*, 15 (Summer 1996): 19–32.

48. Adapted and condensed from David E. Bowen and Edward E. Lawler III, "Total Quality-Oriented Human Resources Management," *Organizational Dynamics*, 20 (Spring 1992): Exhibit 1, 29–41.

49. "Judge Orders Ford to Replace Faulty Device," *USA Today* (April 15, 2001): 1B.

50. Richard J. Schonberger, *Japanese Manufacturing Techniques: Nine Hidden Lessons in Simplicity* (New York: Free Press, 1982), p. 35. Also see Barry Berman, "Planning for the Inevitable Product Recall," *Business Horizons*, 42 (March–April 1999): 69–78.

51. Kevin Maney, "Dell Business Model Turns to Muscle As Rivals Struggle," *USA Today* (January 20, 2003): 2B.

52. For contrasting views, see Christopher W. L. Hart, "The Power of Internal Guarantees," *Harvard Business Review*, 73 (January–February 1995): 64–73; and Thomas A. Stewart, "Another Fad Worth Killing," *Fortune* (February 3, 1997): 119–120.

53. Geoff Colvin, "The 100 Best Companies to Work For: 2006," *Fortune* (January 23, 2006): 90.

54. Richard S. Teitelbaum, "Where Service Flies Right," *Fortune* (August 24, 1992): 115. Also see Michael S. Garver and Gary B. Gagnon, "Seven Keys to Improving Customer Satisfaction Programs," *Business Horizons*, 45 (September–October 2002): 35–42.

55. See Darrell K. Rigby, Frederick F. Reichheld and Phil Schefter, "Avoid the Four Perils of CRM," *Harvard Business Review*, 80 (February 2002): 101–109; Jena McGregor, "A Real Stake In Your Customers," *Business Week* (June 19, 2006): 70; Norm Brodsky, "We All Like to Think We Listen to Our Customers—But Do We Really Hear Them?" *Inc.*, 28 (July 2006): 55–56; and Michael Fitzgerald, "CRM Made Simple: New Software to Supercharge Your Sales," *Inc.*, 29 (January 2007): 46–47.

56. Andy Reinhardt, "Meet Mr. Internet," *Business Week* (September 13, 1999): 136. Another customer-centered manager is profiled in David DuPree, "First-Class Operation," *USA Today* (December 21, 2001): 1C–2C.

57. Based on discussion in Richard J. Schonberger, "Is Strategy Strategic? Impact of Total Quality Management on Strategy," *Academy of Management Executive*, 6 (August 1992): 80–87. For insights about Toyota, the *kaizen* pioneer, see Darius Mehri, "The Darker Side of Lean: An Insider's Perspective on the Realities of the Toyota Production System," *Academy of Management Perspectives*, 20 (May 2006): 21–42; and Charles Fishman, "No Satisfaction," *Fast Company*, no. 111 (January 2007): 82–92.

58. See D. Keith Denton, "Creating a System for Continuous Improvement," *Business Horizons*, 38 (January–February 1995): 16–21; and Thomas Y. Choi, Manus Rungtusanatham, and Ji-Sung Kim, "Continuous Improvement on the Shop Floor: Lessons from Small to Midsize Firms," *Business Horizons*, 40 (November–December 1997): 45–50.

59. Edward E. Lawler III, "Total Quality Management and Employee Involvement: Are They Compatible?" *Academy of Management Executive*, 8 (February 1994): 68–76.

60. Sashkin and Kiser, *Total Quality Management*, p. 42. Six Sigma, another set of quality improvement tools, is discussed in Michael Hammer, "Process Management and the Future of Six Sigma," *MIT Sloan Management Review*, 43 (Winter 2002): 26–32; Margery Weinstein, "Something Better Than Six Sigma?" *Training*, 43 (September 2006): 14; Margery Weinstein, "Six Sigma and Lean: Working Together," *Training*, 43 (November 2006): 13; and Roger O. Crockett, "Six Sigma Still Pays Off at Motorola," *Business Week* (December 4, 2006): 50.

61. Based on discussion in Mary Walton, *Deming Management at Work* (New York: Perigee, 1990), p. 16.

62. See Marta Mooney, "Deming's Real Legacy: An Easier Way to Manage Knowledge," *National Productivity Review*, 15 (Summer 1996): 1–8; and Pamela J. Kidder and Bobbie Ryan, "How the Deming Philosophy Transformed the Department of the Navy," *National Productivity Review*, 15 (Summer 1996): 55–63.

63. W. Edwards Deming, *Out of the Crisis* (Cambridge, Mass.: MIT Press, 1986): p. 5. Also see Oren Harari, "Beyond Zero Defects," *Management Review*, 88 (October 1999): 34–36.

64. Ken Western, "No Matter What It Takes, I'll Do It," *Arizona Republic* (August 1, 1993): F1.

65. See Figure 5 in Deming, *Out of the Crisis*, p. 88.

66. Daniel Roth, "Craig Barrett Inside," *Fortune* (December 18, 2000): 260.

67. Adapted from discussion in Deming, *Out of the Crisis*, pp. 23–96; and Howard S. Gitlow and Shelly J. Gitlow, *The Deming Guide to Quality and Competitive Position* (Englewood Cliffs, N.J.: Prentice-Hall, 1987). Also see M. R. Yilmaz and Sangit Chatterjee, "Deming and the Quality of Software Development," *Business Horizons*, 40 (November–December 1997): 51–58.

68. Deming, *Out of the Crisis*, p. 59.

69. The debate is framed in Paula Phillips Carson and Kerry D. Carson, "Deming Versus Traditional Management Theorists on Goal Setting: Can Both Be Right?" *Business Horizons*, 36 (September–October 1993): 79–84.

70. Deming, *Out of the Crisis*, p. 24.

Chapter 9

1. Jack and Suzy Welch, "So Many CEOs Get This Wrong," *Business Week* (July 17, 2006): 92.

2. From *HR Magazine* by Ann Pomeroy, "She's Still Lovin' It" December 2006. Copyright © 2006 by Society for Human Resource Management (SHRM). Reproduced with permission of Society for Human Resource Management (SHRM) via Copyright Clearance Center.

3. See Gary Kaufman, "How to Fix HR," *Harvard Business Review*, 84 (September 2006): 30; Stephen Covey, "Redefining HR's Role for Success," *Training*, 43 (October 2006): 56; James C. Wimbush, "Spotlight on Human Resource Management," *Business Horizons*, 49 (November–December 2006): 433–436; and Robert J. Grossman, "Measuring the Value of HR," *HR Magazine*, 51 (December 2006): 44–49.

4. Drawn from "Peterson Thrives on HR Challenges," *HR Magazine*, 43 (September 1998): 98, 100.

5. See Robert J. Grossman, "HR's Rising Star in India," *HR Magazine*, 51 (September 2006): 46–52.

6. As quoted in Jeff Greenfield, "Views From the Top," *HR Magazine*, 51 (November 2006): 83.

7. See Patrick M. Wright, Timothy M Gardner, Lisa M. Moynihan, and Mathew R. Allen, "The Relationship Between HR Practices and Firm Performance: Examining Causal Order," *Personnel Psychology*, 58 (Summer 2005): 409–446; and Jack and Suzy Welch, "A Twisted Chain of Command," *Business Week* (September 18, 2006): 116.

8. Bill Leonard, "Straight Talk," *HR Magazine*, 47 (January 2002): 46–51. Also see Carla Joinson, "HR's Seat on the Selection Committee," *HR Magazine*, 45 (April 2000): 82–90.

9. Data from Lin Grensing-Pophal, "Taking Your Seat 'At the Table,'" *HR Magazine*, 44 (March 1999): 90–96. Also see Lin Grensing-Pophal, "What's Your HR Creed?" *HR Magazine*, 46 (June 2001): 145–153.

10. Brian E. Becker, Mark A. Huselid, and Dave Ulrich, *The HR Scorecard: Linking People, Strategy, and Performance* (Boston: Harvard Business School Press, 2001): p. 4.

11. For more, see Nancy R. Lockwood, "Talent Management: Driver for Organizational Success," 2006 SHRM Research Quarterly, *HR Magazine*, 51 (June 2006): 1–11; Robert E. Ployhart, Jeff A. Weekley, and Kathryn Baughman, "The Structure and Function of Human Capital Emergence: A Multi-Level Examination of the Attraction-Selection-Attrition Model," *Academy of Management Journal*, 49 (August 2006): 661–677; and "Human Capital Leadership Awards," *HR Magazine*, 51 (November 2006): 51–68.

12. "The 100 Best Companies to Work For," *Fortune* (February 4, 2002): 84. For more stories about companies helping schools, see George Anders, "The *Re*education of Silicon Valley," *Fast Company*, no. 57 (April 2002): 100–108.

13. As quoted in John Huey, "Outlaw Flyboy CEOs," *Fortune* (November 13, 2000): 246.

14. Data from Jeffrey Pfeffer, *The Human Equation: Building Profits by Putting People First* (Boston: Harvard Business School Press, 1998); and Jeffrey Pfeffer and John F. Veiga, "Putting People First for Organizational Success," *Academy of Management Executive*, 13 (May 1999): 37–48. Also see James P. Guthrie, "High-Involvement Work Practices, Turnover, and Productivity: Evidence from New Zealand," *Academy of Management Journal*, 44 (February 2001): 180–190; and Becker, Huselid, and Ulrich, *The HR Scorecard*, Table 1-3, pp. 16–17.

15. Jacqueline Durett, "R-e-s-p-e-c-t: Find Out What it Means to Employees," *Training*, 43 (June 2006): 12. Also see "Most Stay at First Job Less Than 2 Years," *USA Today* (October 31, 2006): 1B.

16. See Jim Collins, *Good to Great: Why Some Companies Make the Leap and Others Don't* (New York: Harper Business, 2001); and Jim Collins, "Good to Great," *Fast Company*, no. 51 (October 2001): 90–104.

17. Data from "HR Challenges," *USA Today* (November 2, 2006): 1B. Also see Margery Weinstein, "Bad Hires and Poor Promotions Take Toll Across the Organization," *Training*, 43 (June 2006): 12; and "High Cost of Bad Hire," *USA Today* (July 25, 2006): 1B.

18. For example, see Barbara De Lollis and Roger Yu, "Marriott's Looking Forward—and Up," *USA Today* (December 14, 2005): 6B.

19. As quoted in Ruth E. Thaler-Carter, "Diversify Your Recruitment Advertising," *HR Magazine*, 46 (June 2001): 95.

Cialdini, "Harnessing the Science of Persuasion," *Harvard Business Review*, 79 (October 2001): 72–79; Gary A. Williams and Robert B. Miller, "Change the Way You Persuade," *Harvard Business Review*, 80 (May 2002): 64–73; and Gardiner Morse, "How Presidents Persuade," *Harvard Business Review*, special issue: Motivating People, 81 (January 2003): 20–21.

4. See Gary Yukl and Cecilia M. Falbe, "Influence Tactics and Objectives in Upward, Downward, and Lateral Influence Attempts," *Journal of Applied Psychology*, 75 (April 1990): 132–140. Also see David Kipnis, Stuart M. Schmidt, and Ian Wilkinson, "Intraorganizational Influence Tactics: Explorations in Getting One's Way," *Journal of Applied Psychology*, 64 (August 1980): 440–452; and Chester A. Schriesheim and Timothy R. Hinkin, "Influence Tactics Used by Subordinates: A Theoretical and Empirical Analysis of the Kipnis, Schmidt, and Wilkinson Subscales," *Journal of Applied Psychology*, 75 (June 1990): 246–257.

5. Adapted from Yukl and Falbe, "Influence Tactics and Objectives in Upward, Downward, and Lateral Influence Attempts." Also see Gary Yukl, Cecilia M. Falbe, and Joo Young Youn, "Patterns of Influence Behavior for Managers," *Group & Organization Management*, 18 (March 1993): 5–28; Randall A. Gordon, "Impact of Ingratiation on Judgments and Evaluations: A Meta-Analytic Investigation," *Journal of Personality and Social Psychology*, 71 (July 1996): 54–70; Bennett J. Tepper, Regina J. Eisenbach, Susan L. Kirby, and Paula W. Potter, "Test of a Justice-Based Model of Subordinates' Resistance to Downward Influence Attempts," *Group & Organization Management*, 23 (June 1998): 144–160; William D. Crano and Xin Chen, "The Leniency Contract and Persistence of Majority and Minority Influence," *Journal of Personality and Social Psychology*, 74 (June 1998): 1437–1450; and Barbara Price Davis and Eric S. Knowles, "A Disrupt-Then-Reframe Technique of Social Influence," *Journal of Personality and Social Psychology*, 76 (February 1999): 192–199.

6. For research insights, see George F. Dreher, Thomas W. Dougherty, and William Whitely, "Influence Tactics and Salary Attainment: A Gender-Specific Analysis," *Sex Roles*, 20 (May 1989): 535–550; Herman Aguinis and Susan K. R. Adams, "Social-Role Versus Structural Models of Gender and Influence Use in Organizations," *Group & Organization Studies*, 23 (December 1998): 414–446; and Margery Weinstein, "What a Girl . . . and Guy Want," *Training*, 44 (January–February 2007): 6. For a practical example, see Arlene Weintraub, "Making Her Mark at Merck," *Business Week* (January 8, 2007): 64–65.

7. See Mahfooz A. Ansari and Alka Kapoor, "Organizational Context and Upward Influence Tactics," *Organizational Behavior and Human Decision Processes*, 40 (August 1987): 39–49. For more on ingratiation, see David B. Yoffie and Mary Kwak, "With Friends Like These: The Art of Managing Complementors," *Harvard Business Review*, 84 (September 2006): 88–98.

8. Dean Tjosvold, "The Dynamics of Positive Power," *Training and Development Journal*, 38 (June 1984): 72.

9. See Toddi Gutner, "A 12-Step Program to Gaining Power," *Business Week* (December 24, 2001): 88.

10. Morgan McCall Jr., "Power, Influence, and Authority: The Hazards of Carrying a Sword," *Technical Report*, 10 (Greensboro, N.C.: Center for Creative Leadership, 1978), p. 5.

11. For more on these three effects of power, see Anthony T. Cobb, "An Episodic Model of Power: Toward an Integration of Theory and Research," *Academy of Management Review*, 9 (July 1984): 482–493. Also see C. Marlene Fiol, Edward J. O'Connor, and Herman Aguinis, "All for One and One for All? The Development and Transfer of Power Across Organizational Levels," *Academy of Management Review*, 26 (April 2001): 224–242.

12. Based on Edwin P. Hollander and Lynn R. Offermann, "Power and Leadership in Organizations: Relationships in Transition," *American Psychologist*, 45 (February 1990): 179–189. Also see the following for practical implications of power: Margery Weinstein, "Alpha Male on Your Hands: Here's How to Deal," *Training*, 43 (October 2006): 16; Gail Edmondson, "Power Play at VW," *Business Week* (December 4, 2006): 44–45; and James B. Thelen, "Smelling Smoke," *HR Magazine*, 51 (December 2006): 105–111.

13. See Harold J. Leavitt, "Why Hierarchies Thrive," *Harvard Business Review*, 81 (March 2003): 96–102.

14. See John R. P. French Jr. and Bertram Raven, "The Bases of Social Power," *Studies in Social Power*, ed. Dorwin Cartwright (Ann Arbor: University of Michigan Press, 1959), pp. 150–167. Also see Arthur G. Bedeian, "The Dean's Disease: How the Darker Side of Power Manifests Itself in the Office of Dean," *Academy of Management Learning and Education*, 1 (December 2002): 164–173.

15. John P. Kotter, "Power, Dependence, and Effective Management," *Harvard Business Review*, 55 (July–August 1977): 128. For related research, see Sydney Finkelstein, "Power in Top Management Teams: Dimensions, Measurement, and Validation," *Academy of Management Journal*, 35 (August 1992): 505–538; and Herminia Ibarra, "Network Centrality, Power, and Innovation Involvement: Determinants of Technical and Administrative Roles," *Academy of Management Journal*, 36 (June 1993): 471–501.

16. For a revealing case study, see John A. Byrne, "Chainsaw," *Business Week* (October 18, 1999): 128–147. Also see Julie Scelfo, "10 Power Tips," *Newsweek* (September 25, 2006): 78. Jonathan Alter, "Citizen Clinton Up Close," *Newsweek* (April 8, 2002): 34–42.

17. Patricia Sellers, "What Exactly Is Charisma?" *Fortune* (January 15, 1996): 68. Also see Daniel Sankowsky, "The Charismatic Leader As Narcissist: Understanding the Abuse of Power," *Organizational Dynamics*, 23 (Spring 1995): 57–71; Holly Dolezalek, "The Dark Side: When Good Leaders Go Bad," *Training*, 43 (June 2006): 20–26; and Marshall Goldsmith, "Now Go Out and Lead!" *Business Week* (January 8, 2007): 72–73.

18. See Steve Bates, "Unique Strategies Urged to Keep 'Emerging Leaders,'" *HR Magazine*, 47 (September 2002): 14; Carol Hymowitz, "The Confident Boss Doesn't Micromanage or Delegate Too Much," *Wall Street Journal* (March 11, 2003): B1; and Christopher D. Zatzick and Roderick D. Iverson, "High-Involvement Management and Workforce Reduction: Competitive Advantage or Disadvantage?" *Academy of Management Journal*, 49 (October 2006): 999–1015.

19. As quoted in Laurel Shaper Walters, "A Leader Redefines Management," *Christian Science Monitor* (September 22, 1992): 14. For Frances Hesselbein's ideas about leadership, see Roundtable Discussion, "All in a Day's Work," *Harvard Business Review*, special issue: Breakthrough Leadership, 79 (December 2001): 54–66.

20. See W. Alan Randolph, "Re-Thinking Empowerment: Why Is It So Hard to Achieve?" *Organizational Dynamics*, 29 [Fall 2000]: 94–107; W. Alan Randolph and Marshall Sashkin, "Can Organizational Empowerment Work in Multinational Settings?" *Academy of Management Executive*, 16 (February 2002): 102–115; and Brook Manville and Josiah Ober, "Beyond Empowerment: Building a Company of Citizens," *Harvard Business Review*, 81 (January 2003): 48–53.

21. John A. Byrne, "The Environment Was Ripe for Abuse," *Business Week* (February 25, 2002): 119.

22. For a recent sampling, see Kim Lamoureux, "Wanted: Better Leaders," *Training*, 43 (May 2006): 16; Boris Groysberg, Andrew N. McLean, and Nitin Nohria, "Are Leaders Portable?" *Harvard Business Review*, 84 (May 2006): 92–100; Jennifer Vilaga, "New Kids on the Bloc," Fast Company, no. 107 (July–August 2006): 46; Nancy R. Lockwood, "2006 SHRM Research Quarterly: Leadership Development: Optimizing Human Capital for Business Success," *HR Magazine*, 51 (December 2006): 1–12; Alison Stein Wellner, "Eye on the Prize: Secrets of Entrepreneur Athletes," *Inc.*, 29 (January 2007): 40–41; and Holly Dolezalek, "Got High Potentials? *Training*, 44 (January–February 2007): 18–22.

23. Margery Weinstein, "Training Today: q&a," *Training*, 44 (January–February 2007): 7. Also see Larry Bossidy, "The Job No CEO Should Delegate," *Harvard Business Review*, 79 (March 2001): 46–49; Melvin Sorcher and James Brant, "Are You Picking the Right Leaders?" *Harvard Business Review*, 80 (February 2002): 78–85; and Charles Fishman, "Isolating the Leadership Gene," *Fast Company*, no. 56 (March 2002): 82–90.

24. Inspired by the definition in Andrew J. DuBrin, *Leadership: Research Findings, Practice and Skills*, 2d ed. (Boston: Houghton Mifflin, 1998), p. 2. Also see Francis J. Yammarino, Fred Dansereau, and Christina J. Kennedy, "A Multiple-Level Multidimensional Approach to Leader-

ship: Viewing Leadership Through an Elephant's Eye," *Organizational Dynamics,* 29 (Winter 2001): 149–163.

25. As quoted in Oren Harari, *The Leadership Secrets of Colin Powell* (New York: McGraw-Hill, 2002): p. 13.

26. See Gary Yukl, "Managerial Leadership: A Review of Theory and Research," *Journal of Management,* 15 (June 1989): 251–289; Gary A. Yukl, *Leadership in Organizations,* 2d ed. (Englewood Cliffs, N.J.: Prentice-Hall, 1989); and Karl O. Magnusen, "The Legacy of Leadership Revisited," *Business Horizons,* 38 (November–December 1995): 3–7.

27. See David L. Cawthon, "Leadership: The Great Man Theory Revisited," *Business Horizons,* 39 (May–June 1996): 1–4; Nathan A. Forney, "Rommel in the Boardroom," *Business Horizons,* 42 (July–August 1999): 37–42; Thomas A. Stewart, Alex Taylor III, Peter Petre, and Brent Schlender, "Henry Ford, Alfred P. Sloan, Tom Watson Jr., Bill Gates: The Businessman of the Century," *Fortune* (November 22, 1999): 109–128; and Richard S. Tedlow, "What Titans Can Teach Us," *Harvard Business Review,* special issue: Breakthrough Leadership, 79 (December 2001): 70–79.

28. Fred Luthans, *Organizational Behavior,* 3d ed. (New York: McGraw-Hill, 1981), p. 419. Also see Gail Dutton, "Leadership in a Post-Heroic Age," *Management Review,* 85 (October 1996): 7.

29. Ralph M. Stogdill, "Personal Factors Associated with Leadership: A Survey of the Literature," *Journal of Psychology,* 25 (1948): 63.

30. See Daniel Goleman, *Emotional Intelligence* (New York: Bantam Books, 1995); Michaela Davies, Lazar Stankov, and Richard D. Roberts, "Emotional Intelligence: In Search of an Elusive Construct," *Journal of Personality and Social Psychology,* 75 (October 1998): 989–1015; Travis Bradberry and Jean Greaves, "Heartless Bosses?" *Harvard Business Review,* 83 (December 2005): 24; and Stephenie Overman, "Goleman: Develop Emotional Intelligence," *HR Magazine,* 51 (May 2006): 32.

31. Michelle Neely Martinez, "The Smarts That Count," *HR Magazine,* 42 (November 1997): 72.

32. Based on and adapted from Daniel Goleman, Richard Boyatzis, and Annie McKee, "Primal Leadership," *Harvard Business Review,* special issue: Breakthrough Leadership, 79 (December 2001): 49. Also see Daniel Goleman, Richard Boyatzis, and Annie McKee, *Primal Leadership: Realizing the Power of Emotional Intelligence* (Boston: Harvard Business School Press, 2002); and Richard E. Boyatzis, Elizabeth C. Stubbs, and Scott N. Taylor, "Learning Cognitive and Emotional Intelligence Competencies Through Graduate Management Education," *Academy of Management Learning and Education,* 1 (December 2002): 150–162.

33. Data from Judy B. Rosener, "Ways Women Lead," *Harvard Business Review,* 68 (November–December 1990): 119–125. Also see Chris Lee, "The Feminization of Management," *Training,* 31 (November 1994): 25–31; Rochelle Sharpe, "As Leaders, Women Rule," *Business Week* (November 20, 2000): 74–84; and Del Jones, "Many Successful Women Also Athletic," *USA Today* (March 26, 2002): 1B–2B.

34. See "Ways Women and Men Lead," *Harvard Business Review,* 69 (January–February 1991): 150–160.

35. Data from Alice H. Eagly and Blair T. Johnson, "Gender and Leadership Style: A Meta-Analysis," *Psychological Bulletin,* 108 (September 1990): 233–256. Also see Judith A. Kolb, "Are We Still Stereotyping Leadership? A Look at Gender and Other Predictors of Leader Emergence," *Small Group Research,* 28 (August 1997): 370–393; Virginia W. Cooper, "Homophily or the Queen Bee Syndrome: Female Evaluation of Female Leadership," *Small Group Research,* 28 (November 1997): 483–499; and Robert K. Shelly and Paul T. Munroe, "Do Women Engage in Less Task Behavior Than Men?" *Sociological Perspectives,* 42 (Spring 1999): 49–67.

36. Kurt Lewin, Ronald Lippitt, and Ralph K. White, "Patterns of Aggressive Behavior in Experimentally Created 'Social Climates,'" *Journal of Social Psychology,* 10 (May 1939): 271–299.

37. The risks of shifting styles are discussed in Thomas L. Brown, "Managerial Waffling: In Politics—or in Business—Waffling Suggests Bad Leadership," *Industry Week* (January 18, 1993):

34. Also see Oren Harari, "Leadership vs. Autocracy: They Just Don't Get It!" *Management Review,* 85 (August 1996): 42–45.

38. For an informative summary of this research, see Edwin A. Fleishman, "Twenty Years of Consideration and Structure," in *Current Developments in the Study of Leadership,* ed. Edwin A. Fleishman and James G. Hunt (Carbondale, Ill.: Southern Illinois University Press, 1973), pp. 1–40. Also see Vishwanath V. Baba and Merle E. Ace, "Serendipity in Leadership: Initiating Structure and Consideration in the Classroom," *Human Relations,* 42 (June 1989): 509–525.

39. Three popular extensions of the Ohio State leadership studies may be found in Robert R. Blake and Anne McCanse, *Leadership Dilemmas—Grid Solutions* (Houston: Gulf Publishing, 1990); William J. Reddin, *Managerial Effectiveness* (New York: McGraw-Hill, 1970); and Paul Hersey and Kenneth H. Blanchard, *Management of Organizational Behavior: Utilizing Human Resources,* 5th ed. (Englewood Cliffs, N.J.: Prentice-Hall, 1988), p. 171. Empirical lack of support for Hersey and Blanchard's situational leadership theory is reported in Jane R. Goodson, Gail W. McGee, and James F. Cashman, "Situational Leadership Theory: A Test of Leadership Prescriptions," *Group & Organization Studies,* 14 (December 1989): 446–461.

40. See Abraham K. Korman, "Consideration, 'Initiating Structure,' and Organizational Criteria—A Review," *Personnel Psychology,* 19 (Winter 1966): 349–361. Also see Margery Weinstein, "Just Be Nice," *Training,* 43 (September 2006): 14.

41. See Blake and McCanse, *Leadership Dilemmas—Grid Solutions.*

42. See Tom Lester, "Taking Guard on the Grid," *Management Today* (March 1991): 93–94. For a managerial perspective, see Gardiner Morse, "Shut Up and Stop Whining," *Harvard Business Review,* 84 (December 2006): 26.

43. For details of this study, see Robert R. Blake and Jane Srygley Mouton, "Management by Grid® Principles or Situationalism: Which?" *Group & Organization Studies,* 6 (December 1981): 439–455. Also see Robert R. Blake and Jane Srygley Mouton, "A Comparative Analysis of Situationalism and 9,9 Management by Principle," *Organizational Dynamics,* 10 (Spring 1982): 20–43. For another view of leader behavior, see Susan A. Tynan, "Best Behaviors," *Management Review,* 88 (November 1999): 58–61.

44. Fred E. Fiedler, "Job Engineering for Effective Leadership: A New Approach," *Management Review,* 66 (September 1977): 29.

45. For an excellent comprehensive validation study, see Michael J. Strube and Joseph E. Garcia, "A Meta-Analytic Investigation of Fiedler's Contingency Model of Leadership Effectiveness," *Psychological Bulletin,* 90 (September 1981): 307–321.

46. Fred E. Fiedler and Martin M. Chemers, *Leadership and Effective Management* (Glenview, Ill.: Scott, Foresman, 1974), p. 91.

47. Robert J. House and Terence R. Mitchell, "Path-Goal Theory of Leadership," *Journal of Contemporary Business,* 3 (Autumn 1974): 85. An updated path-goal model is presented in Robert J. House, "A Path-Goal Theory of Leadership: Lessons, Legacy, and a Reformulated Theory," *Leadership Quarterly* (Autumn 1996): 323–352.

48. See Steven Berglas, "How to Keep A Players Productive," *Harvard Business Review,* 84 (September 2006): 104–112; and Gary P. Latham and Edwin A. Locke, "Enhancing the Benefits and Overcoming the Pitfalls of Goal Setting," *Organizational Dynamics,* 35, no. 4 (2006): 332–340.

49. Adapted from Robert J. House, "Path-Goal Theory of Leadership: Lessons, Legacy, and a Reformulated Theory," *The Leadership Quarterly,* 7 (Autumn 1996): 323–352.

50. For path-goal research, see Abduhl-Rahim A. Al-Gattan, "Test of the Path-Goal Theory of Leadership in the Multinational Domain," *Group & Organization Studies,* 10 (December 1985): 429–445; Robert T. Keller, "A Test of the Path-Goal Theory of Leadership with Need for Clarity As a Moderator in Research and Development Organizations," *Journal of Applied Psychology,* 74 (April 1989): 208–212; John E. Mathieu, "A Test of Subordinates' Achievement and Affiliation Needs As Moderators of Leader Path-Goal Relationships," *Basic and Applied Social Psychology,* 11 (June 1990): 179–189; and Retha A. Price, "An Investigation of Path-Goal Leadership Theory in Marketing Channels," *Journal of Retailing,* 67 (Fall 1991): 339–361.

51. Leonard D. Schaeffer, "The Leadership Journey," *Harvard Business Review,* 80 (October 2002): 42–43. Also see Dov Frohman, "Leadership Under Fire," *Harvard Business Review,* 84 (December 2006):

124–131; and Gary A. Ballinger and F. David Schoorman, "Individual Reactions to Leadership Succession in Workgroups," *Academy of Management Review*, 32 (January 2007): 118–136.

52. See J. McGregor Burns, *Leadership* (New York: Harper-Collins, 1978). Also see Frederick F. Reichheld, "Lead for Loyalty," *Harvard Business Review*, 79 (July–August 2001): 76–84.

53. See David A. Nadler and Michael L. Tushman, "Beyond the Charismatic Leader: Leadership and Organizational Change," *California Management Review*, 32 (Winter 1990): 77–97; and Burt Nanus, "Leading the Vision Team," *The Futurist*, 30 (May–June 1996): 21–23.

54. Critiques of charismatic leadership can be found in Joshua Macht, "Jim Collins to CEOs: Lose the Charisma," *Business 2.0*, 2 (October 2001): 121–122; Rakesh Khurana, "The Curse of the Superstar CEO," *Harvard Business Review*, 80 (September 2002): 60–66; and Jerry Useem, "Kill Your Career with Charisma," *Fortune* (September 16, 2002): 40.

55. See Joseph Seltzer and Bernard M. Bass, "Transformational Leadership: Beyond Initiation and Consideration," *Journal of Management*, 16 (December 1990): 693–703.

56. For research support, see David A. Waldman, Gabriel G. Ramírez, Robert J. House, and Phanish Puranam, "Does Leadership Matter? CEO Leadership Attributes and Profitability Under Conditions of Perceived Environmental Uncertainty," *Academy of Management Journal*, 44 (February 2001): 134–143.

57. For example, see Taly Dvir, Dov Eden, Bruce J. Avolio, and Boas Shamir, "Impact of Transformational Leadership on Follower Development and Performance: A Field Experiment," *Academy of Management Journal*, 45 (August 2002): 735–744.

58. See Bruce J. Avolio and Surinder S. Kahai, "Adding the 'E' to E-Leadership: How It May Impact Your Leadership," *Organizational Dynamics*, 31, no. 4 (2003): 325–338; Henry S. Givray, "Leadership Lessons from Mom," *Business Week* (May 22, 2006): 106; Justin Fox, "The CEO Stats That Matter," *Fortune* (October 30, 2006): 154–160; and Catherine M. Dalton, "Brandy the Dog on Leadership," *Business Horizons*, 49 (November–December 2006): 429–432.

59. For more on the servant leader philosophy, see Robert K. Greenleaf, *Servant Leadership: A Journey into the Nature of Legitimate Power and Greatness* (New York: Paulist Press, 1977); and Walter Kiechel III, "The Leader As Servant," *Fortune* (May 4, 1992): 121–122.

60. Luci Scott, "21st-Century Teaching Tools," *Arizona Republic* (August 19, 2006): D3.

61. For interesting reading, see Bill George, *Authentic Leadership: Rediscovering the Secrets to Creating Lasting Value* (San Francisco, Calif.: Jossey-Bass, 2003); and Barbara Kellerman, *Bad Leadership: What It Is, How It Happens, Why It Matters* (Boston: Harvard Business School Press, 2004).

62. For more, see Jacqueline Durett, "Mentors in Short Supply," *Training*, 43 (July 2006): 14; and Anne Brockbank and Ian McGill, *Facilitating Reflective Learning Through Mentoring and Coaching* (London: Kogan Page, 2006).

63. Abraham Zaleznik, "Managers and Leaders: Are They Different?" *Harvard Business Review*, 55 (May–June 1977): 76.

64. For details, see Ellen A. Fagenson, "The Mentor Advantage: Perceived Career/Job Experiences of Protégés Versus Non-Protégés," *Journal of Organizational Behavior*, 10 (October 1989): 309–320. More mentoring research findings are reported in Melenie J. Lankau and Terri A. Scandura, "An Investigation of Personal Learning in Mentoring Relationships: Content, Antecedents, and Consequences," *Academy of Management Journal*, 45 (August 2002): 779–790.

65. See Tahl Raz, "The 10 Secrets of a Master Networker," *Inc.*, 25 (January 2003): 90–99; and Betti A. Hamilton and Terri A. Scandura, "E-Mentoring: Implications for Organizational Learning and Development in a Wired World," *Organizational Dynamics*, 31, no. 4 (2003): 388–402.

66. For more, see Kathy E. Kram, "Phases of the Mentor Relationship," *Academy of Management Journal*, 26 (December 1983): 608–625.

67. Holly Peterson and Barbara Kantrowitz, "Leadership for the 21st Century: Lessons We Have Learned—Renetta McCann," *Newsweek* (September 25, 2006): 77.

68. See Susan J. Wells, "Smoothing the Way," *HR Magazine*, 46 (June 2001): 52–58.

69. For more, see David A. Thomas, "The Truth About Mentoring Minorities: Race Matters," *Harvard Business Review*, 79 (April 2001): 99–107.

Chapter 14

1. Dean Tjosvold, *Learning to Manage Conflict: Getting People to Work Together Productively* (New York: Lexington, 1993): p. xi.

2. Excerpted from Om Malik, "The 160-Year-Old Startup," *Business 2.0*, 7, August 2006, pp. 49–51. Copyright © 2006 Time Inc. All rights reserved.

3. Irene M. Kunii, "Japan's Silicon Stampede," *Business Week* (January 20, 2003): 70.

4. See Frank Ostroff, "Change Management in Government," *Harvard Business Review*, 84 (May 2006): 141–147; Thomas A. Stewart and David Champion, "Leading Change from the Top Line," *Harvard Business Review*, 84 (July–August 2006): 90–97; and Kim Cameron, "Good or Not Bad: Standards and Ethics in Managing Change," *Academy of Management Learning and Education*, 5 (September 2006): 317–323.

5. See Carrie R. Leana and Bruce Barry, "Stability and Change as Simultaneous Experiences in Organizational Life," *Academy of Management Review*, 25 (October 2000): 753–759.

6. Adapted from discussion in David A. Nadler and Michael L. Tushman, "Organizational Frame Bending: Principles for Managing Reorientation," *Academy of Management Executive*, 3 (August 1989): 194–204. Also see Loizos Heracleous and Michael Barrett, "Organizational Change As Discourse: Communicative Actions and Deep Structures in the Context of Information Technology Implementation," *Academy of Management Journal*, 44 (August 2001): 755–778; and Peter D. Sherer and Kyungmook Lee, "Institutional Change in Large Law Firms: A Resource Dependency and Institutional Perspective," *Academy of Management Journal*, 45 (February 2002): 102–119.

7. Michael Dell, "How to Thrive in a Sick Economy," *Business 2.0*, 3 (January 2003): 88.

8. See Tom Duening, "Our Turbulent Times? The Case for Evolutionary Organizational Change," *Business Horizons*, 40 (January–February 1997): 2–8.

9. Michelle Kessler, "Cisco's Risky Scientific-Atlanta Buy Pays Off as Quarterly Profit Surges," *USA Today* (August 9, 2006): 2B. Another example of frame bending is reported in Barbara De Lollis, "Ritz Loosens Up Its Tie to Change with the Times," *USA Today* (December 26, 2006): 4B.

10. Kathy Rebello, "Inside Microsoft," *Business Week* (July 15, 1996): 57. For an update, see Jim Frederick, "Microsoft's $40 Billion Bet," *Money*, 31 (May 2002): 66–80. Also see Jim Collins, "Good to Great," *Fast Company*, no. 51 (October 2001): 90–104; Clayton M. Christensen, Mark W. Johnson, and Darrell K. Rigby, "Foundations for Growth: How to Identify and Build Disruptive New Businesses," *MIT Sloan Management Review*, 43 (Spring 2002): 22–31; and Melanie Warner, "Can GE Light Up the Market Again?" *Fortune* (November 11, 2002): 108–117.

11. See Russ Vince and Michael Broussine, "Paradox, Defense and Attachment: Accessing and Working with Emotions and Relations Underlying Organizational Change," *Organization Studies*, 17, no. 1 (1996): 1–21.

12. See Robert H. Miles, "Beyond the Age of Dilbert: Accelerating Corporate Transformations by Rapidly Engaging All Employees," *Organizational Dynamics*, 29 (Spring 2001): 313–321.

13. See Inger Stensaker, Christine Benedichte Meyer, Joyce Falkenberg, and Anne Cathrin Haueng, "Excessive Change: Coping Mechanisms and Consequences," *Organizational Dynamics*, 31 (Winter 2002): 296–312; and Stuart D. Sidle, "Best Laid Plans: Establishing Fairness Early Can Help Smooth Organizational Change," *Academy of Management Executive*, 17 (February 2003): 127–128.

14. For example, see Roundtable Discussion, "Fast Talk: The Old Economy Meets the New Economy," *Fast Company*, no. 51 (October 2001): 70–80.

15. Ichak Adizes, *Mastering Change: The Power of Mutual Trust and Respect in Personal Life, Family Life, Business and Society* (Santa Monica, Calif.: Adizes Institute, 1991), p. 6.

16. See Sandy Kristin Piderit, "Rethinking Resistance and Recognizing Ambivalence: A Multidimensional View of Attitudes Toward an Orga-

nizational Change," *Academy of Management Review,* 25 (October 2000): 783–794; Peter de Jager, "Resistance to Change: A New View of an Old Problem," *The Futurist,* 35 (May–June 2001): 24–27; and Eric McNulty, "Welcome Aboard (But Don't Change a Thing)," *Harvard Business Review,* 80 (October 2002): 32–35. Two interesting non-business example of resistance to change can be found in Barbara Hagenbaugh, "A Penny Saved Could Become a Penny Spurned," *USA Today* (July 7, 2006): 1B–2B; and Devin Gordon, "Attack of the Killer Basketball," *Newsweek* (December 19, 2006): 62.

17. J. Alan Ofner, "Managing Change," *Personnel Administrator,* 29 (September 1984): 20.

18. Peter Coy, "The Perils of Picking the Wrong Standard," *Business Week* (October 8, 1990): 145. Also see Louis Woo, "Speech Technology Can Shrink World," *USA Today* (June 22, 1999): 6E.

19. This list is based in part on John P. Kotter and Leonard A. Schlesinger, "Choosing Strategies for Change," *Harvard Business Review,* 57 (March–April 1979): 106–114; and Joseph Stanislao and Bettie C. Stanislao, "Dealing with Resistance to Change," *Business Horizons,* 26 (July–August 1983): 74–78.

20. Robert Kegan and Lisa Laskow Lahey, "The Real Reason People Won't Change," *Harvard Business Review,* 79 (November 2001): 86.

21. For example, see Arnon E. Reichers, John P. Wanous, and James T. Austin, "Understanding and Managing Cynicism About Organizational Change," *Academy of Management Executive,* 11 (February 1997): 48–59. Practical perspectives are provided in the second Q&A in Jack and Suzy Welch, "Are You a Boss-Hater?" *Business Week* (July 3, 2006): 136; the first Q&A in Jack and Suzy Welch, "Battle Stations in a Dead Calm," *Business Week* (August 7, 2006): 100; and John Kotter and Holger Rathgeber, *Our Iceberg Is Melting: Changing and Succeeding Under Any Conditions* (New York: St. Martin's Press, 2006).

22. As quoted in Del Jones, "Product Development Can Fill Prescription for Success," *USA Today* (May 30, 2000): 7B.

23. See Larry Hirschhorn, "Campaigning for Change," *Harvard Business Review,* 80 (July 2002): 98–104.

24. See Allison Rossett, "Training & Organization Development: Separated at Birth?" *Training,* 33 (April 1996): 53–59; Joseph A. Raelin, "Action Learning and Action Science: Are They Different?" *Organizational Dynamics,* 26 (Summer 1997): 21–34; and Robert N. Llewellyn, "When to Call the Organization Doctor," *HR Magazine,* 47 (March 2002): 79–83.

25. Philip G. Hanson and Bernard Lubin, "Answers to Questions Frequently Asked About Organization Development," in *The Emerging Practice of Organization Development,* ed. Walter Sikes, Allan Drexler, and Jack Grant (Alexandria, Va.: NTL Institute, 1989), p. 16 (emphasis added). For good background information on current OD practices, see W. Warner Burke, "The New Agenda for Organization Development," *Organizational Dynamics,* 26 (Summer 1997): 7–20; Chuck McVinney, "Dream Weaver," *Training & Development,* 53 (April 1999): 39–42; and Ron Zemke, "Don't Fix That Company!" *Training,* 36 (June 1999): 26–33.

26. W. Warner Burke, *Organization Development: A Normative View* (Reading, Mass.: Addison-Wesley, 1987), p. 9. Also see Benjamin Schneider, Arthur P. Brief, and Richard A. Guzzo, "Creating a Climate and Culture for Sustainable Organizational Change," *Organizational Dynamics,* 24 (Spring 1996): 7–19.

27. See Robert H. Schaffer, "Overcome the Fatal Flaws of Consulting: Close the Results Gap," *Business Horizons,* 41 (September–October 1998): 53–60; Cheryl Dahle, "Change Course: That's His Message to the Navy," *Fast Company,* no. 34 (May 2000): 68, 70; and Julia Boorstin, "The Making of a Model Consultant," *Fortune* (January 22, 2001): 158, 160.

28. For example, see Joel Schettler, "Bruce Kestelman," *Training,* 38 (November 2001): 36–39.

29. This list is based on Wendell French, "Organization Development Objectives, Assumptions, and Strategies," *California Management Review,* 12 (Winter 1969): 23–34; and Charles Kiefer and Peter Stroh, "A New Paradigm for Organization Development," *Training and Development Journal,* 37 (April 1983): 26–35.

30. See Robert J. Marshak, "Managing the Metaphors of Change," *Organizational Dynamics,* 22 (Summer 1993): 44–56; Craig L. Pearce and Charles P. Osmond, "Metaphors for Change: The ALPs Model of

Change Management," *Organizational Dynamics,* 24 (Winter 1996): 23–35; and Ian Palmer and Richard Dunford, "Conflicting Uses of Metaphors: Reconceptualizing Their Use in the Field of Organizational Change," *Academy of Management Review,* 21 (July 1996): 691–717.

31. A successful application of Lewin's model at British Airways is discussed in Leonard D. Goodstein and W. Warner Burke, "Creating Successful Organization Change," *Organizational Dynamics,* 19 (Spring 1991): 4–17. Also see Gib Akin and Ian Palmer, "Putting Metaphors to Work for Change in Organizations," *Organizational Dynamics,* 28 (Winter 2000): 67–79; Richard S. Allen and Kendyl A. Montgomery, "Applying an Organizational Development Approach to Creating Diversity," *Organizational Dynamics,* 30 (Fall 2001): 149–161; and Mark Herron, "Training Alone Is Not Enough," *Training,* 39 (February 2002): 72.

32. Susan Berfield, "From One Male Bastion to Another," *Business Week* (May 15, 2006): 38.

33. Grassroots change is discussed in the second Q&A of Jack and Suzy Welch, "The Rumsfeld Conundrum," *Business Week* (September 25, 2006): 144.

34. Bill Breen and Cheryl Dahl, "Field Guide for Change," *Fast Company,* no. 30 (December 1999): 384. Also see Linda Tischler, "Sudden Impact," *Fast Company,* no. 62 (September 2002): 106–118; and Norm Brodsky, "Street Smart," *Inc.,* 25 (February 2003): 44–45.

35. Debra E. Meyerson, *Tempered Radicals: How People Use Difference to Inspire Change at Work* (Boston: Harvard Business School Press, 2001), p. xi. Also see Debra E. Meyerson, "Radical Change, the Quiet Way," *Harvard Business Review,* 79 (October 2001): 92–100.

36. Adapted from "Tips for Tempered Radicals" in Keith H. Hammonds, "Practical Radicals," *Fast Company,* no. 38 (September 2000): 162–174.

37. For practical insights on organizational change, see Scott Kirsner, "How to Stay On the Move . . . When the World Is Slowing Down," *Fast Company,* no. 48 (July 2001): 113–121; Shaul Fox and Yair Amichai-Hamburger, "The Power of Emotional Appeals in Promoting Organizational Change Programs," *Academy of Management Executive,* 15 (November 2001): 84–94; and Robert A. F. Reisner, "When a Turnaround Stalls," *Harvard Business Review,* 80 (February 2002): 45–51.

38. Abraham Zaleznik, "Real Work," *Harvard Business Review,* 67 (January–February 1989): 59–60.

39. For example, see Karen A. Jehn and Elizabeth A. Mannix, "The Dynamic Nature of Conflict: A Longitudinal Study of Intragroup Conflict and Group Performance," *Academy of Management Journal,* 44 (April 2001): 238–251; Margery Weinstein, "Are You Working for an 'Untouchable'?" *Training,* 43 (December 2006): 13; Kerry Sulkowicz, "Sparring Execs Need a Time Out," *Business Week* (December 18, 2006): 18; and Brian Grow, "Out at Home Depot," *Business Week* (January 15, 2007): 56–62.

40. David Drickhamer, "Rolling On," *Industry Week,* 251 (December 2002): 50.

41. Dean Tjosvold, *Learning to Manage Conflict: Getting People to Work Together Productively* (New York: Lexington, 1993), p. 8.

42. Ibid. Also see Allen C. Amason, "Distinguishing the Effects of Functional and Dysfunctional Conflict on Strategic Decision Making: Resolving a Paradox for Top Management Teams," *Academy of Management Journal,* 39 (February 1996): 123–148; Samuel S. Corl, "Agreeing to Disagree," *Purchasing Today,* 7 (February 1996): 10–11; and Deborah Stead, "The Big Picture," *Business Week* (January 8, 2007): 11.

43. For case studies of problems associated with competitive conflict, see Peter Burrows, "What Price Victory at Hewlett-Packard?" *Business Week* (April 1, 2002): 36–37; and Joseph Weber, "The House of Pritzker," *Business Week* (March 17, 2003): 58–65.

44. Walter Kiechel III, "How to Escape the Echo Chamber," *Fortune* (June 18, 1990): 130. For other good material on constructive conflict, see Dean Tjosvold, Chun Hui, and Kenneth S. Law, "Constructive Conflict in China: Cooperative Conflict as a Bridge Between East and West," *Journal of World Business,* 36 (Summer 2001): 166–183.

45. For a good overviews of managing conflict, see Kenneth Cloke and Joan Goldsmith, *Resolving Conflicts at Work: A Complete Guide for Everyone on the Job* (San Francisco: Jossey-Bass, 2000); and Tim

Ursiny, *The Coward's Guide to Conflict: Empowering Solutions for Those Who Would Rather Run Than Fight* (Naperville, Ill.: Sourcebooks, 2003).

46. See "Aggressive Behavior Bullies into Workplace," *HR Magazine,* 44 (February 1999): 30; Rudy M. Yandrick, "Lurking in the Shadows," *HR Magazine,* 44 (October 1999): 61–68; and Kevin Dobbs, "The Lucrative Menace of Workplace Violence," *Training,* 37 (March 2000): 54–62.

47. See Dean Tjosvold and Margaret Poon, "Dealing with Scarce Resources," *Group & Organization Management,* 23 (September 1998): 237–255.

48. See Rhetta L. Standifer and James A. Wall Jr., "Managing Conflict in B2B E-Commerce," *Business Horizons,* 46 (March–April 2003): 65–70.

49. See Kathryn Tyler, "Extending the Olive Branch," *HR Magazine,* 47 (November 2002): 85–89.

50. For related research, see Steven M. Farmer and Jonelle Roth, "Conflict-Handling Behavior in Work Groups: Effects of Group Structure, Decision Processes, and Time," *Small Group Research,* 29 (December 1998): 669–713; and Russell Cropanzano, Herman Aguinis, Marshall Schminke, and Dina L. Denham, "Disputant Reactions to Managerial Conflict Resolution Tactics: A Comparison Among Argentina, the Dominican Republic, Mexico, and the United States," *Group & Organization Management,* 24 (June 1999): 124–154. Practical advice can be found in Marci DuPraw, "Cut the Conflict with Consensus Building," *Training,* 43 (May 2006): 8; and the first Q&A in Jack and Suzy Welch, "Don't Play the Office Cop," *Business Week* (December 4, 2006): 144.

51. Stephen P. Robbins, *Managing Organizational Conflict: A Nontraditional Approach* (Englewood Cliffs, N.J.: Prentice-Hall, 1974), p. 62.

52. See William H. Ross and Donald E. Conlon, "Hybrid Forms of Third-Party Dispute Resolution: Theoretical Implications of Combining Mediation and Arbitration," *Academy of Management Review,* 25 (April 2000): 416–427; Stephanie Armour, "Arbitration's Rise Raises Fairness Issue," *USA Today* (June 12, 2001): 1B–2B; and Patrick S. Nugent, "Managing Conflict: Third-Party Interventions for Managers," *Academy of Management Executive,* 16 (February 2002): 139–154.

53. See M. Afzalur Rahim, "A Measure of Styles of Handling Conflict," *Academy of Management Journal,* 26 (June 1983): 368–376.

PHOTO CREDITS

Chapter 1   p. 2: AP Images; p. 20: Jay Reed.

Chapter 2   p. 28: © Beathan/CORBIS; p. 35: Courtesy of Merrill Lynch; p. 39: © 2004 Gary Markstein. Courtesy of *The Milwaukee Journal Sentinel*; p. 43: AP Images.

Chapter 3   p. 52: Beren Patterson/Alamy Images; p. 56: Photo by David Maxwell.

Chapter 4   p. 74: Martin Barraud/STONE/Getty Images; p. 83: Andre Ramasore/Galbe.com; p. 89: AP Images.

Chapter 5   p. 102: AP Images; p. 107: Paula Bronstein/Getty Images; p. 126: Toby Mellville/Reuters/CORBIS.

Chapter 6   p. 134: AP Images; p. 137: AP Images; p. 147: Bryce Duffy/CORBIS SABA.

Chapter 7   p. 162: STR/AFP/Getty Images; p. 174: Peter Wynn Thompson/ www.peterthompsonphoto.com; p. 185: Jeff Greenberg/PhotoEdit, Inc.

Chapter 8   p. 194: AP Images; p. 198: © Lily Wang All rights reserved; p. 204: Reprinted with permission of Subaru of America, Inc.

Chapter 9   p. 222: Phil Borden/PhotoEdit, Inc.; p. 229: George Rodriguez; p. 233: Ron Ceasar.

Chapter 10   p. 250: Michael Newman/PhotoEdit, Inc.; p. 257: Porter Gifford; p. 268: © Lance W. Clayton.

Chapter 11   p. 280: Reuters NewMedia Inc./CORBIS; p. 285: AP Images; p. 304: Greg Betz.

Chapter 12   p. 312: ColorBlind Images/Getty Images; p. 320: PAXTONsight.com.

Chapter 13   p. 340: Triangle Image /Getty Images; p. 348: Reprinted with permission of The Boston Globe Store.

Chapter 14   p. 366: AP Images; p. 368: Brian Smith; p. 384: Marc Asnin/CORBIS SABA.

Name Index

SUBJECT INDEX